W9-DAI-472

LIFE-SPAN
HUMAN DEVELOPMENT

LIFE-SPAN HUMAN DEVELOPMENT

Dorothy Rogers

State University of New York
College of Oswego

Brooks/Cole Publishing Company

Monterey, California

Brooks/Cole Publishing Company
A Division of Wadsworth, Inc.

Printed in the United States of America

10 9 8 7 6 5 4 3 2 1

Library of Congress Cataloging in Publication Data

Rogers, Dorothy, 1914–
Life-span human development.

Includes bibliographies and index.
1. Developmental psychology.   I. Title.
BF713.R63   155   80-25158
ISBN 0-8185-0389-0

Subject Editor: *C. Deborah Laughton*
Manuscript Editor: *William Waller*
Production Editor: *Joan Marsh*
Cover Design: *Vicki Van Deventer*
Illustrations: *Carl Brown*
Typesetting: *Graphic Typesetting Service, Los Angeles, California*

for
Abigail Dorothy
and
Amanda Elaine

PREFACE

This volume draws together material from psychology, biology, sociology, anthropology, and other disciplines. It treats the life span chronologically, beginning with conception and the prenatal period. The sections that follow deal, in turn, with infancy, childhood, adolescence and youth, young adulthood, middle age, and the later years. Overall, the book provides an integrated study of the entire life span, including interpretation of basic developmental principles, concepts, and issues. Developmental processes are treated at each age level in order to develop an appreciation of their continuity. The last chapter summarizes the various aspects of development, thus providing a better perspective on the life span as a whole.

This book has several features that distinguish it from other life-span texts. Brief anecdotal materials illustrate points and concepts; except where indicated otherwise, they are from the author's own files. All stages of development are pictured realistically in terms of their life-styles, leisure pursuits, and practical problems. In addition, I make conjectures about such topics as prospects for greater longevity and the future of research in the field, an anticipatory glimpse vital in this time of rapid change. An especially distinctive feature is the relatively great attention accorded to adulthood. Life-span texts generally devote most of their content to childhood and adolescence, as though adulthood were an appendage to the earlier periods instead of the longest segment of life. A full chapter in this book is devoted to early adulthood, which is often treated, if at all, in perfunctory fashion.

I am strongly committed to this greater emphasis on adulthood for several reasons. For many years psychologists believed that in infancy and childhood the die was cast for all the years that lay ahead. More recently, studies have produced convincing evidence that significant development and change take place throughout life. While the early years are indeed important, undue emphasis on them may obscure the possibilities for personal growth that remain. Given this lifelong growth potential, it is all the more important that we remain fully aware of it in times of rapid change. We simply do not know enough about what lies ahead to decide, once and for all, what kind of adults children will need to become.

Keep in mind also that students who use this textbook are either older adolescents or adults. They need to know in some detail what being an adult means, from their present life stage onward. Certainly, adulthood is rooted in childhood and adolescence—and the sections devoted to those areas pay tribute to that fact. However, youth and adults provided with life-span books that devote only a small segment to all the years that remain after age 20 may unconsciously absorb the idea that most of life's most significant experience is past. In my view, all of adulthood can be exciting, growth producing, and highly rewarding. And students should be able to relate the ideas in this textbook to themselves and those around them.

People in general have only the haziest ideas about the current and future stages in their adult life. For many years, vast numbers of articles about infants and children, at least some of high quality, have been written for popular consumption. Even today, similar articles about adults are few, though they are gradually increasing in number. Even many college graduates have never had access to courses in life-span or adult psychology. Many of these will be attracted to college courses and textbooks that make up this deficiency. It is hoped that this text will help to fill that need.

The book has other features intended to make it both appealing and teachable. The style is designed to be easy to comprehend, and the content was chosen with students' needs, interests, and perceptions in mind. Lists of annotated readings are found at the end of each chapter, and there is a glossary at the end of the book. The interpretations of significant issues relating to life-span development enhance interest, besides providing perspective on matters of unusual significance today.

I would like to thank the reviewers of this book for their helpful suggestions: Jerry Bruce of Sam Houston State University, Janet Fritz of Colorado State University, and Duane Martin of the University of Texas at Arlington.

I would also like to express thanks to Cherie Blanchard and Ann Hoefer for their help during the various stages of writing and production.

Dorothy Rogers

CONTENTS

1
INTRODUCTION

INTRODUCING LIFE-SPAN PSYCHOLOGY

Definitions

The study of life-span development, observed Rosenfeld (1977), concerns all the biomedical and psychosocial aspects of human development in the context of a person's total environment, taking into account the individual's physiology, psychology, family, home, community, culture, education, religion, race, sex, and economic status, as well as the outside events that impinge upon his or her life. Life-span psychology studies the "inception, growth, progress and ultimate decline of that long, strong thread of individual identity that somehow retains its stability and self awareness as it moves through nonstop change" (p. 32).

Especially critical in studying the life span are the concepts of growth and development. *Growth* indicates quantitative change in size and structure—an increase in magnitude—in body size, intellectual ability, or even social traits. *Development* can be defined as a sequential and continuous process of change in any direction. It is both qualitative and quantitative and involves a complex integrating of functions (Krech, Crutchfield, & Livson, 1974). Development connotes expanding horizons, whereas aging suggests, at least to most individuals, a process of decline or decrement (Kalish, 1975). Development refers not merely to processes that are biologically programmed but also to those in which the organism is changed over time by interaction with the environment (Neugarten, 1977, p. 630).

The study of life-span development involves many disciplines, because life itself is "a complex, multi-dimensional continuum. This continuum is broken into phases or stages, with somewhat abrupt transitions or marker events such as marriage, divorce or retirement" (Rosenfeld, 1977, p. 32). At any point in the continuum life is the "accumulated result" of all that has transpired in the past, with a certain "directional thrust" that influences the future (p. 32). Each stage is concerned with all aspects of development, emerging from the earlier stages and finally blending into those that follow. Each stage of life has its own special tasks and characteristics. These qualities depend partly on maturational factors— for example, **puberty** initiates adolescence—and partly on social circumstance. Old age is partially a matter of being laid on the shelf by society. To comprehend so complex an enterprise, psychology borrows from a host of other sciences. For example, "its marriage with the biological sciences has produced a cumulation of ever more powerful knowledge. So, too, [has] its joint undertaking with anthropology and sociology" (Bruner, 1971, p. 66). Fortunately, psychologists from widely different disciplines are collectively seeking answers instead of attempting to prove their individual points.

Emergence of Life-Span Psychology

Each stage of life has its own image, which varies over time. The Romantics are credited with discovering childhood, and the late 19th century produced the first systematic study of later years. More recently has come recognition of the mid-life transition, just as the bicentennial celebration was a Coming of Age for an entire society (Bridges, 1977).

Until fairly recently attention has focused on segments of the life span, in particular childhood and adolescence. Psychologists tended to neglect older adults because of their relatively small number. At the turn of the century only 28% of Americans were over age 25 and only 3% over age 65, nowadays judged as the beginning of old age (Schaie, 1981). Over the years, as the average life span dramatically increased, the older population multiplied and their problems grew, partly because they began to live apart from their children, interest grew in gerontology, or the study of the aged. This study includes "how some persons may age successfully, how others may experience increasing difficulties, how one person may continue learning and growing while another gets stuck, lost in the past" (Zarit, 1977, p. 11). It became increasingly apparent that old age has roots and cannot be understood without knowing what transpired earlier (Schaie & Gribbin, 1975).

Meantime, at the other end of the spectrum child psychologists became interested in the final outcome of their subjects, especially as individuals they had followed across the years grew up. The logical result was to follow them throughout their lives. After all, older people are the only research subjects for whom we can have longitudinal data for almost the entire life span (Berman, 1975). If their individual development is related to the periods in which they have lived, important insights can be gained into their continuous readaptation in a rapidly changing society. We can also capitalize on what these individuals have learned from their experience about achieving a better quality of life. Moreover, as the better-educated people of today age, they will become more adequate resource subjects. Presumably, they will have better training for evaluating themselves and their environment and for articulating what they have learned.

Psychologists' interest in middle adulthood naturally followed, to close the gap between childhood and old age as well as for other reasons. Until recently adults were primarily concerned with jobs, homemaking, and child care and hence had little time for personal growth. Small wonder that adulthood was portrayed as a homogeneous entity, a "smooth plateau of maturity that goes on and on—barring accident or crippling illness—until the gradual wear-and-tear of our days and years eventually brings on a rapid decline into senility and death" (Rosenfeld, 1977, p. 32).

As work hours declined and as adults became better educated, however, they became more concerned with themselves as persons. As they focused on expanding their experiences, their personalities developed correspondingly. Questions then arose: Should the organism be perceived as biologically programmed merely to maturity and the changes after that regarded as haphazard or as disturbances of an otherwise steady stage? Or are humans simply "programmed toward decline and death" (Neugarten, 1977, p. 630)? Some psychologists still portray changes in adulthood in terms of decline, using a biological model of decrement. But growing numbers speak of developmental changes in adulthood in terms of expansion and actualization, or the realizing of human potential.

The new interest in the middle years is still primarily the property of professionals and has hardly penetrated the popular mind. Most people still think of development as continuing until the mid-20s and declining after age 65, with a sort of "functional plateau" between.

Frames of Reference

Biological versus the psychological approach. The study of life-span development can be approached in various ways, one being biological. Thus, the body's parts, systems, and processes are studied from conception to death. From this point of view no clear subdivisions of adult life can be identified. Although aging is being studied from the cellular to the organismic level, the results have not yet justified discrete life phases. If reproductive maturity were used as a criterion, the life span could be divided into three phases, set off by puberty and the **climacteric.** But this division would be more appropriate for females than males. And these "landmarks" are too few to afford "sufficient rungs on the ladder" to correlate with the significant events and roles of adult life (Katchadourian, 1976).

The psychological, as distinct from the biological, approach deals with humans as thinking, feeling individuals. Psychological age refers to "age-related changes in the person's behavior as a unique individual in perceiving, feeling, thinking, and acting" (Dibner, 1975, p. 69).

Chronological approach. The chronological approach, in which life events are linked to calendar age, is more common. For example, G. Stanley Hall in his book *Senescence* (1922) identified adolescence as ages 25 to 30 and maturity as ages 25 or 30 to 40 or 45, a total of about 20 years for adulthood proper. The rest of life he called senescence. The chronological definition is often employed by society and in courts of law. It is used to determine time for entrance into school, adult legal liability, and the age to receive pension and social security benefits. However, there has been a confusion over when adulthood begins. The states vary in the minimum age they set for such functions as driving a car, voting, and getting married (Jordan, 1976). Only recently do we appear to be focusing on age 18 for most legal purposes.

The chronological model has its strengths and weaknesses. On the one hand, it is clear cut and certain. For example, people can vote at 18—not when,

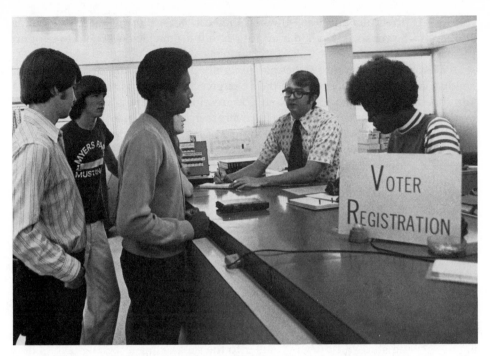

Youths are considered to be politically adult when they are old enough to vote.

according to some hard-to-define criteria, they have proved their readiness for full citizenship. On the other hand, the chronological model can be quite inadequate. Consider the difference between an 18-year-old who is married and has two children and a 28-year-old graduate student who has never held a job (Dragastin, 1975). Chronological guidelines also tell little about individuals, because some people are very active at the age of 75 and others perceive themselves as old at age 50.

The social model. The social model takes into account the roles and values that society attaches to different categories of people at different age stages. In this sense age is a relative matter. When Canadians elected a prime minister who was 48, they thought of him as young; but when he became a bridegroom of 50, they perceived him as old. When people aged 35 or 45 are in a group of teenagers, they are viewed as old; but when they are compared with people of 70, they are thought of as young (Zarit, 1977).

In a complex modern society there is no single system of age status. Neugarten (1977) described how "a system of age norms creates a social clock that is superimposed upon the biological clock in producing orderly and sequential changes in behavior and in self perceptions" (p. 633). Age alone is "an empty variable," because it isn't simply the passage of the years that produces change but also the social and biological events that transpire. For example, youths are considered politically adult at 18, when they can vote. But they are regarded as adult in the larger society when they assume a full-time job and begin to support themselves.

Despite such variations, people generally divide growing up into infancy, childhood, and adolescence. And they perceive adulthood as comprising young adulthood, middle age, and old age. Progression from one stage to another is marked by events in the family cycle and career, changes in health, changes in social responsibilities ("Old age is when you let the other fellow do the worrying"), and changes in psychological characteristics ("Middle age is when you become mellow") (Neugarten, 1971). Concepts of social age vary according to sex and social class. For example, old age is perceived as beginning earlier by working-class people than by those in the middle class.

Society agrees pretty well on the ages when people should get married, be settled in their career, hold top jobs, or be ready to retire. There appears to be a socially prescribed timetable for arranging life's events. Nevertheless, there is greater consensus regarding age expectations in young adulthood than in middle or later years. Meanwhile this normative time-line system serves as a mode of social control that bestows on people various "shoulds."

The personal frame of reference. Individuals also develop their own way of assessing their development over the years. Within the social model described above, they evaluate the current realities of their health, income, and general progress through life. In this way they decide whether they are "on time" (Neugarten, 1971).

Certainly, people do not gauge their progress through life simply by their chronological years. The comment "I am 50 years old" has little meaning. But the statement that "I am 50 years old and further ahead than I expected to be" or that "I'm not as far ahead as others in the same type of work" has much significance. Thus, by assessing their own behaviors and progress according to socially validated time lines and goals, individuals give meaning to the passing of time.

In studies of adults aged 40 to 90 Neugarten and associates (1971) found that people's expectations always involved some "time line" or "age referent." People may say "I'm in better health than others my age" or "Things are perhaps worse than I expected them to be." Or again, an individual who has a heart attack might say "At my age one might expect such a thing." In other words, it seems that people have their own view of the normal life cycle. They set their own goals and assess them according to the time frame set by those expectations.

Aging, Growth, and Development

Closely related to the foregoing frames of reference are concepts of aging. Aging is a process initiated at conception and proceeding continuously until death. As Greenblatt points out, "Life is the continuum of a process known as aging." Anatole France (1844–1924), the French novelist, wrote with great insight that "we are already old when we are born. Aging begins with one's first breath and, surely, with the first lusty cry at birth, as if to be born is to start to die" (Greenblatt, 1977, p. 101). Aging is a relative process. In later years it is often equated, wrongly, with senility and decay. Children who suffer from **progeria** are old by age 13.

The developmental perspective stresses psychological and biological changes associated with aging. Kastenbaum, Derbin, Sabatini, and Artt (1972) employ three concepts of age. Personal age is how old people perceive themselves to be. Impersonal age is how old an individual appears to others. And consensual age is the degree of congruence between personal and impersonal ages. Kastenbaum (1972) also speaks of functional age, or how well an individual performs either on the psychological or biological level. He treats functional aging from the psychological perspective by inquiring of people their personal ages. His older respondents (about 60 years old) depart more from their chronological age in their personal age than did those around age 20. The older subjects said that they looked, felt, and acted younger than their chronological age.

The individual aging process. Not only do individuals age at different rates; physiological functions within the same individual also have their own rates of decline. Certain physical factors, such as blood-sugar level or total blood volume, do not change with age. In general, functions that involve the coordinated activity of more than one organ system—for example, physical work capacity or aerobic capacity—show the greatest decline with years. In fact, under "appropriate levels of muscle strength and endurance, oxygen transport has been widely accepted as the major factor determining the limits of physical working capacity in the young, if the activity lasts more than a minute or two. . . . Cardiac output is determined in turn by heart rate and the volume of blood per beat (stroke volume)" (DeVries, 1977, p. 57). In general, from the third to the sixth or seventh decades, there is a loss of about 26% in cardiac output. Also, there is a gradual decline of about 60% from the late teens to the eighth decade in maximal ventilation, which is attained doing exhausting work. Vital capacity, the volume of air expelled by the greatest possible expiration after the deepest possible inspiration, declines with age. Changes that reflect the aging process appear most often when the organism is under stress because homeostatic readjustment slows with increasing years.

An inherent characteristic of aging is growth, which proceeds at a decelerating rate from birth to maturity, with a spurt at puberty. At all ages the variability of boys' physical characteristics is greater than that of girls. Boys are more extreme in dimensions of height, weight, and bone growth. In consequence, there are more very short men and very tall men as well as very light and very heavy men. They also vary more in tested intelligence (Kagan, 1972).

When any individual's growth is assessed against group norms, certain points should be kept in mind. In the first place, every growth pattern is unique. Norms should also be judged in terms of the population on which they have been established. Certain norms derived from largely Scandinavian stock would be inappropriate for New York City's Puerto Ricans. In any case, we should not be deluded into overestimating our present level of knowledge, including the significance of published norms about growth. Certainly, many questions require further research. For example, what is the significance of minor deviations? Why do some apparently normal individuals follow atypical growth patterns? Perhaps "norms, both psychological and statistical, need recalibration in ways yet to be determined" (Rogers, 1977, p. 81).

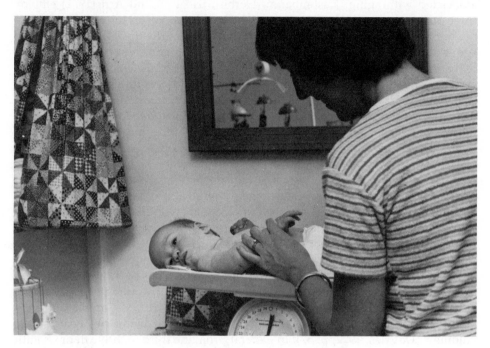

Growth rates are greatly accelerated during the first year of life.

The critical-period hypothesis. Certain experiences at particular periods are presumed to have maximum impact. For example, John Money (1963) argued that early childhood is critical for defining one's sex role. Again, eighth-graders experience more depression than do seventh-graders, indicating that a critical developmental period occurs about that time, possibly because of the greater academic and social demands required by the move into adolescence (Albert & Beck, 1975).

Here Whittaker Chambers (1952, p. 123) recalls an episode from his childhood that proved to be critical.

> Then my mother told me to go and kill the first chicken. The thought of hurting anything so helpless and foolish was too much for me. I said: "I can't." My mother did not even answer me. She took a sharp knife and pressed the handle into my hand. "I will not have any man in this house," she said fiercely, "who is afraid of blood." I knew that she was thinking of my father.

I caught a chicken. I sat down with it in the coop, stroked its feathers and tried to quiet its alarm. It was a sunny day. It was the thought that from the bird's bright eye that world of light must now fade that unnerved me. Why must I darken it? So that the live, free creature could pass through the bowels of a gross person? It made no sense.

I tied the chicken's legs and hung it, head down, from a nail, and as quickly and as mercifully as I could, severed its head. The knife fell as if gravity had jerked it from my hand. Then I hid.

It is commonly presumed that, if certain favorable experiences are not available at critical times, the effects may be irreversible. However, Moltz (1973) suggested that the term *optimum* is better than *critical*. The difference is in not assuming that all is lost if certain learning doesn't occur at a particular time. Still, certain times do seem to facilitate learning more than others.

New concepts of development and change in adulthood. To date it has hardly been recognized that adults are involved in any continuing development processes at all. Instead, "Like a butterfly, an adult is supposed to emerge fully formed, and on cue, after a succession of developmental stages in childhood. Equipped with all the accouterments, such as wisdom and rationality, the adult supposedly remains quiescent for another half century or so. While children change, adults only age" (Gould, 1976, p. 78). This former concept of adulthood as static and as the culmination of growth is no longer appropriate. A more static designation might have been appropriate to a biological model of development, which stresses preservation of the species, than to the psychological model, which focuses on the development of individual potential. A static concept is rational enough in societies where most adults' activities largely relate to child care and obtaining food and shelter. But it doesn't make sense in a complex modern society, where adults can choose from varied life-styles previously reserved for a few (Troll, 1975). Nowadays we look toward a much longer adulthood than formerly.

The most important factor in determining the present concept of adulthood as involving continuous change was rapid social change. Not only do children lead different lives from their parents, but adults' lives also change through time. Already in the early 20th century Henri Bergson (1859–1941) could write: "To exist is to change; to change is to mature; to mature is to create oneself endlessly" (1972, p. 182). Thus, across the years the concept of adulthood has changed from a particular status or condition to a process (Jordan, 1976).

Meantime, an individual's developmental status at any point in adulthood, or at any other point in life, is the product of all that has gone before since conception. That is, at any one time an individual's life can be perceived as representing the accumulated effects of heredity and environment and as having a "certain directional thrust" that guides its course into the future (Rosenfeld, 1977, p. 32). As people look back on their lives in later years, they perceive what they have actually done as well as what they might have done.

Life structure. Levinson (1974) defined an individual's life structure as embracing an "over-all pattern of roles, membership, goals, and the like—particular ways in which a person is plugged into society." Internally, it includes "the personal meanings these [roles] have for the individual, as well as inner identities, core values, fantasies and psychodynamic qualities" (p. 247). Thus, the individual life structure, or pattern, relates to the transactions between self and society (Levinson, 1977). It has three main features. First is the sociocultural world. This world includes the person's family, occupation, race, religion, and specific events and conditions such as prosperity or war. A second aspect is the person's changing roles and relationships as friend, father, citizen, or member of organizations. Finally, aspects of oneself are expressed in different components of one's life, or else at times are neglected in the life structure.

Within any individual life structure certain aspects are central, consuming the greatest energy and time. Others are more peripheral to the basic design of one's life. Within this context, development represents the evolution of life structure. Life structure does not remain static but progresses through a sequence of alternating periods. The stable periods generally last about 6 to 8 years and the transitional ones 4 to 5 years. Although changes do occur during such periods, the basic life structure remains relatively intact. A transitional period is devoted to ending the existing structure and progressing toward a new one (Levinson, 1977).

Models of reality (metaphors). In a different approach Overton & Reese (1973) used **metaphors** to describe world views, or models of reality. The most prominent metaphors that current developmental psychologists hold are those of the machine and the biological organism. The machine metaphor, or **mechanistic** model, is borrowed from physics. It suggests that the world and all its phenomena function as if they were mechanical. Psychologists with this orientation design research as if their subjects reacted mechanically. By contrast, the organismic model is borrowed from the field of biology. It assumes that behavior has a biological basis.

The most significant issue in assessing these two views is whether human beings are primarily active or reactive. According to the mechanistic model,

> The human being is assumed to be a reactive, passive organism, whose natural state, like that of the machine, is to be at rest. All activity (behavior) is the result of external forces originating in the environment. In contrast, the organismic model includes the assumption that the human being is *spontaneously* active. Thus man himself is considered to be the source of change. In the mechanistic model, change is brought about only by external forces [Elias, Elias, & Elias, 1977, p. 26].

According to the mechanistic model, development is simply a matter of stimulus/response sequences. An external force (or stimulus) from the environment changes the organism's behavior (response). All current behaviors are presumed to be explainable and predictable in terms of antecedent conditions or "a knowledge of past S-R [stimulus/response] sequences and present external forces acting on the organism. Consequently, specific antecedent-consequent relationships become the focus of research" (p. 27). Using this model psychologists attempt to analyze behaviors in terms of S-R sequences in order to understand how past and present units produce predictable outcomes.

From the organismic point of view, developmental processes involve qualitative change. The current status of the organism differs qualitatively from its past condition. Gradually, new psychological structures appear, and the relationships among former structures change. This view is based on several assumptions. The first assumption—that specific behaviors have no significance unless they are viewed in terms of total situations—is termed *holism*. This view suggests that the whole is greater than the sum of its parts. The second assumption is that patterns of behavior have underlying psychological structures. Finally, organismic psychologists assume that new psychological structures possess qualitatively different characteristics from old ones. And they assume that the new structures cannot be predicted merely from a knowledge of antecedent/consequent relations (Reese & Overton, 1970).

These two views of the human organism are constantly illustrated in different modes of teaching. The teacher who gives children lists of goods produced in different countries and later, on tests, has them match products and countries is employing a mechanistic model. The teacher who has children compare the climate of several countries and then, in group discussion, consider what crops might flourish there is using an organismic model.

A final way to approach life development is in terms of its stages. This view will be the topic of the next section.

STAGE THEORIES

Background

Origins. By the late 18th century American society had already begun to recognize the various stages of life and to develop institutions that would deal differentially with them. Over the years

> it discovered childhood in the first half of the 19th century and invented adolescence toward the end of it, both emerging into public consciousness as a result of social crises associated with those age groups in a manner similar to the emergence of old age later on. Nevertheless, no clear-cut boundaries for adulthood in America rose until the need to distinguish between the problems of middle and old age [Hareven, 1976, p. 16].

Comparison with learning theory. Against that background, stage theory emerged. This theory views human development as involving relatively discrete,

Children in 19th-century England worked right alongside adults.

hierarchical stages that can be identified psychologically, physiologically, and socially. Stage theories stress the universality of life sequences. Learning theories deemphasize universality on the assumption that learning particular tasks or living through certain experiences makes an individual ready for higher-order, presumably more difficult, tasks (Troll, 1975). For example, Gagné (1968) perceived development as proceeding from simple to complex, as an individual learns successively more complex sets of rules. This process is made easier by transferring what has been learned from earlier, simpler situations to more complex ones. Gagné did not relate stages of development to age, except in that learning takes time and certain abilities must be acquired before others.

General observations. The following outline will place stage theory in clearer perspective. Stages in the life cycle are not decreed by biological nature (Keniston, 1975). Instead, they result from the complex interaction between phases of biological maturation and sociocultural conditions. Stages involve particular biological, psychological, and sociological events characteristic of each. Biological events include the establishment and then diminution of reproductive capacities and physical vigor and the growing probability of disease. Psychological events include progressing through phases of cognitive, psychosexual, and psychosocial development. Among sociological events are entrances into and departures from the most critical areas of social life, including the family, vocation, and social organizations. They also include attaining greater, but finally decreased, positions of responsibility, status, and power within social institutions and networks.

These transitions are referred to collectively as status passages within the life cycle (Bengtson & Starr, 1975). Each stage involves taking on new tasks while at the same time relinquishing modes of behavior that have outgrown their usefulness. While some theorists—among them Havighurst and Erikson—propose that developmental stages continue through adulthood, the process may be somewhat different from that in childhood and adolescence (Havighurst, 1973). Changes during adulthood relate more to sociocultural factors than to physical and cognitive development.

Life events—including marriage, parenthood, the climacteric, retirement, and widowhood—have all been suggested as marking off stages. Still other commonly used markers are the life periods from infancy through old age. Across the centuries new age stages have been added. In the 17th and 18th centuries childhood became a relatively discrete life period, and children were no longer perceived as little adults (Ariès, 1962). Adolescence has been adjudged an invention of the late 19th century (Gillis, 1974). Only within the past few decades, as the transition from childhood to maturity has become increasingly prolonged, has a new period of youth been defined (Panel on Youth of the President's Science Advisory Committee, 1973). Because life experience over time varies with changes in the society, the delineation of life stages also changes. For example, the stage of "trans-adulthood" is emerging as a response to social change. Trans-adulthood (from 18 into the late 20s or early 30s) is a period of trying out different life-styles, of seeking a career, and of testing educational goals. The aim is to remain flexible and ready for change (Greenwald & Danziger, 1975).

Major Stage Theories

Stage theories focused originally on child development. More recently they have been applied to the whole life span. Just as principles govern development from conception through adolescence; so do adults develop by stages, each with its own characteristic tasks. In addition, certain changes occur within each period. However, individuals move from one stage to the next only when they tackle new developmental tasks or restructure their lives. Each structuring can persist more than 7 or 8 years (Levinson, 1974). On the basis of his findings Levinson divides life into five age spans: preadulthood, age 0 to 22; early adulthood, 17 to 45; middle adulthood, 40 to 65; late adulthood, 60 to 85; and late-late adulthood, from 80 until death. The transition from one stage to another is major, requiring several years. Each transition constitutes "both an ending and beginning, a departure and arrival, a death and rebirth, a meeting of past and future" (Levinson, 1977, p. 102).

Better known is Erik Erikson's (1956) portrayal of the life cycle as a series of crises, or conflicts. A **crisis,** according to Erikson, is not some catastrophic

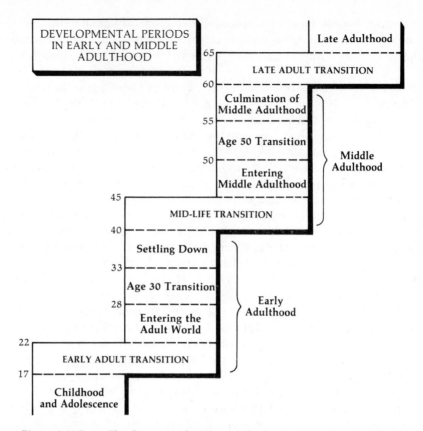

DEVELOPMENTAL PERIODS IN EARLY AND MIDDLE ADULTHOOD

Late Adulthood

65

LATE ADULT TRANSITION

60

Culmination of Middle Adulthood

55

Age 50 Transition

50

Entering Middle Adulthood

} Middle Adulthood

45

MID-LIFE TRANSITION

40

Settling Down

33

Age 30 Transition

28

Entering the Adult World

} Early Adulthood

22

EARLY ADULT TRANSITION

17

Childhood and Adolescence

Figure 1-1. From The Seasons of a Man's Life, *by Daniel J. Levinson. Copyright © 1978 Daniel J. Levinson. Reprinted by permission of Alfred A. Knopf, Inc. and The Sterling Lord Agency, Inc.*

situation but rather a critical period of increased potential and vulnerability. Development proceeds by critical steps, or times of decision between progress and regression. At such intervals either progress is made or failure occurs, leaving one's life situation either better or worse but in either case reintegrated or restructured. Erikson described the developmental issues and adaptive aspects of personality in each period. He related them to the Freudian stages as follows:

1. In infancy (the oral-sensory stage) an individual is preoccupied with the conflict of trust versus distrust. At this stage children should develop a basic sense of trust. From time to time an infant's basic trust is represented as a general feeling of well-being derived from having its needs met. Distrust suggests anticipation of discomfort.

2. During the second year, or anal stage, the conflict is between autonomy on the one hand and sense of doubt on the other. While being trained in basic patterns of sleeping, eating, and toilet use, children must be allowed

CHAPTER 1

14

certain alternatives in order to develop feelings of individual dignity, self-reliance, and freedom.

3. In the next, or genital locomotor stage (ages 4 and 5), children acquire a sense of initiative and overcome feelings of guilt, as they engage in more activities without a direct guidance of the parents.
4. During the latency period, middle and late childhood, they establish a sense of industry.
5. Adolescence is a period of role diffusion during which the sense of identity emerges. The young adolescent decides who he or she is, and the older one decides what to do about it. The danger at this time is self-diffusion, partly because growing genital maturity floods the body with vague new feelings. These feelings must be countered by experiences that will encourage the development of an integrated, healthy sense of self.
6. In young adulthood comes the need for intimacy as opposed to isolation. This is followed by a need for generativity contrasted with a sense of self-obstruction or stagnation. **Generativity** is achieved through caring for and guiding the next generation and through individual experiences and feelings of fulfillment.
7. Finally, in later maturity adults acquire a sense of integrity to counterbalance feelings of disgust and despair (Erikson, 1950).

Jung's concept of life stages derived primarily from his clinical work and psychological theories. His life stages begin with youth, embracing the period from puberty to the middle years. Youth was perceived as concerned with handling sexual instincts, overcoming inferiority feelings, and broadening life horizons. In the next significant period, between ages 35 and 40, people try to carry their youthful selves into the middle years, sometimes developing **neuroses** in the effort. To a certain extent their interests weaken and their convictions, especially those relating to morals, strengthen until they become somewhat rigid around the age of 50.

In the later years Jung saw "deep-seated and peculiar changes within the psyche," with older people changing into their opposites, especially psychologically (1971, p. 14). Older men seem to become more feminine and older women more masculine. In addition, this period inevitably involves a contraction of life activities. Jung was among the first to focus on the second half of life and the need for older people to make their lives meaningful. He was also among the first to portray death as a healthy goal, to be welcomed instead of feared.

Other Stage Theories

Others have attempted to let research speak for itself. Instead of assuming a theoretical position and then seeking to support it, they have analyzed the data to find where significant groupings occur.

Gould and his associates had 524 White, middle-class people of varying ages fill out questionnaires. The researchers found seven distinguishable phases: "[ages] 16 to 17, 18 to 21, 22 to 28, 29 to 36, 37 to 43, 44 to 50, and 51 to 60" (Gould, 1975, p. 76). For most of the questions employed, the responses stabilized between ages 22 and 29 and continued stable from then on. Certain questions evoked distinctive responses even from adjacent age groupings, however, and these questions were used to identify the phases of adult life.

In general, responses of the 16- and 17-year-olds closely resembled the stable patterns of the 22- and 29-year-olds. These adolescents still lived with their families of origin and thought of themselves more as members of the family than as individuals. By contrast, the next older group, the 18- to 22-year-olds, gave replies quite distinct from the just younger or just older group. Members of this group had their own individual psychology and private world. They were especially open to new ideas. But when they again joined the "mainstream" of adult society, after age 22, their responses became typical of those from the rest of the population.

Rhona and Robert Rapoport (1975) divided the life cycle into main stages according to people's preoccupations. Young adults are preoccupied with identifying with social institutions. Adults in the establishment (middle-age) phase are concerned with life investments (productivity, performance, and evaluation). And those in their later years (the retirement phase) stress personal and social integration.

Developmental Tasks

The concept. Robert Havighurst (1953) suggested a somewhat different model for the life span. In this model, the stages become a sequence of developmental tasks. Each period of life requires the completion of certain tasks before those on the next level can be satisfactorily resolved. Moreover, how well tasks are resolved relates to the satisfaction and effectiveness of one's life at that period.

Havighurst (1972) used **developmental tasks** as markers across the life span. Some tasks relate chiefly to biological maturation, others to social role. Each group of tasks has its psychological, biological, and social elements. These tasks follow the same general sequence, but the sequence is neither invariant nor necessarily hierarchical. Nevertheless, there is an optimum time when tasks should be encountered and mastered, as is also true of Erikson's stages. Either failure or delay in resolution of a task retards the successful resolution of the next one.

Definition of tasks. Havighurst (1972) divided the life span into six age periods: early childhood, birth to age 5 or 6; middle childhood, ages 5 or 6 to 12 or 13; adolescence, 12 or 13 to 18; early adulthood, 18 to 25; middle adulthood, 35 to 60; and later maturity, 60 and over. He contended that certain developmental tasks should be mastered during each age period and that failure creates problems in the stages that follow. In infancy and early childhood an individual should learn such tasks as walking, taking solid foods, talking, distinguishing sex differences, and formulating certain concepts of social and physical reality.

In middle childhood developmental tasks include learning an appropriate sex role, acquiring physical skills necessary for playing ordinary games, learning to get along with agemates, developing concepts required for everyday living, and acquiring a conscience and scale of values. The adolescent period is characterized by such tasks as accepting a masculine or feminine sex role, choosing and preparing for an occupation, preparing for marriage and family life, developing new relationships with peers of both sexes, and achieving emotional independence of adults.

In early adulthood an individual chooses a mate, learns how to live with that mate, begins a family, learns to rear children and manage a home, embarks on an occupation, discovers a congenial social group, and assumes some civic responsibility. In the next adult period, middle age, tasks include establishing and maintaining a satisfactory standard of living, developing leisure activities, relating to one's mate as a person, assuming adult social and civic responsibilities, adapting to physical changes, and adjusting to aging parents. Finally, later maturity requires adjustment to decreasing health and physical strength, adapting to retirement and reduced income, adjusting to the death of one's mate, meeting civic obligations, establishing satisfactory living arrangements, and affiliating with one's own age group.

Evaluating Stage Theories

Stage theories have both strengths and weaknesses. On the one hand, sequences of the **life cycle** make better sense within such a framework. Stages indicate how people can be expected to differ at various periods of life; they alert us to crisis points and issues over the years. Nevertheless, such theories are somewhat general and often too idealistic. They do not suggest how such factors as differences in culture, sex, or social class modify the general pattern. Instead, they outline a process that culminates in "human fulfillment" or "successful aging" as defined by the White middle class of society (Kimmel, 1974, p. 26). These somewhat speculative life-cycle theories—for example, that of Erikson— must be tested by applying them to various types of people and conditions of life.

With the exception of Erikson's stages of ego development, conceptualizations of stages have not been especially useful with regard to adult personality (Neugarten, 1977). One reason is that they suggest an invariant and irreversible order, hierarchically arranged. In adulthood there is no clear-cut biological timetable, and life events vary to a greater extent than they do in childhood.

LIFE-SPAN DEVELOPMENTAL RESEARCH

Cross-Sectional Method

Definition and examples. The research methods most commonly employed in life-span developmental psychology are the cross-sectional and the longitudinal. **Cross-sectional research** involves studying individuals of the same or different age levels with regard to specific characteristics and behaviors. Thus, comparisons can be made according to sex, age, and other variables. The samples may be very small populations or, through various sampling techniques, may be nationwide in scope. Views of 8-, 10-, and 12-year-olds about birth and how it occurs might be compared. Implicit in this approach is the questionable assumption that the 12-year-olds held about the same views on the birth process when they were 8 as the 8-year-olds do now. Actually, programs of sex instruction recently introduced into the schools might have made the present 8-year-olds more knowledgeable.

Staff members of *U.S. News and World Report* used a cross-sectional survey of hundreds of young people to draw up a profile of "the new generation" (A new generation, 1976). Often such a study involves other techniques as well. This one used interview and **phenomenological** techniques, the young people being encouraged to tell at length how they perceived themselves and their world.

Critique. This method has both pluses and minuses. On the one hand, such studies are relatively inexpensive and easy to conduct. On the other hand, it is impossible to conclude to what degree group differences are a function of age or of the experiences each group had because of being born in different cohorts or generations (Tobin, 1977). Eighty-year-olds in the year 1978 were not the same as 80-year-olds were three decades earlier. During the interim period there were significant changes in education, pollution, and nutrition. Are the observed changes due to aging or to environmental events?

In other words, subjects in all age groups can hardly be matched regarding all relevant variables, not merely the ones under scrutiny. Nor can the different age groups be matched for education when the norms have changed so much over the years. Obviously, if only college graduates of the older group are compared with young adult college graduates, the older subjects would be far more highly selected than the sampling of young adults. Or consider the common error made in comparing health status at different ages. As Dibner pointed out,

> We would want the age groups to be comparable on health if we are focusing on age differences, and not health differences. But any group of 80-year-olds has already demonstrated that its members are superior physical specimens because they are still alive. A sample of young adults would certainly include many who would not live to the age of 80 [1975, p. 68].

Longitudinal Approach

Definition and examples. In **longitudinal research** the same individuals are examined periodically over the years. The aim is to determine changes in them rather than differences between persons of various ages. This method involves the choice of subjects of one age, who are measured at that time and repeatedly in the years that follow. The focus in the longitudinal study is on age changes (Schaie, 1967).

The earliest longitudinal research of any significance was the Harvard Growth Study, initiated in the 1920s, which followed the same individuals from the early elementary grades. Currently over 300 such studies are in progress.

Among the best known, the Berkeley Guidance Study has followed a sampling of children and their families from the age of 21 months through 18 years, with follow-up studies of the same individuals in their 30s and 40s (Jones, Bayley, McFarland, & Honzik, 1971).

Strengths and weaknesses. Longitudinal studies are viewed as especially useful in developmental research. They concentrate on patterns, facilitating study of the complex interaction of factors influencing development. If the research team is composed of scientists from all relevant fields, a well-rounded picture emerges of how people develop across the years, within changing times and environments.

This approach also raises many problems. Subjects may disappear; the researchers may change; or funds may dry up. When adults are studied, progressively larger numbers die as the years pass. At other times people may simply refuse to continue in the study or may be lost track of. Hence, the final sample will differ considerably from the initial one with regard to such characteristics as health, intelligence, and social class, especially for adults (Siegler, 1975). There is also the danger that the continued study of individuals may itself somehow influence their development. Besides, social changes distort longitudinal research, because they alter the psychological and social contexts in which individuals develop. Finally, changes between time periods may derive as much from environmental effects as from changes within the individual. This problem will become increasingly more difficult because of the tempo of cultural change. However, K. W. Schaie and his associates have devised special techniques for separating out the effects from age and cohort by using both longitudinal and cross-sectional samples (Botwinick, 1973).

Other Approaches

Case method. In both longitudinal and cross-sectional approaches, various methods and techniques are employed, often in conjunction with one another. Maddox (1970) concluded that the most meaningful way of determining life satisfaction among the elderly is through the case method, examining individual life-styles in longitudinal design. In his research, persistence in life-style proved the rule, with 79% of his sample indicating high satisfaction and a high activity level. A mere 14% displayed the so-called disengagement pattern, or high satisfaction with a low activity level. Hence, disengagement proved to be not merely a function of age. For some people it is a lifelong characteristic. Others may assume such a pattern only after a long life of high activity.

Anthropological method. Another approach to studying development is the **anthropological** technique, which involves comparing ways of growing up in different societies. Among the best known of these studies are those by Margaret Mead in the South Pacific. Such studies lend perspective to our own modes of development while yielding insight into widely varying alternatives in life-style.

Biographical method. Levinson used biography to study the life course of 40 men in each of four occupational categories: business executive, academic biologist, novelist, and hourly worker in industry. He followed the sequence of each subject's life appraising behavior and external situation. All aspects of a subject's life that had any significance were assessed, including peer relationships, work, education, marriage, leisure, religion, and politics. The goal was to determine how these aspects were patterned at any particular time, as well as over the years.

In addition to Levinson's "primary sample," a highly diverse "second sample" was selected from varied historical periods, including men's lives as described in autobiographies, biographies, plays, and novels. Overall, the study was multidisciplinary, employing specialists with backgrounds in psychology, psychiatry, sociology, and other fields.

Another version of longitudinal research compares identical twins who grow up in different adoptive families. It is testing hypotheses aimed at unravelling hereditary and environmental factors (Bohman, 1981). The idea is to study subjects separated from biological parents at an early age and reared by nonrelated parents.

A special problem. All the foregoing methods, in varying degree, pose dangers of invasion of privacy and raise ethical issues. Especially in family studies, researchers have the task of balancing the need to penetrate the intimacy of family life against the worth of the knowledge to be gained. Unfortunately, ethical dilemmas in research have not been sufficiently examined or resolved (Larossa, Bennett, & Gelles, 1981).

Critique of Current Research

Gains. In recent years great strides have been made in life-span developmental research. Psychologists are recognizing that development does not end with the onset of adulthood. Research increasingly involves all stages of the life span and the ways they relate to one another. Often, teams of researchers representing different specialties collaborate so that a more complete picture emerges. And the computer is making possible a speed, complexity, and economy of research heretofore impossible. For the first time it has become practical to study large samplings of subjects and to use sophisticated statistical procedures to untangle the complex interrelationships between individuals and the influences that impinge on them. Much of the research today makes the work of the earlier days appear almost primitive.

Weaknesses. Life-span research still has large tasks ahead and continuing problems to resolve. Certain of these problems may be summarized as follows:

1. Understandably, researchers often bypass complex, but nevertheless significant, questions. The vast majority of family research, observed Blood

(1976), is done because it is easy or appealing. For example, it may be concerned with such simple biological characteristics as number of children born or age of oldest child. Or it may deal with popular topics such as sexual studies, perhaps because of their emotional attractiveness. By contrast, there are many areas of relative neglect, including readiness for marriage, the rights of marital partners (what difference it makes if people write their own wedding ceremony), and leisure activities shared by husbands and wives.

2. Researchers often reflect the attitudes and prejudices of their country, subculture, and personal background. Most **developmental psychology** is based on data obtained from urban or suburban subjects interpreted by middle-class professionals. Because of language barriers and deficiencies in research funds, data about adults in many countries of the world are lacking.

3. Researchers may also put their self-image ahead of their discipline. Beigel (1976) cited examples from sex research to show that researchers often appear more interested in promoting their own views than in honestly pursuing the quest for knowledge.

4. Kagan (1977) deplored social scientists' **"fetish"** for debating definitions and creating "too many crusty words that over time have come to have a life of their own—floating free of reality in hallowed halls that seem inviolate" (p. 33).

5. In addition, contended Kagan (1977), social scientists often take for granted that there is a single best function to be found instead of simply admitting that what is best depends on one's perspective.

6. Problems of interpretation are acute and will inevitably remain so. It is difficult to avoid a lag between research studies and the time their results are widely recognized.

7. There is no effective way of projecting into the future so that societies can plan for their people (Hetherington & McIntyre, 1975).

8. Hetherington and McIntyre (1975) hold that the most distinctive feature of developmental psychology is a dearth of satisfactory theories. Some researchers cope with this problem by pursuing only atheoretical studies. Others devise limited theories applying to restricted areas of behavior. Still others busy themselves with "patching, mending, and modifying old theories" (p. 125). Nevertheless, growing efforts are being made to gather and make sense out of theory and research.

9. Some researchers disseminate "conclusions" based on insufficient research. Gollin and Moody (1973) concluded that "elegant discussion" of developmental issues "may be somewhat premature, given the rather uneven condition of the empirical base" (p. 42).

10. In their efforts to be objective, some psychologists ignore their subjects' own expressed views. They should make greater use of individuals as reporting agents, thus combining phenomenological and objective perspectives and determining issues that people consider important to their past, present, and future.

11. Journals that report psychological research on children often provide little information about them except their number, age, sex, and grade. Data about social class, family income, race, and language dialect are ordinarily not reported. If they are, there is no explanation of how the characteristics

were measured. To better interpret developmental research, psychologists need **demographic** variables (McCandless & Geiss, 1975).

12. Conclusions based on generalizations also tend to obscure exceptions to the rule. Although longitudinal stability coefficients of .85 to .95 and heritabilities of .70 to .80 support beliefs in the permanence of mental ability after age 6, McCall (1981) points out that some individuals overcome severe deprivation during their first half year of life. Also, figures supportive of mental stability over the years are based on averages and fail to take note of individuals who demonstrate considerable change as a result of substantial environmental shifts over the years.

13. Most research reports what people are like at a specific period of time, failing to reflect that they are continuously aging. As Nydegger (1981) points out: "We are [all] caught up in time. We are captured and confounded by its irreversibility and diluted by its apparent simplicity" (p.1).

Hetherington and McIntyre (1975) observed that "one comes away from a review of the literature feeling that developmental psychologists, working in different areas, don't talk to each other" (p. 125). While the advice "to get it all together" is demanding the impossible, "the time is ripe to get some of it together." What is needed is "careful analysis, synthesis, and evaluation of the information we now have, and an attempt to evolve theories which [may yield] more systematic and fruitful strategies of research" (p. 126). Also needed are data-gathering surveys on a large scale to provide statistical bases for debate, policy making, and decisions. Such surveys should be systematically repeated and updated. What Brim (1975) said about child development is true of developmental psychology in general—that it "has tried to make its case on the basis of individual children. . . . We must have the information that **macrostructural** [emphasis added] research, using social indicators, can bring to us" (p. 521).

SUMMARY

The discipline of life-span development, which studies all aspects of human growth and development within the context of its environment, is a relative newcomer to the psychological scene. Until recently attention focused on segments of the life span, especially childhood and adolescence. As the older population grew in number and as subjects in childhood longitudinal studies became adults, however, interest in those stages increased. The logical conclusion was to study the entire life span and how its successive segments merge. While the stages may still be studied separately, they are perceived in terms of their relationships to the total life span.

Life-span development can be approached from various frames of reference, including the biological, in which body systems and processes are studied from conception to death. The chronological approach is more common, in which life events are related to calendar age. The social model, used increasingly, focuses on an individual's social roles and interactions throughout life. Finally, the personal frame of reference takes into account individual perceptions, patterns of development, and variations in life-style across the life span.

These frames of reference relate, in turn, to different concepts of aging, the process initiated at conception and concluded at death. Aging can be viewed from a biological, personal, or functional frame of reference, the functional age representing how well an individual performs on all levels collectively.

Certain observations help place life-span development in perspective. People age in different ways with their own personal time clocks. They all continue to grow at a decelerating rate until maturity and to develop throughout life. Meantime, certain experiences have proved significant simply because they occurred at critical, or optimal, times. At all ages, an individual's developmental status is the result of all that has gone before.

There are various ways to organize life-span experience to make it comprehensible and enlightening. Levinson has defined individual life structures in terms of their roles, goals, and personal meanings. Overton has contrasted the mechanistic and **organismic** approaches to explaining developmental phenomena. Freud, Erikson, Jung, and others have viewed the life span in terms of relatively discrete stages, decrete by the interaction of biological and sociological factors. Because the social milieu is evolving, so are the distinctions and boundaries between life stages. Some stage theorists such as Havighurst portray each stage as having its distinctive tasks, which must be mastered if those at the next stage are to be approached successfully.

Stage theories have both their strengths and weaknesses. They provide a framework for ordering the sequences of life and the characteristics that distinguish them from one another. But they are usually overly general, failing to take into account differences of culture, sex, and personality. Especially in adulthood, timetables and experiences defy any neat ordering by stages.

Life-span researchers most often employ the cross-sectional and longitudinal techniques. The cross-sectional approach, which involves comparisons of different age groups, is relatively inexpensive and easy to administer. But the differences discovered, ordinarily attributed to age, may also derive from the different periods in which the age groupings grew up. The longitudinal method, in which the same individuals are studied periodically over the years, is expensive and hard to conduct. It yields significant data concerning individual patterns of development; yet, like cross-sectional research, it confounds age and environmental effects. Some researchers, notably Schaie, use a combination of the cross-sectional and longitudinal methods to reduce this source of error. Various other techniques and methods, such as the case method and anthropological approach, are also employed in life-span research, either alone or with others.

Considerable progress has been made in life-span research, but much remains to be done. It is fast growing, increasingly sophisticated in terms of research design, and comprehensive in problems studied and devices employed, especially the computer. The chapters that follow convey many of the most significant findings to date, and the concluding chapter suggests additional matters for research. Most studies of adults have embraced only a relatively small fraction of the life span. Somehow, research must be integrated in order to yield a valid picture of the total pattern of development and its basic processes. Already it is apparent that the life cycle contains important transactions, or points of passage, as in puberty. Also emerging are pictures of alternative life-styles and evidence of which are the most valid. In time, researchers will derive principles of effective coping and patterns of life-style that can be applied to lifetime strategies. Each stage, including the later ones, will be viewed in its most constructive light, not according to the currently negative **stereotypes** that become a self-fulfilling prophecy (Bridges, 1977).

SUGGESTED READINGS

Bell, R. Q., & Hertz, T. W. Toward more comparability and generalizability of developmental research. *Child Development*, 1976, 47(1), 6–13. Proposes procedures for applying research findings more broadly and making them more comparable.

Block, J. From infancy to adulthood: A clarification. *Child Development*, 1980, 51(2), 622–623. This paper aims to clarify an earlier one about the Berkeley Guidance Study, which has been wrongly construed as suggesting that early character structure has little relationship to later life character structure and outcomes.

Bohman, M. The interaction of heredity and childhood environment: Some adoption studies. *Journal of Child Psychology and Psychiatry*, 1981, 22, 195–200. Adoption studies are reviewed in order to test various hypotheses regarding the relative impact of hereditary and environmental factors, especially their influence on psychiatric disorders.

Booth, A. J. Psychology in a changing world. *AEP* (Association of Educational Psychologists) *Journal*, 1977, 4(4), 11–16. Psychological theories and generalizations have only a moderate life span. They are limited partly by the somewhat elusive quality of the subject matter and partly by the changing perceptions of psychologists. This expanding view of psychology contrasts with the "steady state" view. It recognizes that psychology must always be concerned with evolving processes. Psychology is a vital interacting part of the culture itself.

Carwin, W. C. *Theories of development: Concepts and applications.* **Englewood Cliffs, N.J.:** Prentice-Hall, 1980. Over a dozen of the major developmental theories of current interest in human development are summarized and critiqued.

Cohen, S., Evans, G. W., Krantz, D. S., & Stokols, D. Physiological, motivational, and cognitive effects of aircraft noise on children. *American Psychologist*, 1980, 35(3), 231–243. This study of the effects of aircraft noise on elementary school children offers evidence of the effects of community noise on behavior and examines the generality of laboratory effects in a naturalistic setting.

Elias, M. F., Elias, P. K., & Elias, J. W. *Basic processes in adult developmental psychology.* St. Louis: C. V. Mosby, 1977. See Chapter 3 for a discussion of life-span research, the scope of adult developmental psychology, and the differences in designs for cross-sectional and longitudinal research.

Larossa, R., Bennett, L. A., & Gelles, R. J. Ethical dilemmas in qualitative family research. *Journal of Marriage and the Family*, 1981, 43(2), 303–313. Two basic ethical questions—informed consent and the risk-benefit equation—are evaluated as they relate to qualitative family research.

McCall, R. B. Nature-nurture and the two realms of development: A proposed integration with respect to mental development. *Child Development*, 1981, *52*, 1–12. A conceptual plan for fostering early mental development is suggested in order to optimize contributions of both nature and nurture to cognitive performance.

McCall, R. B. Challenges to a science of developmental psychology. *Child Development*, 1977, *48*(2), 334–344. A critique of conceptual and methodological issues in developmental psychology. The author observes that more research in natural settings is essential.

Papalia, D. E., & Olds, S. W. *Human development.* New York: McGraw-Hill, 1978. Chapter 1 concerns bases for studying and understanding human development. It includes such topics as the history and aspects of development, periods in the human life span, and methods of study.

Parlee, M. B. The rhythms in men's lives. *Psychology Today*, 1978, *11*(11), 82–91. On the basis of relevant research, as well as her own study of men aged 25 to 39, the author reports that males, like females, experience cycles in moods. In both sexes these cycles apparently relate both to hormonal changes and situational factors.

Rosenfeld, A. The new LSD: Life-span development. *Saturday Review,* October 1, 1977, pp. 32–33. The author briefly defines the relatively new discipline that deals with the study of the entire human life span.

Rowe, D. C. Environmental and genetic influences on dimensions of perceived parenting: A twin study. *Developmental Psychology*, 1981, *17*(2), 203–208. A study of identical and fraternal twins and their parents suggested that environmental factors were largely responsible for twins' resemblance in perceptions of parenting behaviors.

Sears, R. R. Sources of life satisfactions of the Terman gifted men. *American Psychologist*, 1977, *32*(2), 119–128. A follow-up of L. M. Terman's study of gifted individuals at an average age of 66 (studied at intervals since 1922) reveals factors predictive of family, vocational, and life satisfaction. The discussion also provides insight into the nature and special advantages of longitudinal research.

Sheehan, N. W., Papalia-Finlay, D. E., & Hooper, F. H. The nature of the life concept across the life-span. *International Journal of Aging and Human Development*, 1980–81, *12*(1), 1–13. A study of people, ages 6 to over 65, determined relationships between ability to categorize animate objects and such variables as age, cognitive style, and classification ability in general.

The new age of genetic screening. *Science 81*, 1981, *1*, 2(1), 32–34. This section, consisting of three articles: "Who shall be born?" by Graham Chedd, "Pregnant pauses" by Michael Gold and "Wrongful life" by Graham Chedd, deals with prenatal checks for defects and the quality control of unborn children.

Vaillant, G. E. How the best and the brightest come of age. *Psychology Today*, 1977, 11 (4), 34–41; 107–108; 110. In this preview of a lifetime study published later in book form (*Adaptation to Life;* Little, Brown), Vaillant tells what happened to a group of men, who had been chosen for their superior characteristics in college, during the 35 years that followed. Some of them dealt creatively with challenges and succeeded, whereas others made little progress or even regressed.

Weiss, J. R. Transcontextual validity in developmental research. *Child Development*, 1978, *49*(1), 1–12. Analyzes the adequacy of research logic and techniques used to find developmental principles that are applicable across eras, cohorts, and settings. Recent methodologies are evaluated within the context of this goal.

2
HUMAN BEGINNINGS

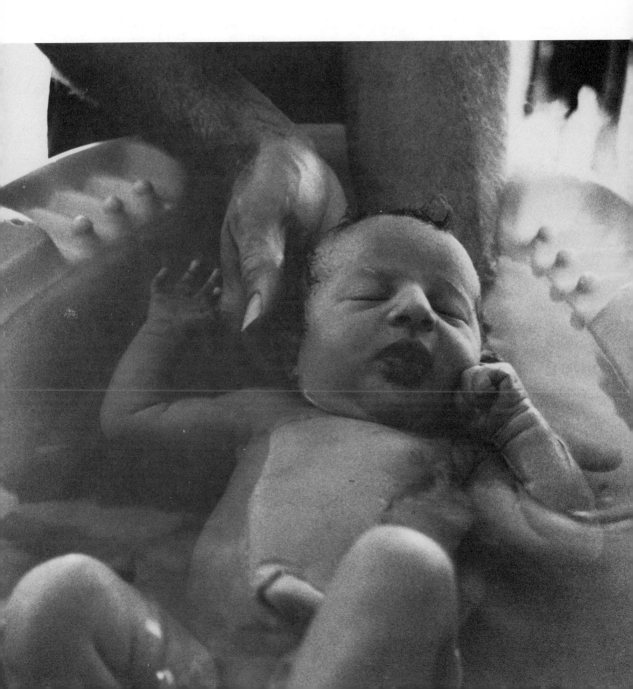

Let us get on with our story of how individuals come to be, grow up, grow old, and eventually die. This chapter will carry the story through the first 2 years of life—infancy.

The preface to the life story lies in heredity, for everyone's origins are as complex and remote as those of the human race. All of us are the genetic heirs of all our ancestors, in ways not yet completely understood.

In former times birth defects were sometimes attributed to the mother's "bad blood" flowing through the veins of her unborn child. An infant's birthmark was the result of some shock the pregnant woman had experienced. Such notions have long since been discarded, and genetics has become a sophisticated science. Significant new findings are emerging from the world's laboratories in a steady stream. Gradually, questions are being answered, though important issues remain.

HEREDITY'S ROLE IN DEVELOPMENT

Heredity versus Environment

A highly debated perennial question has been whether heredity or environment plays the more significant role in development. The environmentalists stress the differences between man and lower forms of life. They view animals as the puppets of their instincts but humans as capable of shaping their own destinies through manipulating their environment. Humans are perceived as having fewer hereditary limitations that limit them to stereotyped responses. Instead, they can learn and adopt infinitely varied behaviors. Other scientists, the **hereditarians,** view each organism as possessing within itself the general outlines of its future.

The common belief today is that genetic factors predispose us to respond along unique channels (Csany, Gervai, & Adani, 1973). Even a small initial genetic difference can set off a chain reaction of responses and thus make a significant difference in an individual's life. Nevertheless, it might be difficult or impossible to detect the genetic factor unless it has been observed from the beginning (Willerman, 1973). Studies of early personality development suggest that genetic factors do appear to play a measurable, sometimes substantial, role in explaining variations in temperament among young children (McDevitt & Carey, 1981; Goldsmith & Gottesman, 1981).

Heredity makes proportionately different contributions to various traits. For example, it plays a more influential role in physical traits than in personality. Its effect is not constant but varies with environmental conditions. Developmental events constitute a part of a long-term plan inherent in the genetic code (Gardiner, 1974). Thus, genetic factors act as predisposing elements in behavioral outcomes and constitute "a varying blend of what was given at conception and the environmental forces that have since operated upon it. The organism's inheritance at times may set limits—often quite broad ones—on how widely a trait can range; but only very rarely does its presence determine the precise nature" (Krech et al., 1974, p. 18).

Genetic Counseling

During pregnancy, various questions about the **fetus** arise that cannot be answered through vaginal examinations. These questions include the possibility of fetal malnutrition, abnormality or death (Laing, 1978). Because X rays can damage the mother's reproductive cells or the fetus, a new diagnostic technique that employs high-frequency sound may be used. This technique "can make visible each part of the fetus as it develops. The head is visible at about 13 weeks of pregnancy and the internal organs after 20 weeks" (Laing, 1978, p. 50). During the last trimester the genital organs can be defined, allowing the radiologist to determine the fetus's sex. While research suggests that this procedure is completely reliable and safe, for now it will be used only when there is doubt whether the pregnancy is normal. More study is needed to dissipate uncertainty about potential long-term side effects.

Amniocentesis. To date the best method of determining fetal abnormalities is **amniocentesis,** which involves a measure of hazard to both mother and fetus. A sample of fetal blood is withdrawn by inserting a long needle into the mother's womb. If the level of a particular protein, alpha fetal protein, proves excessive, the baby is abnormal ("Doctors Sound Out Fetus Monitoring," 1979).

Fortunately, physicians can screen for about 60 genetic defects by this process (Ausubel, Beckwith, & Janssen, 1974). Genetic researchers are also attempting to prevent defects by adding normal genes to cells that carry defective ones. Scientists have already successfully cured genetically defective human cells grown in a test tube. Just what this breakthrough may portend for the future is uncertain.

Because of such progress, genetic counseling has become increasingly popular. Couples often come to genetic counselors because they already have defective children. While well-trained family physicians can handle simple genetic problems, others are so complex as to require a team of experts, working in a genetics center. The center's work with a family may progress through several stages: (1) Diagnosis is made through an evaluation of the family history and laboratory tests. (2) Informative counseling communicates the degree of risk and the options at the family's disposal. (3) Supportive counseling is given if a baby is born defective or if severe disease develops. (4) Follow-up raises the question of who else in the family may be at risk (Fraser, 1976).

Couples often come to genetic counselors because they have already borne defective children—for example, those with tylosis, a rare skin disease, or with testicular feminization, who may appear to be completely normal women, but are not women at all. They have male chromosomes; and instead of a uterus they have a rudimentary sexual organ similar to the testes. Most of them come to the attention of the medical profession because, after marriage, they are always childless and seek to determine why. The truth is that such women are not shes but hes.

Practically all couples choose abortion when amniocentesis determines that the unborn child would have mental or physical defects. Later, some of them develop guilt feelings for having declared a death sentence on their unborn babies. They do not weigh the possible negative effects that bringing up such babies would have on them, the rest of the family, and the marital relationship.

Better-educated parents are more likely than others to take advantage of genetic counseling. In one community where the educational level was low, two doctors examined 2300 families for carriers of **sickle-cell anemia.** The carriers either ignored the information altogether or hid the condition from their prospective mates (Horn, J., 1976, p. 75).

A sampling of geneticists' views. Views about the wisest use of genetic information vary widely. Some well-known geneticists "have proposed sweeping eugenics programs that would purify or improve the national gene pool and thus the human species" (Ausubel et al., 1974, p. 34). They are worried about the ever-increasing "genetic load" that humankind must carry because of scientific advances. Medical improvements now permit increasing numbers of genetically defective persons who formerly would have died to live and reproduce.

Bernard Davis, a professor of bacteriological physiology at Harvard University, has proposed a **eugenics** program to reduce the numbers of those whose genetic heritage would limit their potential for coping with technologically complex environments. While discussions of eugenics are generally unpopular, declared Davis, not many more decades will pass before the population must be stabilized and restrictions placed on the freedom to procreate. Another geneticist, Bentley Glass, has contended that in future, more regulated societies, current genetic types of humans may not adjust. As a result, the presumed rights of men and women to reproduce as they like may be challenged. His paramount consideration is the right of every child to be born with a sound mental and physical heritage.

Some studies have indicated that XYY males—born with an extra Y chromosome—are more likely to manifest criminal or aggressive behaviors. As a result, certain officials have suggested that XYY males be registered at birth and then kept track of across the years. However, the studies in question have been challenged on various grounds. Until better evidence is available, conclusions about XYY males should be reserved (Ausubel et al., 1974).

Cecil B. Jacobsen, chief of the reproductive genetics unit at George Washington University Hospital, has said he believes that parents know what kind of child is best for their marriage. If amniocentesis reveals that the child would be a boy and the parents want only girls, he contended, abortion should be permitted. In this view, parents are "consumers, alternately selecting and rejecting possible variations in children" (Horn, 1975, p. 92).

Genetic Controversies

Sex selection. Sex research suggests that females have biological primacy. "Woman comes out of Adam's rib? No," observed Skovholt (1978, p. 4). All fetuses would simply become female if at particular points in prenatal development certain events did not take place to ensure that some children be male (Money & Tucker, 1975, p. 48). The four critical events "involve sexual chromosomes, sex hormones, the development of external genitalia and the development of internal genitalia. Female is the original sex" (Skovholt, 1978, p. 4).

Some day, considerable controversy may surround the issue of whether to predetermine children's sex. Most scientists agree that a cheap, reliable method of controlling sex will become available. The sex of the fetus may be determined early in pregnancy and undesired children aborted. Or the parents may decide in advance whether to create a girl or boy (Campbell, C., 1976).

Some Chinese physicians have already learned how to identify the sex of a fetus as early as 47 days after conception. The physician "inserts a suction tube into the pregnant woman's cervix and withdraws—or 'aspirates' as the medical term has it—a little clump of sloughed off cells and checks them for the sex of the fetus" (Campbell, C., 1976, p. 86). The Chinese predictions have proved accurate in 93 cases out of 100, and doctors believe the technique will be further improved. In 100 experimental sex predictions and a consequent 30 planned abortions, 29 of the aborted fetuses were girls. The various plans for creating a boy or girl "all exploit the fact that each sperm cell carries either an X-chromosome and produces a female or a Y-chromosome and produces a male if it fertilizes the ovum" (p. 86). These two types differ in various properties, including size, weight, acidity, and speed.

With sex-selection methods apparently near, conjectures are being made about their possibly revolutionary effects. Sex predetermination would please parents, help to eliminate sex-linked hereditary diseases such as hemophilia, and reduce the number of children who are unwanted because of their sex. Women sometimes continue to have children until they get a child of a particular sex. In the meantime, the children of the undesired sex may feel unwanted and rejected. In addition, since most people prefer that the first-born be a son, males would in effect attain a near monopoly on the most favorable ordinal position. First-borns of either sex tend to be more intelligent, successful, and masculine than later-borns. Later-borns prove to have more traditionally feminine traits, such as dependence and sociability. Thus, if a great majority of parents had boys as oldest children, traditional sex-role stereotypes might become stronger than ever before.

Because boys are more often desired than girls, a male surplus might result. On the one hand, this could lead to increased homosexuality, lonely bachelor-hoods, lawless frontier towns, more crime, a more aggressive society, and greater sexual pressures on women. On the other hand, the initial increase in males might result in a baby boom in females, because the shortage of a commodity tends to raise its value.

The right to life. A highly emotional issue in recent years has been the fetus's right to life. Now that increasingly sophisticated means of life support have been developed, the issue arises whether infants with severe medical or physical defects who would otherwise die should be kept alive ("A Right to Live," 1977). The answer is pretty simple in some cases, as when a baby is born without a cerebral cortex. Such children, even with excellent care, will die within a few months and have no prospects of a meaningful future existence. However, there is increasing controversy over letting children with **Down's syndrome,** or "mongolism," die by such means as withholding feeding and treatment of in-fections. Often, these infants have cardiac or gastrointestinal defects that without surgical repair will result in death. On parents' specific requests many pedia-tricians simply neglect the surgery and let the children die. But there is growing opposition to this practice. And when such cases are taken to court, some judges order life-maintaining surgery. In one case, the doctors had decided to let a baby die because it was born with severe facial deformities and a malformed brain. But an emotional appeal in the newspaper about the baby's plight pressured them into resuming treatments ("A Right to Die," 1977).

Despite the availability of amniocentesis, many defective babies are born. They require special treatment if they are to survive. If the parents desire, how-ever, the doctors usually ignore such treatment. For example, at one hospital 43 deformed infants were simply permitted to die during a 30-month period. In these cases both the parents and physicians believed that the babies would not have a future chance of "meaningful humanhood." But what is meaningful life? When Cameron studied people with such severe conditions as muscular disease, blindness, deafness, missing limbs, and paralysis, they proved to be as optimistic and well satisfied as a comparable group of normal people. The handicapped were even less likely than the normal people to have thoughts of suicide. In another survey, mentally retarded children seemed happier than normal ones, according to ratings by parents and teachers (Hall with Cameron, 1976).

FROM CONCEPTION THROUGH BIRTH

Prenatal Period

Fertilization. Whatever a baby's heredity, its life begins with fertilization, when one of about 20 million sperm released by the male during intercourse joins with the ovum in the upper fallopian tube. At this moment much of a human's life is decided, for the chromosomes from father and mother determine sex, eye color, complexion, facial configuration, and body shape. The child inherits 23 chromosomes from each parent, including one sex chromosome from each. Because each new individual's parents gained half their chromosomes from each of their parents, the chances are one in four of duplicating any specific chromosome from a particular grandparent. The chances are one in eight of inheriting chromosomes from a particular great-grandparent, and so on.

After the woman experiences orgasm, the cervix descends and enlarges, thus increasing the size of the path into the uterus and facilitating the sperm's ascension to meet the egg (Newton & Modahl, 1978). Orgasm also has the effect of making vaginal secretion more alkaline. This change allows sperm to move more easily than in the normally acid secretions. While sperm travel a mere .5 centimeters a minute, with the help of muscular contractions and natural hormones and chemicals, they may enter the fallopian tube only minutes after being deposited in the vagina. After its release from the ovary an egg can survive about 72 hours. But it can probably be fertilized only in the first 24.

Stages in the prenatal period. The prenatal period itself is divided into three stages: The ovum-zygote stage lasts from fertilization until the end of the 2nd week. The **embryo** stage extends from the 3rd week through the 2nd month. And the fetal stage lasts from the 3rd month until birth. During the ovum-zygote period the fertilized egg remains almost unchanged in size, because it survives on its own yolk. After about a week it becomes a parasite, obtaining nourishment from the mother. During the 2nd month the embryo grows to about an inch and a half long. Face, neck, fingers, and toes develop—giving the embryo a vaguely human appearance—and sex organs begin to form.

In the 3rd month sexual differentiation continues. The fetus can open and close its mouth, close its fist, and even suck its thumb. In the 4th month the fetus almost doubles in length, and the lower parts of the body accelerate in growth. In the 5th month the fetus wakes and sleeps and sometimes hiccoughs. Skin derivatives appear, including hair and nails. A fetus prematurely born in the 6th month can grasp a rod firmly and cry weakly. It sometimes lives a few hours, or perhaps longer in an incubator. The fetus at 7 months resembles an old person, with red, wrinkled skin. Seventy percent of the fetuses born at the end of 7 months survive. The fetus is very active during the 8th and 9th months, often changing position, and nature applies the finishing touches. Finally, the newborn averages about 20 inches in length and a little over 7 pounds in weight, with a normal range of 5 to 12 pounds.

A baby born prematurely is at some disadvantage, but ordinarily not recognizably so. A comparison of prematurely born but neurologically intact subjects, aged 7 to 9½ years, indicated that the premature children had not caught up with the normally born children but that they were functioning sufficiently normally compared with the general population (Taub, Goldstein, & Caputo, 1977).

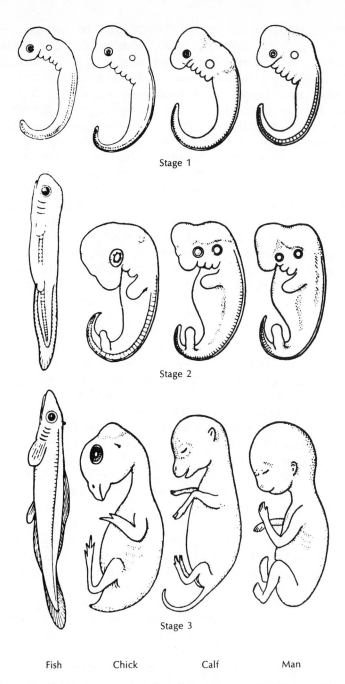

Stage 1

Stage 2

Stage 3

| Fish | Chick | Calf | Man |

Figure 2–1. Similarities in structure of various embryos at three comparable and progressive stages of development. From Child Psychology, *by D. Rogers. Copyright © 1977 by Wadsworth, Inc. This and all other quotations from this source are reprinted by permission of the publisher, Brooks/Cole Publishing Company, Monterey, California.*

Maternal diseases. In general, the fetus is protected against external hazards by the **placenta,** which removes poisonous waste and provides oxygen from the mother's blood. The placenta acts as a barrier between the two bloodstreams, letting nutrients reach the fetus while excluding noxious substances. It safeguards the developing child against most diseases but not always against german measles, gonorrhea, or syphillis, which may produce abnormalities. These diseases, as well as diphtheria, whooping cough, meningitis, scarlet fever, and pneumonia, may leave permanent damage to the central nervous system during this period. If the mother is diabetic, the fetus tends to be abnormally large, thereby complicating the birth.

Endocrine disorders. The maternal endocrine disorders, notably thyroid deficiency, may also have a negative effect on the fetus. A thyroid deficiency may cause **cretinism,** a condition characterized by coarse skin, a protruding abdomen, and intellectual impairment, ranging from slight to serious, depending on the degree of deficiency.

The Rh factor. Some birth defects can be largely controlled with current technology. One of these conditions is the **Rh hemolytic disease,** which arises from genetic incompatibility between mother and unborn baby. The situation results when an Rh-negative mother has an Rh-positive baby. In such cases there is the risk that some of the fetal blood may get into the maternal blood system and thus produce Rh antibodies. If this occurs and any of the mother's later babies are Rh positive, these antibodies can destroy that baby's blood. Since 1968, however, there has been an effective means of prevention. A previously unsensitized Rh-negative woman is inoculated after the birth of an Rh-positive baby with Rh-immune globulin, usually called by its trade name, RhoGam. This treatment prevents the development of the harmful antibodies in the mother's blood.

Nutrition. Nutritive elements diffuse through semipermeable membranes that separate the mother's and fetus's blood. Poor nutrition apparently constitutes the greatest potential hazard in uterine life. Indeed, 70% of all deaths during the first 4 weeks after delivery involve babies 5½ pounds or less. And **metabolic** abnormalities occur three times as often in small as in larger babies (Stickle, 1977). In other words, "Proper nourishment for mothers can add those critical few ounces to birth weight that can spell the difference between life and death, between normal development and retarded physical or mental growth" (p. 208). Yet low infant birth weight in the United States is 16% more common than in Britain, 25% more common than in Japan, and 60% more common than in Iceland or Finland.

In cases of malnutrition, brain development is especially at risk. Brain weight increases faster than that of any other organ, and a lack of nutrients may permanently impair future mental development (Perkins, 1977). During its peak growth period—50 days prenatally and 40 days postnatally—brain tissue grows at the rate of 5% to 6% of its final adult weight every two weeks. At birth the brain is approximately 40% of its ultimate adult weight, and by 4 years of age it is 90%. Clearly, conditions that affect brain development during this period are vital. The effects of severe prenatal and postnatal malnutrition can be reduced by good nutrition early in life. Varying degrees of impairment may well persist, however, depending on the timing, nature, and extent of deprivation involved. Deficiencies cannot be compensated for by normal feeding after the first 2-year spurt of brain growth is over (Lewis, 1975). Typically, affected children have smaller heads than normal.

Effects of drugs. The course of a mother's pregnancy is not directly affected by addiction to narcotics. But her addiction does have important consequences for the **neonate**—it is addicted from birth. Such addicted infants become increasingly less responsive to external stimuli during their first days of life. Inasmuch as cuddling and alertness behaviors provide the chief means by which infants initiate interactions, such infants place unusual demands on the care givers' adaptability (Strauss, Lessen-Firestone, Starr, & Ostrea, 1976).

In other research, (Strauss et al., 1976) narcotics-addicted infants were less able than nonaddicted ones to remain alert or to attend to visual and auditory stimuli, especially at 48 hours of age. The addicted infants were more irritable and resistant to cuddling; but they were as responsive to soothing intervention as normal neonates. Infant addicts were also found to undergo withdrawal symptoms, including tremors, fevers, breathing problems, and convulsions (Brazelton, 1970).

The effects on the fetus of certain other drugs is also clear. Quinine, often taken for malaria, may produce fetal deafness if taken to excess. Drugs administered to the mother during labor or birth may also have detrimental effects on the newborn ("Methadone Addiction in Babies," 1972).

Alcohol, coffee, and tobacco. The mother's use of alcohol, caffeine, and cigarettes can also have adverse effects on the developing fetus. While the effects of tobacco are still uncertain, it seems that expectant mothers who smoke have more unsuccessful pregnancies than do nonsmoking women ("Smoking and Health," 1972). Smoking is believed to be the primary reason for a reduced birth rate among mothers who smoke a pack of cigarettes or more a day (Longo, 1976). The effect on fetal growth relates to the number of cigarettes smoked during pregnancy, not to the cumulative effects of smoking before pregnancy.

The effect of alcohol on the fetus depends on the amount used. Moderate drinking apparently does no damage, but heavy drinking may have an adverse effect. If the mother substitutes alcohol for food, the fetus is deprived of adequate nutrition. In such cases the damage derives not from the alcohol itself but from the mother's failure to eat as she should.

Women themselves are beginning to react to their doctor's advice and to widely publicized reports regarding the adverse effects of heavy coffee and alcohol consumption during pregnancy. In one study (Little, Schultz, & Mandell,

1976) a majority of the women interviewed had cut down on drinking both coffee and alcohol during pregnancy.

Pollution. In a study in Los Angeles County, air pollution resulted in a 314-gram reduction in birth weight when statistically separated from other variables. It also produced a 17% increase in infant mortality. This estimate of increased mortality is conservative, because the data were for people of higher economic status in less polluted areas.

Mother's emotions. The potential effect of the mother's emotional state on the unborn fetus has produced much controversy. Evidence suggests that the developing child is affected, but in ways not exactly clear (Krech et al., 1974). In maternal anxiety or rage various hormones may be liberated, producing chemical changes in the mother's blood. These chemicals, absorbed through the placenta into the fetal bloodstream, may act as irritants with far-reaching effects.

The influence of any specific agent hinges importantly on the developmental stage of the organism. It is the timing, not the agent in itself, that dictates the type of abnormality produced. Whatever parts or limbs are being formed when the harmful agent is introduced are the ones damaged. In general, the younger the organism, the more serious the difficulty or abnormality produced.

Mother's age. From the biological standpoint the optimum period for having babies appears to be between the ages of 21 and 29. Not until the 20s have the sex hormones and reproductive apparatus fully developed. The best time in particular cases is modified by other factors, including the mother's health and family circumstances.

The total effect. In any individual case, the impact of all prenatal influences is modified by their relative strength and how they interrelate. On the basis of a longitudinal study involving 98% of the babies born in Great Britain during a single year, a child-health professor proposed a composite of the ideal pregnant woman: "If I were a baby and could choose my mom, I would have a non-smoking upper-class one about 25 years old, at least 5 feet 5 inches tall, and a bit plump but with a normal blood pressure" ("The Perfect Mom," 1973). While few babies have the good fortune to enjoy an ideal prenatal environment, the wonder is that the vast majority are normal at birth. Normal development is not the same as optimal development, however. The goal should be to maximize each individual's potential through making the prenatal experience as healthy as possible.

Birth

Birth trauma. The sheltered prenatal existence is roughly terminated by birth, usually proclaimed by a loud wail. Birth itself involves physical shock that can modify structures and inherent developmental tendencies. Never again, "in all the rest of the child's life, will there be so sudden and complete a change in

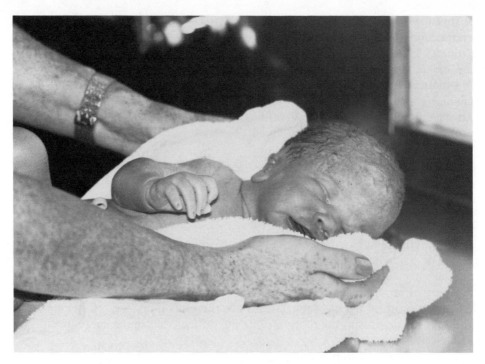

The first hour of this baby's life could be the hardest.

locale; no other journey will ever start from so profound a seclusion" (Rogers, 1977a, p. 42). During labor great stresses and pressures buffet the child's system, which is still dependent on the mother for nourishment and oxygen.

While the fetus is generally secure in its fluid-filled bag and although its skull seems designed to cope with delivery crises, accidents can happen both during and after birth. The lengthy pressure of an unusually slow delivery, the rapid changes in pressure resulting from an excessively rapid delivery, or even the strains of a normal delivery may produce traumatic injuries and rupture blood vessels in the brain. Bleeding within the brain is the most common outcome of such birth **trauma.** One baby in a thousand sustains some brain damage that will prevent the child's ever attaining the mental level of the average 12-year-old.

Injury and illness. The majority of all infants are stunned for a day or two, because of anesthetic effects and pressure on the brain in the birth canal, but ordinarily sustain no permanent damage. Prematurely born infants, those weighing less than 5½ pounds at birth, are more vulnerable to damage than full-term infants. Because their skulls are not fully formed, they are unusually susceptible to injury.

One in five newborns experiences some abnormality or sickness in the hospital after delivery. One in 14 infants weighs 5½ pounds or less; and a quarter of those weighing under 3½ pounds die. Those who survive often suffer abnormalities (U.S. Department of Health, Education and Welfare, 1976). Some nations with fewer resources than the United States have a better record of infant survival (United Nations, 1976).

Special problems arise in the case of teenage mothers, recently an increasing phenomenon. Between the years 1960 and 1974 the number of 16- and 17-year-old mothers in the United States rose by 23%. Births to mothers aged 15 and younger rose by 75%, from 26,000 a year to 46,000 a year. Such mothers are particularly vulnerable because of their physiological immaturity, economic dependency, lack of education, and frequently poor level of nutrition (Stickle, 1977).

Type of birth. Births are of several basic types. The natural, or spontaneous, one allows passage through the birth canal in a head-first position. A breech birth occurs when the buttocks come first, then the legs, and finally the head. In such cases, if the baby is large or the position very awkward, instruments may be necessary. If complications ensue, birth is by **Caesarean section,** or surgical incision through the mother's abdominal wall and uterus.

Each type of birth has its particular hazards. Instrument birth relates to poor coordination, irritability, and hyperactivity, but not necessarily to intelligence. Rapid labor, of less than 2 hours' length, may force oxygen on the infant too abruptly. And unduly prolonged births may result in deprivation of oxygen and degeneration of brain cells. Caesarean-section deliveries increased by 95% in the years 1971 to 1976, accounting for about 20% of all births. Presumably, the aim was mainly to prevent fetal distress. A Caesarean section is a major operation, with half the mothers involved experiencing postoperative complications. A woman's risk of fatality is 5 to 26 times greater from Caesarean than from vaginal delivery. Doctors often resort to it on the merest suggestion of irregularity from fetal monitoring.

Most doctors also oppose home birth, although the infant mortality rate in the United States is twice that in the Netherlands, where, until recently, half the births occurred at home. In the United States home birth services have resulted in very low infant and maternal mortality rates (Corea, 1979).

Questionable obstetrics. In many hospitals, birth can be a stressful experience for a baby. The infant is rudely plucked from its warm, dark world into a brightly lighted, often air-conditioned room and slapped on the rear. The umbilical cord is cut as early as possible. The whole drama is designed for the convenience of the nurses and doctors and involves various questionable obstetric practices, including

heavy reliance on anesthetics which produce drugged babies prone to respiratory distress and apathetic response at birth, the use of instruments which risk brain damage and newborn trauma, obstetric insistence on horizontal delivery tables which prolong second-stage labor because the body is not working with, but against gravity, foot stirrups which stretch the perineal tissue so that physicians feel justified in performing routine **episiotomies**

HUMAN BEGINNINGS

39

[emphasis added] . . . premature cutting of the umbilical cord which robs the newborn of up to a quarter of its blood supply and prolongs the third stage of labor . . . and, perhaps most important from a psychological perspective, the use of general anesthesia which cheats the mother of consciousness at the moment of birth, at precisely the moment when hormonal levels and the euphoria of accomplishment could contribute to a positive experience for the woman and a deep attachment between mother and child [Rossi, 1977, p. 19].*

Traditionally, physicians have complacently believed that the adverse effects on infants of obstetric medication to mothers was transitory. But Yvonne Brackbill reported that they persist in many cases for years. For the period studied, up to 7 years from birth, the negative effects of a few drugs increase. But for others, especially inhalants, the effects continue unabated on mental and motor development. Yet drugs are administered to mothers almost universally, without the women's knowledge of their potential effects. Brackbill advises that mothers be allowed to make a choice after being informed of the risks (Heneg, 1978).

A controversial method. A French physician, Frederick Leboyer, has received much publicity for his technique to take the stress out of delivery. The delivery rooms are softly lighted, and warm, soft music accompanies labor. Newborns are massaged and gently placed in bath water of the same temperature as the amniotic fluid they have just left. And the umbilical cord is not cut until after it stops throbbing. Thus, the baby is eased, instead of rudely ejected, into the world.

Under the auspices of the French Science Research Council, psychologist Danielle Rapoport performed a follow-up study of 120 1-, 2-, and 3-year-olds delivered by the **Leboyer technique** and a similar number delivered in traditional ways. On the average the two groups began talking at the same age. But the Leboyer children walked earlier (13 months compared with 15 months), and they performed better on tests of psychomotor functioning. The Leboyer children's emotional and social superiority was even more impressive, and only eight had even minor feeding and toileting problems. The results could not be ascribed to any extensive preparation or pretraining of the mothers. Indeed, only a third learned of the method during prenatal hospital visits; the remainder had it explained to them during labor (Horn, J., 1977).

Other suggestions. Many critics insist that the conditions of birth could be vastly improved. Doris Hare, president of the American Foundation of Maternal and Child Health, has criticized the forcing of labor, which may result in the death of the infant or brain damage because of oxygen depletion. In addition, the mother may experience a difficult birth, hemorrhage, or uterine rupture. Mothers are also required to maintain a reclining position during delivery instead

*From "A Biosocial Perspective on Parenting," by A. S. Rossi. In *Daedalus*, 1977, *106*(2), 1–32. This and all other quotations from this source are reprinted by permission.

of the more natural, less difficult semisitting position. When forceps are used, as is common, infants may experience intercranial hemorrhage and damage to the facial nerves (Bahr, 1975).

Natural childbirth. In recent years there has been a revived interest in natural childbirth. Doering and Entwisle (1975) reported that women trained in natural-childbirth techniques were more aware of delivery and had experienced childbirth more successfully than women who were anesthetized. Many of the women enjoyed the pushing part of labor, declaring it wonderful or even referring to it as birth orgasm. Women numbed by anesthesia who felt nothing below the waist reported that they had felt detached and that they had been delivered rather than having delivered the baby themselves.

The 1st Day of Life

Research into the 1st day of life is in its own infancy. It is already reasonably safe to assume that parents should have more body and other contact with the new arrival than they are now allowed time for, from the very 1st hour of life (Spezzazo & Waterman, 1977). Babies given to their mothers for an hour during the first 2 hours after birth and 5 extra hours on each of the next three days were compared with those accorded the standard treatment—a short look after birth and about half an hour every 4 hours during feeding. Differences were found in the two groups when they were studied several years later. At the age of 5, children of the extended-contact mothers had higher IQs and language scores (Kennell & Klaus, 1976).

INFANCY

Cognitive Development

A changing view. Birth is the threshold to infancy, the developmental stage when the baby cannot walk or talk or feed itself and is almost wholly dependent on the mother. Most infants are a pretty hardy lot and manage to complete their journey relatively unscathed. In the months that follow they are more competent than was once believed. With regard to their initial comprehension of the world, William James (1842–1910) described it as "one great, blooming, buzzing confusion" (1890, p. 3). But this point of view has changed dramatically. Clearly, the

evidence contradicts the old view of the very young child as an unresponsive vegetable that looks like every other member of the species at that age—an organism that can do nothing except breathe and eat. The new baby learns much the same way an adult learns, from the very first day of his life (Lipsitt, 1971, p. 71).

In fact, cognitive development may not begin at birth. Prenatal life undoubtedly involves conditions and experiences that indirectly modify postnatal cognitive development. At birth the lower noncortical brain centers are well developed, though higher (cortical) ones do not function well for several months. After the noncortical state comes a transitional stage, followed by the cortical stage, in which the cortex is dominant. Thus the infant passes from simple awareness to awareness plus meaning—in other words, to perception. Experience is the **catalyst** [emphasis added] by which the infant ultimately attaches significance to stimuli.

The sensory-response system [in particular] is quite sophisticated even at birth. The neonate is fairly sensitive to touch and temperature. It is more difficult to draw firm conclusions about smell and taste, because physical responses relating to these senses cannot accurately be measured. It was originally thought that infants could smell such substances as ammonia, but now it is believed that they simply react to an irritating quality without perceiving it as a distinct odor. With regard to taste, infants react first to sweetness, only later distinguishing salt, sour, and bitter tastes [Rogers, 1977a, pp. 159–160].

With regard to perception, attention, and conceptualization, humans, like lower animals, have more innately programmed processes than formerly believed. From birth on, however, these innate mechanisms interact with experience throughout the child's total development (Jersild, Telford, & Sawrey, 1975).

Sensory perception. Until fairly recently, opinion about the infant's visual experience was largely speculative. But in the past several years significant data and conclusions have emerged. Newborns' vision is much poorer than adults', and they see fairly well only through the center of the eye. The entire field of view is perhaps a third of an adult's, and they see well only a foot or so in front of their faces. Their lenses are fixed in focus for approximately a month and cannot adapt to varied distances. By 4 months of age, however, their eyes focus normally. And at this age their visual acuity almost equals that of most adults. Even from birth, infants respond selectively to elements of form such as circularity and angularity (Bond, 1972). They also prefer patterns to plain surfaces, and they can discriminate between two- and three-dimensional objects. By the age of 2 months they prefer pictures of a regular face to those with scrambled features, and by 4 months this preference is quite clear.

Not until infants are 2 months old can they discriminate shapes or features or faces. While babies younger than that can see their parents distinctly, the parents appear about the same in size, contrast, and brightness. They are unaware of such details as mouths, eyes, and noses. Thus, "relying on sight alone, a baby less than two months old probably can't tell his mother from his father, nor his sister from the family dog" (Maurer & Maurer, 1976, p. 88). Nevertheless, infants comprehend their surroundings better than these factors would suggest, because they, like adults, use various cues to assist their vision. For example, when a checkerboard grows larger and becomes more clearly focused, they come to understand that it is moving toward them.

"Not only do all normal neonates respond selectively to their environment; they also manifest highly individual modes of response; and they differ in excitability when subject to stress, as indicated by body movement, heart rate, and cries" (Rogers, 1977a, p. 160). In describing specific infants, Brown (1964) portrayed Felicia as quite interactive with her environment, in contrast to Dorothy, who was quite passive. Felicia, who was moderately placid, also differed from Charles, who was tense and active.

Can babies think? Infants are now viewed as somewhat more precocious than was previously thought (Lipsitt, 1977). Indeed, it seems that thought processes are present from birth. With a built-in response repertoire, newborns, instead of waiting for the bottle to touch their mouth, open up when the bottle or nipple approaches. Or the baby will turn its head in the proper direction when placed in the usual feeding position (Zimbardo, 1979). While some psychologists might wish to call these anticipatory gestures genuine thought, they would have trouble designating the exact stage in the development of learning when the onset of thinking occurs. It is "more meaningful to speak of increasing levels of symbolization" (Zimbardo, 1979, p. 255).

Various developmental theorists have postulated stages of cognitive development. Piaget has spoken of developmental transitions that lead to successively higher-level symbolization. In the 1st month the infant's behavior is largely reflexive. From the 2nd to the 4th month, in the stage of primary circular reactions, the infant has a tendency to persist in whatever is especially pleasant or fascinating. After the finger finds the mouth and the mouth sucks the finger, the infant finds it pleasant and leaves it there. In the third infantile stage, of secondary circular reaction, the baby seems to try to make things happen. In this period, from about 4 to 8 months, a certain appreciation of causation appears. If the baby shakes the side of the crib and it rattles, it might tip the crib to make it rattle more.

From age 8 months to 1 year, the stage of coordination of secondary schemes, infants become aware of object permanence and appreciate that, even if an object has gone from view, it still exists. And the infant may search for something that is not in its customary place. In the next stage, of **tertiary** circular reactions—a period of trial-and-error behavior akin to reasoning—the infant explores things and looks at them from various angles. It appears to appreciate that an object is the same even though it looks different from different angles.

Already in the first half of the 2nd year children may also demonstrate "a sense of the symbolic," a competence quite evident when they play with toys (Kagan, 1977, p. 34). At this stage, but not 6 months before, a child may pretend that a piece of clay is a cookie or pour imaginary tea from a small teapot into tiny cups. This newly acquired ability, soon enhanced by language, induces children to apply symbolic labels. Indeed, it is as natural for children as for adults to group similar objects and events into categories. As early as 1 year some children treat toys, foods, shapes, sizes, and colors as belonging to "discrete conceptual categories" (Ross, cited in Kagan, 1977, p. 35).

This child enjoys giving tea parties for her dolls.

Infants differ in the degree to which they focus on objects. For some children, object words make up 80% of their early vocabulary; for others, the proportion is a mere 30%. The object-oriented youngsters may later have academic difficulties in a society that emphasizes verbal understanding. Such children can be helped by relating their nonverbal concepts to language-oriented approaches (Horn, J., 1976b).

Conclusions about overall infant competency. Kassen and Nelson reject the common assumption that infants interpret the world in the same way adults do, though less intelligently. Three words consistently among a baby's first vocabulary are *ball, dog,* and *car,* all dynamic objects that are either self-propelled or moved by the child. Apparently, motion is more important than shapes or color in helping infants organize their environment. Infants analyze their world in terms of what is movable, eatable, or touchable. Yet concepts in their cognitive system, such as "rollability" and "bounceability," do not exist even in adults' functional language system. Even very young infants have a surprisingly well-organized view of their environment that does not require language for comprehension (Horn, J., 1976b).

Lewis (1978) concluded that infants are far more competent than commonly believed. He declared that three major concepts—self-gender, age, and competency—develop early. Infants also gain, in the first months of life, a vast store of information about their world. By 12 weeks of age infants realize whether the mother is talking to them or someone else. At 3 months infants recognize objects as unfamiliar and demonstrate a fear of strangers. By 6 months they show less fear when approached by other children than when approached by adults. Between 9 and 12 months, babies demonstrate some sense of self, and by 18 months they label themselves, saying "baby." Overall, "An infant is far from a mass of confusion. He is a highly sophisticated processor of information" (Lewis, 1978, p. 56).

Such observations should not obscure the wide variations in acquiring competencies that exist within the normal range. All too often, parents who have been told or have read about what to expect of infants fail to realize that such variations are average (Segal & Yahraes, 1978). For example, some infants sleep 10 hours a day, others 23 hours. And some perfectly normal children walk or talk later than others. Parents depend mainly on physicians for advice regarding their children's physical handicaps, yet methods that physicians use to assess infants' mental status has changed little over the past two decades (Kearsley, 1981).

Significance of Infancy

Research underscores the significance of infancy for the years that lie ahead. With regard to personality, an individual who in early years has been inconsistently cared for and loved may feel chronic distrust of others, emotional deprivation, or an incapacity in personal relationships (Shenker & Schildkrout, 1975). Data on the peer relations of 35 boys and 27 girls obtained at age 2½ and again at 7½ indicate sociability to be a quite persistent characteristic. It is also during infancy that the basic foundations of social behavior are laid. In the main, parents begin socializing their babies during the 2nd year. Before that time they have merely played with, fed, and diapered the child. Now they set out to civilize their little savage.

Despite such evidence, a large and growing body of data refutes the traditional view that whatever characteristics the infant develops are difficult if not impossible to change. As we shall see in the next chapter, dramatic changes may follow correspondingly large modifications in the environment.

Attachment

Definition and Significance. I will now move to infants' social, as opposed to cognitive, development. Their first personal relationships take the form of attachments. Attachment refers to affectional bonds between one individual and another. It involves "a range of behaviors exhibited by individuals in a mutually enforcing relationship" (Appoloni & Cooke, 1975, pp. 11–12). The object of one's attachment attains a special psychological significance, for which other individuals cannot easily substitute. Such attachment appears at around 4 to 6 months of age, and even in the 1st month a strong bond develops. The earlier the mother touches the newborn, and the longer is that contact, the firmer is the bond at the end of the 1st month (Klaus, Jerauld, Kreger et al., 1972). Conversely, separation of the mother and infant at birth impairs their relationship and the infant's subsequent development. A longitudinal study of infants from ages 12 to 21 months indicated that those securely attached to the mother at 12 months were significantly more cooperative than were nonsecurely attached children at 21 months (Londerville & Main, 1981).

Some authorities recommend breast feeding, as much for psychological as nutritional reasons. Newton and Modahl (1978) contended that this process proves mutually satisfying and beneficial for mother and infant. The baby's suckling produces sensations that proceed to the mother's pituitary gland, thereby releasing oxytoxin. This substance, in turn, produces contractions in the mother's uterus that help it to resume normal dimensions. The hormone also causes "the grapelike alveoli in the breast, which hold milk, to contract, letting down milk for the baby" (p. 49).

Attachment is believed to be significant partly because it helps infants to feel that their world is secure and comfortable. Cuddling, in particular, stimulates a baby's neurological development, and the lack of such stimulation may intensify any disabilities of premature babies. In one project, psychologist Ruth Rice experimented with 15 premature infants who had just been released from the hospital. The mothers were taught how to provide massaging, stroking, and rocking treatments to stimulate nerve pathways. This treatment was provided four times each day, 15 minutes at a time, for a month. After 4 months, those that had received "touching" treatment had made greater physical and neurological advances than a control group of 15 premature babies not treated this way. The treated infants made higher mental scores, gained more weight, and, more significantly, had greater neurological development (Marcus, 1976).

The infant/caretaker relationship is also portrayed as the foundation for future social relationships. If infants find their contacts with their caretakers satisfying, they more easily establish a basic trust in others (Goldberg, 1977). In play situations securely attached children proved more sociable and positively oriented toward the mother and same-sex peers than did nonattached children (Pastor, 1981). However, the nature of the developmental continuity is not clear (Ainsworth, Bell, & Stayton, 1974). In a study of face-to-face interaction between 26 infants and their mothers, those infants subsequently identified as securely attached were more responsive than infants classified as anxiously attached, and their mothers were more responsive and encouraging of interaction. Later on, the anxiously attached children actively avoided their mothers upon reunion after a brief separation, while the securely attached indicated no ambivalent or avoidant behavior (Bieler, Lieberman, & Ainsworth, 1977).

Rossi (1977) insisted that human infants need bonding to the mother more than do the young of other species, because of their immaturity at birth. In consequence, it is critical for the survival of the human species that infant care be prolonged through an intense relationship between mother and infant. Otherwise, the infant may be neglected. Except under rare circumstances, every known society has employed the mother as the chief caretaker. Indeed, throughout most of human history infants have had close physical contact with their mother, ordinarily about 70% of the day in infancy, decreasing to about 30% in the middle of the second year. Infants today experience a life unknown before, including little touching with their mothers, feeding, being left often in the care of comparative strangers, and sleeping in separate rooms from their parents. They have contact with other humans less than 25% of the day, even in the weeks immediately after birth. This figure soon declines to about 5%, apparently because of the trend away from breast feeding. Lee and DeVore (1976) contend that this trend, as well as the broader deprivation of sensual physical contact with the mother, explains the high frequency of thumb-sucking among infants in the United States and the high level of orality among adults.

Factors influencing attachment. The relative impact of forces determining attachment is uncertain. There is little information about how extremely high hormonal levels during pregnancy contribute to attachment behaviors, especially when women do not touch their babies during the hours after birth when such levels are still high. **Estrogen** levels increase 10-fold in pregnancy and **progesterone** 100-fold, but the effects on maternal behaviors have not been adequately researched (Moltz, Lubin, Leon, & Numan, 1970).

More often, early reciprocal relationships between caretakers and infants are viewed as influenced by mutual encouragement. In other words, to the degree that infants and caretakers find such interaction satisfying and productive of their own feelings of competence and well-being, such interaction is encouraged. However, some babies seem naturally to afford more satisfaction than others. Some of them are cute and easy to cuddle. Others may appear sickly and boney. Some infants respond readily to cuddling; others reject cuddling even when they are tired or ill. Also significant is the compatibility of mother and infant. A calm energetic mother might cope easily with a wiggly, headstrong infant. The same child might be the despair of a nervous mother with low vitality. The sickly child who would strike a note of deep sympathy in one mother might be a source of annoyance, even repulsion, in another. Thus, bonding proceeds more quickly and smoothly if the newborn is not too severe a disappointment to the parent. Young adults have their own ideals of what sort of infants they desire; for example, consider these young women's statements:

> I'd like one with a spirit of its own. I wouldn't mind its crying if it weren't a sickly thing. Of course, you get what you get, and then it's up to you.

> I want a decent-looking baby formed with all parts in good condition. An ugly baby would have a hard time growing up. However, I'd love the baby as much as if it were perfect, even if it wasn't.

> I want my baby to weigh seven or eight pounds, and to be happy, seldom crying, and always smiling and gurgling. I want him to be a fast learner (early in walking, talking, and toilet training) [Rogers, 1977a, p. 327].

Mothers versus others as attachment figures. The concept of attachment in infants has been largely limited to the mother/infant relationship. A more viable concept, the social-network approach, takes into account the infant's dealings with other family members as well as strangers (Weintraub, Brooks, & Lewis,

1977). Fathers, especially, may become important figures of attachment. Evidence from cross-cultural, historical, comparative, and biological sources shows that fathers can play an active role in infant development. Observations of newborns show that fathers are as interested, involved, and **nurturant** as mothers. True, mothers spend more time than fathers in caretaking, but fathers and mothers do not differ in caretaking competence as indicated by sensitivity to infant cues in the feeding situation (Parke & Sawin, 1976).

In other research (Lamb, 1977), observations of 20 infants interacting with their parents at ages 7, 8, 12, and 13 months indicated no preference for either parent, even though the parents played somewhat different roles. The infants responded more positively to playing with their fathers, although both parents initiated similar types of play. Mothers held the infants more during caretaking functions, and fathers more often held them while playing. Lamb concluded that parents have different influences on their children's personality development and that mothers should not be considered the only significant influence on the infants' social and personal development. Children become attached to more than one caretaker and develop a "hierarchy of preferences" that relates more to the quality of interaction than to its duration (Kagan, 1977, p. 36).

The parents, whether father or mother, concludes Kagan (1977), are the most important objects of attachment. He refers to the "mysterious ability" of biological parents in Western nuclear families to remain the preferred adults of attachment even when the children spend considerable time with substitute caretaking adults outside the home. Belsky (1981) warns that it is "no longer acceptable to focus narrowly on parent-infant interaction" (p. 19). Rather, a child's experience must be viewed from the perspective of the total family system. Moreover, the family itself should be examined within the wider ecology in which it is rooted.

Separation anxiety. Any major interruption of parent/child association, such as day care or the mother's working, is commonly viewed as traumatic and a source of separation anxiety. Infants deprived of mothering may become depressed, and those separated from their mothers often exhibit protest and despair (Reite, Short, Seile, & Pauley, 1981). In one study (Kagan, Kearsley, Zellazo, & Minton, 1976), children who had attended a day-care center in Boston for five days a week, from age 3½ months through 30 months, were matched with children being reared at home. When the children were about 20 months old, they were put in an unfamiliar setting with the mother, an unfamiliar woman, and a third person. For the children reared at home, it was a family friend; for the others it was their day-care teacher. During the 45 minutes they were observed, all the children sought the mother for comfort when they were tired or apprehensive. There were no significant differences between the behaviors of the children reared at home and those attending the center.

Once the mother/child bond is established, young children may become disturbed when separated from their mothers.

[For example, for an intelligence test] Timmy [aged 3] was brought by his mother. He began sobbing, "I want Mamma!" the moment his mother left and kept this up for nine minutes in the playroom. He then gradually subsided but kept worriedly questioning the observer, "Mamma come back soon? After num-num (dinner) Mamma come back?" or attempting to bolster up his courage by saying, "No Timmy c'y" (apparently meaning to convey the thought "Timmy will not cry"). But his voice continued to tremble, and his brow never lost its pucker [Murphy, 1962, pp. 48–49].

Researchers report little if any difference in the attachment established between mother and child whether the child goes to a day-care center, remains at home with the mother, or remains at home with a baby-sitter while the mother works (Bronfenbrenner, 1976). Nor do the data suggest that whether or not mothers work when their children are young relates to any later difficulties they may develop. Mental health problems apparently relate to various difficulties between children and parents and not to the maternal employment status. If a mother likes what she is doing, whether at home or at work, children are likely to benefit (Hoffman & Nye, 1974). In other words, "Day care is not the beginning of the end for close family ties. Eighteen months is about the time when children first have nightmares, whether their mothers work or not" (Woolsey, 1977, p. 142).

A footnote. More definitive answers about attachment, observes Rossi (1977), must await better research. To date, in their blending of maternal and infant behavior, researchers have manifested an "exclusive environmentalism" and a neglect of biological factors. In addition, they have focused on the influence of the mother on the child, while overlooking the influence of the child on the mother. The only valid way to study such influences is to consider the interaction of each on the other.

Attachment should also be viewed in relation to detachment, or becoming weaned from the loved object. Both processes proceed throughout the life span. The infant becomes firmly attached to the mother, then to some extent detached in early childhood through peer play and school attendance. A Connecticut psychiatrist, Paul Horton, has contended that children's blankets and stuffed toys constitute transitional attachment objects, helping the child to move from the limited world of the mother to the larger society ("Childhood Attachments," 1979). The attachment to mother persists, though less strongly, until the detachment imposed by her death. At any age death may not produce in one a complete detachment, in the sense that an individual feels watched over and guided by the ideals of the deceased.

Too often, life-span processes, such as attachment, have been viewed mainly in terms of one life stage when only life-span treatment would place them in proper perspective. What varying difference does it make in the long run whether, or how much, an infant attaches to the mother? Will one or more mother surrogates serve as well? How do the functions and dimensions of attachment/detachment behaviors vary across the life span? (Knudsen, 1976). In such terms is infancy, when first attachments are formed, the converse of late old age, when detachments pave the way for the ultimate detachment of death?

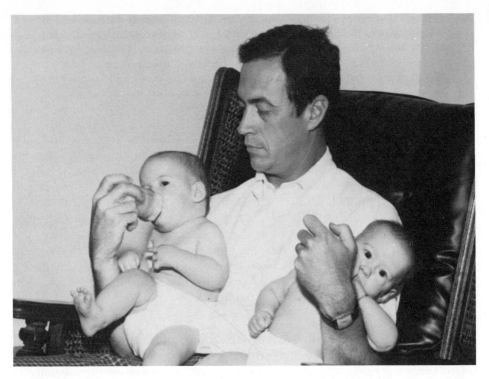

Dads sometimes prefer to let moms to the feeding. The dad here is certainly competent in this role.

A Broader Perspective on Infant Social Relationships

The interpretation of infants' personal relationships is just recently changing in several ways. First, the parent/infant relationship is no longer portrayed as the only important one. Second, as observed earlier, psychologists have ceased to view the infant as "a passive blob, confronted with the task of making sense out of sensory chaos". Now they portray it as "active, capable of organizing complex information, selectively attentive, and capable of rapid learning" (Goldberg, 1977, p. 163). Nevertheless, the view of the infant as competent though immature has been chiefly related to perceptual and **cognitive** skills. Meantime, concepts of infants' social development continue to conform to the "passive-blob" model. While tentative steps have been taken in this area, recognition of infants' social competence is still limited.

The infant's initial concepts of self and other. Recent research yields clues to how infants become conscious of themselves and others. After babies aged 9, 12, 15, 18, 21, and 24 months were placed in front of a mirror, their mothers, in wiping their noses, left red dye on them. When the infants were again placed before the mirrors, there was a clearly defined developmental pattern. The older ones were more likely to touch their noses, indicating that they recognized themselves in the mirror. Only a few infants younger than 12 months responded, compared with 25% of the 15- and 18-month-olds and 88% of the 2-year-olds.

In another study, babies were shown pictures of their mothers, a strange man and woman, strange boys and girls about 5 years old, unfamiliar boy and girl infants, and themselves. The researchers observed how long the babies looked at the slides and how much they smiled. Each time a slide was shown they were asked who it was. While the infants devoted no more time looking at their own pictures than at those of others, the girls looked more at pictures of girl than of boy babies. They also cooed and smiled more at slides of their sex, indicating that a sense of gender emerges along with the concept of self. By the age of 18 months some of the children could label themselves in the slides, saying "baby," and by 22 months they used words such as *me* and *mine*. Babies begin very early to imitate others. Children are twice as likely to imitate audio tapes of themselves as those of unfamiliar babies, and by 1 year this imitation is pronounced.

As early as 9 months, infants apparently recognize their own images in mirrors by waving and fluttering their fingers. They react more to tapes of themselves than to those of strangers. Thus, an infant "at an extremely early young age knows something of who he is and what he can do" (Lewis, 1978, p. 56).

In general, infants are now believed to develop self-awareness during their 1st year and to see themselves as causing events to happen. In addition, various infant competencies suggest that they sense themselves as persons. For one thing, they can tell strangers from parents and children from adults. Babies also learn very early how to control their mother's behavior. For instance,

A baby and his mother look at each other. The baby turns away so the mother looks away. The baby turns back and sees he has lost his mother's gaze. He starts fussing and whimpering and his mother again looks at him. [Thus], babies quickly develop elaborate means of getting and holding their mother's attention" [Lewis, 1977, p. 54].

As early as 3 months of age infants can tell which objects and persons are unfamiliar. They are less fearful when approached by strange children than by strange adults. In order to determine how they make such distinctions, whether their cue is height or facial features, Lewis and his colleagues used midgets. If the infants demonstrated fear of a midget, the face and not height would seem to be their cue. If they seemed to be happy, the cue would seem to be height. To the researchers' amazement the babies seemed neither fearful nor happy but merely surprised, indicating that the midget had "violated" what they had come to expect in normal persons. That is, "The wrong face was on the wrong body" (p. 54).

The infant's own social role. Another development, as suggested earlier, is that infants importantly affect the patterning of their interactions with others. Further, their own constitutional characteristics affect adults, thus modifying the bases of their future socialization and development (Lamb, 1977). It is true that parents still have a larger socializing influence on children than the reverse, partly because parents' behaviors are less malleable and partly because they are more powerful and mature. However, we must acknowledge the infant as actively participating in its own upbringing. The infant experiences significant and qualitatively distinctive relationships with each parent and with **siblings,** all of whom have their special influences on its development.

Meantime, all the individuals in the infant's social world are continually interacting with one another, and the effect of this influence, in turn, impinges on the child. Thus, the quality of the parents' interaction with the child depends somewhat on their relationship with each other. And a sibling may respond more positively to a newborn if the parents have taken measures to prevent sibling rivalry. In short, as Lamb has observed, an understanding of the processes of personal and social development requires an appreciation of "both the depth of infant social competence and the multifaceted complexity of the environment into which the child is integrated" (Lamb, 1977, p. 77).

SUMMARY

Developmental life histories inevitably begin with a consideration of genetic origins and how heredity blends with experience. Parents may seek genetic counseling to find out whether their fetus has an appropriate hereditary endowment, or whether it should be born at all.

Life itself begins with fertilization, when the sperm unites with the ovum in the upper fallopian tube. The period from this instant until birth involves three stages: the ovum-zygote stage from fertilization until the end of the 2nd week; the embryo stage from the 3rd week through the 2nd month, and the fetal stage from the 3rd month until birth. The fetus is protected against external hazards by the placenta, which lets nutrients reach it while excluding most noxious substances. However, it may be negatively affected by such factors as the mother's nutrition, smoking, drinking, and emotional state. Conditions of birth, too, may prove hazardous.

Nevertheless, most infants not only survive but also begin to comprehend and cope with their world earlier than once believed. Their sensory/response system is quite sophisticated even at birth, though their visual images are initially somewhat fuzzy. By the 2nd year a sense of the symbolic can be demonstrated.

The first 2 years, infancy, are critical for later development. The infant forms attachments, or affectional ties, that constitute a basis for future relationships. While the infant's most important attachment object is ordinarily the mother, all family members are significant, in varying degree. But infants are no mere sponges, passively soaking up whatever influences impinge upon them. They interact with and influence their caretakers in ways that modify reactions toward them.

Infants are not only more cognitively developed but also more socially advanced than formerly recognized. By the end of the 1st year they can relate images in the mirror to themselves and have already attained some sense of themselves as persons. They can distinguish children from adults and familiar persons from strangers. Meantime, they sense and respond to a complex material and social environment, including qualitatively distinctive relationships with different family members.

SUGGESTED READINGS

Bayles, M. D. Harm to the unconceived. *Philosophy and Public Affairs*, 1976, 5(3), 292–304. Explores the right to be conceived and standards for whether conceptions should occur. The question arises whether laws should prevent the birth of those who might never achieve a decent quality of life.

Belsky, J. Early human experience: A family perspective. *Developmental Psychology*, 1981, 17(1), 3–23. A study of family relationships shows how infants and parents affect each other, as well as the impact of the arrival of the infant on marital relations.

Blakemore, J. E. O. Age and sex differences in interaction with a human infant. *Child Development*, 1981, 52, 386–388. A study of reactions toward infants indicated significant differences according to both sex and age.

Brown, J. V., et al. Interactions of Black inner-city mothers with their newborn infants. *Child Development*, 1975, 46(3), 677–686. Observations indicate that the infants' behaviors and mother/infant interactions were modified by such factors as birth weights, birth order, sex, and maternal medication.

Caldwell, J. The placental transfer of drugs during childbirth: A possible influence on the newborn. *Journal of Psychosomatic Research*, 1976, 20(4), 267–271. The effects on the child of analgesic drugs used during childbirth are analyzed. The emphasis is on direct effects on the baby, as well as indirect ones arising from changes in the mother's physiology.

Clarke-Stewart, K. A., & Hevey, C. M. Longitudinal relations in repeated observations of mother-child interaction from 1 to 2½ years. *Developmental Psychology*, 1981, 17(2), 127–145. In a longitudinal study of parents and their young children over a period of 12 to 30 months, interactions were analyzed to show developmental continuity or change and individual stability over time.

Dinnage, R. Understanding loss: The Bowlby canon. *Psychology Today*, 1980, 13(12), 56–60. John Bowlby's important contributions to developmental psychology are described and appraised. In the first book of a trilogy, Bowlby dealt with attachment as a basic human drive; in the second, with the crippling effects of separation. In this latest work he focuses on the long-range effects of separation, especially in cases of mourning and bereavement, in both adults and children.

Egeland, B., & Vaughn, B. Failure of "bond formation" as a cause of abuse, neglect, and maltreatment. *American Journal of Orthopsychiatry*, 1981, 51(1), 78–84. A longitudinal study of high-risk mothers indicated that limited contact with the newborn at birth does not relate to later disorders of mothering. Nor did certain indices of bonding failure occur with greater frequency among child-abusing mothers than those providing adequate care.

Elardo, R., Bradley, R., & Caldwell, B. M. A longitudinal study of the relation of infants' home environments to language development at age three. *Child Development*, 1977, 48, 495–503. A study of infants' home environments at ages 6 and 24 months and later at 3 years of age indicates that it is possible to relate early experience to language development. Relationships differed somewhat depending on the sex and race of the child.

Goldsmith, H. H., & Gottesman, I. I. Origins of variation in behavioral style: A longitudinal study of temperament in young twins. *Child Development*, 1981, *52*, 91–103. A longitudinal study of identical and fraternal twins helps to unravel relative effect of genetics and familial influences on behavioral style and temperament.

Goldstein, K. M., Caputo, D. V., & Taub, H. B. The effects of prenatal and perinatal complications on development at one year of age. *Child Development*, 1976, *47*(3), 613–621. Presents a factor analysis of 35 variables descriptive of birth and obstetric complications, prematurity, maternal discomfort, and demographic status. Seven major factors predictive of developmental status at 1 year of age were found.

Jacobs, B. S., & Moss, H. A. Birth order and sex of sibling as determinants of mother-infant interaction. *Child Development*, 1976, *47*(2), 315–322. Data were collected during naturalistic home observations, involving mother/infant interaction and relating to first- and second-born siblings when each was 3 months old. The results suggest that such interaction varied according to the infants' birth order and gender. Interactions between the mothers and their younger infants related to attention-seeking behavior in first-born male and female siblings.

Kearsley, R. B. Cognitive assessment of the handicapped infant: The need for an alternative approach. *American Journal of Orthopsychiatry*, 1981, *51*(1), 43–54. After reviewing current clinical practices in the area of assessment of handicapped infants, the author suggests an alternative approach.

Lamb, M. E. Father-infant and mother-infant interaction in the first year of life. *Child Development*, 1977, *48*(1), 167–181. Twenty infants were observed interacting with their parents at home when they were 7, 8, 12, and 13 months of age. Data were obtained regarding the infants' attachment behavior to their parents and differential attitudes toward each parent, as well as differences in the parents' treatment of an infant.

Lamb, M. E. A re-examination of the infant social world. *Human Development*, 1977, *20*(2), 65–85. A review of the literature suggests that a traditional view of two-person interaction in infant development obscures infants' own participation and their interaction with fathers, siblings, and peers. Progress in understanding children's personal and social development will depend on acknowledging the confidence of infants and the broad dimensions of their social world.

Londerville, S., & Main, M. Security of attachment, compliance, and maternal training methods in the second year of life. *Developmental Psychology*, 1981, *17*(3), 289–299. A longitudinal study of 36 children (in their second year) and their mothers indicated that the child's compliance and cooperation with others related positively to the mother's warmth and gentler physical interventions.

Macfarlane, A. *The psychology of childbirth*. Cambridge, Mass.: Harvard University Press, 1977. A pediatrician summarizes much of the recent research relating to birth and the neonate and discusses such issues as home delivery, induced labor, and bottle versus breast feeding.

McAuliffe, K., & McAuliffe, S. The Gene trust. *Omni*, March 1980, 62–66; 120–122. Examines feats of genetic engineering and anticipated developments in the field of biotechnology, which appear to hold considerable significance for life in decades ahead.

McDevitt, S. C., & Carey, W. B. Stability of ratings vs. perceptions of temperament from early infancy to 1-3 years. *American Journal of Orthopsychiatry*, 1981, *51*(2), 342–345.

A study of the stability of individual differences from early infancy to 1 to 3 years of age disclosed significant correlations.

Meredith, H. V. Somatic changes during human prenatal life. *Child Development*, 1975, *46*(3), 603–610. Section 1 of this paper constitutes an overview of somatic changes that occur during the prenatal period. Section 2 describes the chronological pattern of anatomical modifications during this period from zygote to embryo and from embryo to fetus.

Parke, R. E., & Sawin, D. B. The father's role in infancy: A re-evaluation. *Family Coordinator*, 1976, *25*(4), 365–371. On the basis of cross-cultural, historical, comparative, and biological sources as well as direct observation, it appears that fathers are often as interested, involved, and nurturant as mothers. Although mothers spend more time than fathers in caretaking, parents do not differ in caretaking competence as indicated by sensitivity to infant cues in the feeding situation.

Pastor, D. L. The quality of mother-infant attachment and its relationship to toddlers' initial sociability with peers. *Developmental Psychology*, 1981, *17*(3), 326–335. A study of 37 same-sex, same-age toddler dyads observed between ages 20 and 30 months in play sessions with mothers present demonstrated the consequences of the mother-infant relationship for toddlers' initial sociability and social responsiveness with peers.

Plattner, S., & Minturn, L. A comparative and longitudinal study of the behavior of communally raised children. *Ethos*, 1975, *3*(4), 469–480. Five preschool children living in a commune near a farming community were compared with five others matched for age and sex from nuclear families living in a university community. The commune children proved to be less competitive, more self-reliant, and more cooperative. A year later, when the five commune subjects were attending a public kindergarten, they were still more self-reliant and achieving.

Plomin, R., & Rowe, D. C. A twin study of temperament in young children. *Journal of Psychology*, 1977, *97*(1), 107–113. An assessment of temperament in 91 pairs of twins whose average age was 3.6 years. Of the six traits measured, genetic factors were shown to be implicated in five (sociability, activity, soothability, emotionality, and attention-span persistence). One (reaction to food) reflected no genetic influence but a strong between-family environment effect.

Reite, M., Short, R., Seiler, C., & Pauley, J. D. Attachment, loss, and depression. *Journal of Child Psychology and Psychiatry*, 1981, *22*, 141–169. Research is reviewed regarding the effects on infants of disruption of the attachment bond between mother and infant among both higher primates and humans.

Richards, M. P., Dunn, J. F., & Antonis, B. Caretaking in the first year of life: The role of fathers, and mothers' social isolation. *Child Care, Health and Development*, 1977, *3*(1), 23–36. This follow-up study of children concerns their recollections about the nature and amount of their father's participation in child rearing. The children were also asked about certain of their mother's patterns of behavior toward them, including especially excursions away from home without them.

Shin, E. H. Economic and social correlates of infant mortality: A cross-sectional and longitudinal analysis of 63 selected countries. *Social Biology*, 1975, *22*(4), 315–325. On the basis of data from 63 countries over a 5-year period, an analysis is made of infant mortality and socioeconomic health variables. Comparisons are made between cross-sectional and longitudinal patterns and between developed and developing countries.

Stickle, G. The health of mothers and babies: How do we stack up? *Family Coordinator*,

1977, 26(3), 205–210. Principles and details relating to health conditions of infants and their mothers are presented, along with suggestions for improving the situation.

Sugarman, M. Paranatal influences on maternal-infant attachment. *American Journal of Orthopsychiatry*, 1977, 47(3), 407–421. The literature is reviewed regarding the effects on mother/infant attachment of events during pregnancy, birth, and the postpartum period. For the sake of the emotional well-being of mother and child, recommendations are made for modifying professional practice.

3
DEVELOPMENT IN CHILDHOOD: I

PHYSICAL DEVELOPMENT

Growth and Development

Key definitions. Childhood, like infancy, is a period of conspicuous growth and development. As I noted in Chapter 1, the term *development* suggests sequential and continuous change, both qualitative and quantitative, in functions or structures in any direction (Krech et al., 1974). While *growth* refers to inches and pounds, **development** is a complex process of integrating functions. Another basic term, *maturation,* can be defined as the chemical and anatomical changes in the body that transpire over time, over which an individual has little control. **Maturation** is the "master script writer," outlining the details of future growth. Particular body systems and organs must arrive at certain levels of maturation, or readiness, before they can support various functions. For instance, when the nerves leading from the bladder and rectum are not sufficiently developed, children cannot be conscious of the fullness of these organs and hence are not ready for toilet training.

Principles of growth. Authorities agree on the general principles of growth, one being that changes are relatively uniform, proceeding in some roughly predictable fashion. It can be expected that babies will sit before they walk, and most of them will walk before they talk. Further, the influences of growth are cumulative. Whatever changes occur—whether positive, negative, trivial, or traumatic—will leave residues in their wake. The significance of experience hinges more on their residual effect than on any immediate impact. Furthermore, although change varies in pace, it is continuous and mostly irreversible. Children grow rapidly from birth to age 3 and from ages 11 to 15. The pace slows down in the years in between, but at no time does growth stop. As I expressed it in an earlier text:

> [Note, too, that] "the child is not merely a miniature adult; rather he differs qualitatively and quantitatively from an adult in many of his physical characteristics and behavioral potentials" (Krech et al., 1974, p. 54). The child has a different skeletal structure, proportionately, a different nervous system, and a different hormone and biochemical makeup. These differences are sufficiently significant to forbid generalizing adult behaviors to behaviors of the child.

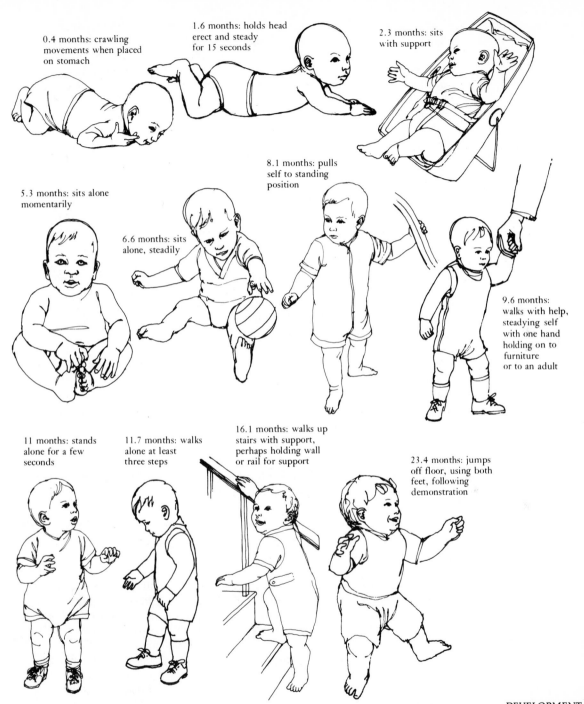

0.4 months: crawling movements when placed on stomach

1.6 months: holds head erect and steady for 15 seconds

2.3 months: sits with support

5.3 months: sits alone momentarily

6.6 months: sits alone, steadily

8.1 months: pulls self to standing position

9.6 months: walks with help, steadying self with one hand holding on to furniture or to an adult

11 months: stands alone for a few seconds

11.7 months: walks alone at least three steps

16.1 months: walks up stairs with support, perhaps holding wall or rail for support

23.4 months: jumps off floor, using both feet, following demonstration

Figure 3-1. Shirley's Developmental Sequences. Mary M. Shirley, The first two years, *vol. II, University of Minnesota Press, Minneapolis. Copyright © 1933 by the University of Minnesota. Reprinted by permission.*

We can get some clues very early about what script the child's growth may follow. **Apgar scores** [emphasis added] (heart rate, respiratory effort, color, muscle tone, and reflex irritability), plus physical growth data obtained at 24 and 36 months, are predictive of later physical growth and mental development (Jordan & Spaner, 1972). Moreover, such development will be gradual; true, "relatively abrupt upsurges and declines in both structure and function can be observed outwardly; but they are merely visible expressions of an actually continuous underlying developmental process. Genetic factors, for example, often must await the culmination of gradual maturational changes before they become expressed and observable" (Krech et al., 1974, p. 54).

Growth is also an integrated, unitary process; however, the various parts of the body have their own growth rates. For example, the head grows rapidly in fetal and infant life and at a diminishing rate during the next ten years, after which its growth all but ceases. By contrast, the sex organs change little during the first decade, but then they grow rapidly and continue to enlarge into late adolescence, even after growth in height has ceased. The heart takes even longer to mature, completing its growth at about age 20.

While a basic pattern undergirds each individual's growth, the various glands affecting that pattern play relatively different roles during childhood and adolescence. Before puberty, the thyroid and pituitary glands are primarily responsible for bone growth and skeletal aging; after puberty, the gonads assume that function [Rogers, 1977a, pp. 78–79].

Physical and motor growth have typically been described as steady, gradual processes; and as individuals develop, they become generally more proficient at various kinds of perceptual and motor tasks. Bower (1976) questioned this assumption, noting that development is somewhat irregular. An infant may have an ability, lose it for a period, and get it back at a later time. For example, newborns have a dramatic aptitude for imitation that demands a considerable degree of coordination between senses and muscles. Newborns can mimic adults who open their mouths or stick out their tongues. This ability soon after disappears and does not return until about the end of the 1st year.

The catch-up mechanism. One unusual phenomenon affecting physical development is the so-called **catch-up mechanism,** which contributes to growth's characteristic target seeking.

The catch-up mechanism is not fully understood yet, but some general assumptions have been made. During the catch-up period, the whole organism grows rapidly and in a proportionate manner; hence, the control probably resides in a central mechanism—perhaps the hypothalamus at the base of the brain (Tanner, 1963). Apparently, there is a time-tally mechanism that represents normal growth so that the organism "knows" when to stop the rapid velocity. This mechanism is significant for several reasons. For one thing, it allows genetically large children to develop in the uteri of small mothers. Since birth size is controlled almost entirely by uterine factors, genetically large children are born small. The catch-up mechanism usually enables them to reach their own growth curves within six months after birth [Rogers, 1977a, pp. 79–80].

Variations according to age, sex, and individual. Physical development varies with age. The rate of growth is most rapid during the prenatal period. The process of acceleration slows down in childhood, picks up at puberty, and slows down after puberty until adult height is reached. Then a relatively stable period ensues, until **senescence** produces a very small shrinkage in overall body size and height. Nevertheless, within this general picture there are large variations. Depending on age of puberty, maximum growth attained, and other factors, some girls reach adult height by age 14, whereas some boys do not reach theirs until 22 or 23 (Krech et al., 1974).

Physiologically, boys and girls differ much less in childhood than after puberty. With regard to most endocrinological and physiological functions, possibly excepting those relating to the pituitary gland, the sexes differ only slightly in early years. Nevertheless, small differences—for instance in skeletal development—exist even prenatally. Sex differences become more apparent around age 7, when girls experience an increase in estrogen function. The subcutaneous layer of fat develops, causing a slight feminine rounding; and by age 10 just a trace of breast growth may appear.

Physical development often varies more widely among individuals than between the sexes. Every individual has a characteristic body makeup and economy, so that body organs differ markedly in size and shape. Body builds also differ, as does the chemical composition of body substances (Williams, 1974). Each individual's saliva is probably as unique as his or her voice, appearance, or disposition. In addition, some people have unusual susceptibility to disease, while others have very strong resistance. The range of these differences, noted Krech, Crutchfield, and Livson (1974), is hardly ever appreciated. For example, "every individual person is endowed with a distinctive gastrointestinal tract . . . a distinctive nervous system, and a **morphologically** [emphasis added] distinctive brain. . . . Can it be that this fact is inconsequential in relation to the problem of personality differences" (p. 651)?

Individual differences make it necessary to reject definitive standards of growth, and while statistical norms are useful, their limitations must be recognized. The term *normality* suggests a wholesome or desirable state, but statistical norms should be viewed simply as describing the current status of the population under consideration. By comparing individuals and groups, we can discover variations and trends. These data, related to such factors as age, sex, race, and nutrition, provide handy reference points for comparing the effects of such variables.

Issues Relating to Physical Development

The worth of special training. One perennially debated issue is whether children's growth proceeds spontaneously, determined by genetics—the so-called maturationist view—or whether it can be accelerated by training. Originally, the maturationists appeared to have the better case. In Mary Shirley's classic study of locomotion, twins were given special training during very early childhood in such activities as roller skating and tricycling. They experienced a deterioration at age 6 in roller skating, in which greater weight is a handicap. But neither twin faltered in tricycling, for which body changes are less important. The results were interpreted as underscoring the significance of maturation. That is, the study appeared to prove that a skill cannot be taught until the stage of maturation permits and that children will spontaneously learn basic motor skills without any special training (McGraw, 1939).

These children are exhibiting some learned basic motor skills.

According to some investigators, however, deliberate exercise of the walking reflex helps an infant to walk earlier than the generally anticipated age of about 14 months (Zelazo, Zelazo, & Kolb, 1972). In this study, deliberately exercised infants began walking at 10.1 months. The more passively exercised walked at

11.4 months. And those not specially exercised began at 12.4 months. In another study, 4-year-olds who were provided special motor training made large gains in complex gymnastic processes as compared with a comparable untrained group. However, there was practically no difference in average gain of the two groups in simple motor abilities such as flexibility, coordination, and balance.

In general, the effectiveness of special training depends on the age of the child and the skill involved. The level of maturation places a ceiling on gains produced by specific practice. This is because the underlying physical factors involved, such as rate of movement or muscular strength, depend on intrinsic growth processes (Piaget, 1973). Apparently, skills of a relatively simple type are acquired through ordinary life activities, relatively independent of special training (Leitwood & Fowler, 1971).

Sex differences. Traditionally, boys have been acknowledged to be so advanced over girls in motor development and so much hardier physically that the sexes have been separated in gym classes and competitive sports. As indicated above, sex differences in potential for developing motor skills seem small, at least in childhood, although some questions are in dispute. For example, it is uncertain which sex is basically more active than the other (Maccoby & Jacklin, 1974). At any rate, there are no sex differences in activity level in infancy. They show up only when children begin social play. Males' greater vigor and activity level can be attributed, to some unknown degree, to societal expectations and environmental opportunities (Chasen, 1974). Certainly, boys are encouraged in far more large-muscle activity than are girls, even today. In any case, the current controversy over girls' participation on a par with boys in competitive sports makes this issue relevant.

Body build and personality. Another issue of long standing concerns the relationship between body build and personality. W. H. Sheldon and his associates (Sheldon, Stevens, & Tucker, 1940) believed that personality traits depend on whether an individual is an **endomorph,** having a round body with small bones; a **mesomorph,** with large bones and well-developed muscles; or an **ectomorph,** with a linear, fragile build. For example, ectomorphic boys were presumed to be quiet, cautious, and hesitant to give offense.

In one relevant study (Staffieri, 1972) boys at several age levels (5 to 6, 14 to 15, and 19 to 20) with two types of body build—average and chubby—assigned items from a check list to pictures of a mesomorph, an endomorph, and an ectomorph. Then they labeled each characteristic as good or bad. At each age level the boys held favorable opinions of the mesomorph, very unfavorable views of the endomorph, and less negative, though still unfavorable, ones of the ectomorph. Staffieri reported similar results for girls aged 7 to 11.

While body type bears little relationship to personality in individual cases, it is obvious why some relationship exists. For one thing, the same genetic factors that limit body build also modify basic **temperament** (typical emotional pattern). In addition, body builds are differentially conducive to developing specific traits.

For example, the lanky ectomorph may not be adept in rough-and-tumble sports and hence become somewhat shy. Finally, individuals may unconsciously conform to the cultural stereotype regarding their body build. The fat girl is expected to be jolly and so at least behaves that way despite what she may feel underneath. Even in a technologically advanced society, where physical strength is apparently of little social or occupational usefulness, physical characteristics influence one's social life greatly (Peevers & Secord, 1973). Besides, large body size, at least among males, may turn out to be an economic, as well as social and personal, asset (Cavior & Howard, 1973).

In any case, all relevant data depend on somewhat questionable categorizations of body build as well as of personality characteristics. The same individual may not always be assigned the same ratio of body components by different, even trained, raters. Moreover, instruments used to estimate such traits as tension, shyness, and joviality are still of questionable validity.

The matter of diet. Also at issue is what diet is best for children. As research underscoring the importance of proper nutrition has proliferated, considerable controversy has developed over the adequacy of what children are offered, or choose to eat, in school lunchrooms. The main problem is that many children themselves prefer snack foods to a balanced diet. "Snacking" is often common in homes where both parents work. In addition, children may become the unwitting victims of whatever diet fads their parents espouse. According to the committee on nutrition of the American Academy of Pediatrics, claims for certain special diets should be subject to careful scientific evaluation. The committee offered the following conclusions where children's special diets are concerned ("Diets and Children's Health," 1977).

1. Although many people have followed vegetarian diets over long terms with excellent results, such diets are sometimes so high in bulk that they may not meet caloric needs or supply sufficient proteins.
2. Long-term research has failed to find any nutritional superiority of the so-called **organic,** natural, and health foods over those grown under usual conditions with chemical fertilizers.
3. While various claims have been made for the worth of large supplements of vitamins C and E, the committee found little or no basis for such claims. People should be cautious about going substantially beyond recommended daily allowances.
4. Excess doses of vitamin A, said to improve visual acuity, prevent infection, and reduce acne, can have serious toxic effects, including increased intracranial pressure and anorexia.
5. Nevertheless, even in the case of extreme dietary practices it is ordinarily possible to escape serious damage by providing dietary balance.

Severe malnutrition in early years will retard the growth rate, both physical and cognitive. However, its effects are reversible through subsequent provision for adequate nutrition. Infants have an unusual capacity to recover from such physical disturbances as well as from psychological stresses, such as that caused by isolation (Kagan, 1978). The degree of recovery from malnutrition depends on its timing, severity, and duration. The effects of less severe, short-term malnutrition are reversible (Herrera, 1979). Consequences of mild under-nutrition for intellectual development is far from clearcut and only weakly associated with intellectual and other forms of development. Nevertheless, consequences of severe malnutrition can be serious, especially when the home environment is also less stimulating, which is often the case (Stevens & Baxter, 1981).

Malnutrition's effects are greatest when growth is normally quite rapid, as during the prenatal period. Males are more susceptible than females to the effects of such environmental disturbances.

Obesity is of special importance for physical health and personal adjustment. Obesity apparently derives from the interaction of genetic and environmental factors in varying proportion. When both parents are overweight, three-fourths of their children are, too. If both parents are thin, only 9 per cent of their children are overweight. When one parent is overweight, so are 41% of the children (Rodin, 1978).

Obesity is not produced by a single gene for fatness, although genes do influence total body weight as well as the relative amount of fat in tissues and its distribution on the body. The amount of fat that the body can store is limited by the number and average size of fat cells. Some authorities believe that the number of fat cells is permanently and genetically determined. Others believe that the number of cells is fixed by nutrition in infancy. Bottle-fed infants often consume more liquid than they need because their mothers allow or encourage them to do so. This excess accelerates the development of fat cells (Rodin, 1978).

Physical appearance. A commonly neglected aspect of physical development is appearance and its impact on adjustment. Research suggests that even in nursery school good looks count. When children aged 4 to 6 were asked to name classmates they liked best, they chose good-looking children and described the homely ones as unfriendly and aggressive (Berscheid & Walster, 1975; Dion 1972).

Early on, children acquire sociocultural concepts of physical ideals from television and reading matter.

> Fairy tales and children's stories, picturing the menacing, hateful characters as having warped bodies and ugly faces, continue to foster the prejudices of children regarding looks. Being nicknamed "baboon face," "eagle beak," "fish mouth," or "donkey ears" may leave a sharp imprint on a child's character [Scheinfeld, 1965, p. 471].

Even teachers evaluate children partly in terms of appearance. Margaret Clifford and Elaine Walster (1975) had 400 teachers look at report cards to which photographs were attached and asked them to evaluate the children involved. The teachers guessed that good-looking children had higher IQs, that their parents were more interested in their education, and that they got along better with their peers than the plain-looking children.

COGNITIVE DEVELOPMENT

Conceptual Stages

Piaget's theory. The most widely accepted view of cognitive development was developed by Jean Piaget and his collaborators, who proposed four main stages. The material that follows is adapted from my earlier text (Rogers, 1977a, pp. 161–163).

Stage 1: sensorimotor activity. The first stage is said to last about 2 years and is subdivided into six phases (Flavell, 1963). During the 1st month, the child shows little besides reflexive behavior. Then, from 1 to 4 months of age, infants' reflexive activities become modified by experience and coordinated with one another. For instance, eye movements and hand movements become increasingly coordinated. From 4 to 8 months, infants begin to anticipate sequences of action toward objects and to notice events outside their own bodies. Moreover, they can intentionally repeat responses that produce interesting results—for instance, kicking their legs to swing a toy that is suspended overhead. In effect, goal-directed activity is beginning.

In the next phase, 8 to 11 months, they begin to differentiate means from ends. If a toy is hidden, they'll search for it and remove the obstacle. The fifth phase, 11 to 18 months, involves active experimentation, variation, and modification of behavior. The child is interested in novelty and manifests curiosity, dropping objects simply to watch them fall. The period from 18 months to 2 years is characterized by emergence of the capacity to respond to or to think about objects not immediately observable. Some degree of problem solving is possible, too. A child may use a stick as a tool for pulling an object nearer, even though he or she has never seen one used for that purpose before.

Stage 2: preoperational thought. This stage is divided into two periods: preconceptual (ages 2 to 4) and intuitive (ages 4 to 7). During the preconceptual stage children are egocentric, using self as the standard of judgment and failing to understand the viewpoints of other people. They also categorize on the basis of single characteristics of objects; for instance, they can't take into account the height and width of an object simultaneously. Moreover, they regard a particular stimulus as representative of other objects. A tree stump may be perceived as a castle, a twig as a machine gun. During both the preconceptual and intuitive stages, the world is magical and perceived in **animistic** terms. That is, children endow inanimate objects with life properties. Contrary to common belief, however, children rarely conceive of objects as knowing or wanting things or as feeling pain.

During the preoperational stage children conceptualize more, construct more complex thoughts and images, and group objects into classes. They use symbols, but they don't yet organize them into broad concepts and rules. A 5-year-old may be able to pretty well describe a car trip, telling about things seen on the way in roughly the correct order, but the child couldn't take a pencil and paper and draw a map of the trip. That is, the 5-year-old has no mental representation of that sequence of events. Henceforth, instead of identifying appearance with true reality, the child acquires the notion of conservation. This notion—that physical qualities are invariant—overrides the way the world looks. Something far away looks small, but a theory has formed, based on cumulative experience, about size as related to distance. In brief, the child's world is reorganized. Old concepts can't even be recalled, perhaps because lower-level ones are simply absorbed by higher-level ones. This cognitive evolution may help account for childhood amnesia.

Stage 3: concrete operations. Even at age 7, the child's theories are still limited in their range of application. Rather than generalizing a theory in so many words, the child must rediscover it in new contexts. For instance, given two balls of modeling clay, one of which is then mashed flat, the child is asked "Which contains more clay?" A young child, impressed by sheer density of the ball, may say the ball holds more; if impressed by visual extent, the child might say the pancake holds more. An older child, however, will say they are equal. But when asked which weighs more, even the older child may not know and may be surprised to find they weigh the same.

During the years 7 to 11, the **concrete-operations** period, reasoning processes begin to be based on logic. Classification at this stage consists not merely in labeling a set of stimuli but in imaginatively combining objects within a class. When asked to sort objects, children find similarities on the basis of perceptual factors such as structural likenesses. They may group all items that have legs or black specks. Later, they shift to conceptual or categorical labels, including "animals," "tools," and the like (Sigel, 1963). The children described below exemplify the concrete-operations period.

Here are some enthusiastic users of Piaget tests.

A group of seven- and eight-year-olds were asked to classify human figures such as fireman, cowboy, and nurse on the basis of similarity. They tended to use labels descriptive of part of the stimuli. For instance, a child might pair the fireman and the soldier because both had uniforms, or the boy and girl because both wore shoes. Also, they sorted familiar objects by functional or class labels. Hammer and saw, for instance, might be paired with cow, sheep, or chicken, because they can be used to build structures in which these animals might live [Sigel, 1961, M2983].

In sum, during the second and third stages, ages 2 to 11, children use logic and reasoning in an elementary way and apply them to the manipulation of concrete objects, but not to verbal propositions. They may order sticks by height but have trouble with a problem such as "Edith is taller than Susan; Edith is shorter than Lily; who is the tallest of the three?" (Mussen, 1963).

Stage 4: formal operations. This final period, during which truly logical thinking emerges, begins between the ages of 11 and 15. Children now take the final step toward abstract thinking and conceptualization. They consider general laws and think about what is hypothetically possible as well as what is real. They can speculate, and speculation is governed by logical rules. By age 15, they use logical operations in an adult manner to solve problems.

Earlier, the child organized knowledge by concrete operations with actual objects. Knowing the rules, the child didn't know how to communicate them. A boy might have been an expert at catching a ball but have been unable to explain anything about its **trajectory.** The girl could ride her bicycle yet be unable to explain the concept "center of gravity." We might say that they knew more than they understood. Now, in the logical stage, the implicit becomes explicit; what is known is understood. Never will everything that is understood become explicit, but the adolescent begins to move in this direction and to codify knowledge.

An application of Piagetian theory. Researchers have tested Piagetian theory in various ways. For example, on the basis of interviews with 60 boys and girls, all middle- and upper-middle-class children in a university community, Anne Bernstein (1976) related children's development of ideas about reproduction to Piagetian stage theory. The children's ages corresponded to certain of the developmental levels proposed by Piaget: a third were ages 3 to 7, a third 7 to 8, and a third 11 or 12.

Piaget stressed that children as philosophers will set about bringing orderliness to their universe. When they gain new information that does not fit their ideas, they simply distort it to fit their level of understanding. Certainly Piaget's view was borne out in this study, as well as his concept of stages.

The children's answers fell into six levels of maturity that indicated a consistent developmental sequence. The structure of the children's answers, not their content, served to distinguish levels from each other. In most cases level-1 children did not understand the laws of cause and effect. They believed that babies had always existed and that the real question was simply where the baby had been before coming to their house. Such children, usually the 3- to 4-year-olds, gave answers such as the following: "You go to a baby store and buy one."

"From tummies." "It just grows inside Mommy's tummy. It's there all the time. Mommy doesn't have to do anything. She just waits until she feels it" (Bernstein, 1976, p. 32).*

Level-2 children, mostly the 4-year-olds, were still quite egocentric, interpreting the world in terms of experiences they had had. As a result they "often fall into the digestive fallacy, and believe that babies are conceived by swallowing and born by elimination" (p. 33). As one girl said, "He [the father] puts his hand in his tummy and gets it [the seed] and puts it on the bottom of the mommy and the mommy gets the egg out of her tummy and puts the egg on top of the seed. And then they close their tummies and the baby is born" (p. 33). As Bernstein pointed out, "This is the level that Henry Ford would have recognized and admired, for these children believe that babies are manufactured by people as if they were refrigerators, TV sets, or automobiles" (p. 32).

Children on level 3 often realized that reproduction involves love and marriage, sexual intercourse, and a union between sperm and ovum. But they had only a limited capacity to put these factors together in an intelligible whole. As one 7-year-old said: "The sperm goes into the mommy to each egg and puts it, makes the egg safe. So if some bump comes along it won't crack the egg. The sperm comes from the daddy. It swims into the penis, and I think it makes a little hole and then it swims into the vagina. It has a little mouth and it bites a hole" (p. 33). Another child who had seen cartons of eggs in the refrigerator explained the father's contribution this way: "Well, the father puts the shell. I forget what it's called, but he puts something in for the egg. If he didn't, then a baby couldn't come, because it needs the stuff that the father gives." (p. 34).

Children in levels 4 through 6, mostly 8- to 12-year-olds, provided mainly physiological explanations. They were able to think logically about people and objects, past and future, and to understand ideas of cause and effect. The level-4 children were aware of the physical facts relating to reproduction, but they did not realize why genetic materials must come together in order to produce new life. One child believed that sperm are "primarily to provide an escort service: 'The sperm reaches the eggs. It looses 'em and brings 'em down to the forming place, I think that's right and it grows until it's ready to take out" (p. 34).

Level-5 children, mostly 11- and 12-year-olds, attempted to explain why the sperm and ovum must join, but most of them still believed that the baby comes already formed from one of the germ cells. As one child said: "The lady has an egg and the man has a sperm and sort of he fertilizes the egg, and then the egg slowly grows. The sperm grows into a baby inside the egg. Fertilize? It means it gets inside the egg, the sperm does. The egg before the sperm goes in it sort of like, well, I guess it doesn't have anything in it to grow. It just has food and I guess a shell on the outside. It's sort of the beginning of the baby. It has to happen, because otherwise the sperm would just die because it has no

*From "Six stages of understanding: How children learn about sex and birth," by A. C. Bernstein. In *Psychology Today*, 1976, 9(8), 31–35: 66. Copyright © 1976 by Ziff-Davis Publishing Company. This and all other quotations from this source are reprinted by permission.

shelter on the outside to keep it alive, no food, nothing. And then the egg has nothing in it to grow, it has no . . . no . . . no living animal in there" (p. 35).

The level-6 children, mostly age 12, provided "exclusively explanations of conception and birth, and realized that both parents contribute genetic material to the embryo" (p. 66). As one 12-year-old expressed it: "The sperm encounters one ovum and one sperm breaks into the ovum, which produces like a cell, and the cell separates and divides. And so it's dividing, and the ovum goes through a tube and embeds itself in the wall of the, I think it's the fetus of the woman" (p. 66). Still others gave a very simple explanation: "the two cells meet and start growing" (p. 66). All the level-6 children included fertilizing the egg or sexual intercourse as a part of the process. Some of them said it was hard to talk about, because the language involved is not acceptable.

The parents of the children, at least for levels 2 through 5, were surprised at the distorted concepts evident in the answers. It was clear that their efforts at sex education had often simply confused the children. One book, suggested for children even as young as 3,

> starts with a pencil dot (to represent an ovum), then proceeds through the sex lives of flowers, bees, rabbits, giraffes, chickens and dogs before it reaches the human level. Very few children can follow any such involved transitions. One 4-year-old boy, who knew a sex education book by heart, declared that some of the mother's eggs never become babies because their daddy eats them. 'It says so in my book,' he said. And so it did, in a discussion of reproduction in fish [p. 66].

Critique of Piagetian theory. Critics of Piaget's stage theory of mental development challenge the concept as misleading or invalid. Ezer (1962) reported that clear-cut stages do not exist. Sequences might vary, and the quality and rate of change depend on the kinds of experience involved (Ausubel, 1957). While Piaget himself admitted the possibility of modifying the pace of developing concepts through provision for appropriate experience, he did not indicate how dramatic such changes might be. Besides, Piaget's straight-line concept of stages failed adequately to take into account earlier learning stages that might somehow relate to later learning, even though on the surface the two might appear quite different. In other words, early concepts may simply serve as bridges for later ones. Finally, stages overlap, producing wide variations within a particular age range. Any random sampling of 5-year-olds would embrace not only very bright but also very dull children, so that the same generalizations would not apply to all. Indeed, many adults still manifest evidence of egocentric speech and preconceptual thinking. Overall, there is an apparent continuity in mental development instead of any distinguishable turning points.

Other authorities believe that Piagetian stage theory establishes too specific and orderly a sequence. Horn (1976) suggested that children can sometimes reach a higher developmental stage and can perform tasks relating to it without having gone through earlier stages, just as some children walk without having crawled. A combination of a particular child's abilities, attitudes, and interests as well as environmental circumstances may produce variations in development of cognitive abilities that the Piagetian model does not adequately explain (Kagan, 1976).

Bower (1976) argues that cognitive development does not proceed in a sequential and orderly fashion. During the first 11 or 12 years children may first master, then lose, the concept of conservation. But they finally attain a stable understanding of it around age 13. There are also fits and starts in children's memory development that do not follow Piaget's model.

Other Studies of Children's Cognitive Development

Bruner's conclusions. Jerome Bruner, like Piaget, has portrayed cognitive development as proceeding by stages. But his emphases are different. Bruner (1973) contends that young children originally represent objects and past events in terms of related motor responses. The baby may drop a rattle, so that it falls out of sight, and then shake her arm as though she were still holding the rattle. Bruner suggests that in shaking her hand the baby is representing the rattle. In other words, the rattle is not simply a plastic object to play with. Instead, it represents shaking the hand and making a noise. Several months later the baby looks over the crib when the rattle drops and becomes excited if an adult removes it. Bruner suggests that this sense of loss shows that the baby carries an image of the rattle in her mind and that she can now tell the difference between shaking her hand and the rattle.

Ultimately, children come to represent things with symbols that do not depend on appearances or images. The word *boy* does not look like a real boy. In arithmetic problems preschool children may use images to arrive at answers. When asked to add two oranges and four oranges a child might draw two circles and then four circles and add them together. In general, Bruner's research indicates that language and conceptual development occur together. At first, children employ words to stand for particular objects or experiences. Later on, they come to use words merely to refer to objects and experiences, but in a symbolic way, to represent large numbers of images and to perform abstract operations.

Concepts of reality. In other research, psychologist Sarah VanCamp questioned 350 kindergarten children to determine their concepts. The children understood that two parents were required to begin a family and that the family could be as small as a mother and child or as large as two parents and ten children. One child described a family as a mother, a daddy, and three children. Another objected that "there doesn't have to be three children. There can be two children and one dog" ("Children's Views of Reality," 1977, p. 28).

The children appeared sophisticated beyond those of earlier generations. Nevertheless, their statements still reflected confusion about matters of probability, sequence, time and place, and cause and effect. They referred to Presidents Lincoln, Kennedy, Ford, and Nixon as though all were still alive. Such events as floods in Europe and earthquakes in Hawaii blended in their minds into one grand confusion. Such confusion arose from the impact of the media, parents' conversations and greater exposure to world events.

Children appear to follow a Piagetian cogitive developmental sequence in understanding age concepts. Such concepts are difficult for elementary children; hence, in the important field of aging the cognitive developmental sequence should be taken into account (Galper, Jantz, Seefeldt, & Serock, 1980–81).

Concepts of death. Concepts of death are limited by the cognitive function and life-style characteristic of each age. Children have already encountered death on television, in reading, and in personal observation, especially with pets. Yet for healthy children, death of the self seems strangely unreal and far away. Their main focus is on everyday activities and people in their immediate environment. They comprehend death in a rational sense but only marginally in an emotional sense (Pattison, 1977).

Children's understanding of death is a gradual process. It takes some time to discover their own mortality, because they relate death to older age. When talking to her 84-year-old great-grandmother, a 4-year-old child said: "You are old. That means you will die. I am young, so I won't die, you know. . . . . But that's all right. Grandmother, just make sure you wear your white dress. Then, after you die, you can marry Nomo (great-grandfather) again, and have babies" (Kastenbaum, 1977, p. 280). It isn't always easy to understand what death means to a child. Often a child is more disturbed by the death of a pet than that of a person.

Factors Relating to Children's Mental Development

Heredity and prenatal factors. Considerable evidence indicates that heredity plays an important role in determining intelligence. When the Wechsler Intelligence Scale for Children was administered to school-age twins and their siblings, monozygotic twins displayed high agreement. But agreement between the nontwin siblings was comparable to that of the dizygotic twins. The brightest siblings achieved somewhat higher verbal IQ scores than the brightest twins, confirming the view that twins are slightly retarded verbally.

Each child's mental development is largely determined by the home environment interacting with inherent biological determinants. Even within the same family, children appear highly diverse in capacities that are never fully understood at birth but are developed through the learning experiences of childhood (Wilson, 1977). Wilson concluded that individual mental differences can never be done away with, because "the variation coded in the **genotype** [emphasis added] is too deeply rooted to be swept aside by special training" (p. 3). Nevertheless, the fullest relization of children's intelligence is a desirable goal, and schools should accord it first priority.

Scarr and Weinberg (1978a) also underscore the role of heredity in intelligence. In comparisons between adoptive and biological children and their siblings or parents, they found no significant differences in IQ between the races. But they did find powerful evidence of genetic determination of intellectual differences between individuals of the same race. They also found dramatic evidence of genetic factors' role in determining attitudes of authoritarianism and prejudice and at least good evidence of genetic relationships to personal and vocational interests.

On at least six measures of personal interests, biologically related family members resembled one another more closely than did adoptive children. Just two correlations proved significant between adoptive family pairs, whereas 15 out of 24 were significant for biological family pairs. In summary the researchers concluded that "the evidence for some genetic influence on intelligence, attitudes, and interest is simply overwhelming" (Scarr & Weinberg, 1978a, p. 35). It is impossible to assign an exact number for the proportion of particular behaviors that are inherited, partly because environment plays greater or lesser roles at different stages of development. Another difficulty is in the tests themselves, because different kinds are used at different ages.

During the prenatal period anything that interferes with the normal development of the embryo or fetus may affect mental potential. For example, individuals who have experienced prenatal malnourishment typically show lower standardized intelligence scores after birth, but the reason is unclear. One theory is that such malnourishment directly impairs intellectual competency through modifying physical growth and chemical maturation of the brain. In any case, the fetally malnourished baby is deficient in socially interactive processes. It emits a characteristic high-pitched cry that may prove grating and induce stress in listeners compared with an infant's normal cry. Besides, parents from economically deprived homes find their frustrations compounded by such an infant. They may, therefore, treat the child in an aversive, nonsupportive manner that contributes to the baby's poor social and mental development (Zeskind & Ramey, 1978). Such infants, when placed in day-care groups especially designed to afford affection and proper nutrition, recover. The annoying cry disappears, and home caretakers become more responsive.

Sex. Although boys and girls have the same overall IQ distributions, they differ in particular intellectual components. The combination of biological and environmental factors responsible is unknown. When observers rated the behaviors of infants whose sex and names they did not know, the sexes differed significantly on three types of activities. The males were awake more often, displayed more facial grimacing, and engaged in more low-intensity activity (Horn, J., 1978, pp. 26–27).

Most authorities believe that differences in the way the sexes are treated account for the vast majority of the differences in their intellectual development and competencies. Although parents do not rate asking parents for help as more appropriate for girls than for boys, they are more likely to react positively when their daughters ask for help (Fagot, 1978). Thus, girls find asking for help a positive experience, whereas boys find themselves criticized and ignored. Girls are treated in a more negative fashion when they manipulate objects; boys are allowed to explore with less interference. Girls are treated more positively when they try to help adults in some task. Hence, it is clear why, by middle childhood, consistent sex differences occur. Although sex similarities are far greater than sex differences, in a few critical areas the sexes are treated differently, with tremendous consequences for the developmental process.

In another study, of parents and their toddlers, parents rated aggressive behavior and rough-and-tumble play as more appropriate for boys (Fagot, 1978). For girls they rated as more appropriate doll play, dressing up, and dancing. Boys were more often left alone by their parents than girls. Girls were given more praise and criticized more by the parents; and both parents were more likely to stop to play with the boys. The mothers did more caretaking than the fathers. The fathers were more concerned about sex-typing the children.

Family factors. Researchers in general believe that mental development is governed by the quality of the home environment in conjunction with "inherent biological determinants" (Wilson, R. S., 1977, p. 215). The home environment provides the necessary potential for realizing inherent abilities and creates a climate of enthusiasm for learning. An analysis of studies of parent/child resemblances in intelligence indicates that much of the difference is not directly related to parent IQ. Some of it may be attributed to other between-family variables (McCiskie & Clarke, 1976). For example, studies were made of four 3- to 10-year-old children who were judged backward by their parents and teachers, despite at least average intelligence. In each case, their mothers had severely denigrated them from earliest infancy. This treatment was focused on one child, usually the oldest, and did not extend to the others. Both the mothers and the presumably backward children possessed a common **pathology,** a very poor self-image and little self-esteem (Berger & Kennedy, 1975).

Another important factor in children's cognitive development is the nature and quality of their verbal interaction with their parents. Parents, such as the mother quoted below, who patiently answer their children's questions help them to sharpen their concepts.

Child: I'm four, aren't I?
Mother: Yes, four years.
Child: What's a year?
Mother: (Explains.)
Child: Is that a long time?
Mother: Quite a long time.
Child: How long?
Mother: It's hard to explain, but it is a lot of days, 365, and that's many.
Child: Well, but how long?
Mother: Well—you know when it was Christmas.
Child: Oh, yes, and I had a tree, and once I had the tree in the corner, and once I had it on the table.
Mother: Well, that was twice, and it takes a year to have Christmas. You see we have Christmas, then the time between that Christmas and the next is a year.
Child: Well, that's a very long, long time. When I was very small we had a Christmas. Is a year a birthday?
Mother: Well, you have one birthday, then the time between is called a year, then you have the next birthday.

Child: Yes, three then four—then five . . . say how old are you?
Mother: Thirty.
Child: How did you stretch up? [Rust, n.d.].*

Two kinds of evidence have heightened interest in possible relationships between intellectual development and family environment. The first is the lower scores of minorities on almost all types of intellectual tasks, coupled with more parental absences, large families, and other adverse environmental conditions. Second, declines in national test scores for almost all groups have related to changes in family configuration arising from the population boom after World War II (Breland, 1977). Zajonc (1976) also ascribes the lower recent scores to the baby boom, for in larger families lower intelligence is often found.

Parents sometimes do not provide their children the encouragement and stimulation they need because of the way their personalities interact. A mother may unconsciously overprotect a child who has from the very first been dependent. The mother who is simply "turned off" by a difficult 4-month-old child may, without realizing it, fail to provide the quality of caretaking and stimulation that would result in competent performance at 30 months of age (Segal & Yahraes, 1978). The dependent child who receives unusual attention from a highly nurturant parent will be rejected by a parent who dislikes such a trait.

Social class and culture. The family's social class seems to be especially significant. One's class and birth order have important effects even in the earliest weeks of life. Naturalistic observations of 2-week-old infants disclosed that first-borns receive more interaction than later-borns in every major category concerned: in periods of play; in verbal, tactile, and caretaking interaction; and in time parents spend looking at the infants. Mothers of high socioeconomic status spent more time talking to the infants, both in a "lulling and [in] a chatting fashion" (Kilbride, Johnson, & Streissguth, 1977, p. 1688). They tended to talk to the infants while caring for them, but mothers of lower social status did not. Infants with the best prognosis for future intellectual development—that is, those of higher social status and the first-borns—were also those who received the largest amount of verbal interaction from their mothers at 2 weeks of age.

A study among 60 South African and Israeli preschool children suggested that socioeconomic status, whether lower or middle class, was the main variable in determining level of imaginative play. It appeared that lower-class children's deficiencies in imaginative play were created not by lack of stimulation in itself but rather by the failure of their parents to help them integrate the stimuli that confronted them in everyday life. Various home background factors important for the development of imaginative play appear to be culture bound, affected by practices within a specific culture (Udwin & Shmukler, 1981).

Television. Opinions vary about how much and in what ways television affects children's cognitive development and how children's programs should be

From "The growth of children's concepts of time, space, and magnitude," by M. M. Rust. Unpublished. Child Psychology by D. Rogers. Copyright © 1977 by Wadsworth, Inc. This and all other quotations from this source are reprinted by permission of the publisher, Brooks/Cole Publishing Company, Monterey, California.

designed. Psychologists Jerome and Dorothy Singer (1979) have objected to the rapid tempo of programs such as *Sesame Street*, believing that it hampers children's capacity to develop imaginative and reflective thinking. While short action sequences are designed to hold children's attention, they may produce shortened attention spans and expectations of excitement and rapid change in the environment. Children need slower-paced programs that leave time for reflection and response. They also require adult models who listen to them and encourage them to think through questions and to express themselves.

Gerald Lesser (1979), psychological advisor to the Children's Television Workshop, disagreed with the Singers. He argued that there is no single best style for teaching young children and that neither longer nor shorter is necessarily better. Lesser pointed out that there is little research evidence supporting the common contention that short action sequences produce adverse effects.

The Singers (1979) also concluded that the program *Mr. Rogers Neighborhood*, with its simple, direct format, was better for teaching facts, whereas the more complex format of *Sesame Street* was more effective in helping children learn inferences or abstract meanings from situations. Their research confirmed this surmise. While the Singers judged the learning of facts to be more important than abstracting meanings, Lesser preferred not to look on different kinds of learning as competing alternatives. Both learning information and making inferences are important to young children. Consequently, diversity in television programs is important. What is needed is an "ingenuity and commitment to children to provide programs in different forms, styles, and moods. . . . Let's leave room to experiment, to discover the range and variety of programs that will most benefit our children" (Lesser, 1979, p. 60).

The IQ Controversy

Intelligence, or the capacity to learn and apply what one learns, can be measured by the **intelligence quotient.** The IQ itself

> is a measure of a child's rate of development up to the age of the testing. It is computed by dividing the mental age (MA)—as determined on a standardized test of intelligence—by the chronological age (CA). Since IQ scores indicate an individual's performance relative to that of others, one can best grasp the significance of a particular IQ score in terms of the number of children in the total population who exceed that score [Rogers, 1977a, p. 146].

The validity of intelligence tests has been seriously questioned, especially in recent years. For one thing, cognitive abilities are too complex to be described adequately by a single measure such as IQ (Carroll & Maxwell, 1979). In addition, intelligence consists of relatively independent primary mental abilities, and individuals with the same IQ can have different patterns of primary abilities. Boys and girls are about equal in global intelligence, or IQ; but girls are higher in verbal abilities and lower on spatial and number abilities. It is improbable that these variations are attributable in any great degree to sex-linked genetic differences. Rather, much of the difference derives from differential treatment of the sexes by their teachers, parents, and even peers (Zimbardo, 1979).

Psychologist Samuel Kohs has concluded that IQ tests do not measure intelligence and that the concept has never even been properly defined. Kohs expresses concern that schools attach so much significance to IQ scores. He points out that nature never produces exact duplicates, whether in apples, pears, or children. Nature likes variety. All human beings have brain power, but each individual is uniquely different, qualitatively and quantitatively, from others ("IQ Irrationality," 1979).

Scarr (1978) calls attention to certain biases of intelligence tests. These tests are samplings of "important aspects of intellectual functioning in a particular cultural context" (p. 338). Certainly the vocabulary and comprehension sections of tests used in the United States would be valueless in completely different cultural and linguistic contexts. The question arises whether U.S. subcultures are sufficiently different to make a different sampling of knowledge essential. To the extent that these subcultures differ, it is wrong to infer that children within them have particular IQ levels based only on culturally biased examinations.

Indeed it is unwise to make inferences from IQ tests regarding general intellectual functioning in any population grouping that differs from the **standardization** sample. And there is even some cultural and environmental diversity within the standardization group. On even the newest and most carefully designed tests, rural children score lower than urban children. However, these tests are certainly a less-than-sufficient sampling of the rural children's skill and knowledge. Scarr (1979) concludes that test scores should be judged to have predictive value only for scholastic and vocational criteria where "skills and knowledge of the majority culture are essential to good performance in these contexts" (p. 339).

Should not society take more note of the plurality of cultures and then devise culturally appropriate ways of assessing intellectual adaptation (pp. 339–340)? While many skills are common in every culture, the relative stress placed on them varies from one group to another. Hunt (1979) observes that simply abandoning any measurement of intelligence does not in itself guarantee equal rights or a redistribution of economic and social benefits. Justice requires that social and economic rewards be allocated to children more even-handedly. Such a reallocation would reduce inequalities in performance and hence make the use of IQ tests less discriminatory.

Language Acquisition

No one has come up with a generally accepted theory of language learning, despite much theorizing. In earlier theories children were viewed as learning language "by associating words with agents and objects and actions, by imitating their elders, and by a mysterious force called reinforcement" (Bruner, 1978, p.

42). Then came Noam Chomsky's LAD (language acquisition device) theory. It held that language is not learned but simply recognized because of inborn mechanisms. When exposed to language, children were viewed as able to extract its grammar because of this innate ability. Both Chomsky and Lenneberg (1966) interpret language acquisition as "instinctive," because children gain the basic elements of their native language during their first 18 months. Lenneberg concludes that language is biologically based. Miller (1977) describes the associationist view as impossible and the naturalistic one as miraculous. Nelson (1981) reports two styles of language acquisition and considerable continuity over time. Some children emphasize single words and simple rules for combining them; others use full phrases and compressed sentences.

According to another theory, the critical-period hypothesis, primary language acquisition must take place during a particular span ending about puberty (Snow & Hoefnagel-Höhle, 1978). This hypothesis also suggests that a second language can be acquired successfully only before puberty. A longitudinal study of English-speaking individuals who learned Dutch in naturalistic settings at different ages disclosed fastest progress during the initial months among adults and those ages 12 to 15. At the end of the 1st year the 8- to 10-year-olds and the 12- to 15-year-olds had gained the best control of the language. The 3- to 5-year-olds scored lowest. Thus, the data do not support the critical-period hypothesis for acquiring language.

Jerome Bruner (1978) explained language learning in terms of problem solving. Even before children speak their first words, they have sorted much of their environment into categories and can distinguish between various objects and actions. As Roger Brown has pointed out, the objects and actions are there just waiting for names. These names are acquired through complex interaction with the mother. Language becomes a joint problem-solving process between mother and infant, as they strive to communicate with each other. At first the communication is nonverbal but capable of conveying intent. This nonverbal, and later verbal, communication is within the context of concrete situations, as when an infant reaches for an object and the mother calls it by name.

The process is social, involving role interaction by mother and child. The mother makes various adaptations by speaking slowly and by following up the baby's responses. Thus,

> When the baby responds to her "Look!" by looking, she follows immediately with a query. When the child responds to the query with a gesture or a smile she responds with a label. But as soon as the child shows the ability to vocalize in a way that might indicate a label, she raises the ante [Bruner, 1978, p. 45].

The communication presumes "shared knowledge" and "a shared script." The child learns words by using them to get things done, not to dig out disembodied rules of grammar. Language learning is not "a solo flight" by a child seeking rules. It is a shared "transaction involving an active language learner and an equally active language teacher" (p. 49).

Like Bruner, Hunt (1979) insists that experience plays a more vital role in language learning than distinct theories suggest. Foundlings reared in institutions with encouragement to communicate orally may be severely delayed in learning language. Simply reducing the infant/caretaker ratio enhances the speed of such children's learning. Indeed, such foundlings, given carefully programmed assistance, make faster progress than children in the average home. It is clear, concludes Hunt (1979), that experience plays a very significant role in children's language learning.

A growing body of research supports Bruner's and Hunt's position. For example, when infants' home environments were appraised at ages 6 months and 24 months, the quality related significantly to the children's language development, assessed then and at 3 years of age. Items measured on the HOME scale (home observation for measurement of the environment) focused on six types of environmental influence: the mother's emotional and verbal responsiveness, her avoidance of punishment and restriction, environmental organization, adequacy of play materials, the mother's involvement with the child, and variations in daily routines. Verbal progress was measured on the Illinois Test of Psycholinguistic Abilities (ITPA). The results suggested that environmental factors strongly affect verbal development in the first 2 years of life.

Children's overall cognitive development is associated with an organized, responsive environment in which appropriate learning activities are provided for the 1st year or so of life. Especially important is the mother's emotional responsiveness to and involvement with the child in language development, as well as provision of proper play materials (Elardo, Bradley, & Caldwell, 1977). Both parents model their infants' development of nonverbal communication skills, especially the daughter's. Parents interact more closely with their daughters than they do with their sons (Brody & Stoneman, 1981).

EMOTIONAL DEVELOPMENT

Pattern of Development

Emotional development follows a cyclical pattern linked to the child's saturation cycle (Silverman, R. E., 1974). The average 3-year-old can accurately identify laughter. But children cannot judge surprise until about the age of 11. Certain emotions are learned more easily than others. While there is no firm evidence, children apparently become more accurate in judging emotions as they approach adulthood, perhaps because they are increasingly able to experience complex emotions (Krech et al., 1974).

Emotional patterns originate early and tend to persist. Children's behavioral and temperament profile is already apparent at 2 or 3 months. In a longitudinal study of 141 children from birth to their mid-teens (Thomas, A., & Chess, 1977), two-thirds displayed three general temperaments. The children in one category (about 40%) were characterized by adaptability, regular body function, and positive mood. A second, difficult group (10%) tended to withdraw from new situations, was generally negative in mood, and adapted but slowly to environmental change. These children displayed intense body reactions and had

Table 3-1. The Development of Some Basic Human Emotions[a]

Month	Pleasure-Joy	Wariness-Fear	Rage-Anger	Periods of Emotional Development
0	Endogenous smile	Startle/pain	Distress due to: covering the face, physical restraint, extreme discomfort	Absolute stimulus barrier
1	Turning toward	Obligatory attention		Turning toward
2				
3	Pleasure		Rage (disappointment)	Positive affect
4	Delight Active laughter	Wariness		
5				
6				Active participation
7	Joy		Anger	
8				
9		Fear (stranger aversion)		Attachment
10				
11				
12	Elation	Anxiety Immediate fear	Angry mood, petulance	Practicing
18	Positive valuation of self-affection	Shame	Defiance	Emergence of self
24		Intentional hurting		
36	Pride, love		Guilt	Play and fantasy

[a]The age specified is neither the first appearance of the affect in question nor its peak occurrence; it is the age when the literature suggests that the reaction is common. (From "Socioemotional Development," by L. Alan Sroufe. In Joy D. Osofsky (Ed.), *Handbook of Infant Development*. Copyright 1979 by John Wiley & Sons. Reprinted by permission.)

irregular body functions. A third, slow-to-warm-up group (15%) was also slow to adapt and somewhat negative in mood, and it was extremely low in activity level. Each of these categories adapts best to a particular mode of handling. The adaptable children react favorably to varied life-styles. The difficult ones require patient, consistent treatment. And the slow-to-warm-up children must be allowed to get used to their environment at their own pace.

Sometimes, children's temperaments may change, at least on the surface, because of environmental circumstances (Thomas, A., et al., 1975). Routine situations may obscure basic temperamental characteristics that nevertheless assert themselves in new situations. One 10-year-old girl who had appeared well adjusted in class became extremely anxious and fearful after moving from a small school to a large, more formal one. Researchers found that she had displayed withdrawal reactions in new situations earlier in life.

Emotional Maturity

Standards. It is important, of course, that children make satisfactory progress toward emotional maturity. P. G. Coleman (1972) judged children's maturity in terms of progress toward attaining certain standards. The first advance is from dependency to self-direction, including the acquisition of competencies and values. A second trend is from pleasure to self-control and reality. A third trend, from ignorance to knowledge, suggests that an individual must be sufficiently knowledgeable in dealing with common problems in order to feel adequate. The fourth trend, from incompetence to competence, involves mastering certain social, intellectual, and emotional skills desirable for life adjustment. A fifth trend is from diffuse sexuality to heterosexuality. It is important not only that trends be in the right direction but also that children keep pace with standards appropriate for their age.

Threats to emotional health. Certain hazards to children's emotional welfare are often cited. The complexity, anonymity, and pace of modern society are presumed to produce feelings of anomie, helplessness, and frustration. The mother's absence due to work theoretically makes them feel abandoned. Television, too, is widely condemned for its fare of violence and overstimulation. Earle Barcus's study of weekend children's television programs in major cities revealed a commercial every 2.9 minutes, more violence in cartoon comedies than live action shows, and a focus on threats of violence and an atmosphere of excitement. Over 60% of the children's programs involved at least one overt act of violence, and 33% were "saturated" with aggression. Indeed, there was little other than violence underlying the programs' themes (Horn, J., 1976d).

Despite all the furor, research has failed to determine conclusively just how the foregoing factors affect individual children. The degree of television violence that may overstimulate one child may actually benefit a more passive one who needs to be more aggressive. Children of some working mothers may feel abandoned, but the vast majority fares as well as those whose mothers remain in the home. Children whose home and school climates are healthy appear relatively secure.

Invulnerable children. In contrast with the earlier preoccupation with emotional problems and their related therapies, a growing emphasis is being placed on the identification of factors associated with emotional health and progress toward emotional maturity. An example of this more positive approach is longitudinal research that has disclosed certain so-called invulnerable children. Such studies, now in progress in both the United States and other countries, involve children deemed likely to make a poor adjustment in life because of exceptionally poor home conditions. These children are followed across the years, and efforts are made to distinguish the factors that differentiate those who turn out as expected from the "invulnerables." The latter appear to defy all known rules of development and turn out exceptionally well despite having the cards stacked against them.

In Norman Garmezy's comparison:

> It's as if you have three dolls, one made of glass, one of plastic, and one of steel. Then someone comes along with a hammer and hits each doll on the head with the same force or blow. The first doll breaks down completely. The second one is dented—one might say scarred—for life. And the third doll just gives off a fine metallic sound, for it is made of steel [Pines, 1979, p. 54].

The steel doll symbolizes the "superkids," or invulnerables. The plastic doll represents children who are psychologically hurt when small and continue to have some difficulties, despite generally adequate functioning. The third doll fully reflects the impact of a hostile early environment.

The superkids, who appear almost immune to their hostile environment, share several traits. They appear fully at ease around others and make other people comfortable, too. They easily make friends. They know how to win over adults and attain their support. They are not overdependent yet rely on adults when it is appropriate. Very often adults—including teachers, baby-sitters, relatives, and others—play an important role in their lives and compensate for some of the lack of support from their parents. They actively seek to cope with their environment and have a feeling of their own competence.

One little girl, whose father was dead and whose mother was too depressed to prepare lunches for her to take to school, would simply make a sandwich out of two pieces of bread with nothing between. In this way she had something to eat when she sat down with the other children. The invulnerables also feel so competent that they often help others who have fewer personal resources. They think for themselves and are highly autonomous from early in life. The children as a whole are achievers, and they do exceptionally well at most things they undertake. They score well on tests of divergent thinking and creativity, occupying themselves with activities such as writing essays and short stories, painting, and sculpting.

It is uncertain how much of these children's strength derives from any specific genetic environment, but at least three conditions appear essential for becoming invulnerable. First, the children have a healthy relationship with at least one parent, especially in early years, a condition that helps establish what Erik Erikson has called basic trust in life. Despite the worst of circumstances, some people are good parents. The significant factor is having some other human being who cares for one in a very particular way. The second qualification is that children require challenges and a measure of benign neglect. That is, children should receive neither too much nor too little attention and assistance. Adults in the environment should be around when the children need them but let them "tough out" the really hard situations alone. Third, the child must not face too many risk factors at once. When any two major factors occur together, the risk rises fourfold. Even the strongest child will break down from experiencing too many major risk factors at once.

Longitudinal research has yet to find certain answers. It isn't known when intervention is most effective or whether there "is a point of no return beyond which no intervention will help" (Pines, 1979, p. 63). The current research began with very young children who are now in their teens; and the point of greatest risk for breakdown is between ages 15 and 45. The aim is ultimately to manipulate environments so as to develop a similar resistance in other children and to prevent breakdowns among at-risk children (Pines, 1979).

PERSONALITY DEVELOPMENT

Growth of Self-Concept

All the foregoing aspects of development relate to and influence children's personality and self-concept. At birth, children lack any feeling that might appropriately be called self-concept. Instead, the "original sense of self is simply a composite sense of either well-being or stress. It is indistinct, amorphous, and largely physical in nature" (Rogers, 1977a, p. 114). Gradually, however, a self-concept develops, the first apparent step being the discovery of the body. Thus,

> An infant has pleasant experiences putting its thumb in its mouth and discovering that the thumb is part of "self." It places other objects in its mouth that produce a different sensation and gains the concept of "other." The infant is called by name and is treated in fairly consistent ways by others, and so the baby comes, in however rudimentary a fashion, to attach value to itself [p. 114].

A child's self-concept develops through interaction with certain reference groups, especially the family, peer group, and neighborhood. Expressions of favor or disfavor from significant others produce corresponding self-attitudes of approval or disapproval (Monge, 1973).

Age can influence children's self-concept either positively or negatively. On the one hand, adults ordinarily treat infants and very young children kindly, making them feel accepted. On the other hand, young children perceive themselves as less powerful than older siblings and hence vaguely inferior. In any case, during middle childhood self-approval may decline. No longer is the child the cute little thing, petted and spoiled by adults. Now there is competition, even failure, at school and often insensitive treatment by peers.

Growth of Personality

Foundations. Personality, like self-concept, develops gradually through the interaction of genetic influences and environmental variables. An individual does not inherit biological characteristics such as extroversion or introversion as such. Rather, one inherits some organic characteristic that somehow affects, and is in turn affected by, the environment. While it is unpopular to suggest that human beings come not only in different colors but also with different temperaments, research indicates that not only animals but also human babies "begin life along developmental pathways established by their genetic inheritance" (Freedman, 1979, p. 36). For example,

A child may inherit a physiological makeup that leads him to be overactive. This overactivity puts him more in touch with his environment than is an underactive child. If he is very overactive, he may cause people in his environment to react negatively. His parents may even punish him to make him limit his activity. He, in turn, may become increasingly aggressive as a reaction to these restraints. The aggressiveness itself, then, is not an inherited trait, but the result of a genetic tendency to activity [Silverman, R. E., 1974, p. 419].

Even from birth infants manifest many individual differences: "One baby curls quietly in an adult's arms; another squirms and kicks with remarkable energy. One sleeps through a rock concert in the next room; another wails when a dog barks two houses away. One baby feels almost limp when picked up; another is always tense and rigid" (Morris, 1979, p. 78). It is generally assumed that these individual characteristics reflect inborn temperament.

Similarly, different races are apparent from the first weeks, days, and even hours of life (Freedman, 1979). Newborns of the Australian aborigines will struggle strongly against cloth placed over the nose, as will Caucasian babies. The Australian babies have strong necks, and some can even raise their heads and look around, movements that Caucasian infants cannot perform until they are about a month old. The aborigines' babies are quite easy to calm, somewhat like the easy-going Chinese infants. It is clear, observes Freedman, that children of different ethnic backgrounds are not born alike.

In other research Thomas, Chess, and Birch (1970) categorized babies as generally difficult, easy, or slow to warm up. They concluded from a follow-up study 14 years later that most of the children had maintained the same general temperament from birth through adolescence. The easy children seemed to be quite adaptable and relaxed even from birth; and in later years they were agreeable and found it easy to make friends. The difficult children were somewhat tense and moody and reacted violently to new people and situations. Slow-to-warm-up children were relatively slow to react, withdrawn, and reluctant to express themselves. In later years they had considerable difficulty in social and competitive situations.

Other psychologists hesitate to categorize babies in this way. They say that the same baby can go through all these states within one day. And while one style may dominate during the day, that typical style may change. About a third of the infants in the study cited above did not fit any of the three categories. These psychologists attribute such differences in infant behaviors as may exist mostly to variations in mode of child care.

Genetic differences are accentuated by differences in mode of child care. When Navajo and Anglo mothers were asked to get the attention of their infants, all under 6 months of age, differences in both babies and mothers were dramatic. The Caucasian babies were relatively active, the Navajos passive. The Navajo mothers were practically silent, using their gaze to gain the babies' attention; the relatively passive infants reacted by simply looking back. The Caucasian mothers addressed the babies, speaking as though the infants could understand them; the babies responded by waving their arms and legs (Freedman, 1979).

Stages. Erik Erikson (1963) portrayed personality as developing by successive **stages,** each involving a conflict. These levels, as related to Freudian stages, are the following: During the 1st year (the oral-sensory stage), the individual is concerned with the conflict of trust versus mistrust. At this stage the child must develop a basic sense of trust. Infants periodically feel discomfort from cold, hunger, or pain. If they discover that they can rely on older people to restore comfort, they develop confidence, both in others and in themselves. If they find the world unstable and confusing, they feel helpless and insecure. Basic trust is interpreted as a general feeling of well-being derived from having one's needs met. Basic mistrust implies anticipation of discomfort or danger. The critical period for developing trust is during the 1st year, when the infant is completely dependent on others' reactions. Whatever degree of trust or mistrust the infant establishes will tend to persist, although modifications will occur with later experience. Of course, the child who does not retain an element of mistrust may become victimized by others. In other words, in all characteristics there should be a sense of balance.

During the 2nd and 3rd years, the anal stage, the conflict is between autonomy and doubt. While being trained in basic patterns of eating, sleeping, or toilet use, children must be allowed some alternatives to acquire feelings of freedom, personal dignity, and self-reliance. During the following genital-locomotor stage (ages 4 and 5), children acquire a sense of initiative and should overcome a sense of guilt. During the next stage of industry versus inferiority, in middle childhood, children learn the basic skills and work habits of their society. The alternative to mastering this task is coming to feel inadequate and inferior. Erikson also perceives this stage as a period of relative sexual and physical latency but rapid cognitive growth.

Two Major Issues

Constancy of personality. Much controversy focuses on the question: How persistent are personality traits? Robson (1972) concluded that prediction of subsequent behaviors from those manifest in infancy has been disappointing for several reasons. The behaviors studied may be insignificant. Or the context in which they occur may be neglected. Or behavioral consistencies may simply rupture at certain levels of strain. Besides, some early behaviors may form the

Gaining a feeling of mastery is an important aspect of personality development.

foundations of later ones that, nevertheless, appear somewhat different. That is, certain early personality characteristics represent potentials, which gradually find expression and assume final form as the result of the interplay of hereditary and environmental factors. Thus, an infant born with unusual reactivity to external stimuli may evolve into an adult who immediately overreacts to every new crisis. Or that same individual may become exceptionally responsive to new situations, reacting to them with alert curiosity. Krech, Crutchfield, and Livson (1974) decided that at least certain personality characteristics are enduring. The mother who insists that her child was stubborn from his 1st day on earth may be speaking the truth (p. 652).

Most researchers, however, report considerable consistency, at least for core traits. Subjects in the Berkeley Longitudinal Study proved quite stable in such dimensions as introversion versus extroversion, impulsivity versus self-control, activity versus passivity, attentiveness versus inattentiveness, and degrees of task orientation (Hunt, J. V., & Eichorn, 1972). In addition, a disposition to smile at discrepant events in infancy appears to be hereditary. And Chinese and Caucasian infants tend to smile differently at auditory and visual events from age 5 months to 29 months. Thus, there appears to be a temperamental component in infant smiling in certain situations. In addition, there is some tendency for slow tempo at play to persist, especially among girls. However, a child's disposition to be either impulsive or reflective at age 10 does not seem to relate in any way to dispositions in infancy. The Hunt and Eichorn study supported "both those who believe in a slim thread of continuity as well as those who hold that infancy provides a minimal preview of the future" (Kagan, Lapidus, & Moore, 1978, p. 1005).

The critical-period question. The **critical-period hypothesis,** which has also produced much controversy, suggests that certain experiences have a far greater effect at some periods of life than others. Such a period may span some months or even an entire life stage. Because maturational changes continue to occur in humans until adulthood, critical periods that relate to them may occur at least until that time and even later. For instance, puberty may be a critical period for the establishment of heterosexuality, and early adulthood may be critical for the organization of the adult life-style.

The concept of critical periods suggests that "golden times" for learning exist at various times in life, the specific time being dependent on the type of learning concerned. For instance, certain aspects of vision are forever impaired if visual experience is lacking during some critical period, perhaps during birth and between birth and age 4 (VonSenden, 1960). Nevertheless, the effects of environmental deficiencies at critical periods may not be irreversible. In a small village in Guatemala, Kagan (1973) observed infants who were kept in windowless huts without toys and with little attention from their mothers. On mental and maturational tests they lagged 4 or 5 months behind U.S. children. These children recovered, however. Older children in the village appeared happy and alert and performed better than American children on culture-fair tests. The challenge is to determine the types of experience necessary to reverse negative effects produced by environmental deficiencies in critical periods.

Child Rearing and Personality

Skolnick (1978) pointed out that two models of child rearing predominate in the United States, both deriving from the 20th-century belief that the good parent should listen to the experts' advice. The Freudian model has produced the image of the vulnerable child, emotionally fragile and requiring lavish support and affection. The second, or **behaviorist,** model derives from the view that parents can shape the child at will. In both models the parents play an omnipotent role. If the child fails, it is because they have failed.

Current research has disclosed flaws in both models. Both grossly exaggerate the parents' power and the child's passivity and pliability. They assume that parents and children interact in a sociocultural world, immune to other influences. They also presume a one-way influence, of parent on child, when the effect is one of complex interaction. Children themselves differ, as do their parents, and the effects of various modes of child rearing will differ accordingly.

The Freudian model of the vulnerable child has fared poorly. The effects of various approaches to basic habit training in feeding, eating, and toileting have few, if any, demonstrable effects later on. The popular concept of an emotionally damaged adult as the inevitable product of childhood trauma has derived from the "methodological flaw" of tracing adult problems to their roots instead of following the same individuals over time. The fact that an individual has experienced trauma and develops anxieties as an adult is no proof of a causative connection. While some persons who suffer trauma as children become troubled adults, others turn out well. Among 200 individuals studied from infancy through adolescence and at age 30, two-thirds of the predictions proved wrong (1964).

Only recently have environmental influences begun receiving the attention they deserve. A child with an uncaring mother may receive support from the other parent, a grandparent, or a street gang (Skolnick, 1978). Children who have come by any means to perceive themselves as able to cope can sustain unusual trauma, because they do not feel hopeless.

Skolnick concluded that parents will profit from coming to realize the limitations on their own power and on the family's perfectibility. They can behave more naturally if they do not perceive in their every act a potential for forever stunting the child's emotional development.

Sometimes children experience the impact of their own influence on their parents. Parents of highly active children tend to intrude physically or get into power struggles and competition with them. In contrast, parents' interaction with less active children is more harmonious (Buss, 1981).

Cultural Differences in Personality

A large and increasing body of research confirms the influence of culture on personality. Among these, a study in Israel of children aged 12 to 14 who had been educated in the Soviet Union, in the United States, and in Israel showed the American and Israeli children to be more open minded, more internal in their feelings of locus of control, and more creative in their thinking. A greater degree of locus of control by Israeli and American children was reflected in their greater willingness to assume responsibility for their achievements in life. Thinking styles characterized by belief systems intolerant of opposing beliefs are associated with rigid child-rearing patterns. Western children are generally encouraged to think independently, and parents and teachers exert relatively little pressure to impose belief systems on them. By contrast, Soviet children are strongly encouraged to embrace norms set by their collectives and are rewarded for conformity at home and at school.

Locus of control reflects the degree to which individuals perceive their behaviors to be under their own control rather than being controlled by fate or the dictates of others. Internal locus of control ordinarily relates to permissive child-rearing, which encourages independence of thinking from the early years. Because American children are taught to control their environment and to initiate their own behaviors, whereas Soviet children are encouraged to subordinate their behaviors to the group, American children typically attain greater internal locus of control. With regard to creative thinking, authoritarian control hinders intellectual development, especially the capacity to deal with novel problems.

By contrast, creative thinking relates positively to permissive child-rearing patterns. American children are typically more creative than Soviet ones, because nonconformist ideas and free expression are accepted, even encouraged, in the West, whereas Soviet children are pressured to absorb approved ideas. Israeli children more closely resemble the Americans than the Soviets because of their Western-oriented society.

Nevertheless, observed Avrim and Milgram (1977), such data do not mean that Soviet children are somehow inferior to their Western counterparts. Considering their sociocultural environment, their behaviors are appropriate. It is realistic that Soviet children perceive their behaviors as largely determined by others and that they find it more adaptive to embrace approved ideas than to initiate novel ones. It should be noted that the populations of all three countries are heterogeneous. Hence, generalizations do not apply to every segment of their respective societies.

Perspective on Personality Research

Most of the main conclusions about personality cited in this section are supported by considerable research. However, it is important not to ascribe to personality research a degree of definitude it does not deserve. For "the truth is, [such] research is unbelievably complex and still in its infancy. The concepts involved, such as self and traits, are inherently elusive and complex" (Rogers, 1977a, p. 138). Nor is there any conclusive agreement about what traits are desirable or undesirable. Nevertheless, data are slowly being collected and fitted together in ever more sophisticated ways.

SUMMARY

Growth and development proceed in orderly, predictable fashion, according to recognized principles. Despite overall similarities, physical development varies somewhat according to age, sex, and individual. It seems safest, at present, to make these conjectures: (1) Early training helps most in developing more complex skills. (2) Sex differences in motor potential are few in childhood, and girls' inferiority in this area apparently derives from sociocultural factors. (3) Body build has some indirect effect on personality, chiefly because of variations of social approval toward different builds. (4) Children do need to eat a balanced diet, with less snacking, and should be exposed to special diets only after their effects have become understood and critically examined.

The effect of physical appearance has been generally ignored by researchers. Nevertheless, it is of considerable significance. Children's peers, even their teachers, react to them, at least partly, on the basis of how they look.

Cognitive development is construed by Jean Piaget and others as proceeding to successively higher stages. Nevertheless, some critics question whether clear-cut stages exist. In general, researchers have discovered increased sophistication with age in coming to understand concepts such as "reality" or "death." Progression through these stages and cognitive development in general vary mainly according to biological endowment coupled with familial influence. Social class, too, has an important effect on whether children gain the proper foundations and attitudes to progress in cognitive tasks. While compensatory education for disadvantaged children has been widely judged a failure, different or more adequate modes of evaluation might disclose benefits.

Emotional development follows the same broad pattern among all children. Optimally, it reflects progress toward emotional maturity. While various factors, such as television violence and the mother's absence, have been cited as threats to emotional health, little proof exists regarding their effect on individuals.

Personality, including self-concept, is a gradual accretion developed by stages, according to Erikson and Piaget. Some researchers have reported little persistence of traits observed first in infancy, but the majority have found that core traits tend to endure across the years. It is also generally agreed that "golden moments" exist for learning at specific periods in life. But Kagan believes that the effects of deficiencies suffered at such periods may not be irreversible. In any case, the sociocultural environment has proved to be significant in determining what characteristics an individual acquires and the variations that distinguish people in one country from another.

SUGGESTED READINGS

Aviram, A., & Milgram, R. M. Dogmatism, locus of control and creativity in children educated in the Soviet Union, the United States, and Israel. *Psychological Reports,* 1977, *40*, 27–34. A study in Israel of children aged 12 to 14 years old indicates that the U.S.- and Israeli-educated children were more open minded, more internal in feelings of locus of control, and more creative in their thinking than the Soviet-educated children. These findings are attributed to differences in socialization.

Baruch, G. K., & Barnett, R.C. Competence-related behavior of preschool girls. *Genetic Psychology Monographs,* 1981, *103*, 79–101. Analysis was made of the determinants of preschool girls' competencies, including parental attitudes and behaviors and the preschool environment.

Buss, D. M. Predicting parent-child interactions from children's activity level. *Developmental Psychology,* 1981, *17*(1), 59–65. A study of 117 preschool children and their parents indicated that highly active children have important effects on the way their parents treat them.

Cicirelli, V. G. Mother/child and sibling/sibling interactions on a problem-solving task. *Child Development,* 1976, *47*(3), 558–596. Interactions were analyzed on the basis of sex and family size. The subjects were eight first-graders with third- or fourth-grade siblings.

Fox, A. M. Review: The special education needs of physically handicapped children. *Child Care, Health and Development,* 1976, *2*(1), 45–71. Educational needs of the children are discussed in terms of school setting, personal and academic problems, roles of professionals, and specific types of handicap involved.

Friedrich, W. N., & Boriskin, J. A. The role of the child in abuse: A review of the literature.

American Journal of Orthopsychiatry, 1976, *46*(4), 580–590. After reviewing theories regarding child abuse, the writers consider the role of the child in such abuse. Emphasis is placed on identifying children who may be at risk.

Galper, A., Jantz, R. K., Seefeldty, C., & Serock, K. The child's concept of age and aging. *International Journal of Aging and Human Development,* 1980–81, *12*(2), 149–157. A study of children from preschool through grade 6 disclosed that concepts of age and aging follow a Piagetian cognitive-developmental sequence.

Gardner, H. Children's art: The age of creativity. *Psychology Today,* 1980, *13*(12), 84–96. Children's art work is discussed in terms of its aesthetic value and artistic worth, and as a means of working through complex problems in their lives. Detailed analyses are made of the drawings of a boy and a girl as they progressed through childhood.

Glasberg, R., & Aboud, F. E. A developmental perspective on the study of depression: Children's evaluative reactions to sadness. *Developmental Psychology,* 1981, *17*(2), 195–202. A study of 5- and 7-year-old children indicated certain developmental changes in depressive reaction as well as individual differences in emotional expression.

Goleman, D. 1,528 little geniuses and how they grew. *Psychology Today,* 1980, *13*(9), 28–43. A follow-up six decades later of high-IQ children first studied in 1921—the famous Terman study—indicates how well these individuals have fared over time in terms of their careers, marriages, and family lives. Factors that account for differences between the most and least successful ones among them are identified.

Goleman, D. Still learning from Terman's children. *Psychology Today,* 1980, *13*(9), 44–53. On the basis of data obtained from successive follow-ups of high-IQ children originally studied 60 years ago, the current directors of the Terman study identified clues to the relationship between early experience and happiness in adulthood. They discuss the purposes of the study and indicate that it will continue as long as the subjects live.

Greenfield, P. M., & Schneider, L. Building a tree structure: The development of hierarchical complexity and interrupted strategies in construction activity. *Developmental Psychology,* 1977, *13*(4), 299–313. The construction of a "tree"—a mobile of plastic construction straws—was examined in order to determine the development of tree representations in areas other than language. The results support the concept of a level of cognitive organization common to action and language. They also afford new data on the nature and development of complex action patterns.

Harre, R. What's in a nickname? *Psychology Today,* 1980, *13*(8), 78–84. An analysis of children's nicknames indicates that children use them to distinguish acceptable from unacceptable children, to establish status hierarchies, and to make clear norms of behavior. Children's social behaviors in this area are very similar to those of adults.

Koch, R., & Koch, J. H. Retarded children. *Psychology Today,* 1976, *10*(7), 88–92; 100. Ways are discussed for reducing the numbers of retarded children. These include better care of fetuses, newborns, and the prematurely born and the avoidance of births that carry high risk of genetic mental defects.

Madden, J., Levenstein, P., & Levenstein, S. Longitudinal IQ outcomes of the mother-child home program. *Child Development,* 1976, *47*(4), 1015–1025. Low-income families participated in an intervention program that focused on modeling verbal interaction between mother and child around selected toys and books. The results suggest that the amount of IQ difference between groups depended on the amount of program intervention within the range of the conditions examined.

McAskie, M., & Clarke, A. M. Parent-offspring resemblance in intelligence: Theories and evidence. *British Journal of Psychology*, 1976, *67*(2), 243–273. Analysis of data indicates that much of the difference between parents and children is not directly related to parent IQ and that some may be attributed to other between-family variables.

Nelson, K. Individual differences in language development: Implications for development and language. *Developmental Psychology*, 1981, *17*(2), 170–187. An effort is made to explain differences in children's styles of language acquisition and usage, as identified in recent research.

Olejnik, A. B. Effects of children's sex and age on achievement evaluations by adults. *Personality and Social Psychology Bulletin*, 1980, *6*(1), 68–73. Sex and age of a child were found to affect its achievement evaluation by adults. It was concluded that age trends in achievement are due not only to actual cognitive developmental changes but also to differential socialization practices of adults.

Plionis, E. M. Family functioning and childhood accident occurrence. *American Journal of Orthopsychiatry*, 1977, *47*(2), 250–263. Family assessment is suggested as a means of identifying children prone to repeated accidents.

Schwarz, J. C. Childhood origins of psychopathology. *American Psychologist*, 1979, *34*(10), 879–885. Origins of serious emotional problems in childhood are discussed in terms of genetics, sex differences, and family interaction. Implications for the welfare of children are considered.

Solkoff, N. Children of survivors of the Nazi holocaust: A critical review of the literature. *American Journal of Orthopsychiatry*, 1981, *51*(1), 29–42. A critical evaluation of studies of children of survivors of the Nazi holocaust discloses methodological inadequacies and suggests more adequate approaches to future research.

Stevens, J. H. Jr., & Baxter, D. H. Malnutrition in children's development. *Young Children*, 1981, *36*(4), 60–71. The past 15 years' research regarding malnutrition and its impact on child development is summarized and its implications discussed.

Udwin, O., & Shmukler, D. The influence of sociocultural, economic, and home background factors on children's ability to engage in imaginative play. *Developmental Psychology*, 1981, *17*(1), 66–72. A study of South African and Israeli preschool children of lower- and middle-class economic status in unstructured play situations shows how cultural, socioeconomic, and home background factors influence fantasy development.

4
DEVELOPMENT IN CHILDHOOD: II

MORAL DEVELOPMENT

Stage Theory

Kohlberg's theory. This chapter will look at the child's moral, social, and sexual development. Kohlberg's (1977) interpretation of stage theory as applied to moral development is the best known. Kohlberg has been more interested in the understanding of morality than in the development of moral behaviors. He has been less concerned with what people do when faced with moral problems than what they believe to be morally proper.

Kohlberg has categorized people as being at one of seven stages in moral development, each stage being characterized by its particular beliefs about morality, such as reasons for being moral. People normally progress through these stages in a fixed sequence from 1 through 6, while a still higher stage 7 is still theoretical. The rate of moving through different levels of morality varies among children and societies. And some individuals never reach the upper levels. Kohlberg has admitted never finding a Stage 7 individual among those he has tested, but he has said that persons such as Socrates and Martin Luther who died for their principles had a strong Stage-7 orientation.

Kohlberg has interpreted moral development in terms of three main levels and their six stages, as follows. At Level 1, preconventional morality, children respond to cultural labels of "good" and "bad" but interpret them in terms of pleasant or unpleasant consequences. This level, in turn, has two stages. In Stage 1, the punishment-and-obedience orientation, behaviors are judged good and bad in terms of their physical consequences, regardless of their value. Deference to power is valued in itself, not in terms of real respect for the moral order. In Stage 2 (the instrumental-relativist orientation), human relationships are interpreted in terms of the "marketplace," or reciprocity ("You scratch my back and I'll scratch yours").

At Level 2, or conventional morality, meeting the expectations of one's society is viewed as worthy in its own right, regardless of the apparent consequences. The attitude is merely one of conforming to the social order and of actively supporting it. This level has two stages. In Stage 3—the interpersonal concordance, or good-boy/nice-girl orientation—behaviors are judged by intent ("He means well"). Good behavior is what pleases or helps others and is approved by them. In Stage 4, the law-and-order orientation, direct behaviors consist of doing one's duty, respecting authority, and maintaining the social order for its own sake.

At Level 3 (postconventional, autonomous, or principled morality), there is a distinct effort to define moral values and principles on their own merit apart from the authority of groups and people holding these principles.

Most children under age 9, some adolescents, and many adolescent and adult criminals are at the preconventional moral level. Most adolescents and adults are at the conventional level. Only a minority of adults arrive at the postconventional level (Kohlberg, 1977). The child who does not steal the cookies because he fears his parent is at the preconventional level. The youth who does not steal from the store because it is a matter of law is at the conventional level, subordinating individual needs to those of the group. The physician who allows a patient with no prospect but suffering to die has defined for herself what is right and wrong. She is at the postconventional level of morality.

Siegal (1980) concluded that Kohlberg's theory is little better than Piaget's. Kohlberg's methods rely too heavily on responses to moral dilemmas with which subjects are largely unfamiliar, but Kohlberg's stages 4 and 5 do help to characterize types of moral reasoning.

Critique of Kohlberg and related theories. Trainer (1977) deplored the uncritical acceptance of such theories of moral development. He concluded that Kohlberg has "hopelessly confused" age changes in moral development and concepts of good moral thinking. If progression toward higher levels of moral thinking is interpreted as identical to achieving progressively better moral thinking, who is to decide what constitutes good moral thinking? Considering the highly diverse moral standards among different societies, and even within the same society, views concerning the higher morality will inevitably differ.

Both laymen and stage theorists such as Kohlberg tend to judge the goodness of people's acts by their intent, not by their outcome. Mischel (1973) agreed that analyses of morality must take into account personal judgments about moral behavior and not simply the consequences of moral behaviors. But how can one, for sure, determine what an individual's intent was? Subjective values attached to behaviors vary according to social class, race, and other factors.

In addition, the conditions in which behaviors occur raise questions about whether the age-related sequence of moral judgment is invariable (Garbarino & Bronfenbrenner, 1976). Kohlberg and Kramer (1969) reported that some of their subjects, judged to have been mainly at Stage 4 in high school, manifested a considerable amount of Stage-2 thinking in their college years. Kohlberg and Kramer explained this apparent regression as produced by the pressures of college life. However, Turiel (1973) portrayed such behaviors as responses to changing values, models, reference groups, personal contingencies, and individual life-styles. That is, he contended, the students were merely responding to a relativism they experienced in a liberal college atmosphere and were neither regressing nor experiencing disequilibrium in their progress through a series of predesignated stages.

Finally, Piaget indicated that an individual's verbal rationale for holding certain moral attitudes—not overt behavior reflecting those attitudes—is what is undergoing developmental change (Inhelder & Piaget, 1958).

The matter of age and the development of prosocial behaviors is a complex one. One might anticipate that certain factors would

increase the likelihood of compassionate responding as children grow older (for example, greater competence, greater capacity for empathy and role taking, more emphasis on behaving responsibly toward others, and the like). Other factors, such as emphasis on individual achievement and competition, or right to privacy, would tend toward inhibiting or decreasing prosocial responses [Yarrow, Waxler, & collaborators, 1976].

Hence, age alone is a poor predictor, and the conditions of socialization may well define age trends for different children.

Three Special Influences on Moral Development

The family. Most theories of moral development stress the influence of family. Because parents regard such values as critical, they ordinarily assert a strong hand in this area. Cottle (1974) describes his own parents' influence in these words: "Even today, when annunciating my own values, I hear the voices of my parents coming from my mouth as though they lived inside me" (p. 267).

High forms of moral reasoning are related to fathers' greater attention.

A follow-up study of adults, originally studied as children 25 years ago by Sears, Maccoby, and Levin (1957) at Harvard University, indicated that the number of statistically significant relationships between child-rearing practices and adult outcomes little exceeded what might be anticipated from chance. It did seem that maternal affection made some long-term difference. And there was a slight negative correlation between punitive treatment in childhood and adult maturity. Somewhat more damaging to adult maturity was strictness, because it inhibited a child's need or tendency to be aggressive or noisy or to act out feelings. Adults who had had a strict upbringing had more-than-average difficulty in valuing and judging. If the strict parent had also been loving, however, there was little long-term ill effect.

Thus, the quality and quantity of parental love holds some significance. Children whose fathers are affectionate are likely to show tolerance and understanding. Strong mother love also contributes to sharing, tolerance, and understanding. But it negatively affects the highest forms of moral reasoning. In contrast, a father's love, even when great, appears to promote high-level moral functioning.

Oddly enough, those individuals who function at the highest, or reasoning, level of maturity seem in a sense less moral, or concerned about others. They will even hurt others if they feel some higher principle is involved.

In general, parents who were easy going and loving had the most mature children. Those who insisted that children toe the mark had conforming children, at the cost of their fuller development. The

> paradox is that promoting maturity leads first to a decrease in moral behavior, as a person . . . moves away from reliance on external authority . . . Only at the highest stage, when people become genuinely and emotionally aware of the feelings and viewpoints of others, do they again begin to behave less antisocially and more prosocially [McClelland, Constantian, & Regalado, 1978, p. 53].

Parents may shape children's moral behaviors in many ways, both obvious and subtle—by rewards and reprimands, by positively reinforcing the behaviors that they favor, and by modeling the desired behaviors. In a study of intrafamilial patterns of moral reasoning that involved 382 parents and children (the offspring ranging in age from 10 to 30 years), wives' and husbands' moral stages related positively though modestly. The siblings' moral stages proved independent of each other. And parents' and sons', but not daughters', moral stages related positively to each other. Nevertheless, these patterns rose to chance levels among the older sons, suggesting that the relationship between the morals of sons and their parents decreases with the years. The even smaller relationships between the morals of daughters and their parents contradicts the common assumption that parents have a greater socializing effect on their daughters. Among the offspring, the moral level of all but the youngest age group of females was lower than that for the males. That is, more of the males employed principled rather than morally conventional thinking (Haan, Langer, & Kohlberg, 1976).

Television. A presumably detrimental influence on moral development is television violence. But tests of this thesis have been neither consistent nor conclusive (Fredrich & Stein, 1973). One problem is that the definition of violence varies (Holden, 1972). In three studies of television violence, football was overlooked in one, judged highly violent in a second, and judged nonviolent in a third.

Television violence appears to have a detrimental influence on moral development.

Another problem is that such findings represent generalizations, and the effects undoubtedly vary with the child. A child who is unhealthily submissive might benefit from identification with more aggressive characters. Because most girls are brought up to be somewhat inhibited and because a measure of aggression—more than most girls possess and less than many boys possess—appears optimal for personal and intellectual development, they might well profit from a moderate diet of aggressive programs. (Of course, girls would probably identify more easily and profitably with *Bionic Woman* or *Wonder Woman* than *Gunsmoke* or National Football League games.) But children with high levels of antisocial aggressiveness might be negatively affected by the very same programs (Eron, Huesman, Lefkowitz, & Walder, 1974).

Culture. The moral values portrayed on television programs or taught by parents are inevitably colored by those of the larger **culture.** Culture includes all the learned behaviors of a people—its patterns of thought and language, its art and technology, its values and customs. With regard to children, culture is the social heritage that determines how they will be reared. As Cottle (1974) expressed it, "The observation of a single life is also an inspection of the human condition and its place in some evolutionary scheme" (p. 278). North American children are socialized into such values as efficiency, achievement, practicality, upward mobility, materialism, and technology.

To gain a better perspective on the child's own society and its ideals, cross-cultural comparisons are useful. They help researchers determine how much people can change without risking their psychic unity. Eisenberg (1972) declares that children's personalities should be changed to whatever degree required and practicable for them to become fully human. Cross-cultural studies indicate how cultures encourage or suppress the development of specific behaviors. For example, Anglo-American children demonstrate more rivalry than do Mexican-American children, probably because of the greater stress on autonomy and independence in middle-class urban, Anglo cultures. This emphasis interferes with developing cooperative relationships (Jones, P. A., & McMillan, 1973).

The individual factor. Whatever impact moral influences have on individual children is modified by their own special needs and dispositions. Besides, they are not exposed to consistent patterns of influence but often to contrasting or contradictory ones from which they must choose. Therefore, "A better metaphor for the process of socialization than a sponge soaking up influence would be that of a selective filter. Each of us is an evaluating, searching being. Our experiences are constantly being filtered through a perceptual and cognitive sieve in accordance with our requirements and unique judgments" (Lazarus, 1974, p. 165).

Facilitating Healthy Moral Development

A practical question arises: How can children be helped to arrive at the highest moral level? Bronfenbrenner (1977) recommends that children learn responsibility, for "the inutility of children in America is a striking fact. We don't let our children do anything important. Maybe they take out the garbage, but that's it. They are useless because we have made them useless" (p. 46). He suggests that school-children learn to care for others—not in books but by actually taking care of them—other children, old people, and the sick.

Aversive versus positive modes of socialization. Other suggestions can be summarized as follows: It is generally agreed that stress must be placed on socialization processes and child rearing. But the issue of whether moral development should be fostered by anxiety conditioning is also a popular one. Bettelheim (1977) argued that adults will never achieve a mature morality unless they have "been subject as children to a stringent morality based on fear and trembling"

(p. 87). Even at the level of complex moral principle, observes Aronfreed (1976), anxiety must serve as the "internal cognitive monitor" required to motivate moral behaviors.

Burton (1976) asserts that everywhere in the world behavior control is utilized far more often than **positive reinforcement.** But he admits that a strategy of total positive reinforcement has never been fully tested. Burton cites research indicating that moderate punishment, especially when accompanied by reasoning, is far more effective than major punishment. Excess punishment may reduce approved behavior by increasing anxiety to a level that focuses attention on the self and thus interferes with distinguishing good from bad behaviors. Punishment is more effective within a general context of warmth and love, especially since a strong ego and feelings of security constitute the "affective underpinnings of prosocial behavior" (Lickona, 1976).

Others largely oppose aversive forms of control, including withdrawal of love, in favor of encouraging morality based on consideration for others. Proponents of this point of view would reject a morality derived from mere conformity to rules that authoritarianism and punishment appear to support. Saltzstein (1976) rejects the behavioristic approach as simply a way of training children in particular behaviors. Such training, he contends, will not necessarily produce spontaneous altruistic and moral behaviors. Cognitive-developmental theorists, such as Kohlberg and Hoffman, prefer long-range preventive procedures for developing moral behaviors. They believe parents should stress children's role taking and opportunities to become sensitive to others' feelings and attitudes. Hoffman emphasizes that punishment arouses anxiety and resentment, focuses attention on the self instead of others, affords punitive rather than altruistic parental models, and fails to provide children actual experiences in helping others (Hoffman, 1977).

Some generally accepted principles. Most theorists, observes Lickona (1976), agree on many basic principles of socializing moral behaviors. First among these is that parents should be consistent and practice the precepts they preach (Burton, 1976). And the content of these moral lessons should be appropriate to the child's cognitive capacities (Aronfreed, 1976). Children should also be instructed how to be good, not just how not to be bad. Television, especially, could provide highly effective models for learning **prosocial** behaviors (Liebert & Poulos, 1976). Modeling has the virtue of contributing to moral competence by demonstrating specific ways of helping others in particular situations. This process has been employed effectively even with preschool children (Yarrow, Scott, & Waxler, 1973). Both the behaviorist and cognitive-developmental theorists recommend catching the child being good (Lickona, 1976) and reinforcing the behavior through appropriate rewards and demonstrations of approval. Burton (1976) specifically recommends helping children to understand that a variety of moral situations may fall into the same category to which a certain moral judgment is applied. "The idea is to develop in children an integrated moral functioning" (Lickona, 1976, p. 26).

SOCIAL DEVELOPMENT

Pattern and Context

Stages. Children's social growth tends to follow a broad, general pattern. The child influences and is influenced by others in a dynamic interaction initiated early in life (Silverman, R. E., 1974). Initially, however, the infant is asocial, and reactions to others are ill-defined and vague. Children at this stage focus on their own wishes and needs. The second stage, a presocial one, is characterized by indiscriminate attachment behavior. At this stage, which begins as early as the 1st month, infants pay others a certain passive attention, moving their arms or legs or following someone with its eyes. In the third stage, at around 3 or 4 months, infants begin clearly to react to others. And a month or so afterward they may even assume social initiative by smiling at familiar persons, whether or not the other smiled first.

In fact, children interact with their peers from a very early age, and from 18 months to 2 years they engage in parallel play. That is, when children are

Very young children often engage in parallel play; they may not talk together, but they will go through similar motions with their playthings.

together, each plays alone but performs actions similar to those of others. One child may take a pile of blocks and shortly knock it down; another child, peripherally aware, may do the same. Meantime, the children have not exchanged a word.

Four observations of toddlers at play over a 7-month duration indicated that parallel play, instead of simply reflecting inadequacy in early peer relationships, provides a naturally conducive context for social development. When the care givers, though present, responded to toddler overtures just briefly, the toddlers turned to familiar toys and not to the unfamiliar peer who was present. Each toy became more interesting when its use by another child drew children into social interaction. Also, at this stage boys engage in rough and tumble play in greater amounts and with more intensity than girls (DiPietro, 1981).

In a society in which leisure activities are gaining increasing recognition, children's play assumes a new significance as a foundation for the years ahead. At the same time, the significance of play as a foundation for progress in cognitive development is becoming increasingly recognized. The games children play afford excellent opportunities for learning many of the concepts involved in the basic school subjects, such as "space," "quantity," "proportion," and a host of others. In addition, children learn to get along with others in situations where they can test their own roles and skills and come to appreciate those of their playmates.

Thus, in time they begin to form friendships, which relate more to specific interactions between a pair than to any overall social competencies. Therefore, general interaction patterns affecting sociometric status should be distinguished from specific interactions that influence friendships (Masters & Furman, 1981).

Sharing versus egocentricity. Young children were formerly portrayed as selfish and egocentric, only gradually becoming socialized into concern for others. In laboratory play situations, however, children 18 months and even younger share with others completely on their own initiative without any praise or prompting. Such sharing refutes the egocentricity so commonly ascribed to young children and "reveals them instead as already able contributors to social life" (Rheingold, Hay, & West, 1976, p. 1157).

Influences on Social Development

Family experience. In Chapter 2 we saw how the foundations of children's social development are laid in the home, through mutual attachments with parents and siblings. In studies of face-to-face interaction between mothers and their infants, those mothers who are somewhat matter of fact and impassive less often elicit positive responses from their babies, and their interactions tend to be brief. The result is that their children later experience anxiety about their attachment. It may be that interaction during these early weeks of life is critical for subsequent social life (Blehar, Lieberman, & Ainsworth, 1977). Maternal behaviors that more strongly relate to positive infant responses are playfulness and pacing of interaction, as manifest in mothers' concern for their babies' present state and the activity in progress.

This influence sometimes operates in an indirect, somewhat devious fashion. Especially in families where parents establish a climate of passive neglect, children are forced to seek affection and approval elsewhere (Condry, 1974). In cases where parents are extremely permissive, children may become socially exploiting and domineering (Lorber, 1971); and the higher the social exploitation rating, the higher is the parents' permissiveness rating. That is, the children use others for their own advantage and try to manipulate them for their own purposes. Hence, while a measure of permissiveness may be desirable, it may reach some point where it discourages optimum socialization. Parents may control intergroup contacts by implicitly or explicitly indoctrinating their children. Mrs. Jones, a social climber, may lead Sally to believe that the neighborhood children are not good enough for her. As a result, Sally strives for, but fails to achieve, friends in an upper-class group who possess the money, manners, and clothes that she lacks.

The impact of the family on social development varies with several factors. A study of 2957 children in Texas examined the relation between birth order and peer status (Roff, Sells, & Golden, 1972). The most favored position with regard to peer status was the younger of two children. The next best was the younger children in a family of three or more. The least favorable position was in the middle of four or more children. While these differences were definite, they were not large. With regard to family life, only harmony and cohesiveness improved peer acceptance. Mothers' employment outside of the home showed no special relationship to the child's social status, but a tense or unstable family climate related to poor social adjustment.

Let me add this cautionary note. It is commonly assumed that the nuclear family is the only satisfactory milieu for a child's social development. However, in a study that compared adolescents in Israeli kibbutzim with those reared according to more traditional family patterns, the kibbutz youth had higher self-esteem and closer interpersonal relationships. Thus, it seems that the greater separation of child from parents in the kibbutz hurts neither parent/child relationships nor personality development (Long, Henderson, & Platt, 1973; Rogers, 1977a, pp. 394–395).

Day care. Day care is often represented as superior to home care in fostering social development, but much depends on the quality of the home situation. A comparison of Chinese-American and Caucasian children, aged 3½ months to 30 months, disclosed that home-reared children were no more or less attached to their mothers than day-care children and that the day-care children were no more social (Kagan, Kearsley, Zelazo, & Minton, 1976). Indeed, at the age of 29 months the home-reared toddlers were a little more sociable than the day-care ones.

Ethnicity and social class related more to learning ability in the young children than did home or group rearing. At 20 months the Caucasians typically had higher English language scores than the Chinese, and the middle-class children scored higher than the working-class children. Thus, this study confirms others that show day care to have little measurable effect on mental or social development of children, the exception being children from less privileged, poorly educated families. During the first years of life such children show better cognitive development than those without day care. However, even this advantage tends to disappear with the years (Bush, 1976).

In a distinct departure from his earlier statements, Jerome Kagan has concluded that constant mothering is not critical for a child's development. A study of children who attended quality day-care programs, with a low child-to-adult ratio and plentiful mastery experiences, disclosed a picture of normal, if not superior, infant development. The day-care children were also no more likely than other children to experience separation anxiety because of absence of the mother. Nor were the day-care children any more aggressive or competitive than home-reared children. The day-care children were superior to home-reared children on the nonverbal portion of the Bayley Scale of Infant Development. The key is in quality day care. Day-care centers "can be incredibly enriching experiences or they can be horrible, threatening, degrading places" (Norman, 1978, p. 22). The same extremes can be found in child care at home.

Society's influence. Certain characteristics of present-day society can be interpreted as contrary to children's best social development. Jensen and Moore (1977) concluded that the competition, so prevalent in our society, produces negative interpersonal consequences. Hence, adults responsible for socializing children should stress cooperative modes of interaction in order to offset the competitiveness within the culture. In addition, today's society is so preoccupied with selfishness that the consuming question simply becomes "What am I getting out of it? Society's fascination with self-aggrandizement makes many young people judge all relationships in terms of winning and losing points. For both sexes in this society, caring deeply for anyone is becoming synonymous with losing" (Jensen & Moore, 1977, p. 28).

Children are also exposed from their earliest years to social hierarchies. In a study of working- and middle-class students in West Virginia and California, Herbert Wilcox reported that children at all ages recognize such a **hierarchy.** As early as 5 children display some ability to interpret organizational relationships, and by the second grade such concepts are often well established. Children's understanding of the hierarchy structure is reinforced by the age-related power they see wielded by upper-grade children in school and older siblings at home ("The Organized Child," 1978).

Sex. Social behavior is also, in considerable measure, a function of sex. This link was demonstrated in a study of previously unacquainted pairs of 33-month-old children, brought together in same-sex and mixed-sex pairs in a laboratory playroom (Jacklin & Maccoby, 1978). Among the girls social play was reduced when they were with boys. When girls played with girls, they displayed much social behavior, and boys playing with boys showed almost as much.

Children of both sexes were more likely to stay close to their mothers or cry when they were paired with a boy; but the effect of being paired with a boy was far stronger for girls. When paired with a boy, a girl cried more than when paired with a girl and also behaved more passively. She often sat quietly watching her partner play, sometimes merely holding a toy but not playing with it. The same girls, when paired with girls, were less passive than boys paired with boys or boys paired with girls. Already they had absorbed the existing stereotypes of what should be expected of partners of the other sex.

In other research among kindergarteners and first- and second-graders, boys proved more oriented to the same sex than girls did in terms of games, television characters, and occupational preferences. This difference is undoubtedly due to the greater flexibility in girls' sex roles. Both sexes preferred same-sex playmates, a preference that increased from kindergarten to first grade. While girls were more flexible in their choice of activities, they nevertheless preferred playing these games with girls (Marcus & Overton, 1978).

Personality factors. An especially important factor in social interaction is the child's own personality. It both modifies and shapes, and in turn is shaped by, the quality of others' responses. In a study of young women interacting with children aged 7 to 10, the children had a profound effect on the women's behavior (Cantor & Gelfand, 1977). When children behaved in a socially responsive, lively way, the women rated them as more attractive, skillful, and intelligent than when they were not responsive. More responsive children were also rated as easier to work with, attractive, and more likable, though not as more intelligent. The women also responded differently to boys and girls. They gave girls more help when they were friendly and talkative rather than taciturn, but they gave boys equal amounts in both conditions. Thus, pleasant children become over-rated, while socially more withdrawn children may be underrated.

It is easily apparent to any observer that children vary greatly in the quality of social response they generate. Children who are low on peer interaction and peer acceptance are typically defined as socially isolated. However, a study of children in eight Head Start classrooms disclosed no relationship between peer acceptance and frequency of peer interaction. On the basis of **sociometric** measures several types of children were identified: sociometric stars, named by many children; sociometric rejectees, commonly disliked; children who interacted often with their peers; and children who were tuned out. The tuned-out children were shy, anxious, fearful, and ignored by their peers—neither accepted nor rejected (Gottman, 1977).

While children's social development is best promoted by the healthy interaction of all factors that impinge on them, deliberate efforts to help them may yield some success. When third- and fourth-grade, socially isolated children were coached in social skills, they received higher ratings from their peers than a control group. The coaching consisted of instructions from an adult in the skills associated with making friends, playing games with their peers in order to practice these skills, and a review session with the coach. A year later the coached children had proceeded further toward being included by their peers, although intervention produced no lasting change in their peer status (Oden & Asher, 1977).

A final word. Two observations may help place children's social development in better perspective. First, rugged individualism, such an important part of North American tradition, has in considerable measure become outmoded. In modern society, work and play are largely a matter of people interacting. Those who lack social skills are often denied promotions on the job or acceptance in the community. Second, unless growing children, in spite of that, retain a healthy self-concept and strong identity, they can easily become manipulated by others and overly dependent on their approval.

SEX-ROLE DEVELOPMENT

Biological Sex Roles

Stages in psychosexual development. Children's sexual behavior can be thought of in terms of biological sex roles and social sex roles. On the one hand, feminine and masculine attitudes emerge as biological consequences of sex awareness, sex interests, and sex drive. Social sex roles, on the other hand, involve patterns of behavior judged appropriate for each sex.

With regard to biological sex roles, cultural patterns are so organized that most individuals follow the same general stages in psychosexual development. According to Freud and his followers, in the first of four stages—birth to age 3—the child is narcissistic. Sensual satisfaction is derived from the infant's own body: from the mouth (nursing), from the anus (bowel movements), and from the sex organs (masturbation). Most children arrive at the point where they prolong the toilet experience, presumably for sexual pleasure. Babies also discover pleasant sensations when handling their sexual organs.

According to a contrasting view, infantile sexuality is mainly erogenous, with sensuality indulged in for its own sake. Sensual pleasures relating to anal and bladder evacuation, sometimes perceived as having erotic significance, play no role in adult sexual expression. When genital activities do gain greater significance in later years, adults retrospectively superimpose sensual interpretations onto infants' anal and urethral sensuality.

From ages 3 to 5 comes the phallic stage, when the child's interest focuses on his or her own genital organs. At this stage the child presumably becomes jealous of the same-sex parent while focusing attention on the opposite-sex parent. The boy focuses sexual feeling on his mother while envying his father—the so-called **Oedipus complex.** Conversely, the girl identifies with her mother, though blaming the mother for her lack of external genitals, an emotion termed penis envy; collectively, these feelings are called the **Electra complex.**

Several factors militate against the validity of the Oedipal hypothesis. The mother is the preferred parent of the majority of children of both sexes, undoubtedly because she attends them more often. Nor does any hard evidence exist that children's emotional response to the parent of the opposite sex is sexual in character. Finally, if a sexual component does exist, it is likely to have initiated with the parent, whose biological sex role has matured, rather than the child, who lacks the hormonal base to support it.

The following conversation between a mother and child illustrates sex concepts in young children:

Child: When I'm thirty will I be a mother?
Mother: If you have a baby you will.
Child: Do all womans have babies?
Mother: No.
Child: Why?
Mother: Some are not strong enough, some are too busy doing other things— some . . .
Child: Well, in three or six weeks when I'm thirty, I shall have a baby—where do babies come from?
Mother: Seeds.
Child: Where do the seeds come from?
Mother: The father and the mother.
Child: Where does the father keep him?
Mother: They are in his body.
Child: Oh, is he keeping them warm same as the mother does the baby?
Mother: He doesn't have them there to keep them warm, but because they belong there.
Child: Well, when I'm six I'll marry you because you're so cute.
Mother: But—(Father comes in.)
Child: Hello, Daddy. Did you buy me something? (No further questioning) [Rust, n.d.].

The genital, or heterosexual, stage is initiated after puberty and usually persists through life. After years of being conditioned to a sexually dichotomous society, most people pursue this pattern after hormonal changes provide the support for it. Heterosexual activity presumably provides greater reduction of tension, especially for the male. Complementary anatomical features encourage heterosexual compatibility on the physical level. And societal demand and the institution of the family support it on the sociopsychological level. However, arrival at the heterosexual stage does not automatically signify good adjustment. Note, for example, the man who molests small girls.

On the final, heterosexual, level it is commonly assumed that a new and mature sexual morality has taken hold. It may have or not, but the situation defies simplistic description (Dreyer, 1975). Today's adolescents have been less conditioned to concepts of marriage derived from the "cult of virginity." In fact, only 23% of young males aged 16 to 19 maintained that a woman's virginity at marriage is important (Sorensen, 1973). In their study Miller and Simon (1974) found that 48% of girls younger than 17 had engaged in light petting, and by age 17 the figures had risen to 69% for the girls and 73% for the boys. In another study Sorensen (1973) reported the modal age of first intercourse to be 15 and the median between 15 and 16.

A critique. Sexual development does not proceed as neatly as the above outline would suggest.

> It is doubtful that everyone goes through all four of the foregoing stages, or in the order given. . . . Probably only through sociocultural sanctions and the prospect of related rewards . . . do such a large majority manage to "muddle through" and establish reasonably satisfactory marriages. A sizable number never attain a mature heterosexuality, presumably because they have become arrested at some early stage. Individuals who are arrested in the narcissistic stage may seek sexual partners solely to please themselves. Individuals who never move beyond the Oedipal stage may remain with their parents the rest of their lives, unable to make a break [Rogers, 1977a, p. 254].

Children have obtained little direct help from adults in achieving healthy sexual adjustment. Informal polling of college students by the author indicates that fewer than a fifth of them rate as adequate the sex education they received at home or school. Even those adults who attempt to give help have trouble finding suitable printed materials on the subject. A study of 31 books on sex education for adolescents disclosed that the books discussed moderately, minimally, or not at all the topics that most interest adolescents—especially sexual intercourse, its context, and its consequences. About 20% of the books presented information impartially, 50% with moral overtones, and 30% with Christian moral precepts, the last giving about half as much information as the others. The authors with a medical degree wrote no more informative books than did the others. In general, the books were inadequate.

The books with moral overtones could be classified as having fig-leaf morality or hidden morality. The fig-leaf books completely ignored sexual intercourse and the genital organs. One of them gave detailed descriptions of every part of the body except the sexual organs, although the jacket proclaimed it to be an anatomy book for children who are curious about their bodies. Another fig-leaf book, *His and Hers: Dating Manners*, considered various aspects of dating, including necking, but did not even hint that sexual intercourse is possible. The hidden-morality books were presumably impartial but actually quite moral.

The Christian books insisted that sexual intercourse be restricted to marriage and that its role is to serve God—instead of to promote a couple's spiritual and physical union. In recent years there has been no apparent decline in Christian sex-education books but growing numbers of impartial books (Rubenstein, Watson, & Rubenstein, 1977).

Only rarely do parents or even sex educators fully recognize that sex education is largely indirect in its more significant and basic aspects. Healthy sexual adjustment is a matter not merely of sex information as such. It also involves feelings and attitudes toward oneself and toward others of the same and the opposite sex. Sexual maturity is a function of total maturity, although progress in other areas of personality by no means guarantees a wholesome status in this one.

Social Sex Roles

Definitions. The social sex role relates to those behavior patterns and psychological characteristics appropriate to each sex. It represents society's ideal of what males and females should be. Sexual identity includes one's sense of being male or female, one's behavior as a male or female, and one's orientation to a sexual partner (heterosexuality, bisexuality, or homosexuality). Sex-role adoption refers to assuming the behaviors of one sex or the other, including manners, mode of dress, and choice of toys and games. Sex-role preference refers to the perception of one or the other sex role as more desirable. Susie may perceive the male sex role as more advantageous (sex-role preference). Yet she may have come to play her role in traditionally feminine ways because of maternal pressures (sex-role adoption). Internally, she is ambivalent, identifying mostly with the stereotypically female but also somewhat with the male sex role (Lynn, 1959).

Biological foundations. A variety of factors, including the biological, contribute to social sex identity. These include prenatal hormones, early sex differences in behavior, the presence of sexually typical or atypical parents, and cultural factors. The administration of the male hormone **androgen** prenatally to the fetus may influence postnatal aggression and interest in babies and dolls (Green, 1975).

Research by Money and Ehrhardt (1972) suggests that gender identity is confirmed at an early age and that the sex assigned an individual at birth is far more important for establishing this identity than is gonadal or genetic sex. Nevertheless, hormonal activity during fetal development has persisting effects that increase the brain's capacity to adapt to the sex of assignment. For instance, in the so-called "testicular-feminizing syndrome" a genetic male has male internal gonads, but external female genitalia, because of a failure of androgen secretion from the testes during a critical phase of fetal development. Such an infant, reared as a girl, may adapt rather easily to female gender identification. This adaptation is ordinarily interpreted as proof that culture has greater influence than biology. But this point of view overlooks the fact that the syndrome was caused in the first place by a biological lack of the male hormone (Rossi, 1977).

Ehrhardt, Epstein, and Money (1968) raise the question of whether the failure of androgen secretion in these genetic male fetuses increases the brain's capacity to adapt to the requirements of the female sex role. They observed that "a counterpart syndrome among genetic females with internal female organs but masculinized external genitalia" raises the same issue. The condition occurs because the mothers took a drug having an androgenic effect in order to prevent miscarriage in early pregnancy. Such babies, when defined as male at birth, acquire a male gender identity. When surgically corrected to remain female, they acquire a female identity. In the latter case such girls depart in some ways from the typical female profiles. They have less interest in girls' activities, more preference for older children, and less responsiveness to babies.

Reports of sex differences, even in infants, would seem to support the view that such distinctions are biologically based. In a study of two groups of newborn full-term infants (14 uncircumcised males, 15 females), the males showed greater levels of wakefulness, facial grimacing, and low-intensity motor activity (Phillips, King, & DuBois, 1978). The uncircumcised males were also slightly more irritable than the females and consequently more active. Earlier theorists suggested that males' innately higher activity level gives them an advantage, especially in the competitive work world. However, heightened activity, especially if it becomes hyperactivity, may prove a disadvantage. Longitudinal studies are needed to determine the persistence of spontaneous activity in newborns and its relation to later life.

Caution should be exercised in interpreting research into sex differences when observers know the sex of the infants being rated. In one study, 204 male and female subjects rated the same infants' emotional responses, half being told that they were observing a boy and the other half a girl. Identical infants in particular situations were judged as showing completely different emotions, depending on the sex attributed to the child, the sex of the raters, and the raters' previous experience with young children. This study underscored the fact that people in the infants' world treat them differently according to their sex (Condry & Condry, 1976). Even from infancy boys and girls live in different social worlds, exposed to contrasting attitudes and expectations.

Parental influence. It is a matter of common observation that parents' differential expectations of their sons and daughters derive from sex-role stereotypes. In order to assess the influence of such stereotypes Atkinson and Endsley (1976) had 40 pairs of college-educated parents react to hypothetical situations in which a son and daughter (aged 4 and 6) interacted with their parents or other persons in ways more typical of one sex than the other. In general, both parents encouraged sex-appropriate behaviors in their children. At the same time, to some extent, they encouraged behaviors characteristic of their own sex in both children.

In other research that involved home observations of children, girls played more often with dolls and soft toys at age 1 or 2 years, whereas boys more often engaged in active play, play with transportation toys, and play forbidden by the parents. No substantial differences were observed in the way parents treated their sons or daughters. Nor did sex differences in the children's behavior increase noticeably from 1 to 2 years. Finally, no correlation was found between parents' sex-role stereotypes and the degree to which children exhibited sex-typed behavior (Smith & Daglish, 1977).

Fathers' and mothers' roles in children's sex-role development are viewed as somewhat different. Daughters of mothers who work outside the home perceive their roles differently from those whose mothers are not thus employed. Such characteristics as competence, competitiveness, and independence, ordinarily attributed to working fathers, are attributed to working mothers as well (Marantz & Manfield, 1977).

Nevertheless, the father may have a greater influence on sex-role perceptions, because he makes a greater distinction in his treatment of sons and daughters. And it is the paternal, not the maternal, role that supports heterosexuality in children of both sexes, according to Johnson (1975). In father/daughter relationships, his superior power is in accord with the superior power granted in the family to husbands. Thus, he fosters her independence from the mother. The early primacy of the mother in the son's experience, however, means that the son must shift his relationship with women from one in which she has greater power as a mother to one in which he himself has greater power as a father and husband. The father encourages heterosexuality in both son and daughter, by serving as a model to his son and by playing the role of "husband" to his daughter.

Therefore, it is incorrect to perceive masculinity and femininity as simply complementary to each other. Because both children initially identify with the mother, the maternal aspect of femininity gives rise to the common humanity of both sexes. However, the sex-differentiating principle derives from the father. (Johnson, 1975).

In cases where homosexual or **transsexual** parents are involved, the question may arise whether their children should be placed in other homes or, in divorce custody cases, be automatically awarded the sexually normal parent. In a study of 37 children reared by female homosexuals or by persons who had changed their sex, 36 had a conventional sex preference or were moving in that direction and had neither transsexual nor homosexual fantasies. The majority of these individuals, aged 3 to 20, were aware of their parents "atypical sexual identity." Only one of the children did not indicate a clear heterosexual pattern. When asked to draw a person, the girls drew females first, and the boys drew males. It appears, suggests Richard Green, who conducted the study, that the parents' unconventional sex preference has little impact on the child's sexuality, partly because of other factors in the environment. Children devote much time to reading and watching television and are exposed to conventional sex models among their peers and others. Green tentatively concluded that children reared by homosexual and transsexual parents differ little from those reared in more conventional family situations (Cohen, 1978).

Sociocultural influence. Parents treat boys and girls differently everywhere in the world, but in different ways and degrees in different areas. For example, in almost all countries parents prefer sons to daughters, with varying emphases (Williamson, 1977). A moderate preference for sons is found in the United States, Israel, Turkey, and Lebanon; a strong one is found in rural areas of Algeria, Egypt, and Tunisia. Only in extremely rare, somewhat obscure, cultures are daughters preferred. Catholics and Jews tend to have stronger preferences for sons than do Protestants, and men stronger ones than women. In individual families, the sex of previous children is the best predictor of current sex preference.

The school as a factor. Schools tend to reinforce whatever sex-role stereotypes their society accepts. They have not been in the vanguard of recent sex-role modifications. Observation of children in preschool classrooms indicates that sex typing among 3- and 4-year-olds changed little from 1968 to 1976, the period over which these data were gathered. Girls who sometimes engaged in masculine-type behaviors received no disapproval from their peers and little from their teachers. By contrast, boys who attempted feminine sex-stereotyped behaviors such as dressing up, doll play, and kitchen play were often criticized by their peers. Especially in the case of dressing up, the teacher also made critical comments. For behaviors such as playing with blocks, which teachers judged as appropriately task related, boys received greater reinforcement from teachers than did girls engaging in exactly the same behaviors (Fagot, 1977).

Children are not so sex typed at certain less traditional schools. A comparison of children in a traditional and in an open nursery school that minimized sex differences disclosed that children in the traditional school more often played in same-sex groups and those in the open school in mixed-sex groups. Of course the results could, to a degree, have been contaminated by the fact that parents probably choose schools with values like their own (Hayes, 1978).

Play. Play activities assume a more important role in sex-typing boys than they do for girls. Fagot and Littman (1975) conjectured that girls are permitted greater latitude in play because such behaviors are irrelevant to societal stereotypes of femininity. Instead, the way girls relate to significant people in their lives is the relevant variable for displaying femininity.

In contrast, boys learn masculine values of competition and achievement on the playground. The little boy entering school is egocentric, out to do things for himself. Hence, he is on a collision course with other children of both sexes on the playground, in the classroom, and going to and from home. Boys' play is saturated with competition, which provides training for their later achievements through competition in school, sports, and the work world. In play they learn the rules of the game, designed not to encourage cooperation but to provide fair competition. Often, boys learn not simply the rules of the game but how to get around them. At home they are constantly prodded to excel, and in the mass media they see glorified the male who becomes "number one" (Fagot & Littman, 1975, p. 11). As they grow up, they come to feel that they have little real worth as individuals if they are not number one in some activity—especially sports, and most desirably contact ones. Meantime, they learn that above all they must avoid playing with girls or playing girls' games (Fitzgerald, 1978).

Effectiveness of sex-role socialization. Because girls and boys, from birth, are treated differently, they learn their lesson early. Even as young as 2 years of age children possess a considerable knowledge of sex-role stereotypes. In a study of 2- and 3-year-olds, both sexes believed that girls

> liked to play with dolls, liked to help mother, liked to cook dinner (three year olds only), liked to clean house (three year olds and two year old girls only), talk a lot, never hit, say I need some help. Boys, but not girls, believe that girls: cry sometimes, are slow (three year olds only), say you hurt my feelings, say you're not letting me have a turn (three year olds only). . . . [Both sexes believed that boys] like to play with cars (three year olds and two year old

boys only), like to help father, like to build things (three year olds only), say I can hit you. Girls but not boys believe that boys like to climb a tree (three year olds only), like to fight, never cry (two year olds only), are mean, are weak and so forth [Kuhn, Nash, & Brucken, 1978, p. 447].*

Both sexes believed that boys, and not girls, when they grow up

will be boss, mow the grass. Boys, but not girls, believe that boys rather than girls, when they grow up, will: be governor, be a doctor, fly an airplane. . . . Both boys and girls believe that girls rather than boys when they grow up will clean the house, be a nurse, be a teacher [p. 448].

In general, the girls believed negative things about boys, and the boys negative things about girls. The girls believed that boys would fight and be mean, views that the boys did not share. And the boys said girls would cry and be slow, views that the girls did not share (Kuhn, Nash, & Brucken, 1978). Somewhere along the line both sexes come to value masculine attributes more highly.

A Concluding Observation

For a better perspective on children's sex roles, consider these observations: (1) In childhood, sex roles are a bit more distinctive than in infancy but less distinctive than in adolescence, after puberty has occurred. (2) Even those parents who feel that sex roles are too confining and inhibiting conform to the traditional stereotypes in rearing their own children. They hesitate to jeopardize their children's opportunities for personal and social adjustment in a world still attached, on basic levels, to traditional sex roles. (3) Certain changes have taken place that may, to some extent, modify children's sex roles. These include the drive to delete sexism from children's books; the emergence of women, in vast numbers, into the work world; and the emphasis on the fathers' role in the home.

SUMMARY

Stage theory has been applied to the aspects of development discussed in this chapter, as to those discussed earlier. Kohlberg depicts moral development as involving three main stages: preconventional, conventional, and postconventional (principled, autonomous). Some authorities warn against the uncritical acceptance of such theories, indicating that standards of morality—hence, what constitutes lower or higher morality—differ.

Among the greatest influences on children's moral development, however it may be measured, include the culture (including television) and the family.

*From "Sex role concepts of two- and three-year-olds," by D. Kuhn, S. C. Nash, and L. Brucken. In Child Development, 1978, 49(2), 445–451. © 1978 by the Society for Research in Child Development, Inc. This and all other quotations from this source are reprinted by permission.

Children themselves do not simply soak up the morals to which they are exposed but modify them to meet their own special inclinations and needs. Authorities agree on many basic principles of socializing children in appropriate moral standards and behaviors, but they differ over the specific modes of teaching to be employed.

In social development, too, children's progress is gradual, from asocial behaviors in infancy to socially adept ones later on. Children are strongly influenced in their social development by their experiences with others, in the family and at play. Unfortunately, certain characteristics of modern society, such as competitiveness and self-aggrandizement, negatively influence children's social values.

Children's sex behaviors can be viewed in two contexts. Biological sex roles concern the emerging of feminine and masculine attitudes as consequences of sex drive. Social sex roles embrace those psychological traits and behavioral patterns characteristic of each sex and include behaviors that society defines as appropriate to one's status as female or male. They constitute the abstracted concepts of the ideal female and male within that culture.

According to Freud, biological sex development proceeds through distinct stages: narcissistic, phallic, Oedipal, and latency-homosexual to the genital-heterosexual stage. Realistically, however, not everyone goes through all these stages or proceeds in the order given.

Social sex roles derive from a variety of influences, mainly biological, sociocultural, and familial. From birth, boys and girls are treated differently, according to social stereotypes varying somewhat with parental interpretation. Fathers apparently have a greater impact, in this matter, than do mothers, because they differentiate more between their daughters and sons. Both sexes are aware of these expectations from early years, although girls are permitted somewhat greater latitude in their role. How much, or in what way, children's sex roles will change in the future is uncertain. Even those parents who favor broader, less confining sex roles adhere, at least broadly, to traditional standards in rearing their own children. Nevertheless, certain factors, such as reduced sexism in textbooks and women's *en masse* trek into the work world, will undoubtedly diminish stereotypes.

SUGGESTED READINGS

Arcus, M. E. Value reasoning: An approach to values education. *Family Relations*, 1980, *29*(2), 163–171. An analysis of the value reasoning approach to values education, in which students are encouraged to reason clearly about values issues. Such an approach helps adolescents think logically about values issues and deal sensibly with value conflicts.

DiPietro, J. A. Rough and tumble play: A function of gender. *Developmental Psychology*, 1981, *17*(1), 50–58. Rough-and-tumble play among preschool children was analyzed and discussed in terms of sex differences and potential influence on long-term development.

Dunn, J., & Kendrick, C. The arrival of a sibling: Changes in patterns of interaction between mother and first-born child. *Journal of Child Psychology and Psychiatry*, 1981, *21*, 119–132. A study in 41 families of interaction between mother and first-born child before and after the birth of a second child indicated that changes in patterns of association between maternal and child variables were mainly the result of changes in individual differences in child behavior.

Etaugh, C., & Ropp, J. Children's self-evaluation of performance as a function of sex, age, feedback, and sex-typed task label. *Journal of Psychology*, 1976, *94*(1), 115–122. After 80 third- and 80 fifth-graders performed tasks that were either sex-appropriate or sex-inappropriate, they were told by prearrangement whether they had succeeded or failed. The children evaluated the importance of their effort, their ability, the difficulty of the task, and luck in accounting for their performance. The successful boys stressed their ability more than luck, but the successful girls did not. The girls, but not the boys, attributed their failures to poor ability more often than they attributed their success to good ability. The sex-typed labeling of the task itself did not influence the performance or the attractiveness of the task to the children.

Flerz, V. C., Fidler, D. S., & Rogers, R. W. Sex-role stereotypes: Developmental aspects and early intervention. *Child Development*, 1976, *47*(4), 998–1007. In an experimental study of 122 children, aged 3 to 8, some aspects of sex-role stereotypes were apparent at age 3 and more at ages 4 and 5. Films proved more effective than picture books in reducing such stereotypes.

Green, R. One hundred ten feminine and masculine boys: Behavioral contrasts and behavioral similarities. *Archives of Sexual Behavior*, 1976, *5*(5), 425–446. A comparison was made of 60 boys referred for cross-gender behavior and 50 boys with typical gender-role behavior. Differences in the activities and backgrounds of the two groups were identified.

Gross, B., & Gross, R. (Eds.). *The children's rights movement: Overcoming the oppression of young people.* Garden City, N.Y.: Anchor, 1977. This collection of papers contains a representative view of what is being taught these days about child advocacy and rights. Topics include child abuse, the development of the children's rights movement, children and youth as their own advocates, and a bill of rights for children.

Kohlberg, L. The cognitive-developmental approach to moral education. *Phi Delta Kappan*, 1975, *56*(10), 670–677. The director of Harvard's Center for Moral Education analyzes his own concept of the course of moral development, explores the aims of moral and civic education, and describes the center's research program. See also Peters's "A Reply to Kohlberg" that immediately follows.

Lewis, M. Early sex differences in the human: Studies of socioemotional development. *Archives of Sexual Behavior*, 1975, *4*(4), 329–335. Research is reviewed regarding sex differences in infants' behaviors, differences in the way parents treat boy and girl infants, and the relationship of sex gender to early development of personality.

Loevinger, J. Origins of conscience. *Psychological Issues*, 1976, *9*(4, Mono 36), 265–297. Psychoanalytic concepts of conscience are discussed, along with the origins of conscience and the relation of growth of conscience to ego development.

Lynn, D. B. Fathers and sex-role development. *Family Coordinator*, 1976, *25*(4), 403–409. A study of 90 8- to 11-year-old sons suggests that sons are no more likely to copy their father than they are to identify with a male stranger or with their mother. However, they are more likely to imitate male than female strangers. In general, fathers are more concerned than mothers with sex-typing their children, especially the boys, although they often have the effect of exaggerating their daughter's femininity. A son's masculinity relates not to his father's masculinity but to a combination of the father's dominance, nurturance, and participation in the son's care.

Masters, J. C., & Furman, W. Popularity, individual friendship selection, and specific peer interaction among children. *Developmental Psychology*, 1981, *17*(3), 344–350. Observations of the social reactions of preschool children, including identification of reinforcing, neutral and punishing behaviors, identified factors contributing to popularity or rejection, as well as choice of friends.

Oden, S., & Asher, S. R. Coaching children in social skills for friendship making. *Child Development*, 1977, *48*, 495–506. When third- and fourth-grade socially isolated children were coached in social skills, the coached children made gains in friendship nominations. A follow-up a year later indicated that the children who had received coaching made continued progress in their sociometric ratings.

Peters, J. J. Children who are victims of sexual assault and the psychology of offenders. *American Journal of Psychotherapy*, 1976, *30*(3), 398–421. Peters argues that many Freudian psychiatrists have been too prone to interpret genuine cases of sexual assault in childhood as products of children's fantasy. Such assaults may seriously affect children's emotional health and become the root of psychiatric problems in adulthood.

Rushton, J. P. Socialization and the altruistic behavior of children. *Psychological Bulletin*, 1976, *83*, 898–913. Research is reviewed regarding children's altruism, cognitive-developmental variables in children's role taking, the role of models, training in role taking, and verbal socialization procedures.

Scheibe, K. E., & Spaceaquerche, M. E. The social regulation of responses to neutral dilemmas among Brazilian school children. *Journal of Cross-Cultural Psychology*, 1976, *7*(4), 439–450. When procedures developed by Bronfenbrenner were used for assessing Brazilian children's responses to moral dilemmas, the general level was higher than for any sample obtained in the Western Hemisphere. Boys' responses were more moralistic than girls'.

Selman, R. L., Jaquette, D., & Lavin, D. R. Interpersonal awareness in children: Toward an integration of developmental and clinical child psychology. *American Journal of Orthopsychiatry*, 1977, *47*(2), 264–274. Proposes a five-stage developmental sequence of awareness of interpersonal issues such as peer-group loyalty and trust in friendship. The degree of children's impersonal or interpersonal awareness was assessed in terms of their success in peer relations in order to clarify the function of social awareness in clinical contexts.

Siegal, M. Kohlberg versus Piaget: To what extent has one theory eclipsed the other? *Merrill-Palmer Quarterly*, 1980, *26*(4), 285–297. Analysis and comparisons of the Kohlberg and Piaget theories of moral development indicate Kohlberg's theory to be only a small improvement over Piaget's, and both to be of real worth in studying moral development.

5
THE CHILD: IN FAMILY, SCHOOL, AND SOCIETY

THE CHILD IN THE FAMILY

Significance of Family Experience

Researchers have concluded overwhelmingly that "the child's psychological development is profoundly and significantly influenced by the kind of care he or she receives" (Clarke-Stewart, 1977, p. 85). For all but 2% of U.S. children such care is within the family. The Carnegie Council on Children has insisted that "families—and the circumstances of their lives—will remain the most critical factors in determining children's fate" (Keniston & The Carnegie Council on Children, 1977, p. xiv).

The impact of particular family experiences has typically been interpreted in entirely too simplistic a fashion. In reading the research that follows, one should keep in mind that the effects of variables discussed will differ according to their context. And that context, in turn, is a complex amalgam of many factors that are often difficult to identify. The context is continuously changing. Also, little effort has been made to examine the ways that children's relationships with their families change over time (Dunn & Kindrick, 1981).

In other words, environmental factors influence all family members' experiences and their reactions with one another. These extrafamilial factors include

> the characteristics and physical features of the immediate neighborhood; the family's employment status and socioeconomic circumstances; the family social network and degree of social-cultural isolation; social and institutional structures such as the schools, communication and transportation facilities, mass media, and government agencies; and the society's cultural ideological patterns and values [Davis, 1979, p. 91].

Social planning should take all these factors into account in devising family-support systems.

Factors Affecting Child's Family Role

Each child plays a role in the family that is based partly on custom and partly on circumstance. More specifically, the child's role is modified by such factors as sex, age, birth order, family size, and social class.

The only child. It was formerly theorized that having siblings produces the positive traits of cooperation and sharing as well as the negative ones of competition and aggression. The only child has traditionally been perceived as unfortunate, selfish, and somewhat maladjusted.

After reviewing others' research, Falbo (1977) concluded that the only area in which reliable and consistent results about the only child are available is intelligence. Median IQ scores of only children are found between the first-borns from small families and later-borns from large families. The common explanation of why only children do not score as well as one might expect from their small family size is that they lack younger siblings to tutor. However, parents in larger families are too busy to provide much in the way of individual encouragement and assistance to younger children.

Falbo's own research (1977) sharply contradicted common views of the only child. In a study of almost 300 people, aged 17 to 62, who had been only children, Falbo found that most of them had a combination of characteristics typical of first-borns. These traits included high achievement motivation and intelligence and certain positive attributes of last-borns such as trustworthiness and independence. In laboratory situational tests, only children proved more likely than those with siblings to be cooperative and trusting, partly because they had grown up without constant competition from siblings and hence had learned to trust other people. Nor did the only children differ from those with siblings in terms

The youngest child occupies a secure position in the family, being loved and cared for by parents and older siblings.

of how many friends they had, how close their friends were, or how popular they believed themselves to be. Birth order made no difference with respect to such personality characteristics as introversion/extroversion or **neuroticism.**

Only children were no more happy or unhappy than children with siblings. They proved more independent in departing from a group decision; and girls rejected group decisions more than boys. While they belonged to fewer organizations, they were more likely to hold offices, suggesting that they had a greater capacity for leadership. In addition, only children and first-borns scored higher than middle- and last-borns on verbal IQ and effectiveness as leaders. The only children may have obtained better verbal IQs because of spending more time with parents during their formative years and learning more adult-like ways of thinking and behaving. Forty percent of them, compared with a mere 3% of children with siblings, named their parents as the single strongest influence in "making me the person I am today" (Falbo, 1976).

Size of family. For the child who has siblings, the number is important. After the post–World War II baby boom, which lasted about 15 years, the average mother today will have between two and three children. Growing up in families of four children is quite different from growing up in families of one or two. The larger the family, the more time children spend interacting with one another. The smaller the family, the more time they interact with their parents, whose conversation and views differ widely from those of siblings. In addition, the parents' relationship to each other will be affected by the reduced demands of having two rather than four children (Glock, 1977).

Larger and smaller families have their respective advantages and disadvantages. The child in the typical small family of today experiences the impact of family crises more sharply and is more likely to be overprotected or to have an exaggerated feeling of importance. Further, in today's families with their close child spacing, sibling rivalries tend to develop; and the older child may have good reason for being jealous of a new arrival. Children may compensate to some extent by attendance at growth centers where there is no hierarchy of age. Children learn to shift for themselves among those with similar power to theirs (Rossi, 1977).

The situation was quite different in earlier years. When larger families, often including grandparents and other kin, lived in the same household, pecking orders less often existed. Also, when several years separated births, older children often played with their friends in the neighborhood or at school and hence were less dependent on their mothers.

Nevertheless, in general, small-family children are fortunate. In smaller families children's births are more likely to be planned in order to reduce the negative impact of childbirth on the mother's health and to limit the amount of time she must spend in child bearing. Moreover, couples can provide more adequately for the needs of each other and for their growing children (Glock, 1977). In addition, the family atmosphere is normally democratic, with the children taking part in decision-making. Stress is on achieving a full life through participating in many cultural and social activities and through ultimately achieving social and vocational mobility. The major reasons for limiting family size are to provide more opportunities for the children and a higher standard of living for the family.

By contrast, children in the large family often experience certain disadvantages. They normally receive less encouragement for inquiry and exploration. And as family size increases, opportunities for interacting with adults decrease, producing less identification with the parents and less internalization of their values (Thompson, 1974).

Factors operating together may have a different effect from factors experienced separately. For instance, the first-born boy in a large family is often better adjusted than the male first-born in a small family (Swanson, Massey, & Payne, 1972). In the larger family the oldest boy possesses a certain status and authority, partly because the father is often too burdened with economic worries to maintain an active family role. By contrast, the oldest girl in such families ordinarily has exceptional burdens of child care without being conceded the status that the oldest boy's masculinity allows.

Nevertheless, many large families provide a wholesome, happy climate. Lazarus (1974) cited a family of 18 children, aged 5 months to 22 years, who presented a picture of general well-being and pride. The older children had part-time jobs after school, and the others helped with household chores. Large-family children often develop a feeling of teamwork and feel special security in having more family members on whom to rely.

Ordinal position. Birth order among the siblings is a significant factor. Research by Croake and Olson (1977), which employed 10 basic scales of the Minnesota Multiphasic Personality Inventory (MMPI), disclosed that oldest and youngest siblings more often scored in the direction of maladjustment but that none of the sample groupings might be classified as maladjusted. Adler (1959) viewed the effects of ordinal position as secondary to an individual's own estimation of the family situation. Adler argued that individuals interact with their world according to their own assumptions. Such assumptions, in turn, are influenced by the family structure in which an individual operates. In contrast, Toman (1959) placed greater stress on such structural aspects of the family group as spacing and sex distribution of siblings. He ignored the creative self within the individual. There were also considerable differences between specific sibling categories as classified by Toman. Thus, Croake and Olson's results gave strong support to Adler's position and some to Toman's.

Kagan (1977) contrasted the roles of first- and later-born children. Because first-borns for a time have an exclusive relationship with the parents, they come more easily to introject parental standards. Because they identify with parental models, they feel they hold a privileged status. And because they are the eldest, they are anxious about rejection by the parental authority. This situation causes first-borns to have higher standards with respect to skills and characteristics valued by the parents. The first-borns of middle-class U.S. parents, who especially value success in school, pursue that value more vigorously than do later-borns and make higher grades. In a random sampling of 2,523 high school students who were administered reading-comprehension tests, only and first-born children whose fathers had at least completed high school made higher scores than others (Glass, Neulinger, & Brim, 1974).

The birth of a second child threatens first-borns' exclusive relationship with their parents. In families of first-born girls in which, before the second child arrived, the mother-daughter interaction had involved frequent play and maternal attention there was little positive interaction between the daughter and her new sibling 14 months later. In contrast, no such association was found among first-born boys with second-borns. The questions arises whether girls are made to feel more dependent on their mothers than boys and hence more likely to resent the second child when the mother's attention is diverted (Dunn & Kendrick, 1981).

Later-borns have several advantages. They feel adequate in comparison with older siblings, especially if the age difference is more than 2 years. If the gap between them and older children is sufficiently great, they perceive the older ones as being in an altogether different category and feel no need to compete.

The mere existence of older or younger siblings is a potent force in the development of a child (Kagan, 1977). The "catalyst of change is simply the introduction of another, like the introduction of a crystal into a cloud to precipitate rain. The other is the catalyst that creates uncertainty in the child. In response to that uncertainty, the child alters his beliefs, behaviors, and roles" (p. 53). Kagan reported that differences between middle- and lower-class children show dramatic similarities to those between first- and later-born children. Like the later-borns, lower-class children arrive at certain conclusions about themselves based on the conceptions of the middle-class child. Middle-class children, like first-borns, seek to differentiate themselves from lower-class children after recognizing their existence, probably during the lower grades (Kagan, 1977).

The youngest child, in many ways, occupies a favorable position. He or she is usually sheltered from the financial stringencies experienced by older children. And such children also receive help from older siblings. Older siblings also provide role models, in some ways more appropriate ones than parents, who represent another generation. Typically the youngest child becomes self-confident, persevering, and striving—not the stereotypical spoiled brat (Rogers, 1977a).

Conclusions about children's family roles. Tentative conclusions about children's roles in the family can be summarized as follows: (1) Although the child in the small family may feel the impact of family crises more acutely than one in a large family and be more likely to be overprotected, on the whole such a child is fortunate. Limitation in family size permits greater opportunities and higher standards of living for children. Hence, such children are ordinarily superior in emotional, physical, and social adjustment to those from large families (Thompson, 1974). (2) While only children often say they would like to have a brother or sister, they have certain advantages. They may be more advanced intellectually, because from birth on they interact more with adults than do children with siblings. And, as in the case of members of small families, they have more opportunities. There is no evidence that they are more selfish, domineering, or egotistical than others. (3) First-borns share certain advantages of only children and are likely to be more self-sufficient and achievement oriented than later-borns. They also have the advantage of being looked up to by younger children and are thus encouraged to examine their own values more closely.

Alternative Family Situations

The number of supposedly typical nuclear families is rapidly diminishing as alternatives correspondingly increase. Kenneth Keniston (1979) advises that due recognition be given to the transformations in families. Even in these times, for many individuals "the ideal American family is still the Dick and Jane family— daddy breadwinner, mommy housewife, two children and probably Spot the dog and Puff the cat" (p. 14). This stereotype would be appropriate now for only 1 in 16 families. Although new types of families are often perceived as somehow threatening, they, too, are genuine families with the capacity to establish loving relationships between their members.

Children of divorce. Growing numbers of children live in family situations that are the product of divorce. Across the years, most laypersons have assumed that children of divorce and remarriage suffer serious emotional and social consequences. Maddox (1975) asserts that one atypical category, stepchildren, never experience a truly normal family situation. Parents in "stepfamilies" have separate pasts, and the "ghosts" of former marriages hover over them despite their new situation. In this view, **reconstituted** families do not ever truly become single entities but, to a certain degree, retain individual identities rooted in their past.

Although nine in ten of these children are in the sole custody of the mother, growing numbers of divorced parents are working out joint-custody arrangements. Advocates of joint custody argue that the almost automatic assignment of children to the mother in divorce cases is based on outmoded sex-role attitudes—for example, that mothers should stay at home and that fathers are poorer at rearing children. Actually, about 60% of divorced women have jobs outside the home, and a growing number of fathers are coming to insist on and to enjoy a significant role in bringing up children.

In general, most judges have insisted that children should not be shuttled back and forth between parents; and psychiatrists have agreed. Recent research is challenging that view. Christine Rosenthal's study of 127 joint- and sole-custody fathers indicated generally favorable situations, even among those men who had remarried. In a New York study of 40 divorced men, the joint-custody fathers were closer to their children, happier, and got along better with their ex-wives than did noncustodial fathers ("One Child, Two Homes," 1979).

Joint custody works best under certain conditions. The parents should be sufficiently affluent to have their own bedrooms separate from the children's and should live in the same school district or general neighborhood. They should be able to separate child rearing from any resentment between themselves and be willing to negotiate. One joint-custody child, Lisa, had "two homes, two wardrobes, two sets of rules, and two sets of friends, neither of which has fully accepted her because of her part time living. Yet both parents feel joint custody is working" ("One Child, Two Homes," 1979, p. 61). The head of the American Bar Association's special committee on joint custody has predicted that by the end of the 1980s joint custody will be the rule and not the exception.

Gettleman and Markowitz (1976), both clinical social workers, rejected the myth of the child damaged by divorce. They contended that divorce may liberate children from the "suffocating relationships" often found in nuclear families. Mother/child relationships may also improve after divorce. Both spouses, after an initial stage of depression and confusion, practically always look and feel better than before.

Wilson, Zurcher, McAdams, and Curtis (1975) concluded that children in broken homes or in "reconstituted families" may have "a predominantly positive, predominantly negative, or mixed experience," depending on many factors (p. 535). Certainly, their data conflict with the common stereotype of "the evil stepfather", nor may it be categorically assumed that environments in step-parent families are less healthy than in natural-parent families.

Popenoe (1976) quoted Elizabeth Oaa's suggestions regarding divorce and its effect on children. Children should not be isolated from the parents' difficulties before the breakup. Instead, they should be given simple, honest explanations. No one should be blamed, least of all the children. Nor should the children be asked to determine the parent with whom they should live. However, they should be thoroughly assured that both parents love them and be given a chance to express any disturbed feelings.

Adopted children. Adopted children typically adapt quite well, partly because the new parents especially wanted to have children. Even cross-racial adoptions work out successfully in 77 per cent of cases ("Transracial Adoptions," 1975). At least 30 states and the District of Columbia have passed legislation that subsidizes the adoption of especially hard-to-place children who may be physically or mentally handicapped, difficult to manage, or much older than adoptees usually are ("Editor's Note," 1975).

Sometimes, adoptions do not work out, and children must be withdrawn from the families in which they were placed, a circumstance called disruption (Rooney, 1979). In Los Angeles County the Department of Adoptions reported a disruption rate of 13% in 1977–1978, compared with only 2% in 1970–1971. Increases like this are largely due to the fact that a decreasing availability of infants for adoption has led many couples to accept children who are older and more difficult to place. After their withdrawal from a home, such children are reassured that appropriate families will ultimately be found. The chances of successful placement for difficult children is vastly increased if adoptive parents have access to workshops, hot lines, and social workers specially trained for dealing with this problem. Children are sometimes best placed with a single parent, as when they have been rejected or abused by a biological or foster father.

Children of working mothers. Children whose mothers work outside the home are rapidly increasing in number. Over half of women with school-age children are now working, including a third of women with children under age 3 (Bronfenbrenner, 1976).

Bronfenbrenner has asserted that fewer and fewer parents are taking adequate care of their children and that substitute care facilities are still all too few. In consequence, growing numbers of children come home from school to empty houses, often with nothing to do but watch television or join other children in an ugly peer group culture, "a culture of destroy, of break, of act out. The essence of it is anomie, a social and emotional disintegration, inside and outside" (Bronfenbrenner, 1977, p. 41). Bronfenbrenner (1977) contended that every child needs at least one person who has "an irrational involvement with that child, someone who thinks that kid is more important than other people's kids, someone who's in love with him and whom he loves in return" (p. 43). If children are brought up only by their mothers, 24 hours every day, the result is likely to be both sick children and sick mothers.

Bronfenbrenner recommended that both parents work part time on flexible schedules and that they share child rearing. He suggested that neighborhoods should become informal support systems, so that each family relies on the others and neighbors help with child care. He observed that fathers can be as adept at taking care of children as mothers.

Research evidence about the influence on children of mothers' working is complex and sometimes conflicting, but it is mostly favorable or neutral. In a comparison of 10-year-olds with employed or nonemployed mothers, the working mothers were far more content with their sex roles. And their children had the more equalitarian concepts of sex role (Gold & Andres, 1978). In most cases in which the mothers worked, the two parents behaved somewhat similarly in domestic activities and child care. They also expressed greater content with the wife's role and more feminist attitudes.

In general, sons of employed mothers are as well adjusted as those of nonemployed mothers. Those who do have adjustment difficulties are usually in the working class. Such boys are more often perceived negatively by their fathers, are more nervous and shy, distinguish more sharply between sex roles, and make lower grades. The reason may not be the mother's employment per se but the father's attitude. Working-class men are far more likely than middle-class men to feel their egos threatened by the wife's employment. Such men normally have little status on the job. Traditionally, they have achieved feelings of self-respect from being the sole providers in the home. And when working wives take that prop away, they may feel less adequate and take out frustrations on their sons. Because of their attitude they also make less satisfactory role models for their sons and impede their developing a satisfactory gender identity.

In another study, of middle-class girls (aged 5 to 11) in New York City, each girl was shown a line drawing of a mother leaving home and waving good-bye to her daughter. Then the subject was asked "How does the little girl in the picture feel about her mother going to work?" Each girl was also asked "What do you want to be when you grow up?" and whether she would give the same answer if she were a boy. Change of mind on the basis of sex would suggest holding a stereotype (Marantz & Mansfield, 1977). The daughters of working mothers had more flexible perceptions and fewer stereotyped responses. More often than the homemakers' daughters, they indicated that both husbands and wives go to work and earn money and perceived homemaking and child care as appropriate for both sexes. Daughters of working mothers also saw women as more competent, competitive, less easily hurt emotionally, and less in need of security. The degree to which the father shared household responsibilities made little difference.

Age was a significant determinant of responses, the older girls being more flexible. They also questioned males' prerogatives in earning money, giving orders, and being a boss, scientist, or doctor. Also, with greater age there was a growing tendency to favor masculine occupations. The mothers' own vocational status had some effect, daughters of mothers with feminine occupations tending to choose feminine careers more often than those with unorthodox occupations. However, only 16% of the girls aspired to the same occupation as did the mother.

Children in communes and other countercultures. Although only a small fraction of children live in **counterculture** situations, they are significant because they represent, in effect, experiments in child rearing. Contrary to popular opinion children fare well in many such situations. Rothschild and Wolf (1976) observed children in various countercultures, including urban and rural **communes,** religious communities, and the drug-rehabilitation organization, Synanon. Children in the rural communes proved to be unusually healthy, and when they were not they had simply more old-fashioned ailments than did urban children. The rural children often wandered about unsupervised, yet the incidence of injuries among them was normal. Because they were accorded unusual freedom, they developed superior self-reliance.

While life in communes proved somewhat hazardous for marriage, children coped with their parents' realignments and breakups better than did children of divorce in more conventional situations. Only among so-called "Jesus freaks" groups and Hare Krishna homes were children abused or neglected (Rothschild & Wolf, 1976). Nor did early sexual experimentation produce any apparent negative effects. Such children had higher-than-average self-reliance, independence, interpersonal adeptness, confidence, ease in dealing with adults, and trust in adults generally. In at least one type of commune, the farm, the most significant feature is a single standard of behavior for adults and children.

In other research, Kanter, Jaffe, and Weisberg (1975) found that children in middle-class communes were regarded as miniature adults and established affectional relationships with other adults as well as their parents in the commune household. Nevertheless, 4- to 12-year-olds experienced considerable confusion from what Kanter termed the "Cinderella effect," or a stream of directions and corrections by several unrelated adults. Such children may also create some problems for parents, especially mothers of young children, so that eventually parents come to reserve the right to protect and punish their own children.

Parental Roles

The mother's role. The roles of mother and father are distinctively different. The mother has been designated by society as the child's chief caretaker and agent of socialization. Because many mothers feel it essential to work outside the home, either to augment the family income or to promote their own self-realization, they may find the caretaker assignment an imposition and feel unconscious hostility toward their children. Others may organize their whole lives around the mother role and create in their children unhealthy feelings of dependency. Mothers must somehow organize their lives to permit themselves to thrive and their children to flourish through warm and efficient, but not excessive, mothering. To do so may well require revisions in the traditional father role.

The father's role. For their part, fathers play their roles in widely varied ways. A study of 190 families in San Diego County, California, revealed four main styles of fathering. The autocratic fathers demanded achievement and organization. Children portrayed these fathers as punitive and controlling. They avoided them as much as possible and spent much of their time among their peers. Typically, they were troublemakers at school, power assertive and antisocial in their behavior. The second style of father, the patriarch, governed his family from a moral or religious frame of reference and had the final say. Such fathers were often from blue-collar backgrounds, and their children did well in school and normally gave little trouble.

A third style, the detached providers, spent little time with their children except during weekend outings or family vacations. They often had upper-middle-class jobs and a good education and income. Their children did well in school and were pretty well adjusted. The expressive leaders (style four) were warmly involved with their family and rated themselves as competent fathers. Their children's morals and school achievement were excellent, and power confrontations rarely occurred. In the home there was a spirit of give and take and general harmony. Any particular individual's fathering style depended on such factors as his own father's style, his on-the-job adjustment, and his marital stability (Broderick, 1977).

Modes of Child-rearing

Effects of parental attitudes and specific practices. Considerable research has focused on the effects of specific parental attitudes and behaviors. To a considerable extent, observes Kagan (1977), the effect depends on the child's own perception of the parents' motive. In the 17th century, colonial parents were admonished to punish their children in order to curb the evil forces born within them, and even well-meaning, well-educated parents subjected their children to severe punishment. For example, Samuel Byrd of Virginia required a child to drink "a pint of piss" because of wetting his bed (Plumb, 1975). Because such severe treatment was common, parents did not regard themselves as cruel and children probably did not feel rejected. In other words, judging parents as either rejecting or accepting cannot be determined purely in terms of their behavior, because rejection is "in the mind of the rejectee. It is a belief held by the child, not an act performed by the parent" (Kagan, 1977, p. 41). This assertion may be true; nevertheless, there is more to such behaviors than is suggested by this conclusion. Even though children who are frequently beaten or talked to harshly may not interpret such behaviors as outright rejection, there may be highly negative effects such as anxiety, reduced ego strength, and undue passivity.

Other researchers have related specific parental practices and attitudes to particular child characteristics. For example, accepting parents tend to have children with high self-esteem (Sears, 1940). Responding to a distressed infant does not, as ordinarily believed, produce spoiling (Ainsworth, 1972). Indeed, refusing to respond to a child to avoid spoiling tends to have just the opposite effect. A close relationship exists between the degree of severity of physical punishment experienced by children aged 2 to 12 and the degree of severity of antisocial aggression they display later on in adolescence (Welsh, 1974).

Corporal punishment is still very common in the average family, although more extreme forms of violence are relatively rare. Mothers are a little more likely than fathers to employ violence against children (see Table 5-1). And sons are punished slightly more often than daughters. It may be that sons commit more punishable offenses or that violence is more appropriate in the socialization of boys than girls (Gelles, 1978).

Table 5-1. Parent-to-Child Violence By Sex of Parent[a]

| | IN PAST YEAR | | EVER | |
INCIDENT	FATHER	MOTHER	FATHER	MOTHER
Threw something	3.6%	6.8%*	7.5%	11.3%*
Pushed/grabbed/shoved	29.8	33.4	35.6	39.5
Slapped or spanked	53.3	62.5**	67.7	73.6*
Kicked/bit/hit with fist	2.5	4.0	6.7	8.7
Hit with something	9.4	16.7**	15.7	23.6**
Beat up	0.6	1.8	4.0	4.2
Threatened with knife/gun	0.2	0.0	3.1	2.6
Used knife or gun	0.2	0.0	3.1	2.7

[a]Reports of 523 fathers and 623 mothers; figures for all incidents represent at least 520 fathers and 619 mothers. (From "Violence toward Children in the United States," by R. J. Gelles. In *American Journal of Orthopsychiatry*, 1978, 48(4), 588. Copyright 1978 by the American Orthopsychiatric Association, Inc. Reprinted by permission.)
*$x^2 \leqslant .05$
**$x^2 \leqslant .01$

Effects of total pattern. Some studies have analyzed the effect of the total child-rearing pattern on children's development. On the basis of home observation of mothers and their young children, Harvard University researchers sought to determine (1) what type of home environment produces the most competent children and (2) the parent's role in the child's development (Harvard

Study Group, 1974). They concluded that the competent child has relatively free access to areas within the home and that the mother should be available at least half the child's waking hours to provide support and assistance required. Mothers should be enthusiastic, afford encouragement, and seek to understand what their children are trying to do. They should talk with the children as often as feasible, encourage "pretend" activities, and use words to provide related ideas. Parents should discipline their children firmly and consistently. They should avoid confining children for long periods and should provide plenty of activities and materials for play.

However, child-rearing methods do not always have the straight-line effects suggested above. Among 400 famous and creative individuals, reported Goertzel and Goertzel (1972), 300 had had family-related problems in childhood. While 74 of 85 writers of fiction and drama and 16 of 20 poets had early histories characterized by "simulated warfare," the early homes of scientists, physicians, and some statesmen were comparatively normal. The families of almost all the 400 individuals were free of major mental disorders. Nevertheless, concluded the researchers, "We haven't the vaguest idea what goes into a healthy family. . . . Not all children of broken homes are misfits and not all children of broken homes turn out to be good boys and girls" (p. 559).

Other researchers have reached the same conclusion; the secret of optimum child rearing is elusive. To date, the results are inconclusive and confusing. "We may as well admit," confessed Farson, "that no one even yet knows how to grow people" (1974, p. 67). Korner (1971) observed that "we are forever looking for the method to raise children, to care, or to educate. However, parents should behave flexibly, taking account of each child's vulnerabilities and strengths" (p. 3). Parents should be encouraged to "tune in and to trust their own intuition in dealing differentially with what their children present as separate individuals" (p. 618). In other words, certain general principles may indeed hold for child rearing. Beyond those broad generalizations, however, considerable flexibility is required to meet the unique demands of individuals within particular situations. Some decades ago parents were given quite specific rules about the art of child rearing. Now parents are advised to learn the general principles and then to decide the details for themselves (Newson & Newson, 1974).

Because of the highly varied and complex factors that enter into all human relationships, concludes Kagan (1976), it may not be possible to identify accurately the relationships between particular parental practices and specific child behaviors except in extreme cases. An example would be persistent and unusual physical maltreatment that produces intense stress. Nevertheless, the cumulative effect of many less-extreme situations may have far more to do with determining the direction of children's growth. Just as the odor of a small portion of perfume may be quite pleasant and a large amount extremely unpleasant, so at some point increasing degrees of otherwise sound parental practices may become negative in effect. The critical question is at what point this negative effect is reached.

Certain parental actions have greater impact in infancy than they do later. Maternal protectiveness in the first 3 years relates more to sons' passivity at ages 6 to 10 and to their achievement at ages 10 to 14 than does similar maternal

THE CHILD: IN FAMILY, SCHOOL, AND SOCIETY

129

treatment during later childhood (Crandall, 1972). Nevertheless, modes of parental behavior remain important throughout a child's journey to maturity.

The trend toward institutionalized care. Finkelstein (1973) deplored society's growing practice of turning over large aspects of child rearing to agencies outside the family. As a result, children's individuality and sense of identity may be threatened, he asserted. He concluded that no solutions have been devised that promise any more to the children than they obtain from family rearing. Nevertheless, note that various alternatives to the nuclear family, such as communes and the Israeli kibbutzim, have proved quite effective for rearing children. A changing world calls for constant monitoring of, and modifications in, modes of child rearing.

Children's Impact on Parents

In the past most attention has been paid to the impact of parents on children. A rapidly growing accumulation of evidence demonstrates children's effects on their parents (Bell & Harper, 1977). Characteristics having special impact on the parents include the children's sex, temperamental styles, tendencies toward assertiveness, impulsiveness, and sensorimotor competencies and impairments. Often other factors affect the mutual impact, including all conditions in which parent/child or sibling interactions occur. For example, the effect of father absence or maternal employment may be conditioned by the mother's feelings about her work, the father's attitude toward her working, and the family's socioeconomic circumstances.

Also note that all family members "exert reciprocal influence. Together they form a system, characterized by interdependent, reciprocal interaction. While it may be useful and even appropriate at times to study isolated elements of this system, exclusive reliance on this level of analysis will limit our understanding of family dynamics" (Davis, 1979, p. 90).

THE CHILD AT SCHOOL

Significance of School Experience

While family background is of primary importance in children's development, the school's influence is significant, too. Because of the knowledge explosion and the complexity of modern life, the school carries an unusual burden. Today's children must master "techniques for acquiring new information, learning how to attend to relevant cues and ignore irrelevant cues, how to apply hypotheses and strategies and relinquish them when they are unsuccessful" (Rogers, 1977b, p. 307). Thus, schools help children to prepare for life in a complex, constantly changing society. According to Eisenberg (1973), "Our challenge is no longer transmitting solutions that have been successful in the past, but helping our children to acquire attitudes and sets for problem solving that will enable them to meet undreamed-of challenges to their capacities" (p. 222).

Early Childhood Education and Day Care

Definitions. In recent years, attention has focused increasingly on children's early care and education. Early-childhood education deals chiefly with cognitive development and is viewed as a downward extension of schooling. Day care ordinarily embraces all arrangements made to take care of children during all or most of the day. Thus, the goals of day care are broader than those of early-childhood education. When the goals of early-childhood classes are compared with those of quality day-care programs, the difference is that all the child's needs—nutritional, physical, social, motivational, and intellectual—are included in day-care service. Schools for infants and young children occupy a brief part of the day and hence embrace fewer types of situations.

Day care. Day-care programs are increasingly common and in demand. Almost 7 million children under age 6 have gainfully employed mothers, and other millions would certainly profit from the experiences that quality day-care provides. Fourteen million more children, age 6 to 13, have working mothers, and a large percentage require after-school care. Yet licensed family day-care centers currently care for only 1.5 million children of all ages. Nor does the possession of a license necessarily signify quality care. Much day care is purely custodial, and in many cases it is outright harmful. With any day-care center, much depends on the quality of day care and on the child's age, characteristics, and family background (Rutter, 1981). Nor is any one type of day care necessarily superior to others. A flexible variety of arrangements is needed to meet the various needs of different children and their families.

Very early day care or childhood education has been criticized on the ground that it deprives children of their mothers. However, the evidence suggests that they are not adversely affected. Typically, children initiated into day care at 9½ months display less tension than those who enter at 3 or 4 years of age (Schwartz, Krolick, & Strickland, 1973). Saia (Evans & Saia, 1972) concluded that children in quality day-care programs have advantages over those reared exclusively at home in their earliest years. They have more opportunities for developing language skills and for associating with different kinds of people. They are intellectually challenged through story telling and stimulating games. Bronfenbrenner (1976) found that day-care children tend to be more physically active, peer oriented, and aggressive than children reared almost exclusively at home.

Relationships between day care and the home environment or school should be explored. The effects of child experience on the parents' marital relationship and neighborhood relationships should also be examined, as well as how these factors, in turn, impinge on the child. Finally, the impact of day care should be related to society's attitudes toward child care, women's roles, and the role of the family.

Because of its nearly exclusive concentration on the direct effects of day care on the child, available research is completely inadequate to evaluate the overall influence of alternative child-rearing arrangements on the child, the parents, or society. Therefore, "To even say that the jury is still out on day care would be in our view both premature and naively optimistic. The fact of the

Children in well-organized day-care centers may fare better than children kept at home.

matter is, quite frankly, that the majority of evidence has yet to be presented, much less subpoenaed" (Bronfenbrenner, p. 946).

Early education. Nursery school and kindergarten have also assumed increasing importance in recent years. The recognition that early education is critical in the ultimate realization of personal and intellectual potential has created concern for its quantity and quality of such schooling.

While the long-term value of early-education programs for the disadvantaged has not been demonstrated, Caldwell (1974) reported positive effects. The usual evaluation, purely in terms of changes in IQ scores, is too narrow and ignores important gains in children's social attitudes, feelings about learning, and nutrition. Nevertheless, early training, to be most effective, should be reinforced in later years.

Special Problems

Exceptional children. Concern for **exceptional children** is growing. Exceptional children are all those for whom regular school programs must be considerably adapted if they are to achieve their potential. They include the over 9 million physically or mentally handicapped children and youth in the United

States. They include the talented and gifted, who somehow survive the traditional classroom but cannot be sufficiently challenged there. They include the tens of thousands of neglected or abused children, whom educators should try to protect from further injury while undoing damage already done. And they include minority-group children, whose educational problems are aggravated by schools' failures to compensate for their cultural and linguistic problems.

In general, the trend is away from using disparaging labels and rigid categories and toward focusing on children's learning characteristics and the accommodation of school programs to those characteristics (Lance, 1976). Another currently popular practice is **"mainstreaming,"** or integrating exceptional children with their normal peers in both social and instructional programs. Proponents of mainstreaming believe that these children, when segregated, become labeled and are denied normal interaction. Opponents, presently in the minority, believe that segregation for at least part of the day is necessary to ensure that children are provided the specialized techniques required for their optimal development.

Sex disadvantages. Many writers, among them Tooley (1977), have asserted that girls thrive in elementary school and boys do not. Tooley concluded that boys are involved in approximately three-fourths of the strife and difficulty in school. Certain characteristics normally associated with the masculine sex role conflict with those required by their student role (Chapman, 1978). If the boy behaves in all-boy fashion, as society says he should, he may become designated as an academic and behavior problem.

Actual observations of women teachers and 3- to 5-year-olds during free-play periods indicated that the sexes received equal amounts of attention but that the teachers related to both sexes in terms of feminine, not masculine, activities (Fagot, 1978). While this experience did not seem to feminize the boys, Fagot conjectured that encouraging boys in more feminine activities might account for their somewhat more negative attitudes toward school. It should be added that girls suffer as much from such treatment as boys. It tends to confirm certain unhealthy aspects of the female role, especially passivity, overconformity, and overdependency.

Girls have also been hindered by sexist reading materials in the schools. A study of prize-winning children's books (Weitzman, Eifler, Hokada, & Ross, 1971-72) disclosed that women were grossly underrepresented in main roles, titles, and illustrations and that males outnumbered females by 11 to 1. When women did appear in stories, they were represented in a stereotyped, passive manner, whereas males were active. Females were likely to get into difficulties from which males finally rescued them. In a study of elementary-school readers ("Women's Own Words," 1972) stories featuring boys outnumbered girl-featured stories by 5 to 2, and even in fantasy and folk stories males predominated 4 to 1.

Educational television. Schools have tried to capitalize on children's fascination for television, with varying success. Paulson (1974) compared classrooms of 3- and 4-year-olds who viewed *Sesame Street* an hour a day for a season with classrooms of children without such viewing. Those who had viewed the program displayed significantly more cooperative behaviors than the controls in situations that were quite similar to those portrayed in the program. However, there was no evidence of any further generalization.

In other research, Sprafkin, Leibert, and Poulos (1975) showed elementary schoolchildren episodes from *Lassie* displaying a dramatic helping example. The children's willingness to help increased in a closely parallel situation. Nevertheless, conclusions about the influence of television should remain tentative. For one thing, we do not know the long-term effects. For another, studies of the influence of the media on social behaviors are virtually nonexistent. Even in areas where media portrayals have been studied extensively, their social effects have been considered only in the most superficial manner. Finally, many of the studies to date are "sadly deficient from a methodological point of view" (Liebert & Schwartzberg, 1977, p. 142).

THE CHILD AND SOCIETY

Social Trends and Effects on Children

Age grading. The ways that a society affects its children are so complex and subtle that they sometimes go unnoticed. The effects of recent trends, especially, are likely to creep up on children before their impact is recognized or understood. In terms of age grading, childhood may no longer be judged the distinctive entity that it has in the past. Increasingly, authorities are recommending that children not be isolated from adults and that they become a part of the life of the larger world. The idea is not that they should become "instant adults," but rather that they should work alongside older generations in genuinely meaningful activities ("Talking with Dorothy Kispert," 1973). Presumably older people, especially the very old, are cheered up by the youth in their midst. And the young attain a sense of the continuity of life and of what the future may hold from older generations.

Nevertheless, society is in some ways becoming more age-graded than before. Children spend less time in family pursuits and more with peers. Young adult couples often gravitate together in the suburbs. Older people often live in their own housing projects or mobile-home parks and like it that way. Perhaps the best answer is age integration for certain activities. It must be recognized that most people prefer being with their age contemporaries most of the time.

Rugged individualism versus social orientation. Children today are encouraged to be individuals, despite society's growing trend toward working, playing, and living in teams or groups. The capacity to perform effectively as a team may be insufficiently valued in a society that has always stressed individuality.

MacMahon (1974) called attention to "the hidden costs of unqualified glorification of idiosyncratic man. Paramount among these costs is the potential threat that the man-as-unique image poses to the human capacity for identifying with others" (p. 619).

However, certain trends may exact too heavy a toll on people as unique individuals. Technological advances can reduce an individual's feelings of personal responsibility and worth. People are relatively inefficient in many pursuits as compared with machines. The proliferation of population reduces an individual's life space and makes it more difficult to preserve a reasonable degree of privacy or feeling of selfhood. While children, and most adults, are hardly conscious of these forces, they nevertheless absorb their impact.

Pluralism. The increasing trend in North America toward **pluralistic** values and forms of life is also having its impact on children. Children from different racial and ethnic backgrounds are encouraged to maintain whatever is best about their culture instead of simply becoming depersonalized in the melting pot. No single mode of child rearing is considered to be infallible, nor is any single mode of life judged best for all children (Greenbaum, 1974). In recent years more attention has focused on the child's status in society, and the concept "child as citizen" has gained support from the civil-rights movement. Bereiter (1976) interpreted this movement as concerned with the child as a person whose individual freedom should not be infringed on, either by parental or official authority.

The pace of society. Children must also adapt to society's complex time system. In leisure matters, people are urged to slow down, in the work world, to speed up. A host of inventions, such as calculators and spaceships, have changed concepts of time. Children, meantime, must adapt their internal time-reference system to external timing. An individual's timing system probably has a physiological base derived from certain internal rhythms. Nevertheless, developing children must learn to transcend their own rhythms in order to become properly integrated into their society. Children must learn "when to say please, when to eat, when to go to the toilet, and when to sleep" (Ashton, 1976, p. 625).

On the basis of his extensive research with young children, Burton L. White (1975) concluded that a child's basic social orientation is complete during the first 2 years and that after this time it is progressively difficult to change. White pointed out that "nowhere in child development research have we demonstrated a strong capacity to alter early personality patterns, or early social attitudes" (p. 258). Nevertheless, White advised that we keep trying where changes seem desired. However, because change is so difficult to achieve, greater attention should be paid to preventing difficulties and to maximizing potential from the time of birth.

Effects of social class. Even in so-called democratic societies, social stratification exists and leaves its mark on children. The family's social class is related to biological and psychological deficits at birth, specific child-rearing practices, and the child's identification with social class. Because of such factors lower-class children have less confidence in their talents than do middle-class children. Many studies have also confirmed a positive relationship between children's social class and such indices of cognitive function as IQ and achievement-test scores, richness of memory and vocabulary, grades in school, and inferential ability. Middle-class U.S. children have greater confidence of success in intellectual situations—for example, at school—and are more reflective than lower-class children (Kagan, 1977).

Families unconsciously communicate to their children their own confidence about the children's ultimate mastery of such skills. On the one hand, parents who have power in the community and feel at home within their society find it easier to motivate their children to acquire socially valued skills and abilities than those who somehow feel "disenfranchised." On the other hand, lower-class parents unconsciously communicate their sense of disenfranchisement within the larger society and their feelings of powerlessness and inadequacy, thus producing in their children less optimistic feelings about chances of succeeding in the larger world (Kagan, 1977).

Children's identification with social class is profound and difficult to change. And while they may tend to deny their feelings of impotence, lower-class children gradually come to realize that they have little that their culture really values. They react to their disadvantage by a readier disposition to take risks, to be aggressive, and to blame their failures on external events rather than themselves (Kagan, 1977). There is no evidence, however, that growing up in poverty produces irreversible psychological damage. And even among children who may have been hurt somewhat by an environment of depression and economic hardship, status in childhood years is not a good predictor of psychological status in adulthood. Nor is there any firm evidence that the welfare system produces children who become "permanently dependent pathology-ridden people" (Macaulay, 1977).

Housing, neighborhood, and social class. Chilman (1978) concluded on the basis of scanty research that a heterogeneous neighborhood may not necessarily produce neighborliness and a better understanding of all types of people. Forbes (1974) recommended instead that the larger community be heterogeneous, with blocks planned for people with heterogeneous status. Bronfenbrenner (1973) recommended that housing developments be planned to encourage mixing of people of all ages, so that the young can get a sense of the life span and the old can share the buoyancy and enthusiasm of the young. However, many older people prefer to live away from noisy children and simply see them when they visit relatives or friends.

The suburbs are commonly perceived as good places for rearing children. The noise and speed of the city are missing, and nearby malls and playgrounds are available. However, sociologist E. A. Wynne has expressed doubts that the suburbs are the utopia for rearing children they are often portrayed to be. Suburban children are sheltered from reality and diversity and prevented from learning the coping skills they need. They are denied the maturing effect of having diverse experiences and mingling with people from varied ethnic and socioeconomic backgrounds. Because of this homogeneity they share common values among themselves and fail to develop negotiating skills ("The Sheltered Life," 1978).

Child Abuse

Neglect. In a sense, child neglect is a form of abuse having its own distinctive features. Child abuse suggests physical and psychological injury to children under age 18; neglect refers to damaging the child through lack of guidance or supervision.

Three major models have been employed to study child abuse and neglect. The first focuses on the caretaker's personality characteristics. The second, or sociological, model focuses on the social environment. A third approach presumes that neglectful and abusive child-rearing practices can best be explored through analyzing external environmental events as they affect families—the social-psychological model. In this approach all interactions within the family are studied, as well as the way the environment impinges on them.

Comparisons of homes in which children are abused, neglected, or neither abused nor neglected indicate distinctively different patterns (Burgess & Conger, 1978). Abusing parents typically interacted less frequently with their children than did controls, and neglecting parents had few positive interactions with their family. Abusing parents were negative toward their children, but neglecting parents were even more so. Abusing mothers showed little verbal or physical contact with their children, and the neglecting mothers showed even less positive interaction. While fathers in the neglecting group tended, like the mothers, to neglect their children, fathers in the abuse group did not differ much from fathers in the control group.

In the neglecting group the husbands tended to be more withdrawn from the children than the wives. While parents in the problem groups differed from controls in interaction with children, they did not tend to treat each other differently. This contradicted the theory that cold husband/wife relationships account for child abuse (Burgess & Conger, 1978). It seemed that children in the neglected sample were just as likely to suffer as those in the abused group. This factor, along with the much higher incidence of neglect than abuse, indicates that concern with abuse should not be allowed to obscure the problem of neglect.

Definition and incidence of abuse. The U.S. Child Abuse Prevention and Treatment Act of 1973 (Public Law 93–237) defines child abuse as "the physical or mental injury, sexual abuse, negligent treatment, or maltreatment of a child under the age of 18 by a person who is responsible for the child's welfare, under circumstances which indicate that the child's health or welfare is harmed or threatened thereby" (Gelles, 1976, p. 139). Other definitions of abuse include in them the child's failure to thrive, abandonment, or emotional mistreatment.

Estimates of child abuse and neglect range from 10,000 cases a year to as high as 10 million. The truth is, it is simply impossible to determine how many cases of child abuse occur. According to Gelles (1976),

> The proportion of unknown child abusers may be at least 100 times greater than the number of cases known. A great many doctors, parents, friends, and clinicians are hesitant to latch the stigma of child abuser on to any particular parents. Parents themselves may not seek help, because in doing so they lay themselves open to being labeled child abusers [p. 3].

Precipitating factors. Child abuse is commonly portrayed as resulting solely from parental frustrations and personality disturbances. However, only one child in a family is typically abused and certain children, on removal from their families, are also abused in foster homes where children have not been abused before (Gil, 1970). Children who cry a great deal in an irritating way or who manifest other exasperating behaviors tend to arouse negative reactions. It is not solely the parents who respond this way but also foster parents, social workers, and, sometimes, even the researchers. That is, the children's characteristics, including their constitutional factors, can stimulate abuse somewhat independently of the parents' personal characteristics or their manner of treating children.

Ordinarily, if by the end of the 3rd month children's fussing and crying does not decline according to the pattern of most infants of that age, maternal attachment to the babies weakens (Robson & Moss, 1970). Abused children are ordinarily those who were, as infants, "irritable, colicky, fretful, and difficult to feed, satisfy or diaper" (Segal & Yahrees, 1978). The single most important infant characteristic predictive of future abuse is birth weight, possibly because the scrawny infant so completely violates the parents' hopes and expectations.

Other factors that contribute to child abuse include unwanted pregnancies and economic hardships. Child abuse occurs more frequently in the lower socioeconomic classes and more by mothers than fathers. In general, abuse stems from two main factors. One is structural stress involving low income, poor education, and low occupational status. Another factor is the cultural norm that permits parents to be violent toward children. Indeed, "In contemporary American families violence toward children is perhaps more common than is love" (Gelles, 1976, p. 139). A third of a national sampling of parents admitted spanking their children frequently, and in-depth interviews disclosed that 96% of parents hit their children, 45% of them quite regularly (Gelles, 1974, p. 54). It appears that violence is not only "culturally acceptable, [but] culturally mandated (Spare the rod and spoil the child)" (p. 139). Gelles stressed that the child abuser is not ill and that the abusing caretakers should be viewed as victims of circumstances that cause their emotions to get out of hand.

Child abuse, unfortunately, is far more common than we would like to think.

Dealing with abuse. Gelles observed that the usual pattern for treating child abuse is to remove the child from the home. Nevertheless, he concluded that placing children in a succession of foster homes may produce more ill effects than the potential physical risks of leaving them with their parents. Adoption may be the best alternative; perhaps society should not be so reluctant to remove children from sick parents.

The child-rearing process should be restricted to those adults who are clearly capable of such a complex art. There are a great many adults who could and would become excellent adoptive parents of abused children. If such a policy became common, parents would be less trigger-happy in discharging their frustrations on their children. While efforts should first be taken to cure abusive parents of their sickness, it should be clear that they are well, with minimal danger of relapse, if they are to be permitted to keep their children. After reports of abuse are duly confirmed, a judge might order the child placed in a foster home until social workers felt reasonably sure that the offending parent would no longer abuse the child. The tensions that precipitated the child's abuse might have arisen from a conflict between the parents, a parent's alcoholism, mental disturbance, anxiety over money, or the child's own behaviors and personality. Therapy might involve marriage counseling, psychiatric help, and social programs that improve the lot of the family in general.

Social agencies themselves should become more skilled, and they should be given more adequate resources for dealing with child abuse. Because U.S. society in general, and its institutions in particular, sanctions assaultive behavior against children, Maurer (1976) recommends that children's advocates take children's part against old-fashioned, unsound ideologies and against institutional neglect and abuse.

Child Advocacy

The need. Unfortunately, the average citizen does not actively look out for children's needs in general. On the basis of interviews with 90 child-care specialists—including scholars, child advocates, legislators, and practitioners—Milton Senn (1977) concluded that most people are largely indifferent to other people's children. Public neglect may derive from the privatism and individualism of the culture and the practice of viewing families as self-sufficient. Hence, most citizens feel little real concern about neglected or abused children. For another thing, children have no political power, and their caretakers often do not know how to take effective political action. Child specialists are ordinarily somewhat politically naive, and public policies are defined by people who know little about children. Most of those interviewed believed that the best way to help children is to improve conditions in families—including housing, economic security, and support by community and public agencies—and to provide better-quality day care.

Specific suggestions. Bennett and McDonald (1977) warned against espousing children's rights purely for their own sake and against the wholesale application of adults' constitutional rights to children. Rights should be defined from the child's point of view. They should be balanced against the need to view the child as a developing person, with emphasis on maximizing his or her potential. In this respect, children have a right to receive parental guidance, to be educated, and somehow to participate in choices that significantly affect their future. An area not yet clarified is how to resolve issues in which the rights of children and parents conflict.

Other authorities have sought to propose an integrated, overall pattern of services for children. A sampling of their suggestions follows. Rossi (1977) contended that the concept of child care should be displaced by that of supportive environments. The notion of taking care of children in a custodial sense, purely to compensate for an impoverished home background, should yield to the idea of development centers that contribute creatively to children's growth in ways that even the best home cannot ensure.

Bronfenbrenner recommends that local studies be made to determine local needs. He urges efforts to find specialists as well as nonprofessionals in the community who can provide mutual caretaking, for example, in the home. He also recommends that researchers focus more on the typical experiences of children—especially informal caretaking in homes and neighborhoods by parents, friends, and relatives—and less on laboratory preschools in universities. While researchers may alleviate some suspicions about the negative emotional impact of day care, they do not yield prime evidence that children's development is significantly improved by any one form of such care (Woolsey, 1977).

Woolsey agrees with Bronfenbrenner, asking why the chief method of child care employed by working mothers within the child's household or among the extended family, especially grandmothers, has received so little attention. It is merely "an illusion" that extended-family relationships have disappeared, especially in the lower classes, she wrote.

Programs for helping children have had varying success. For example, research into the effect of child-development centers is somewhat conflicting (Woolsey, 1977). Significant short-term gains in applied skills and cognitive abilities have been reported in a few experimental projects using structured sequences of learning activities (Stearns, 1971). Training experiments, in conjunction with child-development centers in which mothers are educated in child care, may also produce short-term effects (Robinson, 1973). However, techniques have not been developed for translating such highly supervised projects into large-scale programs. In general, there is little relationship between early progress in preschool environments and later progress in school—or between school achievements and success in later life. Children's experiences are simply too varied and the influences on them too complex for preschool programs to immunize them against later problems.

Bersoff (1976) suggests that children's own perceptions of their situation be given greater regard. While **child advocacy** has increased the power of professionals to act on children's behalf, he observes, it is not always clear what their best interests are. Bersoff suggests that children's rights be adapted to developmental stages, arguing that their decisions prove no more damaging to them than those of adults. He cites the placement process in special-education programs as an example of the manipulation and deceit perpetrated on children. And he suggests that children and their parents be incorporated into the decision-making process. While expansion of children's rights would indeed limit the power of parents and the state, there is no evidence that society would suffer.

Status of Parent and Child in Society

Revised attitudes toward parenting. As suggested elsewhere, many adults no longer consider parenthood an obligation. They decide to have children only when they conclude that parental gratification will outweigh the inevitable problems and frustrations. Children themselves thereby benefit, because they are more likely to be wanted.

To date, society has tacitly accepted the right of any adult, however unfit, to parent children. This concept, however, may change. Intimations of this idea are already appearing in various professional publications, although society as a whole has continued to play ostrich with it. Eventually, the population problem may force this issue onto the public agenda of reform. The problem is already acute in certain countries. Whatever else may awaken society to the need for upgrading parenthood is uncertain.

Children's present status. In certain ways the status of children has changed radically from that in former times (Boli-Bennett & Meyer, 1978). In colonial times, children worked alongside their parents in many enterprises. Today, children are mainly segregated from adults in most activities. Children have increasingly come under the jurisdiction of the state, reflecting the state's concern for socialization of its members. The aim is to ensure that citizens will effectively transact their roles and further the nation's development and progress. Certain state-managed programs have transcended their national boundaries, as in the United Nations. They are evolving "institutional recipes" for the care and rearing of children (p. 810).

It is questionable whether this development will help or hurt children. On the one hand, it tends to encourage in them a certain dependence and to formalize the distinction between their roles and those of adults. On the other, state-managed programs foster better protection for children and equality of opportunity. Thus, "In one sense children are less equal to adults than they used to be; in another sense they are more equal (p. 797)."

Other aspects of children's current status in society can be summarized as follows. (1) As Brim (1975) pointed out, "We are in this nation moving into an era that may be historically the most precarious for America's children" (p. 3). Couples with children experience greater stress than childless couples do (Campbell, A., 1975). (2) Nowadays, children are more likely to be treated as individuals in their own right and not merely as contributors to the family economy. (3) Because couples choose to have fewer children, each child has more advantages. Besides, children are more likely to be planned for and are hence accorded a better reception.

Perspective on Child-Development Research

Despite the vast accumulation of child-development research, many questions remain to be answered. For example, there are numerous how-to-rear-children books, but "there is not a single proven set of procedures for childrearing during the first three years" (White, 1977, p. 3). Clarke-Stewart (1977) concluded that available data "indicate nothing about ways to structure society so as to permit, support, or enhance caregiving" (p. 120).

A second major deficiency is in determining the extent and ways that children differ and how to adapt research findings to individual children. For instance, although practically all children react positively to certain environmental characteristics, such as having supportive parents, some individuals react well to environmental factors that harm others. An illustration is the disease phenylketonuria (PKU). Normal children require the amino acid phenylalanine in their foods if they are to be healthy, but children with PKU are poisoned by this acid. The same nutrition that helps normal children is "deadly" to children with this particular genetic deficiency (Scarr & Weinberg, 1978a, p. 29). For a more common illustration, note that some children are overstimulated by the complex, varied environments that challenge others.

There are several reasons for the continuing uncertainties about optimum factors in children's development. First, although professionals are mainly interested in children's enduring environments, Bronfenbrenner (1977a) reported that "between 1972 and 1974, of all the studies published in *Child Development*, *Developmental Psychology*, and *The Journal of Genetic Psychology*, 76% employed a laboratory paradigm [and] 17% used paper and pencil techniques, while only 8% . . . employed direct observation of behavior" (p. 87). Hence, the bulk of current developmental-psychology research is "the science of strange behavior of children in strange settings with strange adults for the briefest possible period of time" (p. 513).

It is also hard to apply research findings to practical problems, because studies ordinarily deal with "what and why questions, rather than the how-to questions such as how to organize and structure environment and experience in order to accomplish particular results" (Clarke-Stewart, 1977). Yet some efforts are being made. For example, investigators have initiated a number of large-sample longitudinal studies, specifically for facilitating children's long-term adjustment to divorce (Kalter & Rembar, 1981). In addition, a large amount of socialization research has been designed according to certain "grand theories" of human development, including social-learning, cognitive-development and psychoanalytic theories. Such theories afford alternative and often incompatible assumptions about human nature and development. To the degree that any one of them is incomplete, research generated by them will fail to produce fully valid conclusions.

Research results are also contaminated by the use of questionable techniques and atypical situations. Mothers have been asked to fill out questionnaires regarding child rearing and to rate members of their family on certain dimensions under review—ratings that are subject to distortions of memory and judgment. In other cases parents have been observed directly in home and laboratory settings. But do parents behave in their usual ways in the university laboratory, or even in their homes when observers are there (Davis, 1979)?

Researchers themselves often involuntarily bias conclusions. Most studies have been done by middle-class researchers whose own values and points of view become unconsciously reflected in the design and interpretation of their experiments (Davis, 1979).

SUGGESTED READINGS

Anderson, J. G., & Evans, F. B. Family socialization and educational achievement in two cultures: Mexican-American and Anglo-American. *Sociometry*, 1976, 39(3), 209–222. Data were collected from 69 Mexican- and 33 Anglo-American junior high school students and their families. An analysis was made of the effects of family socialization practices on children's self-concepts, achievement orientation, and academic success.

Bell, R. Q. Parent, child, and reciprocal influences. *American Psychologist*, 1979, 34(10), 821–826. Suggests ways in which the well-being of children may derive from greater recognition of children's effects on parents and their reciprocal relationships.

Belsky, J. Child maltreatment: An ecological integration. *American Psychologist*, 1980, 35(4), 320–335. After reviewing alternative models proposed to eliminate child abuse, the author proposes a framework that draws upon Bronfenbrenner's theory of the ecology of human development. Child maltreatment is portrayed as a social-psychological phenomenon determined by factors within the individual, the family, the community, and the culture.

Bruner, J. S. Poverty and childhood. *Oxford Review of Education*, 1975, 1(1), 31–50. Focuses on education of the very young and its influence on intellectual development in infancy and early childhood. Special emphasis on the effects of poverty.

Buriel, R. Cognitive styles among three generations of Mexican-American children. *Journal of Cross-Cultural Psychology*, 1975, (6)(4), 417–429. The study compares second- and third-graders randomly chosen from first-, second-, and third-generation Mexican-American and Anglo-American populations. The Anglo-Americans proved the more field independent and showed the smallest sex differences on a rod-and-frame test, followed by the second-, first-, and third-generation Mexican-Americans. The results are interpreted in terms of selective immigration and community acculturation processes.

Children Today, 1975, 4(3). This entire issue is devoted to articles on child abuse. It affords an excellent picture of the extent and status of the problem today.

Derdeyn, A. P. Child custody contests in historical perspective. *American Journal of Psychiatry*, 1976, 133(12), 1369–1376. In child-custody disputes, the father was given prior rights in the 19th century, whereas mothers' claims have taken precedence in the 20th. More recently, courts have begun to focus more on children's emotional needs. It is likely that they will increasingly call on mental-health professionals for advice in making child-custody decisions.

Edelman, M. W. Who is for children? *American Psychologist*, 1981, 36(2), 109–116. Psychologists are challenged to assume responsibility for helping to develop state and national networks of services for children with special needs in such areas as health care, day care, foster and institutional care.

Etaugh, C. Effects of nonmaternal care on children: Research evidence and popular views. *American Psychologist*, 1980, 35(4), 309–319. Although child-care books and magazine articles have presented a somewhat negative view of nonmaternal care of preschool children, a review of the research indicates that quality care deserves a better reputation. Within the past decade a more favorable attitude has developed toward working mothers and nonmaternal child care.

Goodman, N., & Andrews, J. Cognitive development of children in family and group day care. *American Journal of Orthopsychiatry*, 1981, 51(2), 271–284. A comparison of different educational programs and delivery systems on 52 preschool children in family day care disclosed significant differences in impact on cognitive performance.

Hallinan, M. T. Friendship patterns in open and traditional classrooms. *Sociology of Education*, 1976, 49(4), 254–265. A comparison of open and traditional classrooms indicates that the situation is less hierarchical in the more flexible situations, with fewer isolates and leaders.

Hughes, M., Mayall, B., Moss, P., Petrie, P., & Pinkerton, G. *Nurseries now: A fair deal for parents and children*. Harmondsworth, U.K., 1980. The authors examine the evidence regarding the quality of nursery schools in England and suggest ways for improving early education and child care.

Jacobson, D. S. Stepfamilies. *Children Today*, January–February 1980, 9(1), 2–6. Recent research regarding stepfamilies is reviewed in terms of relationships within such families, major issues, tentative conclusions, and educational groups for stepfamilies.

Kalter, N., & Rembar, J. The significance of a child's age at the time of parental divorce. *American Journal of Orthopsychiatry*, 1981, 51(1), 85–100. Evaluations of 144 children of divorce, ages 7 to 17 years, revealed the child's age at divorce to relate to certain constellations of emotional-behavioral difficulties but not to overall level of adjustment.

Northwood, L. K. The impact of urban removal from a child's point of view. *Journal of Sociology and Social Welfare*, 1975, 3(2), 224–241. A longitudinal study covering 3 years was made of the impact on children of a move forced by urban renewal. Factors are identified that related to poor adjustment in such situations.

Raz, S. M. Growing up in a multi-ethnic community. *Journal of Social and Economic Studies*, 1974, 2(1), 43–55. Patterns of socialization, including child-rearing practices and personality differences, were studied in a village in India. Such details as toilet training, obedience training, learning job skills, and self-sufficiency are included.

Rogoff, B., Sellers, M. J., Pirrotta, S., Fox, N., & White, S. H. Age of assignment of roles and responsibilities to children: A cross-cultural survey. *Human Development*, 1975, 18, 353–369. Cross-cultural data are examined in order to determine the ages at which children in each of 50 cultures assumed responsibility or were assigned more mature social, sexual, and cultural roles. Such assignments were made for various functions at different ages in these cultures. It seemed that, in certain respects, diverse human cultures assigned new roles and responsibilities in the 5- to 7 age range.

Seefeldt, C. *Teaching Young Children*. Englewood Cliffs, N.J.: Prentice-Hall, 1980. This book deals with the historical background and philosophies for early-childhood education, strategies for teaching and curriculum, as well as resources and projects.

Seymour, S. Caste/class and child-rearing in a changing Indian town. *American Ethnologist*, 1976, 3(4), 783–796. Among a sampling of upper-middle-class households, child-rearing practices were found to differ significantly according to the parents' social status.

Strom, R., Rees, R., Slaughter, H., & Wurster, S. Child-rearing expectations of families with atypical children. *American Journal of Orthopsychiatry*, 1981, 51(2), 285–296. A study is reported of the child-rearing expectations of 101 Australian parents of intellectually handicapped children and means of identifying parents who would be most and least successful teachers in a home-based language training program.

Taylor, R. L. Psychosocial development among Black children and youth: A reexamination. *American Journal of Orthopsychiatry*, 1976, 46(1), 4–19. Recent research studies suggested alternative conclusions about the quality and level of Black self-esteem. They contradicted common interpretations of earlier research.

Wallerstein, J. S. & Kelly, J. B. California's children of divorce. *Psychology Today*, 1980, 13(8), 67–76. An in-depth study of 60 families after the parents divorced showed that 37% of the children from these families were depressed, 29% were doing pretty well and 34% were happy and thriving. The children appeared, on the whole, neither better nor more poorly adjusted after the divorce. The most important finding was that children need to maintain a relationship with both of their natural parents and that parents should share responsibility for their child after the divorce.

Weisberg, D. K. The Cinderella children. *Psychology Today*, 1977, 10(11), 84–86; 103. Life for children in urban communes is described as posing certain problems. The presence of many bosses, as in the case of Cinderella's stepsisters, can be confusing to children. But they have certain advantages; for example, they play a part in decision making and learn to share responsibilities.

6
ASPECTS OF ADOLESCENT DEVELOPMENT

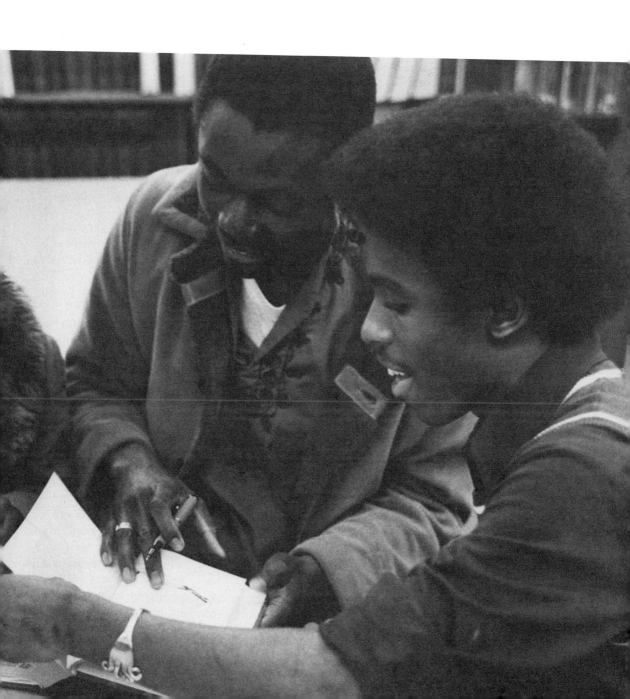

INTRODUCTION

Definitions

Adolescence. In time, the child arrives at the next life stage, *adolescence,* a term derived from a Latin verb meaning to grow into maturity. The concept "adolescence as process" suggests its transitional status between childhood and adulthood. In the total life span adolescence embraces the years from puberty until maturity. *Pubescence,* also called preadolescence, refers to the period in physiological development during which the reproductive system matures, including changes in both secondary sex characteristics and genital organs. Pubescence ends with the achievement of reproductive ability and the appearance of all the secondary sex characteristics that distinguish mature males and females. Puberty is characterized in girls by menarche (menstruation) and in boys by the presence of live spermatozoa in the urine.

Early adolescence, which extends from the onset of the pubescent growth spurt until about a year after puberty, when mature biological functions are pretty well established, can be distinguished from late adolescence, which lasts until maturity. No firm boundaries exist between adolescence and adulthood, because people mature at different rates. And even within the same individual different functions become established at different rates. According to Sheehy (1976), adolescence lasts until that point in the 20s when one takes hold of a "provisional identity" (p. 35).

Youth. Recently a new stage has been defined. *Youth* is more inclusive than adolescence, referring to "those ill-defined years between partial and complete independence relative to the family of origin, a time span that has increased over the past 20 years through the expansion of higher education" (Elder, 1975a, p. 3). The "newcomer is a post-Sputnik creation, born of the union between technology and high education, somewhere between the late teens and mid-20s, and is variously called 'youth' or 'subadult,' or no particular name because his or her status has not yet jelled. Such individuals are clearly not 'teenagers'; nevertheless, for various reasons, they have yet to assume a full-fledged adult role" (Rogers, 1978, p. 5).

Elder (1975a) used the terms *adolescence* and *youth* interchangeably to refer to the years from about the seventh grade to complete independence from the family. Others have portrayed this period as an extension of adolescence, suggesting that youth have simply failed in resolving the developmental tasks of adolescence, especially "abandoning narcissistic fantasies and juvenile dreams of glory" (Keniston, 1975, p. 7).

Conger (1976) proposed a four-group classification of youth that constitutes the basis for the four categories that follow: First, there are those youths who model after their elders and neatly fit into the society. These individuals, by definition, are not alienated. **Alienated** youth themselves include those who try to *reform society*, those who *turn away from society* and try to create a satisfactory culture of their own, and those who are *hostile to society* and try to destroy or redesign it. The reformers rely on politics, and their forum is the campus. Such youths were effective catalysts for the country's political issues during the late 1960s. The escapists include drug users, commune dwellers, and transient "street people." Those alienated youths who turn against society include radical protestors, who advocate revolution rather than evolution, and juvenile delinquents. In certain respects adolescent-young adults, ages 15 to 24, and the retired aging or young-olds, ages 65 to 74, have similar characteristics (Chellam, 1980–81). Both age groups view life as good and feel unaware of their potential worth. Their ideological and spiritual urgings reach a peak at these stages despite problems with their environment. Neither group tends to project plans very far ahead, partly because things seem uncertain in such periods of transition.

Keniston has contrasted adolescence, which suggests residual traces of childish immaturity, with youth, which connotes greater responsibility and maturity. Most individuals at the youth stage have already put behind them the period of adolescent rebellion and have attained a reasonable sense of identity. But they differ considerably from young adults of the same age who have married, settled down, perhaps become parents, and may be committed to a specific occupation.

Significance of Adolescence and Youth

The main task of adolescence. Many writers have commented on the significance of adolescence. It is most often portrayed as critical for establishing an identity. The self-concept is an individual's total view of self, whereas identity indicates feelings of distinctiveness from others. Sense of identity connotes awareness of self as a unique individual with a distinctive life-style. It can be a healthy identity, as in the case of a young person with unusual leadership ability who aspires to be an executive. Or it can be unwholesome, as in the case of a teenager who gains a feeling of distinctiveness from reckless driving. And it can be a **negative identity,** as when an adolescent becomes a revolutionary, showing complete disdain for socially approved roles.

Nevertheless, the identity crisis may have been exaggerated, argued King (1972). Most students, when faced with problems, merely cope in ways that worked in the past. They relate well to others, share feelings with them, and satisfactorily work through feelings of depression. By college graduation many of their earlier self-doubts have already begun to disappear as they feel greater self-confidence, competence, and power. In some situations, as in Amish communities, most adolescents have few identity problems. Each individual knows his or her roles and what society expects (Finkelstein, 1973). However, some Amish adolescents have an identity problem associated with the decision to join or not join the church community. For some of them this task is equivalent to a crisis.

Most young people report that adolescence has been a significant period for them, at least in certain ways.

> I feel it has helped me relate and deal with the pressure of socializing with other individuals (man, age 21).

> I have found it very significant. Mostly in the past 4 years I have felt myself maturing and handling responsibilities—taking charge of my life and interests (woman, 21).

> I have found it to be significant in that it's a period in time when you experience more in one period than ever again, including different sexes, college, high school, puberty, etc. (woman, 21).

> Adolescence has been a primary "warmup" for the real world. One must learn to successfully interact and live with one's peers, and it seems as though these interactions are crucial for later development (man, 20).

Significance of youth. Various writers have commented on the significance of youth. The central characteristic of youth, observed Keniston (1975), is "the tension between selfhood and the existing social order" (pp. 3–4). He perceived in the lengthened transition between childhood and adulthood an opportunity for the individual to achieve a more advantageous position relative to society, in becoming more integrated on the one hand and more differentiated on the other.

Braungart (1975) observed that during this stage young people expand their intellectual horizons and define their relationships to themselves and their society. Baumrind (1975) contended that, if youth is to serve its purpose, society must permit young people a moratorium period for deciding how they can make their own best contribution to society. In societies that have lost their bearings, however, such a moratorium, instead of constituting a bridge to mature commitment, results in a "prolonged wallowing nihilism and escapism" (p. 119).

This period also holds significance for the lifetime that lies ahead. Habits of smoking and drinking that become firmly established in youth may continue to plague some people the rest of their lives. In addition, decisions made now with regard to marriage, career, and personal health habits are critical for all the years that follow.

Images of Youth

The positive view. Sometimes adolescents and youth are jointly termed youth, and they will be so treated in discussing image. The image of youth is no one thing, but many faceted, sometimes confused, and often conflicting. Some people assume a rosy-hued view of youth, warning that a distorted image stressing deviancy becomes a self-fulfilling prophecy. As teenagers may come to embrace and act out this distorted view, it is important to focus on what is good about adolescents.

Robert Coles, a Harvard psychiatrist, detected trends among young people toward healthy ideas about race, sex, and social class. He found them more mature and worldly wise than other generations ("Kids Today Are Pretty Levelheaded," 1976, p. 49). A nationwide survey supported Coles's conclusions. Only an insignificant minority used hard drugs, and most engaged in fewer sexual activities than commonly believed.

Less favorable views. Other authorities—for example, Keniston (1975)—have taken a less rosy view of youth. Youth's advocates, observed Keniston, portray them as zealously idealistic and emotionally healthy, overlooking their potential for "viciousness, immorality, and psychopathology" (p. 22). Similarly, Hendin (1976) asserted that the romanticism of youth—the picture of them as possessing the zest for living and an unusual freedom "that simply is not born out by knowing them—says more about the dissatisfaction with life of the older generation than it does of the joy of the younger" (p. 28).

To view youth realistically, advised Hendin, is not the same as pessimism. Instead, it simply focuses on youth's relationship to the larger society. For, as Bruno Bettelheim expressed it, whenever the older generation has lost its bearings, the younger generation is lost with it (Hendin, 1975, p. 28). That is, the mood of youth is a reflection of the mood of the larger society, of which it is an inextricable part. Some people look to the young to free us from ourselves, to remove us from our present-day materialism. But youth are part of us all.

Causes of distortion. Various factors unite to distort the image of youth. For one thing, youth are constantly changing, reflecting the rapidly changing times and the complexity of society. No single image could ever embrace the varieties of youth in the multiple cultures and subcultures of our times. Images that emerge from the most valid data would be hopelessly out of date before society came to accept them. Hence, youth must adapt to images that have been earned by the young who preceded them. Perhaps the most valid and currently relevant assessment can be gained from continuing discussions among groups that include youth and adults representing the various subgroupings of society.

The image of youth is also elusive because it varies according to such factors as time and social class. Veysey (1976) contended that recent changes in society have been exaggerated and that we should not overreact to constant cries of "crisis." A broader perspective would help to distinguish "confusing momentary (if dramatic) symptoms [from] deeper, quieter tides of change that are less easily defined" (p. B1).* Note the alarm that even sophisticated professionals manifested regarding the youth of the late 1950s, branding adolescents a "van-

*Reprinted by permission of *The National Observer,* © Dow Jones & Company, Inc. 1976. All Rights Reserved.

ASPECTS OF ADOLESCENT DEVELOPMENT

151

ishing breed." At that juncture it appeared that youth had adopted a grown-up style, both academically and in courtship. They went steady at 13 and simply absorbed, without unusual criticism, the world their elders bequeathed them. While middle-class youth sought success, they did so "within a bland, monotonous landscape of muted expectations. The hunger for adventure had evaporated somewhere in the early 20th century, leaving only a pathetic craving for security, intensified by parents' memories of the Great Depression" (p. B1).

Only a few years later the youth climate dramatically changed, and "a strident counterculture, at once pleasure-oriented and desperately apocalyptic, appeared to leave adults somewhere far behind" (p. B1). A housewife who lived near Kent State University recommended that all students who went barefoot should be shot. They were portrayed as "so alien as to be scarcely human" (p. B1). Instead of disappearing, as forecast in the 1950s, "adolescents seemed about to take America over. Youth had transformed into anarchists, ruthlessly spurning all the slots the established institutions offered, meantime grouping themselves communally to carry on an ever-ceasing celebration of unreason" (p. B1). Then again the scene changed, so rapidly as almost to produce disbelief. The soberness of the '50s reappeared, and the crisis of values of the 1960s became a crisis of "ways and means" of the 1970s.

Veysey took issue with the **psychoanalytic** image of adolescence for its failure to take into account the powerful bureaucratic organization that transcends all the shifts and rhythms outlined above. It "remains the arbiter of how one spends a 40-hour chunk of one's weekly waking existence, as well as the provider of sustenance for the whole of one's time on earth" (p. B2). Thus, "far-reaching institutional structures," which the majority created between the Civil War and World War II, have become the most vital factor in determining what we do, stronger in their effect than even family and religion. Moreover, their enormous power to shape destiny, to hand us the roles that we must play, makes the psychoanalytic concept of youth as a distinctive stage of life "relatively superficial or beside the point" (p. B2).

This Freudian concept, popularized by Erik Erikson, embraces the idea of the life cycle and of youth's identity crises as an inherent aspect of it. While disregarding the sociocultural context, neo-Freudians portrayed youth as a period of "almost mystical withdrawal from the real world, a moratorium during which the person unconsciously gathers strength and gains a sense of direction for future engagement. The model here is actually that of the eventual leader, or 'great man'—Luther, Gandhi, the Harvard student" (p. B2). However, concluded Veysey, the identity crisis is more likely to "be a luxury affordable only by the upper-middle class." For the vast majority of youth in the United States and everywhere else, "adolescence is more likely to be shaped by relatively mundane pressures, and by dreams and fantasies, that are earthier, less transcendental" (p. B2).

The picture of youth peddled by writers and professionals during these past several decades has focused on middle-class, sometimes upper-middle-class, youth. It became the model for the pictures of youth that appeared in the professional and popular literature. The radical youth of the 1960s came chiefly from the upper classes. And these same classes, the college students, are responsible for the picture of the youth of the 1980s anxiously seeking jobs in the professions. True, the proportion of college students has increased from 14% in 1940 to over 40% in the 1970s. Nevertheless, even today a small majority of young people does not share the college experience. Some youths are still mainly overlooked—for example, young Black females who may simply be lumped together with minorities or females in general (Smith, 1981).

PERSONALITY

Background

Basic concepts. Adolescent image refers to the picture created in others' eyes; adolescent **personality** represents what one is really like. *Personality* represents the unique pattern of an individual's traits. *Traits* are behaviors that have become habitual and consequently characteristic of the individual. Traits, in turn, become organized into patterns appropriate to one's *roles*—that is, socially expected patterns of behavior relating to functions in various groups. Adolescents play their most important roles in the family, school, and peer group. And in the process of playing their roles they experience successes or failures that mold their *self-concepts*, or pictures of themselves. Coextensive with the self-concept is an *ideal self*, which represents what they would like to become and acts as a compass to provide direction to their efforts. Henceforth, their feelings about themselves tend toward inertia and persistence, unless they have to cope with status-challenging situations (Rosenberg, 1975).

Most adolescents themselves, with some exceptions, believe that their personalities have changed in some way since early childhood.

> My basic personality really hasn't changed since my childhood except for maturity. Of course, I am much older now, and I feel I have grown up both mentally and physically, but my basic personality really hasn't changed (man, age 21).

> My personality has changed in several ways. I have become more open to people, more altruistic, and more enthusiastic (woman, 21).

> There is a slight change in my personality since age 6 or 7 in that I am more open with others and confident in myself, but I still have little personality traits that prevail (woman, 21).

> My personality has changed to some extent in that it has matured, but generally I think I still possess the same with a few more added traits (woman, 20).

Ego identity. Erik Erikson has employed another term, **ego identity,** to indicate "a persistent sameness within oneself and a persistent sharing of some kind of essential character with others." An individual's social identity "consists of the groups, statuses, collectives or social categories by which he is socially recognized and classified in the society" (Rosenberg, 1975, p. 99). These social categories include religion, race, sex, social class, and occupation. Over some of these, of course, an individual has no control.

Adoptees' search for their origins symbolizes the significance of youth's need to define their identity. A study of the outcome of 11 cases of reunion between adoptees and their birth mothers indicated that the majority benefited from the reunion, despite disappointment in some cases. Adoptees feel the need to search for their parents for a variety of reasons, especially to develop a more adequate sense of identity. A growing number of adoptees insist that they have a right, as adults, to the sealed birth records that would disclose the identity of their natural parents (Sorosky, Baron, & Pannor, 1974).

Factors Contributing to Adolescent Personality

Genetic factors. Both genetic and environmental factors contribute to the adolescent's personality and to its components discussed above. Genetic factors are often overlooked, especially in postinfancy stages, partly because we want to believe that youth's dreams will not be thwarted by hereditary limitations. In the United States we are committed to believing that humans are created equal and that, given appropriate experience, anyone can become a well-adjusted, effectively functioning individual. By adolescence, early behaviors have often assumed different forms and become a sort of overlay that masks the more fundamental traits that lie below (Robson, 1972). In other words, earlier behaviors may constitute the foundation of later ones, which nevertheless assume somewhat different form in adolescence.

Experiential and social factors. Some aspects of adolescence are critical in shaping personality. Peskin and Livson (1972) studied relationships between prepubertal and pubertal behaviors and later personality. They concluded that the transition from prepuberty to postpuberty is critical for shaping an individual's sense of safety or of danger toward instinctual expression and curiosity.

Broader social influences have both positive and negative effects on youths' personality. On the one hand, they sometimes contribute to their individual feelings of powerlessness and insignificance. On the other hand, such influences may have the effect of producing new personalities able to function effectively in a postindustrial society. Thus, Buchen (1974) perceived emerging a different kind of person, one who no longer "embodies the traditional image of a fixed identity" (p. 189). He saw individuals as both "more dependent and interdependent," in that they realize they cannot be as effective alone as cooperating with others.

Adolescent Roles

Common roles. In their continuous efforts to develop the selves they desire to be, adolescents try on various roles: the sophisticate, the social butterfly, the athletic hero, and the life of the party. Such roles often relate to adult goals, an example being the aspiring journalist who edits the school newspaper. However, for the time being the student role dominates all others, as youth seek to establish their autonomy. Their family roles have weakened, and they have not yet defined their adult roles. Indeed, school is the place society has designed especially for its adolescents (Coleman, J. S., 1974).

Boys' versus girls' roles. Students' school, family, and work roles often relate little to their future family and career. Lowenthal (1976) found that most boys' jobs were not the type from which careers might develop. The girls were even more limited in roles than the boys, the majority being restricted to home, school, and a "weakened social life." Few of the girls were involved in club activities such as the YWCA or Girl Scouts, which communities more often provided for boys than girls. Hence, it may be simply difference in opportunity that limits girls to a more diffuse, less complex life-style than boys. Both sexes appeared unrealistically optimistic about the future, speaking of "making it big" and of early retirement. Most of the girls perceived work as simply a means of

Traditionally the focus in girls' sex-role socialization was on becoming ladylike and passive. Currently their ideal is perceived as more balanced, incorporating a blend of nurturant and independent behaviors, such as participation in sports.

marking time between school and marriage, taking no thought of some future time when they might reenter the workaday world.

By contrast, boys are not prepared for their adult role as parents. Their failure to act out the role of father in their work or play in childhood certainly contributes to the awkwardness many men display as fathers. Fortunately, this situation is changing, at least among college youth. Later, as young adults, they are coming to accept, even to insist on, their roles as fathers. They share child-rearing tasks and enjoy close relationships with their children. While men in the lower classes remain somewhat apart from their children, the distance is diminishing somewhat.

The search for identity. A major task of adolescents is somehow to integrate their various roles. In the process, a measure of self-diffusion may occur when genital maturity floods the body with vague, unfamiliar feelings. These feelings may be balanced by experiences that encourage development of a healthy, integrated sense of self.

The quest for identity, or integration of roles, attains intensity at this developmental stage, because teenagers are confronted with difficult sexual, social, occupational, and value decisions. This quest presumably produces crises, stress, turmoil, and disturbance of identity among most individuals, especially during late adolescence. Nevertheless, the little research that might shed light on this question yields contradictory results. Monge (1973) reported a high degree of consistency and self-image structure between the ages of 12 and 18, thus contradicting the idea that adolescents reorganize their self-concept. In another study of 11-, 13-, 15-, and 17-year-olds, J. S. Coleman (1974) reported that some of the adolescents at each age level held a negative self-image, but this proportion proved fairly constant for the age groups tested. While some of them did express uncertainties about themselves, there was no developmental change between the ages of 11 and 17.

It is strange that none of the research cited above considered a projection of the self-concept into the future. Yet in research by Coleman, Herzberg, and Morris (1977), which involved 80 boys aged 12 to 16, the young people spoke of the future in such terms as "dreary," "dead," "black," "terrifying," "pointless," or a "dreaded age" (p. 73). The adolescents were undoubtedly projecting their own futures. Thus, questions are raised about the youth's prospects for ready adjustment to the adult world.

Concern for the present self, indicated by a proportion of all the boys, proved no higher at one age than at another. But concern for the future self increased consistently and sharply with age. Only a minority experienced a disturbance of identity with regard to the present, and that disturbance existed equally at different age levels. Overall, Erikson's concept "identity versus diffusion" (see Chapter 1) applied only to a highly restricted sampling, "probably to those who were most likely to present themselves in clinical situations" (p. 73). In another study, a large majority experienced the greatest modification in current self-image between ages 8 and 11. Older adolescents underwent the greatest developmental change in future self-concept (Simmons, Rosenberg, & Rosenberg, 1973).

Girls may have a more difficult time establishing an identity than boys. They have fewer role models recognized by society as having been successful, such as military and political figures. Girls also absorb from earliest childhood the idea that women's role is to help men achieve their identity and her task is mainly to be supportive. This situation is changing, but not nearly so fast as many people believe. Psychological researchers themselves, being predominantly male, have focused on the identity crises of boys, ignoring girls' identity problems almost completely. While there has been some work in this area in recent years, the most widely publicized studies have pertained to males.

Maturity versus immaturity. The following research, described in some detail, differentiates between youths who are role diffuse, lacking in a true sense of identity, and those who appear to be making satisfactory progress toward adulthood. A comparison of 7th- and 12th-grade boys who scored highest and lowest on a psychosocial maturity inventory indicated personality factors that differentiated the two groups. In general, the low-maturity boys were neither very self-aware nor introspective (Josselson, Greenberger, & McConochie, 1977). They lived in the present, their world being composed of "sports, cars and motorcycles, girls and their vicissitudes, adults who yell at you, friends who like you or put you down hard, the complexities of staying out of trouble and the concomitant temptations of drink, dope, and reckless driving which, for them, are the main paths to trouble" (p. 35).* These boys were not ambitious, although some of them expected to attend college, a decision usually imposed on them by others. They relied on external forces to shape their lives, expecting others to obtain jobs for them or entrance into college. Rather than taking charge, they often simply hopefully waited for something to happen to provide the breaks they needed.

Passivity in such matters contrasted with their enthusiasm for "hyper-masculine" activities, including motorcycling and sports. They had problems with impulse control, often getting into fights, acting tough, and getting angry. They counted on others to hold them in check. Their ego ideal was the "hard, self-assured athletic star," and they gained most self-esteem from any evidence of being liked by others. Because they had an unusual need for approval, they viewed making friends as their major task and were extremely susceptible to group pressures.

Ordinarily, they felt that they had not lived up to their parents' expectations. They viewed their parents as quite demanding but believed that the demands were justified. Psychologically, they were intimately tied up with family. While they might rebel, they also had strong dependency and regressive needs. They usually saw their fathers as "either weak or tyrants" and dominated by the mother. They liked and needed their parents, and their struggles for autonomy were quite mild. Their composite goal in life was "to have a good job, a family, a house, a car, and lots of money. They defined themselves by what

*From "Phenomenological aspects of psychosocial maturity in adolescence, Part I. Boys," by R. Josselson, E. Greenberger, and D. McConochie. In *Journal of Youth and Adolescence*, 1977, 6(1), 25–55. Copyright 1977 by Plenum Publishing Corporation. This and all other quotations from this source are reprinted by permission.

they could amass around them. They were little concerned with what to become themselves" (p. 38).

One of the immature boys, Leonard, was pursuing a college preparatory course but had not even thought about a school or course of study. He was merely going because his father wanted him to go so that he could get a better job. He was pessimistic about his future and feared that he would end up like his father, a skilled laborer working 10 hours a day, 6 days a week. He focused now on sports, hanging around with his friends, and going to dances. He had several girlfriends, yet complained that they interfered with the time he spent with his other friends. He constantly spoke of people, especially authority figures, who made demands on him. He was ambivalent about authority, both resenting it and approving it. He doubted that either parent trusted him, and he said they would not let him drive because his brother had got drunk and wrecked the car. He had a part-time job, which he disliked but kept for the money. His own dreams related to material things: a car, a home, and money. Because he couldn't seem to win his parents' approval, he relied on seeking esteem from his friends.

The mature boys were chiefly concerned with personal success and increased self-differentiation. They, too, were active in sports and liked girls and cars, yet attached less importance to them. More often than the immature boys they were concerned about school, individual hobbies, and religious interests. They were more highly varied, more complex, and generally more diversified. They were not so preoccupied with hyper-masculine activities or so concerned about social approval. Because they were ambitious, they were prone to realistic self-analysis; and they had the ego strength to report some measure of self-doubt. They admitted their own shortcomings and pursued their goals vigorously. Because they believed in themselves, they could sustain a measure of failure. They also had a feeling of being individuals and were fully aware of, and capable of, accepting human differences. Their friendships were somewhat intimate, which helped them to communicate and to support one another emotionally.

Yet few of the boys had even once dated seriously or gone steady; and they had rarely established deep heterosexual relationships. While these boys were not "square or overly inhibited," they nevertheless viewed somewhat critically those teenagers who "run wild, take dope, or goof off in class" (p. 42). While they might have "sown their wild oats," they felt they had learned from their mistakes. In general, they were perceptive and aware. In telling what makes a person mature, one cited "knowing the difference between right and wrong for yourself. And if what's right for you is wrong toward the society or something, then you yourself have to change because you can't go against the society" (p. 43).

While some of the boys had close relationships with their parents and others had ambivalent ones, they generally manifested an

empathic differentiated conception of their parents as people. . . . For example, "My father and I don't get along too well. We always get in arguments.

It might be his fault. His mother died when he was young and his father never listened to him. Used to beat him up all the time. That might be one reason" [p. 43].

The boys' parents encouraged them to make their own decisions. For instance, regarding what their parents desired for their future, these replies were typical: "My father advised me to go to college, but he's not pushing me." "My parents and I don't really sit down and talk—they just tell me I should do what I want, but I know deep down it does matter to them" (p. 44). The parents granted considerable autonomy but nevertheless set limits. These boys, unlike the immature boys, respected their parents' rules, showing little need to test their limits. For example:

"My parents don't set a rule about what time I should be home yet I'm usually home around 11 o'clock. I guess if it was 4 or 5 they'd start noticing and set rules." "They always let me make my own decisions. They're stricter if I do anything that was bad for me—I'd be too scared to get caught with dope or something" [p. 44].

Overall, the boys found their parents' rules less significant than their understanding of the kind of people that they—the boys—were in the process of becoming.

The boys had also achieved a certain balance in their lives:

Family, school, friends, work, fun, intimacy, doubt, and resentment [are] all in evidence, but none overwhelms [them]. Thus, they are beginning to sense the possibilities of the world beyond their immediate sphere and are moving, with some trepidation, to explore it. They are less preoccupied by security than the low maturity boys and more ready, perhaps, to fall flat on their faces if necessary [p. 44].

Nevertheless, their lack of rebellion, unusual self-control, excessive concern for moralistic values, and impulse constriction suggested that genuine ego autonomy had not yet been achieved.

Theorists have typically focused on two major developmental tasks of adolescence: the achievement of sexual identity and personal autonomy. In this study, the mature and immature boys manifested quite different patterns of heterosexual development. The low-maturity boys participated in far more heterosexual activity, and the majority of them went steady. The high-maturity boys appeared only tentatively to be undertaking relationships with girls, and none had gone steady. From the standpoint of most theorists the psychosocially more mature boys were less mature in their psychosexual development.

There are two possible explanations. The first is that the immature boys' relationships did not have any real depth and that these boys were thus no more advanced than the mature boys. Second, the mature boys had focused on the early aspects of the identity stage, preoccupied with what they desired to become and testing their talents against the standards of the world. Hence, their lack

ASPECTS OF ADOLESCENT DEVELOPMENT

159

of concern about sexual identity did not actually imply sexual immaturity. Instead, their "resolution of sexual identity rests more on solid identifications with masculine objects" (p. 11).

Females have difficulty establishing maturity, partly because maturity connotes independence, a characteristic encouraged more in boys than in girls. Society propels boys steadily in the direction of independence, whereas girls, even these days, are more sheltered. Even though girls mature physically faster than boys, boys are granted adulthood sooner. This fact is symbolized by the common practice of labeling males men far earlier than females are called women.

PHYSICAL ASPECTS OF ADOLESCENCE

Puberty

Criteria of puberty. Personality changes in adolescence are subtle, often being little suspected by observers. In contrast, physical changes accompanying puberty are clearly visible. Puberty itself is the period during which the reproductive organs attain functional maturity. The most commonly employed criteria for determining the onset of puberty among boys include growth of the testes and scrotum, a surge in height, and ejaculation. For girls, the first menstruation is often regarded as the beginning of puberty. While it does signify a mature state of uterine growth, it does not mean attainment of full reproductive function. For 12 to 18 months after **menarche** there is ordinarily a period of infertility. And for the next 4 to 6 years conception is less likely to occur than after full maturity has been reached.

Age of puberty. By age 13½, the average age of U.S. girls' puberty, menstruation begins. By contrast, boys undergo no comparable rhythmic variations or hormonal changes. The age of menarche steadily declined during the last century but has not changed now for three decades, at least in Western countries (Katchadourian, 1976). Among girls in a Boston suburb the age of menarche ranged from 9.1 years to 17.7 years (Zacharias, Rand, & Wurtman, 1976). Early menarche was associated with stoutness and, oddly enough, blindness. The amount of light reaching the retina relates to age of sexual maturation (Gaylin, 1976c).

Except during adolescence, growth is a quite regular process. But during puberty it accelerates—the so-called adolescent growth spurt. For both sexes weight increases until about age 18 and then tapers off. Between ages 12 and 15 most girls are taller and heavier than boys. But they are caught and passed by the boys at about age 15. Thereafter, the gap widens, because the boys grow for 3 to 4 more years.

Early versus late maturity. In general, adolescents who mature either extremely early or late are disadvantaged; even lesser degrees of late maturing can be disturbing. But early maturing—if not extreme—is an advantage. Late maturers are more likely to be treated as children by family and the larger society after their earlier-maturing contemporaries are being treated as almost adult. Individuals who are generally well adjusted compensate pretty well for problems of late maturing, but the less well-adjusted find that this circumstance makes their total adjustment more difficult.

Table 6-1 indicates the patterns of sexual maturation. There is a wide variation among individuals in age of puberty and sequence of growth.

Secondary sex characteristics. Physical traits that differentiate the sexes without being directly involved in reproduction are called secondary sex characteristics. Those traits directly related to propagation, especially the genitalia, are termed primary. Secondary sex characteristics are significant because they are clearly visible and emphasize distinctions between the sexes. Among such characteristics are change of voice and patterns of hair growth. The girl's voice becomes somewhat more feminine, and the boy's deepens. Boys lose some head hair, which produces an indentation of the hair line on either side of the upper forehead. Both sexes develop pubic hair, which becomes coarser, kinkier, longer, and darker. Facial features also change, especially among boys, whose jawbones become more prominent.

Another common feature of adolescent growth is asynchrony, or disproportion, which may involve differences in timing of growth spurts of parts of the body—in particular the arms, nose, feet, legs, and chin (Eichorn, 1975). That is, people do not grow all of a piece, in simple straight-line fashion. Boys in particular show greater disproportion in facial features than do girls; for example, the nose may be temporarily too long before the jawbone catches up. While most of these asynchronisms tend to disappear, left/right symmetry is never completely accomplished, as becomes evident when separate photographs of the left and right halves of the mature face are compared (Rogers, 1978).

Physical Image

Appearance. Adolescents cannot remain unaware of the rapid changes in their physical image. After all, their bodies constitute the external presentation of themselves to the world, and other persons constantly remind them of it. Even well-adjusted adolescents are concerned about even normal changes in their bodies. In their eyes every blemish becomes exaggerated, and even minor illnesses may take on the proportion of severe disease. Therefore, they seek endlessly to conform to and support the image or picture they want to present to others (Rogers, 1978).

A survey of research indicates that good looks have a far more important influence on youth than they would generally admit (Wilson & Nias, 1976). Psychologist Elaine Walster and her colleagues paired students on a random basis, except that the man was always taller. They had rated all participants in advance in terms of appearance, social skills, personality, and intelligence. After these pairs had attended a dance, they were asked to rate their partner on

Table 6-1. Normal Maturational Sequence in Boys

Phase	Appearance of Sexual Characteristics	Average Ages	Age Range*
Childhood through preadolescence	*Testes* and *penis* have not grown since infancy; no *pubic hair*; growth in *height* constant; no spurt.	—	—
Early adolescence	*Testes* begin to increase in size; *scrotum* grows, skin reddens and becomes coarser; *penis* follows with growth in length and circumference; no true *pubic hair*, may have down.	12-13 years	10-15 years
Middle adolescence	*Pubic hair*—pigmented, coarse and straight at base of penis, becoming progressively more curled and profuse, forming at first an inverse triangle and subsequently extending up to umbilicus; *axillary hair* starts after pubic hair; *penis* and *testes* continue growing; *scrotum* becomes larger, pigmented, and sculptured; marked spurt of growth in *height* with maximum increment about time pubic hair first develops and decelerates by time fully established; *prostate* and *seminal vesicles* mature, spontaneous or induced *emissions* follow, but *spermatozoa* inadequate in number and motility [adolescent sterility]; *voice* beginning to change as *larynx* enlarges.	13-16 years	11-18 years
Late adolescence	*Facial* and *body* hair appear and spread; *pubic* and *axillary hair* become denser; *voice* deepens; *testes* and *penis* continue to grow; *emission* has adequate number of motile *spermatozoa* for fertility; growth in *height* gradually decelerates, 98 percent of mature stature by 17¾ years ± 10 months; indention of frontal *hairline*.	16-18 years	14-20 years
Postadolescence to adult	Mature, full development of *primary* and *secondary* sex characteristics; *muscles* and *hirsutism* may continue increasing.	Onset 18-20 years	Onset 16-21 years

*The normal range was accepted as the first to the ninth decile (80 percent of cases).
From "The body and the body-image in adolescents," by W. A. Schonfeld. In *Adolescence: Psychosocial Perspectives*, by G. Caplan and S. Lebovici (Eds.). Copyright 1969 by Basic Books, Inc. Reprinted by permission.

whether they wanted to see him or her again. A student's interest in his or her date related solely to the date's attractiveness and not at all to intelligence, personality, and social skills (Wilson & Nias, 1976). In other research Landy and Sigall (1974) asked male college students to rate an essay accompanied by photographs of women rated as attractive or plain. They found that the men rated the essay according to the attractiveness of the author.

In general, sex appeal is determined largely by differences in appearance between males and females. "While a moustache or beard can add to a man's appearance, the slightest facial hair on a woman is as unappealing as acne" (Wilson & Nias, p. 97). Girls appear less concerned than boys about the appearance of prospective spouses, but nevertheless have their preferences. They care little about "large biceps or a bulging crotch." They generally prefer slim males with "thin legs, a medium-thin waist and a medium-wide chest, producing a kind of V look. Girls' preferences differ somewhat according to their own personalities. For example, "Extroverted, sporting women like muscular men, while neurotic drug-using women prefer thin figures. Older more traditional women prefer brawny males while younger more liberated women like the lean types" (Wilson & Nias, 1976, p. 98).

Despite these preferences, good looks do not guarantee happiness. When psychologists Eugene Mathes and Arnold Kahn had outsiders rate students' attractiveness, handsome boys proved no better off with regard to self-esteem and sense of well-being than did ugly ones. But beautiful girls did rate slightly higher than did unattractive ones on happiness, self-esteem, and well-being.

Strength and body build. The effect of body build is modified somewhat by age of maturing. As they moved through high school, the mesomorphs in Clausen's study (1975) were perceived as assertive, posed, and adept at interpersonal relationships. By contrast, boys with high endomorphic ratings had difficult peer relationships, especially in the junior high school years. They were often the butt of the group's jokes, had trouble finding friends, and tried to gain peer acceptance in any way they could. Meantime, the ectomorphs continued to be rather submissive, especially in the working class, although negative correlates of ectomorphy, including lack of assertiveness and social poise, decreased in senior high school years. At this time it is the late maturer instead of the ectomorph who becomes least proficient, according to the values of working-class males.

Youths' reaction to their own body build depends largely on their general adjustment. Sometimes a "97 pound weakling may work to build his strength by using Dr. Sampson's barbell and [possibly] become a Wee Geordie, Olympic hammer-throwing champion" (Clausen, 1975, p. 35). However, such a reaction is far less common than is compensation or seeking satisfactions in other areas where one has greater potential. That is, humans more often compensate for weaknesses in other ways than specifically attempting to overcome their handicaps.

Working-class youths value physical prowess far more than do middle-class ones. Both in the working and the middle class, boys who are perceived as highly active or fighters and leaders are typically mesomorphic in body build; but this is more pronounced in the working class. For one thing working-class males more often use muscles in their occupation. In general they are more physical in their behavior. Hence, the working-class ectomorph—the relatively

Working-class youths greatly value physical prowess in adeptness in sports activities.

weak, skinny boy—is perceived far more negatively. The lower-class boys perceive him as a follower, avoiding fights and afraid rather than daring. By contrast, the middle-class ectomorph is not significantly undervalued by his peers (Clausen, 1975). Corresponding research about adolescent girls is lacking.

Clothing. Adolescents use clothing as best they can to enhance their physical appearance. Clothing styles convey certain of their new attitudes toward life; for example, looser clothing permits freer body movement. In general, youth are more concerned about feeling and appearing natural and real than simply putting on a false front. The body itself is perceived "less as an object to be decorated, corseted, and changed to conform to some norm of beauty, than it is to be accepted and presented in its natural state" (Dreyer, 1975, p. 196).*

*From "Sex, sex roles, and marriage among youth in the 1970s," by P. H. Dreyer. In *74th Yearbook of National Society for the Study of Education, Part I,* 1975, 194–223. This and all other quotations from this source are reprinted by permission of the National Society for the Study of Education.

Physical fitness. Adolescent boys and girls differ somewhat in their physical fitness. Tests administered in 1975 to 12 million young people aged 10 to 17 indicated little change for boys from the previous decade. For girls, fitness scores improved steadily until the ages of 13 or 14, when performance reached a plateau. The boys' fitness scores continued to rise as they grew older. After puberty little effort is expended on encouraging girls to maintain their physical fitness. But vigorous sports are encouraged for boys throughout high school and, to a lesser degree, in college.

It has been conjectured that both sexes had come close to realizing their potential in 1965. However, Simon McNeeley, program officer for the 1975 performance tests, reported higher fitness scores then by those schools that emphasized vigorous physical-education programs (Horn, J., 1976c).

Causes of mortality. Among youth aged 15 to 24, automobile accidents are the primary cause of death. The automobile itself is important to them, because it symbolizes autonomy, power, and status among one's peers. According to psychoanalytic theory, it is a sex symbol "able to thrust, penetrate, and conquer space. At the same time, it is a warm and comfortable place" (Tabachnick, 1973). It also represents maturity, because it is associated with adult life and privilege. Factors contributing to accidents are multiple. They include alcohol and youth's feelings that they are omnipotent, that fatal accidents cannot happen to them.

Of next importance as a cause of mortality are malignant tumors, a condition usually associated with aging rather than with youth. The decrease in mortality in a variety of infectious diseases has changed the position of malignancy as a cause of death from disease from eighth to second place (Shenker & Schildkrout, 1975).

Physical Problems

Adolescence has its own characteristic physical problems, one is being overweight. Obesity accounts for 15 to 20% of the major medical pathology of this period (Shenker & Schildkrout, 1975). This condition ordinarily begins in early childhood, the very 1st year being critical. By age 10 to 15 the number of fat cells is permanently fixed; and, once their final number is attained, they can be removed only through surgery. Psychologically, adolescents' eating is influenced by varied factors such as peer-group pressures, family eating patterns, or eating habits established early in life.

A related problem is nutrition—it is easily observable that many adolescents eat a highly unbalanced diet. Another common problem is fatigue, deriving from excess competition, overstimulation, inadequate rest, fast growth, and emotional strain. Fatigue is often expressed in headaches, irritability, sleeplessness, and even overactivity.

Drugs

Cigarettes. The most publicized physical problem of modern youth is their widespread use of cigarettes and drugs. The American Cancer Society reported that the number of teenage girls aged 13 to 17 who smoke rose from 22% in 1969 to 27% in 1975, a mere six years later. The percentage of girls smoking a pack or more a day more than quadrupled during the same period. While three-fourths were fully aware that smoking is harmful, the fact that so many of their peers smoke seemed to counteract this knowledge. Parental influence was also evident, 84% of the girls indicating that their fathers smoked and 64% that their mothers did. Over half the students reported that their schools had special areas where smoking was permitted (Horn, P., 1976a).

Alcohol. Most authorities rate alcohol as a greater threat to youth than the more publicized marijuana. Here is a summary of recent findings. (1) A survey at the Research Triangle Institute indicated that one in four junior and senior high school youths are moderate to heavy drinkers. These 13- to 18-year-olds average from 2 to 12 drinks at least once a week. (2) A national survey sponsored by the National Institute on Alcohol Abuse and Alcoholism indicated that only about one in four (27%) of 7th- through 12th-graders are abstainers. The most popular drinks are beer, wine, and hard liquor, in that order. (3) The incidence of drinking is greater with age, and total abstinence decreases from 38% at age 13 to 17% at age 17. (4) Youth in the South, because of the Bible Belt influence, and those in blue-collar and farming families drink somewhat less than the average. (5) Both parental habits and peer pressures importantly affect teenage drinking. Six of ten teenagers whose close friends drink are themselves moderate to heavy drinkers. (6) While it is presumed that alcohol is displacing marijuana, it seems that many pot smokers also drink (Horn, P., 1976a).

Authorities view youth's drinking with alarm, partly because alcohol is becoming their drug of choice (Brickman, 1974). It often carries no social stigma; and it is easily available. Also, for a time youth may seem to "get by" with the habit, but long-term abuse produces serious effects (Shenker & Schildkrout, 1975). Among these, drinking is "a factor in half of the homicides and a third of the suicides all over the country" (Brickman, 1974, p. 165). Long-term, irreversible effects include "cirrhosis of the liver [and] cerebral, cardiac, and other organ degenerations" (Shenker & Schildkrout, 1975, p. 76).

Hard drugs. The so-called hard drugs, such as **LSD** and heroin, have lost out in popularity with most youth ("A New Generation," 1976). Nevertheless, some youths continue to become addicted to heroin. In New York City the typical age of first use of the drug is 16, and the average age of death of addicts is 26 years (Shenker & Schildkrout, 1975, p. 73). In fact, heroin abuse killed more people in the 15-to-35 age group than did any single other cause, including automobile accidents.

After studying over 1000 college students and young military recruits, Singer (1976) reported that hard-drug users fell into two categories. One grouping wanted to escape from external stresses by achieving a numbness through using **barbiturates** or other "downers." The second group, who sought new sensations, preferred "uppers" and **amphetamines**. Both groups employed a slightly disorganized, pleasure-oriented, "hang-loose" life-style.

Interviews with youths on the Pacific Coast about their experience with LSD indicate that they proceeded through a series of phases with both desirable and undesirable outcomes. The youths classified drugs as either mind drugs or body drugs, depending on the effect. They judged the character of an LSD experience according to five sets of circumstances: the state of mind when taking the drug, the setting in which the experience occurs, the amount of LSD experience they have had, the chemical composition of the drug, and the interaction of the drug with other substances used immediately before or during the experience (Stoddart, 1974).

Marijuana. The problem with **marijuana** is both greater and less than with hard drugs. Far greater numbers use it, but the effects are much less serious. A nationwide survey of high school seniors indicated that the vast majority opposed using any unlawful drug except marijuana. Over 90% frowned on using cocaine, heroin, LSD, barbiturates, or amphetamines regularly, and over 80% disapproved of trying them even once or twice. Two-thirds said they had never used any illegal drug except marijuana, and the third who admitted having tried such a drug had done so only once or twice. By contrast, the use of marijuana was rising. In 1975, 6% said they smoked grass every day, and in 1976 8% did so ("The Young Moderates," 1977).

Youth may use drugs for a variety of reasons, such as achieving "altered states of consciousness [or] making the user feel euphoric, soporific, or tension free" (Shenker & Schildkrout, 1975, p. 73). Some youths try them simply out of curiosity, others because of peer pressure. Also important is the extensive advertising extolling the virtues of drugs for solving all sorts of problems, including anxiety, lack of concentration, and sleeping.

A comparison of drug users and nonusers affords insight into the reasons for taking drugs. LaDriere, Odell, and Pesys (1975) compared the responses of 100 male and female high school students (50 users and 50 nonusers) regarding marijuana usage with answers obtained from a college sampling in an earlier study (LaDriere & Szczepkowski, 1972). The results indicated considerable differences in motivations and profiles between users and nonusers. Every one of the high school users and 70% of the college users mentioned the pleasure of the "high" as a reason for drug use. Fewer than 12% of the high school students—and 12% of the females but 40% of the males on the college level—cited need for escape and a desire for expanded awareness as reasons. Only three students in all gave as a reason that they desired to be "in" with the group. Users in both groups viewed marijuana as "very pleasant, very moral, and very good" (p. 304). It appeared that the "drug culture" was a "fact of life" for these young people (p. 305). Nevertheless, they sometimes refrained because of the risk of being caught or a fear of harmful effects.

Among the nonusers 50% of the male and 24% of the female high school students believed that using marijuana was bad, and 44% of the males and 28% of the females felt that it might have physically harmful effects—an even more pronounced trend than in the college population. Other important reasons that high school, but not college, students gave for not using marijuana included family pressure (32% of the males and 24% of the females) and the risk of being caught (32% of the males and 24% of the females). A few students on both levels cited such reasons as cost, religion, or the fear of drug use per se. The majority of nonusers believed they would never use drugs, although a small percentage said they might try them sometime. On the high school level 36% did not have friends who were users. But of the 64% of nonusers who did have user friends, over half were tolerant of others who used drugs, and the same was true among the college students. The nonusers portrayed using marijuana, not so much as immoral but as simply not making any sense. They especially stressed harmful aftereffects on health rather than moral consequences. They accepted users without referring to morality and considered marijuana as a fact of social life.

Determining the longtime effect of drug use is not easy, and research is inconclusive (Kandel, 1974). Some people contend that the effects of and motivations for the use of marijuana and alcohol are different. They believe that marijuana heightens sensitivity, whereas alcohol depresses it. They believe that marijuana and LSD, used by about 4 million youth in the late '60s, produce completely new emotional, spiritual, and intellectual experiences. And they view that use as an inseparable part of a totally different life-style, focusing on different values from those held by older Americans (Bengtson & Starr, 1975).

Marijuana has been alleged to be a factor in such varied conditions as chromosome damage (birth defects), reduced immunity response, tendency toward crime, and impairment of sexual activity, and it has been called a general health hazard. After reviewing the charges against pot, the most researched drug to date, psychiatrist Norman Zinberg (1976) concluded that "marijuana is a remarkably innocuous substance" (p. 102). Although "drawing any hot substance into the lungs cannot be good for anyone, . . . we should remember that no marijuana smoker in this country uses as many cigarettes today as tobacco smokers do" (p. 104). In addition, while marijuana is an intoxicant, an individual who is high on marijuana performs better at driving than someone high on alcohol. Of course, having been influenced by any intoxicant is a danger. Those under age 18 should avoid all intoxicants, whether they contain alcohol or marijuana, because youth attempting to deal with a highly complex society need "as clear a head as possible." While no one can argue that marijuana is absolutely harmless, it is certainly one of the "least toxic drugs known to modern medicine" (p. 106).

Treatment. Treatment of drug users may be either short term for acute emergencies, or long term for compulsive low-dose and high-dose users and high-dose intermittent users. Methods of treatment vary according to the specific individuals involved. The most important factor in helping people is often the degree of motivation, and former addicts can be the most effective in producing such motivation in others. Especially beneficial are group programs concerned with increasing individual self-esteem, providing peer-group support, and helping individuals to arrive at satisfactory personal and vocational goals. It helps if the program also provides realistic vocational opportunities. Certainly, the problem permits no easy solution. A study of over 2000 high school students indicated that adolescent drug and alcohol use is a complex phenomenon influenced by the psychosocial context. Patterns of drug dependency consist of many elements including family problems, peer pressures, the larger society, the values of the culture and individual psychopathology (Jalali, Crocetti, & Turner, 1981).

ADOLESCENT EMOTION

Typical Problems

Adolescents, both well-adjusted and poorly adjusted, have their characteristic problems, including the frustrations involved in being not quite adult. Youth eagerly await their productive roles in society, yet the need for lengthened education means putting off these goals. Another category of problems relates to school. Students feel anxious about their grades, concerned about courses or majors, and worried lest they fail their parents, who are making sacrifices to send them to school. A third area of concern is sex. Despite all the talk about sexual freedom, adolescents may worry over setting boundaries for their own behavior.

Also contributing to some adolescent's problems are family relationships. Parents sometimes delay granting their children, usually their daughters, the autonomy usually accorded the age group. They may be at odds with their adolescent sons and daughters on such matters as sex, drugs, and religion. Other problems of adolescence derive from the social and physical stresses of that period and changing societal expectations. Thus, "In a society that provides no blueprint for what adults should be, teenagers may become anxiously preoccupied with attempting to fit together the jigsaw of their own personalities and with deciding when they should be grown up" (Rogers, 1978, p. 198).

Bailey (1976) ascribed many of youth's emotional difficulties to sociocultural influence. Disturbances derive from the breakdown in traditional values, the decrease in functions of the family, the problem of finding satisfactory jobs, the "fragmentation of the psyche by wanton technologies of sound and motion [and] . . . the knowledge-rich, action-poor biases of the present educational system" (p. 37). Problems ultimately come down to the individual level. Particular adolescents experience varying combinations of youth's current problems, inevitably in highly idiosyncratic ways.

The Concept of Stress

Storm and stress. Authorities attach different meanings to the stress produced by such problems. Bandura (1964) once observed that "if you were to walk up to the average man on the street, grab him by the arm, and utter the word 'adolescence,' it is highly probable . . . that his associations with this term will include references to storm and stress, tension, rebellion, dependency conflicts, peer group conformity . . . and the like" (p. 224). Others support this view. Adolescents manifest a compulsive need for all possible experiences, asserted Bailey (1976). They attempt "to stuff all experience, no matter how exotic and bizarre, into the tiny time capsule of late adolescence when, for the first time in human history, they have six or seven decades in front of them" (p. 37). "The adolescent is literally taken over by inner acceleration in development, accentuated further by sexual imagery. He experiences, even without drugs, rapid alteration of consciousness and mood which he cannot monitor" (p. 118). Merely to relieve their inner stresses, adolescents may yield control to "demagogues, gurus, and drugs" (p. 118).

Hendin (1976) observed that the suicide rate among young men and women had increased more than 250% during the previous two decades. This "fascination with death is often the climax of having been emotionally dead for a lifetime" (p. 28). Youth's risk taking with regard to cars, motorcycles, and drugs reflects their mood of depression, in which at least for some youth "only the excitement of daring death produces a sense of life. Yet this is a sign of a capacity for emotion and pleasure already so damaged that it will only respond to the ultimate stimulus" (p. 28).

Table 6-2. Proportional Frequency (%) of Suicide Methods by Age and Sex, United States, 1972

Method	10–14 Years		15–19 Years		20–24 Years	
	Males ($N=80$)	*Females* ($N=40$)	*Males* ($N=1106$)	*Females* ($N=278$)	*Males* ($N=1862$)	*Females* ($N=612$)
Poisoning:						
Solid, liquid ...	5	30	7	36	13	35
Gases.............	0	0	8	5	8	4
Hanging, strangulation, suffocation	35	20	20	7	13	9
Firearms, explosives	60	35	58	41	60	43
All other	0	15	7	11	6	9

Young people aged 18 to 25 report more loneliness than any age grouping of adults (see Figure 6-1). Feelings of loneliness are subjective and do not inevitably accompany the circumstance of being alone.

Figure 6–1. From "Loneliness," by C. Rubinstein, P. Shaver and L. A. Peplau. In Human Nature, *1979, 9(2), 60. Copyright © 1978 by Human Nature, Inc. Used by permission of the publisher.*

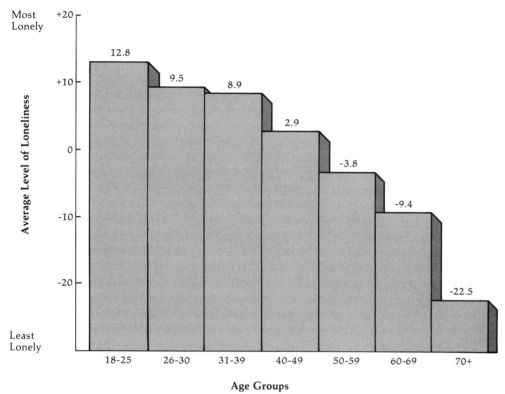

Obviously, no one model applies to all adolescents. Adolescents typically stabilize increasingly over time. And among third- to eighth-graders Pawlicki (1974) reported a developmental trend toward increased feelings of control over the environment with increased maturity (p. 158). A minority is antisocial, depressed, anxious, and disturbed—the classic picture of storm and stress. Some of them never completely overcome the stresses of adolescence and experience adjustment problems for the rest of their lives.

Desirability of stress. Down the decades, observed King (1972), various authorities have indicated that without turmoil and stress progress toward maturity is doubtful. Some psychologists and psychiatrists—for example, Anna Freud—view stress in adolescence as normal and even desirable. The question, then, becomes how much stress do growing individuals need in order to learn to handle their difficulties?

Such theories, wrote King (1972), assume that "an accurate picture of healthy functioning can be obtained from a study of disturbed functioning" (p.

355). A related assumption is that sound emotional health is merely the "absence of disease and that health does not involve any new conceptions of functioning that are absent in illness" (p. 355). These assumptions are open to question. While a minority of adolescents experiences real stress, and while the period itself is indeed one of considerable change, storm and stress do not necessarily accompany adolescence. Instead, argued King, the following conclusions are justified: (1) In contrast to the usual picture of adolescence as highly stormy, identity crises are rare and stress-laden conflicts only moderate. (2) Although there is some rebellion toward parents, relations with them are usually favorable. (3) Emotionally healthy adolescents usually have good peer relationships, high feelings of self-regard, feelings of adequacy, and few self-doubts. Most adolescents do not experience unusual depression and have developed mechanisms for overcoming depressed moods. (4) Adolescents typically deal directly, instead of evasively, with problems, and they share feelings with others. Often they simply turn to other activities, sometimes physical in character.

Long-term prediction. The question also arises whether adolescent stress is predictive of future turmoil. Longitudinal research reveals that personality development is complex and generalizations hard to develop. The Guidance Study of the University of Human Development, initiated in 1928 and involving intensive study of subjects from birth until the present, suggests that adult psychological health is only minimally predictable from behaviors at ages 5 to 7, 8 to 10, and 14 to 16. However, adults' health does relate to behaviors at ages 11 to 13, during preadolescence. That is, those individuals who are relatively healthy during this period will probably be so as adults (Peskin & Livson, 1972).

Nevertheless, some of the individuals in this study were far healthier emotionally at age 30 than might have been expected from their preadolescent behaviors. Such individuals included males from essentially stable, happy families with a close relationship to their father and females who were especially close to their mother during the early years of life.

The Good Side

Not all emotion at adolescence is negative—much of it is positive. There is the excitement of young love, of participating in sports, and of going away to college. There is the quiet satisfaction of growing bigger and stronger and of being treated more as an adult. There are the experiences of wonder and awe at gaining new ideas and being exposed to the achievements of the human race.

Other experiences may be ambivalent in effect or positive for one youth and negative for another. Adolescents often react to an imaginary audience that they imagine to be observing them (Elkind, 1967). If they suspect that this audience (the people around them) is finding fault, they suffer from humiliation and self-deprecation. If they believe it to be admiring, they enjoy the feeling that they are being watched.

Not all emotion is negative—there is the excitement of young love.

MORALITY AND RELIGION

Moral Status at Adolescence

The stage theory. It will be recalled that Lawrence Kohlberg (1975) portrayed moral development as involving three main levels. In the preconventional stage of moral thinking (prior to age 10), children simply respond to cultural labels of behavior as desirable or otherwise. In the conventional level, from age 10 until adult morality is achieved, children and adolescents conform to others' expectations merely because they feel they should follow the rules. On the postconventional, mature, level they progress toward autonomous moral principles that have validity apart from the authority of those who express them. On this level an individual thinks of moral rightness and duty in terms that suggest ideals and universality.

Kohlberg suggested that as many individuals as possible should arrive at a postconventional personalized morality, but the vast majority does not. Fewer than 40% of middle-class college-educated individuals and a smaller fraction of the working class have proceeded beyond the conventional level by age 24. In other words, progression through the hierarchy of moral stages does not proceed automatically.

Forty-four male subjects, aged 13 to 18, were led to believe that each was a member of a group of four students to be rewarded for their work. After working for an hour, each subject was asked to distribute $5.60 among the group members. Analysis revealed that the subjects' orientation in terms of Kohlberg's hierarchy of moral status significantly affected their manner of distribution, whereas the age of the subjects did not (Gunzberger, Wegner, & Anooshian, 1977).

Status of values. It is difficult to assess youth's values, partly because they are complex abstractions that can hardly be translated into quantifiable terms. In any case, youth's values vary according to the times and culture of which they are a part. In the 1950s Jacob (1958) concluded that U.S. college students were gloriously contented about themselves and their future outlook. They were unashamedly self-centered and were concerned chiefly about material gratification for themselves and their families. In the late 1960s many young people developed a concern for others and for their world. Disenchanted about the society they had inherited, they set about redesigning morals for a more enlightened era. While the vast majority of students probably maintained something of the privatistic views of the 50s, a minority of icon smashers placed their stamp indelibly on the time.

In the 1970s three main categories of values emerged, reported Yankelovich and Clark (1974). The first category established new guidelines in matters of public and personal morality, including "more liberal sexual mores; a lessening of automatic obedience to, and respect for, established authority; less reliance on the church and organized religion as a source of guidance for moral behaviors; and less automatic allegiance to my country right or wrong" (p. 64). The second category involved changing attitudes toward family, marriage, and work. And the third involved "a search for self fulfillment, and conviction that there must be more to life than making a living, struggling to make ends meet, and being concerned with the needs of others" (p. 64).

A study among Canadian youth would confirm this view. It reveals a shift away from the predominant value system of the industrial world toward one that is more humanistic and expressive. Contributing to this change in values is increased economic productivity, which permits diversion from purely survival tactics to less materialistic values (Quarter, 1974).

Perspective on youth's morals and values. A nationwide survey of young people disclosed that many youths in 1976 were quite idealistic. They were "continuing a stream of idealism that runs very broadly throughout this nation's history" ("For American Youth," 1976, p. 60). Churches, schools, and homes were again the chief sources of youth's morality and education.

In short, most young people are still rather traditional. It cannot be assumed that a changing morality is necessarily a declining morality. Girls have a healthier feeling about their own sexuality than formerly, when women were taught not to acknowledge sex as pleasurable. Both sexes are more likely to perceive sex as a mode of intimate communication between individuals who respect each other (Dreyer, 1975). The common practice of **cohabitation** and testing sexual aspects of their relationships may reflect a growing respect for the seriousness of marriage. That is, young people do not want to undertake so important a relationship until they feel reasonably certain that they are ready for it. In any case, the vast majority of youth tend ultimately to seek their happiness within the nuclear family. And a large majority (75%) believes that monogamous marriage accords the most satisfying type of heterosexual relationship.

Space limitations prevent dealing adequately with certain other aspects of youthful sex.

Influences on Youth's Morality

The parental factor. Baumrind (1975) found that the parents of more-traditional adolescents firmly and without ambivalence cling to traditional values; they behave firmly yet warmly toward their children. In another study, 7 of 272 university students judged by four psychiatrists to be mentally "superhealthy" were studied with regard to their earlier life history. All seven were from intact homes and described their parents as healthy and well balanced. Five were first-borns, and none had experienced severe trauma during childhood. Yet in many respects these young people would not be regarded as exceptional. It was concluded that being brought up by well-balanced parents in an open, warmly secure environment is the most important contributor to "superhealth" (Holmstrom, 1974).

Other influences. Also affecting youth's morals is the division among adults themselves regarding society's goals and ideals. This conflict produces competing values in families, schools, and all other institutions concerned about youth. Urie Bronfenbrenner of Cornell University has declared that "it is this progressive breakdown in mutual support between structures that has led to the disintegration within them" ("A New Generation," 1976, p. 45).

Finally, a factor that may account for the growing discontentment of non-college youth is that social values have emerged so rapidly that they have outpaced the institutional capacities for accommodating them (Yankelovich & Clark, 1974).

Suggestions for Improving Youth's Morality

Kohlberg recommended that schools design programs for moral instruction. He contended that teachers should be taught how to conduct moral discussions, which would become a fundamental part of the curriculum.

Baumrind (1975) recommended that youth be treated as mature and held responsible as such. In her view, reciprocity is the foundation of moral principle. The relationship of youth and adults should be one of social contract. Because making contracts presumes the liberty of the contracting parties, adolescents who do not perceive themselves as morally free will also not feel it imperative to abide by contracts, either with their parents or with society. Moreover, unless adolescents respect adult authorities as appropriate moral agents, they will not feel ethically obligated to abide by their regulations.

YOUTH AND RELIGION

Historical Perspective

Children in 17th-century England were perceived as strong, vigorous, sinful, and susceptible to peer pressure. Because of the ever-present possibility of death, early conversion was common, and youth were urged to go through rigorous self-examination and self-discipline to achieve salvation. The religious approach may have produced anxieties, but it nevertheless helped youth to deal with their sexuality and to face the very real dangers of death (Smith, 1975). For some youth, religion is still a matter of fundamental faith, while for others it is "a quasi-intellectual" matter. Perhaps about a third of college students attend church ("A New Generation," 1976, p. 45).

Most students resemble their parents in religious views, although there are some atheists and cultists. At the University of California at Davis, students and parents were generally similar in religious commitment. And religious students perceived their families as warmer, more accepting, and happier than did non-religious students. The reason for this relationship was not determined.

Youthful Religious Cultists

The minority of youth who have joined various religious cults has been much publicized. The research psychiatrist James Gordon related young peoples' enthusiasm for cults—such as the Krishna Consciousness Movement, the Divine Light Mission, and the Unification Church—to the anxieties and uncertainties produced by such events as the Bay of Pigs debacle, the Vietnam War, and subsequent instabilities in government and the economy. In order to sort out their own feelings and events in the world around them, they seek definite answers. In addition, they seek a sense of sisterhood and brotherhood in times when parental authority is often questioned and sometimes discredited. They often find in communal situations a sense of family that they otherwise lack. Searching, lonely, anxious youths, especially, find sanctuary in religious communities, where they are fed and housed without question and where they learn to support rather than to compete with one another.

Some young people have become disillusioned with the leaders of the establishment and uncertain of the values in their society. The vacuum thus

Searching, lonely youths can find sanctuary in religious communities, away from the anxieties of contemporary life.

created has produced feelings of anomie and anarchy. Such adolescents gain a sense of certainty from religious leaders who speak with conviction, presumably from divinely guided directives.

One of the chief lures of the cults is the sense of community they afford. Every talent and task is devoted to the common welfare, and everyone's efforts, no matter how small, are appreciated within their private circle. Members also participate in "divinely ordered" tasks, which give them a feeling of personal commitment and significance.

Participants in certain **nontheistic** movements, such as **Transcendental Meditation** and Erhard Seminars Training (EST), display some of the same messianic dedication, perceiving themselves as "activist vanguards in the evolution of human kindness, and divinely appointed healers of all the divisions which plague the earth" (Gordon, 1977, p. 26).

Adults opposed to such cults perceive their members as victims of seduction and brainwashing. Nevertheless, most of these young people are over 18 and hence legally adult. If parents are granted responsibility over them at this age in such matters, their control may easily come to extend to all behaviors, promoting general dependency. Many psychiatrists speak of youth involved in such cults in terms of ego defects and even schizophrenia.

It is true, concluded Gordon, that young people join cults at times of heightened anxiety, their problems often stemming from society itself. Hence, their search for meaningful experiences and an effective way of life should be guided instead of classified as unnatural and deserving of restriction.

ASPECTS OF ADOLESCENT DEVELOPMENT

177

Young people are affected in different ways by cult involvement, depending on their own personalities and the quality of the experiences involved. Some of them "to all appearances have become more loving, productive and happy. In other cases, the belief system and structures of these groups seem to have exacerbated the rigidity and effectiveness of these young people, to make them ever more fearful and contemptuous of those with whom they disagree" (Gordon, 1977, p. 27).

In any case, wrote Gordon, defections from traditional religions can be viewed as criticism of family and societal belief systems. Moreover, if those who join groups find such communal experience satisfying, it behooves us to reexamine the effectiveness of their family lives. With regard to youths who join cults that offer simple and flexible solutions, we should inquire why they acquired habits of thinking that make such systems attractive.

Other factors should also be kept in mind, one being that currently traditional religious organizations were once cults themselves. Moreover, these same organizations at times display dubious goals and destructive behaviors. Finally, many people who urge legal conservatorship or mental hospitalization of young cultists have no first-hand evidence of what specific cults are like.

SUMMARY

Adolescence, the period from puberty until maturity, can be distinguished from youth, a more inclusive, socioculturally defined stage from the late teens until adult roles are assumed. The main task of adolescence is presumed to be the definition of identity, and of youth to make ready for a mature adulthood.

Images of youth are conflicting. Indeed, no single image would reflect the many variations according to social class, philosophical bent, or the times. Popular images relate mostly to middle-class youth, with little regard for the subdivision in this category.

Adolescents' personalities, which represent what they are really like, derive from genetic factors interacting with all life experiences to date. They determine how and how well adolescents play their various roles. Some adolescents manage to transact and integrate these roles very well; others remain uncertain of their roles, victims of role diffusion. Little attention has been paid to how well adolescents project their self-concepts into the future.

While personality development is often subtle, physical changes associated with puberty (the period during which reproductive organs attain maturity) are quite obvious. Such changes are in primary characteristics related to propagation (primarily the genitalia), or in secondary traits such as voice, hairline, or other features that distinguish the sexes. Such changes naturally influence adolescents' images of themselves and their choices of clothing.

Over the years boys maintain their physical fitness somewhat better than girls; and both sexes achieve higher fitness scores in schools that stress vigorous exercise. The chief causes of mortality at this age are automobile accidents, suicide, and malignant tumors. Many adolescents experience problems of overweight and drug use, especially involving cigarettes, alcohol, and marijuana. Authorities agree that youth's excessive use of any drug is bad, creating problems for the future, but they disagree over the potential harm of marijuana.

Authorities also disagree about stress. Some perceive the period as stormy for adolescents in general, some for only the minority. Some portray stress as natural, even desirable, in compelling an examination of one's status and goals in life. In any case, adult psychological health relates somewhat to an individual's emotional status at preadolescence, but only minimally at adolescence.

Controversy also surrounds the matter of adolescents' morals and values. Although Kohlberg has portrayed most adolescents as arriving at a postconventional level of morality, it is questionable how many do. Youth's standards may have greater worth than is often assumed, because changing morals are often confused with declining morals. In any case, youth are strongly influenced by their parents' morality, but they become confused when adults cannot agree among themselves. Many authorities believe that youth's moral development should not be taken for granted and that moral education should be consciously planned.

Youth tend to resemble their parents not only in moral standards but in basic religious views. Most adults view religious cultists as victims of seduction and brainwashing. However, the effect of cult involvement on individual youth may prove constructive.

SUGGESTED READINGS

Broughton, J. M. The divided self in adolescence. *Human Development*, 1981, 24, 13–32. Interviews with adolescents indicate that they possess a certain dualism of the true inner self and an outer false appearance. This dualism is not to be confused with seriously alienated states as in schizophrenia.

Cox, H. Eastern cults and Western culture: Why young Americans are buying Oriental religions. *Psychology Today*, 1977, 11(2), 36–42. On the basis of lengthy, though somewhat informal, research the writer considers why so many young Americans are participating in the neo-Oriental revival. He assesses to what degree it is satisfying their needs and examines its relationship to the U.S. culture.

Eldred, C. A., Rosenthal, D., Wender, P. H., Kety, S. S., Schulsinger, F., Welner, J., & Jacobsen, B. Some aspects of adoption in selected samples of adult adoptees. *American Journal of Orthopsychiatry*, 1976, 46(2), 279–290. Common assumptions about adoptees are examined on the basis of data relating to three groups of adoptees: biological parent schizophrenic or manic depressive; adoptive parent schizophrenic or manic depressive; and biological parent with no psychiatric history.

Etaugh, C., & Ropp, J. Children's self-evaluation of performance as a function of sex, age, feedback, and sex–typed task label. *Journal of Psychology*, 1976, 94(1), 115–122. After 80 third-graders and 80 fifth-graders performed tasks labeled either sex appropriate or sex inappropriate, they were advised of their success or failure. The children evaluated the importance of effort, ability, task difficulty, and luck in accounting for their performance. Girls blamed their failures on lack of ability more than did the boys, who simply called it bad luck. Successful boys emphasized ability more than luck. Successful girls simply believed that they were lucky.

Finn, P., & Brown, J. Risks entailed in teenage intoxication as perceived by junior and senior high school students. *Journal of Youth and Adolescence*, 1981, 10(1), 51–76. A survey of 1269 junior and senior high school students indicated that a large majority recognized the dangers of intoxication. Implications for concerned educators, counselors, and parents are explored.

Fischer, J. L. Translations in relationship style from adolescence to young adulthood. *Journal of Youth and Adolescence*, 1981 10(1), 11–24. A study of transitions in friendship styles from middle to late adolescence disclosed four major relationship styles, as well as differences according to age and sex.

Frankland, E. G., Corbett, M., & Rudoni, D. Value priorities of college students: A longitudinal study. *Youth and Society*, 1980, 11(3), 267–293. An investigation of value priorities of students at a midwestern university from 1975 to 1978 disclosed a distinctive clustering of postmaterialism/materialism responses. Most students had mixed values and were not materialists but postmaterialists; the postmaterialists were not of a higher socioeconomic background than the materialists.

Hakstian, A. R., & Cattell, R. B. An examination of adolescent sex differences in some ability and personality traits. *Canadian Journal of Behavioral Science*, 1975, 7(4), 295–312. Almost 300 11th- and 12th-graders were administered a battery of ability and personality measures. The aim was to determine sex differences on these factors and to determine whether such differences exist on recently identified primary traits.

Jalali, B., Jalali, M., Crocetti, G., & Turner, F. Adolescents and drug use: Toward a more comprehensive approach. *American Journal of Orthopsychiatry*, 1981, 51(1), 120–130. Data from a survey of 2131 high school students regarding drug and alcohol use indicated a need for preventive measures and social psychiatric approaches, with psychiatric care advised for compulsive users.

Johnson, M. M., Stockard, J., Acker, J., & Naffziger, C. Expressiveness reevaluated. *School Review*, 1975, 83(4), 617–644. A study of college students indicates that those women who especially valued the need to achieve also highly valued the nurturing characteristics traditionally associated with women. It is conjectured that, as women gain higher status, men may no longer need to reject traits associated with women, such as sympathy and affection.

Josselson, R., Greenberger, E., & McConochie, D. Phenomenological aspects of psychosocial maturity in adolescence (Part 2: Girls). *Journal of Youth and Adolescence*, 1977, 6(2), 145–167. A comparison of girls who scored at the high or low extremes of the Psychosocial Maturity Inventory indicates that ability to tolerate anxiety and effective social behaviors were basic to their identity formation.

Justice, B., & Duncan, D. V. Running away: An epidemic problem of adolescence. *Adolescence*, 1976, 11(43), 365–371. The problem of runaways is discussed with regard to its prevalence, contributing factors, kinds of families and adolescents involved, and ways of coping with such situations.

Kline, S. A., & Harvey, G. The incongruous achiever in adolescence. *Journal of Youth and Adolescence*, 1974, 3(2), 153–160. In schools that employ highly divergent and idiosyncratic teachers, students have a better chance to find special relationships that will motivate them in pursuing their educational goals, especially when supports outside the school are weak.

Kness, D., & Densmore, B. Dress and social-political beliefs of young male students. *Adolescence*, 1976, 11(43), 431–442. A comparison of conservatively and sloppily dressed college males indicates that the conservative dressers attached status symbolism to clothing, had greater concern for clothes and were more conservative in their social and political beliefs. Indeed, it proved possible from this sample to be accurate 76% of the time in predicting students' beliefs simply by looking at their dress.

Lerner, R. M. Adolescent development: Scientific study in the 1980s. *Youth and Society,* 1981, *12*(3), 251–275. Appraisal is made of the current status of the scientific study of adolescent development and projections suggested about future theory and research.

Lerner, R. M., Orlos, J. B., & Knapp, J. R. Physical attractiveness, physical effectiveness, and self-concept in late adolescents. *Adolescence,* 1976, *11*(43), 313–326. When 124 male and 219 female undergraduates rated 24 body characteristics in terms of physical attractiveness and how physically effective these parts were, they also responded to a self-concept scale. It appears that attractiveness contributed more to the self-concepts of the females than did the effectiveness attitudes; the opposite was true of the males.

Levine, A., & Crumrine, J. Women and the fear of success: A problem in replication. *American Journal of Sociology,* 1975, *80*(4), 964–974. Some years ago Matina Horner concluded that women have a motivation to avoid success, especially when they compete with men. However, other researchers have failed exactly to replicate Horner's findings. In a duplication of the Horner study at the State University of New York at Buffalo, a content analysis of student's stories indicated that most of them contained fear-of-success imagery. But there were no significant differences in the numbers of women and men respondents who included such imagery in their stories.

Rachman, A. W. *Identity group psychotherapy with adolescents.* Springfield, Ill.: C. C. Thomas, 1975. This book constitutes a theoretical framework for practicing group psychotherapy with adolescents, based on Erik Erikson's concepts of ego identity.

Rierdan, J., & Koff, E. The psychological impact of menarche: Integrative versus disruptive changes. *Journal of Youth and Adolescence,* 1980, *9*(1), 49–58. Male and female human figure drawings, made by 49 premenarcheal and 45 postmenarcheal girls and scored for sexual differentiation, sexual identification, and anxiety, disclosed the impact of menarche to be primarily integrative rather than disruptive.

Rybash, J. M., Roodin, P. A., & Lonky, E. Young adults' scores on the defining issues test as a function of a "self" versus "other" presentation mode. *Journal of Youth and Adolescence,* 1981, *10*(1), 25–32. A study that involved 100 college students helped define the role of affective factors in the evaluation of moral problems involving the self versus hypothetical others.

Savin-Williams, R. C. Dominance hierarchies in groups of middle to late adolescent males. *Journal of Youth and Adolescence,* 1980, *9*(1), 75–85. Studies of early, middle, and late adolescents in camping situations indicated that the older adolescents maintained a stable status originally supported by such characteristics as intelligence, crafts skill, and popularity rather than athletic skill.

Stanton, M. Moral judgments among students: A cross-cultural study. *Adolescence,* 1980, *15*(57), 231–241. A cross-cultural comparison of moral judgments of students in England, Grenada, Mauritius, and Nigeria indicated considerable agreement but sufficient variation to refute the claim for the universality of moral judgments.

Wallerstein, J. S., & Kelly, J. B. The effects of parental divorce: Experiences of the child in later latency. *American Journal of Orthopsychiatry,* 1976, *46*(2), 256–269. On the basis of data from an ongoing clinical study, an assessment is made of the impact of parental divorce on 31 children in later latency, as observed shortly afterward and again one year later.

White, K. M. Problems and characteristics of college students. *Adolescence*, 1980, *15*(57), 23–41. The impact of the college experience is examined in terms of its developmental impact on the student's cognition, ego identity, ethics, sex role, political behaviors, and generational unit.

7
BASIC ROLES OF ADOLESCENCE

Adolescents play various significant roles. This chapter will examine their sex role and their position in the family, school, and society.

SEX ROLE

Biological Sex Role

The sexual revolution. In terms of their biological sex role, as defined earlier, adolescents have changed sharply. In the years 1900 to 1920, there was no change in the level of premarital coital experience. Since the 1930s, however, there has been increasing experience with premarital intercourse at ages 15 to 19, the largest changes occurring between 1955 and 1975 (Udry, Bauman, & Morris, 1975).

Has there been a true sexual revolution? The truth is, that the changes have been more revolutionary for women than for men. The number of young men who have had sexual intercourse prior to marriage has increased little in the past 25 years. Among women aged 15 to 25, however, such numbers have increased dramatically. In 1975, there was practically no difference in the proportion of men and women who practiced such behaviors (Dreyer, 1975). In fact, Kantner and Zelnick (1973) reported that 14% of unmarried 15-year-old girls and 46% of those age 19 had had sexual intercourse.

On the basis of a nationwide random sampling Morton Hunt (1973) reported that about 80% of single White men under age 25 and 75% of single White women under age 25 had had sexual intercourse. These figures indicated a slight increase since the early 1950s for men but were far increased for women, only a third of whom reported premarital sexual intercourse in 1953. The incidence of premarital sexual intercourse among noncollege men under age 17 was 66% in the early 1950s and 75% two decades later. However, the percentage of young men 18 to 24 having relations with prostitutes dropped from 33% in 1953 to 3% in 1972 (Hunt, M., 1973).

The incidence of extramarital sexual relationships for married men under age 25 increased a little in the previous two decades, with 32% reporting these behaviors. Meantime, there was a dramatic increase among young wives in extramarital intercourse—from 10% in Kinsey's sample in the early 1950s to 24% two decades later.

The incidence of homosexuality among youth changed little over the two decades. Among young women aged 18 to 24, 10% reported having had homosexual relationships, compared with 20% of the young men. It is hard to express the significance of such findings, because many of the respondents had had only a short homosexual episode in early adolescence.

Males versus females. It is difficult to sort out sexual reactions in terms of what may be natural for people and what has been taught. Don Stauffer and Richard Frost had 100 college students rate features from either *Playboy* (for the men) or *Playgirl* (for the women). More than twice as many males as females (88% compared with 40%) highly approved the centerfold, which focused on frontal nudity of the opposite sex. A large majority (75%) of the men found the female nudity sexually stimulating, whereas an equal number of the women were not aroused by male nudity. Almost all the men were acquainted with *Playboy*, but half the women had never read *Playgirl*. Almost all (84%) of the males said they would buy an issue of *Playboy*, whereas 80% of the women said they would not buy *Playgirl*.

Because 80% of the males believed that people would approve of their reading *Playboy*, compared with 34% of females who would feel approval for reading *Playgirl*, the young women still felt strongly traditional pressures regarding sex. While it has been customary to ascribe such findings to actual differences between the sexes, one cannot discount the sharply different environments in which the sexes are reared (Gaylin, 1976a).

High school versus college youth. Far greater change is apparent on the college level than in high school. While high school students' attitudes toward sexuality changed little in the 1960s, college students' attitudes liberalized considerably (Offer, 1972). The majority of both sexes finds premarital sexual intercourse acceptable if the partners care about each other, a norm called permissiveness with affection. This attitude does not represent a lowering of morality or a disregard for the meaning of sex. Rather, it indicates that adolescents perceive sex as a way of communicating love.

Gender Roles

The female role. The psychological behavior patterns and characteristics judged appropriate for each sex become especially important in adolescence. Girls today have broader horizons than did their grandmothers. The modern girl is not looking forward to becoming either "a robot-like helpmate or an incarnation of the cave woman. . . . Girls are not becoming imitation males; nor do they cling to some outmoded version of femininity" (Rogers, 1978, p. 110). All except an insignificant fraction expect one day to marry and have children, and the great majority intends to combine marriage with working outside the home. They anticipate gaining their chief life satisfaction from their mother role, but they likewise expect to gain personal satisfaction as well as monetary gain from outside employment. Meantime, they expect the family role to be different from that of their mothers before them. They anticipate a more equalitarian relationship and, if employed, expect their husbands to help with the children and household chores.

The male role. Some males feel constantly challenged to prove their masculinity and remain anxious lest they fail to present the image of the all-competent male. They may experience a continuing need to manifest a

> degree of initiative, accomplishment, emotional suppression, and courage that exceeds either their personal inclination or capabilities or both. Some males become so preoccupied with proving themselves as men that they fail to realize their potential as people, and their typically male prerogatives of power, deference to females, and sex initiative may be purchased at considerable expense to their personality development [Rogers, 1978, p. 111].

Recent trends. The abolition of artificial distinctions between the sexes, so that both might express the full range of their potential, is called androgyny. Thus both sexes learn that expressiveness, tenderness, and gentility are human, not merely feminine. Likewise, such traits as decisiveness, directness, and executive ability are also not simply masculine. According to a similar concept, "biculturalism," sex-role subcultures are not interpreted as mutually exclusive.

In recent years the sex roles have become more similar, and history affords perspective on this trend. In early times,

> mere subsistence required a sexual division of labor; for example, in hunting societies tasks assigned each sex differed more than in other societies. This differentiation may have derived partly from the male's greater physical strength and partly from his greater mobility. Males were the hunters and warriors because their mobility was not interrupted by pregnancy and breast feeding, and because they possessed more physical stamina for combat and the hunt.
> However, biological differences between the sexes have lost much of their significance. Each sex can perform the vast majority of present-day jobs about as well as the other, and new inventions will make biological sex distinctions less important still. Increasingly, machines will simply compensate for what either sex may be poorly equipped by nature to do [Rogers, 1978, pp. 112–113].

In the late 1970s, despite the above overall trend, there were glimmerings of a certain return to traditionalism. The feminist movement had lost much of its momentum. Symbolically, dresses were making a comeback. While there seemed to be little chance of a regression to the highly polarized status of earlier times, the trend toward unisex was wavering. Moreover, a nationwide study (Bayer, 1975) indicated that a certain number of college freshmen were still sexist (16.1% of males and 6.6% of females). They agreed with such statements as "the activities of married women are best confined to the home and family" (p. 392). Such students also attached higher importance to marriage and family, were more conservative politically, had a higher regard for authority, and opposed legalizing marijuana. The typical sexist student was "more likely to be a male, although a substantial proportion of women also endorse traditional women's roles" (p. 397). They were also older than their peers, from lower socioeconomic backgrounds, from nonurban areas, and less successful academically. More often than nonsexist students, they had low educational aspirations and majored in business education or the health professions.

Dating

Historical perspective. At any rate, sex roles remain sufficiently polarized in adolescence to support the dating practice. Vreeland (1972) examined dating over the previous several decades. In the 1930s adolescents took their dates to public places "like the malt shop, football and basketball bleachers, and the fraternity dance, or the rumble seats of second-hand cars" (p. 65). Girls preferred dates with fraternity boys who had plenty of money and a car and talked a good line. Boys chose girls who were physically alluring, popular with other males, and generally charming. There was a barter, or bargaining, relationship as the girls "exacted expensive goods and services in exchange for granting even limited access to their bodies; boys paid willingly, to establish minimum locker room credibility" (p. 65).

In postwar years the situation changed, for the young men returning from the war were no longer awkward adolescents. Dating assumed a going-steady pattern and constituted a means of mate selection. It constituted a period when

Nowadays dating is often as much a matter of companionship and fun as of sexual satisfaction.

couples came to know each other, prior to the more serious commitment of courtship. In the '50s came still another pattern of dating, a sort of "emotional therapy; and the playgrounds of earlier periods did double duty as therapists' couches. Going steady was passé—social affairs became interpersonal relationships that ran a scale from casual to meaningful" (pp. 65–66).

The next decade, the '60s, brought dramatic changes to heterosexual relationships. As college administrators relaxed rules governing the presence of women in men's dormitories, and vice versa, "Dating finally moved out of the parking lot and into rooms with closed doors. . . . Girls, asserting their rights as human beings, began to take the pill" (p. 66). Overall, dating became more informal and certainly less exploitive. Young people in their concern for their own and others' humanity, began to act toward their dates as human beings and friends, rather than as subjects of conquest or even as marital partners, at least for the immediate future.

Certainly, Waller's concept of the rating-dating complex, that high school and college youth take prestige dimensions strongly into account in the choice of dates no longer holds, if it ever did (Gordon, 1981). Although such values may have prevailed in the 1920s they have not at other times, especially today when more humanistic values prevail. Heterosexual relationships are more searching, profound, and sincere, although good looks, popularity, and good grooming still count. Nevertheless, men still expect more sexual intimacy on dates and after a fewer number of dates than do women. Few daters feel that their partners share their own feelings about sexual behaviors (Knox & Wilson, 1981). In other respects, dating relationships are not especially distinctive. In a longitudinal study of 231 dating couples disagreements were the same as those found in other types of relationships. Background factors did not relate to the dating couples' differing perceptions; and each partner appeared to see these discrepancies somewhat differently (Hill, Peplau & Rubin, 1981).

In Table 7-1, high school students rate the characteristics most important in a date.

Cohabitation. A growing practice, especially on college campuses, has been for members of the opposite sex to live together over a period of time. Some of those involved view the situation as strictly temporary; others intend to marry when the situation permits. The vast majority reports the benefits as surpassing the disadvantages in such relationships. In a study by Macklin (1972), 80% found the experience maturing and pleasant. No one judged the experience as extremely unpleasant, not at all maturing, or quite detrimental to the persons involved. While most students overwhelmingly endorse the practice, it is too early to determine its long-term significance.

Anticipation of Marriage

New goals. Youth today have reasonably clear ideas about what they expect of marriage. They place more emphasis on the chances for individual growth and satisfaction than on social stability and continuity. While youth place a high

Table 7-1. High School Students' Dating Choices

Characteristics Important to Respondents' Peers	*Characteristics Important in a Date*	*Characteristics Important in a Mate*
1. Is pleasant and cheerful.	1. Is pleasant and cheerful.	1. Is pleasant and cheerful.
2. Is neat in appearance.	2. Is dependable.	2. Is dependable.
3. Has a sense of humor.	3. Is considerate.	3. Is considerate.
4. Is dependable.	4. Has a sense of humor.	4. Is honest, straightforward.
5. Is popular with the opposite sex.	5. Is neat in appearance.	5. Is affectionate.
6. Is natural.	6. Is honest, straightforward.	6. Is natural.
7. Is affectionate.	7. Is natural.	7. Is neat in appearance.
8. Is considerate.	8. Is affectionate.	8. Has a sense of humor.
9. Has a car or access to one.	9. Has good sense, is intelligent.	9. Has good sense, is intelligent.
10. Knows how to dance.	10. Thinks of things to do.	10. Is a good listener.
11. Is willing to neck on occasion.	11. Is appropriately dressed.	11. Is a good sport.
12. Thinks of things to do.	12. Is a good sport.	12. Thinks of things to do.
		13. Is appropriately dressed.

From "Dating Choices of High School Students," by S. L. Hansen, In *Family Coordinator,* 1977, *26,* 135. Copyright 1977 by the National Council on Family Relations. Reprinted by permission.

value on love and family, they do not widely agree on the value of marriage or the effectiveness of the traditional family. In fact, in the early 1970s 34% of the college youth questioned agreed that marriage is obsolete, compared with 66% disagreeing (Yankelovich, 1974). A growing minority of youth does not have traditional views regarding marriage and is interested in exploring alternative life-styles (Dreyer, 1975).

Traditionally, marriage was perceived as a way to achieve certain goals, including parenthood, adult status, and independence from parents. It was also a way for society to attain certain goals, including its survival, the socialization of children, the stabilization of the population, the control of sex impulses, and the preservation of social customs. The effort to find new meaning in marriage is a reflection that it is no longer the social requirement that it once was. Nowadays two people can live together, have sexual intercourse, and have children— either their own or through adoption—and still be accepted by certain groups as fully adult without having been legally married. While certain benefits of

BASIC ROLES OF ADOLESCENCE

189

marriage, including "joint ownership of property, protection from liability, increased credit, inheritance guarantees, and dependency protection for wives and children, may not be found outside marriage, such benefits do not seem extremely important to young people today" (Dreyer, 1975, p. 221).

For youth seeking a new significance in marriage, it represents ways of achieving "personal identity, psychological intimacy, mutual pleasure-giving, the promise of continued personal growth, and a transcendent relationship between two human beings" (p. 221). In the process of this commitment, the partners' different life-styles are not restricted but are opened up to greater development and opportunities for expression. Marital partners are committed not only to each other but to themselves, so that each plays those roles most practical or convenient. Stereotyped family roles dissolve in such marriages, because both partners may be either in school or working. Hence, both must share the roles of homemaker, breadwinner, and child socializer. In these marriages children are not necessities but options that may be desired.

Critics of this new attitude toward marriage believe that it "tends to glorify hedonism and selfishness with a highly romanticized and unrealistic set of attitudes about the nature of society today" (Dreyer, 1975, p. 222). Nevertheless, observed Dreyer, the new emphasis on marriage as personal growth is not "so much a representation of unrealistic romanticism as it is a sensitivity to the rapidly expanding opportunities for human development which are present in contemporary society" (pp. 222–223). Young people who look at marriage in this way view it in a "cool and rational fashion." They perceive it as a viable alternative among various life-styles or means for seeking personal fulfillment. They are neither "star struck [nor] love sick, but are cautious and deliberate, choosing marriage only when it appears to be the only form of commitment which will be satisfactory to the mutual identity, intimacy, and continued growth of two individuals" (p. 223).

THE ADOLESCENT IN THE FAMILY

The Generation Gap

Why it happens. In earlier chapters the general functions of the family in human development were analyzed; the present discussion will be limited to certain issues involving youth and family. Much has been made of the so-called gap between youth and their parents. According to Erikson (1959), youth's search for identity often involves revolt against parental values and domination. Young people are forward looking and often view their parents' values as having little relevance for modern society. In such cases, concluded Erikson, youths' critical views of their parents may assume the form of a negative identity. Instead of trying to benefit from their elders' well-meant advice, they try to be everything they are told not to be, for to do otherwise is simply to buckle under, to conform. In such a situation, advised Erikson, parents should not retreat. Unless youth have leadership, their struggles for truth may become irrelevant and diffuse.

How big is it? The generation gap is far smaller than is commonly assumed. For one thing, parents and youth live in the same era, subject to the same influences. And while the young are learning from their elders, so are the older ones learning from the young. In rapidly changing societies all generations must learn together as changes produced by technology alter the whole social system (Lerner, Karson, Meisels, & Knapp, 1975).

The influence of parents on youth has long been recognized as important.

> I was raised in a normal family, strong in social beliefs, religion fairly normal (female).

> I was brought up in the "Old World" way, where the father had a definite say in what his family did—made all the decisions. Children were a necessary part of life (female).

> My mother "left" when I was 10 days old and I was raised by my father and sometimes my grandparents. I am very independent because of this (male).

> My grandmother lived in the house for 8 years; this placed considerable strain on my brother, and it was like having two mothers. She would go looking for my brother when he was out with his friends and embarrassed him a great deal (female).

Two studies give a greater insight into youth/adult relationships. A study of high school seniors and their parents (average age 50) in a large Western city revealed no significant generation gap. In general, the seniors perceived the older generation more accurately than the parent sample did the younger. The perceptions that each held of the other were benevolent. While conflict was frequent, it was rarely severe. The students accurately perceived their elders as attaching more importance to family responsibilities, security, and contentment. They overestimated their parents' regard for material achievement and failed to realize their concern with personal worth. They generally approved of their elders' values, demonstrating a certain continuity of generations. As one of them said, "I doubt my goals will be any different. . . . I can't see why there should be a difference. . . . When they were my age they thought the same, only customs were a little different" (Thurnher, Spence, & Lowenthal, 1974, p. 314). The seniors accepted security as an appropriate goal for middle-aged people. They also perceived themselves as different from their parents but as tolerating alternatives. Very few actually condemned the goals of the older generation.

The parents expressed some apprehension about their children, perhaps because they needed to justify the success of their own child rearing. They were especially concerned about the occupational and economic success of their children. Some of their concern related to their own stage in life. They viewed the completion of their parental responsibilities with relief. Nevertheless, they were concerned about what success they had had as parents (Lowenthal & Chiriboga, 1972).

The mothers were considerably more accepting of the youth than the fathers. Perhaps, theorized Thurnher, Spence, and Lowenthal (1974), because men are expected to be especially concerned about success and because the achievement of aspirations is less critical for women, the latter can more readily admit that there are alternative value systems.

To some extent the adults had been socialized by their own children (Thurnher et al., 1974). In some cases they had simply adopted values of the young that were congenial to them already. In other cases they perceived these values as new but palatable ideas. As one said, "They want peace. . . . They're farther along in their Utopian goals [and] they've thought about it more than we did." Another said with regard to youth's political activism, "I used to think that going to jail was a horrible thing, but for the courage of convictions, no" (p. 316).

In general, each group was quite benign concerning the other. Nevertheless, there was some conflict. Sources of dispute included "use of the family car, keeping one's room and clothes in order, time to be home from dates, and length of hair" (p. 317). Few reported conflict over politics or values. More often, disagreements related to life-styles, and the young people resented their parents' "insistence on instrumental, goal-oriented activity." As one boy put it in discussing his problems with his mother: "She's **Protestant ethic,** [emphasis added] she doesn't understand changes" (p. 317). The authors concluded that values are changing less than is commonly believed, not enough to bring about any permanent or dramatic changes in the social or political order (Thurnher et al., 1974). While youth indeed are moving somewhat away from social responsibilities, political involvement, and career orientation and are attaching more importance to personal satisfaction in family life, recreation, and avocation, the same may be said of their parents.

Another study, of college adolescents and their parents, suggests that the concept of a generation gap is overly simplistic and that the term *generation gaps* is more relevant (Lerner et al., 1975). In this study, students perceived a wide generation gap, but their parents detected only a slight one. Moreover, the gap between children and their parents may be less than that between the parents and their own parents. The parents of today's youth also grew up in a technological age and during their own formative years were exposed to many of the same influences as their sons and daughters.

In any case, traditional relationships between youth and their parents are changing. Youth are granted a higher status than before relative to the older generation. In addition, today's parents appear to envy the life of their offspring, instead of the other way around. Because of such factors there has been a partial reversal of the traditional socialization pattern, which involved the older generation's socializing the younger ones (Gunter & Moore, 1975). In a rapidly changing society youth "may well represent the parents' linkage to the changing world in their attempt to keep current and with it" (p. 203). Researchers have paid little attention to the impact of siblings on adolescents and youths. However, most young people indicate that there is a significant effect.

I was affected most by my next older brother. I looked up to him, because he always seemed to have a good head on his shoulders for making decisions. I think I tended to listen to his ideas more so than my oldest brother (female).

I was very sensitive to my older brother's comments. If he didn't like my shirt, I'd change it. I always looked up to him. He stuck up for me and I stuck up for him. (female).

I feel that my brother or sister had no or very little effect on me. My brother and I were never close. My sister did help me when I had problems. My friends had more of an effect on me, because I was around them more than my brother and sister (male).

I was influenced mainly by my older brother and two of my older sisters. The three of them went to college, and I did because of their own experiences. My other two sisters never went away (female).

Permissiveness

The call for firmer control. A second issue concerns how permissively youth should be treated. There is an increasing assault on the idea of great permissiveness in the home. Critics have called this child-rearing method "a makeshift response to social and economic changes of the postwar decades—and disastrous in its effects" ("Permissiveness," 1976, p. 54). Such excess permissiveness, in this view, may have accounted for rootlessness among some youth of the 1960s as well as the rise in youthful crime. Ann Jernberg, a therapist, declared that "a family is not a democracy. . . . Children need a time to be babied, a time to be told how to live" (p. 55).

Baumrind (1975) agreed, but distinguished between *authoritarian* and *authoritative* control. Authoritarian parents merely establish arbitrary restrictions, which frustrate their children's attempts to initiate activities on their own. By contrast, authoritative parents control their children rationally, consistently, and firmly, explaining reasons for their demands. They listen to what their children say but do not automatically submit to the children's wishes.

A warning. The trend toward cracking down can proceed too far. Only an insignificant minority of young people is irresponsible and delinquent. The great majority is more "sophisticated, mature, and concerned about society than were former generations, whose parents ruled supreme. When permissiveness is firmly tied to responsibility, the combination can pay rich rewards. It should be added that discipline and control are a very personal matter—a function of the persons involved. What works with one youth may prove a disaster with another" (Rogers, 1978, p. 126).

Effects of Working Mothers and Divorce

Two issues already discussed with regard to children are the effect of mothers' working and the effect of divorce. Certain authorities advise against excessive parental absence, observing that at least half of all mothers of school-age children work outside the home ("Permissiveness," 1976). However, in general, teenage children of working mothers fare as well as those of mothers who remain at home. An exception is that daughters of employed mothers are more likely to become sexually active and are less knowledgeable about basic methods of birth control than daughters of unemployed mothers (Hansson, O'Connor, Jones, and Blocker, 1981). Such adolescents are more independent and perhaps assume the adult role earlier.

Also generally unfounded are fears regarding adolescent children of divorce. No significant differences are found between adolescents of broken and unbroken homes. Too much is made of the divorce rate, declared Coles. The increase in broken marriages is more a reflection of the availability of divorce and alternatives for the woman than of growing tensions within the family ("For American Youth," 1976).

THE ADOLESCENT AT SCHOOL

Social and Personal Adjustment

The school youth culture. Adolescents' role in school is significant, for social as well as academic development. It is commonly overlooked that they participate in special youth cultures at school. Within the framework of their own peer values, students elect class officers, decide what clubs to reject or join, choose seats in the cafeteria or classroom, and form social groups. On the basis of 6 months' experience as a participant observer within a large high school, Cusick (1973) described what this peer culture within the school was like. While the staff treated the student body pretty much as an undifferentiated entity, youth maintained

> their own underground modes of counter aggression (truancy, passive resistance, disregard of rules); and they compensate for the disappointments and indignities they sustain as students within their school peer groups, which overlap, but do not exactly duplicate, those outside it. The school itself promotes such group formations by producing within students a need for them and providing the time for them to pursue their group activities [Rogers, 1978, p. 147].

Groups sorted themselves into various **cliques,** having little to do with each other, including a drama clique, a power clique composed mostly of cheerleaders, and an athletic clique. There were strata groupings corresponding to the classes in the larger society as well as isolates who spent most of their time alone.

The specific way that such lines are drawn and the forms that cliques take depend somewhat on the school and its particular students. In general, schools place little demand on students' time and efforts except during the school day itself. And when peer-group and school obligations clash, peer-group demands win out. The vast majority simply submits to school as a necessity, putting a minimum of effort into academic requirements.

Athletics are an important feature of the high school culture, especially for boys. In the late 1950s, research by James Coleman indicated that athletic prowess was the single most important criterion for the male's social status in high school. Questionnaires submitted to a random sampling of high school students in the 1970s suggest that athletics remained very important in adolescent boys' status system. The strongest support for Coleman's earlier view was found among sons of the uneducated, those in small and suburban high schools and schools with restricted authority structure, and students at the center of the schools' activities. Because trends in the opposite direction are becoming stronger, however, Eitzen (1975) predicted that enthusiasm for sports will probably decrease.

Boys' versus girls' adjustment. Schools are commonly judged to be better adapted to girls' needs than to boys'. In Detroit high schools, however, psychologists Douvan, Kulka, and Locksley found the reverse to be true. The girls indicated a much greater gap between their personal abilities, expectations, and needs and the opportunities provided for them than did boys. Among both sexes, academic achievement proved the major indicator of overall adjustment, more than either popularity or success in athletics. Boys who obtained high grades were less aggressive, experienced less stress, and possessed higher self-esteem than did those who made lower grades. Girls had to achieve "A"s in order to feel as positively toward themselves as boys did who obtained "B"s. In general, concluded the researchers, the schools did not adequately meet student needs, especially those of girls. The girls rated future success in vocation as equally as important as successful marriage, and fewer than 10% expected only to be wives and mothers. Nevertheless, the schools treated them as though they believed 90% desired to be "career housewives" (Gregg, 1976).

Violence in school. The school fails even more to meet the needs of a certain minority who react with various forms of violence. During a 3-year period in the early 1970s, assaults on teachers rose 77.4%, assaults by students on other students 85.3%, robberies 36.7%, rapes or attempted rapes 40.1%, homicides 18%, and weapons confiscated 54.4% (DeCecco & Richards, 1975, p. 51). The common ways of dealing with such problems—avoidance, simply overlooking them, and force—have not worked. Either cracking down on the one hand or simply giving in to the students on the other simply produces more conflict. Instead, DeCecco and Richards recommended the kinds of negotiations employed in labor disputes, politics, and international diplomacy. That is, the parties concerned state their side of the issues, come to a common understanding of those to be negotiated, and bargain so that each side makes gains and concessions. The persons involved will be all those concerned, including teachers, parents, and educational administrators.

Academic Achievement

Declining achievement-test scores. The schools have also been chided for lowering their academic standards, as repeatedly demonstrated on standardized tests. As a result, a nationwide survey disclosed a reaction against permissiveness and a determination to reverse the trend toward lower test scores, poorer discipline, and school vandalism. In other words, parents and their children wanted a "leaner and more disciplined approach to learning" (Scully, 1974, p. 50).

Other ideas taking hold include minimum competency requirements, illiteracy clinics for helping dropouts to learn basic skills, special tutoring programs, and stress on morality and ethics (" 'Three R's' in Schools Now," 1976).

Vocationalism. Growing numbers are calling for a more traditional curriculum and reduced stress on vocational training. Because of the change in the economic situation, youth of the 1970s embraced a new vocationalism with an emphasis on practicality. Richard W. Lyman, president of Stanford University, pointed out that in the '60s we were "greatly over-supplied with amateur rhetoricians and street-corner moralists. Now there seems a danger of our becoming once again over-supplied with careerists and technocrats" (Scully, 1974, p. 37).

In this vocational class, students are learning the workings of various gas meters.

Suggestions for reform. The controversy over the schools' performance precipitated certain major studies, and all concluded that radical reform is required (Passow, 1975). The Coleman Panel suggested that students move into the work force earlier than formerly in order to prepare more effectively for adulthood and to gain outlets for idealism and constructivism. Others suggested that schools tighten their standards and return to fundamentals. As one school superintendent declared: "The classroom has to be a place where you can come to learn and where you can't do your own thing" (" 'Three R's' in Schools Now," 1976, p. 51). The trend in today's schools "is a new realism and an invitation to stop coddling youth, to focus on quality education, and to enforce firmer discipline and higher standards; to provide greater structure and to stress the fundamentals and the three Rs" (Rogers, 1978, p. 134).

In recent years students themselves have become increasingly critical of their schools, especially on the college level. In years past, they were concerned about such matters as housing, rules, or food. Nowadays, they live where they desire, and the *in loco parentis* concept is defunct (McIntyre, 1973). Meantime, they protest the poor quality of their education, declaring that their classwork is not stimulating (Goodman & Feldman, 1975). They complain about the impersonality of their large universities and the aloofness of their professors. While complaining about soft education, they also object to regimentation. In random interviews with 300 students from over 50 colleges and universities, students complained that their grades were determined by tests and written papers. Typical comments included: "Our school is called Zoo U." "In our fraternity we wager to see which courses could be passed without doing anything" (p. 372). Another source of discontent is the grading policy, which students often perceive as "arbitrary, imprecise, unreliable, and, the ultimate condemnation, meaningless and irrelevant" (McIntyre, 1973). Nevertheless, youth's protests are muted grumblings, a faint shadow of those of the late '60s. They have become less interested in academic reform than in obtaining diplomas that, they hope, will help them to obtain jobs.

The Gallup survey. A national sampling of adults was asked what the most important requirements are for graduation from high school for students not planning to attend college. The results are listed in descending order in Figure 7-1.

YOUTH IN SOCIETY

Society's Impact

Advantages and disadvantages. Youth are often portrayed as an adjunct to society, but they are a part of it and absorb whatever is constructive or destructive within it. On the negative side, youths must adapt to a large-scale, complex, impersonal society, and they must somehow define themselves despite

What requirements, if any, would you set for graduation from high school for those students *who do not plan to go on to college* but who plan to take a job or job training following graduation? I'll read off a number of requirements, and then you tell me how important each one is as a requirement for graduation for these students. We would like to know whether you think it is very important, fairly important, or not important.

	Very Important	Fairly Important	Not Important	Don't Know/ No Answer
How important is it that these students . . .	%	%	%	%
. . . be able to write a letter of application using correct grammar and correct spelling?	90	9	*	1
. . . be able to read well enough to follow an instruction manual for home appliances?	86	12	1	1
. . . know enough arithmetic to be able to figure out such a problem as the total square feet in a room?	84	14	1	1
. . . know the health hazards of smoking, use of alcohol, marijuana, and other drugs?	83	14	2	1
. . . have a salable skill, such as typing, auto mechanics, nurse's aide, business machines?	79	17	3	1
. . . know something about the U.S. government, the political parties, voting procedures?	66	30	3	1
. . . know something about the history of the U.S., such as the Constitution, Bill of Rights, and the like?	61	31	7	1
. . . know something about the major nations of the world today, their kind of government, and their way of life?	42	46	10	2
. . . know something about the history of mankind, the great leaders in art, literature?	30	48	21	1
. . . know a foreign language?	16	32	50	2

*Less than 1%

Figure 7-1. From "The 10th Annual Gallup Poll of the Public's Attitudes Toward the Public Schools," by G. H. Gallup, In Phi Delta Kappan, 1978, 60(1), 40. © 1978, Phi Delta Kappan, Inc. Reprinted by permission.

the depersonalizing effects of growing populations and mechanized, computerized economies. They must sort out their values while being continually bombarded by an endless stream of diverse, often conflicting, ideas.

On the positive side, youths have more opportunities than ever before. They have more disposable income for enriching their experience, as in travel. Most colleges and many communities provide programs of cultural activities. Few youths suffer any more from grinding poverty. The very complexity of society results in vastly multiplied opportunities for diverse experience. Current youth are among the first in history who can look ahead to a long life of rich leisure pursuits, because technology has reduced the manpower required to support people's needs.

For another thing, observed Robert Coles, society is taking a better attitude toward youth; it does not rush them prematurely into adult society ("For American Youth," 1976). Adults have also adapted well to certain changes in youth culture, including its music, dress style, sexual experimentation, and use of the milder drugs. That is, the U.S. culture as a whole is showing a certain resiliency and a capacity to accommodate to new trends. One result is that radical youths have almost disappeared; and the activists of the 1960s now have their own homes and the mature responsibilities of adults.

Changing role in society. The role of youth is constantly shifting, and social history sensitizes us to changing patterns in the youth culture. Over time, economic cycles produce variations in the birth rate and, as a result, different socialization experiences for youth. In the Great Depression the drop in the birth rate resulted in a smaller cohort of youth later on. Thus, there were fewer job seekers and better job opportunities. As these youths entered the labor market of the '50s and the early 1960s they had an easy time finding jobs. Meantime, those youths still in college took material success for granted and had time for meditating negatively about the very technology that freed them for meditating. After all, prolonged dependency is a luxury of affluent societies. By contrast, in the depressed '30s the young adult often assumed adult responsibilities (Elder, 1975).

Cities and suburbs. Society's impact on youth varies widely according to the subculture concerned. Most youths live in the cities and suburbs, each with its advantages and weaknesses. In cities youths have many cultural opportunities and a chance to become acquainted with people of diverse backgrounds. But the speed, large numbers of people, and complexity of life may impinge too insistently on them, so that they can hardly feel in touch with themselves. In the suburbs youth have the advantages of good schools, nice neighborhoods, and a friendly personal atmosphere, yet many suburbs are relatively homogenized, not reflecting the diversity of more pluralistic settings.

Rural settings. While the vast majority of youth today lives in cities and suburbs, village and rural youth, such as those in Appalachia, constitute a sizable minority. These youth are often portrayed as disadvantaged because of discontinuities between their own values and those of the larger society. They are also described as "backward" or as "yesterday's people." Nevertheless, rural youth have certain advantages, one being that the family provides them with security against hardship in society. They may have little economic or political power, but they love their land and feel proud of it. Their very lives are saturated with the history of their family and their land. Nevertheless, they have not fully adjusted to the feelings of impotence with regard to the larger society.

Rural youth face special vocational problems. Rural occupations will continue to decline as agricultural work becomes increasingly mechanized. Overall, these youth persist in their "patterns of trust, love, dependence, autonomy" (Manning, 1975). Their true situation can only be appreciated by understanding their "inner person," an almost impossible challenge to those who have grown up elsewhere.

The Youth Culture

The concept. Youth themselves create their own culture within the larger society. The concept of a **youth culture,**

> as a segment of the larger culture, suggests a small, relatively independent, society. Its most significant reactions are within itself, and it maintains somewhat tenuous connections with the larger society. This subculture has its own values (including conformity, fun, and popularity), distinctive behaviors, speech, and styles of dress. The youth culture does not mean a completely homogeneous way of life that all youth share. Rather, it signifies those activities which, collectively, are indulged in more by youth than by adults. Actually many young people are preoccupied with getting ready for adulthood and participate little in the youth culture [Rogers, 1978, p. 142].

Characteristics and content. Despite its apparent independence the youth culture reflects to some extent the larger society. But the adolescent subculture does have its distinctive features: its own hot line of communication, its own social system, and norms regarding clothes, sex relations, academic work, music, and many other matters (Coleman, J. S., 1974). It may be most truthful to say that several subcultures exist, not merely one. They reflect variations in socioeconomic, ethnic, religious, and philosophic backgrounds among their members. But the concept of a youth culture does help to point up ways that teenage activities do or do not reflect those of the larger society. In any case, almost all adolescents belong to the youth culture, but fewer than half remain in it during their later teens (Coleman, J. S., 1974).

The youth culture has both its material and nonmaterial aspects, which youth groups share in varying degree. The characteristic material props include their own favorite selections of cars, cosmetics, records, and clothes.

The nonmaterial characteristics of youth culture include rock music and customs such as dating and assembling at teen hangouts that are the focus of the adolescent's social life. . . . "Popular gathering places are drug stores, pizza parlors, sub shops, shopping centers, drive in restaurants, beaches or parks. A major feature of many such hangouts is rock music" (Rogers, 1978, p. 143). Such music provides an important source of identification and mode of communication within the youth culture.

In addition, James Coleman (1974) identified certain psychological characteristics of the youth culture of the 1970s, one being "inward-lookingness" (p. 113). Youth have their own pop singers, rock bands, and other popular entertainment. Another characteristic is the psychic attachment of youth to their contemporaries. They have their most intimate relationships with one another.

People are becoming sensitive to the need to enjoy their environment, to keep it clean and beautiful, and to exploit its benefits for improving the quality of life.

Peer relations are very important to adolescents and youths of both sexes, although a very close relationship with a friend is more common among girls. In a study of changes in relationship styles from middle to late adolescence females showed more intimate styles of relating compared to males' more uninvolved styles. Women also developed earlier competence at intimate relationships than did males. Moreover, college women reported close friendships with those of the same sex and intimate relationships uncharacteristic of males in either high school or college (Fischer, 1981).

I have had a lot of friends through my life, and I'm sure they have had an influence on me. Some of them have influenced me the wrong way, and I've learned from that. Others influenced me the right way, and I'm glad for it (male).

I've had a very close friend (female) for all four years of college, but recently the friendship is getting more distant ever since I started seeing a guy more regularly. My friend has always been a feminist in her attitudes and behaviors. I respect her feelings, and this loss of closeness makes me feel lonely at times. I hope our relationship will get closer again (female).

I have basically had the same types of friends since elementary school. Most of my friends from high school were my friends in elementary school. I have a large number of friends, although only a few are really close friends. Friends mean a lot to me. They are an important part of my life and I like a lot of them, with some variety (female).

Friends are important to me. I usually don't have a large number at one time, usually about two or three closer relationships. The friends help me share my thoughts and develop and interact with each individual's ideas. They help me grow. (male).

Alienation and Counterculture

Alienation. Although symptoms of youth's alienation from society are far less apparent now than they were in the 1960s, certain segments of youth, in all periods in history, have felt alienated from society. Alienation suggests "a sense of rootlessness, of not belonging" ("Alienation and Education," 1974, p. 20). Youth express their alienation by retreating into narcotics, by running away, by repudiating the school, or by refusing to express any interest in their work. Meantime, young people in the mainstream of society are affected by those who are more clearly alienated, so that "increasingly, an entire youth generation feels itself alienated from organized adult society and its institutions, including schools; it questions all authority, including the authority of teachers; and is unable to believe in the dependability and sincerity of those who attempt to teach them and to supervise their activities" (p. 21).

Counterculture. The related concept "counterculture" suggests the formation of a way of life distinct from, and in opposition to, the major culture. Over the past decade or so a substantial minority of youth developed their entire life-style around counterculture values: (1) Sensory experience, rather than conceptual knowledge is emphasized. (2) The mystical, unknown, and mysterious elements of nature are celebrated. (3) Cooperation, rather than competition is stressed. (4) Direct experience, involvement, and participation are emphasized, as opposed to detachment and objectivity as means of seeking truth. (5) Mastery over nature is rejected and harmony with nature emphasized (Yankelovich, 1972).

Juvenile delinquents. Most counterculture youths' activities are relatively harmless, though often incomprehensible to their elders. A more dangerous breed, the serious disrupters and habitual lawbreakers, include only a small minority, but they constitute a major hazard to society. As a school principal in Los Angeles expressed it, "Only 2 or 3 per cent are the real donkeys, the gang kids" ("Getting Young People to Learn about Real Life," 1976, p. 53).

Except for a small fraction, gang members are from racial or ethnic groups that have recently migrated or from poorly educated, low-income families. Even among Chinese youth, long reputed to be law abiding, the rate of juvenile delinquency has surged.

In several ways current gangs differ from those of the 1950s. Instead of large-scale rumbles, guerrilla activity is the rule. Small numbers, usually in cars, cross the rival territory, attacking enemy gangs with shotguns and handguns. In slum areas roving gang members wantonly destroy property, leaving the "burned out shells of apartment buildings that make the ghetto streets look like Viet Nam villages after a B52 strike" (p. 56).

Recommendations about remedies conflict sharply. Some authorities assume a soft approach, believing that the only way to stamp out gang crime is to eliminate poverty in high-crime areas, find jobs for deprived youths, and help them to achieve an honorable status within the larger society. However, such efforts have tended to fail. In addition, they are long term, and their results are difficult to assess. In the short run, officials are increasingly advocating hard-line police policies and intensive supervision. Leaders of minority groups are talking less of police brutality and calling for a crackdown. Proportionately, minorities themselves are the gang members' most frequent victims, although victims and opportunities to get money are sought wherever they can be found.

LOOKING TOWARD ADULTHOOD

Youth and Vocation

Attitudes. Youths' attitudes toward work and vocation have changed. At one time, work was considered character building, good for its own sake, and people took for granted that it would involve such sacrifice and drudgery. In a 1974 study of college seniors in Pennsylvania, the majority still held positive attitudes toward work. They perceived it as far more than a means for making money or for gaining social status. Instead, they believed that it should be personally satisfying and result in some real contribution to society. They did not view it as distinct from other aspects of their lives. It was felt to be an essential part of their life-style, but not the most important one. Neither personal nor family relationships should be sacrificed in order to become vocationally successful. Instead, vocational and interpersonal relationships were expected to fuse in some meaningful way (U.S. Department of Labor, 1974).

The relationship between work and leisure has also changed. The main value of attending college was to ensure financial security and a high-status job.

Meantime, off-the-job time was reserved for leisure, when people retreated into their private world, embracing their garden, car, and family. Now, however, this dichotomy no longer exists, at least in youth's ideals. Today's students are trying to integrate their private and career goals and attempting to synthesize self-fulfillment and a successful career. Meantime, youth no longer anticipate that their off-the-job hours will be simply time to kill or rest up. They expect leisure, like their job, to contribute to their personal development.

Variations in outlook. Of course, not all youth approach matters of future vocation in the same way. Based on Eriksonian concepts, Marcia (1966) described four types of people and their different ways of dealing with occupational choice and ideology. One category, the identity-achieved individuals, had undergone a crisis period of testing alternatives and had established fairly definite commitments. The **foreclosure-status** individuals had "leap-frogged" the crisis period, but had nevertheless arrived at commitments. Those in the moratorium status were still exploring alternatives in their search for commitments. Finally, the **diffusion-status** persons, whether or not they had had crises, were not exploring alternatives and had no commitments.

Various studies indicated that college males in the achieved or moratorium status earned higher positive scores on various measures. The foreclosure and diffusion youths performed much more poorly (Raphael, 1977). Specifically, Raphael's (1976) research with high school senior girls suggests "that the moratorium period has adaptive value." The moratorium-status girls made significantly higher scores than did the foreclosure and diffusion girls in tolerance of ambiguity, intelligence, and cognitive complexity. For both sexes, experiencing a moratorium period of testing alternatives proved adaptive.

Transition to Adulthood

The final task of youth is to prepare for and make the transition to adulthood. The discontinuity between life in the youth culture and what society expects of adults constitutes something of an obstacle to attaining maturity. Other obstructions are the mass media, with their distorted pictures of adults. While television programs may portray the problems of adulthood, they barely suggest imaginative solutions.

One problem in achieving higher developmental stages lies in an individual's own past. In every stage in life linger the "active remnants of earlier developmental levels, conflicts and stages; hence, no one can ever be said to be completely in one stage of life in all areas of behaviors and at all times" (Keniston, 1975, p. 23). That is, no conflicts are ever completely resolved or problems settled once and for all. For example, any particular individual, ordinarily perceived as a "youth, will also contain some persistent childishness, some not outgrown adolescence, and some precocious adulthood in his makeup" (p. 23). Thus, all that can be said is that earlier stages can be "relatively outgrown" (p. 24).

More often than formerly youth leave their home environs in pursuit of jobs; however, although young men who migrate to different locales in pursuit of jobs have been believed to hold superior qualifications for economic success there is little support for this view (Howell, 1981). It may be conjectured that young peoples' permanent departure from home will have varied emotional impact, but too little research exists about parent-child attachment during adolescence to reach firm conclusions (Moore & Hotch, 1981).

Youth's readiness for maturity may be defined in various ways—for example, in terms of developmental tasks, or the acquisition of those attitudes, habits, and skills required to function effectively as an adult. The youth's progress toward maturity may also be defined in normative terms, or how one's own progress corresponds with that of others of the same age. For perspective on criteria of maturity, it is well to keep in mind that no one criterion is adequate and that a composite of measures might best be used. We must remember, too, that estimates are subjective in nature, depending upon value judgments of the individuals who devise them, as well as the culture or subculture concerned [Rogers, 1977b, p. 501].* Most college seniors look toward their next life stage with anticipation.

My feeling about moving into the real world is that of excitement and adventure. I feel good about it. Moving into middle age is a little more scary, and I would rather not see it come. Old age is the same (man, age 21).

I am apprehensive about what my life will be like. I can handle middle age, but I don't want to live past 60 or 65 (woman, 20).

I'm excited about the new challenges and acquaintances after college. As far as being middle-aged and older, my feelings are dull, since I haven't given it much thought in those two areas. I will accept it when the time period comes (man, 21).

I'm looking forward to getting out in the real world where I can finally do something with my life. Middle age and old age will be okay, as long as I keep my health. I don't think I'll live very happily without it (woman, 21).

Perhaps because of the uncertainties of today's world most young people (with some exceptions) focus on the time just ahead, with little thought for their own later years.

I think about every day as it comes but tend not to think about the future too much. It makes me worry too much (woman, age 20).

I don't usually look more than a year into the future, because things can change so quickly (woman, 20).

I am not the kind of person who thinks about the future (years from

*From *Psychology of Adolescence, Third Edition*, by D. Rogers. Copyright 1977 by Prentice-Hall, Inc., Englewood Cliffs, New Jersey. Reprinted by permission.

now), but I am conscious of my immediate future. I am concerned about my health. I just want to make the most out of life while I can (man, 21).

When I look into the future it seems as if there is not much time left. Every day I feel that time is going by faster and I'm getting too old to do everything that I want to do. I am working for the future, but the future will soon be here (woman, 21).

SUMMARY

College youth carry out their biological and social sex roles quite differently from formerly. In general, they are sexually more permissive but also less exploitive of each other. Sex is perceived as a mode of natural, healthy enjoyment and as a means of communication. Social sex roles are becoming less confining, and both sexes are more fully developing their full humanhood, with diminished anxiety about trespassing on the domain of the other sex. True, both basic differences between roles and pockets of sexism persist, but changing social conditions will inevitably effect modifications.

Meantime, dating practices reflect changing sex mores and roles. The physical aspects of dating relationships persist, but there is growing emphasis on mutual respect and companionship. Some youth prefer cohabitation. Almost all eventually plan to marry, anticipating that it will permit intimacy, companionship, and personal growth.

Authorities agree that the adolescent's family role is significant but disagree about certain issues. They also agree that the generation gap is closing but differ somewhat over the definition and nature of the gap, or gaps. Many authorities believe that parental permissiveness has gone too far, but some of them fear that the reaction against it can also go too far. Youth are also often perceived as the victims of neglect because of the growing number of working mothers and divorced parents. In most cases, however, such fears prove unfounded or at least exaggerated.

The school is especially important in its influence on adolescents, notably in social and academic development. Life at school, both inside and outside the classroom, has its hazards and rewards. These differ somewhat for the sexes. The schools meet some youths' needs so poorly that they resort to various forms of violence against school property, teachers, and peers. Many critics agree that schools should get back to basics and perhaps reduce the degree of vocationalism that has crept into the curriculum. Meantime, student activists have insisted on their say in what mode reform should take; however, students' criticism cooled in the '70s, because of their preoccupation with preparing for and finding jobs.

Youth is an integral part of the larger society and shares its opportunities and adversities. Youth may find it somewhat difficult to retain a clear view and to attain a healthy identity in a technocratic, impersonal, complex society. But that same society affords them rich and varied opportunities not available to former generations. Because such conditions are continuously changing, so does youth's role in society also change.

Not all youth participate in the same subcultures of society or in the same ways. Youths in various environments—city, suburb, or rural areas—share the correspondingly different strengths and weaknesses of those environments. Meantime, young people also participate in their own culture within the larger society, with its own distinctive values and characteristics. Some youths cannot seem to integrate all their roles and become alienated from society, with their own counterculture. In a minority of cases they become serious law-breakers. Thus far the problem of youth delinquency has defied solution, or even significant reduction, despite various recommendations.

Except for severely alienated or delinquent individuals, youths take a serious view of vocational choice and preparation. They approve of work not as an end but as a means of personal fulfillment. They expect, as adults, to integrate their work and leisure roles into a life-style that promotes their personal happiness and continued growth.

A final task of youth is to effect the transition to adulthood, a process not without its obstacles and frustrations. Some adults believe most youths are not adequately prepared; others see them as having matured early. In any case, proving one's maturity is no one-time achievement but a lifelong process.

SUGGESTED READING

Braddock, J. H. II. Race, athletics, and educational attainment: Dispelling the myths. *Youth and Society*, 1981, 12(3), 335–350. Examination is made of evidence from a national longitudinal survey of high school seniors relating to the relationship between athletic participation and athletic attainment for black and white males.

Cain, L. D. The young and the old: Coalition or conflict ahead? *American Behavioral Scientist*, 1975, 19(2), 166–175. An examination of the relevance of the two-generation versus three-generation perspective on modern society. The author perceives more conflict than coalition between the old and the young.

Chess, S., Thomas, A., & Cameron, M. Sexual attitudes and behavior patterns in a middle-class adolescent population. *American Journal of Orthopsychiatry*, 1976, 46(4), 689–701. A study of 91 adolescents, followed from infancy, and their parents. The adolescents indicated a healthier, less fearful, more matter-of-fact attitude toward sex than did the older generation. They were no more prone to casual sexual encounters than the parents had been at their age.

Clayton, R. R., & Voss, H. L. Shacking up: Cohabitation in the 1970s. *Journal of Marriage and the Family*, 1977, 39(2), 273–283. A nationwide sampling of men born between 1944 and 1954 indicated that 18% had lived with a woman for a half-year or more without being married. For some of the men cohabitation was merely a prelude to marriage. For others it was either a temporary or permanent alternative to matrimony.

Cohen, J. The impact of the leading crowd on high school change: A reassessment. *Adolescence*, 1976, 11(43), 373–381. A test of James Coleman's theory about the significant influence of the leading clique was made among 1040 working-class students in a suburban school. It indicated that this group has far less influence than Coleman suggested.

Dornbusch, S. M., Carlsmith, J. M., Gross, R. T., Martin, J. A., Jennings, D., Rosenberg, A., & Duke, P. Sexual development, age and dating: A comparison of biological and social influences upon one set of behaviors. *Child Development*, 1981, *52*, 179–185. Data from a national health survey of 12- to 17-year-olds indicated that social pressure related more closely than level of sexual maturation to age of beginning dating.

Estep, R. E., Burt, M. R., & Milligan, H. J. The socialization of sexual identity. *Journal of Marriage and the Family*, 1977, *39*(1), 99–112. A test of certain theoretical descriptions of the impact of early socialization on adult behavior, with emphasis on theories by Freud, O. G. Brim, and J. H. Gagnon and W. Simon. No one theory was found to adequately explain the data. The significance of postchildhood experiences for the personality trait of sexual self-esteem raises questions about theories stressing the primacy of early experiences in personality formation, especially in sexual matters. Such models explain variance in sexual vulnerability better than they do coping ability.

Garbarino, J. Some thoughts on school size and its effects on adolescent development. *Journal of Youth and Adolescence*, 1980, *9*(1), 19–31. A review of the literature suggests that school size matters up to a population of 500, after which increase on size has no appreciable effect. Recent trends are regarded as conspiring against adolescents in compelling ever larger numbers of academically marginal students to attend schools beyond the optimal size.

Hansson, R. O., O'Connor, M. E., Jones, W. H., & Blocker, T. J. Maternal employment and adolescent sexual behavior. *Journal of Youth and Adolescence*, 1981, *10*(1), 55–60. This study of female adolescents of high school age disclosed associations between the mother's employment status and the daughter's sexual attitudes and behaviors.

Heilbrun, A. B., Jr. *Human Sex-role Behavior*. Elmsford, N.Y.: Pergamon Press, 1981. The author questions, on the basis of two decades of research, some of the currently popular views about the liabilities of conventional sex roles and the advantages of androgyny.

Hite, S. *The Hite report: A nationwide study on female sexuality*. New York: Macmillan, 1976. Based on responses of 3000 women across the country to a questionnaire regarding their sexuality. A new theory of female sexuality is advanced that places sex within its historic and cultural context.

Keith, P. M., & Brubaker, T. H. Adolescent perceptions of household work: Expectations by sex, age, and employment. *Adolescence*, 1980, *15*(57), 171–182. Data obtained from college undergraduates indicated which spouse should assume major responsibility for each of ten household tasks in four age and employment situations and in their projected households. The young women expected more shared responsibilities than the men, and both sexes endorsed greater sharing in marriages other than their own. There was no anticipation of greater sharing when the wife worked full time.

Kelly, J. A., & Worell, L. Parent behaviors related to masculine, feminine, and androgynous sex role orientations. *Journal of Consulting and Clinical Psychology*, 1976, *44*(5) 843–851. A study of 481 college undergraduates classed into four categories—masculine typed, feminine typed, androgynous, and indeterminate. Sex-role orientation related distinctively to reported child-rearing practices. Measurements of parental affection primarily differentiated the male groups. Parental cognitive and achievement encouragement differentiated the female sex-role categories.

Kemper, T. D., & Bologh, R. W. The ideal love object: Structural and family sources. *Journal of Youth and Adolescence*, 1980, *9*(1), 33–48. After obtaining preferences of 227 college students regarding the characteristics of their ideal love objects, the authors identify and discuss the most important predictors: sex, religion, mother's marital happiness, and father's education.

Kidwell, J. S. Number of siblings, sibling spacing, sex, and birth order: Their effects on perceived parent-adolescent relationships. *Journal of Marriage and the Family*, 1981, *43*(2), 315–332. The results of this study indicate that the effects of birth order on parent-adolescent relationships depend on such factors as number, spacing, and sex of siblings.

Knox, D., & Wilson, K. Dating behaviors of university students. *Family Relations*, 1981, *30*(2), 255–258. A study of the dating behaviors of a random sampling of 334 university students—including how they meet, what they do, and where they go–disclosed the nature of parental involvement and differences between the sexes in such situations.

Lueptow, L. B. Social structure, social change and parental influence in adolescent sex-role socialization: 1964–1975. *Journal of Marriage and the Family*, 1980, *42*(1), 93–103. Reports a study that was designed to add to available evidence regarding sex-role socialization by comparing the relative influence of mothers and fathers and relating the evidence obtained to current theories of sex-role socialization. No evidence of change in sex-related patterns of socialization over the 1964–1975 decade was found.

Mathis, J. L. Adolescent sexuality and societal change. *American Journal of Psychotherapy*, 1976, *30*(3), 433–440. Sexual behaviors are portrayed as having increased because of social change. Adolescents handle the resultant anxiety by relying on their equally naive peer group for support. While psychoanalytic theory suggests that such behaviors will interfere with progress toward healthy psychosexual maturity, some authorities disagree.

Moore, D., & Hotch, D. F. Late adolescents' conceptualizations of home-leaving. *Journal of Youth and Adolescence*, 1981, *10*(1), 1–10. A study of college students' conceptualizations of home-leaving disclosed relationships between these results and elements of ego development.

Offer, D., & Offer, J. B. *From teenage to young manhood: A psychological study.* New York: Basic Books, 1975. A follow-up study was made of middle-class young men whom the authors had reported on previously. Of the total sample, 79% were characterized by a continuous growth pattern, 35% by a surgent growth, and 21% by tumultuous growth. A detailed case study is given of the individual in each group whose profile was closest to the group mean.

Peplau, L. A., Rubin, Z., & Hill, C. T. The sexual balance of power. *Psychology Today*, 1976, *10*(6), 142–147; 151. In this study college couples described details of their dating relationships, with emphasis on the matter of power. Follow-ups at 6 months, 1 year, and 2 years later provided a picture of how their relationships had changed.

Roper, B. S., & Labeff, E. Sex roles and feminism revisited: An intergenerational attitude comparison. *Journal of Marriage and the Family*, 1977, *39*(1), 113–119. A comparison among undergraduates' sex-role attitudes in 1934 and in 1974 indicates more-egalitarian attitudes. However, this trend is modified by a tendency for both generations to be more approving of feminist views about women's economic and political status and less so toward domestic status and conduct.

Scales, P. Males and morals: Teenage contraceptive behavior amid the double standard. *Family Coordinator*, 1977, *26*(3), 211–222. Reviews the literature regarding teenage contraceptive behaviors and decision making. The persistence of the sexual double standard is linked to a lack of communication about contraception among young people. The author considers the implications of authorities' neglect of the male's contribution to contraceptive behavior.

Smith, E. J. The career development of young black females. *Youth and Society*, 1981 12(3), 277–312. A review of the literature identifies the psychological and economic variables that contribute to the career development of young black females.

Tittle, C. K. *Careers and family: Sex roles and adolescent life plans.* Beverly Hills, Calif.: Sage Publications, 1981. Data are presented for determining how young people make future plans, sex differences in decision-making, values involved, and effective modes of counseling regarding such matters.

Tooley, K. M. "Johnny, I hardly knew ye": Toward a revision of the theory of the male psychosexual development. *American Journal of Orthopsychiatry*, 1977, 47(2), 184–195. The author argues for a change in traditional hypotheses about male psychosexual socialization. The so-called current psychology of women is portrayed as merely a weak negative of the psychology of men, which can only be properly reformulated if male psychology is changed. While male theorists and practitioners have viewed as positive the harsh realities of male socialization, such conditions have had unfortunate effects on the male ego and the culture as a whole.

Walters, J., & Walters, L. H. Trends affecting adolescent views of sexuality, employment, marriage and child rearing. *Family Relations*, 1980, 29(2), 191–198. Discusses research and opinion regarding adolescent views on changing sexual standards, occupational goals of the sexes, and changing standards of child rearing. Also considered is what can be expected of youth in the next decade and how this projection relates to continuities and change in their views of the family.

8
YOUNG ADULTHOOD

TASKS

General Tasks

Representative views. The major tasks of early adulthood have been variously defined. As observed in Chapter 1, Erikson (1959) outlined successive stages of the life cycle representing choices, or crises, for the expanding ego. After the ego-identity crisis of adolescence comes the development of intimacy in early adulthood, or the ability to merge oneself with another. Otherwise, one becomes isolated and self-absorbed, with little concern for others.

The Grant Study would seem to confirm this view, because its young adults' chief problems related to difficulties in establishing intimacy. During this period (ages 20 to 30) adolescent friendships are replaced by more mature relationships that respect individual differences (Vaillant, 1977). More-successful individuals achieve stable marriages and maintain them. To marry very young, before a capacity for intimacy has been achieved, provides a poor prognosis for successful marriage. Between ages 25 and 35, men work hard, integrate their careers, and spend much time with their families. Meantime, they tend to forgo play, seeking to get ahead. Sheehy (1976) concluded that, at least until recently, the majority of both sexes felt that their lives would be completed by either a career or a mate.

In addition to the need to establish intimacy Neugarten (1977) named as tasks adapting to the work world, becoming a parent, and involving oneself in the lives of a relatively few significant others. Frenkel-Brunswik (1968) differentiated between the tasks of the earlier and later part of this period. The first two phases, until the middle and later 20s, involve establishing an independent life-style. The next phase, from the late 20s until middle age or the late 40s, is characterized by vocational stability, social involvement, and community participation.

Selected Tasks Analyzed

Entering the adult world. According to another authority, Daniel Levinson (1977), the period from ages 17 to 22 is when one questions one's preadult role and modifies the relationships associated with it. Crossing the threshold into adulthood occupies the years from about 22 to 28. This stage involves two main tasks, observed Levinson. The first is to explore alternatives of adult life while avoiding commitments so strong as to preclude further options. A complementary task is to establish a stable life structure, to "settle down, become responsible, and make something of my life" (p. 103). Constructing a life within this exciting new world becomes an exhilarating and often confusing process.

Each individual must establish a balance between flexibility and commitment during these years. Some people remain quite open, testing one job after another while forming only transient relationships. They absorb little of the world into themselves; nor do they invest much of themselves in the world. Some compromise between stability and change, making tentative commitments while keeping their options open. Others keep their options open until ages 25 or 26 and then set about forming a more settled life. Still others form firm commitments from the beginning, assuming that their life structure will last. Such individuals make marital and vocational choices that they intend to follow the rest of their lives.

Most young adults feel considerable optimism about the future, as indicated in these replies to the question "Is your feeling about the future one of hope, fear, dread, resignation—or what?"

> The future is now. Hope is great but desire and persistence are better. Anything that is humanly attainable, I can, if I so choose, attain (man, age 28).
>
> My feeling is of hope. When you've been down, where else can you go but upward? Life is hard, but great. We're only here for a short time—make the most of it (woman, 37).
>
> Hope (man, 33).
>
> Hopes, high ones (woman, 26).

Launching a career. Establishing a career remains a significant task, but with a difference. For one thing, fewer young adults these days believe that hard work always pays off. They are willing to work, but not just for material security. Instead, they want self-fulfillment, self-expression, and interesting work. However, a mere 30% perceive their jobs as having an adequate future. Moreover, about two out of three (63%) perceive a lack of higher education as an obstacle to obtaining a "good, meaningful" job.

Men generally take their vocation more seriously than do married women, although most women take for granted that they will work full or part time, except when the children are young. In a poll by the Roper organization (1974) three out of five women under age 30 favored combining marriage, children, and career. The majority rejected the concept of alimony in situations where the woman is capable of earning a satisfactory income; only one in four believed that custody rights should be automatically granted to mothers. A large majority looked on employment as a means of ensuring economic security—and some of the desirable extras—in times when inflation was the norm.

Those were the attitudes of the middle class. In a study of blue-collar wives, the younger women expected to return to work after their two children—and they expected to have only two—were in school. Moreover, the woman desired a career more personally satisfying than the mundane job she had before she got married. The peak of her future experience, as she anticipated it, would be after the children left home, so that she and her husband could travel and indulge in their special interests to their hearts' content (Gardner, 1974). Gardner concluded that these changes in working women's attitudes are significant, and that these women will never retreat to their former position, as nonemployed housewives.

In both middle and blue-collar classes a woman still puts her husband's work-related problems ahead of her own (Lowenthal, 1975). She must also somehow cope with others' feelings about her working. Her mother and often her husband may oppose such a move. As Sheehy (1976) pointed out, there is only one way for a woman to find out whether she is refraining from going to work because her husband stands in her way or because she distrusts her own abilities. That is simply to make the move. If she is not genuine in her need to break out of her shell, she can easily retreat and blame her decision on her obligations to children and husband. The recent drive for woman's autonomy is cutting across class, race, and age lines. It is sending a ripple through the comfortable, traditional patterns in which women so long took refuge, escaping the discomforts and strains of feeling compelled to compete in the larger society.

For his part, the husband becomes increasingly tied to his job after the children begin to arrive and economic problems grow. Often he becomes so married to the job that he has no room for any other real commitment through his 30s and often until the mid-40s.

It is still often the case that the husband becomes committed more and more to his work and less and less to his family.

A survey of *Psychology Today* readers, who tend to be younger, better educated, and more heavily concentrated in the professions than the general population, indicated a significant gap between what they considered important in a job and how well their own work fulfilled those requirements. This survey is reproduced in Figure 8-1.

Respondents were asked to choose among different degrees of importance and satisfaction for each job feature. Based on averages of their responses, the numbers rank each from 1 (most important to the group or most often satisfying) to 18 (least important or least often satisfying).

	Importance	Satisfaction
Chances to do something that makes you feel good about yourself	1	8
Chances to accomplish something worthwhile	2	6
Chances to learn new things	3	10
Opportunity to develop your skills and abilities	4	12
The amount of freedom you have on the job	5	2
Chances you have to do things you do best	6	11
The resources you have to do your job	7	9
The respect you receive from people you work with	8	3
Amount of information you get about your job performance	9	17
Your chances for taking part in making decisions	10	14
The amount of job security you have	11	5
Amount of pay you get	12	16
The way you are treated by the people you work with	13	4
The friendliness of people you work with	14	1
Amount of praise you get for job well done	15	15
The amount of fringe benefits you get	16	7
Chances for getting a promotion	17	18
Physical surroundings of your job	18	13

Figure 8-1. From "What you really want from your job," by P. A. Renwick, E. E. Lawler, and the Psychology Today *staff. In* Psychology Today, *1978, 11(12), 56. Copyright © 1978 by Ziff-Davis Publishing Company. Reprinted by permission.*

In any case, young men often become dissatisfied with their work at a reasonably young age (from ages 25 to 30) and then want to change their careers. The difficulty arises partly because many young adults narrow their choices too soon. Sometimes they feel they have no option, because of their family responsibilities, except to continue in their present work.

Attaining mastery through work and leisure. Lowenthal (1977) portrayed young adulthood as a time for attaining mastery. And by that stage most males have become committed to efforts at mastery, especially regarding career. Researchers have mostly ignored women on this score (Lowenthal, 1977). The question arises whether, for either sex, attaining mastery through leisure is as satisfying as achieving it through work. In research by Lowenthal, Thurnher,

Chiriboga, and associates (1975) high school seniors—males especially—and newlyweds were almost as concerned with testing leisure styles as with exploring work commitments. Young adults had already achieved strong and intimate interpersonal commitments, and the outlines of mature leisure patterns were beginning to take shape. The individuals quoted here, like young adults in general, differ widely in their choice of recreational activities.

> Chess, listening to interesting people, making money (man, age 28).

> I like sewing, crocheting. I enjoy creating things. I watch TV sometimes for diversion, sometimes for escape. I also like to read (woman, 33).

> I bowl, play tennis. I like to knit, hook rugs, and cook. I also read all the time (woman, 37).

> I like the movies, social activities of the One-Parent Family Council, travel, music, and sex, when it's with a longtime close friend (woman, 29).

An overall task of young adults is to integrate all aspects of their lives into a life-style appropriate to their current stage in life. These patterns are somewhat different in premarriage years than they are after marriage. Until children arrive, today's young people try to have certain experiences, especially travel, that they could not afford until they went to work and that they might have neither the time nor the money for afterward. Increasingly greater numbers plan to delay marriage for this very purpose.

While the children are small, fathers are mostly preoccupied with making ends meet and establishing a beachhead for their careers. Mothers focus mainly on child care and homemaking, and recreational activities dwindle. Parents participate jointly in social affairs normally expected of young marrieds in the job, in community and church roles, and in relations with relatives and neighbors. With regard to companionship, young marrieds associate both with persons of their own sex who have similar interests and with other couples, often because of the husbands' jobs or interests. While they may socialize most often with these other couples, such friends may not be the most intimate ones of either husband or wife (Hess, 1972).

Lower-class couples have fewer mutual friends than do middle-class ones. Most blue-collar married people interact chiefly with groups of their own sex and especially with neighbors or relatives. To some degree young adults of both social classes pursue personal interests, as in sports, cultural activities, and hobbies—a holding operation until these pursuits can be resumed with greater fervor in later adulthood, especially after retirement.

In Table 8-1, based on a study of four stages of adulthood, individuals report more friends at the newlywed period than any other.

Tasks of transition and assessment. In the late 20s comes transition, as individuals appraise their status and achievements to date. During this transition, from about 28 to 33, life is restructured on a new and presumably more sound basis. In effect, one is saying "If I want to change my life—if there are things in it I want to modify or exclude, or things missing I want to add—I must now

Table 8-1. Friendship Networks by Life Stage and Sex

	High School	Newly-wed	Middle-Aged	Preretire-ment	Men	Women	Total
Mean number of friends	4.8	7.6	4.7	6.0	5.2	6.3	5.7
Percent reporting contact:							
Daily	75	24	33	26	38	37	33
Weekly	19	52	44	41	36	34	38
Monthly/less	6	24	23	33	26	29	29
Percent reporting duration of friendship:							
At least 5 yrs.	73	53	12	7	30	39	35
More than 6 yrs.	27	47	88	93	70	61	65
Friend considered important to spouse (%)	NA	61	81	82	79	70	75
Percent of respondents who have an opposite-sex friend:							
Among 3 friends listed	62	66	30	18	39	46	43
For closest friend only	9	12	0	5	8	4	5
Age of closest friend (%):							
Younger	3	3	2	12	6	2	5
Same	94	90	93	85	90	94	90
Older	3	7	5	3	4	4	5
High friendship complexity (%)	38	56	37	70	46	56	46

From *Four Stages of Life,* by M. F. Lowenthal, M. Thurnher, D. Chiriboga, and Associates. Copyright 1975 by Jossey-Bass Publishers. Reprinted by permission.

make a start, for soon it will be too late" (Levinson, 1977, p. 104). For some people this transition is somewhat stressful; for others it is relatively smooth. It assumes the proportions of crisis when an individual finds the current life structure unbearable but perceives no adequate substitute. The majority of men in Levinson's study underwent a moderate or severe crisis during these years. The age-30 transition is also characterized by marital difficulties and divorce, settling down after trying a variety of jobs, and the changing significance of various aspects of one's life.

Sheehy argued that the unsettling that occurs around age 30 is necessary to growth. Those individuals who settle down too soon into a safe marriage and are too unimaginative, or too selfish, to broaden themselves may simply continue to live in the same rut without developing. In order to cope with a certain restlessness they may indulge in certain purely superficial changes, while staying in their safe rut. Or they may build a better house or move into a finer area in the suburbs.

Tasks of the 30s. The period from age 17 or 18 until 32 or 33 is the "novice" phase of early adulthood. The next life structure takes form at age 32 or 33 and lasts until 39 or 40. This stage involves two chief tasks: to establish a niche in society and thus become a contributing member of one's social world and to progress satisfactorily along the timetable of North America's version of success. An individual also becomes a full-fledged adult, defining a life plan while anticipating the future. Essential to this settling-down period is the concept of the ladder, which reflects the realities of society and represents stages of advancement in power, income, rank, quality of family life, and the like. Toward the end of the settling-down period, at age 36 or 37, individuals become their own persons, with a measure of authority. This period is particularly critical in most people's lives. By young adulthood each individual has already reached important conclusions about life.

> I'm not the only one with major problems. People are worse off than myself. I am lucky in so many ways. I have a wonderful son, great family, good health (woman, age 37).
>
> The more I give of myself, the more I receive in personal happiness. It's important to be assertive (woman, 29).
>
> Be thankful for good things you have and try to make the best of your situation. Be happy instead of brooding over your predicament or what you don't have (woman, 35).
>
> Whatever you desire or want in life is possible if you will just meticulously write down on paper what it is you want and when, and how much, and go like hell after it (man, 28).

In addition, Sheehy (1976) portrayed the 30s as the time for settling down and developing an orderly life-style. This decade is one of accomplishment. It is during this period that fantasies are being transformed into realities, and the hard work of the 20s begins reaping some rewards. People tend now to concentrate on building both home life and career.

Redefining Values

Major values. Young adults' decisions about how to establish priorities among all the demands on their resources are determined by their values. Those who do not attend college probably reflect little on their major goals, at least on the way they relate to each other and a total life plan. The vast numbers who do now attend college spend a considerable time doing just that, albeit on a relatively impractical level and unaided by the wisdom that only reality testing brings. For example, they often accept the notion that sincere efforts will pay off, failing as yet to comprehend how much sheer politics (whom you know and how good you are at buttering up the boss) pay off. Inevitably, as they move into adulthood, young people's values become to some degree redefined, although remaining essentially the same.

The following replies to the question "What helps you the most in making life adjustments," are illustrative of two broad categories of young adults: those who rely on some power outside themselves for help and those who depend on themselves.

My partner's [wife's], and my own, desire to achieve (man, age 28).

Believing in God. He's gotten me through many situations. Don't let yourself feel sorry for yourself all the time (woman, 37).

Resolving problems internally (man, 33).

Prayer and faith in God (woman, 29).

Few researchers have explored young adults' values in depth. Among these few, psychologist Robert Gordon determined which resources contributed most to their happiness, how much of each resource they had had as children, how much they were receiving at the time, and how happy they were. The resources measured included love (warmth, affection), status (respect, esteem), information (advice, knowledge), money, goods, and services (work, labor). Love accounted for three-quarters of the effect that all the resources had on the young people's happiness. Services, feeling financially secure, sex, and information explained the rest. Beyond these factors additional status, goods, and money had no significant effect on happiness.

Those individuals who had grown up receiving little love placed much more value on money than did those who received much love as children. Those adults who felt they were not then receiving much love ordinarily valued goods highly, perhaps to compensate for the lack of love. Such persons tended to avoid intimacy and those who would be most likely to provide them the love that they need. Among the resources named, money and goods become the most usual substitute for love, although some individuals used information or ideas instead. One prototype was the "cold-blooded intellectual" who deals with everything abstractly because it is simpler to manipulate ideas than to deal with people and their feelings (Horn, J., 1976).

Changes in outlook with age. What people value varies somewhat across the years. The 20s have their illusions, but these illusions may not necessarily be undesirable. Instead, they may be necessary to vitalize early commitments. There is a certain amount of self-deception at this age, but it may be desirable. Unless an individual really has a feeling of power about what he or she will become, the effort will hardly seem worth it. Instead of hope, feelings of self-doubt will emerge that undermine effort. Many people in their 20s believe that what they are doing constitutes the one true course in their lives (Gould, 1975). During this period an individual is hardly aware of **defense mechanisms** and conflicts from the past.

When young adults take stock, as they often do at ages 29 to 34, they begin to question why they are doing what they are doing. In the process, they discover deeper motivations within themselves that had been submerged during the busy 20s, when developing a "workable life structure" had been the most significant task. This reflection leads to a certain urgency in the years 35 to 43. Now the not-quite-so-young adults recognize that time is not infinite, and they scurry about to make changes in their life-style and vocational goals. Now they may be capable of a broader perspective—for example, in perceiving their children not just as cherished extensions of themselves but as respected individuals whom they are ready to help change into young adults (Gould, 1975).

Many people in middle age, on looking back, wish that they had had different values in their 20s and 30s. A man in his 40s may wish that he had not been so narrowly concerned with his ambition during his 20s, realizing that it deprived him of "irreplaceable experiences" with his family. As one man said, "If I had only known then what I know now about what is important in living. It takes such a long time to find out what it is all about" (Gould, 1975, p. 74). Thus, an individual's values evolve, to some extent, throughout adulthood. The direction of change is "toward becoming more tolerant of oneself, and more appreciative of the complexity of both the surrounding world and of the mental milieu" (Gould, 1975).

Social class relates significantly to values, in ways that change over time. For both college and blue-collar youth, success means "self fulfillment and quality of life rather than money and security" (Yankelovich & Clark, 1974, p. 64). Noncollege graduates' problem is the gap between their desire for interesting jobs and kinds of work that they can obtain.

Young-Adult Sex Roles

The female role. Young adults' values are reflected in their interpretations of sex roles. According to Dreyer (1975) young women today possess clear-cut concepts of sex-role orientation. The first group, the role synthesizers, combine elements of the traditional feminine and masculine roles into a life-style stressing high levels of personal achievement. They seek careers in professional fields or sports and plan to combine these careers with marriage and children. They have a strongly feminine sex-role identity; and they are warm, sensitive, and introspective. Nevertheless, they perceive men as serious competitors and fear such struggles. In marriage they seek husbands who will support their achievement aspirations and share family roles.

Another group, the role innovators, seek new responsibilities, activities, and status as women. They have practical goals, including seeking a good job, making something of themselves, and having enough money for happiness. They perceive their feminine role attributes as means to accomplish these goals. And they perform well in jobs that require loyalty, responsibility, and self-discipline and that yield short-term rewards. Unlike the role synthesizers they are confident, self-accepting, poised, and lacking in conflict about their roles. Ordinarily they work, in order to help out with the family finances. They do not seek or expect equality with men in job situations, because they feel that they accomplish more by seeming feminine (Dreyer, 1975). This role is extremely common among working women today.

A third group are the role traditionals, who conform to the stereotype of the extremely domesticated woman. They seek a husband who will be loving and a good provider and father. They have limited educational and occupational goals and perceive school and work as simply preludes to marriage, when they can focus all their attention on husband and family. Such women are contented and self-assured, and they adopt behaviors that help them to establish and maintain a happy marriage and family.

The fourth group, the role diffused, are uncertain about their role in life. Often they have past histories of considerable ability and confidence; however, they become overwhelmed when choosing among alternatives. They are somewhat traditionally feminine, often because it is the easiest pattern of behavior to follow. Some of them appear immature, cling to their parents, and may be described as experiencing a psychosocial moratorium. Some of them become seriously confused and seek professional help.

Many young women are defining their sex roles in new ways. They still feel the conflict between the traditionally feminine and modern roles, but they are no longer choosing between these roles. Instead, they are developing a role combining career and homemaking. In order to perform this dual role, a woman must be resourceful and creative. She lacks adequate role models, because former generations did not synthesize sex roles. Nevertheless, in the present affluent society women are experimenting with roles, and the outcomes may have broad consequences.

A concomitant of young women's sex-role innovations has been that men's roles are also changing. As the economy shifts in emphasis toward service occupations requiring interpersonal skills of expression and as women begin assuming work formerly considered more appropriate for men, the boundaries demarking sexually appropriate occupational roles become more diffuse. Earlier distinctions in job roles, based on physical strength, simply become irrelevant in times when machines do much of the heavy work. The result is a dissolution of many of the older ideas about sex differences and sex-related vocational requirements.

The male role. Sheehy (1976) contrasted the male and female roles. Traditionally, the masculine sex role has involved initiating and directing activities, and the female's role has been to respond to others' needs and wishes; the same is generally true today. Young men have struggled and worked hard through their 20s, and by age 30 the well-educated ones, at least, have made satisfactory progress toward career goals.

A poll of 28,000 subscribers to *Psychology Today* revealed little basic change in such values (Tavris, 1977). It should also be noted that these respondents were generally younger, less religious, better educated, more liberal, and more affluent than average Americans. The fact that such people are in the vanguard of social change adds weight to their answers, which can be summed up as follows: (1) Neither sex admires the "macho male who is tough, strong, aggressive, and has many sexual conquests" (p. 25).* (2) Both sexes are striving for an androgynous ideal but have not yet achieved it. They approve of men's attempts to free themselves from their "emotional strait jackets." Women want men to be "more gentle, romantic, and expressive than the men themselves do . . . [and] men want to be more warm and loving than they feel they are" (p. 35). (3) In general, women have a higher regard for their men than they do for themselves.

The two male members of this household perform traditionally female tasks.

(4) Men have more trouble defining masculinity than women do. At least women recognize it when they see it and believe their own men to be more masculine than they themselves do. (5) Masculinity represents a complex of desirable

*From "Men and women report their views on masculinity," by C. Tavris. In *Psychology Today*, 1977, *10*(8), 34–42; 82. Copyright © 1977 by Ziff-Davis Publishing Company. This and all other quotations from this source are reprinted by permission.

qualities also appropriate for women, instead of "a set of merit badges that must be earned and rewon." That is, the majority does not believe that men must constantly scurry around engaging in "daring feats of faucet-fixing or hand-to-hand combat" in order to prove their manhood. Indeed, many young people today insist that there is no distinctive dichotomy of masculinity and femininity, but rather only humanity (Tavris, 1977).

The men, asked when they felt most masculine, mentioned spending money on women, saying something witty, accomplishing something that others believed impossible or extremely difficult, or in some cases drinking much liquor. For some of them masculinity was chiefly a matter of how they appealed to women; for others the standard was established in terms of other males. Some of them felt most masculine when involved in work, achieving a major competitive goal, or successfully defeating an opponent. In such cases masculinity was the reward for having struggled against odds and then proved oneself.

Fewer than 10% of either sex believed that men lose masculinity by performing traditionally female occupations or by not working, as when living on welfare or dropping out of the system and remaining at home as "house husbands." The only occupations mentioned that would cause any considerable number (just under 20%) to question a man's masculinity were go-go dancing and prostitution. And the only one that any substantial number (30% of the males and 30% of the females) believed should be restricted to men was armed combat. Nevertheless, men in more traditionally feminine jobs said that they were often assumed to be unmasculine and something less than a real man. Table 8-2, comparing married and cohabiting college males' performance of household tasks, indicates that young men still largely adhere to the traditional roles.

Both sexes in the magazine poll still wanted some sex differences to remain; and substantial numbers of the women wanted to look up to their men. The men were more likely than the women to believe it totally acceptable for the wife to have higher status, be more intelligent, and earn more than the husband. Almost 90% of the men believed it acceptable for their wives to earn more money, but few of the wives earned more. If such a situation is unlikely to arise, it is hard to know how men would function in such real-life situations. The researchers concluded that there are as "many styles of masculinity as a man could want" (Tavris, 1977).

LIFE-STYLES

Young Marrieds

The pluses and minuses of family life. Young adults' overall task is to organize their activities into life-styles or patterns "in terms of [their] use of time. . . . investment of energy and . . . choice of interpersonal objects" (Bengston, 1973, p. 37). Young couples today organize their life-styles and activities around the family. A family can be a source of comfort and "psychic relief," a place where an individual can vent feelings of hostility, depression, and despair that must

Table 8-2. Comparison of Married and Cohabiting Males on Actual Performance of Household Tasks

Task	Percent Always Marr.	Cohab.	Percent More Marr.	Cohab.	Percent Equally Marr.	Cohab.	Percent Less Marr.	Cohab.	Percent N.A. Marr.	Cohab.
Cook	3.7	0	0	12	18.5	36	77.7	52	0	0
Dust	0	0	3.7	0	14.8	48	70.3	40	11.1	12
Dishwashing	3.7	0	3.7	8	40.7	52	48.1	40	3.7	0
Vacuum	3.7	0	0	4	25.9	52	62.9	36	7.4	8
Laundry	11.1	0	3.7	4	18.5	44	66.6	48	0	4
Scrub	7.4	4	3.7	4	25.9	32	55.5	40	7.4	20
Cut lawn	26.8	28	18.5	12	3.7	12	22.2	4	26.6	44
Feed pets	11.1	16	33	0	14.8	36	7.4	16	33.3	32
Pull weeds	14.8	12	22.2	8	3.7	16	22.2	4	44.4	60
Wash car	37	44	26	12	7.4	36	11.1	0	18.5	12
Wash pets	3.7	16	0	4	25.9	28	29.6	12	40.7	40
Finances	22.2	28	18.5	12	33	44	22.2	4	3.7	8
Repairs	44.4	36	37	24	7.4	20	3.7	4	7.4	8
Garbage, trash	29.6	24	40.7	16	14.8	44	7.4	12	7.4	4
Diaper baby	0	0	0	0	18.5	8	18.5	0	62.9	92
Bathe baby	0	0	0	0	29.6	8	7.4	0	62.9	92
Feed children	0	4	0	4	22.2	8	11.1	0	66.6	84
Clean garage	29.6	20	3.7	8	14.8	8	3.7	0	48.1	72
Wash windows	3.7	4	7.4	8	7.4	20	11.1	40	3.7	28
Discipline child	0	0	14.8	0	14.8	8	0	4	70.3	88
Pick up after child	7.4	0	14.8	0	0	8	7.4	4	70.3	88
Menu planning	3.7	8	0	4	44.4	40	37	44	14.8	4
Snow shovelling	44.4	28	22.2	16	0	16	14.8	0	18.5	40

From "The division of labor among cohabiting and married couples," by R. Stafford, E. Backman, and P. DiBona. In *Journal of Marriage and the Family*, 1977, *39*(1), 51. Copyright 1977 by the National Council on Family Relations. Reprinted by permission.

be suppressed outside the home. Within an increasingly impersonal and often suspicious world, families provide adults chances to be useful and to feel needed (Kagan, 1977). When young college students were asked to forecast their life-styles in 1985, the majority included marriage, children, home ownership, a car or two, and a reasonably well-to-do life-style (Stein, 1976). In broad outline most young marrieds follow such a plan.

Despite the advantages of family life, early adulthood constitutes the greatest danger for marriage. During the last half-century, Americans have been most likely to end their unions when the husband is about 30 and the wife 28 (Sheehy, 1976). Over the years just preceding, the problems have been building up, and extramarital relationships may occur. Yet such affairs do not signify a careless disregard for marital ties; instead, they are symptoms of breakdown in marriage. These affairs were judged a major trespass on commitment and trust, and then generally resulted in divorce. In one study, fewer than 2% of the young marrieds under age 25 engaged in such practices as swinging and mate swapping (Hunt, 1973).

In any case, there were gradual decreases in companionship, affectionate demonstrations, and sexual relations between the couple themselves. Instead of developing closer companionship, couples come to have fewer common interests and agree less on their basic opinions. Nevertheless, this cooling-off period after the initial romantic glow does not necessarily signify an unhappy marriage or dissatisfaction regarding it, for marital satisfaction tends to rise again after the children leave home. The earlier pattern of initial romance and intimate emotional interaction, followed by a gradual cooling pattern, proceeds at an even more accelerated rate when couples marry during their teens (DeLissovoy, 1973). They become disenchanted after a mere 18 months of marriage instead of the typical 20 years.

It should be noted that the original relationship involved only two persons. But when children come, the different configuration effects a subtle change, for better or worse, in the spouse relationship. That is, as any individual is added to the household, whether it be a mother-in-law or a child, the quality of life in that household is modified.

Class differences. While the middle and working classes share similar satisfactions and problems, their family life-styles differ. On the basis of a thousand hours of in-depth interviewing with husbands and wives in working-class families, Breslow-Rubin (1976) drew a picture of young-adult, working-class couples' lives. For comparison the researcher also interviewed 25 middle-class families that were matched with the blue-collar families in every respect except education. The two groupings differed considerably, beginning with their childhood. Few of the working-class subjects reported a happy childhood. Yet they expressed no resentment toward their parents, despite cases of parental alcoholism, divorce, or desertion in half the families. All had endured the pain of poverty due to parents' layoffs from work, illness, and other unpredictable events.

The working-class subjects also recalled having had very limited goals as children compared with those of the middle-class respondents. Among the working-class boys, work was not planned but simply occurred. The girls anticipated early marriages in order to achieve the desired status of adults. In contrast, the middle-class respondents had been encouraged by their parents, both with words and resources, to realize their goals. Working-class couples married early and continued to experience poverty. Although they were now free of the disliked demands and supervision of their own parents, they were shortly bogged down with responsibilities for their children, who often arrived in the first year of marriage.

Most of the working-class couples were still struggling to pay for items that they had hoped would let them participate in the type of life they saw portrayed on television. They had purchased considerable leisure equipment, including boats, campers, and cycles, paid off gradually on the installment plan with money earned in overtime work. As a result they had too little leisure time to make much use of what they had purchased.

Both working- and middle-class wives expressed a desire for better communication with their husbands, and the husbands were somewhat confused over their wives' discontent. Nevertheless, there were differences. The working-class woman often described her husband "as a steady worker; he doesn't drink; he doesn't hit me." But not a single middle-class woman mentioned such items.

The decision whether to have children. Traditionally, women of all social classes were socialized to believe that their primary life role was that of mother. Only recently has there been any real effort to relieve this pressure and make motherhood voluntary (Bernard, 1975). The vast majority of women still want children; however, a small minority does not. Of all women who marry, at least 1 in 20, perhaps as many as 1 in 10, never become mothers (Veevers, 1972). The older the age at first marriage, and the longer the interval between becoming married and having a child, the smaller the number of children (Marini, 1981).

Reasons for having children have changed sharply over the years. In preindustrial times children provided certain economic benefits by helping in the fields or caring for younger children. Later, as children gradually lost their economic utility and became an economic burden, they became valued more in terms of "sentiment" or because they could raise the family's status by their own accomplishments. As a result, parents began to identify with their children because of their potential accomplishments (Plumb, 1975). Besides, because parents viewed offspring as extensions of themselves, they could compensate for their own failure by taking satisfaction in their children's achievements. The obvious danger here is that they might unconsciously impose on their children too heavy an obligation to accomplish.

In more recent times, when children are more likely to be planned, they are desired for still other reasons. Parents can dedicate themselves to "a mission that transcends the self—the opportunity to beget and raise a child" (p. 14). Most "are eager to test their effectiveness as a sculptor of new life" (p. 34). Child rearing also lets parents "validate" the value system that they themselves have developed. This system may have been largely acquired from their own parents. Or it may be a "radical transformation, struck from intense childhood pain and carried to adulthood in a vow not to visit upon the next generation the destructive practices and philosophies that scarred their lives" (p. 34). In any case, parents have an opportunity to test the usefulness of ethics and standards that they have gradually carved out and created over the years. Thus, they are practical scientists, testing their individual views of human development with their children (Kagan, 1977).

Only under certain circumstances does having children help to hold a marriage together. The divorce rate is highest for individuals with no children or with relatively large families, while those with moderate-sized families have the lowest rate. That is, childless couples feel less pressure to remain together than do unhappy couples with children. The problems of marriage increase as the number of children grow. At some point the strains of the marriage may exceed the need to maintain it on account of the children (Thornton, 1977).

For a number of reasons, growing numbers of couples decide not to have children. Adults have come to expect more of life today than mere subsistence. In some cases the rewards of child rearing do not, according to their values, offset the obligations and limitations normally involved. Today childless couples have more discretionary time as well as more freedom to travel and participate in outside-the-home activities. In former times they had neither the money nor the opportunity to play Sunday golf, spend the evening at the theater, or travel to Europe. Now such options are common. In addition, women's wages are now high enough and living expenses great enough that the loss derived from remaining home to have children becomes a consideration (Sawhill, 1977). Some adults simply do not enjoy children. Others buy household pets and use them as inexpensive substitutes for children. In any case, as the commodity of time becomes more scarce because of the many demands placed upon it and the expense of rearing children increases, the demand for children decreases.

Another reason for not having children, or for limiting their number, is the world population explosion. In the United States in this century, only 17% of women on the average have remained childless, but the figure has varied greatly. This average includes 11% of women who marry but remain childless, and 6% who never marry and also have no children (Glick, 1977). Veevers (1973) suggested encouraging some women not to have children and rewarding rather than punishing them for the decision.

Some adults may not qualify for becoming parents for genetic or psychological reasons. In some cases, they should not have children because of their own ineptness, or potential for bearing genetically defective children. Or they may want children for the wrong reasons: to help out with household chores, to look after them in their old age, or to carry out specific goals that they themselves have been unable to attain, thus enhancing their status (Veevers, 1974). Nevertheless, society has done little to discourage such people from becoming parents. Traditionally, the privacy of family life and the right of parents to make such decisions purely in terms of their own welfare have been sacrosanct. But the time has come to consider the effects of this **laissez faire** policy and to debate whether the practice of nonintervention may be unduly detrimental (Sawhill, 1977).

In any case, the childless marriage is becoming a viable option, at least among younger, more sophisticated individuals. Young couples who remain childless by choice appear relatively indifferent to the social pressures that beset them (Veevers, 1975). Yet many people are still appalled at such an irreversible commitment to remain childless, especially by couples who have been married only a brief time or are still young. The same persons, observed Veevers, almost never pause to consider that having a child is also an irreversible decision, unless the parents decide to put the child out for adoption or to commit infanticide.

The decision when to have children. Couples who do want children prefer to have them at convenient times. Ordinarily, all a couple's children are born to mothers in their 20s. And during this century the average length of time between first marriage and the birth of the last child has been 10.4 years. The median age of females at first marriage has averaged 20.9 years, and the median age of mothers when the first child was born has varied between 21.5 and 23.5 years. Meanwhile, the mother's median age when the last child was born has declined from a high of 32.9 years to 29.6 years (Glick, 1977) (see Table 8-3).

Table 8-3. Median Age of Mothers at Selected Stages of the Family Life Cycle

Stage of the Family Life Cycle	80-Year Average	*Period of Birth of Mother*							
		1880's	1890's	1900's	1910's	1920's	1930's	1940's	1950's
		Approximate Period of First Marriage							
		1900's	1910's	1920's	1930's	1940's	1950's	1960's	1970's
Median age at:									
First marriage	20.9	21.4	21.2	21.0	21.4	20.7	20.0	20.5	21.2
Birth of first child	22.6	23.0	22.9	22.8	23.5	22.7	21.4	21.8	22.7
Birth of last child	31.3	32.9	32.0	31.0	32.0	31.5	31.2	30.1	29.6
Marriage of last child	53.5	55.4	54.8	53.0	53.2	53.2	53.6	52.7	52.3
Death of one spouse	62.8	57.0	59.6	62.3	63.7	64.4	65.1	65.1	65.2
Difference between age at first marriage and:									
Birth of first child	1.7	1.6	1.7	1.8	2.1	2.0	1.4	1.3	1.5
Birth of last child	10.4	11.5	10.8	10.0	10.6	10.8	11.2	9.6	8.4
Marriage of last child	32.6	34.0	33.6	32.0	31.8	32.5	33.6	32.2	31.1
Death of one spouse	41.9	35.6	38.4	41.3	42.3	43.7	45.1	44.6	44.0
Difference between:									
Age at birth of first and last children	8.7	9.9	9.1	8.2	8.5	8.8	9.8	8.3	6.9
Age at birth of and marriage of last child	22.2	22.5	22.8	22.0	21.2	21.7	22.4	22.6	22.7
Age at marriage of last child and death of one spouse (empty nest)	9.3	1.6	4.8	9.3	10.5	11.2	11.5	12.4	12.9

In any case, age 35 brings into view the "biological boundary," when the woman foresees the end of her childbearing years not far ahead. The childless woman has to face that she must have a child soon or never have one. The largest number of single-person adoptions are by women between the ages 35 and 39 (Sheehy, 1976).

Only in comparatively recent years have briefer intervals between births become the trend in Western societies. During much of human history, breast feeding served to control the spacing of births, "for lactation, together with physical activity and a low sugar and carbohydrate diet, kept body fat low enough to prevent **ovulation** [emphasis added], and hence to assure a child-spacing of three or more years, the number depending on the cultural norms that govern the duration of breast feeding" (Rossi, 1977, p. 20). Because of our enriched diets, however, lactation no longer serves to delay ovulation. In addition, breast feeding has become the exception rather than the rule. These factors, along with parents' desire to space children closely and to have done with child rearing, have introduced a source of stress both to mothers and to children. Such closely spaced births place an undue strain on the mother, both physically and emotionally. And children spaced closely together experience greater jealousies.

Problems associated with child rearing. Even the best of parents experience problems with their children, partly because they become unduly anxious about their responsibilities, feeling responsible for whatever happens to the child. Thus,

> Every childish caper becomes a crisis and a threat to the parents' self-image. Given this illusion of **omnipotence** [emphasis added] they set about manipulating the child, with the aim of creating a perfect individual. . . .
> Parents also have the problem of adjusting to their children, the quality of which adjustment, in turn, affects the child. [For example, by preempting the mother's affections the child can alienate the father, who may then ignore or behave negatively toward the child. . . .]
> Whatever the parents' feelings about their roles, these roles will change subtly over time. When the children are small and helpless, some parents gain satisfaction from their dependency. Inevitably, however, children come to depend on their parents less and less, sometimes making them feel rejected. And since children change more than parents do, the parents' adjustment may be the more difficult one [Rogers, 1977a, p. 361].

Parenthood is not automatically rewarding. Sometimes there is a "crisis of parenthood" that results in considerable problems of social adjustment (LeMasters, 1957). Most first-time parents are somewhat awkward and unskilled in caring for the baby. They often become exhausted from lack of sleep. They must adapt their daily schedules, revise their division of labor, and otherwise reorganize their lives to accommodate the baby's needs.

Some parents often unwittingly dehumanize the child-rearing process. Parental work time is so valuable, alternative attractions are so varied, and modern life's demands on time are so complex that many parents simply deliver their children to day-care centers, buy them records and books, or sit with them in front of television sets instead of singing, talking, or reading to them.

Young adults should be made aware of such hazards and either avoid parenthood or prepare for it properly. Unfortunately, most people have had very little training along this line. In one study more than half the teenagers questioned believed it was all right to spank a 1-year-old for dropping or throwing things. And fewer than a third realized that a lack of love during the 1st year can be damaging for a child. Better training for parenthood is needed on the high school level and in adult educational programs, for both fathers and mothers (Horn, P., 1975).

The young mother's role. Despite such problems, all but 7% of women want to marry and have children. Yet women's self-esteem is higher when they have no children (Sorensen, 1973). By contrast, men's self-esteem is higher when children are present (Bortner & Hultsch, 1974). The young mother's problem is not role conflict—she believes she should be at home—but work overload and isolation in the home. Even if day-care facilities are available, they are typically planned and justified on the basis of developing the child's potential, not for the purpose of helping the employed woman (Roby, 1973). Mothers may also become unduly anxious about how well they are performing their role, because society holds them primarily responsible for their children's upbringing. As a result, they may become anxious, even resentful, regarding their role.

The father's role. Only recently have fathers begun receiving the attention they deserve. Their role has come to be recognized as dependent somewhat on the amount of time they spend at home and their own interpretations and transactions of that role. Fathers interviewed about their first newborn described their baby in great detail, often saying the infant resembled them (Greenberg & Morris, 1974). They enjoyed looking at, holding, and playing with it. Some were even delighted that the baby appeared alive and believed that its opening its eyes in their presence indicated a need to communicate with them. The majority had already established a bond with the newborn during the first 3 days, some of them even earlier.

In the years that follow, middle-class, college-educated fathers, especially, take their parenting role very seriously. They have absorbed enough of the literature on child-rearing to believe that fatherhood constitutes both an obligation and a privilege. Especially as young mothers are reentering the work world in greater numbers, often when the children are still small, fathers are sharing increasingly in the care for children.

The Young Singles

General information about singles. Singles' life-styles are distinctively different—but who are the singles? Stein (1975) defined them as those not currently married or involved in an exclusive homosexual or heterosexual relationship. However, they are defined here as those who are legally single. Their alternatives include couples living together, whether heterosexual or homosexual, single parents, single individuals living alone, and groups living communally.

As implied above, singlehood exists for varied reasons. There are more single-parent families nowadays because of higher rates of divorce, separation, and premarital childbearing (Glick, 1977). Many young people are also delaying marriage. Young women, in particular, may ultimately decide not to marry at all. By age 30, women not yet married are beginning to acquire considerable economic independence and to invest more of themselves in their work. They also take advantage of sources of social and personal satisfaction in many areas other than family and marriage (Adams, 1974). Young women tend to have far more intimate same-sex friendships than men (Hacker, 1981).

Living arrangements. Formerly, most individuals remained with their parents until they themselves got married. Today, however, 25% of males and 17% of females, aged 18 to 24, live in households alone or with roommates or live in group quarters, such as army barracks or dormitories.

Because women marry earlier than men, there are more young single male adults. Of young men aged 18 to 24, over two-thirds lived with their families in 1940; but fewer than half that age group were in their parental homes in 1970. In 1970 a quarter of the 18- to 24-year-old males were living apart from the family, as compared with 16% in 1940. In fact, singles of both sexes are living outside the family in growing numbers, usually alone. An individual who is neither a child nor a spouse is unlikely to live with relatives. Living within a family is most typical of the childhood and marriage years.

Alternative Life-Styles

Major categories. The young-married and single life-styles are most common; a smaller number of couples live together in a quasi-familial relationship without marriage (Carter & Glick, 1976). This small fraction may engage in variant or experimental marriages and families, including single-parent households, dual-career couples with or without children, cohabitating heterosexual couples, swinging or swapping sexual relationships outside marriage, and others. Participants in such variant relationships ordinarily do not regard them as so permanent as do partners in traditional nuclear families. Rather, they expect them to last only as long as they afford benefits for their members (Cogswell, 1975).

One widely publicized arrangement is the commune, in which the excessively intense relationships and loneliness of nuclear families can be countered to some extent by collective living arrangements. Marciano (1975) depicted communes as resembling monastic retreat houses, or places where people can go for reintegration, renewal, or fresh experiences during certain phases of life. Some young couples use communal households as halfway houses between the time they marry and when their first child arrives.

Children seem to fare well in communes, where they are treated as individuals and persons in their own right, with both privileges and responsibilities.

However, child custody may be denied parents who engage in communal life-styles. Consider the wife who moved into a **Synanon** community with her month-old daughter. It was based on efforts to rehabilitate former heroin addicts but also included many non-drug-addict residents. Later on, after she filed for divorce, she lost custody of her daughter, because the court questioned the commune's worth as a home (Weisberg, 1975).

Cohabitation. There is some evidence that, for certain groups, living together for extended periods of time is replacing the simple premarital explorations of a generation ago (Silverman, 1974). Cohabitating couples tend not to come from families that are radical in either their ideologies or life-styles. However, the couples themselves are usually somewhat liberal in sexual norms, religious beliefs, and political ideologies and less conforming than are most people (Croake, Keller, & Catlin, 1974). Nevertheless, the women typically perform the traditionally female tasks, even though 40% of one sample said that they shared mealtime chores (Kieffer, 1972).

SUMMARY AND COMMENT

Young adulthood involves a variety of significant tasks, including leaving adolescence behind, developing intimacy, getting married, defining one's commitments, launching a vocation, and making satisfactory progress toward life goals. Men and, increasingly, women take their vocational careers seriously and want their jobs to provide not only economic security but also opportunity for personal growth. Young adults are beginning to take their leisure lives seriously, too, although child care and jobs limit their discretionary time.

In order to establish hierarchies among the demands made upon them, young adults rely on their values, which evolve somewhat, though remaining basically the same. In general, they place a high value on love and their own personal development. But men, especially, are also committed to getting ahead in the world, to a degree they may later deplore. As they take stock in later years, they may regret having not committed themselves to more basic values.

Young adults' values become reflected in their varied interpretations of sex roles. Women may combine elements of the traditional male and female roles, become role innovators seeking a new status for women, or conform to the traditional stereotype of the domesticated auxiliary to husband and children. Still others are diffused, or uncertain, about their roles.

Men's roles complement women's and have also changed in certain ways. The better educated, at least, reject the macho role in favor of becoming more rounded and expressive persons. Nevertheless, both sexes want some sex differences to remain. Unfortunately, males still feel called on to prove their masculinity in ways that women secretly deplore and that men themselves dislike.

With regard to life-styles, or overall patterns of activities, all but a few young adults still choose marriage and family life. Within the family they find security and a haven within a complex world. Yet, after the bloom of the early marriage years has faded, many unions dissolve in divorce. The problem is not usually a careless unconcern for marital ties but recognition that their current relationship has soured, often because of the wife's preoccupation with child rearing and the husband's with his career.

The middle and working classes share the same marital satisfactions and problems, although their life-styles differ somewhat. Working-class adults grew up with more limited advantages and goals, and the young women, especially, married young to escape parental domination. Often, however, they simply traded one set of problems for another as children arrived and monetary problems persisted.

Married couples of all social classes must decide whether to have children and how to space them. While the vast majority desires children, a still small but growing minority elects to remain childless because of various attractive alternatives. More-traditional people still believe it a duty for married couples to have children; but childless marriage is becoming an increasingly acceptable option.

Even the most devoted parents encounter problems during the course of childrearing. Mothers, especially, become anxious about how well they are discharging their role. Fathers are taking their parental role more seriously and, as their wives move into the work world, assuming more of the child-care chores. Eventually, young parents muddle through their parental crises very well and, as they emerge into middle age, come to appreciate their **progeny** as persons.

The lifestyle of single young adults is distinctively different from that of the young marrieds, as they seek satisfaction in areas other than family. They either live alone or with other singles with similar interests and status.

Some young adults, both single and married, adopt less traditional life-styles, at least for a time. Such alternatives include living in a commune, maintaining a single-parent household, and cohabiting, unmarried, with a member of the other sex. Most participants in such alternatives view them as temporary but feel they have profited from the experience. Children in single-parent households fare much better than generally expected, and children in communes often reap benefits unavailable in the nuclear family.

SUGGESTED READING

Bolton, E. B. A conceptual analysis of the mentor relationship in the career development of women. *Adult Education*, 1980, 30(4), 195–207. This analysis of the mentor relationship as one aspect of women's career development and social learning, deals with the modeling process and the mentor relationship as aspects of social learning. Mentor relationships are discussed in terms of both sexes, and reasons are suggested for the current lack of mentor.

Chellam, G. Intergenerational affinities: Symmetrical life experiences of the young adults and the aging in Canadian society. *International Journal of Aging and Human Development*, 1980-81, 12(2), 79–92. The theory is examined that adolescent-young adults (ages 15 to 24) resemble the young-old (ages 65 to 75) in terms of "psycho-social propensities" and "social location."

Cherlin, A. Postponing marriage: The influence of young women's work expectations. *Journal of Marriage and the Family*, 1980, (42)(2), 355–365. This study of reasons that some women plan to postpone marriage suggests that future career plans influence such postponement. The implications of this and other aspects of the transition to marriage are discussed.

Clarke-Stewart, K. A. Popular primers for parents. *American Psychologist*, 1978, 33(4), 359–369. The characteristics and reactions of readers of child-care books are analyzed in terms of demographic factors, the context of social conditions that helps to produce interest in such books, and the quality of the advice that is offered.

Cosby, A. G., Thomas, J. K., & Falk, W. W. Patterns of early adult status attainment and attitudes in the nonmetropolitan South. *Sociology of Work and Occupations*, 1976, 3(4), 411–428. A study in the Deep South indicates that youth's aspirations for future employment were unrealistic in terms of available opportunities and only marginally related to current attainments. Both White and Black students were unduly optimistic.

Daniels, P., & Weingarten, K. Postponing parenthood. *Savvy*, 1980, 1(5), 55–60. Interviews with 72 couples in three generations who had their children either early (at age 22 or younger) or later (at age 28 or older) in the life cycle indicated that there is no best time to have children, but that lengthy postponement may produce something of a crisis in the late 30s.

Ebaugh, H. R. F., & Haney, C. A. Shifts in abortion attitudes: 1972–1978. *Journal of Marriage and the Family*, 1980, 42(3), 491–499. In the United States attitudes toward abortion became increasingly liberalized from the 1960s until about 1975 when the trend assumed a slightly more conservative direction. These changes seem to be functions of selected demographic variables.

Edwards, J. N., & Booth, A. The cessation of marital intercourse. *American Journal of Psychiatry*, 1976, 133(11), 1333–1336. Even among young married couples intercourse is not always taken for granted. In a sampling of 365 young adults who had been married an average of 11 years, about a third had not experienced marital coitus in about two months.

Fein, R. A. Men's entrance to parenthood. *Family Coordinator*, 1976, 25(4), 341–348. Interviews of 30 husbands who attended childbirth-preparation classes before and after the birth of their first child. The interviews suggest the need for more adequate research into men's preparation for parenting, their involvement in the birth process, and ways they can participate more effectively in family life.

Galinsky, E. *Between Generations: The Six Stages of Parenthood*. New York Times Books, 1980. On the basis of interviews with 228 parents from varied backgrounds, a psychologist derives a theory of parental growth based on changes in the parents' self-images. Parents are portrayed as going through six stages, somewhat defined by the age of the child, and as being at several parental stages simultaneously when their children are of different ages.

Glick, P. C., & Spanier, G. B. Married and unmarried cohabitation in the United States. *Journal of Marriage and the Family*, 1980, 42(1), 19–30. A profile of married and unmarried cohabitation in the United States, presented along with demographic factors that differentiate men and women in such alternative living arrangements.

Gordon, H. A., & Kammeyer, K. C. W. The gainful employment of women with small children. *Journal of Marriage and the Family*, 1980, 42(2), 327–336. An analysis of effects of employment of mothers of small children, based on data from the second stage of a longitudinal study of 735 women, disclosed variables that encourage such women to enter or leave the labor force.

Griffore, R. J. Toward the use of child development research in informed parenting. *Journal of Clinical Psychology*, 1980, 9(1), 48–51. An analysis of popular books on child rearing and their potential effects on parental practice suggested that parents might benefit more from effectively presented knowledge about child development.

Henderson, C. Living the simple life. *Human Resource Management*, 1977, *16*(3), 23–29. A review of relevant writings and research indicates that the United States may be slowly shifting from its emphasis on consumption and economic growth to simpler life-styles, preservation of resources, and protection of the environment. While about half of all Americans approve of such values, only a small minority so far practices them. The trend is away from a materialistically oriented culture to a satisfying, simple life-style, psychologically instead of materially oriented.

Hogan, D. P. The transition to adulthood as a career contingency. *American Sociological Review*, April 1980, *45*, 261–276. The hypothesis that men who order their life transition events in a non-normative fashion achieve less than average occupational status and earnings was tested on a population of 18,370 white males, ages 20 to 65.

Jaffe, S. S., & Viertel, J. *Becoming Parents: Preparing for the Emotional Changes of First-time Parenthood*. New York: Atheneum, 1980. Inteviews with 12 young adults, held before the birth of the child, a week after its birth, and at 3-month intervals during the child's first year, disclosed no single pattern, except the finding that the child helps the parents to achieve maturity.

Kressel, K. Patterns of coping in divorce and some implications for clinical practice. *Family Relations*, 1980, *29*(2), 234–240. Characteristic patterns of response to the stresses of divorce are described, based on a 3-year research project on the social-psychological aspects of divorce and recent studies of the divorcing process. Also considered are implications for clinical practice, including the therapist's role in the decision-making process and forms of assistance advised.

Leahy, R. L., & Eiter, M. Moral judgment and the development of real and ideal androgynous self-image during adolescence and young adulthood. *Developmental Psychology*, 1980, *16*(4), 362–370. A study of 116 individuals at ages 13, 17, and 20, disclosed an increasing appreciation of feminine characteristics. College-age females preferred more masuculine than feminine traits, whereas younger ones indicated no preference.

London, P. The intimacy gap. *Psychology Today*, 1978, *11*(12), 40–45. Old patterns of intimacy in friendship, love affairs, and marriage are perceived as emerging and sexual values as changing among the sexual revolution's "laboratory generation." The young adults (under age 35) are compared with older generations in terms of their needs, attitudes, and behaviors.

Marasco, M. J. Childbirth: Issues and trends. *Family Life*, January & February 1980, *XL*(1), 2–10. Several authorities committed to the practice of prepared childbirth are interviewed on major issues surrounding the topic and on the matter of adjustment to the newborn.

Miller, B. C., & Sollie, D. L. Normal stresses during the transition to parenthood. *Family Relations*, 1980, *29*(4), 459–465. The longitudinal study reported here was designed to determine how and to what extent personal and marital stresses increased or declined before and after the first child arrived. Parents' own modes of adaptation are compared with coping strategies recommended in the literature.

Parelius, A. P. Change and stability in college women's orientations toward education, family, and work. *Social Problems*, 1975, *22*(3), 420–432. A comparison of college women students in 1969 and in 1973 indicates that the more recent subjects were more feminist than the earlier ones in general attitudes toward sexual equality. Both groups were strongly committed to marriage and motherhood. Yet more of the 1974 students anticipated a "double-track" career/homemaking pattern, and fewer expected to interrupt their careers for child rearing.

YOUNG ADULTHOOD

235

Perrucci, C. C. Gender and achievement: The early careers of college graduates. *Sociological Focus*, 1980, *13*(2), 99–111. Longitudinal data from a national sampling of college graduates indicate relationships of sex and grades to level of achievement in young adulthood.

Rossi, A. S. The biosocial side of parenthood. *Human Nature*, 1978, *1*(6), 72–79. A sociologist argues that men and women should play distinctively different roles as parents because of basic differences in their biology. Otherwise, the quality of marital relationships and child rearing will suffer, the author contends.

Scanzoni, J. H. *Sex roles, life styles, and childbearing*, New York: Free Press, 1975. Sex-role norms are examined in terms of their influence on decisions to have or not to have children. Children themselves are viewed as involving costs and rewards, especially for women.

Singh, B. K. Trends in attitudes toward premarital sexual relations. *Journal of Marriage and the Family*, 1980, *42*(2), 387–393. Data from five national surveys indicated that approval of premarital sex relations increased in the 1970s and that differences in views of segments of the population had narrowed. Implications of this trend are considered with regard to such matters as pregnancy and abortion.

9
THE MIDDLE YEARS

INTRODUCTION

Definition and Significance

Middle age defined. Although the term *middle age* is used frequently, it cannot easily be defined. Chronologically, middle age is usually interpreted as beginning sometime in the early 40s and lasting until 65, when retirement normally begins. In the biological sense no initial marker exists, although the climacteric might be judged to herald its conclusion. In the sociocultural sense, middle age is defined in terms of one's social roles after the family-making and status-seeking functions have stabilized. It ends on retirement. Phenomenologically, middle age is a matter of how people perceive themselves. Many people viewed as "young-old" by society still look on themselves as middle-aged.

Divisions, dimensions, and variations. In research by Neugarten and associates, middle-aged people in a Midwestern city saw adulthood as comprising four main periods, each with its distinctive behavior patterns: young adulthood, maturity, middle age, and old age (Neugarten & Peterson, 1957). This progression, in turn, involved five basic dimensions: health and physical vigor, the career line, the family cycle, psychological attributes ("Middle age is when you become mellow"), and social obligations ("old age is when you take things easy and let others do the worrying") (p. 44).

Interpretations of middle age vary according to social class and sex. In the upper middle class, middle age is ordinarily experienced as a stage of major reward and great productivity, the prime of life. For blue-collar workers, middle age arrives earlier and is often perceived in terms of decline such as growing physical weakness, slowing down, or turning into a has-been (Neugarten & Peterson, 1957).

Issues and Roles

Still others define middle age in terms of issues and roles. Peck (1968) perceived the middle years as involving four developmental issues that must be resolved if good adjustment is to ensue. An individual must come to value intellectual activities, seek social relations free of sexual connotations, maintain flexible social investments, and value new experiences.

Certain middle-age issues pertain to new family roles—for example, assuming responsibility for aging parents and defining the boundaries of authority and relationships between self, parents, and children. Middle age also brings the personalization of death, in that more of one's loved ones begin to die. For women there is the "rehearsal for motherhood" and for men "the rehearsal for illness" (Neugarten, 1977, p. 638).

The Tasks of Middle Age

General tasks. Middle age carries its own characteristic tasks, one being the broadening of emotional and friendship ties beyond the immediate family (Gould, 1975). Middle age also requires increased responsibility, judgment, and perspective. The middle-aged adult must be responsible both for younger and older adults, exercise authority, and overcome such youthful excesses as over-conformity, rebelliousness, and impulsiveness. Moderately decreased biological capabilities may be offset by enhanced psychosocial capacities to contribute to society in numerous ways.

Variations by sex. Middle age poses different developmental tasks for the sexes. Women must adapt to their growing children's autonomy and departure from home and, sometimes, to reemployment outside the home. In some cases they are left widowed or must cope with the daylong presence of husbands who retire early. For both sexes, a conscious reorientation toward others and life outside the home begins. The couple may come closer to each other than before the children left home. Or, after years of having been held together because of the children, they may now decide to call it quits. In any case, now that their minds are no longer consumed with the task of child rearing, both parents more realistically assess their own lives. While children regard the future as vague and practically limitless, the mid-life reassessment produces the realization that life and time have definite limits.

Levinson (1977) derived his theory of adult male development—and tasks—from biographical data obtained from 40 men aged 35 to 45 representing four occupational groups. The information was obtained in several interviews and a follow-up session two years later.

1. Leaving the family constitutes the bridge between adolescence and the adult world.
2. Getting into the adult world, which extends from the early 20s to age 27 to 29, is concerned with developing an initial life structure, entering an occupation, and tackling the ego-stage issue of intimacy versus aloneness.
3. The age-30 transition, which embraces 4 to 6 years, affords a chance to identify the provisional first structure performed in the 20s.
4. Settling down extends from the early 30s to age 39 to 41 and involves the development of a second, more stable framework for the early adult life. Efforts are directed toward becoming one's own person.
5. The mid-life transition spans the gap between early and middle adulthood and involves a reappraisal of the life structure of the late 30s, a rediscovery of certain neglected aspects of the self, and choices for developing a new life construct.
6. Restabilization, which takes place during the mid-40s, becomes a time for establishing a living within a first provisional framework for middle adult-hood.

Characteristics of Middle Agers

Here are some of the words and phrases that young adults named as descriptive of adults: *mature, knowledged, intelligent, disciplined, independent, responsible, grown, big, all-knowing, caring, working, routinized, reserved, hurried, prime of life, and competent.* The characteristic most often mentioned suggested a picture of people who are responsible, mature, intelligent, and self-controlled. There was no suggestion that people at this stage have fun or excitement.

Personality traits. People do not assume a succession of new personalities as they progress through their life stages. Personality characteristics at any point are the result of interactions between genetic potential and all of life's experiences to date. Nevertheless, roles shared by people at particular age stages tend to suppress certain behavioral tendencies and to enhance others. The increasing mellowness of many persons in their late 40s reflects a sense of relaxation and growing freedom from the pressures of child rearing and vocational competition. At this age they concentrate on what they have achieved to date, and they no longer sense the urgency of their 30s (Gould, 1975).

Certain popular concepts of the middle aged are false. For example, contrary to popular opinion, people do not inevitably grow more conventional and traditional as they grow older. Unconventional thinking is one of the most stable characteristics from earlier to later years, as indeed are the related characteristics of rebelliousness and sex-typed behaviors (Haan & Day, 1974).

The middle-aged do not become as passive as sometimes believed. A study of recalled dreams by 58 well-educated men, ages 27 to 64 indicated that there was a slight age-related decline of aggression and dreams. Otherwise, dreams demonstrated no middle-age change toward greater passivity or lower ego energy (Zepelin, 1980–81).

Sex differences in mastery motive. A certain degree of sex reversal also occurs with regard to the mastery motive. Middle-aged men are moving toward interpersonal commitments, whereas middle-aged women are seeking greater self-assertion. However, women may lack adequate opportunities for self-realization (Lowenthal, 1975). Both sexes express a need for commitment in areas other than those to which traditional sex roles have confined them, thus supporting Jung's hypothesis that the second half of life compensates for what was missed in the first (Jung, 1960). In order to arrive at Erikson's final stage of integrity, conjectured Lowenthal (1977), an individual must feel fulfilled with regard to both mastery and interpersonal commitments.

Morals and Values

Developmental changes in moral judgment. Apparently, moral judgment does not progress in straight-line fashion from lesser to greater maturity. Rather, the pattern of moral judgment becomes semistructured during college days, ambiguous during the 20s, semistructured again in the early 30s, ambiguous again in the late 30s and early 40s, and semistructured again in the late 40s and 50s. The semistructured egalitarianism of the early 30s suggests an effort at establishing one's selfhood. The ambiguous period of the late 30s and early 40s may represent a compromise between generativity and stagnation, which gives rise to the virtues of production and care, as well as a certain authoritarianism, sometimes because of revived encounters with adolescent sons and daughters. In the late 40s and 50s a semistructured egalitarianism is recovered, reflecting some resolution of matters of self-concept. In other words, the 50s represent the true beginnings of maturity, or a favorable ratio between ego integrity and despair, from which arise the basic virtues of renunciation and wisdom (Erikson, 1950).

Table 9-1 shows how value themes vary at different life stages.

Table 9-1. Value Dilemmas at Various Life Stages.

Life-Cycle Stage; Approximate Ages or Timing	Major Dilemma of Value-Theme Differentiation and Integration		
	Security	*vs.*	*Challenge*
I. Infancy 0-12 months	affective gratification	vs.	sensorimotor experiencing
II. Early childhood 1-2 years	compliance	vs.	self-control
III. Oedipal period 3-5 years	expressivity	vs.	instrumentality
IV. Later childhood 6-11 years	peer relationships	vs.	evaluated abilities
V. Early adolescence 12-15 years	acceptance	vs.	achievement
VI. Later adolescence 16-18/20 years	intimacy	vs.	autonomy
VII. Young adulthood or youth 19/21-29 years	connection	vs.	self-determination
VIII. Early maturity 30-44 years	stability	vs.	accomplishment
IX. Full maturity 45 to age of retirement	dignity	vs.	control
X. Retirement retirement age to onset of severe illness	meaningful integration	vs.	autonomy
XI. Disability onset of severe illness to death	survival	vs.	acceptance of death

From "Role and value development across the life cycle," by C. Gordon. In *Role: Sociological Studies IV,* by J. W. Jackson (Ed.). Copyright 1971 by Cambridge University Press. Reprinted by permission.

Influences on moral judgment. Family is a more important influence on moral judgment than age. On such matters young adults and their middle-aged parents are more similar than are people of the same generation. Moreover, the similarity is about the same regardless of the sex and social class of those involved (Troll, 1975).

Education relates little to morality in adulthood. In a study of adults representing stages throughout the life span, moral development proved not to have been significantly influenced by educational attainment. Apparently, older people compensate for a lack of education by what they learn from experience and hence catch up with the higher moral levels manifested by college students. Only the very oldest persons demonstrate a decline in moral level compared with other adult groups (Bielby & Papalia, 1975).

PHYSICAL CHARACTERISTICS OF MIDDLE AGE

Age Changes

In the mid-life years the body begins losing its reserve capacity. Common physical changes can be summarized as follows:

1. The heart at age 40 pumps about 23 liters of blood a minute under stress, as compared with 40 liters at age 20.
2. Sexual capacity declines, the prostate enlarges, and bladder problems begin to appear.
3. The chest decreases in order to compensate for the weakening of the diaphragm.
4. The kidneys lose a certain reserve capacity for concentrated waste.
5. The gastrointestinal tract secretes fewer enzymes, increasing indigestion and constipation.
6. Hearing acuity declines and eye lenses gradually lose elasticity. Poor vision is increasingly common after age 45, especially among women. While the losses are small and gradual, they convey "an emphatic message of human mortality" (Schanche, 1973).
7. It is generally agreed that maximal strength for most muscle groups is reached between the ages of 25 and 30. During maturity, strength decreases slowly, with the decline being somewhat faster after age 50. Even at age 60, however, the total decrement does not ordinarily exceed 10 to 20% of maximum.
8. The fatigue rate is significantly greater among older persons (DeVries, 1977).

Incidence of Accidents and Disease

With regard to the most common acute illnesses, respiratory ailments account for 72 out of 100 cases by age 45 and 46% after age 65. Second come accidental injuries, accounting for 21 and 16 of each 100 episodes among middle-aged and older people, respectively. The third most common acute condition is diseases of the digestive tract (Hendricks & Hendricks, 1976).

With regard to death among both middle-aged and older people, heart diseases, cancer, and **cerebrovascular** lesions, especially strokes, are the most common causes, collectively accounting for about 70% of deaths among those over 45. Over 40% of fatalities come directly from heart disease alone. Among the middle aged, violent deaths from accidents, suicides, and homicides claim a significant number. For older persons these causes are fewer than those resulting from diminished physiological defenses (Hendricks & Hendricks, 1976).

After age 30 the cardiac output declines at the rate of about 1% a year, the result being a loss in reserve capacity and in the heart's ability to respond rapidly under stress (Freeman, 1965). Cardiac degeneration among the middle aged is characterized by slow decay of the heart muscles. Both functional and structural changes occur that eventually produce tissue death in the muscle.

Even when they are not fatal, heart diseases are incapacitating; and about 20% of all the disabilities of middle-aged men and 15% of those of middle-aged women derive from heart problems (Hendricks & Hendricks, 1976). After a heart attack has occurred, survivors' ability to make a comeback depends somewhat on their personal security and relationships with significant others (Croogl, 1968). Despite a small, recent decline, middle-aged American men have about one chance in five of developing **cardiovascular** problems before retirement, and the incidence is three times greater than among middle-aged females.

Arthritis and rheumatism occur among about half the middle aged and four-fifths of those in their 70s, and the incidence is higher for women in later years and great old age (Hendricks & Hendricks, 1976). The highest incidence of fatal cancers occurs between ages 40 to 60, more often among women in the younger years and men in the older ones.

Selected Health Problems and Concerns

Teeth. While a wide variety of health problems exists, only selected ones will be discussed here, each of special importance at middle age. One of these, dental problems, is exceptionally common from middle age on. While improved care may upgrade dental health in the future, a quarter to a half of today's middle-aged and older people have lost all their teeth. Among these, about three-fourths of the middle aged and over half of the elderly have dentures. Among 45- to 64-year-olds, slightly fewer than half the permanent teeth still remain; and among people 65 to 79 an average of 25 teeth are missing (Hendricks & Hendricks, 1976).

Nutrition. It is estimated that middle-aged men and women should at most use about 2400 and 1700 calories a day, respectively. Each decade after this time this amount should be reduced by about 7 to 10%, for a total reduction of over a third between ages 55 and 70 (Hendricks & Hendricks, 1976). Meantime, a proper balance of protein and carbohydrates and essential minerals and vitamins is critical. While almost 40% of younger people exceed the required consumption of protein each day, older people do not eat enough (Hendricks & Hendricks, 1976).

A wit once remarked that adulthood is when one quits growing at the end and begins growing in the middle. In North America overweight is a common problem, especially in middle age and to a lesser extent in old age, because of the shorter life span of the obese. Freeman (1965) concluded that an average of 4 years could be added to life expectancy at birth if food overindulgence could be prevented. As mentioned above, middle-aged men and women should consume 2400 and 1700 calories a day, respectively. Yet the average food consumption in the United States is about 3300 calories. In contrast, in sections of Kashmir and the Caucasus, where unusual longevity is common, the average daily food consumption is between 1200 and 1900 calories (Leaf, 1973).

Smoking. Cigarette smoking is a major factor in cancer and probably in pulmonary deficiencies, cerebrovascular disease, and coronary heart ailments. Hence, the chance of coronary heart disease is about 70% greater among smokers than nonsmokers, with two-thirds of smokers dying earlier than they might otherwise. In fact, on the average, cigarette smokers die a decade earlier than otherwise comparable nonsmokers; and for men in their 60s smoking is the single best predictor of remaining life expectancy (Granich, 1972).

Heavy coffee drinking. Coffee addiction, so common among adults, may produce heartburn but otherwise is harmless. After examining the coffee-consuming habits of 2350 adults in a rural Georgia County and the relative incidence of heart disease and other causes of death among them over 4½ years, Dr. Siegfried Heyden of Duke University reported no significant differences in death rates between high coffee consumers (five or more cups a day) and low consumers, who drank four or fewer cups a day. More diseases have been popularly attributed to coffee use than to alcohol and cigarette usage combined, observed Heyden. Yet studies linking coffee with bladder cancer, coronary heart disease, and other conditions often fail to take into account the amount of smoking ("In Your Cups? Okay, if It's Coffee," 1977).

Physical appearance. A neglected, but nevertheless important, aspect of physical status at middle age is appearance, a fact underscored by research. When 128 students were shown slides of men and women and asked to speculate about their personal characteristics, they judged the attractive persons to be more successful in their careers and social lives. They judged pretty women as richer, smarter, more successful, more intelligent, and better educated than unattractive ones; the "plain Janes" were judged to be happy homemakers (Bush, 1976).

In another study, Berscheid & Walster (1975) compared the happiness of middle agers with their earlier attractiveness as revealed in photographs from college days. Women who had been beautiful at that age were less happy than those who had been plainer, and the beauties were also less well adjusted and less well satisfied with their lives than were the plainer women. The men's happiness, on the other hand, appeared unrelated to attractiveness.

In conclusion, it seems that physical attractiveness does importantly affect one's life. "It helps shape personality, influences who will be friends, lovers and spouses, limits success in school and career, and may even affect the outcome of a trial. The better looking a person is, the easier life will be; but a plain face does not necessarily mean a miserable life" (Wilson & Nias, 1976, p. 103).

The climacteric. Another middle-age phenomenon, undoubtedly accentuated by changing physical self-image, is the climacteric, marked by hormonal imbalance in both sexes and also menopause in women. This phenomenon, which occurs in most individuals in their 40s and 50s, is signaled by menopause in women, by hair loss in men, and by weakened eyes in both sexes. For some individuals this period is one of maximum accomplishment; for others it is simply one of "depression and drift" (Bailey, 1976, p. 38). Note in soap operas and women's magazines

> the stereotypes of middle age: . . . . the bored housewife, children grown, neurotic about the hot flashes of menopause; the slowed-down business man who suddenly realizes he will never make vice president of the company; vanity panics in both sexes as paunches begin to protrude and the will to contain them recedes; a sudden sense of mortality and **existential** [emphasis added] futility, often accompanied by graceless chasing after sexual reassurances; drinking more and enjoying it less; lingering with the horror of the morning mirror [p. 38].

Kimmel (1974) cited evidence that the sexes are more alike in many functions, including sex, than was once believed. For example, it has been thought that a basic distinction between the sexes is that women have a monthly menstrual cycle involving

> periodic shifts in hormonal level, periodic times of fertility, and monthly menstruation, while men are constantly able to produce sperm and were thought to produce hormones at constant rates. To be sure, women's menstrual cycle is a uniquely female characteristic; but recent evidence has suggested that men may also experience cyclic fluctuations in hormone production [p. 139].

The research regarding the effect of menopause on women is somewhat conflicting. A study of 50 parous women 30 to 40 years old indicated mean premenstrual depression scores to be higher than those obtained at mid-cycle, but much lower than those of patients with psychiatric disorders (Golub, 1976). This presumed relationship between estrogen and behavioral change in middle age is commonly called the "menopausal syndrome." Among physicians themselves the belief is widespread that menopause in large measure accounts for physical and psychological stresses at this time. However, a review of the research casts serious doubt on this view. It suggests instead that "the menopausal syndrome" may simply be an artifact of the practice of taking clinical case histories and directing patients' attention to particular symptoms (Eisdorfer & Raskind, 1975). Men as well as women undergo fluctuations in mood.

Much of the disturbance that women ascribe to menopause may come from other sources. Menopause comes at a period in life when other crises often develop. A woman's parents may be getting old and creating problems for her. Her husband may need her help with crises in his own life. With her children about to leave home, she may be concerned about how she will spend the rest of her life.

Remediation and Prevention

Medical care and aids. By middle age many people become increasingly concerned about their health, taking varied assortments of productive and counterproductive approaches. Some adults monitor their health habits with a clear understanding of their long-term consequences. Many go for regular checkups to their physicians, in consequence often detecting incipient physical problems before they become serious.

Health "care" can produce highly negative results, however. Ivan Illich (1976) declared that the "hospitalization of America . . . turns sucklings into babies, puberty into a critical stage, adulthood into a constant multiple patienthood always dependent on specialists" (p. 66). He referred to three types of **iatrogenesis,** or doctor-caused disease: clinical, social, and cultural. Clinical iatrogenesis comprises "those clinical conditions that are created by the remedies or medicines administered by physicians and hospitals" (p. 66). He cited, especially, unnecessary surgery—for example, 90% of tonsillectomies—as well as the "sickening side-effect of medicines." In fact,

> Every 24 to 36 hours, from 50% to 80% of adults in the United States and the United Kingdom swallow a medically prescribed chemical. Some, like **thalidomide,** [emphasis added], tranquilizers, and probably birth control pills, have long-term effects that may be disastrous. Some drugs are addictive, antibiotics alter the normal bacterial flora, and often induce a super infection [p. 66].*

Illich acknowledged that chemotherapy has helped to reduce mortality from infectious diseases such as scarlet fever, syphilis, and pneumonia and that immunization has reduced the incidence of measles, whooping cough, and

*From "Medicine is a major threat to health," by I. Illich with S. Keen. In *Psychology Today,* 1976, 9(12), 66–77. This and all other quotations from this source are reprinted by permission of the author.

polio. But he questioned the contribution of medicine to treating noninfectious diseases. He attributed the reduction in mortality rate from such diseases to a better environment, including cleaner water, sewage treatment, better working conditions, better nutrition, and better housing. Illich also deplored the dramatically rising costs of medical care, so that 5 to 7 weeks of the average worker's earnings each year are required to pay for medical services. This situation enhances stress, thereby increasing illness. Modern medicine has succeeded in creating patient roles, and patients are being converted into "passive consumers, objects to be repaired, voyeurs of their own treatment [sapping] the will of people to suffer their own reality. It destroys our autonomous ability to cope with our own bodies and heal ourselves" (p. 75).

Nutrition and exercise. Middle agers' growing concern for proper nutrition and adequate exercise is encouraging. Despite a plethora of ill-advised diets, adults are growing more knowledgeable about what constitutes a balanced diet. Regular exercise is equally important, because of commonly sedentary life-styles. In a study of 36 men aged 40 to 58 who were at high risk of coronary heart disease, improvement of physical fitness produced no change in adjustment, self-confidence, or body image; but it did decrease feelings of anxiety and depression (Folkins, 1976). For all people, exercise is important for preservation of sound physical health.

This winner of 60 sports trophies symbolizes women's growing interest in athletics.

EMOTIONAL HEALTH

Factors Relating to Emotional Health

Physical Conditions. All the physical disorders discussed above take their toll on the emotions. And as such ailments grow more frequent and sometimes chronic, anxieties deepen, and attention focuses more on the self. Among subjects aged 45 to 69, who were randomly selected from lists of a health-insurance association, self-ratings of health proved the single strongest factor in life satisfaction. The second most important was activity in organizations (Palmore & Luikart, 1972). Certain factors frequently presumed to relate to life satisfaction, such as marital status and age, actually related little if any. Even such life crises as widowhood related little to life satisfaction, at least during middle age (Noberini & Neugarten, 1975).

In a follow-up of this sample, longitudinal research disclosed that earlier life satisfaction was the best predictor of present life satisfaction. For those whose life satisfaction changed, the most significant causal factors were self-rated health, sexual enjoyment, social contacts, and employment (Palmore & Kivett, 1975). Hence, activity in itself appears to be a poor predictor of life satisfaction during middle age. Feelings of life satisfaction and the relationship between satisfaction and social interaction apparently increase with age.

Heavy responsibilities. The middle aged are in the driver's seat, both in the family and in society and hence carry a heavy burden. They are caught in the middle, responsible for the young and the old. At the peak of their vocational careers, they often play decision-making roles; and on the job they suffer various hazards, including boredom, constant pressure in the managerial classes, and competition from those younger. They are also constantly called on to help in community affairs, whether social, political, or religious.

Assessment of own feelings. Middle age is the time when most people begin to think of how much time remains to live. Hence, they begin to wonder whether they will ever realize their life goals. They must face the fact that vocational aspirations not yet reached probably never will be. It is depressing to realize that an unhealthy marriage can hardly be redeemed after all these years and that retirement and the children's leaving home will leave the couple more exposed to each other than before.

Several middle agers name the most important conclusions they have reached about life to date.

> Not to be afraid to take a chance, to explore every avenue. Like a book there's always something we learn now. Nothing is impossible if you really want it (woman, age 58).

> I always thought the phrase "Life begins at 40" meant things would be much better and always considered the author of the phrase a little

shortsighted. Now I think from age 40 on one's life is put through a wringer of emotions and problems (woman, 51).

Don't cry—pray. Don't worry. Leave it up to God. All things are possible with him. Accept people the way they are and don't be shocked if you are deserted by husband, children, or friends. We see it happen to others (woman, 61).

Your energy slows down after middle age. Make the most of every day. Thank God always for the blessings we do possess (woman, 53).

Such feelings of depression in the 40s sometimes stem from an honest acknowledgment of one's own feelings, a reawakened consciousness of one's special needs. At this stage some individuals who admit that their marriages are unhealthy are simply viewing them more realistically than they did during their 30s (Vaillant, 1977).

Here, several middle agers name their most serious problems.

Not being able to think or do as fast as I used to (woman, age 58).

Coping with monetary problems; raising a teenager; and loneliness (woman, 51).

Already I have experienced being treated by my children like I'm senile, but their children do the same thing to them, too (woman, 61).

Locating in a good retirement community (man, 63).

Aging. Another subtle, but often significant, cause of depression is the growing awareness of one's own aging, reinforced by many subtle and not so subtle reminders. Fading looks, losing one's teeth, the graying of the hair, and becoming a grandparent are constant reminders of the passing years. The aging process itself may involve retiring, early signs of hardening of the arteries (discernable in almost all people 30 and older), endocrine-gland disturbances, weakening of sexual power, and the recurrence of earlier anxieties and conflicts (Rogers, K., 1974).

The middle aged vary considerably in their reactions to aging, as these testimonials show.

I don't mind growing old. In fact, I look forward to the day I will be gray all over my head. I dislike the attitude of our society toward older people (woman, age 51).

I don't really mind. I don't want to ever go to a nursing home and ever need complete care (woman, 54).

I don't like it. If I can be in control of my faculties and get around, and do for myself, I wouldn't mind (woman, 58).

I am striving to "age gracefully" and find that the fact that I am older than I was 10 years ago does not per se alarm me. What does alarm me somewhat is the prospect that old age will adversely affect my ability to actively participate in sports—tennis in particular (man, 51).

When asked to identify their most satisfying period in life to date, the middle aged typically name the 30s or the present.

When my children were old enough to realize that we did the best we could for them—and now, of course, because I am doing what I like and feel satisfying (woman, age 54).

Current—because it is here and now (man, 51).

Present, because I have reached some of the goals that were set at an earlier age. My children have adjusted well and this is one of the main things that I wished for. They are well rounded, happy, and adjust to new things (woman, 43).

Perhaps middle age because I feel I'm accomplishing more. However, it's been more a matter of higher brief periods at each stage, rather than a whole life stage (woman, 62).

The Mid-Life Crisis

Why and how. Problems characteristic of middle age collectively produce the so-called **mid-life crisis,** when the realization of one's situation may precipitate a variety of actions. Five interrelated studies (two in London, two in Nassau County, New York, and one in New York City) examined the critical years at the middle of life. The studies, which involved 2500 respondents, compared differences in middle-age problems according to backgrounds, culture, and time periods. The data revealed strikingly similar manifestations of a mid-life crisis. Sometimes the effects were largely internal, involving a soul searching and reevaluation of philosophies and goals. Sometimes the crisis produced overt action: a change of job, extramarital affairs, or divorce. If the crisis is properly resolved it can be a healthy growth experience; without such a resolution an individual may stagnate or drift.

Contributing factors. Some people experience greater crises than others. Radloff (1974) reported that separated women seemed more depressed than single women. The reverse was the case among men, the single men reporting more depression than either the separated or divorced ones. The women singles seemed more depressed than the men, however. In a survey of research, Bernard (1972) found that married women had poorer mental health than did either single women or married men. Moreover, it was the housewife who identified closely with her home and had no gainful employment whose mental health suffered most.

Overall, sex role is an important factor in emotional health. But life-course projections and the delineation of developmental tasks, as proposed by Freud, Buhler, Erikson, and Peck, do not take into account sex differences. Yet in most cases sex differences are greater than those between developmental stages themselves (Lowenthal, 1975). Women experience fewer health-related and occupational stresses than do men. But they must cope with new opportunities for self-expression and with becoming free of family obligations (Neugarten, 1968). Lowenthal wrote that middle-aged women face more critical stresses than do men, but in later years they leave many of these anxieties behind and take on new developmental tasks. Middle-aged men are especially anxious over their future financial situation and current occupational boredom. By retirement age, they have developed more immediate, **hedonistic** interests.

A Yale University researcher, Dr. Daniel Levinson, observed that the middle-aged individual

> wants desperately to be affirmed by society in the roles [he or she] values most. At about age 40—somewhere in the age 39 to 42 interval—most of our subjects fix on some key event in their careers as carrying the ultimate message of their affirmation or devaluation by society. This might even be a promotion or a new job, or a particular form of success, like writing a best seller [cited in Schanche, 1973, p. 60].

Levinson concluded that the inevitable result of such crisis is change. For even if nothing in the external situation changes, the individual does. One cannot either remain within, or return to the earlier life structure. And even when this structure remains relatively intact externally, internal changes inevitably lend it a different meaning.

Evidence about such mid-life transitions during a 10- to 20-year period—involving aspirations, endocrine changes, confrontation with death, family relationships, and social and role changes—does not support the notion of age-specific crises. Instead, such transitions simply assume crisis proportions when accompanied by several simultaneous demands from personality change. That is, the mid-life stages do not involve an invariant progression of events. Instead, changes merely represent transitions from one reasonably steady state to another.

Overall Emotional Health

Regardless of problems and crises, the emotional health of most middle agers is relatively good most of the time. They lead a calmer, more secure life than either young adults or the very old. They feel reasonably good about their lives after reevaluating their standards of what constitutes success. In a study of six age groups, ranging from 20–25 to 60–75, the oldest subjects had higher real and ideal self-concepts than did the youngest group as well as greater feelings of satisfaction.

Although some middle-age marriages are unhealthy, most are reasonably successful. In a study of upper-middle-class couples who had been married from a short time to more than 24 years, out of a possible score of 20 on a composite index, 63.7% of the husbands and 64.9% of the wives rated their marital happiness as 17 or better. In four of five periods the husbands' level of satisfaction was a little higher than that of their wives. The largest difference in scores was in the first five years of marriage, when wives became disenchanted earlier than husbands (Orthner, 1975).

Especially in late middle age, growing life satisfaction reflects rapidly declining responsibilities. For both sexes retirement is in sight; for women, looking ahead provides a "glimpse of freedom at the end of the tunnel" (Sheehy, 1976). After mothers have determined that they have had their last child, they look forward to increased freedom as their children grow older. Some look forward with dread, wondering whether they can find something to replace the children, others with eager anticipation, and the majority with some relief.

COGNITIVE OPERATIONS

Uneven Progression

Earlier views of cognitive development have been seriously questioned and in certain respects refuted. Development was commonly portrayed in straight-line fashion, partly because the aggregation of many individual scores tended to level out irregularities. The truth is that irregularity, varying widely among individuals, is the rule. For example, people in their early and late 20s demonstrate a lower level of formal operations than do individuals in late adolescence and college age. The data indicate a temporary regression in cognitive operations during the 20s.

By the early 30s, however, there has been restoration to a level somewhat above that of secondary school students, and this recovery persists through the 30s and early 40s. Then, in the late 40s and continuing into the 50s, there is a significant increase in the level of cognitive operations. While the data suggest that the plateau of the late 40s and 50s persists into the 60s before declining, this is unproved. Thus, the data suggest that adults "do, in fact, tend to think like adults" (Peatling, 1977, p. 304). Indeed, the data strongly indicate that adults during their 30s, 40s, and 50s are cognitively advanced and think abstractly.

Contrary to popular belief creativity does not peak in young adulthood. In a study of subjects ages 18 to 84, middle-aged adults scored highest on measures of divergent thought (creativity) and self-esteem. Self-esteem related significantly to expression of divergent thinking in both middle-aged and older adults (Jaquish & Ripple, 1981).

The debate over decline. It is still unclear to what extent basic intellectual factors decline in adulthood and to what extent performance is simply a matter of the accretion of experience. It is commonly agreed that speed of reaction diminishes with age, but much of this decrease can be attributed to the caution born of experience. The middle aged may also learn more slowly, at least the sort of things included on mental tests. But they have not, in the interim since leaving school, practiced learning such things.

At any rate, authorities generally agree that the declines reported by earlier researchers were grossly exaggerated, and some doubt that any meaningful declines occur for most people. They also agree that there is considerable variability from one person to another. After reviewing relevant research, Papalia and Bielby (1974) concluded that "there is considerable variability in adulthood cognitive functioning" (p. 438). Some adults never attain the ability to think formally or to make the highest types of moral judgments. Others continue to show gains into middle age and sometimes beyond.

Much of the confusion surrounding this topic derives from deficiencies in the modes of research commonly employed. Those who doubt that aging inevitably produces decline point to inadequacies in earlier research. The traditional concept that cognitive development is tied in unilinear fashion to maturation was based on cross-sectional and longitudinal studies that had serious flaws. For example, if tests of cross-sections of people at ages 20, 50 and 80 suggest that progressive decrements in reasoning and memory have occurred it might be inferred that such changes inevitably derive from the aging process. But the subjects in each of these age categories grew up in different historical periods. The older ones had a poorer education and thus are less familiar with the concepts used in such tests.

Longitudinal changes among individuals originating from the same **cohort** are minor, and such cohorts maintain characteristic performance levels through the adult years. Nevertheless, there are systematic differences in successive cohorts. Thus, it seems that "in the past, we might have collected data for a psychology of generational differences rather than for a psychology of aging" (Schaie & Gribbin, 1975, p. 65). In any case, research data are contaminated by the fact that, as people grow older, less hardy specimens in the sample drop out by reason of death (Rogers, 1980).

SEXUALITY AND SEX ROLES

Studies of Adult Sexuality

With regard to adult sexuality the data from the oft-quoted Kinsey studies (Kinsey, Pomeroy, Martin, & Gebhard, 1948, 1953) are completely out of date. Most studies indicate that, for example, women today are far more liberal than were their counterparts of the Kinsey years. A third have had extramarital affairs and another 36% have orgasms, usually within 10 minutes; almost all have engaged in and enjoyed oral sex, and almost 65% masturbate. Most of them have discarded the role of passive sex partner and freely enjoy sex. Seven out of ten rate their husbands as good or very good sex partners, and even 30% of those who never experience orgasm rate them that way. Very religious women, it appears, find their sex lives more satisfactory than do less religious ones, perhaps because the clergy teach that sexual compatibility is essential to a good marriage (Gagnon, 1975).

Social class differences. Sexual practices differ significantly for middle- and working-class adults, as clearly shown in Rubin's (1976) in-depth interviews with 50 White, working-class couples and 25 middle-class ones in the San Francisco Bay area. While working-class men have traditionally been portrayed as "little more than boorish, insensitive studs" who care nothing about their partners' needs, the men Rubin interviewed expressed a desire for free, full enjoyment of sex, urged their wife to attempt new techniques, and were often concerned about their wife's achieving an orgasm.

There is always a "time lag between the emergence of new cultural forms and their internalization by the individuals who must act upon them" (p. 44). Certainly, the statement is true regarding sex. The middle-class women in Rubin's study ordinarily had their first experiences in college in a general atmosphere of sexual freedom. Both middle-class and working-class couples engaged in approximately the same sexual behaviors. Nevertheless, the working-class wives were more discontent than were the middle-class ones with their sexual experience. For example, 26% of middle-class women and 70% of the working-class ones engaged in oral sex. Yet fewer of the working-class wives enjoyed it or did not feel guilty about it. Ordinarily, they gave in, often with feelings of guilt and revulsion, from a sense of duty, resignation, or powerlessness. While they disliked both cunnilingus and fellatio, they were less resistant to the former, partly because fellatio required that they assume an active role, contrary to their early sexual learning.

Women still reported that their husbands took pride in their "naiveté" in sexual activities and liked to believe that they had taught their wives everything that they knew. They wanted to feel that their wives were completely innocent before meeting them. Hence, even those women who would have enjoyed letting go hesitated to do so. When women assume the initiative, they may feel they are not behaving in a feminine enough manner.

Working class women, more often than middle-class ones, were somewhat isolated with regard to sex. While middle-class women might talk freely with their friends regarding sex, working-class women were more inhibited about discussing such matters. In addition, middle-class husbands were more understanding of their wives' sexuality. Nevertheless, middle-class women were not without their inhibitions. On all class levels most women feel comfortable about participating with their husbands in coitus. But when it comes to other behaviors such as oral sex, many women, especially in the working class, feel uncomfortable.

Especially in the working class, couples had difficulty communicating with each other about sex. The woman wanted something more than sexual demonstrations of love, while her husband felt that such behavior was the best demonstration of his love. Because the emotional side of his personality had been stunted, he compensated by expressing his feelings indirectly in sex. Ordinarily the women simply submitted, believing that it was their duty as wives. Yet the husband was often frustrated because he wanted not simply to release his own sexual tension but to sense her active involvement.

Unfortunately, sex is usually thought of in terms of meeting the husband's needs. While psychologists express concern about the performance demands placed on men, they say little about the effects of performance demands on women. Orgasm has now become not simply a privilege for women but a "requirement." As one woman said, "Tom's always coming after me with that gleam in his eye. Then, it's not enough if I just let him have it because if I don't have a climax, he's not happy" (p. 92).

It is true that more women have orgasms than formerly and that most of them enjoy sex more than women did in years past. However, a husband's insistence upon his wife's orgasm can become a burden. Besides, women come to feel that the orgasm is more for their husbands' pleasure than for theirs. Unless their wives have an orgasm, husbands feel that they failed in their manhood. And "for women of the working class, who already have little autonomy and control over their lives, this may well be experienced as the ultimate violation" (p. 92). Rubin concluded that "it will take time for women to work through centuries of socially mandated denial and repression. It will probably require that they also first be freer in other beds as well" (p. 92).

Age differences. In all social classes sexual activities gradually decline in frequency over the years. In one study, of a large number of variables studied— among them couple dominance, degree of privacy, and occupational and educational status—the one factor most significantly influencing coital frequency was age (Edwards & Booth, 1976). However, there may be some revival of sexual enjoyment and activity, though not to early-adult levels, after menopause occurs.

Shedding Light on Common Sex Issues

Penis envy. There is much folklore surrounding sex, one aspect of it being that females envy the penis. Such feelings are rare, observed Chilman (1974). Women have completely adequate reproductive facilities of their own and little reason to envy men's equipment. What they may envy is the male's more favored social, economic, and political status and his greater independence, even in today's world. Women's resentment about being female derives not so much from any neuroticism or immaturity as from a healthy and realistic reaction against the injustices that often accrue to their sex (Chilman, 1974).

The double standard. A second issue is the double standard, which allows males greater sexual freedom than females. There is considerable conjecture about the impact that the women's movement has had on this traditionally common value. It has certainly not disappeared but will continue to decline, predicted Yorburg (1973). It will not die out until the sexes have equal status and responsibility for child-rearing and family support. The double sex standard has declined most in those social classes and in those stages of life, especially before marriage, in which women are not independent. As women become more independent of men economically, their sexual behaviors lose their nature as commodities to be traded or withheld for extrinsic rewards. Meantime, sexual activities become freer and more pleasant to women, just as they have been for men.

It has often been argued that men should have greater license for their sexual behaviors, because they have a stronger biological sex urge. There is no firm proof on this point. Apparently androgens are the "erotic hormones" for both sexes. Androgen therapy affects men's sexual motivation only if the androgen secretion level is below normal at the time of treatment. By contrast, women undergoing androgen therapy experience a strong increase in sexual desire (Sopchak & Sutherland, 1960).

The ovaries and adrenals supply androgen to the female, and women who have had these organs removed experience a dramatic drop in orgasmic response and clitoral sensitivity (Waxenberg, 1969). There is also increasing evidence that androgen is not an aggression-inducing hormone and hence does not explain sex differences in such feelings.

Middle-aged couples gain intimacy and fulfillment through a broad spectrum of interactions.

Sex norms in middle age. Sexual activity is just as appropriate in middle age as in earlier years, though it may be less intense and demanding. Cleveland (1976) concluded that both traditional and new norms of sexual behavior are inappropriate for middle age and later years. The newer norms, which stress the naturalness and acceptability of a wide variety of sex behaviors for older as well as younger couples, may prove more demanding than liberating. The preferred alternative would not be performance oriented. Instead, the goal would be to gain intimacy and mutual fulfillment through a broad spectrum of sensual/sexual interactions.

Social Sex Roles at Middle Age

Social sex roles have already been considered in relation to earlier ages, and they will be dealt with again in the next chapter with regard to husband/wife roles in the home. The present discussion will be limited to two topics: the current status of adult sex roles and common recommendations.

Present status. In general, sex roles are becoming less rigid and polarized (Hornung & McCullough, 1981). However, the wide publicity given to the women's movement has tended to portray changes as greater than they are. In one comparison, students and parents appeared to be more favorable toward feminism in 1974 than they were in 1934, especially the women. Both sexes were more inclined to sanction political, legal, and economic rights of women, though being somewhat less approving of feminist views in the conduct and domestic categories. Both sexes are still somewhat traditional concerning the sex-role division of labor within the home (Roper & Labeff, 1977). Attitudes regarding speech, feminine dress, and moral behaviors remained as traditional in 1974 as they were in 1934. Both generations have conflicting, somewhat confused, attitudes regarding the issues posed by feminism. In general, the higher the education of students and their parents, both in 1934 and in 1974, the more approving they were of feminist views.

Women are apparently less inclined than formerly to assume an inferior role to men. In much-quoted research, Matina Horner (1972) reported that women who had had experience with success and scored high on measures for need for achievement nevertheless inhibited their achievement behaviors when competing against men. She termed this behavior "fear of success," observing that for women academic success often produces negative consequences, such as feelings of guilt, peer conflict, and social disapproval.

A follow-up study by Hoffman (1974) indicated that 60% of the women did indeed show fear of success; but an even larger number of men (over 70%) also showed this fear. Komarovsky (1976) determined that women in the 1970s were much less likely to hide their abilities than women two decades previously. When asked how often they had pretended to be intellectually inferior to the man on dates, 32% of women in 1950 said very often, often, or several times; 26% said once or twice; and 40% said never. In the early 1970s, the comparable figures were 15%, 30%, and 55%.

While women themselves have become somewhat more assertive, men have become less so, in the aggressive sense. They have also come to be expressive in their roles. Formerly, they were largely **instrumental,** concerned with running the world and its institutions. The focus was on getting things done, not the human relationships involved. Nowadays, with the shift to a postindustrial era has come a shift from stress on technical production skills to the ability to deal with words, people, and ideas (Douvan, 1975). In other words, the expressive behaviors formerly associated with the home are now becoming more appropriate in the work place.

Nevertheless, there is some evidence that the sex roles have merely become more flexible and fluid and are still a long way from becoming homogenized. The great majority of women still expects to place the wife/mother role somewhat ahead of the career role. Men, meantime, are still reluctant to accord women equal chances for leadership and status. Osmond and Martin (1975) reported that women may meet strong resistance to those sex-role changes that would involve their assuming decision-making, leadership roles outside the family. The men in this sample were least willing to approve women in these roles, whereas the women were equally adamant that they should achieve such positions and could perform them as well as men. It would seem, in view of the men's attitudes, that women will have trouble achieving top-level decision-making positions to any significant extent. To date in the United States, there has been no woman president. Until 1981 there has also been no woman justice on the Supreme Court, and there are fewer women college presidents than formerly.

The sexes are also still portrayed in traditional ways on television. Psychologists Sherry Finz and Judith Waters analyzed three soap operas—*The Guiding Light, The Doctors,* and *General Hospital*—for 8 weeks. In general, the men characters were more directive than the women and were found more often in office settings, except when talking with women in the home. The women were typically nurturant and displayed more avoidance behaviors and hopelessness. In *General Hospital* the women talked frequently, reflecting the stereotype of the "chattery" female. The women, even nurses and doctors, were more often shown in the home. On the job, these women professionals spent most of their time being supportive and nurturant to males ("Out-of-Step Soap Operas," 1977).

Meantime, the women's movement has stumbled along, with the so-called radical feminists taking sharp issue with a newer, milder breed. According to some critics, although the original movement produced more vocational opportunities for women, it failed to arouse sustained mass support (Laudicina, 1973). But many advocates feel that the new feminism is not "an organized movement; nor does it hold meetings or press conferences. It is an all-pervasive rise in female awareness that has permeated virtually every level of womanhood in America, at all ages. Today women believe they have more options, that they can do things that will change their lives" (Adler, N. E., 1975, p. 114).

Meantime, the changes in men toward fuller personhood have stabilized somewhat at a point some distance from the rugged, stoic, masculine model of former times. These changes have not been produced by any concerted effort by men to throw off their yoke but by sociocultural changes that simply nudged them in that direction.

In a survey of *Psychology Today* readers, who are, on average, somewhat younger and better educated than the average adult, respondents indicated what they believe to be important in the ideal individual of both sexes. Table 9-2 reports the findings.

Table 9-2. Traits Important in the Ideal Man and Woman

How important or unimportant is each of the following traits to your concept of the ideal man and the ideal woman?	IDEAL MAN		IDEAL WOMAN		SELF	MATE
	Men	Women	Men	Women	Men	Women
	Percent saying trait is "very important or "essential" to ideal:				Percent of men saying trait is "highly characteristic" of themselves:	Percent of women saying trait is "highly characteristic" of their spouse or lover:
Intelligent	71	84	70	83	—	—
Self-confident	86	86	76	87	32	43
Physically strong	19	21	4	7	15	37
Tall	7	11	4	2	39	40
Physically attractive	26	29	47	32	21	50
Successful at work	54	66	41	60	40	53
Competitive	38	27	18	22	26	33
Aggressive	30	28	16	21	16	23
Takes risks	34	25	21	26	21	25
Stands up for beliefs	87	92	82	90	57	58
Fights to protect family	77	72	72	70	59	52
Able to love	88	96	92	97	54	60
Warm	68	89	83	88	40	54
Gentle	64	86	79	86	42	55
Soft	28	48	63	62	16	25
Romantic	48	66	64	67	33	34
Able to cry	40	51	50	58	—	—
Skilled lover	38	48	41	44	25	46
Many sexual conquests	5	4	4	5	—	—
Sexually faithful	42	67	56	66	45	57

From "Men and women report their views on masculinity," by C. Tavris. In *Psychology Today*, 1977, 10(8), 37. Copyright © 1977 by Ziff-Davis Publishing Company. Reprinted by permission.

Recommendations. Psychologists generally agree that both sex roles have their unhealthy features, and certain recommendations have become common. Sandra Bem (1975) concluded that "we need a new standard of psychological health for the sexes, one that removes the burden of stereotype and allows people to feel free to express the best traits of men and women" (p. 59). Extremely feminine traits, in the traditional sense of femininity, consistently correlate with "high anxiety, low self-esteem and low self-acceptance. And though high masculinity in males has been related to better psychological development in adolescence, [it was] often accompanied during adulthood by high anxiety, high neuroticism, and low self-acceptance" (p. 59). The ideal, maintained Bem, is to free people from their rigid sex roles and to allow them to be androgynous (*andro* and *gyn* from the Greek for male and female). The result would be greater flexibility, fewer inhibitions on what one can do, and a greater chance for realizing one's full potential. The aim, explained P. C. Lee and Gropper (1974), is not to produce feminized males and masculinized females but to let all people be their most natural selves, as individuals.

Laudicina (1973) recommended broadening the scope and meaning of the women's movement in order to make it relevant to the legitimate needs of many more women as well as men. Through redefining task allocations, conventional work roles, and the time demands of occupations, women could assume an equal position in the work world while at the same time retaining the satisfactions of family and home life. Meantime, men could be freed from the excessive occupational demands that have limited their paternal role within the family.

A final comment. Despite the significance of middle age for all aspects of development, including sex role, society has done little to further an understanding of it or to help people cope with it successfully. Technological advances have established a need for fully effective middle-aged people. But this need has exceeded our understanding of middle age. As Kerckhoff (1976) pointed out: "It is not so much what happens to us in middle age as it is what we do with what happens to us; that's what counts." Moreover, "this fascinating time period" should be treated "with the respect it deserves instead of viewing it as a kind of big people's latency" (p. 10).

SUMMARY

Middle age can be defined in chronological, biological, social, and phenomenological terms. It can also be interpreted in terms of distinctive developmental tasks and roles. At this age, people assume special responsibilities for both older and younger generations and for the conduct of society. Such tasks and roles vary according to age, sex, and the individual concerned. They produce pressures that result in change, thus refuting the common concept of adulthood as a long plateau.

The middle-age personality emerges from earlier personality stages, and basic characteristics, once stabilized, tend to persist over the years. Nevertheless, certain characteristics do change somewhat with age; for example, women show greater self-assertion in middle age than earlier. For both sexes moral judgment matures and stabilizes about this time, forming the foundation for wisdom.

Most middle-aged people experience a slow and gradual decline in the senses and other body systems and functions and become increasingly suscep-

Women many times show greater self-assertion in middle age.

tible to respiratory ailments, heart-related diseases, and cancer. Changes in physical appearance become threatening to the ego, especially among those who relied on their good looks for status in the past. Both sexes, women more dramatically than men, experience disturbances arising from the climacteric, or change in sex-hormone balance, with wide variations among individuals. The specific nature and extent of such effects are in dispute.

In their efforts to improve and preserve their health, the middle aged employ both dubious and constructive measures. On the one hand, they may become habitual pill poppers and diet faddists. On the other, they may engage in wholesome, well-balanced nutrition and exercise programs.

Emotional, as well as physical, health at middle age depends mainly on its earlier underpinnings, and it is tested by a variety of problems. The middle aged may become so concerned about such matters as impending old age and whether they have made adequate progress toward their long-term goals that they experience the so-called middle-age crisis. Such crises, properly resolved, produce growth; otherwise they result in stagnation. Despite such problems, most middle agers' emotional health is relatively good.

The status of cognitive operations at middle age is in dispute. The question is whether decline is the inevitable concomitant of aging or the product of experiential and situational factors. In any case, authorities agree that the degree of such decline was exaggerated by earlier researchers.

Views about the status of sexuality at middle age are also changing. While there is an inevitable decline in frequency and intensity of sexual experience, middle agers find their sexual relationships satisfying. Women are less puritanical and naive than in earlier years and accept their own right to enjoy sex experiences. And their husbands show them more consideration than in former years. Nevertheless, various problems and misconceptions remain regarding such matters as the false conception of penis envy, the sometimes poor communication between couples, and the now crumbling double standard, under which males were traditionally allowed greater sexual license than women.

Social sex roles, like sexual behaviors, are changing, becoming less rigid and polarized. While both sexes tend to view the female as relatively more nurturant and the male as more instrumental, they now view the roles as broader and less exclusive. More aggressiveness in females and expressiveness in males is now tolerated, even encouraged, than in former years. Psychologists view this trend as healthful in allowing individuals to realize their potential uninhibited by artificial sex-role boundaries.

SUGGESTED READINGS

Baltes, P. B., & Schaie, K. W. On the plasticity of intelligence in adulthood and old age: Where Horn and Donaldson fail. *American Psychologist*, 1976, 31(10), 720–725. Baltes and Schaie argue that much of the decline in intelligence ascribed to aging stems from cohort effect. They stress the plasticity of intelligence as reflected in large individual differences.

Clemente, F., & Sauer, W. J. Life satisfaction in the United States. *Social Forces*, 1976, 54(3), 621–631. A study of 1347 adults assesses the relative impact on life satisfaction of race, age, socioeconomic status, social participation, and perceived health.

Fried, J. J. Mind and body: The inseparable link. *Science Digest*, Spring 1980, 50–53. A review of evidence from various scientific studies indicates that personality stresses and life experiences are important factors in the etiology and course of disease.

Goldberg, H. *The hazards of being male: Surviving the myth of masculine privilege.* New York: Nash, 1976. The major theme of this analysis is that men have lost touch with themselves, their emotions, and their bodies because of the expectations placed on them and the powers accorded them by society.

Hayslip, B., Jr. Relationships between intelligence and concept identification in adulthood as a function of stage of learning. *International Journal of Aging and Human Development*, 1979–80, 10(2), 187–202. When three groups of participants—ages 17 to 26, 39 to 51, and 59 to 76—were asked to solve certain concept problems in order to identify intellectual correlates of concept identification as a function of learning stage, comparisons both within and between age groups indicated a dynamic picture of interaction among task-related and organismic variables.

Hite, S. *The Hite report: A nationwide study of female sexuality.* New York: Macmillan, 1976. This book, based on a nonrandom sampling of 3019 women, reports their sex practices in some detail. While the results are often startling, they cannot be taken as typical of all women in the United States today.

Horn, J. L., & Donaldson, G. On the myth of intellectual decline in adulthood. *American Psychologist*, 1976, 31(10), 701–719. While a positive sampling bias and wishful thinking in the conduct of research may tend to produce optimistic results, the truth is that decrements in at least some of the significant aspects of intelligence will eventually occur. It is best to acknowledge the possibility of the decrement hypothesis.

Jaquish, G. A., & Ripple, R. E. Cognitive creative abilities and self-esteem across the adult life-span. *Human Development*, 1981, 24, 110–119. A study was made of 218 subjects, ages 18 to 84, to explore the relationship between divergent thinking and self-esteem in age groups across the life span.

Kennedy, M. S. Surviving ambition and competition. *Savvy*, 1980, 1(5), 32–38. A dual-career workshop is described in which couples at the Harvard Business School are helped to gain insight into their particular situations, to discriminate among alternative forms of partnerships, and to develop potentially satisfactory solutions. The situations of several couples are examined in some detail.

Lewis, H. B. *Psychic war between the sexes.* New York: New York University Press, 1976. Basing her conclusion on recent work in various disciplines, the author examines Freudian, Marxist, and feminist views of human relationships and the effects of internalized conflicts between affectionate and exploitative values.

Mackie, M. The impact of sex stereotypes upon adult self imagery. *Social Psychology Quarterly*, 1980, 43(1), 121–125. An analysis of data from a sampling of Western Canadian adults indicated only a weak relationship between sex stereotypes and self-image. Differences in results between this and related research are attributed to variations in modes of measurement employed.

Murphy, J. M., & Gilligan, C. Moral development in late adolescence and adulthood: A critique and reconstruction of Kohlberg's theory. *Human Development*, 1980, 23, 77–104. An alternative conception of postconventional moral development is found to fit existing data on late adolescent and adult moral development better than Kohlberg's concepts of higher stages. Real-life data on the same subjects suggest a progression relating to actual experiences of moral conflict and choice that result in a more dialectical mode of moral judgment.

Richardson, M. S., & Alpert, J. L. Role perceptions of educated adult women: An exploratory study. *Educational Gerontology*, 1976, 1(2), 171–185. Women experienced greatest conflict over their marriage role, followed by the motherhood role, and the work role.

Roberts, J. I. (Ed.) *Beyond intellectual sexism: A new woman, a new reality.* New York: David McKay, 1976. A selection of 21 articles treats various aspects of women's roles, including biological intervention, the self and social interaction, female/male equality in social institutions, cultural change, women and education, and sex-role innovations.

Sharpe, L., Kuriansky, J. B., & O'Connor, J. F. A preliminary classification of human functional sexual disorders. *Journal of Sex and Marital Therapy*, 1976, 2(2), 106–114. This preliminary classification of functional human sexual disorders involves five categories that relate to the behavioral, psychological, and informational components of sexual functioning in both individuals and couples. A study of 20 couples who sought marital therapy and another 20 who sought sexual-dysfunction therapy is related to the discrepancy in the way that a husband and wife view the same marriage. Such discrepancy can apparently become an important source and indicator of stress, greater for the marital-therapy patients than for those in sexual therapy.

Snyder, E. C. (Ed.) *The study of women: Enlarging perspectives of social reality.* New York:

Harper & Row, 1979. This collection of original scholarly articles, summarizing what is currently known about women, is of special interest in areas of sociology, psychology, and interdisciplinary women's studies programs.

Socarides, C. W. Beyond sexual freedom: Clinical fallout. *American Journal of Psychotherapy*, 1976, *30*(3), 385–397. Socarides interprets radical changes in sexual customs as threats to psychological well-being, family structure, and social cohesion. He portrays as especially damaging the gradual erosion of gender role and sexual identity, the downgrading of mothering, and the rejection of the medical model for treating psychiatric disorders in favor of a sociopolitical one (in which emotional disorders are perceived as a matter of social definition). He also deplores the perception of "severe sexual disorders" such as transsexualism and exclusive homosexuality as simply alternative modes of sexual functioning.

Stoltenberg, J. Future genders. *Omni*, May 1980, 66–73; 116. Discusses views of certain authorities on the subject of sexuality in terms of the establishment of gender, identity, treatment of transsexuals, and future alternatives for dealing with gender.

Spreitzer, E., Snyder, E., & Larson, D. The relative effects of health and income on life satisfaction. *International Journal of Aging and Human Development*, 1979–80, *10*(3), 283–288. A measurement of the relative effects of income and health on life satisfaction, based on data from three national surveys, disclosed financial status to be a stronger predictor of life satisfaction for people under age 65, whereas health status proved a stronger influence for individuals over that age.

Vaillant, G. E. *Adaptation to life*. Boston: Little, Brown, 1978. Vaillant selected 100 men from the original Grant Study, in which 268 of the most promising male undergraduates of a prestigious Eastern university were selected in order to follow the course of their lives. On the basis of interviews and vignettes of 40 of these individuals, Vaillant derives certain conclusions about how people mature through adulthood, especially those in the somewhat superior category represented here.

Zacks, H. Self-actualization: A midlife problem. *Social Casework*, 1980, *61*(4), 223–233. People approaching age 40 tend to reevaluate their lives as they become increasingly aware of the time limitation on their life spans. An educational program is suggested for dealing with problems and issues typical of this life stage.

Zepelin, H. Age differences in dreams. I: Men's dreams and thematic apperceptive fantasy. *International Journal of Aging and Human Development*, 1980–81, *12*(3), 171–180. An investigation of age differences in recalled dreams among men ages 27 to 64 indicated some age-related decline in aggression but not in other ways.

10
MIDDLE-AGE LIFE-STYLES

MIDDLE AGE IN THE NUCLEAR FAMILY

Family as an Institution

The most common life-style in middle age is within the nuclear family. Legal marriage between a couple who share the same household with their children is still extremely popular, despite certain minor countertrends. Data from six national surveys indicated that most adults' happiness depends upon having a good marriage more than on anything else (Glenn & Weaver, 1981). In 1975, 84% of all families followed this pattern, and majorities of women (57.5%) and men (63.1%) were both married and living with their spouses (Bernard, 1975; U.S Bureau of the Census, 1976a). However, the proportion of adults living with spouses is slowly declining.

Portent of change. There is even some evidence that the nuclear family may not prove to be a permanent fixture of civilization. Passin (1973) argued that traditional marriage is neither inevitable nor even necessarily optimum. People may prefer a relationship that stresses companionship rather than children and family. Nor need that relationship be exclusive, heterosexual, or permanent. Instead, increasing numbers are either delaying or rejecting marriage in favor of independence. Among a population of unmarried college women, 39% felt that traditional marriage is growing obsolete, and 25% agreed with the statement that the traditional nuclear family of father, mother, and children living in one household no longer works (Stein, P. J., 1973).

Contrary evidence. Every generation, observed Hareven (1977), seems to predict the family's imminent collapse. Even in the past, family behaviors were not simple but were characterized by "diversity and flexibility, a kind of controlled disorder that varied in accord with pressing social and economic needs" (p. 69). In today's complex society, families are even more diverse and flexible. Indeed, history shows that such families can cope with conflicts between their collective needs and the needs of their members under shifting circumstances. It is unrealistic, concluded Hareven, simply to turn back the clock and take refuge in a kind of a family that probably never existed.

It is also a myth that the nuclear family is isolated from its kin. The decreased number of adults in the household may obscure the still-functioning kinship networks. Even today, extended families may maintain separate, but nevertheless closely tied-together, households. It is often pointed out that current mobility has broken up such extended-family relationships. When the poor and the working class move, however, it is ordinarily within the same area. The probability of long-distance moving rises dramatically with educational and income status (Woolsey, 1977).

Marriage at Middle Age

Categories of marriage. Medley (1977) described three types of marriage. In the first type, couples focus on "the intimate and shared nature of their relationship." Marriage revolved around the wife and husband roles, though not to the exclusion of other roles. And the couple's own interaction has proved to be the most rewarding aspect of their married life. In the second type, one spouse behaves as a parent and the other as a child. The "parent" spouse acts in a protective, nurturant, somewhat dominant manner, and the "child" spouse behaves submissively and dependently. Such relationships often develop when one partner has become somehow incapacitated. The third type of marriage includes those couples who are "more or less friends" and who experience greatest satisfaction outside their more intimate relationships. The relative satisfaction that each spouse experiences in any of these marriages depends on their respective needs and how well the two complement each other.

Roles in marriage. In any marriage wives and husbands gradually work out their respective roles. For example, a study of 350 families indicates that each marriage partner still had a clearly defined role regarding areas in which he or she had greater influence on purchase decisions (Shuptrine & Samuelson, 1977). In another study, which involved a random sampling in Utah, spouses assessed their partner and themselves in terms of satisfaction derived from performing various family roles: housekeeping, providing, therapeutic (emotional support and personal help), kinship (maintaining contact with relatives), recreational, sexual, and child care. In general, the husbands evaluated their wife's performance as superior to their own for every role except that of provider. The wives rated their own performance higher on housekeeping, kinship, and child care, and equal on teaching and disciplining the older children. The husbands apparently believed that maintaining contact with the relatives was mainly the wife's role, while their wives were less willing to accept this responsibility.

Overall, the couples appeared relatively satisfied with their mates and their marriages, and they saw both themselves and their spouses as fulfilling significant marital roles rather well. In general, they agreed about which spouse should be responsible for which roles and on how adequately each performed family responsibilities. And they were satisfied with their choice of a mate and their distribution of roles (Chadwick, Albrecht, & Kunz, 1976).

Most authorities believe that those marriages are happiest that permit the maximum self-realization of both spouses and that personal needs should transcend sex-role boundaries (Lee, P. C., & Gropper, 1975). According to this view, with which I agree, any distribution of duties in marriage should relate to the situation and the characteristics and needs of the persons involved. By contrast, Rossi (1977) argued that the central function of family systems is "human continuity through reproduction and child rearing" (p. 2). She insisted that popular views of sex equality and variant marriage and family forms, which she preferred to think of as deviant, obscure basic human characteristics firmly rooted in biology. Unless the biosocial fundamentals are allowed for, she concluded, the current trend toward sexual equality at work in the home, along with joint child rearing, may simply prove to be an episode in history like many other social experiments.

Most of the middle aged say that their marriage has improved over the years.

> Our relationship has probably become more realistic in our expectations of each other (man, age 41).

> It has not changed. [We have always had] good communication. We are most compatible (woman, 58).

> I've always enjoyed our marriage. The rough times were small in comparison to the nice times. With regard to change, I'm less dependent, so we enjoy each other more (woman, 41).

> It has improved with the years as we have held each other up during many problems with his family and mine; and we have become stronger and more loving and mature. Now we have a good relationship and hope we have time to get away by ourselves for a few days (woman, 53).

Characteristics of successful marriage. In any case, those couples thrive best who are supportive of each other. A study of 189 couples disclosed that those having greatest satisfaction with life also had achieved more effective helping relationships with each other. They trusted each other more as confidants, more highly valued each other's helpfulness, and depended less on other people for help. In addition, those pairs who expressed greater satisfaction with their jobs described their spouses as more satisfactory confidants and helpers. Overall, it appears that the husband/wife helping relationship is a significant factor in determining the quality of married life (Burke & Weir, 1977).

Another characteristic of successful marriage is adaptive capacity across the years. The relationship must be flexible if both parties are to continue to grow and to adapt to all the changing facets of their lives. Thus, Medley (1977) portrayed marriage as "a dynamic process—as compared to a static state or condition" (p. 6).

Marriage partners should also perceive their roles as equitable. In a random sampling of couples there was a tendency for marriage partners to perceive more equity than inequity in performing their roles; moreover, this feeling of equity increased over the family life cycle. When married partners did perceive inequity, typically it was in their own favor. However, wives more often than husbands perceived inequity unfavorable to them (Schafer & Keith, 1981).

Finally, each party to the marriage must be not simply a good spouse but an effective personality. Kerckhoff (1976) observed that a better marriage for middle-aged persons depends not "on the improvement of the marriage so much as on the improvement of the human beings in it" (p. 10).

Another factor in marital happiness is health. People with the most serious health problems are also those most likely to have unsatisfactory marriages (Renne, 1970, p. 63). The well spouse has the responsibility of taking care of the unhealthy one in terms of both home responsibilities and finances. Moreover, illness reduces the satisfactions obtained in work, travel, sex, and social relationships.

In general, marital satisfaction varies across the life cycle, being highest early and late in the marriage. Such satisfaction tends to lag during the middle years, perhaps because of the presence of children, changing family roles, and a "wearing off" of the newness of marriage (Rollins & Cannon, 1974).

Gender differences. Husbands and wives inevitably experience the marriage differently because of their different roles. After studying adaptational patterns of men and women at the "empty-nest" and retirement stages, Lowenthal, Thurnher, Chiriboga, and associates (1975) reported that differences between the sexes were more significant than those between the youngest and oldest of either sex. For most women, the family cycle is more important than the work cycle, whereas changes in job status may be more important to men.

Because vocational success is so important to men, those having the greatest chances of achieving satisfaction in marriage are the well-to-do with promising vocational prospects and, often, favorable personality characteristics. This combination makes them attractive candidates for marriage, and they can choose from the best potential wives. Such men, in the upper socioeconomic levels, do indeed have the longest-lasting marriages. In contrast, the best-educated women with the highest income are the least likely among their sex to marry or to maintain their marriages. Such women ordinarily desire greater fulfillment than the more limited perspective of the home or the exacting dual role of marriage and career allows (Glick, 1975).

Although marriage is ordinarily portrayed as more important to women than to men, Bernard (1972) concluded that marriage in the United States is a boon to husbands but not to most wives. She added that alternatives open to young women may be equally undesirable. However, it may be unwise to advise a woman against marriage based purely on evidence derived from comparisons of married and unmarried women. Many unmarried women never wanted to marry at all. Hence, simply advising women to remain single might produce in those with a real desire to marry a feeling of not being fulfilled.

On the basis of data from national surveys, Glenn (1975) reported that married people experienced greater personal happiness than did the divorced, widowed, separated, or never married. The differences were greater for women than men. Married women experience greater stress than others, but women perceive the benefits of marriage as sufficient to outweigh the negative effect of stress. Overall, it appears that women experience both more stress and satisfaction in marriage than men.

The Two-Career Household

Happier or unhappier? As growing numbers of wives enter the work force, speculation has grown about the effect of this development on marriage. In a study of 89 couples, among whom 28 per cent of the wives worked part or full time, the working wives were better satisfied than the nonworking wives. But the husbands of the nonworking wives were better satisfied than those of the working wives (Burke & Weir, 1976). The working wives actually communicated with their husbands more than did the nonworking wives. By contrast, the housewives talked to their husbands more about their children and about their own activities and work. The housewives experienced poorer physical and mental health, more often had had an ulcer, perceived themselves as the worrying type, and described their overall morale as lower.

The picture for husbands of working wives was somewhat different. They reported less happiness with their marriage than did those of nonworking wives. But they agreed more with their wife in terms of various behaviors and values such as display of affection, sexual relations, and friends. They were also more likely than the husbands of nonworking wives to resolve problems with their spouse by a mutual give-and-take rather than by one of them simply giving in. The husbands of working wives were more concerned and worried over housing problems, getting in a rut, money, and problems of communication with and showing affection for their wife. But they actually communicated with their wife more than the husbands of housewives.

Burke and Weir attributed the increased stress of the working wives' husbands to several factors. For one thing, when women work outside the home, their husband loses a significant portion of their support system. Women simply have less energy and time to devote to their husband's social, physical, and emotional needs. The comforts that a husband has come to anticipate when his wife functions as "a servant," homemaker, and mother are necessarily reduced because of the wife's increased responsibilities. Moreover, the husband finds himself assuming more of the tasks in the home, chores which have less status than men's tasks in the society. To a certain degree he finds himself behaving in a supportive role to his wife's goals. Thereby, his position of dominance in the family is, to a considerable extent, reduced. As a result, the husband may have a feeling of reduced self-worth at the same time that his wife's ego improves. Overall, concluded Burke and Weir, men's roles in two-career families hardly produce feelings of fulfillment. Men do derive some benefits from this role, however, such as having better relations with their children, seeing their wives blossom and develop, and learning to deal in practical fashion with home and family life.

Such husbands may also experience difficulty, because they are not experienced in transcending traditional sex roles. While women may have worked before they got married, men have usually been restricted to traditional male tasks from an early age. They have been socialized to fill an instrumental role in society and have rarely been encouraged to develop attitudes and skills needed for homemaking, child rearing, or supportive emotional roles.

In the same study the two types of couples were compared on such characteristics as inclusion, or making efforts to become involved with other people and activities; control, or attempting to take charge or influence other people and things; and affection, or efforts to become close to people. The two-career couples had lower needs in all three areas. The working wives less often sought fulfillment through relating to others and more often valued control over their own destiny. Husbands of working wives also sought less gratification through relations to others and expressed less need to control others than did housewives' husbands. Overall, the two-career couples, as compared with single-career ones, were more self-sufficient and self-reliant. And while working wives were more self-assertive than housewives, their husbands were less assertive and less concerned about power than were the housewives' husbands. The housewives were more submissive than their husbands or than the working wives or their husbands. They were more willing to concede authority to others and indicated greater preference for others to make decisions. The housewives' husbands were more competitive and power seeking than were the working wives' husbands. Consistent with traditional views of the female role, the wives in general were more often passive recipients of interaction than were their husbands. However, the housewives were considerably more passive than were the working wives.

With regard to personality, only in desire to control others did working women differ significantly from working men and more nearly resemble the housewives. Otherwise, the personality structure of working wives is more nearly like that of working husbands than that of housewives. What is not clear is how much this difference reflects personalities originally brought to the job and how much is the function of having been in the work world (Burke & Weir, 1976).

Class differences. The marriage experience also varies according to social class. Breslow-Rubin (1976) found that, even if they worked, middle-class wives were expected to help out with their husband's vocational progress through their own social relationships, entertaining, and community activities. In contrast, the working-class family was removed from the husband's work and perceived as a refuge for him. While true equality was rare for either group, the working-class husband's authority was more readily acknowledged and real, whereas more of the middle-class correspondents at least professed an ideal of equality.

The middle-class and working-class men also differed with regard to vocational security and household tasks. The working-class man was often uncertain that he could provide adequately for the family and perceived his wife's working as a threat to his masculinity and a sign to others that he is not fully a man. The middle-class man was more secure in his job, possessed more status there, and believed in his ability to support his family. In neither social class did the husbands of working wives share household tasks equally, although middle-class women were more likely to hire a domestic. Working-class women workers simply succumbed passively to performing two jobs—outside and inside the home.

Who comes first? A major problem in some two-career marriages is what to do when the spouses' job interests conflict. A survey of *Psychology Today* readers, who are somewhat younger and better educated than the average adult, indicated that both sexes still give the husband's work priority. (See Table 10-1.)

Table 10-1.

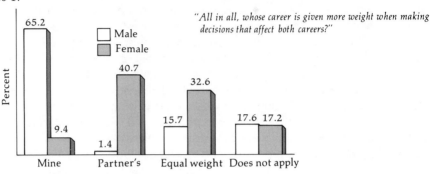

"All in all, whose career is given more weight when making decisions that affect both careers?"

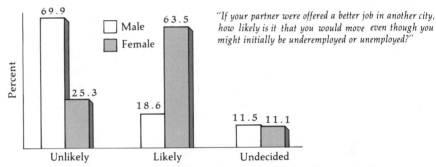

"If your partner were offered a better job in another city, how likely is it that you would move even though you might initially be underemployed or unemployed?"

From "What you really want from your job," by P. A. Renwick, E. E. Lawler, and the *Psychology Today* staff. In *Psychology Today*, 1978, 11(12), 60. Copyright © 1978 by Ziff-Davis Publishing Company. Reprinted by permission.

Middle Agers and Their Children

Children continue to be a significant part of a middle-age couple's family career. The children, now in their middle and later teens, perform varied functions, depending partly on the family involved. In inner cities vigorous teenagers

"familial turf" (Schnaiberg & Goldenberg, 1975). In lower-class families children may perform various services, such as helping to supplement the family income or performing tasks that more-affluent parents might pay outsiders to perform. Lower-class children, through the school situation, may afford contact with the large middle-class community. In addition, children who are successful in classes or athletics may help some parents to compensate for their own lesser status within the society. If parents have come from a foreign country, their children, by means of skills that they learn among their peers and at school, may help to induct them more easily into the language and institutions of their adopted country. Especially in middle age both middle- and lower-class parents gain feelings of reflected prestige and status through their own grown children's occupational achievements.

A father may now try, for the first time, to warm up to his children, just as they are declaring their independence of their parents. He has passed his prime on the job, without having found an adequate substitute for work. Because men typically form fewer intimate friendships outside the family, they may, after work obligations decline, seek closer relationships within the family. The relationship is more between equals now, especially after the children leave home for college or marriage.

THE DIVORCED AND THE REMARRIED

The Divorced

Separation. A third of all first marriages ultimately dissolve, most often in the couple's 20s or 40s. Couples often separate for varying periods. Robert Weiss (1976) defined separation as "the erosion of love and the persistence of attachment," and it can be merely an incident in a marital relationship rather than its termination. This view explains such strange postmarital behaviors as the spouses' continuing to have sex or the man's continuing to repair the house from which he has been evicted. Couples often take refuge in some standard account of why their marriage failed. While it might not conform closely to the facts, it at least provides a rational and orderly way for them to look back on it.

Causes of divorce. Divorce itself is mainly caused by increased tolerance of the practice and by women's increasing ability to support themselves ("Rising Divorce Rate," 1976). It may be "best viewed as reflecting a disequilibrium in a relationship, a point at which costs and benefits are out of line" (Sawhill, 1977, p. 121). Actually many changes in family relationships and behaviors transpire across the life cycle. It would seem, therefore, that divorce should not necessarily be considered a failure. Rather, a particular marriage no longer serves the best interests of the parties involved because it obstructs rather than supports their continued development. Just as different groups and friends enhance our development and happiness at particular periods, the same may be true of our mates.

Divorce also grows out of the fact that many marriage partners come together by chance and often never meet the ideal partner. If they do, it is often too late. Considering the somewhat "haphazard manner" in which mate selection occurs, as well as the "many frailties of human adults, the surprise may be that the proportion of marriages that last—to a happy (or bitter!) end—is as large as it is" (Glick, 1975, p. 22).

Aftermath of divorce. Divorce undoubtedly leaves its scars for both parties. In general, divorced or separated women are more depressed than men in such circumstances. Either men or women with children are more depressed than those without, and those living with their children are more depressed than those who are not. In addition, the younger their children, the more depressed they are (Radloff, 1974). Even when they have children, divorced women are far less likely than formerly to go home to mother. They make it on their own, either because they desire to be independent or because their parents are more reluctant to invite them in (Bernard, 1975).

In one study, 72 middle-class married couples were compared with an equal number of divorced couples in which the mother had child custody (Hetherington, Cox, & Cox, 1977). Not a single case of victimless divorce was found; that is, in every case someone had suffered. The fathers suffered three special problems: organizing practical day-to-day tasks; meeting the strains to, and changes in, self-concepts; and relating with their former wives and their children. The divorced men often sought frantically to establish a new identity. The

Relationships between fathers and children sometimes improve after a divorce.

formerly conservative types might break out in open shirts, wear beards, have long sideburns, and drive flashier cars than formerly. Many of them plunged into a round of social activities. In general, they felt somewhat "shut out," rootless, and at loose ends. They needed to busy themselves with social activities, even those that were not always pleasurable. They saw their former wives and children less as time went on, partly because they found it painful to see their children only occasionally. Sometimes, father/child relationships improved, especially when the home life had been unhappy before. In the 1st year after divorce some of the men enjoyed diverse sexual experiences. However, what they really desired was a long-lasting, more meaningful relationship.

For her part, the divorced mother often reported "feeling helpless [and] physically unattractive" and said she had "lost the identity associated with her husband's status" (p. 42). Such women had less contact with other adults than did their former spouses and found themselves "locked into a child's world," especially in the case of nonworking mothers (p. 45). The working mothers fared somewhat better, because their relationships with coworkers often led to social events. By the end of 2 years the mothers had more influence on the development of their children than did their husbands. Nevertheless, the fathers continued to act as a stabilizing factor. Both fathers and mothers coped more poorly at the end of a year than immediately after the divorce, but they experienced a marked readjustment during the 2nd year. Both parents also experienced financial stress because of the necessity of supporting two households, and both suffered feelings of loss of competence and confidence. They felt that they had failed as spouses and parents and questioned their ability to make a success of future marriages.

In order to run away from reality and to compensate for the loss of self-esteem, the parents, especially the men, became quite socially active during the 1st year of separation. However, they did not find their new social lives very satisfying. They came to realize that socialization in this society is organized more around couples than singles and that single women with children, especially, have limited social opportunities. While at first their married friends were helpful, gradually they themselves turned to single, divorced, and separated people with whom they shared more interests. After about 2 years the parents had made a relatively good adjustment and felt better about their sex lives. However, both sought more sustained, meaningful relationships than were possible in superficial encounters.

For both sexes the 1st year was more stressful. By the end of the year 29 of the 48 men and 35 of the 48 women believed that the divorce might have been a mistake. By the end of the 2nd year, however, only 12 of the 48 mothers and 9 of the 48 fathers believed that they had made a mistake. The researchers concluded that the concept of a romantic divorce is a myth but that divorce is the best solution when conflict has destroyed family harmony and prevents stabilizing the home. Certainly, a "stable home situation in which parents are divorced can be better for family members than a troubled intact family" (p. 46). Nevertheless, few divorced persons are fully prepared for the stresses and traumas that they experience before they reintegrate their lives.

Remarriage

Problems. Approximately three-fourths of women and five-sixths of men who divorce remarry, on the average after 3 years. And about one-half to two-thirds of those who remarry remain together as long as they both survive (U.S. Bureau of the Census, 1976b). Despite this record, there are problems in second marriages, to some extent different from those of the first. These include problems involving stepchildren and the financial and emotional obligations to more than one family.

Lillian Messinger, a social worker at the Clarke Institute of Psychiatry, interviewed 70 remarried couples. She discovered that our culture has not devised means of preparing people adequately for remarriage. The remarried people named their spouse's immaturity, a lack of marital readiness, and sexual difficulties as the major problems in their first marriage, placing money and children last. However, money and children became the chief source of difficulty in their second marriage.

In second marriages children constitute a permanent, often difficult, link to the former spouse and can create a conflict between roles played in the earlier and the later marriage. In addition, before remarriage single-parent families sometimes become "closed systems" to which the new partner finds it difficult to adjust. Children themselves sometimes find it hard to adapt to a new household with a somewhat different life-style and a comparatively strange adult in an authority role. The marriage partners are often caught in the conflict between a desire to please their children and a desire to cater to the new spouse. Financial problems often arise because of the debts remaining from the first marriage. The woman may feel uncomfortable about the financial burden her children impose on her new husband, and the man may feel too proud to reveal the inadequacy of his resources. A major danger between a newly remarried couple is a tendency simply to avoid rather than face problems that arise.

Compensations. Nevertheless, there can be compensation for these problems in the marital partners' greater maturity and more realistic expectations. A comparison of the marital happiness of divorced and remarried people with the never divorced disclosed that men have about as great a chance of happiness in the second marriage. About two-thirds (68%) of the remarried men described their second marriage as very happy, compared with 71% of the never divorced ones. Among the women, 61% were very happily married, compared with 70% of the never divorced women. The lesser satisfaction of the remarried women may derive from the double standard of aging, whereby older women become less marriageable. Hence, many older women may remarry partners below their standards. On balance, remarriages appear to be almost as successful as intact unions (Cohen, 1977).

MIDDLE-AGED SINGLES

The Widow

Although widowhood is most often associated with older people, half of all widows are under age 60, a figure that does not include those who have remarried. In 1975, there were 90,000 widows in the United States under age 45, and half of these were under the age of 60, because women often marry older men. The younger widows are often lonelier than older ones, who are more likely to become friends with people in similar straits. Besides, older people are better prepared mentally for widowhood because they have had occasion to rehearse the event through the widowhood of a friend or relative (Troll, 1975).

Single Parents

Categories and incidence. According to the U.S. census of 1970, over 3½ million families were headed by a single parent, and over 85% of these parents were women (Brandwein, Brown, & Fox, 1974). Single parents include unwed mothers or fathers, divorced parents, and adoptive parents. In addition, aggregate families are appearing, constituted of members from several divorces (Toffler, 1976). Overall, one in seven American children is reared in a single-parent household, and in urban areas the proportion rises to one in four.

Special problems. Single parents share certain problems. Often they are strapped financially yet are unable because of family responsibilities to compete on equal terms in the marketplace. They are also viewed and treated as an anomaly in a society structured for nuclear families. Finally, they are cut off from other supportive adults by the very demands of taking care of their children. In consequence, they often attempt a "desperate search for a new mate instead of cooperative arrangements with other single persons" (Stein, P. J., 1976, p. 99).

In addition, persons who choose alternative family life-styles encounter legal problems over children, inheritance, and taxes. In one case, in which a couple had lived together intermittently for 18 years and had three children, the father was denied custody of the children after his wife died, the assumption being that unwed fathers are unfit to rear children (Weisberg, 1975). Child-custody rights also arise in situations involving homosexual couples (Davidson, Ginsberg, & Kay, 1974). Whether or not the single-parent family is inferior cannot be easily determined because of the many complex variables involved.

To some degree the welfare system serves to retard remarriage because of public aid to dependent children. In any case, one recurring consequence for children of one-parent families headed by women is the chance of growing up poor (Ross & Sawhill, 1975).

The divorced mother. The most common type of single parent, the divorced mother, is often in effect denied head-of-household status. And institutions often deny credit to divorced women or grant it only in their former husbands' name. They may even insist that a woman's ex-husband or her father sign for her and thus attain partial control of her property (U.S. House, 1970). Moreover, landlords may refuse to rent to families without adult males, so that the divorced mother may have to pay more than a man for equivalent housing (Brandwein, Brown, & Fox, 1974).

Society also expects children from broken homes to be poorly disciplined, to experience sex-role confusion, and to be more likely to become delinquents.

Mothers themselves may introject such negative stereotypes and become anxious and insecure about their child-rearing competency. As a result, they may attempt the "super woman" role or take refuge in remarriage.

As heads of households, such women often experience economic problems (Brandwein, Brown, & Fox, 1974). Typically, they have had less job training than men, are concentrated more in low-income occupations, and are less likely than men to have any job at all. Because they ordinarily must work, their on-the-job functions conflict with those of child care and homemaking. Many of them must report to welfare agencies. In short, the families of divorced mothers often suffer severe economic hardships. And because the mother usually keeps the children after divorce, the parent least able to provide for them must shoulder the chief economic responsibility (Brandwein, Brown, & Fox, 1974). If the father keeps the children, his own expenses, like those of divorced mothers, increase, because he ordinarily pays for help with child care and housekeeping (George & Wilding, 1972).

Nevertheless, the divorced mother's ability to take care of the children alone should not be underestimated. Kriesberg (1970) discovered that, on the whole, husbandless mothers do not differ from married mothers in beliefs, values, or conduct that affects the children. In fact, many divorced mothers perceive their state as providing them with increased power and independence. A woman may have greater power as the head of household than she ever had as a dependent in a male-headed household (Gillespie, 1971).

The single father. An increasingly frequent phenomenon today is the single male parent. About half a million families in the United States are headed by men without wives, chiefly widowers or those awarded custody of the children after divorce (Orthner, Brown, & Ferguson, 1976). In general, the men studied found it difficult to work and take care of the children, too. Nevertheless, they said that child rearing had not jeopardized their performance on the job. Most of them preferred to leave their children in nursery schools or day-care centers rather than with baby-sitters or friends. After the children were older, they played alone after school. Ordinarily the men performed their own household chores with help from the children. Some of them expressed concern about their daughters' sex education, especially around puberty, and about the absence of feminine role models. Otherwise, the men derived considerable satisfaction from their father role and believed that they were doing a quite adequate job of parenting. (Of course, there were some exceptions, as there are in two-parent households.) Thus, despite their lack of training for this role, they felt confident of their ability to perform successfully as single parents.

The single foster parent. Also growing in numbers today are adoptions by single parents. Traditionally, the single person has been viewed as the "adoptive parent of last resort" (Feigelman & Silverman, 1977). Such parents have been granted older, minority, or handicapped children whose physical, emotional, and social needs exceed those of other children. While such an attitude may be "consistent with the laws of supply and demand," it seems strange that welfare workers would assign to adults with the least resources those children with the greatest needs. Single parents must also cope with the many discriminations against single individuals in this society. Finally, single parents may have fewer economic resources, because there is only one worker in the family.

Despite such obstacles, single adoptive parents perform as well as adoptive couples, raising questions about certain theories of child development. It has often been maintained that two-parent families are essential to let a child resolve the Oedipus complex and to provide role models for children of both sexes. However, as men and women come to share child-rearing tasks and as sex roles become increasingly mingled, children may learn their roles from either parent.

Singles without Children

Childless singles include heterosexuals, homosexuals, and bisexuals. Some single women become **"paranurturers,"** sublimating their child-caring function through such professions as social work or taking care of the orphaned and retarded. Still others become office wives, taking care of and devoting their lives to the men for whom they work (Sheehy, 1976).

Distinctive features of life-style. Married adults typically depend on each other and their children for their chief support. Singles without children depend primarily on close friends or, sometimes, on members of their family of origin. In fact, a successful single life-style hinges on being socially acceptable and

Childless single people have greater freedom in choosing life-styles.

finding people with whom one can react meaningfully. That is, single people must have a relatively permanent sense of relatedness to others, develop patterns of independence, and feel engaged with their fellow beings (Stein, P. J., 1976). Childless singles have greater freedom to select living arrangements and can decorate their homes, make plans, and spend their money without consultation with others.

Being single also carries disadvantages. The middle-aged single woman is rarely perceived as single by choice. The male single may be viewed as a somewhat irresponsible adventurer. Both are discriminated against in the work world, the woman for being a woman and the man for being less stable than a husband and father. Society discriminates against them in numerous other ways. For example, they pay higher taxes than marrieds, yet they may not be eligible for certain forms of moderately priced public housing and other benefits.

As in the case of minority groups, a constructive ideology coupled with effective organization would probably improve singles' political clout and reduce discrimination (Stein, P. J., 1976). Yet their very heterogeneity makes it difficult for them to develop cohesive objectives. Fortunately, declared P. J. Stein (1975), "Singlehood is emerging as a social movement, overlapping with other liberation movements" (p. 501). Moreover, it is rapidly attaining the status of a valid lifestyle. And growing numbers of middle-aged singles find their status so satisfying that they have long ago discarded marriage as a viable option.

SUMMARY

The nuclear family remains a popular institution despite some modifications and alternative modes of life. Middle-aged husbands and wives transact their complementary roles very well, in general, and judge their mates' marital performance to be successful. In two-career households the picture is a bit less sanguine. Working wives experience greater feelings of self-fulfillment than do nonworking wives but often have trouble coping with the dual demands of homemaking and vocation. Some husbands, especially in the working class, have trouble assuming any meaningful portion of the household duties or admitting to themselves that their own earnings are insufficient. Both middle-aged husbands and wives take satisfaction in their nearly grown, or grown, children, who no longer constitute a drain on their time and energies.

A third of all first marriages ultimately dissolve, partly because many adults these days are unwilling to preserve unions that do not contribute to their continuing growth. After a difficult period of readjustment, a large majority of divorced persons remarries, in most cases successfully. Other candidates for remarriage are the widowed, who may experience special problems at middle age because such a status has not been anticipated that early in life.

Single people pursue quite different life-styles from the married. In general, single parents, even men, perform a far more competent parental role than is commonly recognized, often despite formidable obstacles. Singles without children normally have fewer off-the-job obligations and can indulge their personal fancies and foibles at will. Because they lack the support of a marital partner or children, they rely heavily on close friends. They enjoy certain very real advantages—for example, more discretionary time and funds. But they must cope with the discriminations imposed upon them by a largely married society.

SUGGESTED READINGS

Adams, V. The sibling bond: A lifelong love/hate dialectic. *Psychology Today,* 1981, *15*(6), 32–34; 36–37. This study of sibling relationships in adulthood shows them to be complex, many-faceted, and significant and varying greatly according to individual, family, and situation.

Ahrons, C. R. Divorce: A crisis of family transition and change. *Family Relations,* 1980, *29*(4), 533–540. Normative transitions are perceived as common in cases of divorce, and both stresses and coping strategies relevant to such transitions are identified. Suggestions are made for reducing stresses relating to the complex processes of families-in-transition.

Bell, R. R. Friendships of women and of men. *Psychology of Women Quarterly,* 1981, *5*(3), 402–417. Differences in feelings about friendship and aloneness were determined among four groups, defined according to gender and conventionality versus non-conventionality of values and attitudes toward life.

Bequaert, L. H. *Single women: Alone and together.* Boston: Beacon Press, 1976. Based on research and interviews with single women, the author examines their experiences with parenting, jobs, and community relations; their contacts with cultural institutions (the law, the church); and resources available to them.

Booth, A., & White, L. Thinking about divorce. *Journal of Marriage and the Family,* 1980, *42*(3), 605–616. Interviews with 1364 married persons permitted comparisons between those who were contemplating divorce and those who were not, as well as identification of factors that differentiated the two categories.

Borenzweig, H. The punishment of divorced mothers. *Journal of Sociology and Social Welfare,* 1976, *3*(3), 291–310. Although divorce has become more acceptable in U.S. society, the divorced woman is perceived as a threat to married women and the consumer-oriented social order. Hence, she is subjected to various sanctions.

Bozett, F. W. Gay fathers: How and why they disclose their homosexuality to their children. *Family Relations,* 1980, *29*(2), 173–179. Examination is made of the effects of gay fathers' disclosure of their sexual preference to their children. In general disclosure tended to produce more positive effects than nondisclosure.

Campbell, A., Converse, P. E., & Rodgers, W. L. *The quality of American life: Perceptions, evaluations, and satisfactions.* New York: Russell Sage Foundation, 1976. Variations in life satisfaction are determined for a national sampling of the over-18 population on the basis of class, age, education, and income. Implications for social policy are discussed.

Daniels, P., & Weingarten, K. Postponing parenthood. *Savvy,* 1980, *1*(5), 55–60. Intensive interviews were conducted with 72 couples in three generations who had their children early (22 or younger) or late (28 or older) in the life cycle, to determine what difference it makes, especially in women's lives, when people have children. It was concluded that there is no best time, but that long postponement may create something of a crisis in the late thirties.

MIDDLE-AGE LIFE-STYLES

281

Davidson, S., & Packard, T. The therapeutic value of friendship between women. *Psychology of Women Quarterly*, 1981, 5(3), 495–510. After reviewing the literature regarding friendship for both sexes, the authors describe a study of 42 university women's same-sex friendships and their therapeutic value.

Defrain, J., & Eirick, R. Coping as divorced single parents: A comparative study of fathers and mothers. *Family Relations*, 1981, 30(2), 265–273. A comparison of divorced single-parent fathers and mothers disclosed almost no significant differences on 62 of 63 questions about their feelings, the child's feelings, new social relationships, and so on.

Ehrenreich, B., & Deirdre, E. The manufacture of housework. *Socialist Revolution*, 1975, 5(4), 26, 35–40. A history of how the housework role developed in America over the 19th and 20th centuries and how rationalizations developed to make women satisfied with this role.

Eiduson, B. T. Child development in emergent family styles. *Children Today*, 1978, 7(2), 24–31. A follow-up study of children originally observed 4 years before who are growing up in a variety of family styles. Systematic home observations and detailed interviews disclosed that the children were being socialized in psychologically healthy ways that promote growth.

Elder, G. H., Jr. & Rockwell, R. C. Marital timing in women's life patterns. *Journal of Family History*, 1976, 1(1), 34–53. A study of women born just prior to the Great Depression indicates how age of marriage critically influenced their future life course. It also demonstrates the importance of assuming a lifelong perspective when examining the course of marriages.

Framo, J. L. Friendly divorce. *Psychology Today*, 1978, 11(9), 76–81. A marriage therapist describes the typical difficulties that persons contemplating or already committed to divorce encounter. He suggests types of behavior appropriate in various situations. The points made are amplified by descriptions of actual cases he has encountered.

Glenn, N. D., & Weaver, C. N. The contribution of marital happiness to global happiness. *Journal of Marriage and the Family*, 1981, 43(1), 161–168. Data from six national surveys were used to compare the relative contribution to marital happiness of seven aspects of life, ranging from work to friendship.

Katz, S. N., & Inker, M. L. (Eds.) *Fathers, husbands and lovers: Legal rights and responsibilities.* Chicago: American Bar Association, 1979. This authoritative book of ten articles, all but one by attorneys, deals with changes in medicine and the law that have a significant impact on the American family in all its varied forms, with special relevance to the husband and father. Topics that are treated include rights of the unwed father, the father's legal support duty, property rights of unmarried but de facto spouses, wife battering, and paternity testing.

Kerckhoff, R. K. Marriage and middle age. *Family Coordinator*, 1976, 25(1), 5–11. The author attempts to explain discrepancies between reports that middle-age marriage is satisfying and reports that it is characterized by problems.

Knox, D. Trends in marriage and the family—the 1980s. *Family Relations*, 1980, 29(2), 145–150. A comprehensive view of the literature discloses 39 trends in 15 areas of marriage and the family. Certain trends are well established, others are less certain. Also discussed are implications of these trends for family-life counselors and educators.

Lewis, J. M., Beavers, W. R., Gossett, J. T., & Phillips, V. A. *No single thread: Psychological health in family systems.* New York: Brunner/Mazel, 1976. A long-term study of certain healthy families and how they function. Knowledge of the characteristics of family systems that produce adaptive individuals may be of value to professionals in dealing with less healthy environments.

Maxwell, J. W. The keeping fathers of America. *Family Coordinator*, 1976, 25(4), 387–392. Interviews with and questionnaire responses from 30 middle-class fathers aged 36 to 63 who had an average of 2.9 children yielded certain important conclusions. In general, it seems that fatherhood is prospering and that the nuclear family is still healthy.

Mendes, H. A. Single fathers. *Family Coordinator*, 1976, 25(4), 439–444. Four separated fathers, 7 widowers, and 21 divorces, aged 25 to 59, were interviewed for 3 hours about their single-father role. The results indicated that the single father has not yet been integrated into the U.S. culture and that role clarification is still needed, especially regarding homemaking, emotional support, and supervision of the children. Nevertheless, the fathers believed they were doing a good job and found their role emotionally satisfactory.

Newcomb, M. D., & Bentler, P. M. Cohabitation before marriage: A comparison of married couples who did and did not cohabit. *Alternative Lifestyles*, 1980, 3(1), 65–77. A comparison of couples who had or had not cohabited before marriage disclosed little difference in background but considerable difference in personality. Theoretical implications of the findings are discussed.

Nichols, B. B. The abused wife problem. *Social Casework*, 1976, 57(1), 27–32. Case workers sometimes assume that the wife provokes and even enjoys abuse, an attitude reflecting the Freudian view of feminine masochism. Her behavior, not the husband's, is viewed as inappropriate. Such wives should be accorded case-worker advocacy, knowledge of relevant laws, and sources of help.

Petersen, R. Social class, social learning, and wife abuse. *Social Service Review*, 1980, 54(3), 390–406. A random survey of married women in Maryland disclosed two common causes of wife abuse: that it is due to either sexist social tradition or to sociocultural stress and behaviors learned in the family of origin. The results supported the view that it arises mostly from social cultural stress and childhood learning.

Puglisi, J. T., & Jackson, D. W. Sex role identity and self esteem in adulthood. *International Journal of Aging and Human Development*, 1980–81, 12(2), 129–138. A study of identity and self-esteem in a sampling of over 2000 Ohio State University students, employees and alumni, ages 17 to 89, disclosed significant differences in self-esteem according to sex-role identification and masculinity according to age.

Schaie, K. W. Psychological changes from midlife to early old age: Implications for the maintenance of mental health. *American Journal of Orthopsychiatry*, 1981, 51(2), 199–218. An examination of changes from middle life to old age serves to debunk various common stereotypes about people of this age.

Stein, P. J. Singlehood: An alternative to marriage. *Family Coordinator*, 1975, 24(4), 489–503. Singlehood is portrayed as viable and positive. Surveys indicate the increasing popularity of postponing marriage or deciding not to marry at all.

Zimmerman, S. L. The family: Building block or anachronism. *Social Casework*, 1980, 61, 195–204. Evidence examined from a systems perspective indicates that the family has retained its basic traditional functions while adding significant new responsibilities.

11
WORK AND LEISURE IN MIDDLE AGE

WORK

Significance

Changing attitudes. Traditionally, most people have defined themselves and their roles in terms of work (McDaniels, 1977). That is how such names as Carpenter, Baker, and Miller had their origin. Such an emphasis is understandable when we realize that work formerly involved most of one's waking hours. Identification with work is strong even now, despite later induction into the work world, earlier retirement, and shorter hours (Beck, 1977). In addition, work importantly affects life-styles and dictates the organization of one's life. After retirement people find that they must now structure their own time. Pfeiffer and Davis (1971) reported that from 80 to 90 per cent of their middle-class subjects, 46 to 71 years of age, would prefer to work even if they had sufficient funds without working. Few of them gained more satisfaction from leisure than from work activities.

In some ways the significance of work is changing. A generation ago job security and making a decent living were the most important factors. While they are still important, people now expect their jobs to do still more. Pay is not as important as a feeling of accomplishment and self-fulfillment ("Why Millions Hate Their Jobs," 1976).

Variations in work attitudes. Attitudes toward work vary according to sex, social class, age, profession, and individual. A man's status depends directly on his vocational achievement, whereas a woman is ordinarily ascribed the same status as her husband, regardless of her job. As a result, women have greater mobility, both downward and upward, than men do. And women more readily cross boundaries between the major status groupings of blue collar and white collar (Chase, 1975). There is also a closer relationship between the statuses of fathers and sons than between those of fathers and their daughters.

Feelings about work also vary with the years. By midlife, ages 35 to 45, expectations of work and life-styles have changed. Previously acceptable standards for a job are no longer tenable. The quality of the job and accompanying working conditions have become as important, or more so, than the pay it provides (Vriend, 1977). The concept of mid-career crisis with regard to work applies to women as well as men. Women, like men, may not care for what they are doing but still not know what they want to do; unlike men, they often feel they cannot do anything.

Middle-aged adults may even consider changing their jobs, or even careers, because they dislike their present jobs, find another field more attractive, or need more money. Some couples at mid-life experience severe strain because of children's college expenses. Among others the strain has been eased by increasing salaries, the children's leaving home, or the mortgages being paid off. Even these people may become more concerned about building up reserves for retirement.

A career change may or may not involve a change in life structure. Some people undergo both. Individuals whose personal values change may also develop different ideas about vocational success, perhaps concluding that money is not among the most important things in their life. Others change their career without significantly changing their life structure—for example, the engineer who leaves a corporate job in order to establish a company of his own. These individuals Thomas (1977) called pseudo-changers. Still others, whom Thomas called crypto-changers, remain in the same job while significantly altering their life structure. Almost everything about them may change except the job they hold. Another group, the persisters, change neither their career nor their life structure, giving rise to the question whether an individual can move through mid-life without reevaluating life goals. Such lack of evaluation, concluded Jung (1933), can be devastating, for

we cannot live in the afternoon of life according to the programme of life's morning. . . . The afternoon of human life must also have a significance of its own and cannot merely be a pitiful appendage to life's morning. Whoever carries over into the afternoon the law of the morning (money making, social existence, and so forth) must pay for doing so with damage to his soul [pp. 108–109].

Sheer commitment to work varies considerably by occupation; for example, artists and college professors are usually more committed than are blue-collar workers. In general, those who prefer to continue working find their work experience more meaningful and are more personally involved in what they do (Elias, 1977).

Women at Work

Problems. Women, like ethnic minorities, have special difficulties with career in mid-life. For one thing, they may not have received the educational opportunities that would allow them to follow the career that they desire. Hence, they often engage in activities that do not provide them the greatest potential satisfaction. Further, they may not have enough money to pursue the career of their choice and the training required for it, and they may lack adequate job-seeking skills and labor-market information. They also lack self-confidence because of their lower status in society in general and the work world in particular. Analysis indicates that women do indeed encounter an atmosphere conducive to lower performance and morale (Hagen & Kahn, 1975). This problem becomes more acute for women when they reenter the labor force. Formerly, "Identity was no special problem because a woman was not part of the larger world outside of her home and family, but a woman today needs to know who she is, what her skills are, what she wants and what she thinks is important" (Thom, 1975, p. 129).

Even today there is a wide wage gap of from $3,000 to $4,000 between men and women workers' incomes. Over two-thirds of the country's women workers are in menial, dead-end jobs. Even professional women are confined largely to lower-status jobs in their respective fields (Hall, 1975). Meantime, accepting lower wages will mean fewer Social Security benefits on retirement (Vriend, 1977). As a result, women have trouble setting aside enough money for the future (Rubenten, 1977).

In addition, it is sometimes difficult for married women who have never worked outside the home, or have not done so for a number of years, to go to work. They may feel that their primary responsibility is to their home, husband, and children. Or they may have become so locked in that they are hardly aware of broader horizons (Miles, 1977).

Society itself has not yet readjusted to women's rapidly growing numbers in the work world. Instead, it is organized on the unwritten assumption of the male worker with a wife at home (Holmstrom, 1972). Although half of those in the labor force are now women, their needs are ignored in structuring the conditions of employment. Moreover, family assistance in the form of baby-sitters and maids is relatively rare (Hedges & Barnett, 1972).

Most working women also experience an unequal division of labor in the home. When both marital partners work, the woman still has the far greater part of domestic responsibility. Mainardi (1972) speaks of the "ploys" that men use to "con" their wives into doing most of the housework. And the men are supported in this effort by long-standing prejudices that make of housework the woman's main responsibility. In fact, in one study of modern capitalist, socialist, and communist democracies and dictatorships, the working wife was found to be busier than even the heads of state (Lear, 1973). Instead, men and women should be able to alternate periods of employment, study, work, and leisure over the course of a lifetime ("Working Women," 1977).

There are both advantages and disadvantages to married women's employment. Thomopoulos and Huyck interviewed 171 couples, among which 66 of the wives worked, two-thirds full time. Seventy-eight per cent of the couples testified that the wife's working had had a positive effect on the marriage. Fifty-eight per cent of the men and 71% of their wives believed that the women provided more stimulating companionship because of their work. Fewer than 7% of the families believed themselves neglected. A majority of the working wives (71%) believed their husband had assumed a more active role as a parent, compared with only 42% of the men. On the other side, 70% of the women did not have enough time to adequately perform their dual role as mother and worker. Thirty-three per cent acknowledged neglecting housework, although only 20% of their husbands agreed with them. Twenty-two per cent of the women thought that their husbands did not help enough with child care, and a third acknowledged concern about leaving their children. The working and nonworking wives reported about equal satisfaction in personal and marital happiness, but the working wives expressed greater dissatisfaction than the housewives with the quality of their child care (Gaylin, 1976b).

Variations in adaptation to work role. Of course, women vary considerably in the way they discharge their work role. One group, the super achievers, includes such well-known figures as Margaret Mead, Barbara Walters, and Sophia Loren. Such women are sufficiently successful that they can hire full-time housekeepers to take care of their children while they continue their professional careers (Sheehy, 1976). Another group, the integrators, are women who attempt to combine marriage, motherhood, and career from the early married years on. In many cases, however, they have dispensed with their marriage or their career

In increasing numbers, although still a small minority, women have begun to engage in activities, such as running for political office, that were formerly male dominated.

by their 30s or let someone else, perhaps a grandmother or private school, rear their children. Their husbands often do what they can to get them to return to the traditional pattern and give up their job. Certainly, it is almost impossible to do all three things well. After attempting this three-in-one life for a number of years, some women simply run out of physical and emotional energy to cope with it. Sometimes they simply take a moratorium in order to assess the situation.

Achievement motivation. In 1968 Matina Horner reported that women have a motive to avoid success, especially in competition with men. However, various replications of the study have failed to confirm Horner's results (Levine & Crumrine, 1975). A. H. Stein and Bailey (1973) decided that women are as motivated as men to achieve, but in somewhat different ways. Women seek to achieve in areas that are approved for them and men in lines of work that are considered masculine.

In general, women with a high achievement motivation choose from several options. Sometimes they pursue careers that are not feminine and do not marry; or else they combine job and housewifery (Troll, 1975). At other times they follow a serial career—working, for example, then retiring for a period of child rearing, and then resuming employment after the early-childhood years are over. In some cases women merely obtain their major achievement gratification vicariously, through their children's or husband's successes. In a survey of about 1000 young, college-educated, married women, a majority found their husband's accomplishments more satisfying than their own. This view was far more prevalent among traditional women than the more liberated ones (Lipman-Blumen, 1972).

Men at Work

Problems. Men, too, have their mid-life crisis, when they experience doubts about their identity and sometimes feel disheartened over their unfulfilled dreams and ambitions (Schlossberg, 1977). Hence, it becomes a period for reassessing oneself. The problem is not so much failure but the gap between what they have achieved and what they had dreamed of accomplishing.

In addition, men may become dissatisfied with their jobs at mid-life. Salary increases have tapered off or stopped altogether; chances for promotion have dimmed or disappeared; and the future stretches ahead as much more of the same. For such reasons even relatively successful people, such as middle managers, lose enthusiasm for their jobs. Just

"imagine you are a middle manager. . . . Four supervisors and two specialists report to you, and your total operation consists of 54 people. You've just past your 40th birthday. . . . You will remain in your present job for the next 20 years. At age 60 you will be retired with appropriate ceremony to enjoy your well-earned pension. Remember, you can count on doing the same thing from now until retirement" [Kay, 1974, p. 25].

Basically healthier men often experience more job dissatisfaction than others, because they cannot fit comfortably into organization life, where the chief concern is productivity. Healthy people are active and autonomous, whereas organizations reduce people to submissive, dependent roles. Workers may adapt in various ways: they can climb the organizational ladder, leave it, or simply put in their time. As one individual expressed the dilemma:

> "I'm 45 years old. . . . But I'm not a happy person. The money doesn't mean a God-damned thing. If I could find something else, I'd love to get out of it. Let's say I'm a successful failure. I'm bored with the routine of it all. Basically, it's the same routine" [Chiriboga & Thurnher, 1975, p. 71].

In the traditional American family the husband-father was a provider and the wife-mother the housewife. This situation persisted from the 1830s until about 1980 when the U.S. Census no longer automatically named the adult male head of household. During those years the provider role became competitive, and men were expected to be good providers. More recently, as greater numbers of married women have entered the work force, both the privileges and powers of the good provider have diminished. However, a substitute sociopsychological structure has yet to be achieved (Bernard, 1981).

Some men manage somehow to adapt; others lack coping styles in dealing with on-the-job frustrations. The failure to cope adequately with such contingencies may cause a lasting physiological change and a modification in susceptibility to disease (Friis, 1976). Moreover, "Prolonged dissatisfaction may produce permanent activation of biochemical mechanisms, such as persistent essential hypertension and increased heart rate" (Spekke, 1976a, p. 50).

Men in general suffer from identification with their work role, largely because society has expected it of them. As a result, changes in job status are even more important to men than changes in the life cycle (Back & Back, 1977). Meantime, they devote so much of their time to their jobs that they have little opportunity to develop other aspects or facets of their personality (Gintis, 1972). And if they lose their jobs, their unemployment can prove devastating. This is especially true of older workers, partly because they normally remain out of work from 30 to 70 per cent longer than do younger people (Entine, 1977).

A study of male achievers. Even successful men vary in their capacity to adapt over the course of their work careers. The Grant Study initiated at Harvard in 1938 disclosed how the young male subjects cultivated their confidence and their careers between 25 and 35 and then somehow fell into self-deception and losing touch with themselves. While taking on ever-more-responsible commitments, they failed to grow personally, locked into their destinies.

These **wunderkinder,** or locked-in men, desired to achieve but were willing to take more risks. Ordinarily they had a mentor or someone to encourage them. Their work was their life, their excitement, their dream, and their play. Examples are Einstein, who evolved the theory of relativity at age 35, and Alexander and

Napoleon, who developed empires before they were 30. Productivity is the key to the wunderkind men, often with both fortunate and unfortunate consequences. In general,

> The work is his fix. The dividing line between work and private life is blurred early. . . . He works even at play. The point of the vacation is to recharge his batteries for more work; the point of the golf game is to sew up a business friendship, unless the point of the game is even more basic: to win the championship [p. 90].

Such individuals have unusual energy and unusual capacity for retrieving themselves after failures. Ordinarily they make a utilitarian choice in marriage, possibly having their mistress on the side. In general, "Their wives form a sanctuary which psychologically and literally frees the man to work. [While] the existence of a family may be crucial, their wives and children could be interchangeable" (Bardwick, 1974, p. 93). Such men desire power. They want to become part of the "inner circle," and making money is a secondary motive. They are loath to admit when they have arrived at mid-life, and the crisis is actually triggered by arriving at success.

Of course, there are high achievers who manage to rise above their own success and renew themselves through benefiting society or serving as mentors to the young. All the 20 successful men in a University of Michigan study made abrupt, dramatic career changes or became social activists in middle age. An esteemed academician undertook to modify national social policies (Bardwick, 1974). A physician gave up a middle-class practice in order to establish a clinic for the poor. All 20 denied that they had ever had a middle-age crisis. They were not specially introspective, nor was their work of any great benefit to society; nevertheless they perceived their jobs as having value. Their wives had dedicated themselves to their husbands, yet fully three-fourths of the men did not fully respect them as people, saying instead that they were wonderful women in the sense of their auxiliary role. Nevertheless, the wunderkinder generally do have a mid-life crisis that compels them to take stock of their lives (Sheehy, 1976, p. 223). Only one man in 20 over age 40 is unmarried; and divorced and widowed men remarry sooner than divorced or widowed women do. While men may elect to remain single while under age 35, those over that age tend to dispense with their bachelorhood fast.

Improving the Job Situation

Because of problems already suggested and others, imaginative efforts are being made to cope with worker dissatisfaction. Gerald Sussman of Pennsylvania State University declared that job dissatisfaction is on the rise ("Why Millions Hate Their Jobs," 1976). Much of this discontent derives from a new life ethic, displacing the earlier ethic of ambition and success. The new ethic involves a growing concern for personal satisfaction and development. As a result, some corporate managements are breaking up assembly lines, providing workers a totality of tasks instead of single monotonous competitive ones, permitting workers to set their own hours and organize their own work, and in general treating them as mature individuals. Adjustments are being made in such things as

> time (for example, flexitime), place (for example, work at home), environmental modification of task (for example, changing tasks frequently), broadening tasks to include bundles of tasks, increasing workers' autonomy (through goal setting and task reorganization), and fringes (for example, corporate-paid or state-paid continuing education, with family allowances and release time)" [Weber, 1976, p. 5].

It has also been suggested that work places be redesigned, as in plans initiated by the American Telephone and Telegraph Company a decade ago. And work was arranged so that a particular individual was identified with a particular piece of work. For example, a single individual might be responsible for installing and repairing telephones in a whole apartment complex or airport (Schlossberg, 1977). Some insurance companies are redesigning clerical jobs to permit greater worker satisfaction. Certain coal companies are letting miners make as many decisions as they can on their own ("Why Millions Hate Their Jobs," 1976).

Dissatisfied workers are also being helped to prepare for and find new jobs. It is becoming increasingly apparent that "people start, stop, and restart; that they recycle, that they often feel they need to shift gears" (Schlossberg, 1977, p. 77). One aid to such recycling is continued education. Such programs should be coordinated with students' needs. They must be either part time or full time, permit flexible class scheduling and course requirements, and allow credit for previous learning (Cross & Valley, 1975). Support services for such education include counseling, child care, and career guidance. However, some people are reluctant to participate in such programs. When a training program was offered for adult migrant workers in Arizona, affirmative responses were obtained from only 75 out of 900 families (Belbin & Belbin, 1968).

LEISURE ACTIVITIES

Definition and Significance

The concept of leisure. Work and leisure are sometimes perceived as opposites, and "vacations are all that keep us from being pulverized by the Old Grind. Nevertheless, we also work very hard at our recreation, and 'limp exhausted' back to our offices after vacations, 'back to the salt mines, ha, ha' " (Stegner, 1976, p. 41). Kelly (1977) suggested that leisure can be defined along two dimensions: the extent to which an individual freely engages in a particular leisure activity and the relationship between leisure activity and an individual's occupation.

Leisure can also be defined in terms of time and absence of economic gain. Work is what an individual does for pay, with at least relatively firm deadlines.

Leisure is thought of in terms of free time and, while some monetary gain may be involved, it is not the primary objective. A Geneva symposium concluded that leisure is time at one's own disposal above and beyond work or other obligations. These are only a few of the many definitions for leisure.

Leisure activities can also be differentiated according to the degree of expressive involvement (see Table 11-1).

Table 11-1. Leisure Activities in Increasing Order of Expressive Involvement

I. Relaxation.	
1. Solitude:	Having time to be alone to think, daydream, plan, or just do nothing.
II. Diversion	
2. Television viewing:	Hours of TV watched on an average day.
3. Cultural consumption:	Looking at paintings or listening to music.
4. Reading:	Reading and finishing any book within the last year.
5. Movies:	Going to the movies.
6. Spectator sports:	Watching sporting events either at the game or on television.
7. Entertaining:	Visiting with friends in one's home or going to someone else's house.
III. Developmental	
8. Outdoor activities:	Going to the country, the beach, camping, fishing, walking in the woods.
9. **Travel:**	Taking trips to other cities for reasons other than business.
10. Organizations:	Belonging to social or civic clubs or organizations.
IV. Creativity	
11. **Cooking:**	Cooking, baking, barbecuing—fixing food for oneself, one's family or one's friends.
12. Home embellishment:	Sewing, mending, decorating, fixing, building, or working in the yard.
13. Discussion:	Talking about local or national problems and issues.
14. Cultural production:	Singing, drawing, or painting, playing a musical instrument.
V. Sensual transcendence	
15. Guns:	Using firearms in sports such as hunting or target practice.
16. Participation in sports or exercise:	Vigorous physical activity either inside the home or out.
17. Dancing and drinking:	Going out for an evening to a place where you can dance or drink.

From "Role and value development across the life cycle," by C. Gordon. In *Role: Sociological Studies IV*, by J. W. Jackson (Ed.). Copyright 1971 by Cambridge University Press. Reprinted by permission.

Changing significance. In recent years leisure has gained increasing significance, partly because people have more discretionary funds. Beginning in 1970, for the first time in history, Americans spent less than half their income on basic necessities. Meantime, parents are using leisure activities to socialize their children into proper values (Carisse, 1975).

By mid-life, couples often have more money than before, as their financial responsibilities decrease and available resources increase. Family earning power increases because husband and wife are often both working and the husband has attained a higher status on the job. There is also more available time because of less need for overtime, moonlighting, or working vacations. Now, for the first time, many people have a chance to develop themselves along varied dimensions. They have been too consumed with child rearing or vocation to give much thought to leisure. But after attaining some financial security, they seek to extend their world beyond the sphere of their vocation. Meantime, more opportunities for leisure activities have become available and characteristic of current society. Because of the growing percentage of 35- to 55-year-olds in the population, leisure opportunities are being designed especially for them.

Bosserman (1971, p. 147) perceived leisure as coming to dominate the modern culture, saying that

> [it] is becoming a way of life. To choose life styles implies having discretionary income, time, and hence social behavior. People—youth especially—increasingly want to be identified by their life style and culture taste, rather than by occupation. Technological and scientific advances have made possible these three discretionary features. Their intersection is creating a new world perspective, a new consciousness, which is a hallmark of the "leisured society." More specifically, discretionary income can be spent for those items not considered basic needs; discretionary time means time free from work; discretionary social behavior opens a myriad of life styles to anyone regardless of family, education, age, health, ethnic background, and location. This is a new type of society [p. 150].

Evidence of the new emphasis on leisure abounds. Colleges are offering courses on the topic. Companies that make leisure products have proliferated. A leisure-behavior laboratory functions at the University at Illinois, and there is a center for leisure studies at the University of South Florida (McDaniels, 1977). New publications have appeared such as the *Journal of Leisure Research* and *Travel and Leisure,* and there are sections on life-style and leisure in *Newsweek* and *Time.* Meantime, employers and politicians have produced more leisure by adapting work calendars, increasing vacation periods, and creating more and better-equipped recreational facilities and parks.

Types of Activity

Specific pursuits. Leisure activities have, in a short time, achieved the status of the nation's number-one industry in terms of people's expenditures. This phenomenon embraces a wide variety of activities.

1. Sport activities, including jogging, hiking, bowling, archery, tennis, and boating, attract over 700 million people a year. It is projected that summertime outdoor recreational activities will involve four times as many people in the year 2000 as in 1960.
2. Attendance at sporting events rose 25 million from 1974 to 1976, the most popular events being football, basketball, baseball, horse racing, auto racing, and hockey.
3. Interest in cultural activities has grown dramatically: 78 million Americans visited museums in 1976, and 62 million attended at least one live theater performance.
4. The number of Americans actively involved in hobbies is growing. Major hobbies in 1976, with the numbers addicted to them, were gardening, 36.5 million families; CB radio, 120 million operators; stamp collecting, 16 million; bridge and chess, about 10 million regular players each; genealogy, 10 million researchers; photography, 3 million hobbyists; and coin collecting, 1 million.
5. About 40 million people spend many leisure hours in service activities, often in churches and hospitals.
6. For other millions recreation is mostly secondary, chiefly watching television or going to movies. People in the United States have been increasing their spending every day in pleasure pursuits ("The Boom in Leisure," 1977).

Friendships. The choice of leisure activities to some extent limits an individual's acquaintances. People who focus on particular activities such as skiing, surfing, mountaineering, or bowling in effect gain entry into unique social worlds. These worlds involve different degrees of commitment, skill, and participation and varying patterns of relationship among those involved—the so-called leisure sets (Cheek, Field, & Burge, 1976).

Adults choose friends more on the basis of such similarities in occupational status, duration of marriage, or age of children than on similarity in their own age (Hess, 1972). In any case, most married adults have a reasonably large number of acquaintances among their neighbors and colleagues at work, but only three or four close friends. Moreover, people generally become less sociable as they grow older (Haan & Day, 1974).

Social networks are complex and difficult to analyze. Studies of such networks in the contrasting environments of Los Angeles and Hull, Ontario, just north of Ottawa, indicate that "in modern mobile society primary groups have become functionally differentiated, with kin, neighborhood, and friends serving quite separate social functions with little overlap" (Irving, 1977, p. 88). Those individuals who were kin-oriented in social interactions reported looser-knit social networks among their other associates, and vice versa. Thus, the networks among kin and others represent somewhat distinct phenomena, and "kin and neighbors are not cemented together in an integrated huddle of social familiarity" (p. 88). Contrary to former times, kinsfolk in mobile societies are coming increasingly to represent a separate area of social support from others. However, social networks are surprisingly close knit in widely varied urban environments and remain, in general, dependent on the residential locality (Irving, 1977).

Factors Relating to Choice of Activity

Sex and marital status. Leisure styles in mid-life vary far more according to marital status than to sex differences (Haan & Day, 1974). Such sex differences as exist in adolescence iron out during adult years. With regard to marital status, singles rely more on friends than do couples, who count chiefly on each other; and they have only personal friends, because friends of the extended family are not counted in this category (Hess, 1972). Singles' choice of activities is also more varied, because they have fewer family responsibilities.

Social class. Class interrelates with sex in affecting the choice of leisure activities. For almost every type of pursuit, the participants come mostly from the upper and middle classes, chiefly because they have adequate income to pursue leisure in their free time (Burdge, 1969). Working wives, of both the middle and blue-collar classes, have little free time. Overall, however, econom-

Upper- and middle-class people have more opportunities for leisure pursuits.

ically well-off wives work an average of 3 hours less than the underprivileged classes (Gunter & Moore, 1975). In comparison with blue-collar wives, they engage in more activities with their husbands, whose leisure activities are nevertheless shared largely with their own sex.

Age. It is quite obvious that leisure activities vary with age. In one study (Shulman, 1975), interviews with 347 adults indicated that social relationships and personal networks vary with age in their composition, stability, and degree of involvement. Younger people spend more time with their associates, which increases the probability that those in the network will come to know other network members. By contrast, married people include kin and neighbors in their networks.

At least until the **"empty-nest" stage,** the most important leisure activities of parents are, in this order: personal interaction with spouse or children; family activity—recreational or travel; cultural activity—usually reading or television; recreation—sports, outdoor activity, and the like; home maintenance; and miscellaneous (Kelly, John R., 1975). Also, until the children leave home, a couple's jointly shared activities decrease, and this may be a reason for the usual decline in marital satisfaction. After retirement, however, a reversal occurs, and couples engage in more activities together.

Among those studied, the majority was involved in stable, close-knit networks composed of friends, kinspeople, and, to some extent, neighbors. Single young adults were least likely to include their kin among their closest relationships. The young adults were involved in establishing a career and seeking companionship and a mate. Hence, they associated more with agemates with similar interests. However, older couples and their children became involved in stable sets of networks of kin and neighbors as well as friends (Shulman, 1975).

Individual personality. The relationship between leisure choices and personality characteristics has not been adequately researched. Yet it is easily apparent that people at any life stage vary greatly in choice of activity because of individual differences in personality, life-style, and experiences. Fortunately, the trend toward a more pluralistic society makes room for greater individual choice of activity. In addition, increasing free time makes possible "moving from a style of life in which everything is normative and pre-defined by society, to a life-style where there is more room for choice" (Gunter & Moore, 1975).

Improving Adult Leisure

Various recommendations are being made for improving adult leisure styles. William Glasser, an educator and psychiatrist, offered these observations about recreation in the United States today ("Needed for America," 1977).

1. People should be active in their leisure because humans are "doing" kinds

of beings. Sometimes, of course, people might need simply to lie on the grass and open themselves to thoughts and feelings. Nevertheless, they also need active participation, as in reading a book or playing golf or tennis.

2. Ordinarily, recreation should involve sharing an experience with another person or persons, whether in sailing, walking, or tennis. By contrast, watching television is lonely and inactive; and excessive viewing may cripple creativity and curiosity.

3. The growth of participatory sports, such as jogging, is a very positive development. Growing numbers are becoming active and getting out-doors. They may play shuffleboard, golf, and tennis or relax with chess, checkers, or cards.

4. Activities should be made available that do not depend on organizing people into groups such as softball leagues or orchestras. Organized activities are good but require effort to initiate and maintain. By contrast, activities such as skiing, fishing, bike riding, golf, and jogging provide simpler, less expensive recreation.

5. Such exercises as yoga and meditation may help to provide greater self-discipline. But **encounter groups,** where people "commiserate with each other," may simply substitute "emoting for experiencing." Nevertheless, the worth of any activity depends on the quality of experience of those involved. While some participants do not gain from participation in encounter groups, others report benefits. Much depends on the quality of leadership and the "fit" between an individual and the rest of the group.

6. Recreation can become too grim and exacting. It should not have "much of a goal" but should let the mind be free. Many people who run or jog do so not merely for physical satisfaction. The runners report that their minds "spin out" so that they experience a "high" that provides a renewal of strength and spirit. Indeed, every individual needs to find appropriate recreation that frees the mind and helps one to escape daily stresses in "a deeply felt way, whether through playing golf, painting a picture or camping in the woods. . . . The secret of happiness is to get involved doing something you believe in enough to accept yourself completely in the process' (p. 76).

Glasser deplored conditions that interfere with appropriate recreation. There are not enough opportunities for people to enjoy leisure time. The tennis courts, golf courses, ski slopes, and national parks are entirely too crowded. While well-off people may have their recreational vehicles and country-club, tennis-club, and yacht-club memberships, average people have inadequate access to public recreational activities. Private enterprise simply cannot take care of the job; therefore, the federal government, perhaps through a department of recreation, should look out for people's leisure needs.

In recent years, interest in a wide variety of recreations has been growing all across the United States ("Recreation for All," 1977). Many communities are making active efforts to increase their recreation facilities. In some cases day-care centers and schools are used for recreation during off hours. In one community complex, a recreation center has physical-education classes, jogging, hobbies, and games. In the evening, dance music and drama groups occupy a community theater beside a school.

Despite the growing minority that pursues an active recreational program, a considerable majority is still unwilling to pay the very considerable cost of maintaining adequate facilities. For one thing, most citizens have hardly been alerted to the extent of the need or been sold on the desirability of such programs.

Many communities are making an effort to increase recreation facilities, including places for arts and crafts.

It is necessary to educate the public to realize that recreation constitutes a significant measure for dealing with such problems as drug abuse, alcohol, and crime, 80% of which transpires during off-work hours. Moreover, because of early retirement, high unemployment, and a shorter work week, the destructive instead of constructive use of leisure can become an increasingly serious social problem unless issues relating to leisure are confronted realistically ("Recreation for All," 1977).

SUMMARY

Most people, especially men, have traditionally defined themselves in terms of work, but the situation is changing. Although it is still deemed important for proving oneself and for making money, work is now expected to contribute to personal fulfillment. Of course, attitudes toward work vary according to sex, social class, and individual.

Men and women differ somewhat in their vocational attitudes and status. Women still confront much discrimination in the work world, and the married woman, in particular, experiences additional complications. She may feel guilty about neglecting her children, find her husband unsupportive, or have trouble fulfilling a dual role. For their part, men often fail to reach their vocational goals or focus on work to the detriment of other important values. Nevertheless, adaptations to work are highly variable, and many people of both sexes somehow contrive to achieve considerable personal fulfillment through their vocation. This task is made easier by certain of the many steps being taken nowadays to improve the work environment.

Meantime, leisure is attaining increasing significance because of the greater amount of discretionary time and funds. People develop their own leisure styles, which involve association with others of like taste. Their choice of activities relates to such factors as sex, age, marital status, and personality. These leisure styles will undoubtedly become modified and improved because of the rapidly growing concern for such matters in modern society.

SUGGESTED READINGS

Aneshensel, C. S. & Rosen, B. C. Domestic roles and sex differences in occupational expectations. *Journal of Marriage and the Family*, 1980, 42(1), 121–131. A questionnaire study of adolescents discloses significant relationships between sex roles, domestic roles, and occupational expectations. For males, domestic and occupational expectations are relatively discrete; for females they are complexly interwoven.

Berlinguer, G. Life-styles and health: Alternative patterns. *International Journal of Health Services*, 1981, 11(1), 53–61. An analysis of the working experience in Europe suggests the risk of rejecting technology on the basis of reduced life expectancy and alienation phenomenon. Instead, improved insight into social systems can point the way to improvements in lifestyles and health programs.

Bernard, J. The good-provider role: Its rise and fall. *American Psychologist*, 1981, 36(1)., 1–12. After reviewing the past history of the respective roles of the husband-father-provider and the wife-mother-housewife in America, the author identifies obstacles that must be overcome if a more wholesome realignment of family roles is to be achieved.

Flanagan, J. C. A research approach to improving our quality of life. *American Psychologist*, 1978, 33(2), 138–147. This progress report concerns the following: the empirical definition of quality of life for adults; surveys of 30-, 50-, and 70-year-olds to identify their criteria for quality of life; current attainment of it by adults, and a simulation model for evaluating proposals to upgrade it.

Hoffman, L. W. Maternal employment: 1979. *American Psychologist*, 1979, 34(10), 859–865. The mother's employment is discussed in terms of psychological value to the mother and effects on children of different ages.

Hornung, C. A., & McCullough, B. C. Status relationships in dual-employment marriages: Consequences for psychological well-being. *Journal of Marriage and the Family*, 1981, 43(1), 125–141. Examination is made of the consequences of inconsistency between an individual's status and his or her spouse's status, as well as incompatibilities between wives' and husbands' occupational and educational status.

Jahoda, M. Work, employment, and unemployment: Values, theories, and approaches in social research. *American Psychologist*, 1981, 36(2), 184–191. Ways are suggested for ordering research findings relating to work in order to reduce shortcomings in current understanding of the field.

Kanter, R. M. Jobs and families: Impact of working roles on family life. *Children Today*, 1978, 7(2), 10–15. This analysis concerns such factors as changing work values, adult personal development, division of labor between spouses, and flexible, more autonomous work schedules.

Kanter, R. M. Work in a new America. *Daedalus*, 1978, 107(1), 47–78. The writer analyzes changes in attitudes, values, and practices regarding labor and concludes that significant modifications are taking place. The most important changes are insistence that work become more significant and a more meaningful part of the total lifestyle and insistence that individual rights in the work place be respected.

Kelly, J. R. Outdoor recreation participation: A comparative analysis, *Leisure Sciences*, 1980, 3(2), 129–154. Data from a telephone survey are analyzed to determine demographic variables (age, sex, race, income, and so forth) relating to participation in outdoor recreational pursuits.

Kennedy, M. S. Surviving ambition and competition. *Savvy*, 1980, 1(5), 32–38. Describes a dual-career workshop that tells how couples at the Harvard Business School are helped to gain insight into their situation, to discriminate among alternative forms of partnerships, and to work out potentially satisfactory solutions. The situations of several couples in the workshop are then examined in detail.

Newman, O. Leisure and life style. *Ontario Psychologist*, 1976, 8(2), 28–34. Various definitions and concepts of leisure are discussed, along with the relationship of leisure to work and projected changes in future leisure behaviors. In addition, the significance of television on the choice of life-styles is stressed.

Rice, B. Can companies kill? *Psychology Today*, 1981, 15(6), 78–85. The issue is examined regarding to what extent corporations should be held reasonably responsible for the mental health of their employees and what legal redress should be available.

Shaver, P., & Freedman, J. Your pursuit of happiness. *Psychology Today*, 1976, 10(3), 26–32; 75. An analysis of the results of a questionnaire about happiness returned by over 50,000 readers of *Psychology Today*. The findings indicate factors that either increase or reduce happiness, at least for this category of Americans. Some of the results are surprising.

Weiss, J. A., Ramirez, F. O., & Tracy, T. Female participation in the occupational system: A comparative institutional analysis. *Social Problems*, 1976, 23(5), 593–608. Data from 66 countries are analyzed in order to determine political, social, and economic structures influencing women's participation in the labor force and their employment in high-status positions.

Wilkinson, M. W. Leisure: An alternate to the meaning of work. *Journal of Applied Rehabilitation Counseling*, 1975, 6(2), 73–77. Because many occupations have limitations that prevent them from being especially meaningful for workers, alternatives for self-fulfillment may be sought in leisure activities.

12
A PROFILE OF THE OLDER PEOPLE AMONG US

INTRODUCTION

Old Age Defined

People are ordinarily defined as old at age 65, chiefly for practical reasons. This is the age when Social Security payments normally begin and when many companies traditionally enforce retirement. However, greater numbers are coming to pursue a vigorous life long after retirement. There is a growing tendency to distinguish the "young old," age 65 to 75 or 80, from the "old old," whose decline is more apparent. If the normal life span ever substantially increases, the concept of old age will undoubtedly change again.

Demographic Data

The mushrooming older population. The proportion of older people to the general population has been rapidly changing throughout the century. In 1900, about 4% of the U.S. population were aged 65 or older, but by 1970 almost 10% were in this age group. Life expectancy had increased from about 50 years in 1900 to 71 in 1973. At the turn of the century only 39.2% of White males ever reached 65 years of age, compared with 67.5% in 1973 (U.S. Department of Health, Education, and Welfare, 1975). However, the main cause of this greater average length of life is the decreased infant and childhood mortality rate, with only modest gains in life expectancy for older persons. For instance, an individual aged 65 in 1900 might have expected to live 11.5 more years; the same-aged person in 1973 could anticipate 15.3 years, or a gain of 3.8 years.

The growing proportion of the elderly in recent years is due both to lower death rates and even more to declining birthrates (Bouvier, Atlee, & McVeigh, 1977). The chief reason for a drop from 1973 to 1977 was a sharp decline in heart disease. If there is a breakthrough in other major diseases, that percentage could be much higher. Yet we have hardly begun to learn how to deal with the elderly among us.

According to 1977 projections by the U.S. Census Bureau, by the year 2000 the number of those age 65 and older will increase from about 23 million to almost 32 million, a gain of about 39%. People over age 65 will make up at least 17% of the U.S. population by early in the next century. Meantime, the median age of Americans will climb from 29.4 years now to 37.5 by the end of the century and will perhaps peak at about 38.1 in 2035 ("Profile of an Aging America," 1977).

The older population is itself aging, so that the 75-and-over age group has increased dramatically. In 1900, 25% of older people were 75 or older; in 1990 39% will probably be in that grouping, half of them 80 years or older. This aging of the aging is expected to continue, at least for the years just ahead. It is due to the larger birth cohorts of the earlier 20th century, now becoming quite old, as well as to medical discoveries that have permitted a larger proportion of these age groups to survive (Bouvier, Atlee, & McVeigh, 1977). An unpredictable, yet highly significant, factor is "the nation's fertility rate. This rate—basically the average number of children born to each woman in her lifetime—dropped from a peak of 3.8 in 1957 to 1.8 [in 1977]" ("Profile of an Aging America," 1977, p. 54).

The sex differential in longevity. In recent years the difference in life expectancy between the sexes has increased in the United States. In 1900 the difference was only .7 years, compared with 4.1 years in 1973. In 1970 there were a mere 64 men for each 100 women in the over-age-75 population. The average life span is expected to rise from 77 to 81 years for women and from 69.1 to 71.8 for men in the years 1977 to 2080 ("Profile of an Aging America," 1977). The proportion of women to men in the total population is expected to grow from 51.2% in 1977 to about 52% by 2050.

These sex differentials in longevity are significant for several reasons. For one thing, women are more likely to become widowed than men. Almost three-fourths of men over age 65 are married, compared with fewer than half (37%)

Women are more likely to be widowed than men and less likely to remarry soon thereafter.

of women. And there are three widows for every widower over age 65 (U.S. Bureau of Census, 1976). The average age for becoming widowed is 56 years. Men generally marry within 3 years of the death of the spouse, whereas women, on the average, remain unmarried for 7 years (Cleveland & Gianturco, 1975). Moreover, the remarriage rate for widowers over age 65 is eight times as high as for widows (Treas & Van Hilst, 1976).

The differences in women's and men's life expectancy also relates to living arrangements and economic circumstances. Thirty-six per cent of older women, compared with 15% of men, eventually live alone (Cutler & Harootyan, 1975). Over 45% of divorced, single, and widowed women exist below the poverty level, compared with 33% of men in the same status. In that case, is women's greater longevity really a "blessing"? They less often maintain independent living arrangements; they are more likely not to have the companionship of a spouse; and they typically have very low incomes (Bengtson, Kasschau, & Ragan, 1977).

Longevity also differs according to marital status. Frances Kobrin and Gerry Hendershot have reported that longevity favors married people over single ones and married men over married women (Horn, J., 1977b). In general, women outlive men by about 8 years. Among unmarried men, those who are heads of families live longest, followed by men living with a family without being its head, and finally those living alone. Men living alone have a mortality rate 94% higher than that of married men, compared to 46% higher for nonmarried family heads. The situation for nonmarried women is different. The mortality rate for non-married women, who live in a family that they do not head, is 100% higher than that for married women. For married women who head a family it is 19% higher, and for those who live alone, 27% higher (Horn, J., 1977b).

PERSONALITY AND ADJUSTMENT

Personality Characteristics

Representative findings. There is a considerable body of data, the grea' majority of it from cross-sectional studies, about personality characteristics o the elderly. Some of this research can be summarized as follows:

1. Increasingly with age, sometimes beginning as early as the 50s, individuals become increasingly self-preoccupied. Beginning with the late 60s and 70s, their social interaction declines (Neugarten, 1971).
2. People over age 50 have fewer positive feelings about friends, neighbors, and organizations (Phillips, 1969). In telling TAT stories older people are less intense than younger ones and describe fewer conflicts (Rosen & Neugarten, 1960).
3. There is some evidence that need to achieve is weaker in older people, though age differences are not great. Perhaps their decreasing achievement motivation relates to their diminished effectiveness of performance (Chown, 1977).

4. A tendency to be cautious apparently increases with age. However, older people feel more confident of their cautious beliefs than do younger ones; and caution often vanishes when they are required to make decisions (Botwinick, 1970).

5. Older people perceive themselves as less willing to experience change, and they are perhaps more dogmatic (Chown, 1960; Weir, 1961).

6. Older people are well known for reminiscing or reflecting on the past. In some cases it appears to help them resolve past conflicts and to promote self-integration. At other times it apparently does little toward promoting self-acceptance, and sometimes it may produce depression. An absence of reminiscence, on the one hand, or compulsive reminiscence, on the other, can be a symptom of disturbance (Coleman, P. G., 1972).

7. A certain degree of sexual role reversal is often presumed to occur with age, as men become somewhat nurturant and women grow more aggressive and egocentric. This same underlying pattern of change occurs across cultures, men moving from active to passive modes of mastery as women move from passive to active. That is, women become more instrumental, domineering, and at ease with their own aggressive impulses. Gutmann (1974) explained these sex differences on the basis of roles. First, in early adulthood, the tasks of parenthood differentiate sex-role requirements. Women must suppress their aggressiveness in order to be effective in their child-rearing role, whereas men suppress affiliative needs to succeed in their role as providers. Then, after the demands of parenthood are over, earlier suppressed elements of personality come to the fore with a movement toward the unisex of later life. An alternative explanation might be based on hormonal changes, for after the climacteric the sexes become biologically less polarized as male or female. For example, the woman's voice deepens, and her face becomes hairy; the male's voice contains a higher pitch, and his behaviors become more passive.

Evaluation of research. With regard to the age differences in traits cited above, reports are inconsistent from one investigation to the next. The chief exception is introversion, which typically increases over the years after the 20s (Neugarten, 1977). Even here, age may be a lesser factor than is commonly assumed. If the environment is structured to provide older people with ample and satisfying opportunities for mingling with others, will they not become more externally oriented? Besides, to the degree that they are helped to cope with their problems, they will be able to take their minds off themselves.

Inconsistent findings stem from flaws found in most studies of personality and aging. Hence, conclusions in this area must remain tentative for the time being. Unfortunately, most of the instruments used are of undetermined validity and reliability. Another problem in deciding whether personality changes are a function of aging is the common disregard for events that have intervened over time, such as widowhood or failure to achieve one's career goals. The individual who turns inward may do so, not as an inherent result of aging, but because of a succession of traumatic life events. Still another problem is that, as the years

A PROFILE OF THE OLDER PEOPLE AMONG US

307

pass, those who survive represent an increasingly selective sample. In a study of 47 men in their 70s and of the 19 still surviving 11 years later, the survivors had displayed higher levels of psychological adaptation in the initial study (Granich & Patterson, 1971).

An equally difficult problem is that of comparing the personality characteristics of people reared in different historical periods. Currently, more older than younger people are "hawks" where matters of national war policy are involved. Are we to conclude that older people are more aggressive than younger ones? In this instance, the difference is probably due mostly to the fact that the older generation had concepts of patriotism and respect for the military drummed into them as youths. By contrast, today's young people have grown up during antiwar times, in a somewhat isolationist national environment. When Parham (1976) distinguished age differences from cohort differences among a large sampling of subjects aged 21 to 84, stability rather than change characterized most of the traits examined.

When such factors are taken into consideration, it appears that change is more apparent than real. A study of women aged 45 to 57 that was repeated 10 years later revealed high consistency over time in life satisfaction, psychological and psychosomatic symptoms, coping ability, and degree of gratification with certain attributes of body and self (Noberini & Neugarten, 1975). Sometimes, when personality changes do seem to have occurred, what others see may differ substantially from the way an individual feels. Someone who appears to have become more cautious as a result of age may be reacting to failing vision. In matters where acute vision is less critical, the longer-term dimensions of cautiousness may prevail.

Individual differences. Overall, people in later years, as at all life stages, differ considerably among themselves in personality characteristics and lifestyles. Some of them are task oriented, and others are people oriented; some simply ease through life, and others live quite actively. Among their subjects, Reichard, Livson, and Peterson (1962) found three positive and two negative attitude clusters. The positive people were described as mature (integrated), rocking-chair (passive, liking an easy life), and armored (keeping active as a defense). The negative clusters were aggressive (projecting anger onto the world) and self-hating (projecting anger onto themselves). To date, efforts have focused mainly on identifying differences between age groups, and little effort has been directed toward determining how individual life-styles change over time.

Emotional Health

The role of age: conflicting evidence. It is unclear what role age plays in determining emotional health. Meltzer and Ludwig (1967) found that the relative number of pleasant incidents recalled decreased after the 40s. Cameron (1967) reported that individuals over age 70 had lower morale scores and felt less competent than did 30-year-olds, although the groups did not differ in current feelings of unhappiness. Nevertheless, concluded Kalish (1975), many old people manage to cope with their problems and "to enjoy life as much as, and often more than, younger persons" (p. 21). While older people have their problems, they are often less susceptible than younger ones to "certain anxieties and vanities and social pressures" of earlier years, so that they "can be more free to be themselves, to do what is important to them" (p. 21).

When older people are asked whether they are reasonably happy with their lives to date, they usually have some regrets but are resigned to the fact that they cannot go back.

> My chief regret is that I didn't know more about sex when I married. Our best adjustment came after 50 (man, age 69).
>
> Of course I have regrets (woman, 86).
>
> Because you can't go back, why not accept life as it is (woman, 74)?

In any case, it seems that adjustment is largely an extension of earlier patterns. In Neugarten's studies (1971), measures of psychological well-being did not relate to age. Such variables as being adaptive, purposive, and goal-directed remained consistent over the years.

Factors that influence adjustment. At every stage in life emotional health fluctuates according to various factors. Especially among the institutionalized elderly, it is significant in determining whether people can cope successfully with their chief stresses (Eisdorfer & Wilkie, 1977). There is disagreement about whether relocation produces increased morbidity and mortality. In some cases it produces negative outcomes and in others, positive ones, depending on the results of the move. Socioeconomic factors are especially important in aging. Higher-status people perceive old age more positively than do lower-status ones. Older people of lower socioeconomic status are less satisfied even when other factors such as health are controlled (Alston & Dudley, 1973).

Perhaps personality organization itself is the pivotal mediating factor in determining older people's adaptation. Older people do not simply react to their environment but actively select those activities that are most consonant with their own self-concepts and life-styles. They do not merely adapt to social and biological changes that occur over time but create patterns of life that provide them the most ego satisfaction (Neugarten, 1977).

Some individuals, of course, are more successful in such adaptations than others and hence place a greater value on the time allotted them on earth. In a study of attitudes toward the future, college students aged 18 to 20 and 101 nursing-home residents were asked whether they wanted to live 100 years or longer, how long they wanted to live, and what death meant to them (Moriya, 1975). Only 7.8% of the younger subjects wanted to live 100 years, compared with 30.9% of the older ones. However, half the older sampling preferred to die immediately. Most of the students (75.5%) desired to live to the ages of 60 to 85, 26% preferring age 70. Individuals in both groups who wanted to live as long as possible desired to do so in order to learn what would happen in the future or to get more things done. Death meant the beginning of a new existence to 29% of the students but the end of everything to 41% of them. More of the older than the younger subjects believed in life after death.

Measurement of Emotional Health

The varied estimates of the aged's adjustment derive at least partly from differing criteria regarding what constitutes emotional health. Havighurst (1963) concluded that life satisfaction can best be evaluated by asking people how they feel about their own lives. He proposed that five reactions be considered: enthusiasm for present life, resolution and fortitude, congruence of goals and achievements, positive self-concept, and positive mood tone. According to Schaie and Schaie (1977), the definition of behaviors reflecting successful aging depends on what models are chosen. Such models are usually determined by the middle aged. But a behavior such as disengagement may be adaptive for some people, just as maintaining considerable engagement and activity may be optimum for others. It is often desirable to compare subjects' own feelings with conclusions from objectively derived data (Schaie & Schaie, 1977).

There is also the question of interpretation of data. Observing that certain of the elderly are grouchy and combative, Lieberman (1975) perceived these as survival assets, a sort of "adaptive **paranoia**." He suggested that traditional views of coping with crisis may be appropriate at different life stages. An alternative explanation also presents itself. As each year passes, older survivors encounter increasingly serious problems, which may themselves produce increasing grouchiness.

SEXUALITY IN LATER YEARS

Sexual Activity

Physiological factors. Basic to modifications in sexual activities over time is the physiology of both sexes. Males do not experience an abrupt climacteric. And the testosterone level subsides only gradually, until around age 60 it stabilizes for the rest of one's life (Kaplan, 1974). The reduced testosterone level produces a

> less firm erection [so that] much direct tactile stimulation [is required] for development and maintenance; the production of less ejaculatory fluid, which results in less frequent need to ejaculate; a longer stimulative period preceding ejaculation; fewer genital spasms during orgasm; a lower intensity of orgasm; a qualitative change from an intense genitally focused sensation to a more

diffused and generalized feeling of pleasure; and an increase in the length of the refractory period, during which time the man is unable to ejaculate or possibly to erect [Cleveland, M., 1976, p. 234].*

The decrease in the woman's estrogen level during menopause produces

a delay in the reaction of her clitoris to direct stimulation. The vaginal opening becomes narrower, and there is loss of muscle tone in the vaginal walls. There is less lubrication during excitement. The intensity of her orgasm may be lowered. Estrogen is an anti-androgen hormone, and as her estrogen level drops, the androgen-estrogen ratio in a woman's body changes. This ratio change may result in increased sexual interest [pp. 234–235].

Incidence of sex activity. Because of such changes and other reasons, sexual activity diminishes in later years. Both men and women require longer to reach the point of orgasm or ejaculation, and the experience is not as intense as in earlier years. Other factors include physical or emotional difficulties, chronic illness, or a gradual loss of potency or of desire (Pfeiffer, Verwoerdt, & Davis, 1972). The rates of coitus diminish more rapidly with men's age than with women's, and childless couples maintain higher rates than those who have had children (James, 1974). There is no age limit on women's sexuality; but with each passing decade fewer of them have available marital partners (Pfeiffer, 1974).

Nevertheless, many elderly people continue to maintain an active interest in sex, even into their 90s (Pfeiffer & Davis, 1972). Nor are all older people, males especially, completely monogamous in their sexual relationships (James, 1974). In most retirement homes women greatly outnumber men, and certain of the men enjoy this situation. Wax (1977) described "one hale septuagenarian said to service an unending lineup of elderly lovelies is dubbed 'the stud of Sunset House' by the dietician" (p. 151).

Individual sexual activity varies according to many factors. Among men aged 45 to 69, health status, life satisfaction, and social class relate positively to sexual functions. Use of antihypertensive drugs and concern about physical well-being relate negatively (Pfeiffer & Davis, 1972). Among women, the main determinant of sexual expression in both middle and later years is marital status. Single and married men report approximately the same amount of sexual activity and interests; however, single women report less interest and activity than do married ones. For both sexes the amount of past enjoyment and activity are the chief predictors of sexual enjoyment and activity in later years (Pfeiffer & Davis, 1972). Among 102 married young, middle-aged, and older couples, older lovers rated higher on emotional security and loyalty and lower on sexual intimacy, whereas young adult lovers rated higher on communication. Men had higher

*From "Sex in marriage: At 40 and beyond," by M. Cleveland, Ph.D. In *Family Coordinator*, 1976, *(25)(3)*, 233–240. Copyright 1976 by the National Council on Family Relations. Reprinted by permission.

feelings of loyalty while women rated higher on emotional security (Reedy, Birren & Schaie, 1981).

The frequency of sexual behavior also relates to individual feelings and attitudes. Aging individuals may worry about such matters as failing sexual capabilities or feel guilty that they still have sexual desires, sometimes believing sex activity to be wrong at their age. To some extent such attitudes may be adaptive. For instance, the preponderance after age 65 of unmarried women to men is accompanied by a relatively low incidence of sexual interest in such women. Thus, the decline in sexual interest with age relates to the total socio-psychological situation (Pfeiffer & Davis, 1972).

Changing Attitudes toward Sex in Later Life

Traditional views. In effect, most older people have absorbed society's prejudices against their own sexuality. They are less accepting of unconventional sexual behaviors among the elderly, such as remarriage of a widower age 70 despite his children's objections, than younger people are.

Sexual activity has been associated by society with the young at the child-bearing age. Older couples are viewed as almost asexual: "Physiologically [they] don't need sex. . . Sexual tension is built on physical attractiveness; to be old

Proper health care is of special importance to older people.

is to be ugly and ugly people cannot inspire sexual tension in others. Romantic love can only occur among the young, and sex without romantic love is not quite moral" (Cleveland, M., 1976, p. 234).

Current professional practices. Traditionally, even professionals tend to ignore older people's sexuality; but their views have changed dramatically. "Postparental couples" are advised to maintain a "second-honeymoon" marriage, to "read marital enrichment manuals, [and] to learn new sexual arousal techniques which will make their sex lives as exciting as they had been in the early years of marriage." The question arises whether such advice is any better than old practices, and whether it coincides any better with "physiological, behavioral, and emotional reality" (Cleveland, M., 1976, p. 235).

It is unrealistic to expect that older people can experience sex in the same way they did in earlier years. For this reason, "The new sexual norms devalue aging as much as did the traditional norms. They ignore the physiological changes of aging, implying that youthful sex is the only good sex, thereby urging couples to reach for an impossible goal" (p. 236). Sexual activity in later years should not be "performance oriented, not oriented toward orgasm. Instead, the objective is to gain intimacy, joy, and fulfillment through a broad spectrum of sensual, sexual interactions" (p. 236). Older couples can enjoy "nongenital sensual pleasuring and oral and digital manipulations which may or may not result in actual physiological orgasm and/or ejaculation" (pp. 236–237).

PHYSICAL CHARACTERISTICS

Observable Changes

A sampling of changes. Certain physical changes that relate to age are well known. The height decreases, posture changes, wrinkles appear, facial muscles and skin **atrophy,** and facial profile changes. Ordinarily, too, weight increases with the years. In one sample (Brozek, 1952) there was a mean increase of 27 pounds of fat from age 20 to 55; but fat-free body weight decreased. Even if body weight remains the same, the individual is getting fatter because of losing active protoplasm at about 3 to 5% each decade after age 20 to 25.

Meantime, the aging voice is "characterized by a higher fundamental frequency in men and a lower frequency in women, a smaller frequency range, a change in vocal intensity, and a modification in voice quality" (Corso, 1977, p. 551). After menopause, at about 50 years, the hormonal balance shows a predominance of **androgynous corticoids** from the adrenal glands. Hence, the female voice sounds more masculine and manifests a drop in frequency. The singing voice is affected by age earlier than the speaking voice (Corso, 1977). Among individuals over age 60 vocal strain or fatigue (tired voice) are often encountered (Cooper, 1970).

Alteration of body identity. Because of these extensive changes the individual's own body image becomes modified, in a generally negative direction. Because society views such changes as undesirable, the individual unconsciously devaluates them, too. Much also depends on the type and degree of change, as well as the individual's own perception of such change and overall adjustment.

Changes in body systems. Internally, physical changes are gradual but widespread. The various organ systems and functions in the body decline at somewhat different rates. From age 20 to 103 the speed of transmission of peripheral nervous impulses decreases about 10% and the basal metabolic rate (the amount of oxygen used by cells in the basal state) about 20% (Tobin, 1977). After a peak in early adulthood for both sexes, there is a slow decline in physical working capacity as measured by maximum oxygen consumption, or aerobic capacity. Among men the maximum is reached at about 17 years, followed by a decline to less than half that amount by age 75. For women the maximum is reached between ages 20 and 29, followed by a 19% decrease from 50 to 65 (DeVries, 1977).

The Senses

Losses in vision. Of special significance are changes in the senses, particularly vision. The incidence of blindness and other visual problems increases in later years. Legal blindness increases from about 250 to 500 to 1450 per 100,000 in the age groups 40 to 64, 65 to 69, and over 69, respectively (Fozard, Wolf, Bell, McFarland, & Podolsky, 1977). Poor visual acuity, as determined by conventional clinical standards, also increases with age (Anderson & Palmore, 1974). Visual acuity of 20/20 is optimal; 20/50 or worse is sufficiently serious that some states place a restriction on one's driver's license at this level. A longitudinal study of 21 persons indicated that the incidence of visual acuity of 20/50 or worse in the better eye rose by 13% from age 60 to 69 and 32% from age 70 to 80. It is harder to prescribe glasses properly for older persons, because they may have multiple visual problems, often including those of accommodation, **astigmatism,** refraction, and color vision. While diseases such as **glaucoma** are relatively unusual among older people, they should be identified as early as possible (Fozard et al., 1977).

It is important that visual environments for the elderly be carefully planned. They need a level of illumination greater than that of younger people; but they are also more susceptible to glare. Lighting should be individually controlled, so that illumination for different tasks can be varied independently of lighting for an entire area.

Hearing loss. Among adults the most common source of auditory deficiency is **presbycusis,** or a "progressive bilateral loss of hearing for tones of high frequency due to degenerative physiological changes in the auditory systems as a function of age" (Corso, 1977, p. 535). In the United States about 13% of the over 65 group show advanced signs of presbycusis. And because of the rapidly aging population there may be 80% more hard-of-hearing persons in the year 2000 than today. Such changes in hearing relate to disturbances in the inner ear and related neural pathways. Physiological changes in the auditory system combine to produce functional decrements in distinguishing pure tones, pitch discrimination, and speech discrimination (Corso, 1977).

Decrements in other senses. Age-related changes occur in the other senses as well, including taste and touch. While various investigators have reported decrease in taste sensitivity with age, this conclusion must be viewed tentatively. Not all experiments verify this observation, nor can firm conclusions be drawn about smell. Odor sensitivity is quite stable over age, and observed decreases may result from sex differences, smoking, and disease. Odor preferences change rather early in life, reflecting a combination of maturation and learning, rather than aging (Engen, 1977).

Sensitivity to sensations that arise from stimulation of the skin, the viscera, the muscles, and the joints decreases with advancing age. It is unclear whether the loss is due directly to aging—as in specific **neuropathies** associated with disease or injury whose chance of occurrence increases with age—or is only the indirect result of aging. In any case, the elderly have less capability of coping with extreme environmental temperatures. And they are more susceptible to falls and other complications because of dizziness, muscular weakness, and decreased input from joint and muscle receptors (Kenshalo, 1977). Only about 25% of the elderly experience loss in touch sensitivity, and very few experience impairment of temperature and pain sensitivity.

Sleep Patterns

Often older people, as well as their families, fail to recognize that changing sleep patterns are normal. Many older people complain about sleep disturbances, including trouble in falling asleep, lack of sleep, restless sleeping, or early waking. A distinction should be made, however, between changes in sleep patterns that accompany normal aging and those that reflect emotional disturbances. Older people normally sleep more lightly and awaken more often. They distribute their sleep differently over the 24-hour cycle, taking brief naps of 15 to 60 minutes several times during the day. Such patterns should not be disturbed by using medication to encourage sleep through the night or by preventing older people from taking catnaps during the daytime (Pfeiffer, 1977).

Illness and Disease

Most common disorders. Medawar (Kass, 1971) has defined senescence as "those changes in bodily capacities that accompany aging and that make the individual increasingly likely to die from random causes, since no one dies merely of old age but must also be affected by some other condition" (p. 699).

Because of such conditions, often chronic, more than 40% of noninstitutionalized older people have some limitation on normal activity, compared with 13% of the total population. The most common of such conditions among the elderly are heart disease, rheumatism, and arthritis. Other common problems include visual and auditory impairments, high blood pressure, and mental and nervous disorders (Bouvier, Atlee, & McVeigh, 1977). Acute illnesses, those lasting less than 3 months, are more common among people in general than the elderly. However, such illnesses have a more restrictive effect on older people's activities. For reasons still not fully clear, people with the same degree of impairment manifest different degrees of disability (Shanas & Maddox, 1977).

The health of the two sexes differs somewhat in later years. More older men than older women are unable to perform major activities because of chronic health conditions (Kalish, 1975). Men are more likely to suffer from life-threatening illnesses such as cardiovascular disease, whereas women are more prone to conditions such as arthritis that seldom lead to death (Verbrugge, 1975).

The leading causes—together accounting for almost three-fourths of deaths among older people—are heart disease, cancer, and stroke, in that order. Heart diseases are by far the leading cause, accounting for 46% of all deaths among the elderly. By contrast, cancer and stroke each causes fewer than 15%. In fourth place, influenza and pneumonia together cause fewer than 5% of deaths. Other main causes of death for women are diabetes and **arteriosclerosis;** for men, they are accidents and a combined category of asthma, emphysema, and bronchitis (Bouvier, Atlee, & McVeigh, 1977).

Assessment of seriousness. The above catalogue of disorders sounds grim; but the aging processes alone are less detrimental than is commonly believed. Decrements presumed to result from age may be found in some, but not all, older individuals. For example, arteriosclerosis, ordinarily attributed to aging, is a metabolic disorder that affects only some individuals and is treatable, to some degree, by exercise and dieting. Other presumed decrements of aging— including senile brain damage, personality deterioration, intellectual decline, and, to some extent, impairments in physiological capacity—result from illness or disease rather than aging alone.

DeVries (1977) warned against attributing all functional decline to the aging process, because changes in physical activity are rarely taken into account. Apparently, physiological decrements relate more highly to decreased activity level than to age itself (Wessel & Van Huss, 1969). In fact, most of the age-related changes described above can be produced in young, healthy men by the simple means of enforced bed rest. In one study, after 3 weeks of bed rest, maximum cardiac output decreased by 26%, oxygen consumption by 30%, and maximal ventilatory capacity by 30% (Saltin & Grimsby, 1968). Hence, we can question to what degree observed decrements with age are true functions of aging and how much they are produced by the long-term effects of an increasingly sedentary life-style.

At least one other factor, incipient disease processes often unrecognized and undiagnosed in their earlier stages, may also contribute to losses in function.

For example, occlusion of coronary arteries by fatty deposits, which eventually precipitates a heart attack, may exist even in teenagers. To sum up, of three factors that may account for functional losses—aging itself, incipient disease processes, and inactivity—only the last can be easily reversed by means of properly planned exercise programs. While such treatment should be made available, it is good that most older people retain faith in their physical potential to cope. The aged often underestimate the extent of their health problems. Fewer than 20% of the 1900 people in Osterfeld's (1968) study reported health problems, but physicians concluded that a majority needed treatment.

In national samplings (Table 12-1) it becomes apparent that many older people may find it difficult to perform various everyday tasks. Modifications in household construction and furnishings would considerably improve their ability to cope and might well make the difference between whether they could remain in their homes.

Table 12-1. Percentages Reporting Difficulty in Household Task

	National Sample[a]				National Sample[b]			Low-Income Communities[c]	
	65-69	70-74	75-79	80+	65-69	70-74	75+	Poor	Near-Poor
Doing things around the house					13	28	37		
Bathing self	7	8	13	19	8	11	17	9	8
Household cleaning								28	23 (females)
Doing laundry								32	28
Preparing meals								16	13 (females)
Dressing	8	8	7	13	10	12	12		
Climbing stairs	26	29	33	42	9	18	20		
Going outdoors					7	13	20		
Cutting toenails	14	17	22	34					

[a]Shanas, Townsend, Wedderburn, Friis, Milhøj, and Stehouwer, 1968.
[b]Schooler, cited in *Indicators of the Status of the Elderly in the United States*, 1972.
[c]National Council on the Aging (1971).
From "The impact of the environment on aging and behavior," by M. P. Lawton. In *Handbook of the Psychology of Aging*, by J. E. Birren and K. W. Schaie (Eds.). Copyright 1977 by Van Nostrand Reinhold Company. Reprinted by permission of the National Council on the Aging, Inc.

INTELLIGENCE IN LATER YEARS

Conflicting Evidence

Evidence of decline. A great many studies have found significant losses with age in cognitive performance (Riegel & Riegel, 1972). At least in certain learning tasks, cross-sectional analyses indicate small age changes before age 60 and larger ones thereafter. Age declines also appear in longitudinal comparisons, as shown in the Baltimore Study of mostly well-educated men (Arenberg & Robertson-Tchabo, 1977). For the majority there is at least apparent regression in cognitive functioning during advanced years (Bielby, 1974). After reviewing the literature, Botwinick (1977) concluded that "decline in intellectual ability is clearly part of the aging picture" (p. 580). Recent literature indicates that decline begins later in life than heretofore recognized and may include fewer functions. In some studies scores have risen even to age 50 (Botwinick, 1977).

Brain differences with age have been demonstrated, however, and simple observation of older individuals often shows marked changes in cognitive behaviors. In a follow-up study at age 60 to 74 of persons originally tested in their 20s or early 30s, there was a significant decline in initial learning and retention, but vocabulary scores remained high (Gilbert, 1973).

Overemphasis on decline. It was formerly believed that intelligence rises until early adulthood, remains on a plateau for 10 years or so, and begins a regular decline in the 40s. However, longitudinal studies show that intelligence does not decline as early as that (Baltes & Schaie, 1974). Even then, the decline may be very small. For some intellectual functions, especially those involving speed of response in nonverbal, perceptual, manipulative skills, decline may occur earlier. Much also depends on the individual. On various tests some people in their 40s, 50s, and 60s perform better than do average 20-year-olds. Some older people perform as well as the very best of the young subjects (Schoenfeld, 1977). Typically, older people are slower than younger ones; but some of them are just as fast as the young.

On the one hand, those who perform relatively well in the earlier years also perform well later on. On the other hand, "The performance level when young is no yardstick of whether age decline will be great, small, or neither. Some changes relate to closeness to death, the so-called **terminal drop** [emphasis added], perhaps during the last few months of life" (Botwinick, 1977).

Changes in Response Capability

The process. Welford (1977) explained how age-related changes retard effective response:

> It's one thing to perceive that an event has occurred, another to decide what to do about it, and still another to carry out the action decided upon. . . In the perceptual mechanism, data from the various sense organs are analyzed, coordinated and supplemented from the memory store. The processed data are fed through the translation mechanism, so-called because it translates them into action by triggering decision and computing a response. The orders for this response are passed to the central effector mechanism which programs a phased sequence of muscular actions to execute them [p. 450].

Where older people are concerned, the chief limitation appears to be in the second and third mechanisms in this chain—that is, the translation and central effector links.

Limitation on decision making. The most significant change in motor performance with age is in speed. Larger movements made at maximum speed slow with age, apparently because of muscular limitations (Welford, 1977). However, most movements involved in everyday manipulatory tasks are limited not by muscular factors but by the speed of the decision needed to organize movements. Older people are also more cautious than younger ones in monitoring their behaviors and hence take more time to respond. Industrial and traffic accidents among the aged relate more to slow decision making than to motor or sensory impairment. At least in simpler sensorimotor performances, there is little consistent relationship to such factors as educational level, socioeconomic status, or sex.

Shortcomings in Research

For the time being, firm conclusions about the relation of aging to mental function must remain tentative because of weaknesses in research. Many studies of the 1930s, '40s, and '50s caused researchers to conclude that intelligence increases until early adulthood, arrives at a plateau that persists about 10 years, and begins declining somewhat regularly about the age of 40. Such conclusions were based on cross-sectional studies involving people who differed not only in age but also in generation. That is, samples of people at different ages born at different times have been compared, and it is well known that older people have had less education than younger ones in our society. Hence, measured differences in intelligence might reflect either generational or age differences or both.

By contrast, Baltes and Schaie (1977) and their associates, LaBouvie and Nesselroade, tested the same people (of different ages) at different times. Thus, they might compare subjects age 50 in 1956 with other subjects who were 50 in 1963. A statistical analysis disclosed that differences in scores mainly reflected generational differences, not chronological age. For example, older people functioned more poorly on certain tests than younger ones more because of their limited early education than age differential. Baltes and Schaie concluded that the idea of overall intellectual decline in later years is largely a myth.

Other objections based on problems with research techniques can be summarized as follows:

1. There is no longitudinal study proving conclusively that specific abilities deteriorate in old age, although such inferences have been made from cross-sectional studies (Bielby, 1974). In a longitudinal study spanning the ages 65 to 75, no significant decrements occurred except during the 5 years before death (Riegel & Riegel, 1972).
2. Although learning ability has long been represented as declining with age, observed deficits may reflect differences in performance rather than a decreased ability to learn (Schaie & Gribbin, 1975).
3. Perhaps, too, the abilities of older people may be organized differently from those of the young (Nesselroade, Schaie, & Baltes, 1972). When

A PROFILE OF THE OLDER PEOPLE AMONG US

319

Birren (1969) studied 100 successful professional people's methods of coping with demands, he found that they defined tasks differently from the young. They perceived that their goals had changed and might change again. Thus, they had programmed themselves for a measure of flexibility, in contrast to the rigid conventionality often attributed to older people. They were also aware of limitations imposed by their advancing age and had compensated in a variety of ways, including conserving energy and coming to distinguish between critical and insignificant tasks. In short, when judging the real-life performance of older people, "It is naive to regard them as passive victims of a cognitive degeneration of which they are helplessly unaware. On the contrary, older people may be said both to conserve and to exploit their intellectual resources more fully than do the young, to have a more subtle perception of points at which the complexity of decisions exceeds their capacities, and thereby to avoid unnecessary blunders" (Rabbitt, 1977, p. 623). Therefore, research into older people's performance should also concern modes of adaptation to decrements. While memory and perceptual motor performance indeed deteriorate in advancing age, the correct question is not "Why are old people so bad at cognitive tasks?" Rather it is, "How, in spite of growing disabilities, do old people preserve such relatively good performance?" (p. 623).

4. Age-related decrements in problem solving have been interpreted chiefly in terms of declines in learning and memory. However, we lack models by which to interpret performance on cognitive tasks in terms of a broad range of processes including memory, learning, perceptual integration, attention, and so on (Rabbitt, 1977).

5. Intellectual ability sometimes declines, as a result not of aging but of specific causes. In short, senility is not inevitably the outcome of aging. While a certain slowing of speed and response is somewhat a function of aging, it is also related to environmental deprivation, depression, and declining health (Butler, 1975).

6. Older individuals are apparently especially disadvantaged when their time to respond is short, reflecting age-related difficulties in retrieving stored information. Even under self-paced conditions, age differences in performance are found (Arenberg & Robertson-Tchabo, 1977).

7. Age differences in various human activities often relate to motivation rather than to intellectual or physiological competence (Elias & Elias, 1977). Especially with regard to problem solving, laboratory experiments often confront old people with tasks for which they have little motivation. Nor have they had an opportunity to practice the particular skills that may be involved. A research mode often ignored has been the study of the age of carrying on activities in which they are genuinely interested. In contrast, too much motivation can prove as bad as too little. Overinvolvement and overarousal often impair the performance of older people relative to the young (Elias & Elias, 1977).

8. IQ tests themselves are age biased, focusing on abilities that are most important in early years. Another difficulty is the distinction between an individual's confidence and performance. Handicaps that have nothing to do with an individual's basic ability may influence the way that person performs on a test. For example, the situation may be such that older subjects suffer from fatigue in taking a test. Such tests also vary somewhat

among themselves, and all represent their designers' concepts of what constitutes intelligent behavior. This factor, plus the inevitable flaws in all testing, means that results can vary a bit on different tests and from time to time. It can be assumed that in all cases there is a gap of some unknown dimension between intelligence-test scores and how intelligent a person really is. Nevertheless, it is generally conceded by psychologists that the better intelligence tests do a better job of gauging mental function than any other means we have.

9. Although tremendous sums and efforts have been devoted to overcoming educational discrimination in early childhood, little money has been spent on compensatory programs for older people. Yet even the meager provisions made thus far indicate that such efforts would hold great promise. Certain researchers have tried physical treatments. For example, "hyperbaric oxygen treatment—the breathing of concentrated oxygen for extended periods to increase the oxygen supply to the brain—seems to improve memory for recent events, although the outcome of such research is not at all free of controversy. The treatment of hypertension and conditioning of alpha waves also seems to be promising" (Baltes & Schaie, 1977, p. 70).

Other researchers are experimenting with psychological aspects of learning—different modes of presentation and the use of various kinds of rewards. When trading stamps were used as a reward for faster performance in canceling letters, marking answer sheets, and copying words, even after as little as 2 hours of training women aged 65 to 80 increased in speed as much as 20 to 35%.

Chronic Brain Disease

Extent and character of decline. Senility and chronic brain disease are not inherent parts of the aging process, and they affect only about 5% of the over-65 population. The incidence of brain disorders increases with age, however, although many people have lived to 100 years or over without the dramatic decline associated with senile brain disease, manifest in extreme forgetfulness or incapacity to perform simple cognitive tasks.

As people grow older, two types of change in the brain may occur. The first involves the normal age changes, which produce a continuous decrease in the number of functioning brain neurons across the adult years. Unlike other body cells neurons do not reproduce after the early years; after the cells are damaged or die, they are not replaced. Such changes lead mainly to a decrease in reaction time, which for the majority is minimal except in especially stressful circumstances (Zarit, 1977).

More extensive brain damage, along with the extreme behavior changes called senility, sometimes stems from particular disease processes, as in arteriosclerosis or heart disease. Or it may be caused by extensive deterioration involving the death of great numbers of brain cells for some yet unknown reason. This type of damage is qualitatively different from normal aging and is perhaps of genetic or viral origin.

Acute versus chronic conditions. Such organic syndromes may be either acute (reversible) or chronic, ordinarily referred to as senility. Older people are often incorrectly labeled as having chronic brain syndromes when their condition may instead be acute. **Acute brain syndrome** can be precipitated by factors that will, in turn, produce permanent damage, including brain tumors, strokes, or severe head injuries. In addition, it can be caused by certain transient conditions, including malnutrition, somatic infections, toxic reactions to medications, or even unhappy events such as relocation to a new nursing home. Once the precipitating cause is treated, the individual usually returns to the original level of mental function. Sometimes people with acute brain syndrome are wrongly diagnosed as schizophrenic or senile. Unfortunately, many doctors have neglected the mental status of older people.

By contrast, **chronic brain syndrome** is not, on the basis of present knowledge, reversible. Nevertheless, there is no perfect correlation between the extent

Older persons have the potential for excellent performance in many areas, including athletics.

of brain damage and the capacity to function. Some individuals who displayed little behavioral deficiency have been found in postmortem examinations to have endured extensive brain damage. Occasionally, through psychotherapy or improvements in care, individuals with chronic brain syndrome have made some gains (Zarit, 1977).

General Competence

Unfortunately, the general public still "buys" the notion that older people are less competent simply by reason of aging. Yet a survey of the literature regarding middle-aged and older workers discredits the stereotypes that limit their employment opportunities. In general, older workers are better satisfied, display greater stability on the job, have fewer accidents, and lose less time than younger workers.

Older people also have the potential for excellent performance in other areas—in politics, volunteer work, and leisure activities. In fact, older people have the potential for continuing growth, even to the very end. Many capacities can be maintained throughout life at either full or gradually diminishing effectiveness. There may even be gains, as in personal awareness, esthetic sense, and perspective on the course of human development, a potentially rich resource for helping younger people plan their years ahead. The challenge is to devise programs and forms of assistance that will optimize cognitive and general competence in later life. Older people respond favorably to a variety of ecological and motivational conditions. And their intellectual development is characterized by plasticity instead of inflexibility and decline. Hence, educational opportunities for them should be based on a psychology of development and enrichment and not a purely maturational interpretation (Labouvie-Vief, 1976).

SUMMARY

The older population in North America is mushrooming because of increasing longevity. The aged differ in personality from younger people less than is commonly assumed, and the differences that are found can be attributed largely to changing times rather than to the aging process itself. Estimates of emotional health in later years vary partly because of large individual differences. Despite their many problems, most older people manage to adapt very well. Sexual adjustment in later years is improving in tandem with changing social attitudes toward sexuality among the aging. While older people may not engage in sex activities in exactly the same way as in earlier years, they may find them quite satisfying if adapted to their current physiological status.

The catalogue of physical disorders among the aging sounds grim and involves all parts of the body; but the aging processes alone may be less detrimental than is commonly believed. As medical advances continue and people come to appreciate the importance of healthy life-styles, including proper nutrition and regular exercise, greater numbers will remain in relatively sound physical condition until advanced old age.

Authorities differ over the degree of decrement in intelligence in later years, although they agree that earlier estimates of decline were exaggerated. Some authorities still report considerable decline, but others attribute much of the apparent loss to faulty measurement and interpretation of data. Even senility and brain disease may derive from particular disease processes rather than aging itself. Such conditions may be acute (reversible) or chronic, given the current status of knowledge. General competence, too, declines far less than is often believed, at least until very old age.

The foregoing somewhat optimistic outlook suggests that the social, emotional, and physical status of older people could be vastly improved under optimal conditions. Until death itself is conquered, deterioration will ultimately occur. In the last years preceding death comes the so-called terminal drop, when cognitive and mental condition deteriorates at a more rapid pace than before.

SUGGESTED READINGS

Atchley, R. C. Selected social and psychological differences between men and women in later life. *Journal of Gerontology*, 1976, *31*(2), 204–211. A study of sex differences among 3,630 Midwestern retired teachers and telephone-company employees. It indicates that the women had been as work oriented as the men, took a longer time adjusting to retirement, and reported more negative psychological symptoms.

Beeson, D. Women in studies of aging: A critique and suggestion. *Social Problems*, 1975, *23*(1), 52–59. A critical examination is made of various studies that conclude that aging is more traumatic for men than women. It is then suggested that this finding arises from theoretical assumptions. The author proposes that a phenomenological approach is more adequate for investigating the private sphere in which the woman's experience is defined.

Botwinic, J. *We are aging*. New York: Springer, March, 1981. An authority on the subject of aging summarizes research on social and psychological aspects of later life.

Butler, R. N. The life review: An unrecognized bonanza. *International Journal of Aging and Human Development*, 1980–81, *12*(1), 35–48. Physicians are advised to listen to their patients' life review to understand better the phenomena of aging as well as their physical and mental status.

Butler, R. N., & Lewis, M. I. *Sex after sixty*. New York: Harper & Row, 1976. This guide deals with physical status, typical problems, the special problems of those without sexual partners, and other aspects of the topic.

Cox, H. The motivation and political alienation of older Americans. *International Journal of Aging and Human Development*, 1980, *11*(1), 1–12. This study, which employed a sampling of older Americans and focused on the relationship between their personal orientation and their feelings of anomie, political discontent, and political incapability, suggested that early personal orientation toward problem-solving produces expectations that afford long-range behavioral and motivational patterns.

Cutler, S. J., Lentz, S. A., Muha, M. J., & Riter, R. N. Aging and conservatism: Cohort changes in attitudes about legalized abortion. *Journal of Gerontology*, 1980, *35*(1), 115–123. Analysis of changes in attitudes about the availability of legal abortions over a 12-year period, based on seven national surveys, disclosed increasingly favorable attitudes from youngest to oldest cohort. There was no evidence of growing rigidity, conservatism, or a slower rate of change among the older cohorts.

Fallot, R. D. The impact on mood of verbal reminiscing in later adulthood. *International Journal of Aging and Human Development*, 1979–80, *10*(4), 385–400. Among 36 women, ages 46 to 85, those individuals over age 65 reported no different impact of reminiscing on mood from younger participants, thus calling into question the age-specific nature of this phenomenon as an adaptive function in later years.

Fisher, D. H. *Growing old in America*. New York: Oxford University Press, 1977. The status of the elderly, especially with regard to their political fortunes (and misfortunes), is traced from the favorable climate of colonial times to the less favorable, but improving, situation of today.

Hall, E., & Neugarten, B. Acting one's age: New rules for old. *Psychology Today*, 1980, *13*(11), 66–80. A *Psychology Today* writer, Elizabeth Hall, interviews an authority on the psychology of aging about the economic and social consequences of the rapidly increasing number of older persons and concludes that this age group is having a significant effect on American life.

Hendricks, J., & Hendricks, C. D. *Aging in mass society: Myths and realities*. Cambridge, Mass.: Winthrop, 1977. See Chapter 9, "Dilemmas of Retirement," relating to such topics as embarking on retirement, the retirement decision, pension programs, and making the most of retirement.

Jaquish, G. A., & Ripple, R. E. Cognitive creative abilities and self-esteem across the adult life-span. *Human Development*, 1981, *24*, 110–119. Data obtained from 218 subjects, ranging in age from 18 to 84 years, disclosed a positive relationship between divergent thought and self-esteem but little effect of relationship of age to variance in divergent thinking.

Kalish, R. A. *Late Adulthood: Perspectives on human development, Second Edition*. Monterey, Calif.: Brooks/Cole, 1982. This book, one of three in the Life-Span Human Development Series, concerns ideas, issues, and information currently available regarding the psychology of later years. The aim is to present a realistic picture of older people in a balanced fashion, neither overemphasizing their problems nor falsely presenting the period as one of comfort and pleasure.

Kulys, R., & Tobin, S. S. Interpreting the lack of future concerns among the elderly. *International Journal of Aging and Human Development*, 1980, *11*(2), 111–126. This study of a sampling of 60 individuals, all 70 years old or older, suggests that their lack of concern for the future is not so much a matter of degree of security or avoidance of threat as an acknowledgment that anxiety about future adversities is nonfunctional, involving preoccupation with events that may not occur.

Maletta, G. J. & Pirozzolo, F. J. (Eds.) *The Aging Nervous System*. New York: Praeger, 1980. This book reviews research regarding the nervous system processes in later years, followed by a section on clinical studies.

Mishara, B. L., Kastenbaum, R., Baker, F., & Patterson, R. D. Alcohol effects in old age: An experimental investigation. *Social Science and Medicine*, 1975, *9*(10), 535–547. A carefully controlled comparison of consumers and nonconsumers of alcoholic beverages. It indicates no negative effects of alcohol consumption. On the contrary, those individuals who were allowed alcohol and consumed it improved more than those allowed it but did not consume it.

Nehrke, M. F., Hulicka, I. M., & Morganti, J. B. Age differences in life satisfaction, locus of control and self-concept. *International Journal of Aging and Human Development*, 1980, *11*(1), 25–34. In a study of veterans, ages 50–59, 60–69, and over 70, the older men appeared to have resolved the ego-integrity-versus-despair crisis better than the others, despite having lived for a longer period of time in what is often viewed as a sterile environment.

Neugarten, B. (interviewed by Elizabeth Hall). Acting one's age: New rules for old. *Psychology Today*, 1980, *13*(11), 66–80. A *Psychology Today* writer, Elizabeth Hall, interviews one of the country's major authorities on the psychology of aging regarding the economic and social consequences of the increasing number of older persons among us and finds that this age group is already having a significant effect on American life.

Peterson, D. A., & Eden, D. Z. Teenagers and aging: Adolescent literature as an attitude source. *Educational Gerontology*, 1977, *2*(3), 311–325. A content analysis of books that have won the Newberry Prize for Adolescent Literature from 1922 to 1975. It indicates that older people are shown as not very motivated, complex, or interesting.

Reedy, M. N., Birren, J. E., & Schaie, K. W. Age and sex differences in satisfying love relationships across the adult life span. *Human Development*, 1981, 24, 52–66. A study of 102 happily married young, middle-aged, and older couples disclosed significant age and sex differences in the major characteristics of satisfying heterosexual love relationships.

Schaie, K. W., & Schaie, J. P. Clinical assessment and aging. In J. E. Birren & K. W. Schaie, (Eds.), *Handbook of the psychology of aging*. New York: Van Nostrand Reinhold, 1977. Clinical assessment of older people is discussed in terms of aims, diagnosis, techniques, and the relation of assessment data to the life prospects of elderly clients.

Watson, J. A., & Kivett, V. R. Influences on the life satisfaction of older fathers. *Family Coordinator*, 1976, *25*(4), 482–488. Analysis indicates that 22% of the variance in life-satisfaction scores could be attributed to self-rated health, social class, importance of religion, number of living children, and frequency of visits with children. Health and social class related more closely to satisfaction than did any other variable.

Winefield, A. H., & Mullins, G. P. Probability learning and aging. *Journal of Genetic Psychology*, 1980, *136*(1), 55–64. A study of 48 young adults, ages 18 to 20, and 48 older adults (mean age 78) in a learning task that involved different reinforcement procedures and material rewards indicated for men an increase with age in rigidity and cautiousness and for women a decrease in those qualities.

13
TASKS AND LIFE-STYLES IN LATER YEARS

INTRODUCTION

Tasks

Various tasks have been named as essential to satisfactory adjustment in old age. Erikson (1959) proposed as the chief task of this stage the formulation of a philosophy of life, including full self-acceptance. People see that their life has been their own creation, that it could not have been really different, and that it has been meaningful. The issue is one of ego integrity versus a sense of despair. Older people achieve a successful resolution of earlier crises that leave them ready to accept life for whatever it is. And there is no despair over the inability to begin again or to adjust to change and no acute foreboding over old age and inevitable demise (Erikson, 1963).

A related task is that of life review. The elderly person defines an identity that "integrates the diverse elements of an individual's life and allows him to come to a reasonably positive view of his life's work. Failing this, psychopathology is likely to manifest itself" (Pfeiffer, 1977, p. 651).

Another major task of later life is adaptation—for example, to loss (Pfeiffer, 1977). While losses may occur at any time in life, they are extremely common in old age. The task may be to replace friends or spouse with new relationships or employment with volunteer work. Adaptation also involves "renunciation, the loss of significant others, and the yielding of a sense of competency and authority" (p. 651). Other issues relate to integrity, and the importance of what one has been rather than what one is. Still other issues relate to putting one's store of memories in order.

Life-Styles

Another basic component of later years, life-style, is the byproduct of all prior experience, modified by current circumstance. On the basis of life-history information about people aged 40 to 70, it appears that patterns of aging derive from long-term life-styles. Consistencies in coping styles, not inconsistencies, are typical as people move from middle age into later years. Thus, barring major "biological accidents" or "social upheavals," patterns of aging can be pretty well predicted from knowing individuals in their middle age (Neugarten, 1971). For example, a 102-year-old woman who had worked in the textile mills of Oswego, New York, when she was young, prepared her own meals and read a newspaper every day. She was still mobile, getting around with a cane. Her morale was quite high, and she had a real zest for living (King, n.d.).

There is no single pattern of aging, and people grow old in ways consistent with their earlier life-styles. Nor does aging even out individual differences, except perhaps close to the end of life. In a study by Maas and Kuypers (1974) some of the older men and women had developed a sociable life-style. But the nature of their interpersonal relationship, whether limited to the family or extended beyond it, depended somewhat on whether they were still working and the availability of a family network. Others maintained a more detached style, with frequent interaction but low psychological involvement. The women favoring this life-style were well educated and well off, focusing on groups and formal activities. They did not reject their families but were not especially intimate with them. Men with the detached life-style typically had risen to executive or supervisory positions and knew many people without having close relationships with any of them.

By contrast, men of lower socioeconomic status were often loners, leading lives focused on their home and on leisure-time activities. They did not have intimate relationships with their wives. Women who were not married but were relatively young, employed, and healthy had close relationships with their children and grandchildren. Older women in poor health and no longer married remained somewhat uninvolved with others and felt dissatisfied. Overall, the disengaged, unhealthy, older individuals of both sexes were dissatisfied with their family relationships and held themselves remote from their grandchildren. They had latched onto the sick role and become dissatisfied and negativistic.

THE MARRIEDS

The Typical Pattern

The most common life-style involves marriage. A large majority of older people is married, at least in the "young-old" years. Aging couples are more numerous than single aging individuals. Thirty-two per cent of women and 68% of men over age 65 are still married, and two-thirds of the married do not share their household with others (Black, 1977). Moreover, because of gains in longevity, the number of such couples has continued to increase. The average age of death of the first spouse in a couple increased from 57 to 65 during the decade 1967–1977 because of the lower mortality rate. This 8-year increase in the joint survival of married couples, when added to the 3-year earlier age of the mother when the last child marries, means that the "empty-nest" period has increased in this century by 11 years. Earlier in the century one spouse ordinarily died fewer than 2 years after the last child married. Now couples can look forward to living together for 13 subsequent years, or about a third of the average total of 44 years of joint married life (Glick, 1977).

Most older people report that their marriages are, or were, reasonably happy.

> I married an exciting woman. The most difficult problems in my marriage have resulted from unplanned interference because we—in pursuit of our own interests and purposes—did things to interfere with the actions of our mate (man, age 72).

> Like everyone, we had words, but never carried a quarrel overnight (woman, 74).

> Very satisfying. We were both ignorant about sex and would have been happier in our physical relationship if we had not been so uptight about it. Sex therapists would have helped, but I still believe in traditional moral standards (man, 69).

Marriages often improve in later years. Because marital relationships are secondary to children's demands, couples often grow apart in the child-rearing years. But the couple's interaction increases again in postparental years, especially after retirement. As a result, most older people perceive their marriage positively, and many report increasing satisfaction with the years (Stinnett, Carter, & Montgomery, 1972). Following retirement the husband/wife relationship typically shifts away from the husband's work-oriented, instrumental behaviors to mutually expressive behaviors produced in the domestic divisions of labor.

There are problems, of course. For example, couples who have always rigidly defined their sex roles have greater difficulty adapting. The retired male who has always prided himself on work achievements may have lower morale than the wife who chiefly values interpersonal relations. Wives whose self-esteem has depended on running the household exactly as they liked have trouble if the husband insists on sharing control of domestic affairs (Lowenthal & Robinson, 1977).

Often the most difficult problems of older couples involve conflicting philosophies of life and a lack of mutual interests. Older husbands complain about the presumed lack of respect accorded them by their wives, and wives complain about poor communication. The increased time for interaction that brings some couples closer together simply highlights the incompatibility between others.

Remarriage

An increasing phenomenon among the elderly is remarriage. Until quite recently, older people who wanted to remarry often felt that society, their children, or their friends disapproved (Black, 1977). In the past decade or so, however, the number of women aged 65 and over marrying (the majority for the second time), has practically doubled, and such marriages are proving quite successful. Barbara Venick talked with 14 women who remarried sometime between 60 and 83, all of whom had been married from 2 to 6 years at this time.

Three-fourths of the women were either satisfied or very satisfied with their second marriages. The majority had met their husbands through relatives of mutual friends or else had known them for a long time. Four had met their future husbands at senior citizens' activities. They had married chiefly for companionship, and, second, to take care of someone. With regard to sex, they cared far less for the physical act itself than for caressing and intimacy. Although most of the men had taken care of their own needs while single, after marriage the couples followed the traditional roles, with the husband making household repairs and doing the heavier work and the wives cleaning and cooking. Before marriage the women had socialized with their close friends or their children, but after marriage their husband became their closest companion.

Remarriage is an increasing phenomenon among older people.

Of course, these marriages varied in degree of success. In general, they were more tranquil than either spouse's earlier union, sometimes because of the lack of stress involving inlaws, career ambitions, and child rearing. Those women adapted best for whom marrying again produced no great change in life-style or place of residence as well as those who were used to taking care of someone else. The career-oriented women made a less adequate adjustment. The majority of the women reported that their children and younger relatives approved of their marriage but that their age peers were more skeptical, doubting that the marriage would succeed (Gaylin, 1976b).

Cohabitation

Another recent phenomenon has been an increasing number of cohabiting elderly couples. Almost 20,000 couples over age 65 lived together without benefit of matrimony in 1975. This represented an eight-fold increase (Glick, 1975). In 1970, among men over age 75 who lived with a nonrelative, one in five lived with a female (U.S. Bureau of the Census, 1973). Older people are increasingly living among nonrelatives in new family forms and identifying with such persons. As a result, traditional forms of inheritance may be increasingly modified.

The reason for such cohabitation at this life stage is not some drastic change in the sex ethics of the elderly but in Social Security regulations. If a widow who has been dependent on a late spouse's benefits remarries, she forfeits either 50% of that income—or all of it, if she seeks new payments as a married woman. Collective individual benefits are greater than those allotted to a couple. And because about a fourth of the nation's older people subsist below poverty guidelines and a great many others are on the margin, the desire to get married must often be sacrificed to the survival needs of food, shelter, and medical care.

Companionship, not sex, is the primary goal that most older people seek in living together. Such companionship "means everything from dependable dinner/movies/walk around the block company to fondling and hugging, to nightly re-try-all positions, rapturous unions" (Wax, 1977, p. 148). Some couples do, and others do not, engage in actual intercourse. Wax (1977) told of a lonely widow age 62 who placed an ad in the personal column of the *New Republic* seeking a male pen pal, believing that the type of man she would find interesting would be reading that magazine. After a 3-month "exchange of soul-baring letters" with one respondent the two got together and sublet an apartment, an arrangement that worked out quite well.

THE SINGLES

Living Alone

Despite the foregoing developments, the chief increase in single individuals occurs in later years, and the majority of them lives alone. In fact, although considerable attention has been paid to such alternatives as divorce, communes, and unmarried couples living together, the chief change from living in traditional families is to living alone. Most of those living alone are women, partly because wives are likely to survive their husbands. Indeed, a third of U.S. women over age 65 were living alone or with nonrelatives in 1970, compared with 13% in 1940 (Kobrin, 1976). Women tend to marry men a few years older than themselves, and so there again their chance of being the survivor is greater. Further, men remarry sooner than women, because there is a greater remarriage market for them. In consequence, in 1970 82% of men aged 45 to 74 were living with their spouses, compared with only 65% of women. In ages over 74 the disparity was greater still.

People accustomed to being loners often dislike living in age-homogeneous residence areas, where they are pressured to join in group activities (Hochschild, 1973). Of course, living arrangements alone do not determine life-style, for people who live separately nevertheless may have many ties. Nevertheless, physical separation in living arrangements does create significant differences. It provides greater privacy and, for the young at least, greater independence. By contrast, older people who live alone may, because of their own disabilities, be unable to profit from the autonomy that living alone would otherwise provide. That is, their very disability would create a dependency on others (Kobrin, 1976).

Nevertheless, many older people live alone quite happily until very late years. The preservation of one's autonomy and unique life-style often more than compensate for the problems of greater age. Besides, individuals who have always been alone become quite ingenious at working out solutions.

Widowhood

The live-aloners include many who have been widowed, both women and men. Burnside (1977) reported loss to be the constant theme in her group work with older people, the most difficult loss being that of a beloved spouse. In fact, of the many events that may significantly change an individual's life, concluded Black (1977), the death of the spouse has been rated as the most severe crisis of all. Some people suffer the loss after a marriage of 30 to 50 or more years. One 80-year-old said: "I can still see her. . . I have not gotten over it yet and don't know if I ever will." Men apparently have an even more difficult sense of loss than women.

Problems. The problems associated with widowhood are numerous. One of them is that modern societies, in contrast to simpler ones, have no prescribed patterns for the widowed. Instead, many alternatives are open to them, but they often lack either the resources or the skills to take advantage of them (Lopata, 1973). Nor is there any real preparation in our society, other than some silent consideration, for the inevitable end of marriage when one partner dies (Silverman, P. R., 1977).

In the psychological sense, widowhood does not necessarily coincide with the moment that the spouse dies. Legally, individuals are widowed at that time. But it may be somewhat later that they come to grips with their new social and emotional role. The period immediately after the death of a spouse is one of anomie, or roleless role. Newly widowed people do not understand what the new role means or what to expect of themselves. In the beginning the widow is numb, sustained during the funeral by feelings almost of unreality. But the numbness is replaced by a growing consciousness of the finality of separation. Gradually, the feeling of selfhood changes, along with perceptions of the outer world. Grief does not end completely, and there is no restoration.

Becoming widowed usually demands a new life-style. Hence, surviving spouses must endure not only grief but also the radical reorientation required of living alone. Their new role may involve increased loneliness, the lack of someone with whom to share leisure activities, work tasks, affection, and sex (Parkes, 1972). Meantime, as patterns of friendship change, the older person's interest in cooking, good meals, being well groomed, or keeping an attractive house may diminish.

While widows or widowers often withdraw, at least for the time being, from social life, their acquaintances may also disengage. Thus, seeking companionship except with others of similar status may prove difficult (Parkes, 1972). The extent and direction of change relate somewhat to the part that the marital role had played in their lives. In any case, reality has been dramatically altered, chiefly because they have no one with whom to share all the routines of their daily lives.

The widow. Widowhood is a status that most women ultimately experience, and the number of widows is ever increasing. In 1850 both sexes had a life expectancy of about 40. By the turn of the century the woman's life expectancy for the first time exceeded that of the man. She lived 2 years longer, 48 to his 46. In 1973 half the once-married women aged 70 to 74 were widows, a figure rising to 75% among women aged 75 to 79 (Havighurst, 1973). Today, women live 6 years longer than men, and one in every six women in the United States over age 21 is a widow. If current trends persist, by the year 2000 there will be 40% more women than men in the United States (Sheehy, 1976, p. 373).

The widow has several distinct problems, one being the image she creates. She is generally perceived as a somewhat forlorn figure, and most widows also lack adequate financial resources. In fact, the adverse impact of widowhood on morale and on association with others derives more from economic factors than from widowhood itself—at least among the poverty-level elderly. When widows live with their children, they are expected to help with the grandchildren and the household chores, yet they have no real authority. Almost all of them fear that they are intruding on their married children.

Widows also have less chance than widowers to find companionship among the other sex (Kalish, 1975). In addition, many widows are

> targets of discrimination. They are women in a male-dominated society, and they are old in a society that venerates youth. Many are grieving and lonely in a country that would deny and ignore such unhappy emotions. They are without mates in a social network of couples. . . . They are poor in a wealthy land [Lopata, 1973a, p. 92].

Finally, for a woman who does not have a job, widowhood requires establishing a completely new role. Such a widow feels like an extra whenever she goes out with couples with whom she and her husband had socialized.

On the positive side, a widow still has certain roles of mother, sister, daughter, or friend. And among older widows, she has a ready reference group among those friends who have preceded her in this role. Or she may participate in a Widow-to-Widow program, which involves the already widowed giving assistance to the newly widowed. In this case the helper understands what support is needed and knows that distress may be acute and prolonged. A new widow feels that she is not all alone in her experience and is helped to discover new ways of becoming reengaged in society in acceptable and meaningful roles (Silverman, P. R., 1977).

Widows are better off than the widowers in some respects. They are more likely than men to have anticipated one day losing their spouse and hence may have practiced the widowhood role in advance (Lopata, 1973). Older women also have more friends outside the family than men do. Overall, they have greater emotional involvement and are more active than men in relationships with family, neighbors, and friends (Itzin, 1970).

The widower. The widower also has his distinctive problems. He experiences greater life-style changes, because he must learn to manage affairs for which neither his former activities nor his self-image had prepared him (Borardo, 1970). However, few widowers—or widows—are left entirely alone. They usually have close friends and living relatives, even if they don't live with them. Of the widowed age 65 and over, at least 75 to 80% have children, and 82% have living siblings (Black, 1977).

INTERPERSONAL RELATIONSHIPS

Kinship Ties

Family relationships. Older people, including the widowed, have significant family ties. While social scientists have recently focused on the nuclear family, it increasingly seems that nuclear units interlink within and across generations. In a sense, the extended family is not dead. For example, most older people, especially on the higher socioeconomic level, have frequent contacts with nearby relatives. Some of them live in a complex or multigeneration family household. Ten per cent live with siblings, 36% with their children; and strangely enough, about 5% of people over age 65 live with aging parents (Black, 1977).

Even when parents and grown children occupy different households, they see each other frequently. Sixty-two per cent of people over age 65 have a son or daughter within walking distance; 84% live within an hour of at least one child; and only 7% live any farther away than 24 hours (Black, 1977). Children visit the parents more than parents do the children, often because it is harder for parents to move around.

In times of disaster, older people call on family and kin more than they do friends, neighbors, or service agencies. In fact, they go to the more formalized agencies as a last resort. This helping function works both ways between the generations and consists of providing money and services, both in response to crisis and as a regular part of daily life (Black, 1977). Most often, older parents rely on their children, especially their daughters. If no children are available,

TASKS AND LIFE-STYLES IN LATER YEARS

335

they may turn to siblings (Shanas, 1968). Increasingly, as greater numbers live to old age, more people in their 60s will be confronted with caring for parents in their 80s and 90s. Thus, they will have significant relationships with their parents, their children, and perhaps grandchildren.

Such relationships may also pose problems. Although they are supported by kinship norms and are often gratifying and meaningful, they are also quite "vulnerable." As older people grow more dependent, they may want to contribute to their children yet be unable to do so (Kalish, 1975). In other cases older women who live near a married child with young children often have low morale, perhaps because they are called on too often to baby-sit. In still other cases, either generation may succeed in dominating or making life difficult for the other. The younger generation, like the older, may feel unwanted and in the way, and the older may tyrannize the younger. One 60-year-old single woman, whose widowed mother lived with her, purchased an attractive lot on the edge of a city with a view to building her dream house there. But her mother objected, wanting to live in the city where her friends were. The daughter wistfully gave up her idea and sold the lot; and by the time her mother died the cost of construction had risen to the point that she could not afford to build a house.

As a result of such problems, only about 8% of older people believe it is desirable to live with their children, and 77% would prefer to live somewhere else when they cannot take care of themselves (Black, 1977). Many of them maintain their own homes apart from their children, even after they are widowed. The sibling relationship is the longest lasting, often persisting for seven decades or more; and it is also the most egalitarian and the least studied (Adams, 1981).

Lowenthal and Robinson (1977) found that bonds between opposite-sex siblings are strengthened in later life. Even when siblings lose touch with each other they usually reestablish relationships. Such relationships may be very rewarding or sometimes marked by ambivalence. Whether warm or cool, sibling relationships remain alive when siblings are apart.

The grandparent role. Older people vary considerably in their roles as grandparents. The more traditional grandparenting is found among those over 65. Younger ones sometimes resent their role or care little about it, maintaining considerable distance from the grandchildren. A sampling of grandmothers' role behaviors indicates the relative importance of their activities with grandchildren (see Table 13-1).

Some older people even enjoy being foster grandparents. In one program, 6-, 7-, and 8-year-old children "adopted" grandparents, some of them well past 90, in a nearby nursing home. The children visited them two or three times a week. As a result, the "grandparents" showed more interest in their appearance, had better appetites, complained less, and shared their common interest in children (Whitley, Duncan, & McKenzie, 1976). For their part, children and youth usually have a high regard for their grandparents. Responses obtained

Table 13-1. Grandmother's Role Behavior with Grandchildren (n = 125)

Percentage Distribution

Role Behavior	Activity			Frequency**			Initiator			
	Yes	No	Inapp.*	High	Low	Inapp.	G/P	G/C	Ch.	Inapp.*
Provide gifts	97.6	1.6	.8	23.2	72.0	4.8	97.6	---	---	2.4
Baby-sit with grandchildren	92.0	7.2	.8	55.2	33.6	11.2	35.2	3.2	52.8	8.8
Home recreation	79.2	19.2	1.6	49.6	24.2	26.4	30.4	47.2	---	22.4
Zoo and shopping trips	69.6	29.6	.8	21.6	44.8	33.6	61.6	6.4	30.4	1.6
Drop-in visits	64.8	33.6	1.6	46.4	13.6	40.0	57.6	1.6	3.2	37.6
Relate family history	47.2	50.4	2.4	4.0	40.0	56.0	25.6	18.4	1.6	54.4
Teach sewing	42.4	55.2	2.4	10.4	27.2	62.4	13.6	27.2	.8	58.4
Help with emergencies	39.2	59.2	1.6	7.2	28.8	64.0	23.2	9.6	6.4	60.8
Take grandchildren on vacations	28.4	60.8	.8	2.4	34.4	62.3	22.4	8.8	6.4	62.4
Take children to church	37.6	60.8	1.6	5.6	32.0	62.4	33.6	3.2	.8	62.4
Provide advice on personal problems	29.6	68.0	2.4	5.6	21.6	72.8	16.8	12.8	---	70.4
Provide advice regarding work	24.0	72.8	3.2	4.0	18.4	77.6	17.6	6.4	---	76.0
Provide advice regarding religion	13.6	84.8	1.6	4.8	8.0	87.2	9.6	3.2	.8	86.4
Teach native language	1.6	96.8	1.6	---	1.6	98.2	.8	---	.8	98.4

*Inappropriate refers to those cases in which age, sex, residential proximity, health, and the like preclude such behaviors.

**High frequency: Subjects engaged in behavior once a month or more. Low frequency: Subjects engaged in behavior a few times a year or less often.

From "Grandmotherhood: A study of role conceptions," by J. F. Robertson. In *Journal of Marriage and the Family*, 1977, 39(1), 171. Reprinted by permission of the National Council on Family Relations and the author.

from 86 grandchildren 18 to 26 years old indicated that they did not perceive their grandparents as out of touch or old fashioned and believed that they had been importantly influenced by them. Moreover, they recognized certain responsibilities for their grandparents in the form of emotional support, tangible help when needed, and qualitative as distinguished from merely ritualistic visiting.

Friendships

Significance. For some older individuals, kinship ties are more meaningful than associations with friends; when commitments conflict, kinship receives priority (Hochschild, 1973). Informal friendship groups in the same area prove more satisfying than do family networks. Such friends are important for several reasons. They provide a sense of self-continuity and are generally supportive in times of difficulty. They also serve as confidants and as companions with whom to share mutual interests (Lowenthal, 1975). One may join with friends in various kinds of recreation and in conversation about things of mutual concern. Besides, these days older people are expected to call on younger ones only when necessary, a situation that many of the older generation find hard to accept. In fact, the "old old" today find more difficulty adjusting than will the old old a few years from now, because the latter will have been brought up on different parent/child philosophies. For such reasons friendships in old age tend to boost morale, whereas relationships with children often produce an equivocal effect (Blau, 1973).

Factors limiting friendships. A variety of factors affects the formation and duration of friendships. While some friendships persist into old age, others fade away or end because friends die. Older people may also have trouble getting about and making new friends or maintaining contact with old ones. Certainly, healthy old people are more likely to see their friends than are those in poor condition. In some cases older people make more friends than they did when they were younger, especially when they live in mobile-home parks or retirement communities. People make more friends in a homogeneous social milieu where others are similar to themselves, as in age-segregated housing or in communities where people have common interests.

As noted earlier, men form intimate friendships less often than women, a tendency they may consciously deplore in later years. Among middle-class and less affluent subjects, men's diadic relationships resembled parallel play and were oriented toward work rather than personalities (Lowenthal et al., 1975).

In a study of women's friendships over the life cycle it was found that women in their 20s continued to have their school friends as intimates although women in their 30s lost many of these ties, perhaps because they had developed new friendships in their roles as wives and mothers. Later on, marriage creates family friendships for women—for example, couples associate with the husbands' work colleagues and their spouses (Goldman, Cooper, Ahern, & Corsini, 1981).

COMMUNAL LIVING

Noninstitutional Group Living

Common styles. As suggested earlier, older people often prefer to live among their agemates. Growing numbers of the elderly are forming group marriages and communes, partly because they have seen experimentation among the young in alternative forms of family living. At other times, they devise new groupings that do not require marriage and its obligations, while maintaining with their grown children a certain intimacy at a distance (Somerville, 1972).

Some older people live in mobile-home parks with a special life-style and culture all of their own (Deck, 1972). Others live in retirement communities where the stress is on friendship, recreation, and leisure. Thus, such people might be termed a new leisure class. Such communities are also quite democratic, and people are not especially impressed by the others' former occupation or status (Jacobs, 1974).

Older people often prefer to live among their agemates, in mobile-home parks or retirement communities.

Advantages and disadvantages. Such age-homogeneous places have been viewed both positively and negatively. They are sometimes referred to as **geriatric** ghettos, neglected by society because they are not in view. Others have called them "hedonistic in spirit and devoted only to pleasure, recreation, and leisure activities." Even older people should "remain in the mainstream of life and attempt to remain productive" (Streib, 1976, p. 172). Still others believe that retirement communities have very real advantages for the elderly. They provide older people with an environment where they are buffered against the consequences of loss of status and downward mobility. In this environment they mingle chiefly with people in their same situation. They are not constrained to compete with people younger and more vigorous than themselves. They are not pitied by those around them for being less active than they were. Besides, they ordinarily join such communities voluntarily and can leave them if they like (Streib, 1976). As a woman of Sun City, Arizona, observed:

> Retired people don't belong in a busy working society because they make pests of themselves, so we came to a retirement community where everyone is at leisure. It's nice to have a place to go to have fun and maybe act a little foolish. I never learned how to ride a bike or swim until I came here—and no one will laugh at you because you're older [cited in Streib, 1976, p. 172].

Finally, in such communities one's associates are experiencing the same decline as oneself. For such reasons people living in retirement villages are often happier than those who live in mixed-age groups.

Of course, retirement villages vary in quality and kind. Social activities vary according to the facilities and programs provided (Sherman, 1974). The communities also vary in age restrictions. Some of them limit residence to those over 50. While members of such communities have less contact with family members than those in the general community, they have more available friends and a higher morale (Kalish, 1975).

Retirement life-styles. Sources of satisfaction and modes of adaptation vary with life-style. Retirement life-styles relate to earlier ones; and retirees many times seek to carry out goals that they were unable to attain earlier, when they lived more restricted lives. Among these life-styles, Lowenthal (1972) outlined nine and discussed five in considerable detail. (1) First are those with an excessively instrumentalist style. Such people are very task oriented and compulsively active, even in leisure-time activities. (2) Those who employ an instrumental, other-oriented style have gained special satisfactions from people they knew on the job. (3) People with a receptive/nurturant style have developed "networks of close personal relationships" (Lowenthal, 1972, p. 321). Such people often develop new social networks outside the work situation after they retire. (4) Another group, the autonomous individuals, are creative, initiate their own activities, and simply develop relationships when needed. They are capable of creating their own new roles and developing new capacities. Retirement has less effect on them than on most retirees. (5) People employing the self-protective style have never felt unusual dependency on others; hence, **disengagement** with retirement means nothing new for them.

The foregoing categories suggest that retirement life-styles are varied. Nevertheless, they undoubtedly represent only a small fraction of those actually followed.

Old-Age and Nursing Homes

Institutional living differs so much from the foregoing communal life-styles as to warrant separate treatment. Age-homogeneous living situations, such as age-segregated private and public housing, retirement communities, and trailer camps, are far more satisfying than "old-age" residences and nursing homes (Lowenthal & Robinson, 1977). The former are ordinarily chosen by and voluntarily entered by their residents. The latter are places to which older people are usually sent, often against their wishes. In the one case all the residents are equals, freely associating together. In the other they must interact within the institutional hierarchies of authority and health care. In such situations, authorities often treat certain residents much better than they do others.

Only a small fraction of older people—about 2% of individuals 65 to 75 years old and 8 to 9% of those over 75—are in nursing homes or other such institutions (Bouvier, Atley, & McVeigh, 1977). However, these statistics do not lessen the plight of those who live in such places, especially in the large fraction of substandard ones. The general picture of nursing homes is one of an "overworked, undertrained, and highly harassed staff who are unable to cope with the physical needs of their patients, to say nothing of their psychosocial needs" (Lowenthal & Robinson, 1977, p. 449).

Conditions in residential homes are also often deplorable—small rooms, little or no privacy, unattractive surroundings, and poor food. Especially in the larger-sized homes, residents are almost totally isolated from friends and relatives (Curry & Rutliff, 1973). Nor are the elderly poor visited as often as are richer individuals (Kosberg, 1973). It should also be observed that those who are visited more often receive better care and more attention from the staff. The individuals who always enjoyed their privacy and took special pride in being independent fare worse than others. Those who have been more protected throughout their lives make better patients in old age than do those who have trouble accepting their dependency needs (Lowenthal & Robinson, 1977).

In such situations, an older person's chief security and satisfaction is gained from close friends. Therefore, unless older people themselves desire it, they should be transferred from one residential or convalescent care facility to another only when absolutely necessary. Such changes result in a considerable increase in the incidence of death (Goldfarb, Shahinian, & Burr, 1972). For one thing, they may have some difficulty learning to cope with a new physical environment. For another, there is simply something reassuring about being in a place that is familiar.

RETIREMENT

Reasons for Retiring

People retire for varied reasons, often for a combination of them. The two main ones are, first, the inability to work because of such factors as compulsory age requirements or illness and, second, a decreased need for earning, as in the case of married women (Palmore, 1971). Other reasons for retirement include changes in the nature of the job, difficulty in keeping up with work demands, or time spent commuting to work (Elias, 1977). In other cases, workers may be fed up with taking orders and having to be subservient. Blue-collar workers, especially, often become disenchanted with their jobs. Four hundred white, male, blue-collar workers were asked "If you could retire with as much money as you need for a good pension and not have to work any more, would you do it right away, or would you wait a while?" Two-thirds of the men over age 65 in lower-level tasks said they would retire immediately, and half the men under age 40 said the same thing. Of the men in higher-level work, half of those over age 65 and a third of those under age 40 would choose immediate retirement (Puner, 1977).

Forced Retirement

A large majority of people is against compulsory retirement before age 70—a great many opposing it at any age—and lawmakers have yielded to such views. The case against compulsory retirement is based on several main points: (1) Flexible retirement policies might employ standards of ability and merit already used to determine hiring and promotion within companies. (2) Compulsory retirement compels older workers to leave jobs in which they are entirely competent and to seek work in areas where they are disadvantaged and make a lesser social contribution. (3) Older people only want to compete on the same basis as others. They do not ask for special consideration. (4) Most workers at age 65 still have several years ahead during which they will be quite capable of effective performance. Older people perform as well or better than younger ones on most measures. (5) A majority of those forced to retire lacks an adequate income, and many must subsist below the official poverty level. (6) Finally, and perhaps most importantly, work is the core of some people's lives. Until they feel ready and willing to retire, it may be psychologically healthier for them to continue to work (Palmore, 1977).

Older people themselves have conflicting views on the subject of mandatory retirement.

> Mandatory retirement is much like mandatory schooling at age 5 or 6. Some are ready and some are not. At the college we sometimes hire 30-year-olds who should be retired at 31. A person who really wants to retire has already retired from his work in any case (man, age 72).
>
> Mandatory retirement age limits should continue to be permitted. All holders of public office should be forced to retire at age 70 (man, 69).
>
> Many men are still very able at 65 and have no outside interests. But in "hard" times the young should not be kept unemployed (woman, 86).
>
> The people in the past had to retire. Why not the same as of now? (woman, 74).

There are also cogent reasons for such laws: (1) Compulsory retirement proves face saving for individuals who can no longer perform their work adequately. (2) If older people hang onto their jobs, young people will have an increasingly hard time gaining a foothold in the work world. (3) Older people will block the progress of younger adults into higher-status positions, thus enhancing the friction between generations. (4) Many older people who desire or need to retire need something to nudge them to make the decision.

Problems of Retirement

Various problems may accompany retirement, whether voluntary or forced. These include lack of preparation, especially in learning how to use leisure time, and loss of the work role in society. Retirement also means yielding a formerly respected status with little chance of finding an alternate one equally valued by society (Elias, 1977). It can take years for individuals to overcome the work ethic instilled in them from early childhood. While people might be better prepared for retirement if they were not socialized so thoroughly in the work ethic, society itself might have difficulty maintaining economic progress (Puner, 1977). As a result, older people often feel called on to establish the value of their leisure, so that it will constitute a base for a new social identity (Miller, S. J., 1968). That is, retired people may choose activities that help them to live up both to their own and others' expectations.

In contrast, some people do not derive their primary identity either solely or chiefly from occupational roles. In such cases they may not feel the need for maintaining an achievement orientation equal to their previous work status.

Adaptations to retirement. Individual reactions to retirement vary. People employed in heavy labor, assembly-line jobs, or other tedious work usually want to retire (Sheppard & Herrick, 1972; Terkel, 1974). Others look forward to doing many things that they have lacked time for while employed. Most retirees report greater happiness since retirement, although some of them have mixed feelings.

> I have felt the loss of prestige and feeling of worth, but relief from responsibility and criticism. I've had more time for friends, old and new (man, age 69).
>
> I have neither been happier nor the reverse. I miss my students, but many continue to contact me. And sometimes my colleagues invite me to lecture on favorite subjects so even that loss is modified. I certainly don't run out of things to do (man, 72).
>
> Since retiring I am very happy, because I continue to do part-time work for a wonderful family during the summer. I am also active and find some time for travel (woman, 68).
>
> I've been happier, mostly (woman, 86).

These different attitudes result in correspondingly different behaviors. Some people continue similar work but on a part-time, or even unpaid, basis. Others develop casual hobbies more fully. Still others alter their whole social situation, sometimes by moving into communities that are organized around retirement. The older the individual, the more time is devoted to leisure but the narrower, more sedentary, and more home bound such leisure activities are (Gordon, Gaitz, & Scott, 1977).

Factors relating to successful retirement. Adjustment in the later years relates especially to health, sex, education, and vocational background. The old idea that retirement hastens ill health or even death has been disproved (Streib & Schneider, 1971). On the one hand, people often retire because of loss of health. On the other hand, many times health improves after work stresses are removed. Education is a factor, too, because better-educated individuals can more effectively structure their free time, obtain further work after they retire, and have more economic resources to support their retirement activities. Professional and white-collar workers have also been accustomed to assuming more control over their life situations (Hendricks & Hendricks, 1976).

Women find retirement less traumatic than do men, partly because they "retired" once before, when they became mothers. In addition, they are more accustomed to performing activities in the home. Women who have assumed an instrumental role at home might experience lower morale than women who have emphasized expressive aspects of their role (Lipman, 1961). Women react negatively to retirement if they have not wanted to retire; however they have a capacity not shared by men to transcend their biology and to adapt to life's transitions, even when in ill health. On the other hand, the aging woman appears more vulnerable to social isolation, in consequence of former social expectations (Levy, 1980–81).

DISENGAGEMENT VERSUS ACTIVITY

Disengagement

The concept. The long-held so-called disengagement theory suggests that, in the years following retirement, it is natural for the individual and society to withdraw from each other. It also suggests that older people prefer to become less involved with the external world and with social norms and to become more interested in and preoccupied with their own concerns and philosophy of life. Cumming and Henry (1961) reported that older people play fewer roles and have both fewer and less-intimate relationships with others. When disengagement occurs, it is most common after age 75 or 80, although total disengagement is not inevitable until shortly before death (Palmore, 1969).

In practice, disengagement is neither an all-or-none nor a simple matter. One can disengage from some aspects of earlier involvements while remaining engaged in other areas of life. On the basis of a longitudinal series of interviews, Lehr and Rudinger (1969) reported that 78.8% of the subjects, aged 60 to 75, made few significant role changes over a 4-year period. A mere 7.9% reported fewer social roles whereas 14.3% engaged in more roles.

Factors affecting disengagement. Disengagement views are not confined to the aged. Even young children who are dying display disengagement behaviors.

Spinetta, Rigler, and Karon (1974) presented two groups of children—one hospitalized with leukemia and another hospitalized with chronic but nonfatal illnesses—a scale model of a hospital room and five dolls representing a mother, father, doctor, nurse, and sick child in bed. When the children were asked to put the figures where they most wanted them to be, the fatally ill group consistently placed the sick-child doll figure farther from the bed than did the chronically ill children. Thus, the dying children perceived a greater psychological distance from others and even preferred to maintain that distance.

Disengagement theory is often contrasted with activity theory, which is basically the opposite process. Activity theory proposes that older people have the same social and psychological needs as younger ones. At any age, reduction in one activity, such as employment, will produce dissatisfaction and a disproportioned life-style unless alternative activities of a fulfilling type take its place.

Desirability of disengagement. There is sharp disagreement over the desirability of disengagement. Such withdrawal is often perceived as developmental in character and not merely imposed by society. In this view, an individual chooses to disengage. Cumming and Henry (1961) reported that among people over age 65 those who disengaged had higher morale than those who did not. In a society that encouraged activity among the elderly, however, engaged people might make the better adjustment.

The extent of disengagement also relates to such factors as sex, individual preference, and situation, including role loss. In a longitudinal study of men aged 70 to 93, the men in general reported no decrease over a decade in activities relating to religion, friends, family, or economics. A similar group of women experienced a small but significant decrease in activities relating to friends, family, and leisure but an increase in economic activities and no change in religious activities. Perhaps the decrease in family interaction and increase in economic activity should be attributed to the women's greater longevity (Palmore, 1968).

Personal preference also affects disengagement, as indicated in an 11-year longitudinal study of 24 men, initially aged 65 to 75. The men in general remained stable in the complexity of their daily behavior, life contentment, feelings of satisfaction, extent of social interaction, and degree of activity as distinct from passivity. Nevertheless, certain changes did transpire in interrelationships between these measures. Their greater interdependency reflected an increasing all-or-none social functioning in later years. While a few subjects manifested disengagement behaviors, the majority did not (Youmans & Yarrow, 1972).

Disengagement is not always voluntary. In fact, older people's disengagement from outside activities relates more to their changing situation than to the aging process itself. Rural women over age 75 reduce their outside contacts more often than those in metropolitan areas, probably because of their relative lack of transportation facilities (Youmans, 1967). In society in general, the elderly experience a loss of roles, such as in widowhood and retirement.

Perspective on disengagement. Authorities differ over the worth of disengagement as a process. Some of them assume the "victim approach" in describing the "role portfolio" of older persons, as suggested in the common theme of rolelessness in later years (Rosow, 1974). Others observe that older people are not without roles or without significant others. Ordinarily they have leisure, family, and neighborhood roles. Nor does the loss of some roles necessarily mean the loss of all roles. An individual may be both widowed and retired yet have family and leisure roles.

The truth is that neither disengagement theory nor activity theory satisfactorily explains the behaviors of older people all of the time. Instead, these behaviors are determined by varied factors similar to those that determine people's motivations throughout their lives. Some individuals preferring to maintain a high level of activity and others who have remained somewhat isolated all their lives do not suffer from isolation in old age. In general, voluntary disengagement does not hurt morale, but forced disengagement—whether due to widowhood, retirement, poor health, or low income—reduces social interaction and morale.

Overall, it seems that activity is healthier than disengagement for most people, to the extent that health permits. For people who have never been active, however, considerable disengagement may be optimum, especially given their roleless state. In any case, because activity is healthier for most older people,

Activity is healthier than disengagement for most people.

society should provide situations that are conducive to, and supportive of, diverse activities in later years.

Activities

Work versus leisure. Researchers report that older people's disengagement is less common, and activity more so, than is usually believed. And they are more integrated than isolated in modern, urban, industrial societies. The large majority lives in private households, and at least a majority lives in social and economic security. The elderly also participate in politics and civic affairs much as do other adults. Meantime, 12.8% of men and 9% of women continue working past age 65, at least for a time. And those numbers may grow as age barriers to forced retirement crumble. Older workers may be even more attached to their jobs than younger ones (Meltzer, 1965). For one thing, those most attached to their jobs are most likely to continue working. For another, they no longer take for granted that they can get new jobs and hence cling to what they have.

These older workers face certain handicaps (Hauser, 1976). As far greater numbers of women have entered the labor market, better-trained, young, educated females are often in greater demand than less-skilled, less-well-educated, older workers of either sex, whose skills may be somewhat out of date. Moreover, both education and rapid technological change have placed a premium on the need for updating skills.

Nevertheless, society has, to a certain extent, relieved the adverse impact on the elderly. Technological advances have reduced the hazards of hard physical labor and have reduced the advantage of physical strength. Moreover, the growing power of labor unions, with their seniority rules, have afforded some advantage to older workers. Besides, the government has many programs to aid older people, including old-age pensions, Medicare, and unemployment insurance.

Most older people, however, relinquish their jobs and adapt to leisure. Meyersohn (1972) proposed four functions of leisure. One is to recover from work (respite and restoration). The second function is self-realization, focusing on craftsmanship and activity. A third function is spiritual renewal or contemplation. And the fourth is entertainment, often related to use of mass media and somewhat escapist in effect.

Types of activity. Older people are devoting their leisure time to increasingly varied pursuits, among them extended educational activities. In 1974 about 5% of individuals aged 55 to 64 and 2% of those over 65 were either enrolled in some educational institution or taking courses through a museum or library or by television (Harris & Associates, 1975). Others engage in volunteer work and, in the process, make friends among themselves. However, most older people do not belong to extrafamilial social networks. Those who do, ordinarily belong to only one, one exception being church membership, which is ordinarily maintained well into the 70s (Riley & Foner, 1968).

Those older people who remain actively involved in social networks are ordinarily married and still working. After retirement they ordinarily reduce their involvement in voluntary organizations associated with their occupational role. Meantime, women are more likely than men to maintain their religious activities. And while church groups accept older people's participation, few actually seek it (Atchley, 1978). The majority of both sexes prefers watching religious programs on television, in situations of solitude and peace, to church attendance, which makes demands on their economic resources and physical energies (Lowenthal & Robinson, 1977). In any case, serious disruptions in their life patterns, as through the death of a spouse, often reduce their participation in outside activities (Gubrium, 1972). In general, changes in relationships among older people are not toward greater participation in formal organizations but toward more-intimate relationships, especially within their own families (Brown, 1974). In fact, successful adjustment in later life relates most closely to having such relationships and a secure home atmosphere (Gordon, Gaitz, & Scott, 1977).

What older people do in the home is varied, though usually isolated and sedentary. A study of 206 retired men disclosed that they participated in 57 activities, most of them isolated, and that life satisfaction related to the amount and type of activity (Peppers, 1976). After surveying the research, Hendricks and Hendricks (1976) also reported varied activities. The most common forms of diversion, filling the greatest amount of time, were watching television, reading, and visiting. Older people participated in these three activities more than younger ones, averaging more than 6 hours a day—3 hours with television, 2 hours visiting, and an hour reading. Only about 5% of older people participated regularly in sports, usually in fishing and other somewhat passive activities. The most common forms of exercise, walking and gardening, were less than half as common as simply being idle and contemplating.

Other leisure activities included making home repairs, doing handiwork, attending church, and belonging to social organizations. Few of the elderly went to concerts, the theater, or museums, and almost two-thirds had been to none of them at any time in their lives. They more frequently attended movies but preferred other activities. And, whether because of visual and auditory difficulties or other factors, half of them went less often than they once had. Also, for various reasons, the major one financial, they went on fewer and less-extended vacations and outings after age 65. Despite all that has been written on the subject, fewer than 10% of middle-aged or older people take adult-education courses.

People who reminisce, or review their life, appear to have greater ego integrity. However, it is uncertain to what extent such reminiscing satisfactorily resolves their past life or prepares them for death (Boylin, Gordon, & Nehrke, 1976). In any case it is undoubtedly pleasant and may support their hopes that their life has been worthwhile.

A study of leisure patterns in later years. One of the most comprehensive studies of older people's leisure activities, social attitudes, and certain aspects of mental health was a sampling of adults in Houston from 1969 to 1970. It indicated that, the older the subject, the lower the level of overall leisure activity. The leisure participation among those aged 20 to 29 was almost four times as great as for those over 75. Among the oldest groups, 75 and older, subjects reported decreased participation in such activities as going to the movies, dancing and drinking, participation in sports, outdoor activities, traveling, and reading.

There was about the same frequency of participation among life-span groups in seven leisure categories: television viewing, discussion, spectator sports, cultural consumption, entertaining, participation in clubs and organizations, and home embellishment. By contrast, activities that increased with age ordinarily took place at home with family and friends. They were also more sedentary, with less-intense levels of involvement. Older people had a higher frequency of participation in only two of the leisure categories surveyed—namely, relaxation in solitude and, for the men, cooking.

At all ages men participated more than women in dancing and drinking, sports and exercise, using guns, travel, outdoor activities, discussion of important issues, spectator sports, and membership in clubs and organizations, all relating to institutionalized male sex roles. However, men participated less than women at all ages in cultural activities, television viewing, relaxation and solitude, cooking, and home embellishment.

The lower frequency of reading and listening to music relate to the lower educational level of the older correspondents. As currently better-educated people grow older, participation in such activities in old age will probably increase. For a similar reason—the lack of earlier education in how to utilize personal resources—substantial numbers lead a quite empty existence, often sitting for hours watching television. Though the media provide some "contacts" for the housebound, they may also have a certain tranquilizing effect on those who could become more active (Lowenthal & Robinson, 1977). Many such people also spend several hours a day doing "absolutely nothing." Joseph Spengler of Duke University wrote that no issue is of greater concern than how people use their decreased income and discretionary time. Whole empires tend to crumble in the "soft lap of luxury" (Puner, 1977, p. 136).

Factors affecting leisure patterns. The choice of activities in later years relates to such variables as cultural background, social class, sex, earlier experience, health, and opportunity, including situational factors. In one Jewish center those individuals with a U.S. background preferred participation in activities that permitted them to express their individuality. Those from Eastern European backgrounds were chiefly interested in activities that provided a sense of belonging to a social network (Gutmann, 1973).

Social class is of importance, too. Contrary to the stereotype, leisure roles are apparently not related to age. Individual interests are usually stable over time (Palmore, 1968). However, studies of old people ordinarily involve those who had little leisure time in their youth and, therefore, no long-term patterns of leisure activity to occupy them. As people brought up in today's leisure-oriented society grow old, their retirement problems may be correspondingly reduced.

There are sharp differences in the life course of the sexes. Women tend to lose value earlier than men do, both in the vocational and sexual spheres. Women's life course is constructed more around life events and men's around occupational ones (Van Dusen & Sheldon, 1976). Women attend church more often and more regularly (Britton & Britton, 1972).

The sex differential in activities relates to matters of health and longevity. In the late 1950s the percentage of men over age 65 unable to perform common retirement activities was twice that of women. And in the 1970s the gap widened, so that four times as many men were seriously limited in their activities (Verbrugge, 1976).

Education for Leisure

Although many older people are developing effective leisure styles, the majority might well profit from leisure education. Especially as more people live to great old age, such education becomes imperative. And since leisure patterns persist, such education should be continuous from early years. The present generation of the elderly is unable, either in social or practical terms, to capitalize on its leisure. Two-thirds of the older participants in the Duke Longitudinal Studies reported greater satisfaction in work than in leisure activities. Asked whether they would prefer to continue working, even if they had sufficient funds, the proportion answering positively was as high or even higher among the retired as in any other age group (Pfeiffer & Davis, 1974).

SUCCESSFUL AGING

What constitutes an effective life-style varies with the individual. Nevertheless, certain factors are ordinarily associated with successful aging. One of these, especially pertinent to later years, is finding competent ways to prolong survival and to ensure self-protection (Lowenthal, 1977). Another is to develop alternative sources of satisfying need. Among a random sampling of older people living in the community, Clark and Anderson (1967) reported 61% as being rather well adjusted. Among a hospital sample only 12% could be judged to have adapted successfully; and of the maladapted individuals 54% had problems finding alternative sources of need satisfaction.

A third factor related to successful aging is activity. Among 100 women over age 65, Schoenfield (1973) reported a positive relationship between future commitments to planned activities and good adjustment. Among another sampling, aged 40 through 90, "high life satisfaction" was more typical of people who were socially active and involved than of those who were inactive. But there was great diversity in characteristics of people who had aged successfully, depending on their personality type.

Some individuals, as they grow older, discard certain role responsibilities yet remain quite well satisfied with their lives. Others experience a decrease in both life satisfaction and in social and role interaction. Still others have maintained high satisfaction across the years despite low levels of activity, and this situation continues as they age. Overall, the "pivotal factor" in determining which individuals will age successfully is personality organization and the individual's capacity to adapt (Neugarten, 1977).

It is commonly assumed that high social involvement suggests a good adaptation and relative isolation a poor one. However, low social involvement does not, in itself, produce either poor mental health or low morale. Certain of the greatest scientists, artists, and statesmen have achieved their eminence by freeing themselves from or avoiding intimate interpersonal relationships (Lowenthal & Robinson, 1977). People who suffer most from loss of social contacts in later years are those who were socially inclined at earlier life stages.

Many people seek to offset aging by what Guemple (1969) called "renewal activity," or trying to be and act like younger people. In so doing, older people seek to gain some of the young's status and privileges. Examples of this phenomenon include "May-December marriages" or second families in which a man may become a father at the same time as he does a grandfather. One example was Bing Crosby, who married a much younger woman after his first wife died and then fathered a second brood of children. In other cases, retirees may learn a new job, or middle-aged people may enter college. In such cases much depends on one's motivation. For those who deliberately seek to associate with those younger than themselves, the results can be socially frustrating. But individuals who are quite realistic about their age may simply engage in renewal activities without attempting to become part of a younger social group.

SUMMARY

Adjustment in later years, as at all other stages, requires the effective performance of particular tasks. The tasks at this age level include the formulation of a philosophy of life and a capacity to adapt, because of the unusual range of problems encountered.

A large majority of older people is married, at least in the "young-old" years; although more of this age group are ultimately widowed for varying lengths of time. Among the married, relationships often improve at this stage, partly because responsibilities for child rearing and vocation are past or greatly reduced. Those who become widowed may remarry or, sometimes, cohabit, if remarriage would reduce their essential Social Security benefits.

The singles at this stage include some divorced people and "never marrieds" and many who have become widowed. The widowed may have unusual difficulties adjusting because of having lived so long with the same person and the dramatic readjustment in life-style required. Never-married singles adjust better, because their home life has not substantially changed.

Later years inevitably bring certain changes in family relationships. Nowadays, older people ordinarily live alone or with others of their age in their own homes, in retirement communities, or, ultimately, in nursing homes. Most of them still maintain frequent contact with their children and, when in need, often receive significant support from them. Some of them find great satisfaction in the grandparent role; others, especially younger grandparents, find such a role a reminder of their own aging.

Increasingly, older people are choosing to live in retirement villages or mobile-home parks, designed especially for their age group's needs. While they may miss whatever advantages derive from associating with younger people, they enjoy associating with those who share their own interests and problems.

One feature of later years, retirement, has raised certain significant issues, one being whether people should be retired against their will. While there are arguments for and against, the trend is toward letting people work longer than has ordinarily been permitted in recent years. In any case, retirement requires readjustment, more for men than for women. The popular disengagement theory suggests that in the years following retirement it is natural that the individual and society withdraw from each other. While some people may indeed prefer to withdraw, it appears probable that most people profit from continued activity. Withdrawal, when it occurs, is usually a matter of the older person's situation rather than choice.

Older people's activities are varied and are usually based on earlier interests. Some of the "young old" continue to hold jobs, although many seek early retirement. Older people do a great deal of watching television, reading, and socializing with relatives and friends. Other activities are highly varied, depending on such factors as age, sex, social class, marital status, living arrangements, and personality.

What constitutes successful aging also varies; nevertheless, certain principles seem generally sound. Aging requires alternative ways of satisfying need, ways of ensuring self-protection and prolonging survival, and whatever degree of social activity may be congenial to the individual concerned.

SUGGESTED READINGS

Barrett, C. J. Intimacy in widowhood. *Psychology of Women Quarterly*, 1981, 5(3), 473–487. This exploration of intimate relationships potentially available to the widowed woman includes friends, relatives professional and non-professional associates, even the deceased spouse. The author concludes that resources do not meet the widow's intimacy needs.

Glenn, N. D., & McLanahan, S. The effects of offspring on the psychological well-being of older adults. *Journal of Marriage and the Family*, 1981, 43(2), 409–421. Analysis of data from six U.S. national surveys yielded little evidence that older adults gain significant psychological benefits from the later stages of parenthood.

Golant, S. M. Future directions for elderly migration research. *Research on Aging*, 1980, 2(2), 271–280. An appraisal of directions in future research regarding causes and consequences of elderly migration disclosed several major areas of inquiry: which of the elderly moved and where; reasons for migration and the decision-making processes involved; and environmental context of residential readjustments.

Goldman, J. A.,, Cooper, P.E., Ahern, K., & Corsini, D. Continuities and discontinuities in the friendship descriptions of women at six stages in the life cycle. *Genetic Psychology Monographs*, 1981, *103*, 153–175. This study of female friendships at six stages of life from junior high age until old age deals with individual conceptions of friendship, expectations of friends, and how these concepts and expectations change over the life cycle.

Gubrium, J. F. (Ed.). *Times, roles, and self in old age.* New York: Human Sciences Press, 1976. This collection of theoretical articles examines disengagement theory, role consistency in later years, the chronology of life, retirement, generational roles, and other topics.

Hendricks, J., & Hendricks, C. D. *Aging in mass society.* Cambridge, Mass.: Winthrop, 1977. Chapter 10, "Family Life and Living Arrangements," and Chapter 11, "Aging: Everyday Concerns," deal with older people's family relations, living arrangements inside and outside institutions, social involvement, sex relationships, and other factors affecting their life-styles.

Kimmel, D. C. Life history interviews of aging gay men. *International Journal of Aging and Human Development*, 1979–80, *10*(3), 239–248. Interviews of 14 gay men, ages 45 to 81, about their life histories and experiences of aging, indicated wide diversity in patterns of aging, the presence of certain positive aspects of gay aging, and considerable life satisfaction of many of them—findings that contradict the common stereotype of lonely old gay men.

Kirkendall, L. A. Fulfillment in the later years. *The Humanist*, September–October 1977, pp. 31–33. A professor emeritus of family living tells what he has learned from his own experience about those factors that afford the greatest fulfillment in old age. He mentions especially the need for companionship, intimacy, and continued personal realization through meaningful work.

Koger, L. J. Nursing home life satisfaction and activity participation. *Research on Aging*, 1980, *2*(1), 61–72. A comparison of 22 nursing home residents attending an 8-week writing workshop to produce a magazine and 20 residents not attending discloses a significant increase in life satisfaction for those who worked on the magazine; whereas the others' scores did not change significantly.

Lee, G. R., & Ihringer-Tallman, M. Sibling interaction and moreale: The effects of family relations on older people. *Research on Aging*, 1980, *2*(3), 367–391. This study, which concerned the relationship between the older person's morale and interaction with siblings, revealed no relationship between the two. In terms of interaction frequency, relations with kin did not impact on the morale of the elderly; nor did age differences seem relevant.

Miller, D. B., & Beer, S. Patterns of friendship among patients in a nursing home setting. *Gerontologist*, 1977, *17*(3), 269–275. A study of intellectually intact patients. Seventy-six percent of them named other residents as friends, 76% the staff, and 45% volunteers. The qualities they most admired related, first, to personality and, second, to common interests. The community within the long-term-care institution constituted a nucleus of their network of friendships.

Our surplus citizens: How America wastes its human resources. *Saturday Review*, August 7, 1976. This special report contains three brief articles (pages 16 to 26) about mandatory retirement and its associated problems.

Palmore, E., & Kivett, V. Change in life satisfaction: A longitudinal study of persons aged 46–70. *Journal of Gerontology*, 1977, *32*(3), 311–316. A longitudinal analysis of changes in life satisfaction among 46- to 70-year-olds disclosed no significant changes in average life-satisfaction scores and none between the sexes, despite some individual changes. At the end of a 4-year period, life satisfaction related significantly to initial levels of self-rated health, sexual enjoyment, and social activity.

Roberts, W. L. Significant elements in the relationship of long-married couples. *International Journal of Aging and Human Development*, 1979–80, *10*(3), 265–281. A study of factors in the lifestyle of 50 couples, married an average of 55.5 years, and whose mean age was 79, indicated a relatively high degree of sexual activity and good health for over half the sample. Significant elements in these marriages were qualities of caring, independence, and companionship.

Schultz, N. W. A cognitive-developmental study of the grandchild-grandparent bond. *Child Study Journal*, 1980, *10*(1), 7–26. A study of 74 persons, ages 4 to 22, regarding attachments between grandparents and grandchildren indicated clear developmental trends as well as more numerous and abstract descriptions of the grandparent with whom there was greatest interaction.

Shanas, E., & Sussman, M. B. (Eds.). *Family, bureaucracy and the elderly.* Durham, N. C.: Duke University Press, 1977. These papers, by authorities in the field of aging, represent a pioneering effort to understand the relationships between older people and social institutions.

Toseland, R., & Sykes, J. Senior citizens center participation and other correlates of life satisfaction. *Gerontologist*, 1977, *17*(3), 235–241. A comparison of participants and nonparticipants in activities at the center disclosed no differences between them in life satisfaction. Nor did the findings confirm the researchers' hypothesis that the center served a highly satisfied older population. Instead, life satisfaction related to the respondent's health, financial status, and activity level.

14
PROBLEMS AND PROGRAMS OF AGING

Problems tend to proliferate in later years. And they are often experienced concurrently instead of being spaced over time. Actually, others often expect the elderly to find such problems to be more serious than they actually do (see Table 14-1). But these difficulties—and their remedies—are certainly serious enough to deserve careful attention.

Table 14-1. Differences between Personal Experiences of Americans 65 and Over and Expectations Held by Other Adults about Those Experiences

	Very Serious Problems Experienced by the Elderly Themselves (Percentage)	Very Serious Problems the Public Expects the Elderly to Experience (Percentage)	Net Difference
Fear of crime	23	50	+27
Poor health	21	51	+30
Not having enough money to live on	15	62	+47
Loneliness	12	60	+48
Not having enough medical care	10	44	+34
Not having enough education	8	20	+12
Not feeling needed	7	54	+47
Not having enough to do to keep busy	6	37	+31
Not having enough friends	5	28	+23
Not having enough job opportunities	5	45	+40
Poor housing	4	35	+31
Not having enough clothing	3	16	+13

From "The myth and reality of aging in America," by L. Harris and Associates. Copyright 1975 by the National Council on the Aging, Inc. Reprinted by permission.

There is no point in keeping people alive longer, observed Butler (1975), if they are not able to live a satisfying, effective life. Therefore, efforts should involve not merely extending life but improving its quality. The challenge is both to identify and cope with problems of later years and to design new and imaginative programs for personal enrichment.

Here, several older people name their most serious problems.

> Meeting expenses—34 dollars a day for board and room (woman, age 86).
>
> Concern for my wife's health and for my own sight; concern for the state of the world (man, 72).
>
> Our son, who has a wife and three children, is still not entirely self-supporting, and we have to help him with dental bills and tuition to finish theology school. Our daughter has two children by a husband she divorced after 8 years of debt and mental cruelty. A child by a new husband will have to be supported by our daughter with our help (man, 69).
>
> The unhappiness that has come into the life of one daughter and her children. The husband and father suffered permanent brain damage through a work-related accident (woman, 73).
>
> Having to live away from my own home (woman, 74).

PHYSICAL AND EMOTIONAL HEALTH

Physical Problems

Common disorders and therapies. While the extent of physical impairment among older people varies widely, there is always some increase with age. Among a random sampling of people over 65 years of age in Durham County, North Carolina, 25% suffered from some significant physical impairment (Pfeiffer, 1973).

The chief causes of death for those 45 and older are heart disease, cancer, stroke, and accidents. However, most older people's health problems are chronic, ranging from relatively mild aches and pains to persistent illness and long-term disability (Butler, 1975). About 72 per cent of those aged 45 to 64 and 72 per cent of those 65 and older have one or more chronic conditions.

Several factors should be kept in mind regarding these physical problems. First, 84% of people over age 65 somehow accommodate to them and manage their own lives. With suitable support systems even more could maintain their independence. Second, the elderly must often cope with several physical disabilities and other problems as well, such as loss of spouse or strained finances. The miracle is that they cope as well as they do.

Assistance should be geared more closely to the realities of the situation. The major emphasis should be on supportive systems for those with chronic conditions. To date, care systems have been designed chiefly for people with acute illness, although the vast majority suffer more from chronic and degenerative conditions (Shanas & Maddox, 1977). Finally, it is important not to ignore older people's disabilities as the inevitable consequences of aging or to interpret their expressions of concern as evidence of growing petulance. While assistance should not foster dependency, it should be every bit as available as for any other age group. These conditions, in turn, have a negative effect on morale and adjustment in general. In addition, negative effects have been repeatedly demonstrated from "even mild chronic disease or sensory impairment, especially on psychomotor performance and intellectual functioning" (Abrahams, Hoyer, Elias, & Bradigan, 1975, p. 671).

Alcoholism. Chronic older abusers of alcohol include a few recent recruits; however, most of them were also abusers during their younger years. The problem drinker is sometimes simply trying to cope with basic disturbances such as chronic anxiety or illness. While treatment of the elderly for alcohol abuse is similar to that for the young, older alcoholics have more physical disorders. Hence, alcoholism can have more serious effects in the older person (Pfeiffer, 1977).

Some authorities warn against prescribing alcoholic beverages to help older people relax or sleep better, lest they become alcoholic. However, moderate drinking may be good for them. The psychologists Mishara, Kastenbaum, Baker, and Patterson arranged daily cocktail parties at a residence for the elderly and at a nursing home. At one type of party only nonalcoholic drinks were served; at the other, alcoholic beverages were available, no more than two drinks a person. The researchers measured each participant's mental, emotional, physical, and functional state both before the experiment and again at the end of 9 and 18 weeks. After the first 9 weeks only a few positive effects of drinking appeared. The elderly imbibers seemed more friendly and reported falling asleep more easily at night than did the nondrinkers. By the end of the second 9-week period the imbibers' improvement was noticeable. They were friendlier to each other and the staff, assumed more initiative, and were more physically active.

The atmosphere in the nursing home became more friendly and intimate. In the downtown residence home the benefits were even greater. The residents began to express opinions more strongly and increased the variety of their social contacts and activities. They had reestablished control over their lives. Moreover, the drinkers' pulse rates went down—not below normal but definitely down—possibly due to better cardiac function (Casady, 1975).

Nutrition. A far more common problem than drinking is poor nutrition. Older people may lose their appetite or eat improperly for many reasons, including "loss of teeth, decreased perception, or diminished taste or smell, loneliness, anxiety, or stress" (Lowy, 1975, p. 147). Those who live alone are especially prone to eat in haphazard fashion. In consequence, home visits have been formalized by volunteers, who often perform services beyond those of mere visiting and friendship. For older people generally, Berman (1975) advised that free community nutritional-guidance centers be established and that local tearooms and coffee houses provide nutritious meals at modest rates. Such meals should also be made available in neighborhood restaurants and local community centers, he advised.

Exercise. With advancing years people typically become more sedentary and often put on weight. After studying 350 cases of obesity, Greene (1939) reported that inactivity related to the onset of obesity in 67.5% of the subjects, whereas a history of increased food intake related to only 3.2%. Much research supports the view that a lack of physical activity is the key cause of obesity. Exercise can also slow down or even reverse loss in aerobic capacity, which importantly limits the capacity of the cardiorespiratory system (Dehn & Bruce, 1972; Nunnelly, Finkelstein, & Luft, 1972).

The positive effects of exercise programs have been clearly demonstrated. In one experiment (DeVries, 1977) men aged 52 to 87 (mean age 69.5) volunteered to take part in a vigorous exercise program that involved calisthenics, jogging, stretching exercises, or aquatics for about an hour three times a week. The men improved significantly in oxygen-transport capacity, reduction in body fat, and physical-work capacity. The older men were far more trainable with regard to physical-work capacity than had been expected, and they did not need to have been trained vigorously in early years. In another study, which involved women aged 52 to 79, physical fitness was significantly improved, although they did not show much improvement in the respiratory system.

In other research DeVries and Adams (1972) compared the effects of exercise and meprobamate (a commonly used tranquilizer) on reducing muscle tension in ten elderly, anxious subjects. Treatment with neither placebos nor meprobamate showed any significant effects. But exercise did have a relaxing effect, without the undesirable side effects that may be found with tranquilizers. This point is especially important for older people, who can hardly afford any further decrements in reaction time, motor coordination, and driving performance that may result from using tranquilizers. A quarter of an hour's walk at a moderate rate is enough to produce positive effects that will last for an hour afterward.

To sum up, concluded DeVries, programs of vigorous physical conditioning for older individuals can produce significant improvements in

> the cardiovascular system, the respiratory system (at least in the male), the musculature, [and] body composition; and in general the result is a more vigorous individual who can also relax better. Other health benefits are likely to include a lower blood pressure and lower per cent of body fat, with the concomitant lessening of risk factors for development of coronary heart disease that these factors entail [1977, p. 60].

Psychological Problems

Common problems. The emotional problems of the elderly are so common as to be taken for granted. Many of them relate to forms of loss, including loss of health, an adequate income, home, spouse, or friends. These losses result in feelings of loneliness and social isolation. An especially keen loss is the reduction in mental acuity. Older people are generally quite aware of memory losses and their incapacity to think as clearly or as quickly as before (Burnside, 1977). Other problems include giving up feelings of competency and authority, the significance of what one has been rather than what one is, and setting one's memory store in order, perhaps as a means of getting ready for ending the life story (Neugarten, 1977).

Older people must also cope with the effects of change. The community may change, so that they are living among strangers. If they are moved to a nursing home, their social contacts are limited. They also lack the work relationships that afforded the chief source of new friendships earlier in life. Meantime, the more rapid the changes, the more does the older person's world differ from that in which he or she grew up. Today's elderly were originally socialized into a preindustrial society and have had to adjust as well as they can to a technological mass society.

Pathology of aging. A long-standing issue has been whether normal aging processes can or should be distinguished from pathological ones. Busse (1969) distinguished between primary aging (inherited biological processes that are detrimental and time related but independent of trauma, stress, or disease) and secondary aging (declines in functioning resulting from trauma or chronic disease). Secondary processes do not relate to aging in a directly causative way, although they correlate with age, in that the incidence of accidents and disease increases among older people.

In general, there is a higher incidence of psychopathology in advanced old age. It is especially noticeable after age 75 and dramatically so past 80 (Pfeiffer,

Many old people experience feelings of sadness, isolation, and even depression.

1973). The lowest incidence of psychopathology is found among the married, with greater prevalence among the widowed and still higher rates among the separated and divorced (Pfeiffer, 1977).

The most common functional psychiatric disorders in later years—that is, those with no clear organic base—are the affective disturbances, especially depression. Many old people experience episodes of sadness, lack of interest, and feelings of listlessness as a result of especially stressful life situations. More-persistent depressive reactions are experienced by far fewer individuals, again often in response to significant losses or stressful circumstances (Pfeiffer, 1977). Suicide among the elderly, usually due to depression, occurs at a rate over triple that of the general population (U.S. Public Health Service, 1974). While younger people may often attempt suicide without succeeding, older people who attempt it rarely fail, having decided fully to die (Pfeiffer, 1977).

Most common after depressive reactions are paranoid reactions, or the attributing to other people of motivations that do not exist. Paranoiacs are suspicious of others and often attach false explanations to occurrences around them. While paranoid reactions in younger people often suggest severe psychiatric disturbances, those in later years are more easily explainable. They may represent an effort to "fill in the blank spaces in the cognitive map of the individual regarding his [or her] environment" (p. 656). The next most common psychiatric disorder of later years is **hypochondriasis,** which is characterized by unusual preoccupation with one's own body functioning or with disease in the absence of any significant physical pathology (Pfeiffer, 1977).

Psychotherapy. Butler (1977) deplored the general "atmosphere of futility" that surrounds psychotherapy administered to the elderly. The potential for psychological change may even be greater in later years than in any other period, the motive for such change being the proximity to death. At this stage individuals have their entire past life as a backdrop against which to appraise their successes and failures. Finally, there is the leisure time for efforts that may be lacking in the middle years.

Elderly people do not receive their share of benefits from the mental-health system. In community mental-health centers they account for only about 7% of inpatient services and 3% of outpatient services (Kahn, 1977). Instead, they have been subject to an "emerging custodialism"; that is, the aged are simply being placed in nursing homes. The ostensible purpose is to avoid hospitalization, but such homes are often even more custodial than are hospitals. And removing the elderly from the hospital to the community often represents a new location but the same old custodial philosophy (Polak & Jones, 1973). In fact, such homes have displaced the county and state hospitals as "custodial warehouses" (Kahn, 1977, p. 254).

In addition, mental-health professionals tend to avoid dealing with elderly people, possibly because of their own "unresolved conflicts with parental images and a need to deny [their] own mortality" (Lawton & Gottesman, 1974). According to the concept of custodialism, patients are perceived as different from normal people, difficult to control, and better taken care of in a somewhat rigid setting. The setting itself simply involves caretaking and is maintained by a rigid hierarchy.

According to the completely different concept of therapeutic community, pathology is viewed as often induced within the institution itself, where patients are encouraged to assume a sick role. Advocates of this concept recommend making hospitals democratic and establishing communication between staff and patients.

Kahn (1977) summarized certain recommendations regarding mental health programs for the elderly.

1. The healthy component of the personality should be reinforced rather than the sick role.
2. Psychopathology is not inevitable in aging individuals, even in cases of central-nervous-system dysfunction.
3. Senility is a psychosocial and biological matter. While little can sometimes be done about the biological aspect, social and psychological facts can be modified.
4. Intervention may be harmful as well as helpful. In general, it is best to pursue a policy of minimal intervention, which involves preserving the normal functioning in the usual setting as much as possible. Thus, it is better to provide care in the home instead of the hospital and in neighborhoods instead of the central city. Minimal intervention, however, is not the same as neglect.
5. Both the old person and the family must be taken into consideration. The elderly can sometimes be helped best by providing support for the family.
6. It is well to set specific goals in dealing with the elderly, or matters may simply drift along.
7. It is best to provide services from nonprofessionals and outreach workers, rather than doctors. And it is best if they come from the same neighborhood and age group as the clients concerned.
8. To whatever extent possible, older people's sense of control should be maintained. Otherwise, help results in decreased infantilization and impairment.
9. A guarantee that help will be provided when needed is important.

Certain changes are likely in the future. The elderly will have a higher social status. They will be better educated and will have greater political and social sophistication. As a result, they will be much less willing to put up with custodialism.

LIVING ARRANGEMENTS

Private Housing

Conditions. Federally subsidized lower-cost housing affects only a small fraction of the older population, for about 90% live in neither special housing nor institutions. As of 1976, most older individuals lived in houses of poor quality, one in five of them in substandard housing lacking basic plumbing facilities. Over half lived in units built in 1939 or earlier, often much earlier (Carp, 1976). Most elderly renters lived in older buildings in older parts of cities where rents were low, facilities few, and personal safety uncertain (Carp, 1977). About 600,000 older people, mostly men, lived in dilapidated old hotels and boarding houses. Older women have special problems, one being that two-thirds are widows. A survey in Los Angeles indicated that about 90% of individuals over age 50 disliked their housing arrangements. Nevertheless, few of them moved (Birren, 1977). Some of them were too poor to move, and others simply feared changing to strange though better neighborhoods.

Over 60% of the elderly lived in metropolitan areas, the majority in central cities. Because such areas are often unsafe, the aged tended to be block-bound or home-bound (Carp, 1977). The less impoverished were migrating to the suburbs. Because of poor transportation facilities, they, too, may become mostly home-bound when they grow too old to drive.

The 17% of older people who lived in small towns and the 5% who lived on farms often lacked facilities that others take for granted. These include electricity, plumbing, telephone, central heating, air conditioning, and transportation. The rural elderly were the most impoverished, had the poorest housing and were often isolated for lack of transportation. They tended to have poorer health and more disabilities than do older people generally.

Setting. The majority (70%) of older people lived in family settings; a quarter lived alone or with nonrelatives; and the rest (about 1 in 20) lived in institutions. Increasingly, the elderly are trying to maintain their own independent households instead of living with others. Seven in 10 older people enjoyed the independence of owning a home but often found it a physical and financial burden. Sometimes the neighborhood decayed around them or their homes fell into disrepair. Many needed help in paying the home mortgage or insurance or in making household repairs.

Growing numbers, especially of the lower-middle-class elderly, live in mobile-home communities. Such an environment encourages a sense of community as well as feelings of security and companionship.

Supportive services. While, the historical trend has been toward more institutional services for the elderly, the past 3 decades have seen a growing movement toward helping people in their own homes (Beattie, 1977; Shanas & Maddox, 1977). In larger cities, homemaker and visiting-nurse services and "meals on wheels" may be provided. Also, home-health visits may be arranged by medical personnel through the Medicare and Medicaid programs, after such care is approved by the patient's physician as part of the overall treatment plan. Some old people live at home while receiving regular medical and preventive services at a hospital. These include physical therapy and dental, optical, and podiatric care in an atmosphere that is not illness oriented.

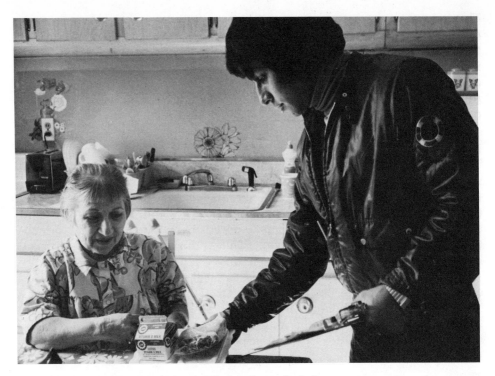

More and more communities provide "meals on wheels."

The Ring-a-Day Service provides that volunteers, often older people themselves, call elderly persons living alone at prearranged times each day. In cases of emergency, or when there is no answer, the caller notifies a doctor, neighbor, or relative.

Two special programs. One pioneering agency, the Minneapolis Age and Opportunity Center, affords supportive services that permit older people to remain in their own homes rather than go to nursing homes. This agency's services are adapted to the particular needs of its clients. For example, for one couple it delivers two meals a day, a hot dinner and a cold lunch, so that the woman need prepare only breakfast. A homemaker arrives once a week to do the heavier cleaning, vacuuming, and changing beds, and a man occasionally cleans the yard. The agency also provides transportation to clinics; personal help when needed, such as financial counseling; and information on particular resources, such as food stamps and legal services. A handyman may build a wheelchair ramp, repair a furnace or other appliance, put up storm windows, or do other odd jobs.

In Orlando, Florida, a nonprofit organization, which in 1977 had 112 older members in eight residences, provides a "halfway house" for the elderly. In these communes people who are no longer completely independent or totally dependent can share a home and have their basic needs supplied. They help each other to deal with the problems of growing old and feel a sense of belonging.

They form family units with legal control over their lives. They also have power over hiring and firing the staff, voting new members in or out, and determining their own entertainment and menus. The businessmen who organized this service believe that older people are better off living with their contemporaries and at the same speed as others their own age. They also believe that old people think somewhat differently and that they simply cannot cope with the attitudes of younger people (Kellogg & Jaffe, 1977).

Nursing Homes

Shortcomings. The number of older people stored away in nursing homes is growing, partly because people are living longer. The trend is also supported by changes in social attitudes and laws. For one thing, children are no longer judged financially responsible for their parents. For another, 80% of nursing-home residents have expenses paid by Medicaid (Margolius, 1977). This program, however, is far from adequate. Although 70 to 80% of nursing-home residents have moderate to severe mental disorders, active treatment programs exist only in state mental hospitals and are rare in old-age and nursing homes. Hence, most mentally ill elderly people who live in institutions are accorded custodial care rather than true mental-health services.

Another shortcoming of nursing homes is the danger of residents being robbed, because they often lack facilities for protecting their possessions. At the very least they need small lockers in which to keep their spending money and most cherished possessions. Indeed, they have room for few personal possessions of any kind. Yet things that are important to an individual are a part of the extended self, contributing to a sense of personal integrity and completeness. Another major loss is a certain sense of dignity. In nursing homes, patients are often treated like children and herded around like cattle. Nor are they listened to or fully respected. A part of this loss of dignity is through a lack of privacy. For example, one man was undressed and bathed by the nurses even though he felt completely capable of taking care of himself.

The loss of familiar surroundings can also create considerable apprehension and disrupt contact with the residents' former world. They miss the familiar routines and familiar places, familiar foods and drinks—perhaps for one person raw cucumbers and another hot biscuits. They may also have to forego wine and beer unless the doctor specifically permits it. Another loss is independence, and although some individuals gladly forfeit their autonomy, others struggle firmly to maintain it, even when to do so might imperil their own safety and health. One 93-year-old woman who had recently broken her hip and had great difficulty walking would sneak off and take a bath by herself rather than have someone attend her. Sometimes the struggle is all the more prominent because of the need to overcome a growing recognition that increased dependence is inevitable (Burnside, 1977).

Suggestions. Certain precautions will at least reduce the negative efforts of institutional care. There should be a national policy regarding such care, and regular inspections should be held. Residents should be consulted about desired modifications. Wherever possible they should be allowed to remain in familiar environments, so that they will not become disoriented. Pastalan and Bourestom (1977) reported a sharply increased mortality among older people required to move from one institution to another. Moreover, those who moved more than 45 miles had a higher mortality rate than those who moved shorter distances. Those who either firmly disapproved of or accepted the move died at a lower rate than those who didn't appear to care. However, this reaction may have reflected an inability to discriminate clearly among the very old, sick, and confused (Bush, 1977).

Best of all, the elderly should be provided for in their own homes wherever possible. Many older people must be institutionalized because their grown sons and daughters cannot care for them during the day. Hence, a new service provides geriatric day hospitals or day-care centers. Such services usually operate five days a week and provide psychiatric, medical, social, rehabilitative, and recreational activities, as well as transportation to and from the older person's residence. Another new form of assistance, called respite service, relieves the primary caretakers of responsibilities for the elderly, especially on weekends or vacation periods (Beattie, 1977). Figure 14-1 indicates how greatly the elderly vary in their capacity to remain in their own homes and the degree to which special assistance is required.

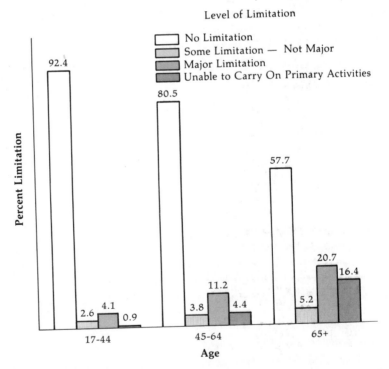

Figure 14-1. *Percentage of adults with various degrees of limited activity, 1970.*

Suggestions Regarding Housing

Upgrading environments. A matter of special concern for the elderly is their lack of privacy in dwelling arrangements. The right to privacy is a significant concern that should not be denied merely because of one's old age (Pfeiffer, 1977). In addition, older people's environment should provide "support in the context of familiar objects and persons." It should allow them to have "both private sanctuary and easy contact with others" (Birren, 1977, p. 130). They should feel a part of the neighborhood in which they live. Unfortunately, the population of a neighborhood changes, so that older people find themselves increasingly surrounded by strangers. They need to have stores, doctors, dentists, and other facilities nearby because of their relative lack of mobility. Many of them do not have an automobile or easy access to public transportation. In short, it is important to view the environment through the eyes of the elderly when considering how well they can adjust. They are often confronted with obstacles that would be no problem for the young: high bus steps, the need to cross wide, busy streets to catch a bus, fast-changing traffic lights, high curbs, and inadequate building labels (Birren, 1977, p. 131). Overall, housing for the elderly should transcend the mere need for shelter and encourage a richer, more meaningful life. Certainly, housing has a significant impact on the life satisfaction and life-styles of people at any age (Carp, 1977).

Age desegregation. A current issue involves the segregation of groups according to age. Butler (1977) strongly recommended mixing all ages, on the ground that old and young benefit equally. The old are presumably invigorated by associating with the young, and the young profit from observing first hand the realities of later years. Others, including this writer, believe that older people benefit by a considerable degree of age segregation. The elderly often feel most comfortable with their contemporaries, because they feel unwanted by younger ones. Or they enjoy sharing life experiences and memories with others who lived through the same period (Kalish, 1975).

OTHER PROBLEMS

Economic Situation

Current status. The median income of families 65 years and older is only about half that of all families. And because these figures include only families having employed persons, the situation is even worse (Medley, 1977). Older people's income level is often low because many of the women never worked outside the home until after the children were grown, and then in low-paying jobs. It is not easy to gain a proper perspective on the elderly's plight. The concept of poverty is relative in a country where not only the bare essentials but also various luxuries, including television sets and automobiles, are taken for granted by practically every family. Thus, a lack of such items is especially hard

PROBLEMS AND
PROGRAMS OF
AGING

367

to bear (Havighurst, 1975). In addition, statistics do not take into account assets and debts, benefits from government services, and tax laws that affect people differently (Schulz, 1977). About half of all male wage and salaried workers and three-quarters of women have no other pension than that provided by Social Security (Fox, 1974; Schulz, 1977).

The situation varies somewhat according to marital status. Half the unmarried elderly have incomes below the poverty level, while only 14% of married couples are in that category. It should be added that married people are often heavily subsidized by their children.

Economic-assistance programs. For the elderly the most important sources of income are retirement benefits, including Social Security and public and private pensions (Bouvier, Atlee, & McVeigh, 1977). At this stage retirement payments constitute at least half the income for most couples and almost two-thirds the income for individuals. About 95% of all the older people in the United States are eligible for Social Security benefits. Second in importance as a source of income for the elderly are wages. Third is income from real estate and investments. The fourth-ranked source is some form of public assistance.

The Social Security program, first instituted in 1935, was not designed to provide a completely adequate income but rather to supplement other resources. In general, it makes absolutely minimum provision for existence; and it must be supplemented if an even reasonably satisfying way of life is to be achieved. Yet there are two chief obstacles to maintaining an adequate supplementary income. First, it is difficult for employees over 65 to obtain work. Second, people on Social Security who annually earn more than a small sum have their payments reduced by a dollar for every two they earn over that amount (Albert & Zarit, 1977).

Government assistance with health expenses takes the form of Medicare and Medicaid. Medicare, a national health-insurance program, pays about 38% of the medical bills of the elderly. Various services are not covered, including treatment for problems with sight, hearing, feet, and teeth. Out-of-hospital prescriptions and psychiatric care, transfusions, and physical rehabilitation are covered only minimally. Various services that could keep old people out of institutions—including homemaker, day-care, and home-health services and various forms of supportive assistance—are ordinarily not covered.

The second major health-assistance program is Medicaid. It is not specifically for older people, yet one in three Medicaid dollars goes for nursing-home care. People are eligible for Medicaid only within certain income limits. Unfortunately, both programs encourage hospitalization and many times result in the exhaustion of an individual's resources before he or she can qualify for Medicaid (Albert & Zarit, 1977).

Vocational assistance. Butler (1975) suggested that programs in continuing education be provided because skills become obsolete. Opportunities should be increased for less efficient or handicapped persons. Even those with lower efficiency can make a positive contribution ("Work in America," 1972).

Progress is also being made in reducing prejudice against workers on the basis of age. It is argued that such policies as forced retirement are unfair, because older workers are often just as competent as younger ones. Besides, people age at different rates, and a specific age for compulsory retirement is purely arbitrary. The country needs human productivity, yet some of its most creative people may be involuntarily put on the shelf.

Among reasons given for maintaining a compulsory-retirement policy are these: (1) It is simple to administer, whereas flexible retirement would necessitate complicated tests, difficult to administer thoroughly or to justify. Thus, compulsory retirement prevents unfair discrimination against individuals. (2) It allows both employers and employees to plan in advance. (3) It also allows advance planning for retirement benefits at particular ages. (4) It reduces unemployment problems by decreasing the number of workers who are competing for jobs. (5) It keeps tenure and seniority rules from preventing the employment and promotion of younger workers.

Intangible Disadvantages

Stereotypes. Older people also suffer from certain more or less abstract disadvantages, among them **euphemistic** labels and erroneous stereotypes. Most older people feel negative or indifferent about the common designation of them as "senior citizens."

> What difference does it make? We are all human beings (woman, age 74).
>
> Growing old is natural and inevitable. It is pleasant to know that former long-ago pupils can still recognize you, even though the mirror indicates increasing old age. Call them anything you like, but *call* them (woman, 86).
>
> Silly euphemisms usually amuse me. This one is no worse than "Internment Director" for Undertaker, which was in a newspaper ad last year (man, 72).

Kalish (1975) prefers the term *older person,* and so do I. Older people are often stereotyped as poverty stricken, ill, and severely depressed, a picture refuted in Maas and Kuyper's 1974 study. Further, according to Butler (1975), 95% of all those over age 65 live in the community and only 5% in institutions; and 81% get around without assistance. Older people are also perceived as having fewer interests, being set in their ways, feeling sorry for themselves, and being oriented toward the past. People with more direct experience with the elderly—and older people themselves—are slightly less negative regarding old age than younger people are (Chown, 1977). The concept of the aged varies somewhat according to the social group or context. At age 48, Canadian Prime Minister Pierre Elliott Trudeau was perceived as somewhat young to embark on so important an office but rather old to be marrying a 23-year-old woman (Schoenfield, 1974).

Older people accurately perceive that their social status and, sometimes, their abilities are declining; and they realize that death lies not far in the future. Hence, they remind the young of the phenomena of old age and death. In consequence, "Their very presence is often upsetting, eliciting responses from younger people that range from condescending humor to bitter anger; many of us resent having to contemplate our own finitude" (Kalish, 1975, p. 74).

Women suffer earlier from the aging stereotype than do men. In the United States women are more often considered old before age 65 than are men, despite women's greater longevity. However, older women do not label themselves as old any more than older men do. In one study 40% of both sexes over age 65 perceived themselves as younger than their actual age (cited in Riley & Foner, 1968, p. 303). However, older women do have a more negative self-image than do men (Pollack, Karp, Kahn, & Goldfarb, 1962).

Ageism. Ageism, or prejudice on the basis of age, is most often directed toward the elderly. It derives from "a deep-seated uneasiness on the part of the young and middle aged—a personal revulsion to and distaste for growing old, disease, disability, and fear of powerlessness, 'uselessness' and death" (Butler, 1977, p. 132).

GENERAL MODES OF ASSISTANCE

Types of Programs

Community services and activities. Programs already available are varied and often praiseworthy. Nevertheless, they are often offered to only a fraction of the total older population. Among the most useful are those designed to help older people find satisfying and meaningful ways to use their time. In some cities social-activity programs have been arranged in varied settings, including settlement houses, hospitals, parks, and recreation areas. A somewhat older service, the senior center, provides opportunities for recreation, creative growth, communal dining, and a broad overall range of functions—social, educational, recreational, and medical (Beattie, 1977).

A great deal of literature is available to older people about how to make the most of their retirement and to use their new autonomy creatively. The American Association of Retired Persons publishes two magazines—*Dynamic Maturity*, for preretirees 50 to 65 years old, and *Modern Maturity*, for all those age 55 and over. This organization and the National Retired Teachers Organization, as well as many other professional groups, publish a great deal of free material offering retirees suggestions about how to "find new jobs or careers, make money, get all available government benefits [and] meet their budgetary, housing, health, nutritional, social, and recreational needs" (Puner, 1977, p. 137). Older people may also participate in training programs designed for older workers.

Senior centers make available social, medical, recreational, and educational services.

Another recent service meets the legal needs of the elderly in matters of protection, civil rights, and guardianship. Such services are essential for the mentally impaired who lack people of integrity to help them (Beattie, 1977).

Continuing education. The lifelong learning movement gains its stimulus from several sources. For one thing, because of the technological revolution, changes are taking place continually and rapidly. Hence, an education that is finished at age 18 to 21 will hardly suffice at 50. Second, women's entrance into the world of work in great numbers requires extensive retraining. In the third place, because of the extension of life expectancy, more Americans will live longer and will need to pursue productive lives for longer years than ever before. Moreover, with the reduced birth rate, there are increasing numbers of educational resources that are not being fully used. For another thing, lifelong learning is also a lifeline for the disadvantaged—women, minorities, youth, the unemployed, the isolated elderly, and workers whose jobs are growing obsolete (Mondale, 1976).

Education for older people should be designed specifically for their needs. Methods for educating younger people may prove quite inappropriate for adults returning to school after years away from academic pursuits. Educational psychologists must then develop ways of motivating and teaching adults that are appropriate to their capacities and needs (Schaie, 1973). Schools and churches often have the best available space in the community for providing special services to the elderly, including recreation, hot meals, and continuing-education programs (Kalish, 1975).

Making Services Available

Certain programs are designed for helping older people avail themselves of such services as may exist. Those most likely to be isolated and unaware of how to utilize helping networks are the poor, the ill, and the unmarried. Such people are also more likely than their opposites to be in institutions. Certain services have been designed to help identify these so-called invisible aging and to make them aware of the type of help available. Another innovation, the registrant service, provides that older people, once registered and identified, be given information about various services on a continuing basis (Beattie, 1977).

Self-Help Activities

Older people can often participate significantly in providing their own services. In Jamaica, New York, the service program for older adults, community organizations, and senior citizens' groups, together provide activity and service programs, with the seniors themselves helping older residents. The Senior Citizens Advisory Council identified special needs and interests, initiated a crime-prevention program, arranged free checking accounts in local banks, and sponsored health seminars. In the Retired Senior Volunteer Program, elderly participants help others with assistance from the Federal Action Agency (Margolius, 1977).

It has been suggested that the elderly, if they bound themselves together could become a significant factor in elections. But the aged, unlike other minorities, do not have a common background. Instead, they are highly diverse in their interests, education, health, religion, and customs. Hence, it is difficult for them to cross various racial, ethnic, and religious lines to associate with and help each other. It is important, therefore, that older people develop effective ways of representing their own interests.

Upgrading Programs

A few suggestions. There is a pressing need to examine present practices and to determine how best to help older people participate more fully and meaningfully in society (Zarit, 1977). First, there is a need to identify and properly train potential advocates for old people. As Kalish (1975) pointed out, "There are hazards involved in intervening in the lives of others" (p. 115). Such advocates may not fully understand the needs of those they are attempting to help, and the latter may dislike having others engineer their lives. In many cases younger people, especially members of a family, get together and decide how to dispose of older family members without obtaining either their opinion or consent.

Any policy discussion should also involve consideration of what roles are best for the elderly in society. In this regard more attention should be paid to the needs of older people from their own point of view, as well as roles that people in the middle years expect to play as they age. Whatever counseling is provided, older people should take into account their overall situation. Individuals and their environment should be viewed as a total system (Fozard et al., 1977). A comparison of 232 widowed and 363 married women, aged 45 to 74 years, indicated that the widows' lower morale related to such factors as poor health, low income, and amount of family interaction rather than from widowhood itself (Morgan, 1976).

As far as living environments are concerned, intervention should be evaluated by the people affected. Public administrators recognize older people's need for accessible health care, economical housing, consumer goods, protective services, and adequate transportation. In addition, older people themselves recommend situations that permit maximum flexibility and choice, consumer-protection programs, reduced transit fares, and expanded bus routes. They often prefer to remain in their present housing but lack access to facilities, especially in larger communities (Risenfeld, Newcomer, Berlant, & Dempsey, 1972).

A factor rarely considered is the congruence between individual and environment. People should not be placed in situations from which they cannot extricate themselves. They may find themselves in environments that are not even reasonably suited to their own life-styles, competencies, goals, or values. In other words, people should be matched to environments, with provision for change in case of mismatch. Those who value privacy dislike residential situations that stress planned activities, whereas the more socially inclined find such opportunities rewarding. Not only should living environments be sufficiently varied to support a diverse range of life-styles, but older people should also be educated about what alternatives are available and how to make appropriate decisions.

Greater emphasis should be placed on rehabilitation programs associated traditionally with physical restoration and more recently with improving psychiatric and mental health. Still more recently there is growing concern for vocational rehabilitation of the elderly (Beattie, 1977).

A summary statement. Berman (1975) summarized items that would be of help to the older population in the United States:

> (1) The right to earn up to two and a half times the funds provided by social security for the first five years after retirement, tax free and without penalty, and thereafter any additional amount but with tax. (2) Experimentation with income maintenance and negative income tax. (3) Provision of adequate hous-

ing with food, with rent and food not to exceed 40 per cent of the individual's social security check. (4) Development of self-contained, mixed, or predominantly "old-age" communities. (5) Provision for adequate (for example, two sets of) clothing per year at a cost not to exceed 10 per cent of the individual's social security check. Clothing and food stamps with merchant's price set at cost (no profit) can be redeemable from the community government. (6) Complete, rather than limited, coverage of medical and nursing expenses and immediate availability of first-rate medical care. (7) Free off-rush-hour public transportation, with rush-hour transportation at a modest cost. (8) Free admission to local theatres at off-peak times. (9) Maintenance by the community of local community centers for the elderly. These centers could be at a lounge area in the local schools, libraries, and even town halls. (10) Arrangement for group travel tours at greatly reduced rates [p. 16].*

There is growing emphasis on consulting older people about programs designed to assist them. Older people themselves often have strong opinions on the subject.

Social Security payments should not be affected by marriage. There should be no limit on work and none for earning income. The wealthy can draw Social Security and keep their income from investments (man, age 69).

Stop entertaining older Americans! Encourage them to give as long as they are physically able. I should add mentally and emotionally able too (woman, 73).

More volunteer work is needed—for example, aid at the hospitals and programs for entertainment and service (woman, 68).

Start to think of them as assets rather than as liabilities, which would make them into assets. Self-fulfilling predictions have more influence on results than any other factor. How this influences the stock market is an obvious similar example (man, 72).

SUMMARY

The elderly suffer from a wide variety of physical and psychological problems, varying greatly by sex, age, and individual. Many suffer from malnutrition and a few from alcoholism, although very moderate drinking may prove harmless or even beneficial. To what extent the higher incidence of psychopathology in advanced old age can derive from normal aging processes or from disease and trauma is debatable. To date, mental-health specialists have done little to meet the special needs of the elderly.

Other major problems of the elderly relate to housing, finances, vocation,

*From "Prologue to Aging: Societal structure and the aged," by H. J. Berman. In *Understanding Aging: A Multidisciplinary Approach*, by M. G. Spencer and C. J. Dorr, (Eds.). Copyright 1975 by Appleton-Century-Crofts, N.Y., p. 16. Reprinted by permission.

and ageism. Many older people must cope with such conditions as living in dilapidated, high-crime, urban areas or in poorly run nursing homes and eking out an existence on a skimpy budget. Those who want to supplement their income by part- or full-time employment confront considerable discrimination. Discrimination on the basis of age is widespread and is based on stereotypes, both negative and undeserved.

Many programs and proposals are being developed to alleviate or dispel such problems. To date, however, they have been poorly integrated and available to relatively few. Modes of assistance include special publications for the elderly, including free material regarding matters of interest to them; supportive home-care and nutritional services for those who live alone; continuing education, including vocational retraining; and many others. Older people's efforts on their own behalf through applying political pressure have been largely ineffective or inconsequential, partly because they have such diverse characteristics and needs. In general, programs devised for helping older people should take into account their diversity, their continuously changing needs, and their own perception and ideas about efforts to help them.

SUGGESTED READINGS

Arling, G. Resistance to isolation among elderly widows. *International Journal of Aging and Human Development*, 1976, 7(1), 67–86. A survey of widows aged 65 to 85 indicated that their ability to resist isolation related mainly to their health and the availability of economic resources. Such factors significantly modified the variety of the widow's daily activities and her contacts with family, neighbors, and friends. The widow's good adjustment also correlated positively with higher education and with rural or small town, rather than urban, environment. Availability or degree of contact with the children bore no apparent relationship to other activities. However, friendship and neighborliness related positively to such activities as taking walks, attending church services and meetings, and shopping.

Bachrach, C. A. Childlessness and social isolation among the elderly. *Journal of Marriage and the Family*, 1980, 42(3), 627–637. Among a national sampling of persons, age 65 and older, a relationship was found between number of children and isolation. Childlessness also related to isolation, although this effect related more strongly to the older person's health and occupation (farm, manual, or nonmanual).

Birren, J. E., & Sloane, R. B. (Eds.) *Handbook of Mental Health and Aging*. Englewood Cliffs, N.J.: Prentice-Hall, 1980. This definitive reference work, composed of original contributions by outstanding specialists, concerns research, theory, and current practices relative to mental health and aging.

Eisdorfer, C. *Annual Review of Gerontology and Geriatrics*. New York: Springer, 1980. This critical interdisciplinary review of research progress, programmed development, and clinical practice relating to gerontology and geriatrics contains contributions by such authorities as James Fozard, Leonard Hayflick, and George Sacher.

Gatz, M., Siegler, I. C., & Dibner, S. S. Individual and community: Normative conflicts in the development of a new therapeutic community for older persons. *International Journal of Aging and Human Development*, 1979–80, 10(3), 249–264. During the establishment of a therapeutic community for geriatric patients in a state mental hospital, contradictory role expectations in staff-staff and staff-patient relationships prevent programs from accomplishing their goals. More realistic humanistic goals, embracing a broad range of patient competencies within a reasonable time framework, are recommended.

Gelfand, D. E. Ethnicity, aging and mental health. *International Journal of Aging and Human Development*, 1979–80, *19*(3), 289–298. The author explores relationships between mental-health problems of older persons and ethnic groups in American society and offers suggestions for guiding future research in this field.

Havighurst, R. J. Education through the adult life span. *Educational Gerontology*, 1976, *1*(1), 41–51. Education is viewed as lifelong, involving both instrumental and expressive aspects. While interest in education is now lower among people over age 60 than among younger adults, older people of future years will probably show more interest in continuing education, because they will have had more education in their youth.

Labouvie-Vief, G. Toward optimizing cognitive competence in later life. *Educational Gerontology*, 1976, *1*(1), 75–92. Evidence is accumulating that decrement in later life may not be pervasive and that older people's intellectual performance responds favorably to a variety of conditions. It appears that a new educational psychology of adult life is needed.

Moos, R. H. & Lemke, S. Assessing the physical and architectural features of sheltered care settings. *Journal of Gerontology*, 1980, *35*(4), 571–583. The Physical and Architectural Features Checklist, which measures the physical resources of sheltered care settings, proved useful for comparing and describing facilities. In general more attractive facilities are those with more flexible physical settings, more staff facilities, and a greater degree of choice for residents.

Newman, E. S, & Sherman, S. R. Foster-family care for the elderly: Surrogate family or mini-institution? *International Journal of Aging and Human Development*, 1979–80, *10*(2), 165–176. A study of a sampling of 100 adult foster homes in New York State indicated the extent to which older clients become integrated into the family. The dimensions used to evaluate such integration were affection, social interaction, performance or ritual, and minimization of social distance.

Orben, C. J. Public housing for the elderly. *Journal of Sociology and Social Welfare*, 1976, *3*(4), 421–436. The author discusses reasons for the housing plight of the elderly, problems that thwart adequate provision of low-cost public housing, and suggestions for improving the situation.

Ross, H. E., & Kedward, H. B. Demographic and social correlates of psychogeriatric hospitalization. *Social Psychiatry*, 1976, *11*(3), 121–126. A comparison of 100 admissions to three Toronto hospitals with the general over-65 population in that area. It indicated that high-risk groups included disproportionate numbers of widowed and separated men, older people living alone, residents of old-age and nursing homes, and women with smaller-than-average families. These findings support the hypothesis that social isolation tends to produce admission to institutions.

Watson, W. H. The aging sick and the near dead: A study of some distinguishing characteristics and social effects. *Omega: Journal of Death and Dying*, 1976, *7*(2), 115–123. A study within a home for the aged indicates how patients' own characteristics cause them to be more or less well treated and to be placed nearer, or farther from, the nursing station.

15
DEATH

ATTITUDES TOWARD DEATH

Traditionally, people in Western culture have denied death through assuming the reality of a life after death and a bodily resurrection. Recently, other alternatives have included living on in the memory of others, through one's works and accomplishments, or through one's own descendants. Another belief system involving denial holds that humans are reincarnated in other earthly forms.

Only since the Second World War has the subject of dying received any important scientific attention. Even recently a survey of professional therapists indicated that 40% had not discussed their funeral plans with anyone and 28% had not written their wills, which suggests that even they had ignored death-related issues (Clarke, 1981). But during the past few years the trickle of articles and books on the subject has turned into a tide. It encompasses such diverse topics as capital punishment, suicide, and abortion. It covers such legal matters as wills and bequests, funerals, and mourning.

Reasons for Current Concern

The United States is becoming obsessed with death, declared Hendin (1975). In general, authorities deplore the country's traditional attitudes toward death and promote a healthier view. To date, observed Holcomb (1975), Americans have failed

> to come to any reasonable terms with death. To die seems indecent, inconsiderate, immoral, unAmerican. . . . Thus our pretenses about death strengthen its power to destroy us while we live. Death is a vital part of life and to reject death is to reject the life that includes death. In the very degree that we strip death of its meaning and dignity, we strip life of meaning and dignity [p. 268].

The alternative, suggested Holcomb, is acknowledging the significance of grief, being willing to endure the pain that death involves, and in the process achieving a "spiritual transcendance that triumphs over both the finitude of life and the infinitude of death" (p. 468).

Lifton (1975) asserted that violence and unnatural forms of death (war, murder, torture, suicide) have displaced sexual repression as a preoccupation in modern society. In trying to comprehend the impact of mass death (as in war or the Jonestown suicides), he argued, it is more valid to speak of psychic numbing than repression. This numbing suggests impairment of clear cognitive function, as demonstrated in the survivors of Hiroshima.

Indicators of interest. One reflection of the growing interest in the topic is death education in seminars for the elderly, in the colleges, and even in grade schools. Children's response is mixed. Among a class of Black inner-city and White suburban children, the latter were far more likely to approve of discussing death in the classroom. Some of the children in both groups opposed such discussions, chiefly because they found them disturbing. However, the attitude of most children about death seems healthier than their elders'. After one small girl's brother had died, her mother recalled, this exchange took place:

> "I will keep your ashes, Mom [after you die], but who will keep mine?"
>
> I say, "Your kids will, if you have kids. Or your best friend."
>
> "Who will keep the ashes of the last person in the world?"
>
> "God will," I say. [Keyser, 1977, p. 97].*

Fear of Death

Death fear defined. The fear of death has been analyzed in terms of particular fears of

> pain, loneliness, abandonment, mutilation and, somewhat more difficult to define, fear of the loss of self . . . a kind of dissociation of the self as a conscious entity (the sense of me-ness one feels) from the self as a particular individual, with his particular history in the everyday world. That individual is one's closest associate and one fears his loss. Although everyone feels a certain fear of death, people react to it in their own unique ways, because people die, as they have lived, as individuals, as suggested in the saying, "Death is terrible to Cicero, desirable to Cato, and indifferent to Socrates" [Powers, 1977, p. 265].

People often fear the dying process more than death itself. They fear it will be painful or that they may be abandoned and left alone. They may fear dehumanization by being transformed into a sort of "plumbing shop." Part of the fear is fear of the unknown.

*Excerpt from "When Wendy's brother died," by Marty Keyser, *Readers Digest*, July 1977, 95–97. Reprinted by permission.

People often fear the dehumanizing aspects of dying more than death itself.

Contrasting reactions. Much of one's anticipatory grief about death surrounds the fear of losing oneself. People may feel that their lives are incomplete and that there are many unfinished tasks. They may feel cheated that they will not know what happens to their family in the future, share with them what goes on in their lives ahead, or know what happens in the world in ages to come. Some individuals appear unwilling to let go because they have a desperate feeling that they have not done what they should have. They cannot accept the kind of life that they have lived and hence are unable to place a final blessing on themselves.

In contrast, some individuals may wish to die, feeling that there is no prospect of any worthwhile life to come. The dying often give up the will to live because they are afraid of humiliation, abandonment, and loneliness (Becker, 1973). In other cases they have become chronically ill and know there is no prospect of cure.

Becker (1973) suggested two other attitudes regarding fear of death. According to the healthy-minded concept, reactions to death are learned. Hence, the fear of death is unnatural. With appropriate training and satisfactory human relationships, death can become viewed as a natural process that does not arouse fear. The morbidly minded attitude suggests that everyone fears death and that it is unnatural. Becker assumed the morbidly minded position, declaring that death fear is so great that people inevitably develop rituals and belief systems to cope with the problem.

However, attitude surveys would tend to refute Becker's conclusions. In a multiethnic sample only a fourth admitted fearing death. And a mere 16% of an institutionalized, reasonably alert elderly group expressed such a fear (Kalish & Reynolds, 1976; Kimsey, Roberts, & Logan, 1972). To what extent can we accept at face value people's statements that they do not fear death? Is it possible that the lower death fear asserted by some older people covers up a more intense fear, through a stronger form of denial?

Typical reactions. The following testimony suggests how varied personal reactions to death may be.

> I resent the idea of death as unfair—a cruel joke. I can't bear to think of not knowing what will happen in all the ages to come (divorced man, age 60).
>
> It is inevitable and must be accepted (separated woman, 51).
>
> As I grow older I am beginning to realize that death is part of living (widowed woman, 54).
>
> I look to death as "peace" at last (married woman, 53).

Factors that limit fear. Fears of death vary according to such diverse factors as religiosity, state of consciousness, and culture. When death-related stimuli were compared for graduate students in psychology and religion, Zen meditators, and users of **psychedelic** drugs, the two altered-state groups indicated far less anxiety, perhaps because such states involve transcendent experiences and blurred ego lines (Garfield, 1974). Thus, the boundary between self and nonself becomes diminished, and the prospect of dying does not suggest a different state.

Religious belief also relates to degree of fear. Becker (1973) asserted that people across the ages have coped with their "physicalness" through religious beliefs that permit them to transcend the physical body that eventually dies and rots. People who have abandoned a belief in life after death may seek **transcendence** through having children or influencing the future, possibly by a book or invention. At any rate, people who are more religious appear to be less anxious about death than those who are less religious. Perhaps some feeling of personal transcendence makes their dying easier (Augustine & Kalish, 1975). Nelson and Nelson (1973) reported the least fear of death among the very religious and only a moderate fear of death among the most nonreligious, including firm **agnostics** and atheists. The highest death anxiety was found among people intermediate in their religiosity. The differentiating factor in this case was a belief system that involved uncertain and confused, rather than specific, religious views, whether pro or con.

Attitudes toward death also vary widely according to culture and subculture. Among a multiethnic sampling Kalish and Reynolds (1974) found that about two-thirds of Blacks wanted to live past 90, compared with only 25 to 28% of Japanese-Americans and Anglo-Americans. However, over half the Blacks and Anglos, about half the Japanese, and a third of the Mexican-Americans would let people die if they so desired. The number of people expressing this view diminished with age. People who favored such permission would include those dying anyway (48%) or in pain (21%). Those individuals who would reject people's own right to die cited the right of God alone to terminate life (48%) or the belief that there might still be hope (32%).

On the worldwide level not all cultures have had a dread of death. The Basques in northern Spain anticipate death as the high point in their life and maintain a complex and lengthy series of mourning rites. The Masai in East Africa have quite simple burial customs, paying more attention to everyday life and having little fear of death (Preston, J. J., 1977). One reason that people fear death in North American society is the lack of familiarity with it, because death usually occurs in the hospital.

Age-related attitudes. Among 434 persons in Los Angeles, causing grief to friends and relatives proved less important to older individuals as a reason for dreading death than it did to younger ones, perhaps because they had fewer dependents. The elderly felt less concerned about giving up experiencing, because they had less future potential for satisfying experiences, qualitatively and quantitatively, than the young. The dying process also involves loss of control. Dying people have little to say about decisions regarding themselves—and older people have lost much of this power already.

Inevitably, the foreshortening of one's personal future requires readjustment of time and resources. During the last part of life people may reorganize their activities. In the first place they know that the ending of life will mean an end to all experiences and possessions. If they could look forward to a never-ending life, they would not have to withdraw from people and things. Second, the finitude of life changes the way an individual uses time. If people had all the time in the world, they would not have to establish priorities. For the elderly, time is a directly limiting factor. When elderly residents of certain rural communities were asked what they would do if they knew they were to die in 30 days, they were far less likely than younger people to say that their activities would change at all (Beck, 1965).

It might be assumed that the elderly fear death more than do the young because it is just around the corner. However, the opposite is true. While older people think of death more often, they are less frightened of it (Kalish & Reynolds, 1975). Overt fear is present in about 30% and denial in another 15%;

adjustment to or realistic resolution of the death problem has occurred in about 55% (Butler, 1977).

Such variations derive partly from the fact that reactions to death are a matter not only of age but also of how age interacts with other variables. A young or middle-aged individual who is living a rich, meaningful life might find the idea of death more terrifying than a person leading a comparatively meaningless existence.

Older people's relatively diminished fear of death can be tentatively explained. The elderly realize their limited futures, often have health problems, and no longer have certain roles which they once found very satisfying. It has been said of older people that "their future is behind them" (Kalish, 1977, p. 490). People in industrialized societies expect to live about 65 to 75 years, women somewhat longer and men a bit less. Hence, they feel deprived if they anticipate a shorter life. If they outlive such expectations, however, they feel that they have been granted more than that to which they were entitled. When people grow older, they become somehow "socialized" to their dying. As their peers die in increasing numbers, they become accustomed to death and hence look forward to their own deaths more realistically.

Most books on developmental psychology, including this one, discuss death near the end, although it occurs at all ages. Life expectancy was around 18 years in prehistoric times, about 20 in the Greco-Roman period, and about 35 in the Middle Ages (Dublin, 1965). Even at the turn of the century few people lived into their 60s and 70s. Nowadays it is mostly the elderly who die; and although old people have always died, "The dying have not always been old" (p. 484).

THE CONCEPT OF DEATH

Definition

Physical criteria. Not only attitudes toward death but concepts of when death has occurred vary. Traditionally, people have believed that death can readily be determined and that the cessation of prior activity signifies that it has occurred. Ordinarily, when people speak of death they refer to somatic death, affecting the whole organism. It involves the death of all the bodily tissues; but people are declared dead before all their tissues have died (Powers, 1977). In fact, the instant of physical death is no all-or-none matter. Certain organs may function even after clinical death has been determined.

The core issue in determining that physical death has occurred is the conflict between the death of the brain and nervous system and that of the heart and respiratory system. The brain is considered to be dead when an electroencephalogram (EEG) is flat; that is, there is no detectable electromagnetic activity in the brain. While this definition appears practical, there is the problem that some patients have, although rarely, recovered after 2 or even 3 days with a completely flat EEG (Powers, 1977). Brain death is generally caused by a lack of oxygen, which in turn is usually produced by failure of the lungs or heart. An ad hoc committee of the Harvard Medical School has proposed that criteria for death include no movements or breathing, unresponsivity and unreceptivity, and no reflexes, all confirmed by a flat electroencephalogram (Cassell, Kass, & Associates, 1972).

Nonphysical concepts of death. Death can be defined in other than purely physical ways. Psychological death refers to the cessation of cognitive function, presumably irreversible. The unique thing about being dead is the lack of ability to experience—that is, "to think, to perceive, to behave, to have feelings" (Kalish, 1977, p. 484). Social death has occurred when others perceive an individual as being "as good as dead." An individual may be judged clinically dead and yet still be talked to and related to by those in the environment. Such an individual is socially alive though both clinically and psychologically dead (Kalish, 1968).

Operational definitions. Operationally, physicians may declare that death has occurred on the basis of criteria that presume, rather than establish, the reality of death. The operational definition may be supplemented by a conceptual definition that links the criteria of brain death to the complete sense of death of the person (Agich, 1976). Thus, the determination of death in specific cases derives from a varying complex of factors. In some cases, physicians may prefer a narrow definition of death, so that they can get on with an urgent organ-transplant operation. More-hasty declarations and less-thorough examinations may also be accorded older people, "the suicide victim, the dope addict, the known prostitute, the assailant in a crime of violence, the vagrant, the known wife beater, and generally, those persons whose moral characters are considered reproachable" (Sudnow, 1967, p. 105).

In sum, it seems that death is many things. It is

a biological event, a rite of passage, an inevitability, a natural occurrence, a punishment, extinction, the enforcement of God's will. . . . It is disruption of the social fabric by removing a significant person from the scene; it strengthens the social fabric by removing those less capable of doing their tasks and by permitting others, who otherwise chafe at being restricted, to move into more demanding roles [Kalish, 1977, p. 483].

But definitions of death and dying can be stretched too far. The process of dying should be distinguished from the process of aging, for "in one sense, we are all dying, that is, we are all being processed toward our death. Living is dying, and dying begins at conception" (p. 484). This concept of dying provides some "food for thought," but it may simply cover up the phenomenological significance of dying in the "real world" (p. 484).

Undoubtedly, criteria for death will continue to vary as long as there are advances in medical science. At one time death was believed confirmed if a mirror held before the patient's mouth did not fog up. Obviously, if death is defined by statute, doctors have to honor that concept until the law changes, despite medical advances that make it obsolete.

The Death Experience

The death trajectory. Each death experience has its own pace, or trajectory. The dying trajectory refers to the pacing of death, whether sudden or slow, regular, or erratic. It may proceed in the same downhill direction, be on a plateau, or involve up-and-down stages. Trajectories may be very different for the individual dying from lung cancer, the one who commits suicide by jumping off of the Golden Gate Bridge, and the one who simply wastes away over a period of years.

Various interventions may serve to retard or accelerate the dying process. Among these are medical techniques, psychological intervention, and assorted others such as voodoo, initially relating to the Haitians' use of magical rites to hasten death. Sudden death may also result from traumatic shocks, perhaps caused by catastrophic stress on the autonomic nervous system (Hinton, 1972). Relocation, especially among the confused elderly, may also hasten death. Another factor is the will to live, referring to individuals' intervention in their own dying trajectory. D. P. Phillips and Feldman (1973) found that more people die shortly after such occasions as birth dates and important holidays than in the same period before such dates. While such results are usually ascribed to a will to live, they might as easily be attributed to the unusual excitement and strain brought on by such occasions.

There is no clear-cut answer to the question of whether it is more desirable to experience a sudden and unexpected death or a more prolonged one (Kalish & Reynolds, 1976). Individuals preferring the quicker death desire to avoid suffering as well as emotional strain on themselves and their loved ones. However, this mode of death can be more stressful for the survivors, partly because they have had no chance to prepare for it. Nor did the deceased have any chance to set his or her affairs in order, to finish some significant undertaking, or to participate in the grieving processes along with the loved ones.

If the dying trajectory is prolonged, loved ones' may work through most of their grief feelings before actual death occurs. Indeed, they may indicate some frustration and irritation that clinical death is so long delayed. When death does occur, they may feel more relief than grief. While others may perceive them as quite unfeeling, they may have worked out their anticipatory grief long ago. By contrast, when sudden death occurs and there has been no chance for anticipatory death, the survivors may afterward discuss times leading up to the death and their feelings about the deceased, in a sense compensating for the lack of anticipatory grieving.

The Stages of Dying

Kübler-Ross's theory. For people who do not die suddenly and who are aware of their impending demise, reactions ordinarily proceed through certain stages. The first stage, observed Kübler-Ross (1974) on the basis of hundreds of interviews, is one of denial, even though the patient may have sought to determine the truth. After coming to realize their plight, dying individuals often retreat into the self in a state of isolation. The second stage is one of anger, especially when the person is young. This hostility may be vented in any direction, against doctors, relatives, or God. After this anger subsides, dying people may attempt to bargain for their lives, making various promises to God. Such bargains have in common that they are almost never kept. The fourth stage is one of depression, often called anticipatory grief, a grieving for oneself and the prospect of losing everyone and everything that one loves. After this depression comes the final stage, one of acceptance (Powers, 1977).

Kübler-Ross (1969) found the acceptance stage of dying to be quite adaptive. It suggests a reduction in an individual's attachments to others, to material possessions, and to ideas. Acceptance of disengagement allows an individual to focus whatever cognitive and emotional powers remain on those remaining attachments that are most vital. The dying stage thus closely resembles the concept of disengagement that is associated with the elderly.

Weisman (1972) suggested that acceptance is not the same as capitulation. That is, an individual can accept impending death without yielding whatever life remains. Moreover, not going gently into that good night, but raging against the dying of the light may be an acceptable mode of dying for the individual doing the dying, even if it is uncomfortable for the survivors and hospital professionals. Indeed, acceptance and raging may not be mutually exclusive; nor should acceptance be confused with wanting to die.

Perspective on death stages. These stages do not occur in unvarying order. Dying people may move from one stage to another, sometimes slowly, sometimes rapidly, and sometimes simultaneously and at varying levels of awareness. Nor does every individual ultimately attain a state of acceptance. Kübler-Ross herself pointed out that most of her patients exhibited two or three stages at the same time and not always in the same order.

At the Brink of Death

There has been much conjecture about what it is like to die. According to one theory, the dying experience involves depersonalization, which serves as a defensive reaction to life-threatening situations. While alerting the organism to threat, it produces an integration of reality and holds in check potentially disorganizing emotions. Meantime, a mystical elaboration of the experience may produce a sense of spiritual rebirth following the near-death episode. According to another theory the dying are often aware but generally peaceful. In recordings of the last moments of great men, over and over the final words indicate a sense of peace and a readiness to go (Powers, 1977).

Other conjecture is based on reports by people who have come very close to dying. These experiences are becoming increasingly common in hospitals' emergency trauma centers. On the whole such people report that the dying process is far less traumatic than commonly believed and sometimes involves considerable ecstasy. In one such report a woman, revived from the threshhold of death after a violent allergic reaction to penicillin, reported first having fought against dying, even though she was not afraid, and then having known that she wanted death. Then came in rapid succession many vivid scenes from her life as well as various fantasies. She pictured herself on a bright red bicycle, on a bright green lawn. There flashed before her a picture of the Taj Mahal, a monument erected by a husband for his wife.

In another case a young teacher, restored after his heart stopped beating, had believed himself in a great supermarket, trussed up like a roast, on a conveyor belt bound for the checkout counter. His experience was somewhere between nightmare and ecstasy and involved both struggle to survive and humor. He recalled saying to himself at one point "Oh no, oh no, they are not going to check me out." On being revived and seeing many doctors around him in white he exclaimed "Christ, there are a lot a clerks in this meat market" (Holcomb, 1975, p. 257).

CARE FOR THE DYING

The Appropriate Death

The ideal is to help people to die in the way they would prefer, what Weisman called an appropriate death. Most individuals die in health-care institutions, the greatest number of these in hospitals. There, "The conspiracy of silence which surrounds the dying patient isolates him when he most needs the support of those closest to him" ("Acceptance of the Idea of Mortality," 1975, p. 216). Instead, most people would prefer dying in their own homes, a desire more common among younger and older adults than those between the ages of 40 and 59 (Kalish & Reynolds, 1976). Most family members would also prefer that their loved ones die at home. Nevertheless, the caretakers' burden is often severe, and in retrospect a third of them are uncertain about the decision to have them die at home (Cartwright, Hockey, & Anderson, 1973). Among newer options as a place for dying is the hospice, where the terminally ill are provided good medical care, unlimited visiting hours, and amelioration of pain when they have only days or weeks to live (Kalish, 1977).

The appropriate death also involves genuinely concerned medical personnel. Unfortunately, some dying patients, especially the old or quite deteriorated, may not receive extraordinary help. Instead, they are perceived as "having earned their deaths" (Glaser & Strauss, 1968, p. 496). Undoubtedly, some doctors become rather careless about life-sustaining machines and a patient's right to live. One physician recalled being asked by a colleague, regarding an emergency case: "Do you mind if this patient dies? The respirator is on the fifth floor and the nurse says it's a pain in the ass." ("A Right to Die," 1977, p. 287).

In the last stages of dying the patient's greatest fear is that of being abandoned, a fear with a very sound base. In most hospitals dying patients are moved into a single room. The nurses, doctors, and even relatives devise various reasons for avoiding their room, often on the pretext of not wanting to disturb them. Doctors and nurses often cut down visits to them, reserving more attention for those whom they believe can still be helped. Families themselves often act as though the person has already passed on (Powers, 1977).

Suggestions for Improvement

Such unfortunate circumstances should certainly be improved. The dying are entitled to doctors especially trained in dealing with them. Through frequent short visits, families, friends, or volunteer workers should assure the dying that they will not be left alone. They may also be provided psychotherapy, both to strengthen their will to live and to prepare them for the worst to come (Kalish, 1977). Patients may be helped to overcome feelings of complete despair and to gain some confidence that their lives have been significant. The prospect of death or its occurrence can even bring a great surge of positive emotional feeling, a reaction not yet systematically documented. Encounters with someone about to die can be enriching (Barrett, 1981).

When individuals approach death, they often experience altered states of consciousness that may improve the effectiveness of psychotherapy. During such states they may experience new insights that they want to share with others. LSD has recently been tried to help the dying experience transcendence. In the process patients may perceive death as a transitional state and not the ultimate end, suggesting the potential for continued consciousness after death.

What to Tell Dying Patients

One issue relating to dying that has involved considerable controversy is whether to tell the dying of their condition. About 80% of patients say they would prefer to be told (Powers, 1977). More people believe that they should be told than are sure that others should be told (Kalish & Reynolds, 1976). Perhaps most of the dying realize their condition anyway.

If given only a designated period to live, people vary somewhat in how they would spend their limited time. In one study (Beck, 1965) people in rural Western communities were asked what they would do if they knew they were to die in a month. The elderly were less likely than younger ones to say that they would modify their activities. Another study (Kalish & Reynolds, 1976), in the greater Los Angeles area, involved three age groups—20 to 39, 40 to 59, and over age 60. The period involved was 6 months instead of 30 days. More of the older persons said they would not change their life-style. Three times as many older than younger ones said they would spend their remaining time in prayer, reading, contemplation, and other activities that signify withdrawal or inner and spiritual needs.

Various reasons are given for and against informing the patient about impending death. About 80% of physicians favor withholding the truth, because it might prove upsetting or destroy the patient's will to live. However, many authorities favor a policy of openness with the patient. In a speech entitled "A Matter of Life and Death," Dr. Thomas B. Hackett, a psychiatrist, declared that people who have learned the truth about their terminal condition sustain fewer psychological traumas than do those to whom the truth has been denied. Weisman (1972) asserted that "to be informed about a diagnosis, especially a serious diagnosis, is to be fortified, not undermined" (p. 17).

Advantages of open approach. Various other advantages are cited to support the policy of openness. Kalish (1977) suggested that patients may desire to set their house in order by going over financial matters, telling of the existence or location of important papers, or completing responsibilities. In addition, they and their loved ones may laugh and cry together over memories that are dear to them. Or they may seek and grant forgiveness for real or imagined wrongs that they have done each other. The patient may even give instructions about funeral or memorial services. Family members often have little if any idea about what the deceased would have wanted.

Mutual awareness between the dying and loved ones also allows them to communicate frankly together. Such relationships, coupled with a significant belief system, may produce a feeling of transcendence that allows dying people to maintain self-esteem and comfortable feelings about their past and future. They feel that their life had meaning and that this meaning extends beyond and transcends their own brief time on earth (Augustine & Kalish, 1975). Even if patients do not want to dwell on death, they may want at least to share their feelings about what these last days and hours are like.

Exceptions to the rule. What should be done about the minority of people who feel, sometimes strongly, that they would not like to be told of imminent death? In such cases, it is best that they make their wishes clear to intimates, in writing, before such circumstances arise. There have been cases when death seemed certain but the patients lived. Was it partly because they still believed they had a chance?

Sustaining Life

Another controversial issue is how long to keep a person alive through the use of heart/lung machines, organ transplants, respirators, and other such measures. Patients who would certainly otherwise have died can now be kept alive, at least technically, for months or even years. One woman in a coma after a cerebral hemorrhage was maintained alive for 6 weeks simply by means of intravenous feedings and a respirator. After the doctor explained to the family that she could remain this way for years without any chance of recovering, they agreed that the respirator should be unhooked ("A Right to Die," 1977).

In deciding whether to maintain life, there are three possible courses of action: to utilize every possible effort to keep the individual alive; to cease taking extraordinary measures but to continue the usual medical procedures; or to take steps that will accelerate death or simply permit the individual to proceed toward it. Such decisions are often made by the physician in conjunction with the family and, occasionally with the dying individual. When elderly people in a veterans' home were asked their preferences—assuming that they were terminally ill, in great stress, and bearing heavy medical expenses—almost half wanted the doctor to try to keep them alive. A fourth favored eliminating unusual methods but rejected efforts to hasten their deaths, while the remaining fourth accepted a speeding up of the process (Preston & Williams, 1971).

A related issue is whether active **euthanasia,** such as deliberately giving an injection to end a patient's misery, may be judged homicide. The only doctors who have come on trial for mercy killings have been exonerated, and many physicians come very close to active euthanasia. In a survey by Diana Crane, a sociologist, 43% of 660 internists questioned acknowledged that they would provide increasing doses of narcotics to cancer patients who were in unusual pain, knowing quite well that the drug would eventually produce fatal respiratory arrest ("A Right to Die," 1977). Certainly, most doctors employ passive euthanasia by not providing certain treatments in apparently hopeless cases. A matter that complicates such cases is that patients who have been totally given up on are sometimes restored to relatively good health. Gruzalski (1981) urges that we abandon the "convenient myth that letting a patient die is not an act of killing" (p. 97). This "unsettling conclusion" raises the question whether letting die is morally any less objectionable than killing.

The Living Will

In recent years the idea of a **"living will"** has been proposed so that patients' desires can be respected. Such a will is drawn up while an individual is still in control of his or her mental capacities, indicating conditions under which extraordinary measures should be applied or withheld. While such documents as yet have no legal force, some state legislatures have initiated proposals to make them legally binding. One problem is that individuals who are facing the imminent prospect of dying may feel quite differently from the way they did when their deaths were further removed. Yet their condition during these later stages may prevent them from changing their living wills.

GRIEF AND RITUALS

Reactions to Death

The recent surge of interest in death has focused growing attention on grief. Grief involves varied responses, including depression and guilt, derived from either real or fantasied feelings of responsibility for the death or from presumed failures in former relationships with the dead. Anger is often accompanied by blaming of those who might or might not have had some role in the death, including physicians, God, or other family members. Anxiety and restlessness are also common; and preoccupation with the image of the departed one is often vividly real (Kalish & Reynolds, 1976). Meantime, others often treat grieving people as sick ones, talking about them in hushed tones and assuming their responsibilities at least for a time (Parkes, 1972).

Grief reactions vary with age. Children are not unaffected by death. On the contrary, death may leave a permanent imprint on their personalities. Often they feel guilty that they have somehow been responsible for the death, perhaps of a sibling or friend. They may be unsettled by the failure of a sibling to be born if they have been told of its imminent arrival. The greatest impact results from the loss of a parent. A British study disclosed that boys age 4 and even younger who had lost their fathers were more than usually susceptible to extreme depression in adulthood (Hill, 1972).

In adult years the loss of a spouse can often bring unusual grief. Aging survivors, especially, may feel vulnerable to what now is perceived as a more "hostile society" (Kalish, 1977, p. 502). Nor are such feelings easily overcome. Among a sampling of widows and widowers, those still depressed a month after the loss were likely to be depressed a year later. For parents who unexpectedly lose a baby, several years may pass without a sense of healing. Such an event may produce lasting ways in which a woman especially relates to her other children and her husband (Rubin, 1981).

Adjusting to Death

Satisfactory readjustment depends on such props as rituals, ceremonies, and grief work, or "the process of working through the disengaging process, becoming free from the relationship that existed" (Holcomb, 1975, p. 251). It involves "working through a complex of deep and distressing emotions and learning to cope with ongoing life without the presence of the person, thing, function, or relationship that no longer exists" (p. 251). Grief work may anticipate, be current with, or take place long after the loss. Individuals may also engage in anticipatory grief work about their own demise, either in the dim, faraway future or at some probable time near at hand. Most writers believe that such anticipatory grief work can be useful. Thus, an individual gets ready for bereavement in smaller doses so that the acute shock of the ultimate reality is somewhat diluted or diminished.

Purpose of ceremonies. The rituals and ceremonies that follow death not only honor the dead but also provide for the psychological needs of the survivors (Kalish, 1977). Presumably, the ceremony helps to make the death more real, thus reducing the "search for the lost object." Nevertheless, research on this point is lacking. Perhaps the abuse often leveled at funeral directors and physicians constitutes a displacement of guilt that survivors feel for having neglected the dead. Still, such feelings are sometimes deserved.

Funerals and rituals may also help survivors at a time when their own affective functioning is reduced. That is, they need the resources provided by

Rituals and ceremonies honoring the dead help the survivors cope with their grief.

others to help them to cope with their grief. Thus, "The wake and the funeral reaffirm the group identity of the survivors" (Lopata, 1973b, p. 53). In other words, sharing the funeral rituals represents "an affirmation of family and community ties at a time of stress" (Kalish, 1977, p. 503).

Changing funeral customs. Nevertheless, death-related ceremonies and rituals are changing. The bereaved often ask that donations to various charities be made instead of sending flowers. Some people request cremation, with their ashes sprinkled over a lake or mountain. Neither the sprinkling of ashes nor a money donation to help survivors get through a period that often involves financial stress should be considered a secularization of death, but simply as a newly emerging sacred ritual.

Growing controversy surrounds the traditional funeral customs of this society. Illich objected that dying is coming to be "managed" by various professionals and that people must be educated to die in the correct sequence. He criticized "the destruction, by a standardized white-coat policy of crisis management, of the 100 ways in which the individual might accomplish in a solemn manner that last expression of health that consists of living it up to the last moment" (Illich with Keen, 1976, p. 74).

Mitford (1977) observed that

funeral transactions impinge on consumers in certain distinctive ways, including the disorientation caused by bereavement, the lack of standards by which to judge the value of the commodity offered by the seller, the need to make an on-the-spot decision, general ignorance of the law as it affects disposal of the dead, [and] the ready availability of insurance money to finance the transaction [p. 289].

The funeral industry recommends that selling be "subtle" rather than "hard sell" and that pricing be according to the family's means, regardless of their wishes. Funeral directors are warned by experts in the field not to be too crass in their manner, as in such remarks as, "I can tell by the fine suit you are wearing, that you appreciate the finer things, and will want a fine casket for your mother" (p. 289).

A growing minority is coming to emancipate itself from the social pressure to accord the dead an impressive funeral. Such people may insist on cheaper funerals or dispense with them altogether, choosing cremation and a memorial service or nothing at all beyond what the law requires.

STATUS OF THE PSYCHOLOGY OF DYING

With the psychology of dying in such a state of furious ferment, it is difficult to assess its current status. Kalish (1977) asserted that the most significant development has been "breaking through the taboo surrounding death" (p. 504). Nevertheless, research into death has still not gone beyond the "toddler" stage and deserves attention on several points (p. 504). First, methods need refinement. For example, simply asking people if they are afraid of dying is hardly a conclusive measure of fear of death. Such answers cannot be quantified; nor do they take into account unconscious factors or the possibility that denial of fear may be a defense mechanism against a very real fear. In addition, the "clichés" in this area deserve testing. For example, it is often assumed that people should be told that their condition is terminal. Most individuals want to know, but some do not. While openness may be healthier than "mutual pretense" for some people, pretense may be more adaptive for others. Again, some people prefer being surrounded by intimates when they die; others prefer to be by themselves. To date, researchers have approached such questions in too global a fashion.

It is important not merely to determine individual differences on such matters but also to understand their significance. They should be analyzed both on the individual level and in terms of such factors as sex, race, religion, family status, class, and age. Death has a different meaning for older than for younger people, partly because society places different values on their death. Studies should also be replicated from time to time and in cultures around the world because of the importance of the historical and social context within which the death occurs.

SUMMARY

In recent years the topic of death has received increasing attention. Fear of death relates to such factors as religiosity and age. Death is also variously defined in physical and nonphysical (psychological and sociological) terms. Because practical matters require that specific criteria be adopted for determining when death has occurred, operational definitions are employed by physicians.

Each death has its own pace, or trajectory, and dying people typically proceed through certain stages. These, however, are not invariable. There has been much conjecture over how it feels to die, and reports from people who have recovered after approaching the brink are assumed to throw some light on the subject.

Interest has also grown regarding care for the dying and problems relating to the death itself. The ideal is to permit each individual to have an appropriate death, the type best for him or her. Programs are also being developed for helping the bereaved and for dealing with the highly varied individual reactions to grief. Meantime death-related rituals are changing. They often include substitution of charitable donations for flowers, cremation instead of burial, and memorial services in place of funerals.

Some of the most controversial issues relating to death concern whether to tell dying people that the end is near, whether to try to sustain an apparently meaningless life, and what death rituals or ceremonies to employ. The trend seems to be in the direction of communicating openly with the dying, not deliberately prolonging life in the hopelessly ill, and having simpler ceremonies. But attitudes on the topic are in a state of flux, and it is uncertain what shape they will take in the future.

SUGGESTED READINGS

Balkin, E., Epstein, C., & Bush, D. Attitude toward classroom discussions of death and dying among urban and suburban children. *Omega: Journal of Death and Dying*, 1976, 7(2), 183–189. A study of 50 Black, inner-city children and 50 White, suburban children discloses their reasons for approving or disapproving of discussions of death in the classroom.

Clarke, P. J. Exploration of countertransference toward the dying. *American Journal of Orthopsychiatry*, 1981, 51(1), 71–77. A comparison of professionals and nonprofessionals revealed no differences in their feelings toward death and the dying.

Coombs, R. H., & Powers, P. S. Socialization for death: The physician's role. *Urban Life*, 1975, 4(3), 250–271. In-depth interviews of medical students regarding the evolution of their feelings about death suggest a five-stage developmental model. Also discussed are the implications of such attitudes for the welfare of patients.

Crook, T., & Eliot, J. Parental death during childhood and adult depression: A critical review of the literature. *Psychological Bulletin*, 1980, 87(2), 252–259. Experiencing a parent's death during childhood is viewed as traumatic and as producing a predisposition to depression when faced with rejection or loss in adulthood. The long-term significance of such loss has received little recognition to date.

Dinnage, R. Understanding loss: The Bowlby canon. *Psychology Today*, 1980, *13*(12), 56–60. John Bowlby's contributions to developmental psychology are described and appraised. In this work on attachment as a basic human drive, he stresses the long-range effects of separation, especially in cases of mourning and bereavement, in both adults and children.

Goodman, L. M. *Death and the Creative Life*. New York: Springer, May 1981. This exploration of the effect of actualization of personal potential on individual attitudes toward death features interviews with 20 artists and scientists.

Gruzalski, B. Killing by letting die. *Mind*, 1981, *XC*, 91–98. The author analyzes the concepts of active and passive euthanasia, including legal and moral implications, and attacks the view that letting a patient die is not an act of killing.

Hall, E., with Cameron, P. Our failing reverence for life. *Psychology Today*, 1976, *9*(11), 104–106; 113. Because of such factors as growing population and shrinking natural resources, psychologist Paul Cameron perceived Americans as becoming more casual about and accepting of death—for example, with regard to euthanasia, suicide, and abortion.

Kurlychek, R. T. Death education: Some considerations of purpose and rationale. *Educational Gerontology*, 1977, *2*(1), 43–50. Various issues are examined that are relevant to death education programs for the elderly.

Marshall, V. W. Organizational features of terminal status passage in residential facilities for the aged. *Urban Life*, 1975, *4*(3), 349–368. A comparison of how older people confront dying within a home for the aged and a retirement village. The situation was found to be superior in the village. There, impending death became a focus for collective involvement and mutual support.

Mills, G. C., Reisler, R., Jr., Robinson, A. E., & Vermilye, G. *Discussing death: A guide to death education*. Homewood, Ill.: ETC Publications, 1976. This book, intended for the death educator, provides curricular content helpful for dealing with children and adolescents. It is stressed that death anxieties are learned and can be averted through appropriate education.

Noyes, R., & Kletti, R. Depersonalization in the face of life-threatening danger: An interpretation. *Omega: Journal of Death and Dying*, 1976, *7*(2), 103–114. Anecdotal evidence is employed to support the theory that depersonalization is a common protective reaction to life-threatening danger. While defending the endangered personality against the threat of death, it stimulates an integration of that reality and, sometimes, a sense of rebirth.

Parkes, C. M. Determinants of outcome following bereavement. *Omega: Journal of Death and Dying*, 1975, *6*(4), 303–323. Interviews with widows and widowers under age 45, shortly after their bereavement and a year later, disclose those factors most predictive of poor adjustment.

Portwood, D. A right to decide. *Psychology Today*, 1978, *11*(8), 66–76. The writer reviews common attitudes toward suicide, considers the unhappy plight of many elderly people, and concludes that society should fully accept the right of the elderly to end their own lives. She cites instances in which individuals have undertaken death by design rather than endure a future that they felt no longer held any meaning.

Schneidmann, E. S. *Death: Current perspectives*. Palo Alto, Calif.: C. Mayfield, 1976. This compilation of recent papers on death and dying reflects personal, social, and cultural perspectives. It treats such topics as concepts of death, its psychological aspects, the demography of it, determination of it, its survivors, and death as a social disease.

Schulz, R. & Bazerman, M. Ceremonial occasions and mortality: A second look. *American*

Psychologist, 1980, 35(3), 253–261. An examination of data regarding the rise or decrease in number of deaths before or after important events fails to disclose conclusive findings.

Sheskin, A., & Wallace, S. E. Differing bereavements: Suicide, natural, and accidental death. *Omega: Journal of Death and Dying*, 1976, 7(3), 229–242. A comparison is made of widows' experiences after their husband's suicide, natural death, or accidental death. Bereavement is discussed in terms of anticipation of death, individual reactions to it, readjustment, and reinvolvement.

Siegel, R. K. The psychology of life after death. *American Psychologist*, 1980, 35(10), 911–931. This article critically reviews the evidence cross-culturally, historically, and currently, regarding life after death.

Veatch, R. M. *Death, dying and the biological revolution: Our last quest for responsibility*. New Haven, Conn.: Yale University Press, 1976. Various issues are considered that relate to the medical, ethical, and legal aspects of death and dying. These include alternative definitions of death and patients' rights to refuse treatment or to be informed of the nature and seriousness of their condition.

Wass, H. Views and opinions of elderly persons concerning death. *Educational Gerontology*, 1977, 2(1), 15–26. Views of the elderly were compared with those of younger ones as obtained from a *Psychology Today* questionnaire. The study indicates a need for a better understanding of how older people feel about death. For example, current funeral practices are not approved of by many older people.

Wood, J. The structure of concern: The ministry in death-related situations. *Urban Life*, 1975, 4(3), 369–384. Interviews with 31 ministers in two communities indicate how they carry out their death work with regard to the dying patient, the funeral, and the bereaved. It is suggested that an overly formalized role may reduce the quality of assistance to the persons involved.

16
CONCLUSION

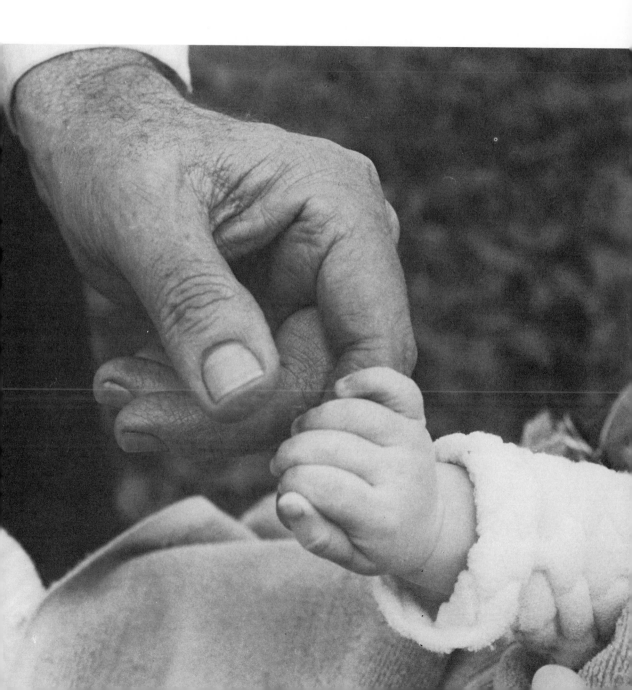

Earlier chapters have been concerned with successive life stages; this one will provide an overview of the entire life span. While it involves a measure of duplication, such a summary of aspects of development for all stages affords a picture of the total pattern. Life-span development is analyzed in relation to environmental factors and future prospects. But first of all I discuss aging, the process that propels every individual through life stages.

AGING

Significance

Daily behaviors. The effects of aging are often subtle and pervasive, even in everyday life. These patterns and related attitudes vary by age groups. Across the years age-related patterns gradually emerge that affect daily behaviors. For example, in natural outdoor conversations younger and older people stand physically closer together than middle-aged people do (Riley, 1976). When Neugarten obtained views from people aged 20 to 60 about appropriate behaviors, the limits for others' behaviors went down as their ages increased. But limits for their own behaviors went up. However, the two estimates converged at age 60, suggesting that older people experience increased restraints on their behaviors (Neugarten, Moore, & Lowe, 1965).

Changing significance. The question arises whether age is becoming more or less significant. On the one hand, age mixing is becoming more common in some areas. It is already usual to see "70-year-old students, 30-year-old college presidents, 22-year-old mayors, 35-year-old grandmothers, 50-year-old retirees, 65-year-old fathers of preschoolers, 60-year-olds and 30-year-olds wearing the same clothing styles, and 85-year-old parents caring for 65-year-old offspring" (Neugarten & Hagestad, 1976, p. 52). As much variability increases around the usual age norms, we may appear to be becoming "an age-irrelevant society." On the other hand, certain distinctions are still highly apparent. We have a variety of age status systems and an increasing number of age differentiations. For example, government programs use chronological age for distinguishing different categories of people.

The significance of aging will undoubtedly be affected by increasing life expectancy. If the average life is increased by only 5 years, observed Neugarten (1973), the effects on society and its institutions will be profound. For example, there will be a growing demand for quality retirement communities, geriatrics specialists, and continuing-education programs. Depending on what adjustments are made, it cannot now be predicted whether the status of the aged will become better or worse in the future as the number of old people increases (Neugarten, 1973).

The Aging Process

Current information. Shock (1977) summed up the current concept of the aging process as embracing so "many diverse phenomena it is clear that no single theory can explain [them] all. . . . A whole spectrum of biological, physiological, psychobiological, and social theories will be needed" (p. 103). On the one hand, biological theories of aging are essentially genetic, the basic assumption being that the life span of the various animal species is programmed by the genes. On the other hand, physiological theories stress the interaction between cells, tissues, and organ systems in their effort to explain overall response to change within the body. While physiologists realize that the final explanation of aging may reside at the cellular level, they stress the importance of relationships between the various organ systems in maintaining the integrity of the organism. Similarly, when bacteria and various microorganisms were originally identified as causal agents for various diseases, medical scientists often searched for single causes. But later research indicated that many diseases have multiple causes, and the idea that a single agent is the only cause of a disease has been generally relinquished.

Prospects for longer life span. Skeptics point out that, while some of the causes of premature death have been eliminated, little has been done to increase basic longevity (Butler, 1975). Most medical advances are simply allowing more people to reach old age rather than increasing old age itself. The change in life expectancy in the United States over the past 2 decades has been almost negligible (Eisenberg, 1977). Hence, the "most optimistic expectations for medical advance are for further postponement, but never the prevention of death" (Berger, Hamburg, & Hamburg, 1977, p. 241).

Strehler (1977) conjectured about the limits of the life span. As people age, many body functions become less effective, so that about 1% of initial capacity is lost each year after age 30. At this rate, the reserve capacity to perform work would give out at around 120. It is hardly surprising, therefore, that the longest fully authenticated life on record is 118 years. While there are claims that persons have lived 2 or more decades longer, these have not been authenticated. Still, the chances of dying do not increase in direct proportion to the extent of function loss.

Some authorities hold out hope that human life can be extended. Kalish (1976) suggested that it may become possible to control, or at least modify, the aging process, either directly by altering the body chemistry or indirectly through better health care and diet. Such knowledge may be available within the foreseeable future, added Kalish, even within the next 3 to 5 decades. Certain research into the deceleration of aging processes in lower animals already shows promise. With such new knowledge, perhaps by the turn of the century several years may be tacked onto current life expectancy. In that case, society's institutions must make corresponding adjustments. For example, consider the impact of a longer life span on mandatory retirement age and population growth.

Katchadourian (1976) agreed in substance, declaring that it may be

> possible to tamper with the biological clocks that regulate the very processes of growth and aging. . . . If and when that time comes, decisions may have to be made about what part of the life cycle to prolong. In a life span of, say, 100 years, would we want to foreshorten childhood or prolong it? If adulthood is to be stretched out, can it occur during our "prime" or will it simply prolong the period of decrepitude [p. 53]?

It seems strange, observed Strehler (1977), that society has not spent more time and money in attempting to comprehend, control, and even reverse the basic causes of aging. Nevertheless, less money has been devoted to the entire area of research in biological aging than to a single moon shot. Undoubtedly, the reason is that people have simply taken for granted that they will die and have believed it impossible that any alternative could exist. Nevertheless, such research, if undertaken in the near future, might even extend the lifetime of current generations.

The control of the aging process would revolutionize the human scene. The same breakthroughs that would extend life spans would probably also greatly improve the body's general condition and function. Individuals who lived for 100 years or longer would be healthier for an even greater percentage of their total lives than now. Even quite old people would have bodies more like those of the young, and their mental content would be vastly enriched because of the expanded time for becoming acquainted with the wonders of the universe. Moreover, because the middle years of life would be doubled, people could spend more time making contributions to society. Educational programs would be thoroughly reorganized, so that life-span education would become the general practice. Meantime, as machines took over more of the burdensome tasks, minds and energies would be freer for decades of truly fulfilling kinds of experience.

Successful Aging

Given the present life span, certain conditions, environments, and behaviors relate to successful aging. Ordinarily, being "on time" in terms of social expectations is important, and those who are not experience some difficulty. Those people who enter college when they are in their 30s or 40s may feel somewhat uncomfortable around their younger classmates. Women who have become widowed comparatively early or men who have retired much younger than their colleagues may find their social relationships difficult. Nevertheless, being "off time" sometimes has fortunate byproducts. Those who retire earlier

Abkhasians work late into life, eat low-calories foods, and have meaningful social lives, all of which contribute to their long lives.

than usual can take advantage of opportunities that they might be unable to enjoy later on. Men who become fathers somewhat late prove more secure and effective in that role than do early or "on-time" fathers, partly because they are no longer preoccupied with the stresses of their early career. In this sense, simply by delaying some role transitions instead of tackling several important ones head on, an individual can avoid role overload.

A second factor in successful aging is the ability to cope, which also presumes adaptability. Such a characteristic is developed in varying degree early in life and tends to persist. Successful aging depends on its underpinnings, constructed in early years.

Other personality traits are significant, too. Studies by Neugarten and her associates (1964) suggest that personality type and organization are critical in determining which individuals will age successfully. Although such factors as economic security, health, and marital status are more important than age in determining successful aging, and although environmental factors contribute to variations in the way people age, personality characteristics are the significant mediating factors.

Environment relates not only to successful life but also to length of life. For example, the Abkhasians are described as long-living people (Benet, 1971). Their longevity may derive from working until late in life, a meaningful social life, and diet. They eat a low-calorie diet, including little meat, eggs, or salt, and few of them smoke; and the elders are well integrated into the larger community.

ASPECTS OF LIFE-SPAN DEVELOPMENT

Physical Development

Changes over time. The most basic aspect of aging and development is physical, beginning with fertilization. In childhood, boys and girls are not simply small adults; they differ qualitatively from grown-ups in biochemistry, nervous system, and skeletal structure. A basic pattern underlies each individual's growth, but the rate varies with age. The most rapid growth is during the prenatal period and again, though less so, toward the end of childhood.

Children's physical problems normally involve such matters as weight, rest and sleep, nutrition, accidents, and familiar illnesses such as measles and influenza. Thus, physical care for children is mainly aimed at improving their nutrition, ensuring that they obtain the proper vaccines, and providing for adequate rest, exercise, and play.

Adolescence is initiated with puberty, which involves changes culminating in the capacity to reproduce. Changes are both primary—in sex organs involved in reproduction—and secondary—affecting voice, breasts, structure, and features. Common physical problems at this stage involve nutrition, fatigue, body image, and the use of drugs, including cigarettes, alcohol, and marijuana.

In the course of development from conception to maturity, growing individuals have trajectories. If the normal growth pattern is deflected from its path by illness, a period of extreme malnutrition, or other circumstances, a not fully understood catch-up mechanism serves thereafter to restore the pattern.

The picture during maturity is one of physical stability in young adulthood, followed by a slow decline in middle age that becomes more rapid thereafter. By adulthood the body has, in the main, attained proportions that change little thereafter. In middle age certain decrements become apparent, varying greatly among individuals, and the body begins losing its reserve capacity. Common physical changes at this stage can be summarized as follows: (1) The heart at age 40 pumps about 23 liters of blood a minute under stress, as opposed to 40 liters at age 20. (2) Sexual capacity declines, the prostate enlarges, and bladder problems begin to appear. (3) The chest decreases in order to compensate for the weakening of the diaphragm. (4) The kidneys lose a certain reserve capacity for concentrated waste. (5) The gastrointestinal tract secretes fewer enzymes, increasing indigestion and constipation. (6) Hearing acuity declines and eye lenses gradually lose elasticity. While the losses are small and gradual, they convey "an emphatic message of human mortality" (Schanche, 1973).

In general, the later years involve considerable loss of physiological adaptability and less capacity for coping with stresses (Timiras, 1972). Over 40% of older people who are not in an institution have some limitation on normal activity, compared with 13% of the total population (Bouvier, Atlee, & McVeigh, 1977). Chronic conditions such as heart disease, arthritis, rheumatism, and sensory impairments are common. The major causes of death are heart disease, cancer, and stroke, in that order, together accounting for almost three-fourths of deaths in later years.

Three observations help to place the foregoing dismal statistics in clearer and more favorable perspective. The aging processes themselves are less detrimental than is commonly believed. Technology is achieving growing successes against conditions often associated with, but wrongly attributed to, the aging process itself. Many people remain quite healthy and vigorous until great old age, and the challenge is to expand this number greatly. The apparently simple preventive and therapeutic effects of regular exercise programs have been demonstrated. At all age stages, the growing fund of knowledge about health, if supported by sufficient funds for its application and enough discretion in its use, would vastly improve human physical resources.

Mental Development

Mental development involves certain basic concepts. *Learning* is the modification of behavior in consequence of experience. *Cognition* indicates the higher mental functions and processes involved in comprehending one's environment. *Intelligence* suggests the capacity for learning to act effectively, but its exact nature is unclear. Heredity defines limits on ultimate mental growth, but experiences are significant in defining the functional level of intelligence.

Cognition from infancy through maturity. Infants' perceptions were formerly perceived as amorphous and all but meaningless. Now infants are viewed as actively and selectively responding to their environment. Piaget and others have portrayed cognitive development as progressing by stages: sensorimotor, concrete-operations, and formal-operations. Others have argued that well-defined sequences do not exist, that sequences vary, and that the rate of change depends upon experience.

Although the pattern is not completely smooth, cognitive operations at the next stage normally change little. Young adults often display a lower level of formal operations than do most individuals in late adolescence and college years. The level is restored in the early 30s and persists through the 30s and early 40s. A plateau appears to persist at least until the 60s (Botwinick, 1977).

Certain of the longitudinal studies on cognitive development as measured by intelligence tests, originated in 1931 with Terman. In that year children aged 2 to 5½ years were administered the Stanford Binet Intelligence Test, and a decade later, in 1941, the majority was retested. In 1956, when the subjects had arrived at about age 30, about half the original sample was tested for the third time. Their IQs did not change in the first decade but increased over the next 15 years from an average of 113 to 124 (Bradway, Thompson, & Cravens, 1958). On the fourth testing, when they were in their early 40s, their average IQ was 130, or an additional 6 points (Kangas & Bradway, 1971). At least during the ages 20 to 50, superior individuals appeared to improve in "knowledge of symbols and abstractions and in ability to use these in relation to each other" (Bayley & Oden, 1955).

Exactly when the peak of intelligence occurs and decline begins is widely debated. There is probably no one peak age for the beginning of such a decline. After reviewing the literature, Botwinick (1977) concluded that "decline in intellectual ability is clearly part of the aging picture" (p. 580). However, certain cognitive functions do not decline before ages 50 to 65 and often little even then. For other intellectual functions, especially those involving speed of response and perceptual, manipulative, and nonverbal skills, decline may occur even earlier. In general, people who performed well when young do so later on. However, the earlier performance level is no reliable predictor of whether the ultimate decline with age will be small, large, or neither. Some changes relate to closeness to death—the so-called terminal drop during the last few months of life (Botwinick, 1977).

Perspective. Much of what has already been said about physical development applies here. Much of the decline in IQ ordinarily attributed to aging can be due to other factors: sensory malfunction, diseases, life stresses, or tests that discriminate against the elderly. Baltes & Schaie (1976) did not totally reject the idea of intellectual decline. But they emphasized the plasticity of intelligence and wide individual differences in intellective functioning at all life stages.

Emotional Development

Emotion in childhood and adolescence. Constitutional differences combined with subsequent experience define emotional patterns. Prenatal factors, including the mother's emotionality, also play a part. At birth, infants already display differences in reactions to frustration and emotional patterns, and such variations remain throughout life.

Children's characteristic stresses and reactions are well known, but their long-term significance is uncertain. Childhood problems commonly derive from tensions within the family and poor adjustment in school and peer group. Recent research rebuts many long-held assumptions about children's reactions to such problems. Thomas and Chess (1980) question the importance of maternal deprivation in early years. While poor care is highly undesirable, environmental factors are viewed as able to minimize or maximize earlier developmental difficulties. In the Grant Study (Vaillant, 1977), certain childhood characteristics— including fingernail biting, early toilet training, mental illness among relatives, and even having a cold, rejecting mother—proved poor predictors of emotionally unhealthy adulthood. However, when the lives of 13 men whose childhood had been desolate and lacking in love were contrasted with those of 23 men whose childhoods had been favorable, four predictions emerged regarding the relationship of childhood to adjustment at mid-life. First, men with unhappy childhoods proved to be unable to play. Second, they were more dependent and lacking in trust. Third, they were more often mentally ill. And fourth, they had fewer friends (Vaillant, 1977).

By adolescence, basic emotional patterns appear to be pretty well established despite somewhat greater instability at this time. This period is often portrayed as turbulent and adolescent behaviors as erratic. Problems at this stage commonly relate to sex, love, school, peer relations, work, and, to a lesser degree, money and parents. The degree of stress varies greatly among individuals, and it typically subsides in college years. But the long-term significance of such variations is unclear. Certain traits apparent in adolescence show little relationship to outcomes at mid-life. In the Grant Study (Vaillant, 1977), adolescents' characteristics that would seem to be predictive of successful adult outcomes—such as liveliness in outward emotional tone, altruistic concern for others, and friendliness—showed little relationship to later emotional health.

Also undecided is the question whether storm and stress is an inherent part of adolescence. Youth disturbances have recurred down the years, perhaps the same in substance though different in form. According to the president of the International Association of College and University Security Directors, "Rip-offs, rapes, assaults, and armed robbery on, or adjacent to, campuses have replaced the protest, vandalism, and student demonstrations of the 60s" ("Protection against Campus Crime," 1973, p. 8). However, such behaviors at least partly reflect the perennial failure to provide youth a meaningful social role.

Dramatic changes in social customs, especially those relating to family life and sexual relations, make it difficult to distinguish behaviors that represent healthy exploration for the purpose of coping with social change from those that constitute individual pathology simply disguised by social change. The tendency is simply to label altered values as deviant. The need is to determine which aspects of behavior are healthy and which are pathological (Alexander & Cohen, 1981).

Adult emotions. Adulthood is a relatively stable period emotionally, at least until later years, despite temporary upheavals relating to change in circumstance, coupled sometimes with adverse physical conditions. Young adults are ordinarily too busy with establishing a family and vocation to be neurotically preoccupied with themselves, despite temporary crises caused by such factors as child-care problems, economic stress, or marital dissatisfaction. In addition, men may worry about getting ahead vocationally, and young women may experience fatigue and frustration because of being tied to young children in the home (Bugard, 1974).

In the 40s and early 50s come the mid-life crises, when people become increasingly aware of the limitations on future time (Gould, 1975). It is costly to have such a crisis, concluded Sheehy (1976), but it can be even more costly not to have it. Not to do so may lock a person for good into a single-track, unrewarding way of life.

Next comes a calmer, mellower stage, when there is no longer the sense of urgency that there was in earlier adulthood. Problems of coping with retirement, the children's leaving home, and making decisions about aging parents may collectively produce periods of depression. But they are ordinarily faced realistically, without great upheaval.

In later years, stresses derive from a growing number of physical and social problems, including failing senses, widowhood, losing meaningful social roles, economic problems, and far more. Nevertheless, most older people adapt quite well, having attained a workable philosophy of life. Stripped of the vanities and elusive goals of earlier years, they are at last free to be themselves.

In a comparison of people at four life stages (see Table 16-1), high school seniors proved to be the least well satisfied, followed by the middle aged. People at the preretirement stage expressed the greatest satisfaction of all. High and low points of satisfaction were distributed throughout life.

Social Development

Social behaviors to maturity. The foundations of social behaviors are laid in infancy through the mutual attachments of the infant and family members, especially the chief caretaker, the mother. From an early age, however, children also take an interest in their peers. Eckerman, Whatley, and Kutz (1975) observed 30 pairs of home-reared children, ten in each of three age groups—10 to 12 months, 16 to 18 months, and 22 to 24 months—in unfamiliar place settings with their mothers. The children made little contact with their mothers, interacting more with their toys and with one another. The older the children, the more they preferred playing with their peers.

Initially, the parents devote considerable time and effort to playing with their infants, but later on peers are more willing than parents to react to a child's playful overtures. Peer behaviors are also more novel and more easily duplicated than those of adults. A child's peer-group role and social orientation are significantly modified by experiences in the home. Children whose family relationships are good, who live in families with a healthy milieu and harmonious social

Table 16-1. Measures of Perceived Well-Being

	High School		Newlywed		Middle-Aged		Preretirement	
	Men	Women	Men	Women	Men	Women	Men	Women
Percent very happy	25	26	48	52	37	33	52	37
Life satisfaction[d]	26.2	28.6	30.9	30.2	29.6	28.1	30.6	29.9
Positive affect[b,c]	8.6	9.2	9.5	10.6	7.6	8.2	7.7	8.4
Top of world[b,c]	1.8	2.1	2.3	2.8	1.7	1.9	1.9	2.0
Excited[b]	2.4	2.4	2.5	2.6	1.7	2.1	1.7	2.1
Pleased	2.4	2.4	2.5	2.8	2.3	2.2	2.2	2.5
Proud[b]	2.0	2.3	2.2	2.4	1.8	2.0	1.9	1.8
Negative affect[a]	7.9	8.6	7.4	7.8	5.8	6.1	5.2	5.4
Lonely[b]	2.0	2.2	1.4	1.8	1.1	1.4	1.3	1.2
Depressed[b,c]	1.7	2.0	1.7	2.0	1.3	1.8	1.1	1.6
Bored[b]	2.1	2.4	2.1	2.4	1.6	1.2	1.4	1.3
Restless[b]	2.1	2.0	2.2	1.6	1.8	1.7	1.4	1.4
Affect Balance[b,e]	13.7	13.7	15.1	15.7	14.8	15.1	15.5	16.0

[a]Higher scores on the negative-affect items imply greater negative affect.
[b]Differences between the stages are significant at $p < .05$.
[c]Differences between men and women are significant at $p < .05$.
[d]Life-satisfaction scores ranged from 10 to 36.
[e]Computed by subtracting negative-affect score from positive-affect score; scores in table have had a constant of 13 added to make all scores positive.
From *Four Stages of Life*, by M. F. Lowenthal, M. Thurnher and D. Chiriboga and Associates. Copyright 1975 by Jossey-Bass Publishers. Reprinted by permission.

relationships, and who are emotionally healthy ordinarily develop sound social roles.

In childhood, individuals focus on their activities more than on one another; in adolescence, the reverse is true. Indeed, peer relations are more prominent in adolescence than at any other stage in life, and personal satisfaction at this time relates strongly to social effectiveness. Peer relations assume the form of friendships, close cliques, and "crowds." These groupings collectively compose the youth culture, or society. It is relatively independent of the larger society and has its own distinctive values and behaviors. Some authorities say that no true youth culture exists, because young people inevitably reflect the values of the larger society. The majority says it does and that it is a useful concept.

Social activities at this stage are extensive and varied. All groups of boys and girls join together in their search for close relationships and security. Other elements in the youth culture are the demand for autonomy, which sometimes produces defiance of adults, and concern for the underdog, as demonstrated in youth's sympathies for civil-rights groups. Meantime, most young people come to perceive their own parents as "multidimensional persons," neither as all good nor as all bad, neither as all powerful nor as possessing "feet of clay" (Keniston, 1975, p. 18).

Interpersonal relationships in adulthood. Social activities sharply diminish after the threshold of adulthood is passed, especially for those who are married. Homemaking and vocational pressures consume most of a young couple's time once the children arrive. Meantime, husband and wife go about socially as a pair, with other couples in the neighborhood or those met on the job.

In later middle age, after the children leave home and retirement has begun, a couple spend more time with each other. Because they have more time now, they may also spend more time with relatives (including aging parents, children, and grandchildren) and friends (especially other retired couples). Meantime,

In later middle age people have more time for relatives, especially grandchildren.

throughout the years the couple's own relationship has continued to evolve. Skolnick (1973) reviewed a national study in which couples were interviewed during their engagement period, 5 years after marriage, and after they had been married 18 to 20 years. During this period there was a decline in physical affection, companionship, interests, beliefs, values, and marital adjustment; beliefs concerning marriage and feelings of loneliness increased. Society, on the one hand, places strains on marriages; on the other hand, it succeeds in holding them together even after they have become empty (Stein, P. J., 1975).

In later years social relations vary greatly with type of residence—alone or with children, in a retirement community or in a nursing home. Social life correspondingly varies from almost none to an almost continuing state. Although some authorities deplore the segregation of the elderly, older people, like those of other ages, chiefly enjoy associating with their contemporaries. Even the new friends that they make are generally among the other elderly. Such persons have experienced what they have; hence, there is a natural empathy.

Biological Sex Role

Child and adolescent sexuality. An individual's psychosexual development results from the interplay of sex drive and experience. It is often portrayed as including four main stages, beginning with the narcissistic stage, when the infant gains sensual satisfaction from its own body. In early childhood, at the phallic stage, the child is presumed to become attached to the opposite-sex parent. In the third, or latency, stage children associate mainly with their own sex, sometimes participating in exploratory sex behaviors. At the genital stage, normally beginning after puberty and continuing from then on, erotic feelings focus on the other sex. However, not all people go through all these stages or in this order.

Children ordinarily have no biological sex problems except those imposed on them by society. Because of adults' ignorance and bumbling, children may be punished for masturbation and exploratory sex behaviors, and they rarely have a healthy sex education. Sex problems in adolescence involve early love, petting, cohabitation, and birth control. Even today adolescents have difficulty deciding on proper levels of intimacy or controlling their sexual impulses. Despite the availability of more-effective contraceptive techniques than existed in former generations, they are often careless or inept in their use.

Something of a sexual revolution has occurred among teenagers. According to a nationwide survey by Johns Hopkins researchers, premarital intercourse among 15- to 19-year-old girls rose by 30% from 1971 to 1976. The median age for initiating sexual activity fell to 16.2 years in 1976, compared with 16.5 years in 1971. Also by 1976 55% of the 19-year-olds had had intercourse, and more young women were using contraceptives. In 1971 only 45% used any contraceptive method at all, and a mere 16% had ever used the pill or an intrauterine device (IUD). Just 5 years later a third of the 63% who used contraceptives employed the pill or an IUD ("Sexually Active Teenagers," 1977).

Meantime, adolescents have come to look on sex as an effective way to get acquainted and a way to develop, rather than merely to express, intimacy (Rossi, 1977). Nevertheless, males are two or three times more likely than females to sanction a somewhat casual attitude toward sexuality (American Council on Education, 1976).

Adult sexuality. Adults' sexual attitudes and behaviors have also changed. The double standard has weakened, so that both partners now participate actively in the sexual relationship. They have intercourse frequently in young adulthood (about nine times a month) and considerably less often in middle age ("How's Your Sex Life?" 1975). Such practices as oral sex and masturbation are increasingly common (Rubin, 1976). The characteristics most predictive of little extramarital sex include a happy marriage, sexual conservatism, and conventional life-style. While extramarital coitus is far more common in unhappier marriages, many women who rate their marriage as very satisfactory also have extramarital intercourse (Bell, Turner, & Rosen, 1975). In the past those who engaged in extramarital activities were considered sinful or even sick. And even today adultery is often associated with the "psychiatric jargon of being immature, narcissistic and neurotic" (Boyer, 1975, p. 375).

Formerly, sex among the elderly was thought of as somewhat deviant or indecent, if it was thought of at all. Now sexual activities for older people are coming to be considered not simply acceptable but even desirable. While certain physiological changes with age produce a different pattern of sexual interaction among older couples, such changes do not suggest an end to the need of sexual activities, but merely a reason for changing patterns in that activity (Cleveland, 1976).

Social Sex Role

Sex roles until maturity. Society and its institutions, especially the family and school, make a host of distinctions between the sexes. As a result, the sexes, in a sense, live in different subcultures throughout life. The acquisition of social sex roles, or patterns of behavior judged appropriate for each sex, probably begins during the 2nd year, and such patterns are well established by age 3. Parents either unconsciously or consciously begin inducting children into their appropriate sex roles from birth, and by the age of 2½ children have considerable knowledge of sex roles (Heise & Roberts, 1970). From birth children are also exposed to myriad sex-related symbols, including ways of wearing the hair, modes of dress, and differential behaviors of fathers and mothers. While concepts of sex roles have not "clearly crystallized by age 6, there is already a considerable overlap between the standards of first-grader and adult" (Rogers, 1977a, p. 263).

During childhood the sex roles are not completely mutually exclusive, or polarized, but after puberty they become sufficiently polarized to support complementary roles of dating and courtship. Even in these situations sex-role distinctions are less rigid than they were in earlier times, especially in college. Girls often call up boys and even help pay expenses on dates, and sexual behaviors on dates reflect a reduction in the traditional double standard. Yet adolescents differ considerably among themselves. In general, males tend to be more androgynous than masculine typed, feminine typed, or interdeterminate if they experienced warm parental affection as children. Females are more androgynous if they were encouraged to achieve (Kelly & Worrell, 1976).

Adult sex-role differentiation. The degree of sex-role differentiation among adults depends on such factors as social class, education, whether the wife works, and the nature of the individual. In general, sex roles are more polarized among the lower classes. When the wife works outside the home, performance of household tasks becomes sexually **depolarized** in varying degrees.

In a cross-sectional study of adults at eight stages in the family life cycle, sex differences fluctuated according to the demands of various life situations. Thus, in grandparenthood, when women were no longer bound up with child rearing or men with making a living, there was a rise in expressiveness for men and autonomy for women. Women demonstrated more tenderness than men at all ages except for grandparents and married childless men (Feldman, Biringen, & Nash, 1981).

Moral Development

Developmental stages. It will be recalled that the best-known theories of moral development are those of Piaget and Kohlberg. According to Piaget, the young child interprets wrong in terms of amount of damage done, the older one in terms of motives and principles. Similarly, at Kohlberg's preconventional level children respond to social rules and labels of "good" and "bad," interpreting them in terms of their consequences (punishment or reward). At the next, or conventional, level children perceive rules as worthy in their own right and as a matter of loyalty to the social order and its agents, primarily parents and teachers. On the third, postconventional, level an individual evaluates behaviors in terms of personal values and principles, apart from the authority of people holding those principles.

Most individuals never progress past the conventional level, and it may be just as well. Society depends for its continuity on a certain cohesiveness and on the masses' respecting its dictates. Modifications in morality and values, made necessary or desirable by changing times, can be effected by the minority who do achieve the postconventional level and who, fortunately, possess greater intelligence and insight than the average person.

In recent years Kohlberg has determined a new stage in his concept of moral development similar to Erikson's stage of integrity. This stage involves coming to terms with the self and establishing interpersonal commitments within the broader social and historical frame of reference. However, this philosophical concept is contrary to empirical evidence. Positive traits often tend to relate to each other. In one study, highly trusting fifth-graders transgressed less often and were more trustworthy than were the moderate-or low-trusting subjects (Doster & Chance, 1976).

Adolescent morals and values. Matters of morality and value attain high significance at adolescence. Teenagers are confronted with many new situations and important decisions, such as those regarding sex and drug use, and are exposed to conflicting value systems, especially in college.

Most youth support their society's basic values, although a minority—the so-called alienated youth—feels estranged from it and constitutes a counterculture. Such alienation may result from society's failure to provide sufficient alternatives, from poor communication, or from society's own deficiencies, such as growing materialism, impersonality, and pseudosophistication. In some cases alienation may simply be a symptom of growing up and testing current values before determining one's own. At the same time, youth are largely insulated from adult guidance within their own groups. They have greater freedom than did former generations and a more complex social milieu; hence, they experience more crises in resolving problems and committing themselves to values. Ultimately, most become effective members of the society they once scorned.

Adult morals and values. There is no abrupt change in value systems on achieving adulthood. An individual's core values, originally learned in the home, tend to persist, although young adults become somewhat more conservative after children arrive—the so-called parenting effect. Because they feel responsible for their children's welfare, they now view the world in terms of the way their children may be affected. In consequence, single people, especially the better educated and upper class, are often more liberal.

Reiss (1981) points out that little change has taken place in the proportion of adults favoring various positions on abortion, premarital sexuality, and pornography, despite the apparent growth of conservatism over recent years. Conservative forces have apparently organized themselves more effectively and made themselves more obvious.

Personality

Pattern of development. Personality embraces all an individual's behaviors as uniquely organized through the interaction of heredity and experience. These characteristic behaviors, or traits, become organized into socially expected behavior patterns appropriate to an individual's roles or functions in life. Self-concept is how an individual comes to feel about how he or she plays roles. It importantly modifies one's goals, mental health, and interpersonal relationships. The status of self-concept fluctuates over the years, partly because society attaches different statuses to successive age roles and partly because of varying success in coping with an endless stream of life tasks and problems.

Meantime, life experiences should be properly patterned and "on time," or else optimal effects will not occur. For example, adolescents are especially concerned with defining an identity and deciding what to do about it. They are given to introspection, appraising where they are and where they are going. As they peer ahead, each sex shapes goals regarding future family and vocational roles. Traditionally, males have been more achievement oriented, attaching greater importance to future vocation, and females more **affiliative,** expecting to find their chief satisfaction as wives and mothers. Although males have become more expressive and concerned about family satisfaction and females more achievement oriented than in other years, considerable distinction still exists.

The vast research regarding personality change across the years is confusing and conflicting, with some researchers, but not others, reporting sharp age differences (Neugarten, 1977). Investigators at the University of Chicago (Neugarten & Associates, 1964) utilized large and representative samples of people aged 40 to 80 and conducted interrelated studies over a 10-year period. They reported change from active to passive mastery in relation to the environment, and from outer- to inner-world orientation, or "increased interiority" (p. 637). Older men proved more receptive than younger ones to their nurturant, affiliative, and sensual urges, and older women responded more than younger ones to their aggressive, egocentric impulses. No age-related differences were reported in various socioadaptive dimensions, such as purposive, goal-directed behaviors, satisfaction with life, or coping styles.

In other research individual differences emerged as more important than aging in accounting for personality traits in later years. The Institute of Human Development in Berkeley, California, which has traced the same individuals from infancy to middle adulthood, has demonstrated important individual differences. Both individuals and types of persons retain their recognizability and, in this sense, demonstrate a continuity of personality over time (Haan & Day, 1974). The best guess at this juncture is that some individuals change more than others and some characteristics are more persistent than others.

Analysis will show that certain personality changes ordinarily attributed to aging derive instead from situational factors. For example, older people's presumed greater cautiousness may result from increased threats from their environment. In the main, basic personality characteristics appear somewhat persistent across the years. For example, few individuals change so dramatically as to shift from active to passive during the course of their lives. Among most individuals, changes in personality with age are minor compared with differences among people generally (Woodruff & Birren, 1972). Schaie and Parham (1976), who administered questionnaire items twice to a large sampling aged 21 to 84, reported stability rather than change in a majority of the personality factors disclosed.

Concepts Relating to Life as a Whole

Life cycle. All aspects of development, collectively, constitute the life cycle. The life cycle, or life course,

> is a way of conceptualizing the aging process: a sequence of statuses and roles, expectations and relationships, constituting, in the broadest meaning of the word, an individual's "career." While the life cycle is universal, it is also infinitely varied. It is shaped by the variety of roles and opportunities available to an individual, as well as by the resources that individual can marshal at various stages of his or her career [Van Dusen & Sheldon, 1976, p. 106].

The aging process of a life cycle involves a succession of roles, the most significant usually being the family role but also embracing student, vocational, and social roles. These role sequences afford "texture" to the life cycle, and the individual's own interpretation of those roles, or the stamp he or she places upon them, is termed the life-style. Particular roles relate to certain ages: the student roles with youth; parental roles with early adulthood; living alone —whether divorced, widowed, or never married—with the middle and later years.

Age cohorts. Historical times and episodes—such as the Great Depression, World War II, the Vietnam War, and the civil rights movement—leave their imprint on people as they move through life and vitally influence patterns of fertility, marriage, employment, and life-style in general. Meantime, successive age groups, or birth cohorts, have unique patterns of experience as they proceed through the life cycle, resulting from the interaction of aging processes and the times (Van Dusen & Sheldon, 1976). For example, the cohort that arrived at adulthood during the 1930s still carries the imprint of the Depression. For another instance, the "baby-boom" cohort is experiencing keen competition for college admission, employment, and varied social services—the results of membership in a group that is larger in size than that which preceded or will follow it.

Life-style or life structure. The individual's own patterning of behaviors throughout the life cycle is termed life-style or life structure. All individuals must somehow integrate demands on them and arrive at some compromise regarding the multiple timetables associated with entering and leaving roles. Some people's life structure is loosely organized; others' is tightly knit and cohesive. Some individuals operate from a long-term, others from a short-term perspective.

The life-style is continuously evolving and represents an individual's endless compromise between personal goals and environmental demands. Certain approaches prove rewarding and become habituated, distinguishing marks of the life-style. Others may be rejected after being given a trial. For example, young people appear to be seeking a kind of community control, in contrast with the erosion of control in the larger society today. Nevertheless, young people who enter communes may find out that they cannot simply unload their upbringing in an affluent, middle-class environment. That is, they bring a "certain emotional baggage . . . into the communes, and hence find themselves unable to produce the sort of environment that native Americans or Chicanos naturally possess because of their own racial traditions" (Coles with Woodward, 1975, p. 67).

Life-style versus life cycle. Life periods become not only socially but also personally defined. That is, people perceive their own positions on the ladder of age, and they relate themselves to the life cycle as they grow older. They decide for themselves on behaviors that are appropriate for each period, and such perceptions affect their self-image and personality. These age-related perceptions differ somewhat according to social class. For upper-middle-class individuals, middle age is commonly perceived as a period of peak productivity, the prime of life. For blue-collar workers, middle age arrives earlier in relation to chronological age and is often perceived as a period of decline, physical weakening, and winding down (Neugarten, 1977).

Modern Society and Life

Effect of selected factors. There is some danger, when tracing developmental histories, of focusing on individuals to the exclusion of their environment. Yet from conception until death the human organism is interacting with, and being modified by, vast numbers of environmental factors, complexly blended together.

Crowding and overpopulation. Among these environmental factors is density of population, or sheer numbers of people. I once drove a jeep through the countries of Southeast Asia and, immediately afterward, around Australia, including the vast, almost empty Outback. The psychological impact of the abrupt change was dramatic.

A certain amount of not-yet-adequate research has been conducted into the impact of crowding. Booth (1976) concluded that crowded family living conditions seldom have any real consequences and that, even when they do, those effects are not significant. In animal research various negative effects of crowding have been reported, including aggression, decreased fertility, and sexual perversion. However, Schaar (1975) observed that "what's bad for a rat apparently isn't all that bad for humans." He cited studies in which college students were placed in different-sized rooms for periods up to 4 hours while tackling mental tasks and participating in discussions. Crowding did not seem to affect their reasoning, but it did influence their social behavior. Boys, especially, found smaller rooms uncomfortable, and the girls sometimes found the interpersonal space in larger rooms too great. Both sexes appeared to accommodate rather well to the situations as they found them. However, this research did not involve the long-term effects of such conditions or individual differences.

Modern versus simpler societies. Family life plays a less important role in modern societies than it did in simpler ones. Relationships become based more on practicality than sentiment. There is also somewhat less security in the nuclear than in the extended family, in which an individual has access to a wide variety of close ties. In addition, older people are valued in simpler societies, for their knowledge is transmitted from one generation to another by word of mouth (Hauser, 1976). In a complex society, in which knowledge is transmitted by various highly specialized institutions such as research centers, schools, and museums, an older individual no longer serves as a source of wisdom. In the sophisticated, urban society, religion also becomes less significant. And recreation becomes increasingly commercialized. Meantime, government interventionism becomes more common as complex, informal organizations and interdependence increase. Bureaucracy, not merely in government but in labor, business, and all associations, organizes life within the society.

Technology. One factor associated with modern society, **technology,** deserves special attention. Swift technological changes have dramatically altered the physical surroundings in which people live and the way people make their living and spend their time. Technology has greatly increased the preparation needed for adulthood, thereby retarding entry. It also produces a rapid obsolescence of vocational skills, thereby increasing one's chance of becoming a technological liability.

Meantime, technology's byproducts have exposed children to masses of information and intellectual stimulation. Many have traveled widely. On television, they have a chance to see how people around the world live. In classrooms, they have far more materials and better-trained teachers than ever before (Chamberlin & Girona, 1976). It has been largely overlooked that television has also had a profound impact on the attitudes and ways of life of people of all ages.

According to Gunter and Moore (1975), the technological revolution, with its byproducts of **cybernation** and automation, has even produced a new stage of life, falling generally between the ages of 17 and 30. Its main characteristics, besides its dependence on technology, include "the disengagement from societal obligations, postponement of entry into adulthood, prolonged preparation for living 'life' through education, prolonged dependence on parents and the state, and an increasing amount of 'free time,' and discretionary income" (p. 200).

In any case, it has only been through technological advances that human beings have the potential, for the first time in history, of doing much more than fighting for survival and living rather simple lives. Nowadays, given the increased free time and resources provided by technology, the richness, complexity, and quality of life can be vastly improved.

Ecology. Certain other influences can be treated more globally or comprehensively. **Ecology** refers to the impact on individuals, both direct and indirect, of the surroundings in which they live (Bronfenbrenner, 1974). It includes all the "objects and life-supporting conditions that affect an individual's behavior" including characteristics of housing, food, clothes, and assorted other things (Proshansky, 1974). Geography and climate constitute important parts of the physical environment. The immediate physical environment includes the neighborhood, the local shopping center, or the corner store. The properties of such settings, whether social, psychological, or physical, serve to foster certain behaviors and to obstruct others.

People have their own special needs for space to call their own and for privacy. Other ecological needs include safety, freedom from stress, and a feeling of control over the environment instead of dependency on it. According to Getzels (1974), "Our visions of human nature find expression in the buildings we construct, and these constructions in turn do their silent yet irresistible work of telling us who we are and what we must do" (p. 538). The ideal type of housing varies with age group (see Figure 16-1).

Here, several middle-aged persons express views about the type of community in which they would prefer to live.

Housing	Family Type		
	Families with Children	Elderly	Working Adults
Single Family	Strongly Recommended	Recommended	Not Recommended
Walk-Up	Strongly Recommended	Not Recommended	Barely Acceptable
Medium High-Rise — With Doorman	Recommended	Strongly Recommended	Strongly Recommended
Medium High-Rise — Without Doorman	Barely Acceptable	Recommended	Not Recommended
Elevator High-Rise — With Doorman	Barely Acceptable	Strongly Recommended	Strongly Recommended
Elevator High-Rise — Without Doorman	Not Recommended	Recommended	Not Recommended

Figure 16-1. Ideal assignment of families to housing. From "Community of Interest," by O. Newman. In Human Nature*, 1979, 2(1), 61. Copyright © 1978 by Human Nature, Inc. Used by permission of the publisher.*

> I enjoy nature a great deal and especially like the water. I like space, and yet I like the stimulation of a metropolitan area, so I would say I would like a secluded seaside home 15 or 20 miles from a city (close to the mountains) (woman, age 41).

> Peaceful and quiet, clean and pleasant. My husband and I love nature and enjoy country living so very much. The beauty of God's works surround us, and we are grateful for this (woman, 53).

> I would prefer to live in a slightly larger community—say, 10,000 to 20,000 people (man, 51).

> Warmer climate and more relaxed life (man, 63).

Culture. Another global influence is the total way of life of the society, or its culture. In China, for example, ancestor worship creates respect and reverence for old age. It also "anchors roots deep in historical time, living and dead" (Black, 1977, p. 167). There are so many cultures around the world and so many complex subgroupings within a culture that it is difficult to move beyond broad generalizations when speaking of life-styles. It is certainly important to recognize that extremely wide variations exist and that, ultimately, every individual represents a unique biosocial model of aging.

Nevertheless, the question of the impact of future cultures and societies on human beings is a matter of conjecture. We are uncertain to what extent people's behaviors are influenced by more subtle forces of environment. For example, has the constant concern for energy resources introduced a basic insecurity into the fabric of the current personality? Or will sheer numbers some day render hopeless the search for individual identity and a place in the sun (Buchen, 1974)?

Changing Times

Examples of change. Examples of change and their impact on human life could be multiplied endlessly. Among these, the influence of changing economic conditions on the life course is dramatically illustrated by comparing age groups now in their 40s with those in their 20s. The small cohorts born during the Great Depression completed their education and became adults during times of economic expansion. Because they were few in number when vocational opportunities were bountiful, their work careers were on a faster-than-usual timetable, and many rose to relatively high positions at comparatively young ages (Elder, 1975b). The cohorts that followed, who were part of the postwar baby boom, became adults and sought their first full-time jobs in times of economic recession. Many such young adults are experiencing frustrations and slowdowns in their work careers and are somewhat behind time in their assumption of work and family roles. Another change in the past decade is from producing products to producing ideas. This trend will, in turn, lead to differences in educational curricula, vocations, and even leisure pursuits.

Also changing is the average age of the population. From 1970 to 1977 the median age of the population in the United States rose by 1½ years to 29.4, and it was expected to climb to 38 over the following 53 years ("End of Youth Culture," 1977). This aging of the population is due primarily to child-bearing cycles—the drop during the Depression of the '30s, followed by the baby boom and then the "baby bust" since the 1960s. These cycles have produced two larger age groups in the generations before and after them. The older of these groups, born over a decade before the Depression, is now retiring by the millions. And the still larger baby boom of young adults is now emerging into an already overcrowded labor market. At the same time, since 1972 the reduction in deaths from heart disease has elevated Americans' average life expectancy by more than a year, to 69.1 for men and 77 years for women. As "these underemployed workers pile up, more and more Americans will find career ladders blocked by a glut of senior employees" ("End of Youth Culture," 1977, p. 55). Because of the consequent competition and decreasing rewards, there may be growing pressures for a welfare state.

When these "baby boomers" begin retiring in about 40 years, the pressures on young and middle-aged adults will vastly exceed those of today. At the same time larger numbers of people moving into old age will produce greater opposition to reducing any benefits for the elderly. Laws have already been passed that would outlaw mandatory retirement for many people until age 70 and would increase the amount that older employees can earn without losing Social Security benefits.

Significance. Matters of change are significant for two main reasons. First, as mentioned in several chapters, people can be judged only in terms of the times their life has spanned. Second, people must learn as children to be flexible if they are to adapt successfully; and they must continuously readapt to a new world constantly in the process of revision. They must also become and remain capable of a broad perspective, prepared for the greatest possible number of future worlds. The pace of change, coupled with increased longevity, means that long-lived individuals will experience a succession of somewhat different worlds.

It is still unclear to what extent the personality phenomena associated with successive cohorts are age related or are the result of having lived through the same historical periods at the same stages in life. The task is to determine whether there are orderly and sequential changes related to age and, if so, if they are significant in accounting for differences in behavior (Neugarten, 1977, p. 632).

Social Programs

Suggested services. Society, via its government, is assuming a more serious role in helping people adapt to complex modern problems. Meantime, psychologists have become increasingly involved in designing and evaluating community programs for promoting personal and social well-being (Kelly, Snowden, & Munoz, 1977). These programs include such services as the following:

1. Consulting specialists provide assistance with mental-health problems, and various kinds of **paraprofessionals** function as advocates, outreachers, and consultants and in other helping roles.
2. Crisis intervention involves providing appropriate services during periods of special stress. Positive resolution of crises often marks a turning point toward increased feelings of mastery and health. The reverse may solidify or induce maladaptive processes.
3. Mental-health centers are increasingly embracing a human-service ideology. Human needs are viewed as requiring comprehensive, integrated, accessible service.
4. Assistance is being differentiated according to the diverse cultures and personalities of clients. Unfortunately, counselors themselves may consciously or unconsciously discriminate against those whom they disapprove of or do not understand, such as unwed mothers, homosexuals, or those differing with them politically.
5. Primary prevention embraces all basic measures taken to attain and maintain personal well-being, thereby reducing or eliminating future problems. The services provided would be wide ranging, including activities so diverse as consideration of the economy's role in human well-being, provision of ombudsmen for handling citizens' complaints, diffusion of mental-health information, and provision for genetic counseling. Other assistance might assume the form of social support systems, as in the widow-to-widow program. Or people might be helped to develop varied skills for academic, leisure, or practical everyday use—for example, gardening, home mechanics, and domestic arts.
6. Environmental psychologists would be concerned about such matters as the effects of noise and crowding on human well-being, community and neighborhood design, including the location of facilities; and the designing of homes and furniture.
7. Congress created an Office of Technology Assessment in 1974 to evaluate the possible social consequences of new technologies before it becomes too awkward to withdraw or change them.

Efforts to anticipate the effects of new technologies derive from unfortunate prior experiences with various technological developments. Pesticides, drugs, and supersonic aircraft have produced unforeseen problems. Unfortunately, certain products, such as birth-control pills and tranquilizers, attain widespread usage before their long-term effects are known.

Perspective on social programs. New programs have certain distinctive characteristics, including built-in design for continued evaluation. A basic aim is to ensure that material and nonmaterial products of the postindustrial order will be utilized for the social good. Denis Gabor, the developer of holography, suggested that society invent its future. However, warned Lakoff (1977), "Despite some merit in this suggestion, it is dangerous to rely too heavily on social manipulation and to believe that any social problem can be solved, given the right government program" (p. 662). Programs are concerned with both current and future impact. High priority is given the dynamic relationship between the social context and the individuals concerned. Second, social policies are formed within a political context, and politicians, in order to ensure their own reelection, are prone to put visible short-term results ahead of long-term welfare. For example, it is popular to gain votes by running up an already colossal national debt while ignoring the legacy of inflation—even the threat of economic collapse—that is left to future generations. The pursuit of quality of life today can, without future perspective, endanger the quality of life tomorrow. Third, each individual should be viewed longitudinally as possessing a past and a future and as preparing for roles that will be molded, in part, according to the shape of the world yet to come. What this world will be like can only be guessed. Observe that the present generation will live to about the age of 90, and those just born could possibly live to be 120 years old (Buchen, 1975). Fourth, people at all stages must therefore be helped to develop anticipatory behaviors and attitudes. In other words, they must come to have the "future in their bones" (Toffler, 1970). They must develop the kind of intellectual processes that will enable them to perceive and deal with new relationships and rapidly changing realities.

Finally, the life-span approach suggests perceiving the impact of programs on individuals, in terms not simply of their present life stage but also of the total stretch of life ahead. For a clearer perspective on present need, past histories must also be taken into account. Meantime, in all such intervention programs the individual's own perceptions must be respected and utilized. Nor must people be overly guided or manipulated, lest they become steered in unwise directions.

LOOKING AHEAD

Futurism

Significance. The pace of change has focused growing attention on the future. One of the hidden clues to successful coping may be a sense of the future. Hence, education itself must reflect such a sense. Too often, schools "act as if the child and the adult . . . exist side by side, simultaneously. One gets the clear impression that schools in the 1970s are attempting to prepare students for adult life in the 1970s" (Kauffman, 1976, p. 4).

The most significant aspect of modern technology is change. It isn't merely a matter of new social and economic relationships displacing old ones but of the new ones being displaced at an ever faster pace. What is new is not change but the rate of change, resulting from the vastly increased rate of scientific advance. Meantime, if people do not become intelligent consumers, somehow remaining abreast of the times, they will miss much that is enriching, exciting, and growth producing.

Predictions. Experts whose concern is the future, the **futurists,** make specific projections. For example, some of them predict that by the 21st century two population corridors in the United States will emerge, from San Francisco to San Diego and from Boston to Washington. Five out of six Americans are expected to inhabit these two areas, and people will be bound together "in specialized housing complexes, grouped by age, marital status, and socioeconomic categories. New life styles will be an integral part of these population clusters" (Spekke, 1976a, p. 50).

Some futurists predict that genetic engineering may ultimately modify the human mind and body. Thus, "Test tube humans may be designed possessing desired physical and mental characteristics; cloning, in a sense, may give us the possibility of eternal life; **cryogenics,** [emphasis added] can put you on ice to cure your ills in another century" (deFries, 1976, p. 596).

Other futurists refrain from specific long-term predictions and project instead a "variety of scenarios and assorted futures" (Lakoff, 1977). The so-called doomsday prophets predict dire outcomes, based on long-term projections of present trends. They have predicted that, if population controls are not somehow established, the earth will in time become hopelessly swamped with people. If careless exploitation of natural resources persists, they say, these resources will become dangerously depleted.

Others of these futurists point out that judicious use of economic policies, conservation measures, and human ingenuity could result in adequate conservation and alternative fuels. They also point out that population projections are uncertain, because such rates rise and fall with changing circumstance (Maddox, 1972). To doomsayers who warn against impending starvation and an environment made unpleasant or even dangerous because of pollution, the critics cite the so-called Green Revolution produced by the introduction of improved crop varieties and measures that could, if enforced, control pollution. In other words, the same advanced technology that has produced problems has the resources to solve them.

Life-Span Developmental Psychology

Current trends. Facing the future, life-span developmental psychology itself is showing healthy trends. (1) It is displaying a certain pluralism, recognizing that generalizations often mask individual and subgroup differences. There are many variations of youth, middle age, and later years; many successful life-styles; and multiple formulas for appraising progress through life. (2) Basic and applied research are increasingly becoming fused, and each will be enriched and lent perspective by the other. (3) Interdisciplinary and multidisciplinary approaches to the complex phenomena of life in modern society are essential if its various facets are to be sorted out and understood. (4) While conceptualizations and analyses of individual development have already attained a respectable base, the study of both immediate and more-remote environments, and of human adaptation within them, is just beginning to receive the respect it deserves.

Life-span developmental psychology has two other positive factors going for it as it moves into the future. (1) There is an ever-increasing body of research, such as longitudinal studies, on which to base future investigation. (2) The growing interest among the citizenry at large in attaining quality of life should produce a supportive milieu for such a discipline. Given such a context, it should be easier to gain adequate research funds and the cooperation of subjects as well as to interest more researchers in this discipline. The vastly increased sophistication of research techniques, devices (especially the computer), and researchers themselves should promote life-span research, which inevitably involves more complex and elusive questions than does a single life stage.

Future tasks. Fortunately, this field is finally winning the attention it deserves, because many challenges exist. A sampling of these follows.

1. Imaginative approaches must be developed to integrate the contributions of people with different theoretical positions. Traditionally, psychoanalytic theory has focused largely on early life through adolescence, partly because it stresses the biologically determined sequence of drives. Adult personality has been perceived as somewhat stable (Neugarten, 1977). It will help, suggested Neugarten (1977), if developmentalists place greater emphasis on descriptive studies of adults, especially those that relate social and biological factors to each other. Then, antecedent/consequent relationships can be distinguished. That is, theory emerges from, rather than precedes, observation. To date, added Neugarten, life-span developmental psychologists have focused chiefly on model building and research designs. They have been more effective in indicating how to study the life span than in deciding what to study about it.

2. Studies should be replicated and updated, but comparisons should take into account interim cultural change. Even over a 2-year period Nesselroade and Baltes (1974) recorded changes in adolescent ability and personality. Cultural change is accelerating to the extent that it must be given consideration when comparisons are made of research results performed at different times.

3. Sameroff and Chandler (1975) suggested a model for developmental process that they called transactional, to stress the continuous interplay and reciprocal influence of organisms and environmental factors over time. One example of this approach is the study of the reciprocal effects of parent/infant interaction (McCall, 1977).

4. There is need for more multi-university projects to be undertaken; to move from descriptive to explanatory research; and to subject parochial findings to cross-cultural tests (Barado, 1981).

The research that we do have clearly negates the long-held assumption that chances for personal growth are largely complete by adulthood. Longitudinal research is documenting the life-styles of individuals whose life becomes increasingly rich and rewarding across the years, even through great old age.

There is growing need for a more global view of whole individuals interacting in total environmental settings. As more cross-disciplinary research emerges, a more reasoned, proportioned image of adulthood will emerge.

CONCLUSION

423

Research is negating the folklore that you can't teach an old dog new tricks.

SUMMARY

This chapter is concerned with integrating insights from the preceding chapters to provide a comprehensive view of the total life span. It also considers the aging process and the aging individual, from birth to demise, in terms of the environment and the future. The aging process itself has been rather well defined, but finding how to control it, or lengthen the life span, remains to be done. Some people view the current life span as genetically determined and resistant to expansion. Others believe that the possibility of longer life exists and that society should accept the challenge to convert it into reality.

The various aspects of human development are generally perceived as progressing by stages, with variations according to sex, social class, culture, and individual. Where individuals are concerned, all these aspects of life development become complexly integrated into life-styles, or structures, which gradually evolve over the life cycle. The life-style represents an individual's own working compromise between individual needs and environmental demands. Such demands today are complex, shaped by a postindustrial technological society. Thus, life involves an endless process of adapting to such problems as crowding and social change.

Because of the pace of change and the phenomenal advances in technology,

CHAPTER 16

424

new developments often outrun the behavioral adaptations required to appreciate and utilize them effectively. The answer may lie in anticipating possible futures and being intelligently prepared for them. Meantime, the growing science of life-span developmental psychology, already characterized by certain healthy trends, must remain future oriented. Only then will it be able realistically to portray the drama of individuals endlessly confronted by a stream of futures merging swiftly into presents, across their life cycle.

SUGGESTED READINGS

Alexander, J. & Cohen, J. Customs, coupling, and the family in a changing culture. *American Journal of Orthopsychiatry*, 1981, *51*(2), 307–316. This paper concerns problems in differentiating forms of behavior that reflect healthy exploration in the process of coping with social change from those that suggest individual pathology.

A prescriptive analysis for the family field in the 1980s. *Journal of Marriage and the Family*, 1981, *43*(2), 249–269. This section consists of four articles relating to family research and theory for the 1980s by Felix M. Berardo, Reuben Hill, Greer Litton Fox, Jaqueline P. Wishman, and Joan Aldous.

Boss, P. G. Normative family stress: Family boundary changes across the life-span. *Family Relations*, 1980, *29*(4), 445–450. Families are described as experiencing stress until their members' tasks and roles are clarified. Family structures require reorganization if their members are to adapt to changing conditions over the life cycle.

Bronfenbrenner, U. Toward an experienced ecology of human development. *American Psychologist*, 1977, 513–531. The ecological approach to research in human development concentrates on "the progressive accommodation, throughout the life span, between the growing human organism and the changing environments in which it actually lives and grows. The latter include not only the immediate settings containing the developing person but also the largest social context, both formal and informal, in which these settings are imbedded. . . . The changing relation between person and environment is conceived in systems terms."

Elder, G. H. *Children of the Great Depression: Social change in life experience.* Chicago: University of Chicago Press, 1974. A longitudinal study of children born in the years 1920 and 1921 and followed since then. It discloses the long-term impact of the Depression on their lives and indicates changes that occur within families and between generations.

Goodlad, J. I. An ecological approach to change in elementary school setting. *Elementary School Journal*, 1977, *78*(2), 95–105. The author discusses the concept of school as a culture operating within the larger environment. A successful project is described in which a number of schools followed a "dialogue-decisions-action-evaluation process in transforming themselves into dynamic cultures."

Kelly, J. G., Snowden, L. R., & Munoz, R. F. Social and community interventions. *Annual Review of Psychology*, 1977, *28*, 323–361. After a review of the literature on social and community intervention, suggestions are made for future directions in such work.

Lesse, S. Factors influencing sexual behavior in our future society. *American Journal of Psychotherapy*, 1976, *30*(3), 366–384. Predictions are made concerning the probable effects of political, social, and demographic factors on the family, sexual relations, and leisure activities.

Lowenthal, M. F., Thurnher, M., Chiriboga, D., and Associates. *Four stages of life.* San Francisco: Jossey-Bass, 1976. A study of high school seniors, young newlyweds, middle-aged parents, and older people about to retire discloses characteristics related to successful coping at these periods of life. The book affords a perspective on changes that occur across the life span.

McAuliffe, K., & McAuliffe, S. The gene trust. *Omni*, March 1980, 62–66; 120–122. Analysis is made of anticipated developments in the field of biotechnology and genetic engineering, which seem to hold significance for life in the future.

Neugarten, B. L. Adaptation and the life cycle. *Counseling Psychologist*, 1976, 6(1), 16–20. Neugarten examines ways in which social change and historical setting influence the timing of major life events and the consequent social expectations regarding age-appropriate behaviors. In spite of changes in the life cycle, certain regularities occur along social, biological, and psychological dimensions. These regularities include increased interiority (saliency of the inner life), changed time perspective, and personalization of death. After reviewing studies of the female climacteric, retirement, death, and widowhood, the author concludes that it is not the anticipated life event that ordinarily assumes crisis proportions; instead, the crises are precipitated by occurrences that upset the rhythm of the life cycle.

Ornauer, H., Wiberg, H., Sicinski, A., & Galtung, J. (Eds.) *Images of the world in the year 2000: A comparative ten-nation study.* Highlands, N.J.: Humanities Press, 1976. A project under the auspices of the European Coordination Center at Vienna, Austria. Samplings of the population aged 15 to 40 were collected in ten countries, and a survey was made of attitudes toward the future as conditioned by the subjects' past experiences and present realities.

Reiss, I. L. Some observations on ideology and sexuality in America. *Journal of Marriage and the Family*, 1981, 43(2), 271–283. Two broad ideologies, the Traditional-Romantic and the Modern-Naturalistic, are derived from an examination of five areas of public controversy over sexuality; (1) abortion, (2) genetic differences, (3) exploitation and pornography, (4) sexual normality, and (5) sexual history.

Shanas, R. H., & Shanas, E. (Eds.). *Handbook of aging and the social sciences.* New York: Van Nostrand Reinhold, 1976, pp. 59–86. Aging and increasing longevity are considered in terms of world population trends. Demographic factors of aging are analyzed for individual countries, and comparisons are made between more- and less-well-developed countries.

Toffler, A. The American future is being bumbled away. *The Futurist*, 1976, 10(2), 97–102. A well-known futurist warns that the government is letting the future be preempted by foreign nations and big corporations. He urges the government to employ futurists to determine long-range options for the American people, so that they can participate in deciding what their future will be.

Yankelovich, D., & Lefkowitz, B. The new American dream: The U.S. in the 1980s. *The Futurist*, 1980, 14(4), 3–16. Having had their faith in progress shaken in recent years Americans have become increasingly pessimistic about their future; however, a new American dream may emerge. That is, from Americans' current ambivalence may arise some other version of the American dream.

GLOSSARY

acute brain syndrome: an organic, sometimes reversible brain disorder, precipitated by factors that may, if not treated, produce permanent damage including brain tumors and strokes.

affiliative: pertaining to establishing positive affective relationships with others.

agnostic: one who believes that it is not possible to know whether there is a God or future life.

alienation: the condition of feeling distinct from, isolated from, and to some degree opposed to the dominant social group.

amniocentesis: perforation or topping, as by a needle, of the innermost membrane of the sac enclosing the embryo.

amphetamines: synthetic drugs customarily used as inhalants, as sprays for head colds, hay fever, etc., and as diet pills. Amphetamine sulfate is a white, odorless powder that acts as a stimulant to the nervous system.

androgen: any substance, such as the testis hormone, that has masculinizing effects.

androgynous: having both masculine and feminine characteristics.

animistic: characterized by the belief that natural phenomena and objects, such as the rocks or the wind, have souls.

anthropology: the comparative study of the chief characteristics of man, including somatic characteristics, social habits and customs, language, and prehistory.

Apgar score: the condition of the newborn based on certain criteria including, among others, color, heart rate, muscle tone, and respiration.

arteriosclerosis: a condition distinguished by thickening, hardening, and diminished elasticity of the arteries.

astigmatism: a structural defect of the eye that prevents light rays from focusing on a single point in the eye, so that indistinct images are produced.

atrophy: a wasting away.

barbiturate: a crystalline acid or salt used as a hypnotic or sedative.

behaviorist: one who believes that observed behaviors constitute the only valid data of psychology.

behavior modification: also called educational engineering, suggests the shaping of behavior through schedules of reinforcement, or reward, of desired responses.

caesarean section: delivery of a baby through a surgical incision in the mother's abdominal wall and uterus when passage of the infant through the birth canal is not advisable.

cardiovascular: pertaining to the heart and blood vessels.

catalyst: an agent having the power to effect change without itself being altered.

catch-up mechanism: an inferred process that restores the normal growth pattern after it has been temporarily altered from its usual course by some abnormal condition such as illness or severe malnutrition.

cerebrovascular: pertaining to the cerebral blood vessels.

child advocacy: action taken by adults on the child's behalf.

chronic brain syndrome: an irreversible brain disorder produced by continuous decrease in functioning brain neurons over the years.

climacteric: the syndrome or pattern of symptoms (somatic, hormonal, and psychic) that characterizes the termination of the reproductive period in the female or the normal diminution of sexual activity in the male.

clique: a close-knit, unisexual social group, most characteristic of early adolescents, especially girls, but occurring sometimes among children as young as eight or nine.

cognitive: pertaining to those processes by means of which an individual becomes aware of objects and situations—for example, reasoning, learning, remembering, and problem solving.

cohabitation: the state of living together, the term is most commonly applied to unmarried couples.

cohort: a group of individuals who share some characteristic such as age or period in history.

commune: a close-knit community of people who share common interests and activities, as in the area of child rearing.

concrete operations: in Piaget's cognitive development theory, the period (between ages 7 and 11) when reasoning processes have begun to appear logical. By this stage the child can perceive structural similarities and categorize items on the basis of perceptual cues.

corticoid: applies to hormones of the adrenal cortex or to any other natural or synthetic compound acting in a similar manner.

counterculture: a culture or way of life that develops within a larger culture and has no real substance of its own; its only function is to criticize the major culture, and its activities reflect reactions to that culture.

cretinism: a chronic condition resulting from a congenital lack of thyroid secretion and marked by arrested mental and physical development and by physical aberrations. The acquired adult form of this disease is called myxedema.

crisis: defined by Erikson as a critical situation or time of increased potential or vulnerability.

critical period hypothesis: the proposal that, if certain experiences occur during specified periods, they will have unusual and lasting effects.

cross-sectional research: research involving a number of persons in terms of one or more variables at a given time.

cryogenics: the practice of freezing the body immediately after death and maintaining it in this state indefinitely, in the belief that, ultimately, means will be developed that allow restoration of life.

culture: the way of life—material and behavioral—of a society, including its customs, knowledge, beliefs, and morals.

cybernation: the process involved in human control functions and the mechanical and electric systems designed to replace them; involving the application of statistical mechanics to communications engineering.

defense mechanism: a reaction intended to maintain the individual's feelings of adequacy and worth.

demographic: pertaining to the study of human populations, including population trends, distribution, and differential birthrates in subcultural groupings.

depolarized: reduced from a status of occupying exactly opposite positions in some continuum.

development: a process involving all the many changes, both qualitative and quantitative, that occur during progress toward maturity. It embraces both changes inherent in the maturing process and those resulting from interaction between the individual and his or her environment.

developmental psychology: the branch of psychology concerned with characteristic behaviors at successive stages of development and the processes involved in moving from one stage to the next.

developmental task: a skill or accomplishment that should be satisfactorily mastered at a particular age/stage if an individual is to be ready for the next stage.

diffusion status: the condition of lacking an integrated distinctive role or sense of self.

disengagement: the mutual withdrawal by aging persons and those in their social environment from each other.

Down's syndrome: mongolism; a condition usually characterized by a final mental age of between 4 and 7, a small brain, a docile disposition, and a very short life span.

ecology: the study of the relationships between organisms and their physical environment.

ectomorph: an individual with a body build characterized by linearity, fragility, and thin muscles.

ego identity: a sense of uniqueness as a person and distinctiveness from others, equivalent to answering the question "Who am I?"

electra complex: the repressed desire of a girl for sex relations with her father.

embryo: the organism in its early prenatal stage—in mammals, until it begins resembling the adult form.

empty nest stage: the period in parents' lives immediately after their grown children leave home.

encounter group: a group characterized by frank, intimate, often emotional interaction.

endomorph: an individual with large accumulations of fat, a large trunk and thighs, tapering extremities, and relatively weak bones and muscles.

episiotomy: surgical incision of the vulvar orifice.

estrogen: any of several estrus-producing compounds, estrus being the sexual excitement, or heat period, of female mammals.

eugenics: the study and arrangement of conditions conducive to improving the mental and physical characteristics of future generations.

euphemism: the substitution of a less offensive word for a more offensive one to convey the same idea.

euthanasia: the practice of "helping," or allowing, a person to die instead of exerting special efforts to maintain life when such life would probably be a meaningless and vegetative existence.

exceptional children: those children for whom regular programs must be adapted if they are to reach their potential.

existential: of, or based on, existence.

fetish: anything regarded with unreasoning devotion.

fetus: the developing young in the human uterus after the second month.

foreclosure status: the state of having made commitments so early as to have prevented exploration of alternatives.

futurist: one who pursues the science of anticipating and planning for years to come.

generativity: the impulse for procreation, interest in establishing and guiding the next generation.

genotype: although originally representing all of an individual's inherited predispositional characteristics, now used more often in the sense of a group sharing a particular predisposition.

geriatric: relating to the curing or healing of disorders of old age.

glaucoma: a disease of the eye characterized by intense intraocular pressure, producing hardness of the eye, atrophy of the retina, and ultimately blindness.

hedonistic: pleasure-seeking.

hereditarian: one who emphasizes the role of heredity, as opposed to environment, in the development of the organism.

hierarchy: arrangement according to rank.

hypochondriasis (hypochondria): a condition characterized by abnormal concern over one's health and, often, imaginary illness and deep melancholy.

iatrogenesis: a doctor-caused disease or condition.

intelligence quotient (IQ): used to describe the relation between a score obtained on a mental test and an individual's chronological (life) age.

instrumental: characterized by goal-directed activity.

laissez-faire: a live-and-let-live philosophy.

latency: the homosexual stage of psychosexual development, ages approximately 8 to 12.

Leboyer technique: a mode of childbirth designed to reduce stresses to the newborn.

life cycle: the complete set of phenomena and events that comprise the total life span.

living will: an individual's expression of desire regarding such matters as whether to maintain life by extraordinary efforts or use of life-support machines at a future time when that individual's condition may no longer allow his making such a decision.

locus of control: the perception of behaviors as being controlled either internally, by oneself, or externally, by others.

longitudinal research: research involving repeated observations of or measurements on the same individuals over a period of time.

LSD: lysergic acid diethylamide, a powerful hallucinogen used illegally by people and also, on a very limited basis, in some types of psychotherapy.

macrostructural research: pertaining to gross structure.

mainstreaming: the practice of placing all children in the general school program instead of in special education classes.

marijuana: the dried leaves of hemp, which have a narcotic effect when ingested.

maturation: development, resulting in changes in behavior, that is due to hereditary factors rather than to learning.

mechanistic: emphasizing the agency or means by which something is accomplished.

menarche: the establishment or beginning of the menstrual function.

mesomorph: an individual with sturdy, upright posture and highly developed skeletal structure—in general, an athletic build.

metabolic: relating to the chemical and physical processes within organisms and cells by which food is built up into protoplasm and broken into simpler substances.

metaphor: a figure of speech in which one thing is likened to another, different from that other, as if it were that other (for example, "All the world's a stage").

mid-life crisis: a critical period during middle age when an individual is induced by the culmination of personal, physical, and social factors to examine his or her life, which may result in important modifications of life style and philosophy.

morphological: having to do with structure or form.

negative identity: a feeling of distinctiveness gained in some unfavorable way.

neonate: the newly born infant.

neuropathy: any nervous disease, especially a degenerative condition of a nerve or nerves.

neurosis: a psychological disorder which significantly interferes with adjustment, is less serious than psychosis, and leaves the personality relatively intact.

neuroticism: a state of excessive emotional or nervous reaction.

nontheistic: characterized by some view other than the belief in one God as the creator and master of the universe.

nuclear family: the family composed only of the father, mother, and children as opposed to the *extended family*, which also includes all the descendants of a common grandparent and all their relatives.

nurturant: supportive—involving warmth and involvement (personal love and compassion).

obesity: condition of being extremely overweight.

oedipus complex: in psychoanalytic theory, excessive emotional attachment, involving conscious or unconscious incestuous desires of the son for his mother.

omnipotence: the state of being all powerful.

organic: constitutional; derived from living organisms.

organismic: relating to living organisms.

ovulation: the process by which a mature ovum (female germ cell) escapes from a ruptured ovarian follicle.

paranoia: a functional psychosis characterized by delusions of persecution or grandeur.

paranurturer: an individual who acts as assistant to trained persons in the helping professions.

paraprofessional: an individual with little or lesser special training who assists the trained professional.

pathology: a diseased or abnormal condition of the organism or its parts.

personality: the total pattern of an individual's characteristic traits, constituting his or her distinctive ways of adapting to the environment.

phenomenological: pertaining to an individual's own perceptions of an object or experience.

placenta: the spongy organ within the uterus that, with the umbilical cord, establishes a connection between mother and child. It acts as a barrier between the two bloodstreams, allowing nutrients to reach the child while keeping out noxious substances.

pluralistic: relating to the conceptualization of a culture or group as composed of relatively distinct subgroups, each with its distinctive life-style and behaviors.

positive reinforcement: the strengthening or stamping in of a particular response by rewarding it whenever it occurs.

presbycusis: the diminished acuteness of hearing occurring in old age.

progeny: offspring; descendants.

progeria: premature old age; a form of infantilism characterized by lack of pubic and facial hair, gray hair, wrinkled skin, and the appearance and manner of old age.

progesterone: a hormone that prepares the uterus for the reception and development of the fertilized ovum.

prosocial: approved by, or favorable to, society in general.

Protestant ethic: a set of ideas about man's spiritual relationships, presumably characteristic of Protestant Christianity, that emphasizes hard work, personal stewardship, pleasurelessness, and individual enterprise.

psychedelic: having the effect of producing extreme reactions including visual stimulation, flights of rapid thought, and hallucinations.

psychoanalytic: relating to psychoanalysis, a systematic approach to human behavior whose broad outlines were laid down by Sigmund Freud. It embraces a theory of personality development and functioning, psychotherapeutic techniques, and research techniques for the investigation of personality functions.

puberty: the time at which the individual's reproductive organs attain readiness to function and secondary sex characteristics develop.

pubescence: the period of about two years preceding puberty, or the time span of physiological development during which the reproductive system matures.

Rh hemolytic disease: a condition produced when the so-called Rh blood (an agglutinating) factor is introduced into Rh negative blood (that lacking Rh), of the mother thus producing pathology in the offspring, including abortions or still births, or possibly mental deficiency.

reconstituted family: the family produced by marriage of formerly married persons, at least one of whom has one or more children.

senescence: the process of growing old.

sibling: offspring of the same parents.

sickle cell anemia: a condition marked by anemia (condition in which blood is deficient in quality or in quantity) and by ulcers in which the subject's red blood cells acquire a sickle shape.

socialization: the process by which an individual learns to behave like, and to get along with, others in his or her society and culture.

sociometric: relating to the measurement of relationships within social groups.

stage theory: the concept that human development proceeds according to sequential and successively more mature stages and that certain kinds of experience are needed for proper development at each of these stages.

standardization: the process of testing a population to obtain norms, or standards, with which the score of an individual can be compared.

stereotype: a preconceived, prejudiced picture of the members of a particular group.

Synanon: a community established for the rehabilitation of former heroin addicts.

technology: a collective term for the by-products (material goods, inventions, means of production, and so on) of the evolution from an agricultural to an industrial economy.

temperament: the emotional, or affective, aspects of an individual's personality.

terminal drop: accelerated decline in cognitive development within the years just preceding death.

tertiary: third; of the third rank.

thalidomide: a drug, at one time administered to a woman prior to pregnancy to prevent spontaneous abortion, that produced deformities in many offspring.

trajectory: path.

transcendence: state of going beyond the limits of human knowledge.

transcendental meditation: a procedure for inducing complete relaxation, ordinarily performed for about 20 minutes each time twice a day, in which one sits with eyes closed, focusing on the rhythm of his or her breathing, and saying some word or number in rhythm with the breathing.

transsexual: one who feels like a member of the opposite sex.

trauma: an experience that inflicts serious physical or psychological shock on the organism.

viral: pertaining to viruses or submicroscopic agents that cause various diseases.

wunderkind: child prodigy; one that succeeds in a competitive or highly difficult field or profession at an early age (plural–wunderkinder).

youth culture: all those attitudes, behaviors, and material objects which characterize, and set apart, persons in their teens and early twenties.

REFERENCES

Abrahams, J. P., Hoyer, W. J., Elias, M. F., and Bradigan, B. Gerontological research in psychology published in the *Journal of Gerontology, 1963–1974*: Perspectives and progress. *Journal of Gerontology,* 1975, *30,* 668.

Acceptance of the idea of mortality. *Intellect,* January 1975, *103*(2362), 215–216.

Adams, M. The single woman in today's society. In A. Skolnick & J. Skolnick (Eds.), *Intimacy, family and society.* Boston: Little, Brown, 1974.

Adams, V. The sibling bond: A lifelong love/hate dialectic. *Psychology Today,* 1981, *15*(6), 32–34; 36–37.

Adler, A. *What life should mean to you.* New York: Putnam's, 1959.

Adler, N. E. Emotional responses of women following therapeutic abortion. *American Journal of Orthopsychiatry,* 1975, *45*(3), 446.

Adler, R. Social factors affecting emotionality and resistance to disease in animals. 3. Early weaning and susceptibility to gastric ulcers in the rat. A control for nutritional factors. *Journal of Comparative Psychology,* 1962, *55,* 600–602.

Agich, G. J. The concepts of death and embodiment. *Ethics in Science and Medicine,* 1976, *3*(2), 95–105.

Ahlgren, A., & Johnson, D. W. Sex differences in cooperative and competitive attitudes from the 2nd through the 12th grades. *Developmental Psychology,* 1979, *15*(1), 45–49.

Ainsworth, M. D. S. Cited in: A scientific look at the origins of infant-mother attachment. *Johns Hopkins Medical Journal,* 1972, *6*(1), 1.

Ainsworth, M. D. S., Bell, S. M., & Stayton, D. J. in M. P. M. Richards (Ed.), *The integration of a child into a social world.* London: Cambridge University Press, 1974, pp. 99–136.

Albert, N., & Beck, A. T. Incidence of depression in early adolescence: A preliminary study. *Journal of Youth and Adolescence,* 1975, *4*(4), 301–307.

Albert, W. C., & Zarit, S. H. Income and health care of the aging. In S. H. Zarit (Ed.), *Readings in aging and death: Contemporary perspectives.* New York: Harper & Row, 1977, pp. 120–127.

Alexander, J., & Cohen, J. Customs, coupling, and the family in a changing culture. *American Journal of Orthopsychiatry,* 1981, *51*(2), 307–316.

Alienation and education: A statement of the Philadelphia Federation of Teachers. *Changing Education,* 1974, *6*(1), 20–21.

Alston, J. P., & Dudley, C. J. Age, occupation and life satisfaction. *Gerontologist,* 1973, *13,* 58–62.

American Council on Education. *The American freshman: National norms for fall 1975.* Washington, D.C.: Author, 1976.

Anderson, B., & Palmore, E. Longitudinal evaluation of ocular function. In E. Palmore (Ed.), *Normal aging.* Durham, N.C.: Duke University Press, 1974, pp. 24–32.

Anderson, R., & Nida, S. A. Effect of physical attractiveness on the opposite- and same-sex evaluations. *Journal of Personality,* 1978, *46*(3), 401–413.

Apollini, T., & Cooke, T. P. Peer behavior conceptualized as a variable influencing infant and toddler development. *American Journal of Orthopsychiatry,* 1975, *45*(1), 4–17.

Arenberg, D., & Robertson-Tchabo, E. A. Learning and Aging. In J. E. Birren & K. W. Schaie (Eds.), *Handbook of the psychology of aging.* New York: Van Nostrand Reinhold, 1977, pp. 421–449.

Ariès, P. *Centuries of childhood.* New York: Random House, 1962.

Ariès, P. The family and the city. *Daedalus,* 1977, 227–235.

Aronfreed, J. Moral development from the standpoint of a general psychological theory. In T. Lickona (Ed.), *Moral development and behavior: Theory, research, and social issues.* New York: Holt, Rinehart & Winston, 1976, pp. 54–69.

Ashton, R. Aspects of timing in child development. *Child Development,* 1976, *47*(3), 622–626.

Atchley, R. C. *The social forces in later life.* Belmont, Calif.: Wadsworth, 1978.

Atkinson, J., & Endsley, R. C. Influence of sex of child and parent on parental reactions to hypothetical parent-child situations. *Genetic Psychology Monographs,* 1976, *94*(1), 131–147.

Augustine, M. J., & Kalish, R. A. Religion, transcendence, and appropriate death. *Journal of Transpersonal Psychology,* 1975, *7,* 1–13.

Ausubel, D. P. *Theory and problems of child development.* New York: Grune & Stratton, 1957.

Ausubel, F., Beckwith, J., & Janssen, K. The politics of genetic engineering: Who decides who's defective? *Psychology Today,* 1974, *8*(1), 30–32; 34–43.

Aviram, A., & Milgram, R. M. Dogmatism, locus of control, and creativity in children educated in the Soviet Union, the United States, and Israel. *Psychological Reports,* 1977, *40,* 27–34.

Back, K. W. Meaning of time in later life. *Journal of Genetic Psychology,* 1965, *109,* 9–25.

Back, K. W. Personal characteristics and social behavior: Theory and method. In R. H. Binstock & E. Shanas (Eds.), *Handbook of aging and the social sciences.* New York: Van Nostrand Reinhold, 1976, pp. 403–431.

Back, K. W., & Morris, J. D. Perception of self and the study of whole lives. In E. Palmore (Ed.), *Normal aging 2: Reports from the Duke Longitudinal Studies, 1970–1973.* Durham, N.C.: Duke University Press, 1974, pp. 216–221.

Bahr, R. The woman who moved medical mountains. *Prevention,* 1975, *27*(10), 123–124; 129–134.

Bailey, S. K. The several ages of learning. *Change,* 1976, *8*(4), 36–39.

Balakrishnan, T. R., Allingham, J. D., & Kantner, J. F. *Family growth study.* Unpublished mimeographed manuscript, University of Western Ontario, 1972.

Baltes, P. B., & Schaie, K. W. Aging and IQ: The myth of the twilight years. *Psychology Today,* 1974, *7,* 35–40.

Baltes, P. B. & Schaie, K. W. On the plasticity of intelligence in adulthood and old age: Where Horn and Donaldson fail. *American Psychologist,* 1976, *31*(10), 720–725.

Bandura, A. The stormy decade: Fact or fiction? *Psychology in the Schools,* 1964, *1,* 224–231.

Bardwick, J. M. Evolution and parenting. *Journal of Social Issues,* 1974, *30*(4), 39–62.

Baumrind, D. Early socialization and adolescent competence. In S. E. Dragastin & G. H. Elder, Jr. (Eds.), *Adolescence in the life cycle.* Washington, D.C.: Hemisphere Publishing, 1975, pp. 117–143.

Bayes, A. E. Sexist students in American colleges: A descriptive note. *Journal of Marriage and the Family,* 1975, *37*(2), 391–397.

Beattie, W. M., Jr. Aging and the social services. In R. H. Binstock & E. Shanas (Eds.), *Handbook of aging and the social sciences.* New York: Van Nostrand Reinhold, 1976, 619–642.

Becker, E. *The denial of death.* New York: Free Press, 1973.

Belbin, E., & Belbin, R. M. New careers in middle age. In B. L. Neugarten (Ed.), *Middle age and aging.* Chicago: University of Chicago Press, 1968.

Belcky, J., & Steinberg, L. D. The effects of day care: A critical review. *Child Development,* 1978, *49*(4), 929–949.

Bell, R. Q., & Harper, L. *Child effects on adults.* New York: Halsted Press, 1977.

Bell, R. Q., & Hertz, T. W. Toward more comparability and generalizability of developmental research. *Child Development,* 1976, *47*(1), 6–13.

Bell, R., Turner, S., & Rosen, L. A multivariate analysis of female extramarital coitus. *Journal of Marriage and the Family,* 1975, *37*(2), 375–384.

Belsky, J. Early human experience: A family perspective. *Developmental Psychology*, 1981, *17*(1), 3–23.

Bem, S. L. Androgyny vs. the tight little lives of fluffy women and chesty men. *Psychology Today*, 1975, *9*(4), 58–62.

Bengtson, V. L. *The social psychology of aging*. New York: Bobbs-Merrill, 1973.

Bengtson, V. L., Kasschau, P. L., & Ragan, P. K. The impact of social structure on aging individuals. In J. E. Birren & K. W. Schaie (Eds.), *Handbook of the psychology of aging*. New York: Van Nostrand Reinhold, 1977, 327–353.

Bengtson, V. L., & Starr, J. M. Contrast and consensus: A generational analysis of youth in the 1970s. In *74th yearbook of National Society for the Study of Education (Part 1)*. Chicago: University of Chicago Press, 1975, pp. 224–266.

Berardo, F. M. Survivorship and social isolation: The case of the aged widower. *Family Coordinator*, 1970, *19*, 11–25.

Berardo, F. M. Family research and theory: Emergent topics in the 1970s and the prospects for the 1980s. *Journal of Marriage and the Family*, 1981, *43*(2), 251–254.

Bereiter, C. The right to make mistakes. *Intellect*, 1973, *109*(2353), 184–190.

Berger, M., & Kennedy, H. Pseudobackwardness in children: Maternal attitudes as an etiological factor. *Psychoanalytic Study of the Child*. 1975, *30*, 279–306.

Berger, P., Hamburg, B., & Hamburg, D. Mental health: Progress and problems: *Daedalus*, 1977, *106*(1), 261–276.

Berman, H. J. Prologue to aging: Societal structure and the aged. In M. G. Spencer & C. J. Dorr (Eds.), *Understanding aging: A multidisciplinary approach*. New York: Appleton-Century-Crofts, 1975.

Bernard, J. *The future of marriage*. New York: Bantam, 1972.

Bernard, J. Adolescence and socialization for motherhood. In S. E. Dragastin & G. H. Elder, Jr. (Eds.), *Adolescence in the life cycle*. Washington, D.C.: Hemisphere Publishing, 1975, pp. 227–252. (a)

Bernard, J. *The future of motherhood*. New York: Penguin, 1975. (b)

Bernard, J. The good-provider role: Its rise and fall. *American Psychologist*, 1981, *36*(1), 1–12.

Bernstein, A. C. Six stages of understanding: How children learn about sex and birth. *Psychology Today*, 1976, *9*(8), 31–35; 66.

Berscheid, E., & Walster, E. H. Physical attractiveness. In L. Berkowitz (Ed.), *Experimental social psychology*. New York: Academic Press, 1975.

Bersoff, D. N. Developing legal theories in child advocacy. *Clinical Psychologist*, 1976, *29*(2), 20–21.

Biegel, H. C. Changing sexual problems in adults. *American Journal of Psychotherapy*, 1976, *30*(3), 422–432.

Bielby, D. D., & Papalia, D. E. Moral development and perceptual role taking egocentrism: Their development and interrelationship across the life-span. *International Journal of Aging and Human Development*, 1975, *6*(4), 293–308.

Birren, J. E. Age and decision strategies. In A. T. Welford & J. E. Birren (Eds.), *Interdispl. Topics Gerontol.*, 1969, *4*, 23–36.

Birren, J. E. The abuse of the urban aged. In S. H. Zarit (Ed.), *Readings in aging and death: Contemporary perspectives*. New York: Harper & Row, 1977, pp. 127–131.

Birren, J. E., & Woodruff, D. S. Human development over the life span through education. In P. B. Baltes & K. W. Schaie (Eds.), *Life-span developmental psychology: Personality and socialization*. New York: Academic Press, 1973.

Black, D. The older person and the family. In S. H. Zarit (Ed.), *Readings in aging and death: Contemporary perspectives*. New York: Harper & Row, 1977, pp. 165–169.

Blau, R. S., & Holmes, D. A. Meeting the mandate to employ youth. *Worklife*, 1978, *3*(1), 3–7.

Blau, Z. S. *Old age in a changing society.* New York: Franklin Watts, 1973.

Blehar, M. C., Lieberman, A. F., & Ainsworth, M. D. S. Early face-to-face interaction and its relation to later infant-mother attachment. *Child Development*, 1977, *48*(1), 182–194.

Blood, R. O. Research needs of a family life educator and marriage counselor. *Journal of Marriage and the Family*, 1976, *38*(1).

Bohman, M. The interaction of heredity and childhood environment: Some adoption studies. *Journal of Child Psychology and Psychiatry*, 1981, 22, 195–200.

Boli-Bennett, J., & Meyer, J. W. The ideology of childhood and the state: Rules distinguishing children in nation constitutions, 1870–1970. *American Sociological Review*, 1978, *43*(December), 797–812.

Bond, E. K. Form perception in the infant. *Psychological Bulletin*, 1972, 77, 225–245.

The boom in leisure—where Americans spend 160 billions. *U.S. News & World Report*, May 23, 1977, pp. 62–69.

Bortner, R. W., & Hultsch, D. F. Patterns of subjective deprivation in adulthood. *Developmental Psychology*, 1974, *10*(4), 534–545.

Bosserman, P. Implications for youth. In M. Kaplan & P. Bosserman (Eds.), *Technology, human values, and leisure.* Nashville, Tenn.: Abingdon Press, 1971.

Botwinick, J. Age differences in self ratings of confidence. *Psychological Reports*, 1970, 27, 865–866.

Botwinick, J. *Aging and behavior.* New York: Springer, 1973.

Botwinick, J. Intellectual abilities. In J. E. Birren & K. W. Schaie (Eds.), *Handbook of the psychology of aging.* New York: Van Nostrand Reinhold, 1977, pp. 580–605.

Bouvier, L., Atlee, E., & McVeigh, F. The elderly in America. In S. H. Zarit (Ed.), *Readings in aging and death: Contemporary perspectives.* New York: Harper & Row, 1977, pp. 28–36.

Bower, T. G. R. The object in the world of the infant. *Scientific American*, 1976, *235*(5), 38–47.

Boylin, W., Gordon, S. K., & Nehrke, M. F. Reminiscing and ego integrity in institutionalized elderly males. *Gerontologist*, 1976, *16*(2), 118–124.

Bradway, K. P., Thompson, C. W., & Cravens, R. B. Preschool IQs after twenty-five years. *Journal of Educational Psychology*, 1958, 49, 278–281.

Brandwein, R. A., Brown, C. A., & Fox, E. M. Women and children last: The social situation of divorced mothers and their families. *Journal of Marriage and the Family*, 1974, *36*(3), 498–514.

Braungart, R. G. Youth and social movements. In S. E. Dragastin & G. H. Elder, Jr. (Eds.), *Adolescence in the life cycle.* Washington, D.C.: Hemisphere Publishing, 1975, pp. 255–290.

Brazelton, T. B. Implications of infant development among the Mayan Indians of Mexico. *Human Development*, 1972, *15*, 90–111.

Breland, H. M. Family configuration and intellectual development. *Journal of Individual Behavior*, 1977, *33*(1), 86–96.

Breslow-Rubin, L. The marriage bed. *Psychology Today*, 1976, *10*(3), 44–50; 91–92.

Brickman, W. W. Adolescents and alcohol abuse. *Intellect*, 1974, *103*(2361), 165.

Bridges, W. The discovery of middle age. *Human Behavior*, 1977, *6*(5), 64–68.

Brim, O. G., Jr. Macro-structural influences on child development and the need for childhood social indicators. *American Journal of Orthopsychiatry*, 1975, *45*(4), 516–524.

Britton, J. H., & Britton, J. O. *Personality changes in aging.* New York: Springer, 1972.

Broderick, C. B. Fathers. *The Family Coordinator,* 1977, *26*(3), 269–275.

Brody, G. H., & Stoneman, Z. Parental nonverbal behavior within the family context. *Family Relations,* 1981, *30*(2), 187–190.

Bronfenbrenner, U. Developmental research, public policy and the ecology of childhood. *Child Development,* 1974, *45*(1), 1–5.

Bronfenbrenner, U. *The experimental ecology of education.* Address before the American Educational Research Association, San Francisco, April 1976.

Bronfenbrenner, U. Toward an experimental ecology of human development. *American Psychologist,* 1977, *32,* 513–531.

Brown, J. L. States in the newborn. *Merrill-Palmer Quarterly,* 1964, *10*(4), 313–327.

Brozek, J. Changes of body composition in man during maturity and their nutritional implications. *Federation Proc.,* 1952, *11,* 784–793.

Bruck, C. Professing androgyny. *Human Behavior,* 1977, *6*(10), 22–31.

Bruner, J. S. The process of education revisited. *Phi Delta Kappan,* 1971, *53*(1), 18–21.

Bruner, J. S. Organization of early skilled action. *Child Development,* 1973, *44,* 1–11.

Bruner, J. S. Learning the mother tongue. *Human Nature,* 1978, *1*(9), 42–49.

Buchen, I. H. The limits to individuality: Past and future mass models. *Intellect,* 1974, *103*(2361), 185–189.

Buchen, I. H. The future of sexuality. *Intellect,* 1975, *103*(2364), 405.

Bugard, P. [Fatigue in the woman and the child.] *Psychologie Medicale,* 1974, *6*(7), 1351–1372.

Burdge, R. J. Levels of occupational prestige and leisure activity. *Journal of Leisure Research,* 1969, *1,* 262–274.

Burgess, R. L., & Conger, R. D. Family interaction in abusive, neglectful, and normal families. *Child Development,* 1978, *49*(4), 1163–1173.

Burke, R. J. & Weir, T. Relationships of wives' employment status to husband, wife and pair satisfaction and performance. *Journal of Marriage and the Family,* 1976, *38*(2), 279–287.

Burke, R. J., & Weir, T. Husband-wife helping relationships: The mental hygiene function in marriage. *Psychological Reports,* 1977, *40,* 911–925.

Burnside, I. M. Loss: A constant theme in group work with the aged. In S. H. Zarit (Ed.), *Readings in aging and death: Contemporary perspectives.* New York: Harper & Row, 1977, pp. 230–234.

Burton, R. V. Honesty and dishonesty. In T. Lickona (Ed.), *Moral development and behavior: Theory, research, and social issues.* New York: Holt, Rinehart & Winston, 1976, pp. 173–197.

Bush, S. Beauty makes the beast look better. *Psychology Today,* 1976, *10*(3), 15–16.

Bush, S. A change of scene can be fatal. *Psychology Today,* 1977, *10*(9), 32.

Buss, D. M. Predicting parent-child interactions from children's activity level. *Developmental Psychology,* 1981, *17*(1), 59–65.

Busse, E. W. Theories of aging. In E. W. Busse & E. Pfeiffer (Eds.), *Behavior and adaptation in late life.* Boston: Little, Brown, 1969.

Butler, R. N. Man does not die, he kills himself. *International Journal of Aging and Human Development,* 1975, *6*(4), 367–370.

Butler, R. N. Age-ism another form of bigotry. In S. H. Zarit (Ed.), *Readings in aging and death: Contemporary perspectives.* New York: Harper & Row, 1977, pp. 132–134.

Butler, R. N. The life review: An unrecognized bonanza. *International Journal of Aging and Human Development,* 1980–81, *12*(1), 35–48.

Caldwell, B. M. A decade of early intervention programs: What we have learned. *American Journal of Orthopsychiatry,* 1974, *44*(4), 491–496.

Cameron, P. Ego strength and happiness of the aged. *Journal of Gerontology,* 1967, *22,* 199.

Campbell, A. The American way of mating: Marriage *si*, children only maybe. *Psychology Today*, 1975, *8*(12), 37–43.

Campbell, C. Economic reality—intruder on the American dream. *Psychology Today*, 1975, *9*(1), 36–37.

Campbell, C. The manchild pill? *Psychology Today*, 1976, *10*(3), 86–88; 90–91.

Cantor, N. L., & Gelfand, D. M. Effects of responsiveness and sex of children on adults' behavior. *Child Development*, 1977, *48*(1), 232–238.

Carisse, C. B. Family and leisure: A set of contradictions. *Family Coordinator*, 1975, *24*(2), 191–197.

Carp, F. M. User evaluation of housing for the elderly. *Gerontologist*, 1976, *16*(2), 102–111.

Carroll, J. B., & Maxwell, S. E. Individual differences in cognitive abilities. In M. R. Rosenzweig & L. W. Porter (Eds.), *Annual Review of Psychology*, 1979, *30*, 603.

Carter, H., & Glick, P. C. *Marriage and divorce: A social and economic study* (2nd ed.). Cambridge, Mass.: Harvard University Press, 1976.

Cartwright, A., Hockey, L., & Anderson, J. L. *Life before death*. London: Routledge & Kegan Paul, 1973.

Cassell, E., Kass, L. R., & Associates. Refinements in criteria for the determination of death: An appraisal. *Journal of the American Medical Association*, 1972, *221*, 48–54.

Cavior, C., & Howard, R. Facial attractiveness and juvenile delinquency among Black and White offenders. *Journal of Abnormal Child Psychology*, 1973, *1*(2), 202–212.

Chadwick, B. A., Albrecht, S. L., & Kunz, P. R. Marital and family role satisfaction. *Journal of Marriage and the Family*, 1976, *38*(3), 431–440.

Chamberlin, L. J., & Girona, R. Our children are changing. *Educational Leadership*, 1976, *33*(4), 301–305.

Chambers, W. *Witness*. New York: Random House, 1952.

Chapman, R. B. Academic and behavioral problems of boys in elementary school. *Counseling Psychologist*, 1978, *7*(4), 37–40.

Chase, I. D. A comparison of men's and women's intergenerational mobility in the United States. *American Sociological Review*, 1975, *40*(4), 483–505.

Chasen, B. Sex-role stereotyping and prekindergarten teachers. *Elementary School Journal*, 1974, *74*(4), 220–235.

Cheek, N. H., et al. *Leisure and recreation places*. Ann Arbor, Mich.: Ann Arbor Science Publishers, 1976.

Chellam, G. Intergenerational affinities: Symmetrical life experiences of the young adults and the aging in Canadian society. *International Journal of Aging and Human Development*, 1980–81, *12*(2), 79–92.

Childhood attachments: Toys that make growing up easier. *Human Behavior*, 1978, *8*(1), 48.

Children's views of reality. *Children Today*, 1977, *6*(4), 28–29.

Chilman, C. S. Some psychosocial aspects of female sexuality. *Family Coordinator*, 1974, *23*(2), 123–131.

Chilman, C. S. Habitat and American families: A social-psychological perspective. *Family Coordinator*, 1978, *27*(2), 105–112.

Chiriboga, D., & Thurnher, M. Concept of self. In M. F. Lowenthal, M. Thurnher, & D. Chiriboga (Eds.), *Four stages of life: A comparative study of women and men facing transitions*. San Francisco: Jossey-Bass, 1975, pp. 62–83.

Chomsky, N. Review of verbal behavior by B. F. Skinner. *Languages*, 1969, *35*(1), 26–58, fn. 48.

Chown, S. M. A factor analysis of the Wesley rigidity inventory. *Journal of Abnormal Social Psychology*, 1960, *61*, 491–494.

Chown, S. M. Morale, careers and personal potentials. In J. E. Birren & K. W. Schaie (Eds.), *Handbook of the psychology of aging.* New York: Van Nostrand Reinhold, 1977, pp. 672–691.

Clark, E. V. Strategies for communicating. *Child Development,* 1978, *49*(4), 953–959.

Clark, M. & Anderson, B. G. *Culture and aging.* Springfield, Ill.: C. C. Thomas, 1967.

Clarke, P. J. Exploration of countertransference toward the dying. *American Journal of Orthopsychiatry,* 1981, *51*(1), 71–77.

Clarke-Stewart, K. A. *Child care in the family: A review of research and some propositions for policy.* New York: Academic Press, 1977.

Clausen, J. A. The social meaning of differential physical and sexual maturation. In S. E. Dragastin & G. H. Elder, Jr. (Eds.), *Adolescence in the life cycle.* Washington, D. C.: Hemisphere Publishing, 1975, pp. 25–48.

Cleveland, M. Sex in marriage: At 40 and beyond. *Family Coordinator,* 1976, *25*(3), 233–240.

Cleveland, W. P., & Gianturco, D. T. Remarriage probability after widowhood: A retrospective method. *Journal of Gerontology,* 1976, *31*, 99–103.

Cohen, D. More young women are smoking and they're smoking more. *Psychology Today,* 1977, *10*(11), 131.

Cohen, D. R. Children of homosexuals seem headed straight. *Psychology Today,* 1978, *12*(6), 44–46.

Coleman, J. S. Comments on responses to youth: Transition to adulthood. *School Review,* 1974, *83*(1), 139–144.

Coleman, J. S., Herzberg, J., & Morris, M. Identity in adolescence: Present and future self-concepts. *Journal of Youth and Adolescence,* 1977, *6*(1), 63–75.

Coleman, J. S., & Others. *Youth: Transition to adulthood.* Chicago: University of Chicago Press, 1974.

Coleman, P. G. *The role of the past in adaptation to old age.* Unpublished doctoral dissertation, University of London, 1972.

Coles, R., with Woodward, K. Survival drill in suburbs: The cold, tough world of the affluent family. *Psychology Today,* 1975, *9*(6), 67–68, 70; 74; 77; 133.

Condry, J., & Condry, S. Sex differences: A study of the eye of the beholder. *Child Development,* 1976, *47*(3), 812–819.

Condry, J., & Siman, M. L. Characteristics of peer- and adult-oriented children. *Journal of Marriage and the Family,* 1974, *36*(3), 543–554.

Conger, J. J. *Adolescence and youth* (2nd ed.). New York: Harper & Row, 1976.

Cooper, M. Voice problems of the geriatric patient. *Geriatrics,* 1970, *25*, 107–110.

Corea, G. Childbirth 2000. *Omni,* 1979, 48–50; 104–107.

Corso, J. F. Auditory perception and communication. In J. E. Birren & K. W. Schaie (Eds.), *Handbook of the psychology of aging.* New York: Van Nostrand Reinhold, 1977, pp. 535–553.

Cottle, J. J. The surviving family: Notes on intimacy, kinship, and maturity. *Youth and Society,* 1974, *5*(3), 259–278.

Crandall, V. C. The Fels study: Some contributions to personality development and achievement in childhood and adulthood. *Seminars in Psychiatry,* 1972, 4(4), 383–397.

Croake, J. W., & Olson, T. D. Family constellation and personality. *Journal of Individual Psychology,* 1977, *33*(1), 9–17.

Croogl, S. H., et al. The heart patient and the recovery process. *Social Science and Medicine,* 1968, 2, 111–164.

Cross, K. P., & Valley, J. R. *Planning nontraditional programs.* San Francisco: Jossey-Bass, 1975.

Csanyi, V., Gervai, J., & Adani, G. Two-time-dependent responses of checks to imprinting stimuli. *Journal of Comparative and Physiological Psychology,* 1973, *83,* 13–18.

Cumming, E., & Henry, W. E. *Growing old.* New York: Basic Books, 1961.

Curry, T. J., & Rutliff, B. W. The effects of nursing home size on resident isolation and life satisfaction. *Gerontologist,* 1973, *13*(3), Part 1, 295–298.

Cutler, N. E., & Harootyan, R. Demography of the aged. In D. Woodruff & J. E. Birren (Eds.), *Aging: Scientific perspectives and social issues.* New York: Van Nostrand Reinhold, 1975.

Cyrus-Lutz, C., & Gaitz, C. M. *Lifetime goals: Age and ethnic considerations.* Houston: Texas Research Institute of Mental Sciences, 1972.

Davidson, K., Ginsburg, R. B., & Kay, H. *Sex-based discrimination: Text, cases, and materials.* St. Paul, Minn.: West Publishing, 1974.

Davis, A. J. Parental influences on young children's personal-social development. Proceedings of the Third Annual Purdue Child and Family Symposium, Child rearing research in the 70s: Implications for practitioners. West Lafayette, Ind.: Purdue University, 1978.

Davis, A. J. Parent-child interaction and the socialization process: A critical analysis of the research. *Contemporary Education,* 1979, *50*(2), 86–92.

DeCecco, J. P., & Richards, A. K. Civil war in the high schools. *Psychology Today,* 1975, *9*(6), 51–56; 120.

Deck, J. *Rancho paradise.* New York: Harcourt Brace Jovanovich, 1972.

Defrain, J., & Eirick, R. Coping as divorced single parents: A comparative study of fathers and mothers. *Family Relations,* 1981, *30*(2), 265–273.

Dehn, M. M., & Bruce, R. A. Longitudinal variations in maximal oxygen intake with age and activity. *Journal of Applied Physiology,* 1972, *33,* 805–807.

DeLissovoy, V. High school marriages: A longitudinal study. *Journal of Marriage and the Family,* 1973, *35,* 245–255.

DeVries, H. A. Physiology of exercise and aging. In S. H. Zarit (Ed.), *Readings in aging and death: Contemporary perspectives.* New York: Harper & Row, 1977, pp. 56–60.

DeVries, H. A., & Adams, G. M. Comparison of exercise responses in old and young men: 1. The cardiac effort total body effort relationship. *Journal of Gerontology,* 1972, *27,* 344–348.

Dibner, A. S. The psychology of normal aging. In M. G. Spencer & C. J. Dorr (Eds.), *Understanding aging: A multidisciplinary approach.* New York: Appleton-Century-Crofts, 1975, pp. 67–90.

DiPietro, J. A. Rough and tumble play: A function of gender. *Developmental Psychology,* 1981, *17*(1), 50–58.

Diets and children's health. *Children Today,* 1977, *6*(4), 30.

Dion, K. K. Physical attractiveness and evaluation of children's transgressions. *Journal of Personality and Social Psychology,* 1972, *24,* 207–213.

Doctors sound out fetus monitoring. *New Scientist,* 1978, *81*(1144), 674.

Doering, S. G., & Entwisle, D. R. Preparation during pregnancy and ability to cope with labor and delivery. *American Journal of Orthopsychiatry,* 1975, *45*(5), 825–837.

Doster, J. T., & Chance, J. Interpersonal trust and trustworthiness in preadolescents. *Journal of Psychology,* 1976, *93*(1), 71–79.

Douvan, E. Sex differences in the opportunities, demands, and development of youth. In *74th yearbook of National Society for the Study of Education (Part 1).* Chicago: University of Chicago Press, 1975, pp. 27–45.

Downs, A. The impact of housing policies on family life in the United States since World War II. *Daedalus,* 1977, 163–180.

Dragastin, S. E. Epilogue: Research themes and priorities. In S. E. Dragastin & G. H. Elder, Jr. (Eds.), *Adolescence in the life cycle.* Washington, D.C.: Hemisphere Publishing, 1975, pp. 291–301.

Dreyer, P. H. Sex, sex roles, and marriage among youth in the 1970s. In *74th yearbook of National Society for the Study of Education (Part 1).* Chicago: University of Chicago Press, 1975, pp. 194–223.

Dublin, L. L. *Factbook on man.* New York: Macmillan, 1965.

Dunn, J., & Kendrick, C. The arrival of a sibling: Changes in patterns of interaction between mother and first-born child. *Journal of Child Psychology, Psychiat.,* 1981, *21,* 119–132.

Eckerman, C. O., Whatley, J. L., & Kutz, S. L. Growth of social play with peers during the second year of life. *Developmental Psychology,* 1975, *11*(1), 42–49.

Editor's note. *Children Today,* 1975, *4*(5), 21.

Ehrhardt, A. A., Epstein, R., & Money, J. Fetal androgens and female gender identity in the early-treated androgenital syndrome. *Johns Hopkins Medical Journal,* 1968, *122,* 160–167.

Eichorn, D. H. Asynchronizations in adolescent development. In S. E. Dragastin & G. H. Elder, Jr. (Eds.), *Adolescence in the life cycle.* Washington, D.C.: Hemisphere Publishing, 1975, pp. 81–94.

Einstein, E. Stepfamily lives. *Human Behavior,* 1979, *8*(4), 63–68.

Eisdorfer, C., & Raskind, M. Aging, hormones and human behavior. In B. E. Eleftheriou & R. L. Sprott (Eds.), *Hormonal correlates of behavior* (Vol. 1). New York: Plenum, 1975.

Eisdorfer, C., & Wilkie, F. Stress, disease, aging and behavior. In J. E. Birren & K. W. Schaie (Eds.), *Handbook of the psychology of aging.* New York: Van Nostrand Reinhold, 1977, pp. 251–275.

Eisenberg, L. The human nature of human nature. *Science,* 1972, *176,* 123–128.

Eisenberg, L. On the humanizing of human nature. *Impact,* 1973, *23*(3), 213–224.

Eitzen, D. S. Athletics in the status system of male adolescents: A replication of Coleman's *The adolescent society. Adolescence,* 1975, *10*(38), 267–276.

Elardo, R., Bradley, R., & Caldwell, B. M. A longitudinal study of the relation of infants' home environments to language development at age three. *Child Development,* 1977, *48*(2), 595–603.

Elder, G. H., Jr. Adolescence in the life cycle. In S. E. Dragastin & G. H. Elder, Jr. (Eds.), *Adolescence in the life cycle.* Washington, D. C.: Hemisphere Publishing, 1975, pp. 1–26. (a)

Elder, G. H., Jr. Age differentiation and the life course. In A. Inkeles, J. Coleman, and N. Smelser (Eds.), *Annual Review of Sociology* (Vol. 1). Palo Alto, Calif.: Annual Reviews, 1975. (b)

Elias, M. F., & Elias, P. K. Motivation and activity. In J. E. Birren & K. W. Schaie (Eds.), *Handbook of the psychology of aging.* New York: Van Nostrand Reinhold, 1977, pp. 357–383.

Elias, M. F., Elias, P. K., & Elias, J. W. *Basic processes in adult developmental psychology.* St. Louis: C. V. Mosby, 1977.

Elkind, D. Egocentrism in adolescence. *Child Development,* 1967, *38,* 1025–1034.

End of youth culture—Changes it will bring. *U. S. News & World Report,* October 3, 1977, pp. 54–56.

Engen, T. Taste and smell. In J. E. Birren & K. W. Schaie (Eds.), *Handbook of the psychology of aging.* New York: Van Nostrand Reinhold, 1977, 554–561.

Entine, A. D. Counseling for mid-life and beyond. *Vocational Guidance Quarterly,* 1977, *25*(4), 332–336.

Erikson, E. H. *Childhood and society.* New York: Norton, 1950.

Erikson, E. H. Identity and the life cycle. *Psychological Issues,* 1959, *1,* 50–100.

Erikson, E. H. *Childhood and society* (2nd ed.). New York: Norton, 1963.

Eron, L. D., Huesman, L. R., Lefkowitz, M. M., & Walder, L. O. How learning conditions in early childhood—including mass media—relate to aggression in late adolescence. *American Journal of Orthopsychiatry,* 1974, *44*(3), 412–423.

Evans, E. B., & Saia, G. E. *The case for infant day care and a practical guide.* Boston: Beacon Press, 1972.

Evans, R. I. *Dialogue with Erik Erikson.* New York: Dutton, 1969.

Ezer, M. Effect of religion upon children's responses to questions involving physical casualty. In W. Allinsmith (Ed.), *The causes of behavior: Readings in child development and educational psychology.* Boston: Allyn & Bacon, 1962.

Fagot, B. I. Consequences of moderate cross-gender behavior in preschool children. *Child Development,* 1977, *48*(3), 902–907.

Fagot, B. I. The influence of sex of child on parental reactions to toddler children. *Child Development,* 1978, *49*(2), 459–465.

Fagot, B. I., & Littman, I. Stability of sex role and play interest, from preschool to elementary school. *Journal of Psychology,* 1975, *89,* 285–292.

Falbo, T. Does the only child grow up miserable? *Psychology Today,* 1976, *9*(12), 60; 65.

Falbo, T. The only child: A review. *Journal of Individual Psychology,* 1977, *33*(1), 47–61.

Farson, R. Birth rights. *Ms.,* 1974, *11*(9), 66–67; 71; 94–95.

Feigelman, W., & Silverman, A. R. Single parent adoptions. *Social Casework,* July 1977, pp. 408–425.

Feldman, S. S., Biringen, Z. C., & Nash, S. C. Fluctuations of sex-related self-attributions as a function of stage of family life cycle. *Developmental Psychology,* 1981, *17*(1), 24–35.

Feldman, S. S., & Nash, S. C. Interest in babies during young adulthood. *Child Development,* 1978, *49*(3), 617–622.

Finkelstein, B. J. The search for identity: An institutional problem? *Intellect,* 1973, *102*(2353), 150–151.

Finn, P., & Brown, J. Risks entailed in teenage intoxication as perceived by junior and senior high school students. *Journal of Youth and Adolescence,* 1981, *10*(1), 51–76.

Fischer, J. L. Transitions in relationship style from adolescence to young adulthood. *Journal of Youth and Adolescence,* 1981, *10*(1), 11–24.

Flavell, J. H. *The developmental psychology of Jean Piaget.* New York: Van Nostrand Reinhold, 1963.

Folkins, C. H. Effects of physical training on mood. *Journal of Clinical Psychology,* 1976, *32*(2), 385–388.

For American youth: "Demands no other generation has had to face." *U.S. News & World Report,* September 6, 1976, pp. 59–61.

Forbes, J. *Studies in social science and planning.* Edinburgh: Scottish Academic Press, 1974.

Fozard, J. L., Nuttal, R. L., & Waugh, N. C. Age-related differences in mental performance. *Aging and Human Development,* 1972, *3,* 19–43.

Fozard, J. L., Wolf, E., Bell, B., McFarland, R. A., & Podolsky, S. Visual perception and communication. In J. E. Birren & K. W. Schaie (Eds.), *Handbook of the psychology of aging.* New York: Van Nostrand Reinhold, 1977, pp. 497–534.

Fraser, F. C. Current concepts in genetics: Genetics as a health-care service. *New England Journal of Medicine,* 1976, *295*(9), 486–488.

Fraternities bounce back—With big changes. *U.S. News & World Report,* March 11, 1979, 46.

Fredrich, L. K., & Stein, A. N. Aggressive and presocial television programs and the natural behavior of preschool children. *Monographs of the Society for Research in Child Development*, 1973, *38*(4, Serial No. 151), 1–64.

Freedman, D. G. Constitutional and environmental interaction in rearing of four breeds of dogs. *Science*, 1958, *17*, 585–586.

Freedman, D. G. Ethnic differences in babies. *Human Nature*, 1979, *2*(1), 36–43.

Freeman, J. T. *Clinical features of the older patient.* Springfield, Ill.: C. C. Thomas, 1965.

Frenkel-Brunswik, E. Adjustments and reorientation in the course of the life span. In B. L. Neugarten (Ed.), *Middle age and aging.* Chicago: University of Chicago Press, 1968, pp. 77–84.

Friedl, E. Society and sex roles. *Human Nature*, 1978, *1*(4), 68–75.

Friis, R. Job dissatisfaction and coronary heart disease. *Intellect*, 1976, *104*(2375), 594–596.

Frodi, A. M., & Lamb, M. E. Sex differences in responsiveness to infants: A developmental study of psychophysiological and behavioral responses. *Child Development*, 1978, *49*(4), 1181–1188.

Frodi, A. M., Lamb, M. E., Leavitt, L. A., & Donovan, W. L. Fathers' and mothers' responses to infant smiles and cries. *Infant Behavior and Development*, 1978, *1*, 187–198.

Gagné, R. Contributions of learning to human development. *Psychological Review*, 1968, *75*, 177–191.

Gagnon, J. H. Sex research and social change. Archives of Sexual Behavior, 1975, *4*(2), 111–141.

Galper, A., Jantz, R. K., Seefeldt, C., & Serock, K. The child's concept of age and aging. *International Journal of Aging and Human Development*, 1980–81, *12*(2), 149–157.

Garbarino, J., & Bronfenbrenner, U. The socialization of moral judgment and behavior in cross-cultural perspective. In T. Lickona (Ed.), *Moral development and behavior: Theory, research, and social issues.* New York: Holt, Rinehart & Winston, 1976, pp. 70–83.

Gardner, W. L. *Psychology—A story of a search.* Monterey, Calif.: Brooks/Cole, 1974.

Garfield, C. A. Psychothanatological concomitants of altered state experience: An investigation of the relationship between consciousness alteration and fear of death. Unpublished doctoral dissertation, University of California, Berkeley.

Gaylin, J. Don't blame the divorce rate on working wives. *Psychology Today*, 1976, *16*(2), 18.

Gaylin, J. More men than women still turn on to nudes. *Psychology Today*, 1976, *10*(3), 19. (a)

Gaylin, J. Someone to care for in your vintage years. *Psychology Today*, 1976, *10*(6), 44–45. (b)

Gaylin, J. The age of first menstruation is stabilizing. *Psychology Today*, 1976, *10*(2), 20. (c)

Gelles, R. J. Demythologizing child abuse. *Family Coordinator*, 1976, *25*(2), 135–141.

Gelles, R. J. Violence toward children in the United States. *American Journal of Orthopsychiatry*, 1978, *48*(4), 588.

George, V. & Wilding, P. *Motherless families.* London: Routledge & Kegan Paul, 1972.

Getting young people to learn about "real life." *U. S. News & World Report*, September 6, 1976, pp. 52–53.

Gettleman, S., & Markowitz, J. *The courage to divorce.* Ballantine, 1976.

Getzels, J. W. Images of the classroom and visions of the learner. *School Review*, 1974, *82*(4), 527–540.

Gil, D. G. *Violence against children.* Cambridge, 1970.

Gilbert, J. G. Thirty-five-year follow-up study of intellectual functioning. *Journal of Gerontology*, 1973, *28*, 68–72.

Gillespie, D. Who has the power? The marital struggle. *Journal of Marriage and the Family*, 1971, *33*, 445–458.

Gillis, J. R. *Youth and history.* New York: Academic Press, 1974.

Gintis, H. Alienation in capitalist society. In M. R. Edwards & T. Weisskopf (Eds.), *The capitalist system.* New York: Prentice-Hall, 1972.

Glaser, B. G., & Strauss, A. L. *Time for dying.* Chicago: Aldine, 1968.

Glass, D. C., Neulinger, J., & Brim, O. G. Birth order, verbal intelligence, and educational aspiration. *Child Development*, 1974, *45*, 807–811.

Glenn, N. D. The contribution of marriage to the psychological well-being of males and females. *Journal of Marriage and the Family*, 1975, *37*(3), 594–601.

Glenn, N. D., & Weaver, C. N. The contribution of marital happiness to global happiness. *Journal of Marriage and the Family*, 1981, *43*(1), 161–168.

Glick, P. C. A demographic look at American families. *Journal of Marriage and the Family*, 1975, *37*, 15–26.

Glick, P. C. Updating the life cycle of the family. *Journal of Marriage and the Family*, 1977, *39*(1), 5–13.

Goertzel, V., & Goertzel, M. *Cradles of balance.* Boston: Little, Brown, 1972.

Gold, D., & Andres, D. Developmental comparisons between ten-year-old children with employed and nonemployed mothers. *Child Development*, 1978, *49*(1), 75–84.

Goldberg, S. Social competence in infancy: A model of parent-infant interaction. *Merrill-Palmer Quarterly*, 1977, *23*(3), 163–177.

Goldberg, S. R., & Deutsch, F. *Life-span individual and family development.* Monterey, Calif.: Brooks/Cole, 1977.

Goldfarb, A., Shahinian, S. P., & Burr, H. T. Death rate of relocated nursing home residents. In D. P. Kent, R. Kastenbaum, & S. Sherwood (Eds.), *Research planning and action for the elderly.* New York: Behavioral Publications, 1972.

Goldman, J. A., Cooper, P. E., Ahern, K., & Corsini, D. Continuities and discontinuities in the friendship descriptions of women at six stages in the life cycle. *Genetic Psychology Monographs*, 1981, *103*, 153–175.

Goldsmith, H. H., & Gottesman, I. I. Origins of variation in behavioral style: A longitudinal study of temperament in young twins. *Child Development*, 1981, *52*, 91–103.

Goleman, D. Meditation helps break the stress spiral. *Psychology Today*, 1976, 82–86; 93.

Goleman, D. Back from the brink. *Psychology Today*, 1977, *10*(11), 56–59.

Golub, S. The magnitude of premenstrual anxiety and depression. *Psychosomatic Medicine*, 1976, *38*(1), 4–12.

Goodman, N., & Andrews, J. Cognitive development of children in family and group day care. *American Journal of Orthopsychiatry*, 1981, *51*(2), 271–284.

Goodman, N., & Feldman, K. A. Expectations, ideals, and reality: Youth enters college. In S. E. Dragastin & G. H. Elder, Jr. (Eds.), *Adolescence in the life cycle.* Washington, D. C.: Hemisphere Publishing, 1975, pp. 148–179.

Gordon, C. Role and value development across the life cycle. In J. W. Jackson (Ed.), *Role: Sociological studies 4.* London: Cambridge University Press, 1971.

Gordon, I. J., Beller, E. K., Lally, J. R., Moreno, R., Rand, C., & Freiberg, K. *Studies in social and emotional development in infancy: A collaborative study* (Office of Child Development Report No. CB-268). Washington, D. C.: U.S. Government Printing Office, 1973.

Gordon, M. Was Waller ever right? The rating and dating complex reconsidered. *Journal of Marriage and the Family*, 1981, *43*(1), 67–76.

Gottman, J. M. Toward a definition of social isolation in children. *Child Development*, 1977, *48*, 513–517.

Gould, R. Adult life stages: Growth toward self-tolerance. *Psychology Today*, 1975, *8*(9), 74–78.

Granich, M. Factors affecting aging: Pharmacologic agents. In P. S. Timiras (Ed.), *Developmental physiology and aging*. New York: Macmillan, 1972, pp. 607–614.

Granich, S., & Patterson, R. D. Human aging 2: An eleven-year biomedical and behavioral study. Washington, D.C.: U.S. Government Printing Office, 1971.

Green, R. F. Age-intelligence relationship between ages sixteen and sixty-four. A rising trend. *Developmental Psychology*, 1969, *1*, 618–627.

Green, R. Sexual identity: Research strategies. *Archives of Sexual Behavior*, 1975, *4*(4), 337–352.

Greenbaum, W. America in search of a new ideal: An essay on the rise of pluralism. *Harvard Educational Review*, 1974, *44*(3), 411–440.

Greenberg, M., & Morris, N. Engrossment: The newborn's impact upon the father. *American Journal of Orthopsychiatry*, 1974, *44*, 520–531.

Greenblatt, R. B. Aging through the ages. *Geriatrics*, June 1977, pp. 101–102.

Greenwald, M., & Danziger, C. Transadulthood: An emerging style of life. Unpublished manuscript, 1975.

Gregg, G. Breaking up: Men suffer more than women. *Psychology Today*, 1976, *10*(16), 45; 114; 116. (a)

Gregg, G. Remarriage: Children and money are the real problems. *Psychology Today*, 1976, *10*(6), 26–28. (b)

Gubrium, J. F. Toward a socio-environmental theory of aging. *Gerontologist*, 1972, *12*(3), Part 1, 281–284.

Guemple, D. L. Human resource management: The dilemma of the aging. *Eskimo Sociological Symposium*, 1969, (2), 59–74.

Gunter, B. G., & Moore, H. A. Youth, leisure, and post-industrial society: Implications for the family. *Family Coordinator*, 1975, *24*(2), 199–207.

Gruzalski, B. Killing by letting die. *Mind*, 1981, XC, 91–98.

Gunzberger, D. W., Wegner, D. M., & Anooshian. Moral development and distributive justice. *Human Development*, 1977, *20*, 160–170.

Gutmann, D. L. .The new mythologies and premature aging in the youth culture. *Journal of Youth and Adolescence*, 1973, *2*(2), 139–155.

Gutmann, D. L. Alternatives to disengagement: The old men of the Highland Druze. In R. A. LeVine (Ed.), *Culture and personality: Contemporary readings*. Chicago: Aldine, 1974, pp. 232–245.

Haan, N., & Day, D. A longitudinal study of change and sameness in personality development: Adolescence to later adulthood. *International Journal of Aging and Human Development*, 1974, *5*(1), 11–39.

Haan, N., Langer, J., & Kohlberg, L. Family patterns of moral reasoning. *Child Development*, 1976, *47*(4), 1204–1206.

Hacker, H. M. Blabbermouths and clams: Sex differences in self-disclosure in same-sex and cross-sex friendship dyads. *Psychology of Women Quarterly*, 1981, *5*(3), 385–301.

Hagen, R. L., & Kahn, A. Discrimination against competent women. *Journal of Applied Social Psychology*, 1975, *5*(4), 362–376.

Hall, D. Pressures from work, self, and home in the life-styles of married women. *Journal of Vocational Behavior*, 1975, *6*, 121–132.

Hall, E., with Cameron, P. Our failing reverence for life. *Psychology Today*, 1976, *9*(11), 104–108; 113.

Hansen, S. L. Dating choices of high school students. *Family Coordinator*, 1977, *26*, 135.

Hansson, R. O., O'Connor, M. E., Jones, W. H., & Blocker, T. J. Maternal employment and adolescent sexual behavior. *Journal of Youth and Adolescence*, 1981, *10*(1), 55–60.

Hardy, J. B., Welcher, D. W., Mellits, E. D., & Kagan, J. Pitfalls in the measurement of intelligence. Are standard intelligence tests valid instruments for measuring the intellectual potential of urban children? *Journal of Psychology*, 1976, *94*(1), 43–51.

Hareven, T. K. The last stage: Historical adulthood and old age. *Daedalus*, 1976, *104*(4), 13–38.

Hareven, T. K. Family time and historical time. *Daedalus*, 1977, 57–70.

Harris, L., & Associates. *The myth and reality of aging in America.* Washington, D. C.: National Council on the Aging, 1975.

Harvard Study Group. Guidelines for successful child rearing. *Today's Health*, February 1974, pp. 52; 61.

Hauser, S. T. Self-image complexity and identity formation in adolescence: Longitudinal studies. *Journal of Youth and Adolescence*, 1976, *5*(2), 161–177.

Havighurst, R. J. *Human development.* New York: David McKay, 1953.

Havighurst, R. J. Successful aging. In R. J. Williams, C. Tibbitts, & W. Donahue (Eds.), *Processes of aging.* New York: Atherton Press, 1963, pp. 299–320.

Havighurst, R. J. *Developmental tasks and education.* New York: David McKay, 1972.

Havighurst, R. J. A cross-cultural view of adolescence. In J. F. Adams (Ed.), *Understanding adolescence* (2nd ed.). Boston: Allyn & Bacon, 1973. (a)

Havighurst, R. J. History of developmental psychology: Socialization and personality development through the life span. In P. B. Baltes & K. W. Schaie (Eds.), *Lifespan developmental psychology: Personality and socialization.* New York: Academic Press, 1973. (b)

Havighurst, R. J. Objectives for youth development. In *74th yearbook of National Society for the Study of Education* (Part 1). Chicago: University of Chicago Press, 1975, pp. 87–89.

Hayes, D. S. Cognitive bases for liking and disliking among preschool children. *Child Development*, 1978, *49*(3), 906–909.

Hedges, J. N., & Barnett, J. K. Working women and the division of household tasks. *Monthly Labor Review*, 1972, *95*, 9–14.

Heise, D. R., & Roberts, E. P. M. The development of role knowledge. *Genetic Psychology Monographs*, 1970, *82*(first half), 83–115.

Hendin, H. The new anomie. *Change*, 1975, *7*(9), 24–29.

Hendricks, J., & Hendricks, C. D. *Aging in mass society: Myths and realities.* Cambridge, Mass.: Winthrop, 1977.

Henig, R. M. The perils of painless childbirth. *Human Behavior*, 1978, *7*(10), 50–51.

Herreta, G. Effects of nutritional supplementation and early education on physical and cognitive development. Paper presented at the West Virginia Conference on Life-Span Developmental Psychology: Intervention. Morgantown, June 1978.

Hess, B. Friendship. In Riley, M. W. Johnson, & A. Foner (Eds.), *Aging and Society* (Vol. 3). New York: Russell Sage Foundation, 1972.

Hetherington, E. M., Cox, M., & Cox, R. Divorced fathers. *Psychology Today*, 1977, *10*(11), 42–46.

Hetherington, E. M., & McIntyre, C. W. Developmental psychology. *Annual Review of Psychology*, 1975, *26*, 97–136.

Hill, C. T., Peplau, L. A., & Rubin, Z. Differing perceptions in dating couples: Sex roles vs. alternative explanations. *Psychology of Women Quarterly*, 1981, *5*(3), 418–434.

Hill, O. W. Childhood bereavement and adult psychiatric disturbances. *Journal of Psychiatric Research*, 1972, *16*, 357–360.

Hochschild, A. R. *The unexpected community.* Englewood Cliffs, N.J.: Prentice-Hall, 1973.

Hoffman, L. W. The employment of women, education and fertility. *Merrill-Palmer Quarterly*, 1974, *20*(2), 99–119.

Hoffman, L. W. Changes in family roles, socialization and sex differences. *American Psychologist*, 1977, *32*(8), 644–657.

Holcomb, W. L. Spiritual crises among the aging. In M. G. Spencer & C. J. Dorr (Eds.), *Understanding aging: A multidisciplinary approach*. New York: Appleton-Century-Crofts, 1975, pp. 222–234.

Holden, C. TV violence: Government study yields more evidence, no verdict. *Science*, 1972, *175*(4022), 608–611.

Holmstrom, L. L. *The two career family*. Cambridge: Schenckman, 1972.

Holmstrom, R. ["Superhealthy" students: On the picture of mental health: 3. The minority of the "superhealthy."] *Psychiatria Fennica*, 1974, 221–230.

Horn, J. When genetic counseling backfires. *Psychology Today*, 1975, *9*(4), 20; 80.

Horn, J. Human abilities: A review of research and theory in the early 1970s. *Annual Review of Psychology*, 1976, *27*, 437–485. (a)

Horn, J. An infant eye view of the world. *Psychology Today*, 1976, *10*(6), 30–32. (b)

Horn, J. Physical fitness, 10 years later. *Psychology Today*, 1976, *10*(2), 26; 30. (c)

Horn, J. A steady diet of commercials, spiced with a dash of violence. *Psychology Today*, 1976, *10*(1), 16. (d)

Horn, J. Easing a baby's way into the world. *Psychology Today*, 1977, *10*(10), 34. (a)

Horn, J. The life-giving properties of marriage. *Psychology Today*, 1977, *10*(8), 20; 22. (b)

Horn, J. Are male infants more active than females at birth? *Psychology Today*, 1978, *12*(4), 26–28.

Horn, P. A new teenage course: Learning to be parents. 1975, *8*(10), 79–80.

Horn, P. Our wayward youth—drinking, drugs and smoking are on the increase. *Psychology Today*, 1976, *9*(12), 32–34. (a)

Horn, P. The new middle-class fundamentalism. *Psychology Today*, 1976, *10*(4), 24–25. (b)

Horner, M. Toward an understanding of achievement-oriented conflicts in women. *Journal of Social Issues*, 1972, *28*, 157–176.

Hornung, C. A., & McCullough, B. C. Status relationships in dual-employment marriages: Consequences for psychological well-being. *Journal of Marriage and the Family*, 1981, *43*(1), 125–141.

Howell, F. M. Residential preferences and life plans. *Youth and Society*, 1981, *12*(3), 351–378.

How's your sex life? *Newsweek*, September 1, 1975, p. 57.

Hunt, J. McV. Psychological development: Early experience. In M. R. Rosenzweig & L. W. Porter (Eds.), *Annual Review of Psychology*, 1979, *30*, 103–144.

Hunt, J. V., & Eichorn, D. H. Maternal and child behaviors: A review of data from the Berkeley growth study. *Seminars in Psychiatry*, 1972, *4*(4), 367–381.

Hunt, M. Sexual behavior in the 1970s. *Playboy*, 1973, *20*(10), 84–88.

Illich, I., with Keen, S. Medicine is a major threat to health. *Psychology Today*, 1976, *9*(12), 66–77.

In your cups? Okay, if it's coffee. *Duke Alumni Register*, 1977, *63*(7), 7.

Inhelder, B., & Piaget, J. [The growth of logical thinking from childhood to adolescence.] (A. Parsons & S. Seagrin, trans.). New York: Basic Books, 1958.

IQ irrationality. *Human Behavior*, 1979, *8*(1), 49.

Irving, H. W. Social networks in the modern city. *Social Forces*, 1977, *55*(4), 867–880.

Itzin, F. Social relations. In A. M. Hoffman (Ed.), *The daily needs and interests of older people*. Springfield, Ill.: C. C. Thomas, 1970.

Jacklin, C. N., & Maccoby, E. E. Social behavior at thirty-three months in same-sex and mixed-sex dyads. *Child Development*, 1978, *49*(3), 557–569.

Jacob, P. E. Does higher education influence student values? *National Education Association Journal*, 1958.

Jacobs, J. *Fun City: An ethnographic study of a retirement community.* New York: Holt, Rinehart & Winston, 1974.

Jalali, B., Jalali, M., Crocetti, G., & Turner, F. Adolescents and drug use: Toward a more comprehensive approach. *American Journal of Orthopsychiatry*, 1981, 51(1), 120–130.

James, W. Marital coital rates, spouses' ages, family size and social class. *Journal of Sex Research*, 1974, 10, 205–218.

James. W. *The principles of psychology* (Vol. 1). New York: Holt, 1890.

Jaquish, G. A., & Ripple, R. E. Cognitive creative abilities and self-esteem across the adult life-span. *Human Development*, 1981, 24, 110–119.

Jennings, F. G. Adolescents, aspirations, and the older generation. *Teachers College Record*, 1964, 65(4), 335–341.

Jensen, R. E., & Moore, S. G. The effect of attribute statements on cooperativeness and competitiveness in school-age boys. *Child Development*, 1977, 48(1), 305–307.

Jersild, A. T., Telford, C. W., & Sawrey, J. M. *Child psychology.* Englewood Cliffs, N.J.: Prentice-Hall, 1975.

Johnson, M. M. Fathers, mothers and sex typing. *Sociological Inquiry*, 1975, 45(1), 15–26.

Jones, M. C., Bayley, N., MacFarland, J. W., & Honzik, M. R. *The course of human development: Selected papers from the Berkeley longitudinal studies.* Waltham, Mass: Xerox College Publishing, 1971.

Jones, P. A., & McMillan, W. B. Speech characteristics as a function of social class and situational factors. *Child Development*, 1973, 44, 117–121.

Jordan, T. E., & Spaner, S. D. Biological and ecological influences on development at 24 and 36 months of age. *Child Development*, 1972, 43, 908–920.

Jordan, W. D. Searching for adulthood in America. *Daedalus*, 1976, 105(4), 1–11.

Josselson, R., Greenberger, E., & McConochie, D. Phenomenological aspects of psychosocial maturity in adolescence (Part 1). *Journal of Youth and Adolescence*, 1977, 6(1), 25–55.

Jung, C. G. *Modern man in search of a soul.* New York: Harcourt, Brace, 1933.

Jung, C. G. *The stages of life. The structure and dynamics of the psyche.* New York: Pantheon, 1960. (a)

Jung, C. G. The stages in life. In *Collected Works of C. G. Jung* (Vol. 8). New York: 1960. (b)

Jung, C. G. The portable Jung (J. Campbell, Ed., & R. F. C. Hull, trans.) New York: Viking, 1971.

Kagan, J. The emergence of sex differences. *School Review*, 1972, 80(2), 217–227.

Kagan, J. Kagan counters Freud, Piaget theories on early childhood education effects. *APA Monitor*, 1973, 4(2), 1–7.

Kagan, J. Emergent themes in human development. *American Scientist*, 1976, 64(2), 186–196.

Kagan, J. The child in the family. *Daedalus*, 1977, 33–56.

Kagan, J. The baby's elastic mind. *Human Nature*, 1978, 1(1), 66–73. (a)

Kagan, J. The parental love trap. *Psychology Today*, 1978, 12(3), 54–61; 91. (b)

Kagan, J., Kearsley, R. B., & Zelazo, P. R. The emergence of initial apprehension to unfamiliar peers. In M. A. Lewis & L. A. Rosenblum (Eds.), *Friendship and peer relations.* New York: Wiley, 1975, 187–206.

Kagan, J., Kearsley, R. B., Zelazo, P. R., & Minton, C. *The course of early development.* Unpublished manuscript, 1976.

Kagan, J., Lapidus, D. R., & Moore, M. Infant antecedents of cognitive functioning: A longitudinal study. *Child Development*, 1978, 49(4), 1005–1023.

Kahn, R. L. Excess disabilities in the aged. In S. H. Zarit, (Ed.), *Readings in aging and death: Contemporary perspectives.* New York: Harper & Row, 1977, pp. 228–229.

Kalish, R. A. *Late adulthood: Perspectives on human development.* Monterey, Calif.: Brooks/Cole, 1975.

Kalish, R. A. Death and dying in a social context. In R. H. Binstock & E. Shanas (Eds.), *Handbook of aging and the social sciences.* New York: Van Nostrand Reinhold, 1976, pp. 483–507.

Kalish, R. A., & Reynolds, A. D. *Death and bereavement in a cross-ethnic context.* Unpublished manuscript, 1973.

Kalish, R. A., & Reynolds, D. K. *Death and ethnicity: A psychocultural study.* Los Angeles: University of Southern California Press, 1976.

Kalter, N., & Rembar, J. The significance of a child's age at the time of parental divorce. *American Journal of Orthopsychiatry,* 1981, *51*(1), 85–100.

Kandel, D. Inter- and intra-generational influences on adolescent marijuana. *Journal of Social Issues,* 1974, *31*(2), 54–64.

Kangas, J., & Bradway, K. Intelligence at middle age: A thirty-eight year follow-up. *Developmental Psychology,* 1971, *5,* 333–337.

Kanter, R. M., Jaffe, D., & Weisberg, D. K. Coupling, parenting, and the presence of others: Intimate relationships in communal households. *Family Coordinator,* 1975, 24(4), 433–452.

Kaplan, H. *The new sex therapy.* New York: Quadrangle, 1974.

Kass, L. R. Death as an event: A commentary on Robert Morison. *Science,* 1971, *173,* 698–702.

Kastenbaum, R., Derbin, V., Sabatini, P., & Artt, S. The ages of me: Toward personal and interpersonal definitions of functional aging. *Aging and Human Development,* 1972, *3*(2), 197–211.

Katchadourian, H. Medical perspectives on adulthood. *Daedalus,* 1976, *105*(2), 29–56.

Kauffman, J. M. Nineteenth century views of children's behavior disorders: Historical contributions and continuing issues. *Journal of Special Education,* 1976, *10*(4), 335–349.

Kay, H. H. *Sex-based discrimination in family law.* St. Paul, Minn.: West Publishing, 1974.

Kearsley, R. B. Cognitive assessment of the handicapped infant: The need for an alternative approach. *American Journal of Orthopsychiatry,* 1981, *51*(1), 43–54.

Kendler, H. S., & Kendler, T. S. Vertical and horizontal processes in problem-solving. *Psychological Review,* 1962, *49,* 1–16.

Kellogg, M. A., & Jaffe, A. Old folks commune. In S. H. Zarit (Ed.), *Readings in aging and death: Contemporary perspectives.* New York: Harper & Row, 1977, p. 247.

Kelly, J., Snowden, L. R., & Munoz, R. F. Social and community interventions. *Annual Review of Psychology,* 1977, (28), 323–361.

Kelly, J. R. Work and leisure: A simplified paradigm. *Journal of Leisure Research,* 1972, *4,* 50.

Kelly, J. R. Life styles and leisure choices. *Family Coordinator,* 1975, *24,* 185–190.

Keniston, K. Prologue: Youth as a stage of life. In *74th yearbook of National Society for the Study of Education* (Part 1). Chicago: University of Chicago Press, 1975, pp. 3–26.

Keniston, K. Meeting children's needs. *The Crisis,* 1979, *86*(1), 13–16.

Keniston, K., & the Carnegie Council on Children. *All our children: The American family under pressure.* New York: Harcourt Brace Jovanovich, 1977.

Kenshalo, D. R. Age changes in touch, vibration, temperature, kinesthesis and pain sensitivity. In J. E. Birren & K. W. Schaie (Eds.), *Handbook of the psychology of aging.* New York: Van Nostrand Reinhold, 1977, 562–579.

Kerckhoff, R. K. Marriage and middle age. *Family Coordinator,* 1976, *25*(1), 5–11.

Kids today are pretty levelheaded. On TV . . . sex . . . drugs . . . family. *U.S. News & World Report,* September 6, 1976, pp. 48–49.

Kieffer, C. *Consensual cohabitation: A descriptive study of the relationships and sociocultural characteristics of eighty couples in settings of two Florida universities.* Unpublished master's thesis, Florida State University, 1972.

Kilbride, H. W., Johnson, D. L., & Strissguth, A. P. Social class, birth order, and newborn experience. *Child Development,* 1977, *48*(4), 1686–1688.

Kimmel, D. C. *Adulthood and aging.* New York: Wiley, 1974.

Kimsey, L. R., Roberts, J. L., & Logan, D. L. Death, dying and denial in the aged. *American Journal of Psychiatry,* 1972, *129,* 161–166.

King, D. Unpublished manuscript. Oswego, N.Y.: SUNY.

King, S. H. Coping and growth in adolescence. *Seminars in Psychiatry,* 1972, 4(4), 355–366.

Kinsey, A. E., Pomeroy, W. B., Martin, C. E., & Gebhard, P. H. *Sexual behavior in the human male.* Philadelphia: Saunders, 1948.

Kinsey, A. E., Pomeroy, W. B., Martin, C. E., & Gebhard, P. H. *Sexual behavior in the human female.* Philadelphia: Saunders, 1953.

Klaus, M. H., Jerauld, R., Kreger, N., et al. Maternal attachment. *New England Journal of Medicine,* 1972, 286–289; 460–463.

Knox, D., & Wilson, K. Dating behaviors of university students. *Family Relations,* 1981, *30*(2), 255–258.

Knudtson, F. W. Life-span attachment: Complexities, questions, considerations. *Human Development,* 1976, *19,* 182–196.

Kobrin, F. E. The primary individual and the family: Changes in living arrangements in the United States since 1940. *Journal of Marriage and the Family,* 1976, *38*(2), 233–239.

Kohlberg, L. Stage and sequence: The cognitive-developmental approach to socialization. In D. A. Goslin (Ed.), *Theory and Research.* Chicago: Rand McNally, 1969.

Kohlberg, L. Continuities in childhood and adult moral development revisited. In P. B. Baltes & K. W. Schaie (Eds.), *Life-span developmental psychology: Personality and socialization.* New York: Academic Press, 1973.

Kohlberg, L. The implications of moral stages for adult education. *Religious Education,* 1977, *72*(2), 182–201.

Kohlberg, L., & Kramer, R. B. Continuities and discontinuities in childhood and adult moral development. *Human Development,* 1969, *12,* 93–120.

Komarovsky, M. *Dilemmas of masculinity: A study of college youth.* New York: Norton, 1976.

Korner, A. F. Individual differences at birth: Implications for early experience and later development. *American Journal of Orthopsychiatry,* 1971, *41*(4), 608–619.

Kosberg, J. I. Differences in proprietary institutions caring for affluent and nonaffluent elderly. *Gerontologist,* 1973, *13*(3), Part 1, 299–304.

Krech, D., Crutchfield, R. S., & Livson, N. *Elements of psychology* (3rd ed.). New York: Knopf, 1974.

Kriesberg, L. *Mothers in poverty.* Chicago: Aldine, 1970.

Kübler-Ross, E. *On death and dying.* New York: Macmillan, 1969.

Kübler-Ross, E. *Questions and answers on death and dying.* New York: Macmillan, 1974.

Kuhn, D., Nash, S. C., & Brucken, L. Sex role concepts of two- and three-year-olds. *Child Development,* 1978, *49*(2), 445–451.

Labouvie-Vief, G. Toward optimizing cognitive competence in later life. *Educational Gerontology,* 1976, *1*(1), 75–92.

LaDriere, L., Odell, R. E., & Pesys, E. Marijuana: Its meaning to a high school population. *Journal of Psychology,* 1975, *91,* 297–307.

LaDriere, M. L., & Szczepkowski, T. Marijuana: Its meaning to a college population. *Journal of Psychology,* 1972, *81,* 173–180.

Laing, F. C. Ultrasound. *Human Behavior,* 1978, *1*(3), 50–56.

Lakoff, S. A. The future of social intervention. In R. H. Binstock & E. Shanas (Eds.),

Handbook of aging and the social sciences. New York: Van Nostrand Reinhold, 1976, pp. 643–663.

Lamb, M. E. Father-infant and mother-infant interaction in the first year of life. *Child Development*, 1977, *48*(1), 167–181.

Lamb, M. E. Interactions between eighteen-month-olds and their preschool-aged siblings. *Child Development*, 1978, *49*(1), 51–59.

Lance, W. D. Who are all the children? *Exceptional Children*, 1976, *43*(2), 66–76.

Landy, D., & Sigall, H. Beauty is talent: Task evaluation as a function of the performer's physical attractiveness. *Journal of Personality and Social Psychology*, 1974, *29*, 299–304.

Lapidus, D. *A longitudinal study of development.* Unpublished doctoral dissertation, Harvard University, 1976.

Larossa, R., Bennett, L. A., & Gelles, R. J. Ethical dilemmas in qualitative family research. *Journal of Marriage and the Family*, 1981, *43*(2), 303–313.

Laudicina, E. V. Toward new forms of liberation: A mildly utopian proposal. *Social Theory and Practice*, 1973, *2*(3), 275–288.

Lawton, M. P. The impact of the environment on aging and behavior. In J. E. Birren & K. W. Schaie (Eds.), *Handbook of the psychology of aging.* New York: Van Nostrand Reinhold, 1977, p. 282.

Lawton, M. M., & Gottesman, L. E. Psychological services to the elderly. *American Psychologist*, 1974, *29*(9), 689–693.

Lazarus, R. S. *The riddle of man.* Englewood Cliffs, N.J.: Prentice-Hall, 1974.

Leaf, A. Every day is a gift when you are over 100. *National Geographic*, 1973, *143*(1), 93–118.

Lear, J. Working wives busiest. *Seattle Post-Intelligencer*, November 12, 1973.

Lee, P. C., & Gropper, N. B. Sex-role culture and education practice. *Harvard Education Review*, 1974, *44*(2), 213–245.

Lee, R. B., & DeVore, I. (Eds.), *Kalahari hunter-gatherers.* Cambridge, Mass.: Schenkman, 1976.

Lehr, U., & Rudinger, G. Consistency and change of social participation in old age. *Human Development*, 1969, *12*, 255.

Leithwood, K. A., & Fowler, W. Complex motor learning in four-year-olds. *Child Development*, 1971, *42*, 781–792.

LeMasters, E. E. Parenthood as crisis. *Marriage and Family Living*, 1957, *19*, 352–355.

Lenneberg, E. H. The natural history of language. In T. Smith & G. H. Miller (Eds.), *The Genesis of Language: A Psycholinguistic Approach.* Cambridge, Mass: MIT Press, 1966.

Lerner, R. M., Karson, M., Meisels, M., & Knapp, J. R. Actual and perceived attitudes of late adolescents and their parents: The phenomenon of the generation gaps. *Journal of Genetic Psychology*, 1975, *126*, 195–207.

Lesser, G. S. Stop picking on big bird. *Psychology Today*, 1979, *12*(10), 57; 60.

Levine, A., & Crumrine, J. Women and the fear of success: A problem in replication. *American Journal of Sociology*, 1975, *80*(4), 964–974.

Levinson, D. J. *The psychological development of men in early adulthood and the mid-life transition.* Minneapolis: University of Minnesota Press, 1974.

Levinson, D. J. The mid-life transition. *Psychiatry*, 1977, *40*, 96–112.

Levy, S. M. The adjustment of the older woman: Effects of chronic ill health and attitudes toward retirement. *International Journal of Aging and Human Development*, 1980–81, *12*(2), 93.

Lewis, M. The busy, purposeful world of a baby. *Psychology Today*, 1977, *10*(9), 53–56.

Lewis, R. A. Social influences on marital choice. In S. E. Dragastin & G. H. Elder, Jr. (Eds.), *Adolescence in the life cycle.* Washington, D.C.: Hemisphere Publishing, 1975, pp. 211–226.

Lickona, T. Research on Piaget's theory of moral development. In T. Lickona (Ed.), *Moral development and behavior: Theory, research, and social issues.* New York: Holt, Rinehart & Winston, 1976, pp. 219–240.

Lieberman, M. A. Adaptive processes in late life. In N. Datan & L. Ginsberg (Eds.), *Life-span developmental psychology: Normative life crises.* New York: Academic Press, 1975.

Liebert, R. M., & Poulos, R. W. Television as a moral teacher. In T. Lickona (Ed.), *Moral development and behavior: Theory, research, and social issues.* New York: Holt, Rinehart & Winston, 1976, pp. 284–298.

Liebert, R. M., & Schwartzberg, N. S. Effects of mass media. *Annual Review of Psychology,* 1977, *28,* 141–173.

Lifton, R. J. On death and the continuity of life: A psychohistorical perspective. *Omega: Journal of Death and Dying,* 1975, *6*(2), 143–159.

Lipman, A. Role conceptions and morale of couples in retirement. *Journal of Gerontology,* 1961, *16,* 267–271.

Lipman-Blumen, J. How ideology shapes women's lives. *Scientific American,* 1972, *226,* 24–42.

Lipsitt, L. P. Babies: They're a lot smarter than they look. *Psychology Today,* 1971, *5*(7), 70–72; 88–89.

Lipsitt, L. P. The study of sensory and learning processes of the newborn. *Clinics of Perinatology,* 1977, *4,* 163–186.

Little, R. E., Schultz, F. A., & Mandell, W. Drinking during pregnancy. *Journal of Studies on Alcohol,* 1976, *37*(3), 375–379.

Lomax, E. M., Kagan, J., & Rosenkrantz, B. G. *Science and patterns of child care.* San Francisco: W. H. Freeman, 1978.

Londerville, S., & Main, M. Security of attachment, compliance, and maternal training methods in the second year of life. *Developmental Psychology,* 1981, *17*(3), 289–299.

Long, B. H., Henderson, E. H., & Platt, L. Self-other orientations of Israeli adolescents. *Developmental Psychology,* 1973, *8*(2), 300–308.

Longo, L. D. Carbon monoxide: Effects on oxygenation of the fetus in utero. *Science,* 1976, *194,* 523–525.

Lopata, H. Z. Living through widowhood. *Psychology Today,* 1973, *7*(2), 86–92. (a)

Lopata, H. Z. *Widowhood in an American city.* Cambridge: Schenkman, 1973. (b)

Lorber, N. M. Permissive home environment and exploitative, domineering, preadolescent peer behavior. *Psychology,* 1971, *8*(1), 12–15.

Lowenthal, M. F. Some potentialities of a life-cycle approach to the study of retirement. In F. M. Carp (Ed.), *Retirement.* New York: Behavioral Publications, 1972.

Lowenthal, M. F. Psychosocial variations across the adult life course: Frontiers for research and policy. *Gerontologist,* 1975, *15*(1), Part 1, 6–12.

Lowenthal, M. F. Toward a sociopsychological theory of change in adulthood and old age. In J. E. Birren & K. W. Schaie (Eds.), *Handbook of the psychology of aging.* New York: Van Nostrand Reinhold, 1977, 116–127.

Lowenthal, M. F., & Chiriboga, D. Transition to the empty nest. *Archives of General Psychiatry,* January 1972, pp. 8–14.

Lowenthal, M. F., & Robinson, B. Social networks and isolation. In R. H. Binstock & E. Shanas (Eds.), *Handbook of aging and the social sciences.* New York: Van Nostrand Reinhold, 1976, pp. 432–456.

Lowenthal, M. F., Thurnher, M., Chiriboga, D., & Associates. *Four stages of life: A comparative study of women and men facing transitions.* San Francisco: Jossey-Bass, 1975.

Lowy, L. Social welfare and the aging. In M. G. Spencer & C. J. Dorr (Eds.), *Understanding aging: A multidisciplinary approach.* New York: Appleton-Century-Crofts, 1975.

Luckey, E. B. What I have learned about family life. *Family Coordinator,* 1974, 23(3), 307–313.

Lynn, D. B. A note on sex differences in the development of masculine and feminine identification. *Psychological Review,* 1959, *66,* 258–262.

Lyons-Ruth, K. Moral and personal value judgments of preschool children. *Child Development,* 1978, *49*(4), 1197–1207.

Maas, H. S., & Kuypers, J. A. *From thirty to seventy.* San Francisco: Jossey-Bass, 1974.

Macauley, J. Stereotyping child welfare. *Society,* 1977, *14*(2), 49–51.

Maccoby, E. E., & Jacklin, C. N. The psychology of sex differences. Stanford, Calif.: Stanford University Press, 1974.

Macfarlane, A. The psychology of childbirth. Cambridge, Mass.: Harvard University Press, 1977.

Macklin, E. D. Heterosexual cohabitation among unmarried college students. *Family Coordinator,* 1972, *21*(4), 463–472.

Maddox, G. L. Retirement as a social event in the United States. In B. S. Neugarten (Ed.), *Middle age and aging* (2nd impression). Chicago: Chicago University Press, 1970, p. 357.

Maddox, G. L. Social determinants of behavior. In F. Hine, E. Pfeiffer, G. L. Maddox, & P. Hein (Eds.), *Behavioral science: A selective view.* Boston: Little, Brown, 1972.

Maddox, G. L. The patient and his family. In S. Sherwood (Ed.), *The hidden patient: Knowledge and action in long-term care.* New York: Spectrum, 1975.

Mainardi, P. The politics of housework. In J. S. Delora & J. R. Delora (Eds.), *Intimate life styles.* Pacific Palisades, Calif.: Goodyear, 1972.

Manning, P. K. Rural "WASP" youth: Structure and sentiments. In *74th yearbook of National Society for the Study of Education* (Part 1). Chicago: University of Chicago Press, 1975, pp. 306–339.

Marantz, S. A., & Mansfield, A. F. Maternal employment and the development of sex-role stereotyping in five- to eleven-year-old girls. *Child Development,* 1977, *48*(2), 668–673.

Marcia, J. E. Development and validation of ego identity status. *Journal of Personal and Social Psychology,* 1966, *3,* 551–558.

Marcus, D. E., & Overton, W. F. The development of cognitive gender constancy and sex-role preferences. *Child Development,* 1978, *49*(2), 434–444.

Marcus, M. Caressing and cuddling helps a baby grow. *Psychology Today,* 1976, *9*(8), 101.

Margolius, S. Aged parents and dependent kids: The middle-aged dilemma. In S. H. Zarit (Ed.), *Readings in aging and death: Contemporary perspectives.* New York: Harper & Row, 1977, pp. 248–251.

Marini, M. M. Effects of the timing of marriage and first birth on fertility. *Journal of Marriage and the Family,* 1981, *43*(1), 27–48.

Masters, J. C., & Furman, W. Popularity, individual friendship selection, and specific peer interaction among children. *Developmental Psychology,* 1981, *17*(3), 344–350.

Maurer, D. M., & Maurer, C. E. Newborn babies see better than you think. *Psychology Today,* 1976, *10*(5), 85–88.

Maxwell, J. B., & Maxwell, S. E. Individual differences in cognitive abilities. In *Annual Review of Psychology,* 1979, 30, 603–640.

McCall, R. B. Challenges to a science of developmental psychology. *Child Development,* 1977, *48*(2), 333–344.

McCall, R. B. Nature-nurture and the two realms of development: A proposed integration with respect to mental development. *Child Development,* 1981, *52,* 1–12.

McCandless, B. R., & Geiss, M. F. Current trends in developmental psychology, In W. H. Reese (Ed.), *Advances in child development and behavior* (Vol. 10). New York: Academic Press, 1975.

McCiskie, M., & Clarke, A. M. Parent-offspring resemblance in intelligence: Theories and evidence. *British Journal of Psychology*, 1976, *67*(2), 243–273.

McClelland, D. C., Constantian, C. A., Regalado, D., & Stone, C. Making it to maturity. *Psychology Today*, 1978, *12*(1), 42–52; 114.

McDaniels, C. Leisure and career development in mid-life: A rationale. *Vocational Guidance Quarterly*, 1977, *25*(4), 344–350.

McDevitt, S. C., & Carey, W. B. Stability of ratings vs. perceptions of temperament from early infancy to 1-3 years. *American Journal of Orthopsychiatry*, 1981, *51*(2), 342–345.

McGraw, M. B. Later development of children specially trained during infancy: Johnny and Jimmy at school age. *Child Development*, 1939, *10*, 1–19.

McGuinness, D. How schools discriminate against boys. *Human Nature*, 1979, *2*(2), 82–88.

McIntyre, J. P. College students in transition. *Intellect*, 1973, *101*(2348), 385–386.

McKeown, T. Determinants of health. *Human Nature*, 1978, *1*(4), 60–67.

McMahon, C. Celebrating human uniqueness. *Phi Delta Kappan*, 1974, *55*(9), 619–621.

Medawar, P. B. *The future of man.* New York: Basic Books, 1960.

Medley, M. L. Marital adjustment in the post-retirement years. *Family Coordinator*, 1977, *26*(1), 5–11.

Meltzer, H., & Ludwig, D. Age differences in memory, optimism and pessimism in workers. *Journal of Genetic Psychology*, 1967, *110*, 17–30.

Menstrual myths. *Human Behavior*, 1979, *8*(4), 60–61.

Meyersohn, R. Leisure. In A. Campbell & P. E. Converse (Eds.), *The human meaning of social change.* New York: Russell Sage Foundation, 1972, 205–228.

Miles, L. Implications for women and minorities. *Vocational Guidance Quarterly*, 1977, *24*(5), 356–363.

Miller, G. A. *Spontaneous apprentices: Children and language.* Seabury Press, 1977.

Miller, G. A. The acquisition of word meaning. *Child Development*, 1978, *49*(4), 999–1004.

Miller, S. J. The social dilemma of the aging leisure participant. In B. L. Neugarten (Ed.), *Middle age and aging.* Chicago: University of Chicago Press, 1968.

Milliones, J. Relationship between perceived child temperament and maternal behaviors. *Chld Development*, 1978, *49*(4), 1255–1257.

Mischel, W. Towards a cognitive social learning reconceptualization of personality. *Psychological Review*, 1973, *80*, 252–283.

Mitford, J. The funeral transaction. In S. H. Zarit (Ed.), *Readings in aging and death: Contemporary perspectives.* New York: Harper & Row, 1977, pp. 289–294.

Moltz, H., Lubin, M., Leon, M., & Numan, M. Hormonal induction of maternal behavior in the ovariectomized rat. *Psychology and Behavior*, 1970, *5*, 1373–1377.

Mondale, W. F. The next step: Lifelong learning. *Change*, 1976, *8*(9), 42–45.

Money, J. Developmental differentiation of femininity and masculinity compared. In S. M. Farber & R. H. Wilson (Eds.), *Potential of woman.* New York: McGraw-Hill, 1963.

Money, J., & Ehrhardt, A. A. *Man and woman, boy and girl.* Baltimore: Johns Hopkins University Press, 1972.

Monge, R. H. Developmental trends in factors of adolescent self concept. *Developmental Psychology*, 1973, *8*(3), 382–393.

Moody, R. A., Jr. *Life after life.* Atlanta: Mockingbird Books, 1975.

Moody, R. A., Jr. *Reflections on life after life.* New York: Two Continents, 1977.

Moore, D., & Hotch, D. F. Late adolescents' conceptualizations of home-leaving. *Journal of Youth and Adolescence*, 1981, *10*(1), 1–10.

Moos, R. H. Social environments of university student living groups. Architectural and organizational correlates. *Environment and Behavior*, 1978, *10*(1), 109–137.

Morgan, L. A re-examination of widowhood and morale. *Journal of Gerontology*, 1976, *31*(6), 687–695.

Moriya, K. Attitudes toward the future: A comparative study of younger and older samples. *Journal of Child Development*, 1975, (11), 39–44.

Morris, C. G. *Psychology: An introduction* (3rd ed.). Englewood Cliffs, N.J.: Prentice-Hall, 1979.

Mueller, E., & Brenner, J. The origins of social skills and interaction among playground toddlers. *Child Development*, 1977, *48*(3), 854–861.

Murphy, L. B., et al. *The widening world of childhood.* New York: Basic Books, 1962.

Mussen, P. H. *The psychological development of the child.* Englewood Cliffs, N.J.: Prentice-Hall, 1963.

Needed for America: "The kind of recreation that frees the mind." Interview with William Glasser. *U.S. News & World Report*, May 23, 1977, pp. 74–76.

Nelson, K. Individual differences in language development: Implications for development and language. *Developmental Psychology*, 1981, *17*(2), 170–187.

Nelson, L. P., & Nelson, V. *Religion and death anxiety.* Presentation to the annual joint meeting, Society for the Scientific Study of Religion and Religious Research Association, San Francisco, 1973.

Nesselroade, J. R., & Baltes, P. B. Adolescent personality development and historical change: 1970–1972. *Monographs of the Society for Research in Child Development*, 1974, *39* (1, Serial No. 112).

Nesselroade, J. R., Schaie, K. W., & Baltes, P. B. Ontogenetic and generational components of structural and quantitative change in adult cognitive behavior. *Journal of Gerontology*, 1972, *27*, 222–228.

Neugarten, B. L. (Ed.), *Middle age and aging.* Chicago: University of Chicago Press, 1968.

Neugarten, B. L. Lecture delivered at the 24th annual meeting of the Gerontological Society, Houston, October 28, 1971.

Neugarten, B. L. Personality change in late life: A developmental perspective. In C. Eisdorfer & M. P. Lawton (Eds.), *The psychology of adult development of aging.* Washington, D.C.: American Psychological Association, 1973, pp. 311–338.

Neugarten, B. L. Personality and the aging process. In S. H. Zarit (Ed.), *Readings in aging and death: Contemporary perspectives.* New York: Harper & Row, 1977, pp. 72–77, 630.

Neugarten, B. L., & Associates. *Personality in middle and late life.* New York: Atherton Press, 1964.

Neugarten, B. L., & Hagestad, G. O. In R. H. Binstock & E. Shanas (Eds.), *Handbook of aging and the social sciences.* New York: Van Nostrand Reinhold, 1976, pp. 35–55.

Neugarten, B. L., Moore, J. W., & Lowe, J. C. Age norms, age constraints, and adult socialization. *American Journal of Sociology*, 1965, *70*, 710–717.

Neugarten, B. L., & Peterson, W. A. *A study of the American age-grade system.* Proc. Int. Assoc. Gerontology, Fourth Congress, 1957, *3*, 497–502.

A new generation: Where it's heading. *U.S. News & World Report*, September 6, 1976, p. 45.

Newman, O. *Defensible space.* New York: Macmillan, 1972.

Newman, O. Community of interest. *Human Nature*, 1979, *2*(1), 61.

Newson, J. & Newson, E. Cultural aspects of childrearing in the English-speaking world. In M. P. M. Richards (Ed.), *The integration of a child into a social world.* London: Cambridge University Press, 1974, pp. 53–82.

Newton, N., & Modahl, C. Pregnancy: The closest human relationship. *Human Nature*, 1978, *1*(3), 40–49.

Noberini, M., & Neugarten, B. L. *A follow-up study of adaptation in middle-aged women.* Paper presented at the 28th annual meeting of the Gerontological Society, Louisville, Ky., October, 1975.

Norman, M. Substitutes for mother. *Human Behavior*, 1978, *7*(2), 18–22.

Nunnelley, Finkelstein, & Luft. In H. A. DeVries, Physiology of exercise and aging, in S. H. Zarit (Ed.), *Readings in aging and death: contemporary perspectives.* New York: Harper & Row, 1977.

Nydegger, C. N. On being caught up in time. *Human Development,* 1981, *24,* 1–12.

Oden, S., & Asher, S. R. Coaching children in social skills for friendship making. *Child Development,* 1977, *48*(2), 495–506.

Offer, D. Attitudes toward sexuality in a group of 1500 middle-class teenagers. *Journal of Youth and Adolescence,* 1972, *1,* 81–100.

One child, two homes. More divorced parents are agreeing to joint custody. *Time,* January 29, 1979, *113*(5), 61.

Organized Child, The: Hip to hierarchies. *Human Behavior,* 1978, *7*(12), 49.

Orthner, D. K. Leisure activity patterns and marital satisfaction over the marital career. *Journal of Marriage and the Family,* 1975, *37,* 91–102.

Orthner, D. K., Brown, T., & Ferguson, D. Single-parent fatherhood: An emerging family life style. *Family Coordinator,* 1976, *25*(4), 429–437.

Osmond, M. W., & Martin, P. Y. Sex and sexism: A comparison of male and female sex-role attitudes. *Journal of Marriage and the Family,* 1975, *37*(4), 744–758.

Osterfeld, A. M. Frequency and nature of health problems of retired persons. In F. M. Carp (Ed.), *The Retirement Process* (U.S. Public Health Service Publication No. 1778, pp. 83–96). Washington, D.C.: U.S. Department of Health, Education, and Welfare, 1968.

Out-of-step soap operas. *Human Behavior,* 1977, *6*(3), 32.

Overton, W. F., & Reese, H. W. Models of development: Methodological implications. In J. R. Nesselroade & H. W. Reese (Eds.), *Life-span developmental psychology: Methodological issues.* New York: Academic Press, 1973.

Ozmon, K. L. Effects of ECS on imprinting in Japanese quail. *Journal of Comparative and Physiological Psychology,* 1973, *82,* 360–367.

Palmore, E. B. The effects of aging on activities and attitudes. *Gerontologist,* 1968, *8,* 259.

Palmore, E. B. Predicting longevity: A follow-up controlling for age. *Gerontologist,* 1969, *9,* 103–108.

Palmore, E. B. Longevity predictors—implications for practice. *Postgraduate Medicine,* 1971, *50,* 164.

Palmore, E. B. Compulsory versus flexible retirement: Issues and facts. In S. H. Zarit (Ed.), *Readings in aging and death: Contemporary perspectives.* New York: Harper & Row, 1977, pp. 138–143.

Palmore, E. B., & Kivett, V. R. *Change in life satisfaction among the middle-aged.* Paper presented at the 28th annual meeting of the Gerontological Society, Louisville, Ky., October 1975.

Palmore, E. B., & Luikart, C. Health and social factors related to life satisfaction. *Journal of Health and Social Behavior,* 1972, *13,* 68.

Panel on Youth of the President's Science Advisory Committee. *Youth: Transition to Adulthood.* Washington, D.C.: U.S. Government Printing Office, 1973.

Papalia, D. E., & Bielby, D. D. V. Cognitive functioning in middle- and old-age adults. *Human Development,* 1974, *17,* 424–443.

Parke, R. D., & Sawin, D. B. The father's role in infancy: A reevaluation. *Family Coordinator,* 1976, *25*(4), 365–377.

Parkes, C. M. *Bereavement: Studies of grief in adult life.* New York: International Press, 1972.

Parlee, M. B. The sexes under scrutiny: From old biases to new theories. *Psychology Today,* 1978, *12*(6), 62–69.

Passin, H. The single past imperfect. *Single,* August 1973.

Passow, A. H. Once again: Reforming secondary education. *Teachers College Record*, 1975, 77(2), 161–187.

Pastor, D. L. The quality of mother-infant attachment and its relationship to toddlers' initial sociability with peers. *Developmental Psychology*, 1981, 17(3), 326–335.

Pattison, E. M. *The experience of dying*. Englewood Cliffs, N.J.: Prentice-Hall, 1977, pp. 105–110.

Paulson, F. L. Teaching cooperation on television. *A V Communications Research*, 1974, 22, 229–246.

Peatling, J. H. Careers and a sense of justice in mid-life. *Vocational Guidance Quarterly*, 1977, 25(4), 303–308.

Peevers, B. H., & Secord, P. F. Developmental changes in attribution of descriptive concepts of persons. *Journal of Personality and Social Psychology*, 1973, 27, 120–128.

Peppers, L. G. Patterns of leisure and adjustment to retirement. *Gerontologist*, 1976, 16(5), 441–446.

The perfect Mom. *Saturday Review of the Sciences*, 1973, 1(3), 86.

Perkins, S. A. Malnutrition and mental development. *Exceptional Children*, 1977, 43(4), 214–219.

Permissiveness: "A beautiful idea" that didn't work? *U.S. News & World Report*, September 6, 1976, pp. 54–55.

Peskin, H., & Livson, N. Pre- and postpubertal personality and adult psychologic functioning. *Seminars in Psychiatry*, 1972, 4(4), 343–353.

Pfeiffer, E. *Multidimensional quantitative assessment of three populations of elderly*. Paper presented at the annual meeting of the Gerontological Society, Miami Beach, Fla., 1973.

Pfeiffer, E. Sexuality in the aging individual. *Journal of American Geriatrics Society*, 1974, 22(11), 481–484.

Pfeiffer, E. Psychopathology and social pathology. In J. E. Birren & K. W. Schaie (Eds.), *Handbook of the psychology of aging*. New York: Van Nostrand Reinhold, 1977, pp. 650–671.

Pfeiffer, E., & Davis, G. C. The use of leisure time in middle life. *Gerontologist*, 1971, 11, 187.

Pfeiffer, E., & Davis, G. C. Determinants of sexual behavior in middle and old age. *Journal of the American Geriatrics Society*, April 1972, p. 157.

Pfeiffer, E., Verwoerdt, A., & Davis, G. C. Sexual behavior in middle life. *American Journal of Psychiatry*, 1972, 128, 10.

Phillips, D. L. Social class, social participation, and happiness: A consideration of interaction opportunities and investment. *Sociology Quarterly*, 1969, 10, 3–21.

Phillips, D. P., & Feldman, K. A. A dip in deaths before ceremonial occasions: Some new relationships between social integration and mortality. *American Sociological Review*, 1973, 38, 678–696.

Phillips, S., King, S., & DuBois, L. Spontaneous activities of female versus male newborns. *Child Development*, 1978, 49(3), 590–597.

Piaget, J. *Child and reality: Problems of genetic psychology*. New York: Grossman, 1973.

Pines, M. Superkids. *Psychology Today*, 1979, 12(8), 53–61.

Plumb, H. J. The new world of children in eighteenth-century England. *Past and Present*, 1975, 67, 64–95.

Polak, P., & Jones, M. The psychiatric nonhospital: A model for change. *Community Mental Health Journal*, 1973, 9, 123–132.

Popenoe, P. Problems of working mothers. *Family Life*, 1976, 36(2), 1–4.

Portnoy, F. C., & Simmons, C. H. Day care and attachment. *Child Development*, 1978, 49(1), 239–242.

Powers, T. Learning to die. In S. H. Zarit (Ed.), *Readings in aging and death: Contemporary perspectives*. New York: Harper & Row, 1977, pp. 263–270.

Preston, C. E., & Williams, R. H. Views of the aged on the timing of death. *Gerontologist*, 1971, *11*, 300–304.

Preston, J. J. Toward an anthropology of death. *Intellect*, 1977, *105*(2383), 343–344.

Profile of an aging America. *U.S. News & World Report*, August 8, 1977, p. 54.

Proshansky, H. M. Theoretical issues in environmental psychology. *School Review*, 1974, *82*(4), 541–555.

Protection against campus crime. *Intellect*, 1973, *102*(2351), 8–9.

Puglisi, J. T., & Jackson, D. W. Sex role identity and self esteem in adulthood. *International Journal of Aging and Human Development*, 1980–81, *12*(2), 129–138.

Puner, M. Retirement and leisure. In S. H. Zarit (Ed.), *Readings in aging and death: Contemporary perspectives*. New York: Harper & Row, 1977, pp. 135–137.

Quarter, J. Shifting ideologies among youth in Canada. *Youth and Society*, 1974, *5*(4), 448–474.

Rabbitt, P. Changes in problem solving ability in old age. In J. E. Birren & K. W. Schaie (Eds.), *Handbook of the psychology of aging*. New York: Van Nostrand Reinhold, 1977, pp. 606–625.

Radloff, L. *Sex differences in mental health: The effects of marital and occupational status*. Paper presented at the American Public Health Association, October 1974.

Raphael, D. Identity status in urban women. *Journal of Youth and Adolescence*, 1977, *6*(1), 57–62.

Rapoport, R., & Rapoport, R. N. *Leisure and the family life cycle*. London: Routledge & Kegan Paul, 1975.

Recreation for all is latest goal in the cities. *U.S. News & World Report*, May 23, 1977, pp. 72–73.

Reedy, M. N., Birren, J. E., & Schaie, K. W. Age and sex differences in satisfying love relationships across the adult life span. *Human Development*, 1981, *24*, 52–66.

Reichard, S., Livson, F., & Peterson, P. G. *Aging and personality*. New York: Wiley, 1962.

Reiss, I. L. Some observations on ideology and sexuality in America. *Journal of Marriage and the Family*, 1981, *43*(2), 271–283.

Reite, M., Short, R., Seiler, C., & Pauley, J. D. Attachment, loss, and depression. *Journal of Child Psychology and Psychiatry*, 1981, *22*, 141–169.

Renne, K. S. Correlates of dissatisfaction in marriage. *Journal of Marriage and the Family*, 1970, *32*, 54–67.

Renwick, P. A., Lawler, E. E., & *Psychology Today* staff. What you really want from your job. *Psychology Today*, 1978, *11*(12), 56.

Rest, J. Developmental psychology and value education. *Review of Educational Research*, 1974, *44*, 241–259.

Reynolds, D. K., & Kalish, R. A. Anticipation of futurity as a function of ethnicity and age. *Journal of Gerontology*, 1974, *29*, 224–331.

Rheingold, H. K., Hay, D. F., & West, M. J. Sharing in the second year of life. *Child Development*, 1976, *47*(4), 1148–1158.

Riegel, K. F. & Riegel, R. M. Development, drugs, and death. *Developmental Psychology*, 1972, *6*(2), 306–319.

Riesenfeld, M. J., Newcomen, R. J., Berlant, P. V., & Dempsey, W. A. Perceptions of public service needs. The urban elderly and the public agency. *Gerontologist*, 1972, *12*, 185–190.

A right to die? In S. H. Zavit (Ed.), *Readings in aging and death: Contemporary perspectives*. New York: Harper & Row, 1977, pp. 283–288.

Riley, M. W. Age strata in social systems. In R. H. Binstock, & E. Shanas (Eds.), *Handbook of aging and the social sciences*. New York: Van Nostrand Reinhold, 1976, pp. 189–217.

Riley, M. W., & Foner, A. (Eds.), *Aging and society* (Vol. 1). New York: Russell Sage Foundation, 1968.

Rising divorce rate. *Intellect*, 1975, *103*(2366), 488.

Robertson, J. F. Grandmotherhood: A study of role conceptions. *Journal of Marriage and the Family*, 1977, *39*(1), 171.

Robinson, M. *An experiment with strategies of intervention and innovation.* Paper presented for a symposium on Parent Child Development Centers at the 1973 meeting of the Society for Research in Child Development.

Robson, K. S. Development of object relations during the first year in life. *Seminars in Psychiatry*, 1972, *4*(4), 301–316.

Robson, K. S., & Moss, H. A. Patterns and determinants of maternal attachment. *Journal of Pediatrics*, 1970, *77*, 976–985.

Roby, P. *Child care—who cares? Foreign and domestic infant and early childhood development policies.* New York: Basic Books, 1973.

Rodin, J. The puzzle of obesity. *Human Nature*, 1978, *1*(2), 38–49.

Roff, M. Childhood social interactions and young adult bad conduct. *Journal of Abnormal and Social Psychology*, 1961, *63*, 333–337.

Rogers, D. *Child psychology* (2nd. ed.). Monterey, Calif.: Brooks/Cole, 1977. (a)

Rogers, D. *Psychology of adolescence* (3rd. ed.). Englewood Cliffs, N.J.: Prentice-Hall, 1977. (b)

Rogers, D. *Adolescence: A psychological perspective* (2nd. ed.). Monterey, Calif.: Brooks/Cole, 1978.

Rogers, D. *The adult years.* Englewood Cliffs, N.J.: Prentice-Hall, 1979.

Rogers, D. *Controversial topics in life-span developmental psychology.* Monterey, Calif.: Brooks/Cole, 1980.

Rogers, K. Crisis at the midpoint of life. *New Society*, 1974, *29*(619), 413–415.

Rollins, B. C. & Cannon, K. L. Marital satisfaction over the family life cycle: A reevaluation. *Journal of Marriage and the Family*, 1974, *36*(2), 271–282.

Rooney, R. When child adoption doesn't work. *Parade*, March 4, 1979, 23; 26.

Roper, B. S. & Labeff, E. Sex roles and feminism revisited: An intergenerational attitude comparison. *Journal of Marriage and the Family*, 1977, *39*(1), 113–119.

Roper organization poll. Ruder & Finn, 110 E. 59th Street, New York, New York, 1974.

Rosen, J., & Neugarten, B. Ego functions in the middle and later years: A TAT study of normal adults. *Journal of Gerontology*, 1960, *15*, 62–67.

Rosenberg, M. The dissonant context and the adolescent self-concept. In S. E. Dragastin & G. H. Elder, Jr. (Eds.), *Adolescence in the life cycle*. Washington, D.C.: Hemisphere Publishing, 1975, pp. 97–116.

Rosenfeld, A. The new LSD: Life-span development. *Saturday Review*, October 1, 1977, pp. 32–33.

Rosow, I. *Socialization to old age.* Berkeley: University of California Press, 1974.

Ross, H. L., & Sawhill, I. V. *Time of transition: The growth of families headed by women.* Washington, D.C.: Urban Institute, 1975.

Rossi, A. S. A biosocial perspective on parenting. *Daedalus*, 1977, *106*(2), 1–32.

Rothchild, J., & Wolf, S. *The children of the counterculture.* Garden City, N.Y.: Doubleday, 1976.

Rubenstein, J. S., Watson, F. G., & Rubenstein, H. S. An analysis of sex education books for adolescents by means of adolescents' sexual interests. *Adolescence*, 1977, *12*(47), 293–311.

Rubin, L. B. The marriage bed. *Psychology Today*, 1976, *10*(3), 44–50; 91–92.

Rubin, S. A two-track model of bereavement: Theory and application in research. *American Journal of Orthopsychiatry*, 1981, *51*(1), 101–109.

Rubinton, N. New careers for adults. *Vocational Guidance Quarterly*, 1977, *25*(4), 364–368.

Russell, G. The father role and its relation to masculinity, femininity and androgyny. *Child Development*, 1978, *49*(4), 1174–1181.

Rust, M. M. The growth of children's concepts of time, space and magnitude. Unpublished manuscript, Teacher's College, Columbia University.

Rutter, M. Social-emotional consequences of day care for preschool children. *American Journal of Orthopsychiatry*, 1981, *51*(1), 4–28.

Salkind, N. J., Kojima, H., & Zelniker, T. Cognitive tempo in American, Japanese, and Israeli children. *Child Development*, 1978, *49*(4), 1024–1027.

Saltin, B., & Grimby, G. Physiological analysis of middle-aged and old former athletes. *Med. Thorac.*, 1968, *22*, 181–187.

Saltzstein, H. D. Social influence and moral development: A perspective on the role of parents and peers. In T. Lickona (Ed.), *Moral development and behavior: Theory, research, and social issues*. New York: Holt, Rinehart & Winston, 1976, pp. 253–265.

Sameroff, A. J., & Chandler, M. J. Reproductive risk and the contination of caretaking casualty. In F. D. Horowitz, E. M. Hetherington, S. Scarr-Salapatek, & G. M. Siegel (Eds.), *Review of child development research* (Vol. 4). Chicago: University of Chicago Press, 1975.

Sawhill, I. V. Economic perspectives on the family. *Daedalus*, 1977, 115–125.

Scarr, S. From evolution to Larry P., or what shall we do about IQ tests. *Intelligence*, 1978, *2*, 325–342.

Scarr, S., & Weinberg, R. Attitudes, interests and IQ. *Human Nature*, 1978, *1*(4), 29–37. (a)

Scarr, S., & Weinberg, R. A. The influence of "family background" on intellectual attainment. *American Sociological Review*, 1978, *43*, 674–692. (b)

Schaar, K. Mead, Bronfenbrenner critique family research. *APA Monitor*, 1975, *6*(5), 8.

Schafer, R. B., & Keith, P. M. Equity in marital roles across the family life cycle. *Journal of Marriage and the Family*, 1981, *43*(2), 359–367.

Schaie, K. W. Age changes and age differences. *Gerontologist*, 1967, *7*, 128.

Schaie, K. W. Reflections on papers by Looft, Peterson and Sparks: Towards an ageless society? *Gerontologist*, 1973, *13*, 31–35.

Schaie, K. W. Psychological changes from midlife to early old age: Implications for the maintenance of mental health. *American Journal of Orthopsychiatry*, 1981, *51*(2), 199–218.

Schaie, K. W., & Gribbin, K. J. Adult development and aging. *Annual Review of Psychology*, 1975, *26*, 65–96.

Schaie, K. W., & Parham, L. A. Stability of adult personality: Fact or fable? *Journal of Personal & Social Psychology*, 1976, *34*, 146–158.

Schaie, K. W., & Schaie, J. P. Clinical assessment and aging. In J. E. Birren & K. W. Schaie (Eds.), *Handbook of the psychology of aging*. New York: Van Nostrand Reinhold, 1977, pp. 692–723.

Schanche, D. What really happens emotionally and physically when a man reaches 40. *Today's Health*, 1973, *60*, 40–43.

Scheinfeld, A. *Your heredity and environment*. Philadelphia: Lippincott, 1965.

Schlossberg, N. K. Breaking out of the box: Organizational options for adults. *Vocational Guidance Quarterly*, 1977, *25*(4), 313–319.

Schnaiberg, A., & Goldenberg, S. Closing the circle: The impact of children on parental status. *Journal of Marriage and the Family*, 1975, 37(4), 937–953.

Schoenfield, D. Future commitments and successful aging. 1. The random sample. *Journal of Gerontology*, 1973, 28, 189.

Schoenfield, D. Translations in gerontology—From lab to life: Utilizing information. *American Psychologist*, 1974, 29, 796–801.

Schonfeld, W. A. The body and the body-image in adolescents. In G. Caplan & S. Lebovici (Eds.), *Adolescence: Psychosocial perspectives*. New York, Basic Books, 1969.

Schulz, J. H. Income distribution and the aging. In R. H. Binstock & E. Shanas (Eds.), *Handbook of aging and the social sciences*. New York: Van Nostrand Reinhold, 1976, 561–591.

Schwarz, J., Krolick, G., & Strickland, R. Effects of early day experience on adjustment to a new environment. *American Journal of Orthopsychiatry*, 1973, 43, 340–346.

Scully, M. G. The job generation. *Intellectual Digest*, 1974, 4(10), 37.

Sears, R. R. Relation of early socialization experiences to self-concepts and gender role in middle childhood. *Child Development*, 1970, 41(2), 167–189.

Sears, R. R., Maccoby, E., & Levin, H. *Patterns of childrearing*. Cambridge, Mass.: Harvard University Press, 1957.

Segal, J., & Yahres, H. Bringing up mother. *Psychology Today*, November, 1978, 90–96.

Senn, M. J. E. *Speaking out for America's children*. New Haven, Conn.: Yale University Press, 1977.

Sexually active teenagers. *Children Today*, 1977, 6(4), 29.

Shanas, E. The family and social class. In E. Shanas, P. Townsend, D. Wedderburn, H. Friis, P. Milhoj, & J. Stehouwer (Eds.), *Old people in three industrial societies*. New York: Atherton Press, 1968, pp. 227–257.

Shanas, E., & Maddox, G. L. Aging, health, and the organization of health resources. In R. H. Binstock & E. Shanas (Eds.), *Handbook of aging and the social sciences*. New York: Van Nostrand Reinhold, 1976, 592–618.

Sheehy, G. *Passages: The predictable crises of adult life*. New York: Dutton, 1976.

Sheldon, W. H., Stevens, S., & Tucker, W. B. *The variables of human physique*. New York: Harper & Row, 1940.

The sheltered life. *Human Behavior*, 1978, 7(10), 61.

Shenker, I. R., & Schildkrout, M. Physical and emotional health of youth. In *74th yearbook of National Society for the Study of Education* (Part 1). Chicago: University of Chicago Press, 1975, pp. 61–86.

Sheppard, H. L. The potential role of behavioral science in the solution of the "older work problem." *American Behavioral Scientist*, 1970, 14(1), 71–80.

Sheppard, H. L., & Herrick, N. *Where have all the robots gone? Worker dissatisfaction in the '70s*. New York: Free Press, 1972.

Sherman, S. R. Leisure activities in retirement housing. *Journal of Gerontology*, 1974, 29, 325–335.

Shock, N. W. Biological theories of aging. In J. E. Birren & K. W. Schaie (Eds.), *Handbook of the psychology of aging*. New York: Van Nostrand Reinhold, 1977, pp. 103–115.

Shulman, N. Life-cycle variations in patterns of close relationships. *Journal of Marriage and the Family*, 1975, 37(4), 813–821.

Shuptrine, F. K., & Samuelson, G. Dimensions of marital roles in consumer decision making: Revisited. *Journal of Marketing Research*, 1976, 13(1), 87–91.

Siegal, M. Kohlberg versus Piaget: To what extent has one theory eclipsed the other? *Merrill-Palmer Quarterly*, 1980, 26(4), 285–297.

Siegler, I. C. The terminal drop hypothesis: Fact or artifact? *Experimental Aging Research,* 1975, *1,* 169.

Sigel, I. E. *Cognitive style and personality dynamics* (Interim progress report for National Institute of Mental Health, M 2983). 1961.

Sigel, I. E. Sex and personality correlates of styles of categorization among young children. *American Psychologist,* 1963, *18,* 350.

Silverman, P. R. Widowhood and preventive intervention. In S. H. Zarit (Ed.), *Readings in aging and death: Contemporary perspectives.* New York: Harper & Row, 1977, pp. 175–182.

Silverman, R. E. *Psychology.* Englewood Cliffs, N.J.: Prentice-Hall, 1974.

Simmons, R., Rosenberg, F., & Rosenberg, M. Disturbance in the self-image at adolescence. *American Sociological Review,* 1973, *38,* 553–568.

Singer, J. L. Fantasy: The foundation of serenity. *Psychology Today,* 1976, *10*(2), 32–34; 37.

Singer, J. L., & Singer, D. G. Come back, Mister Rogers, come back. *Psychology Today,* 1979, *12*(10), 56; 59–60.

Sipple, P. W. Another look at student freedom. *Intellect,* 1973, *102*(2351), 29–31.

Skolnick, A. *The intimate environment.* Boston: Little, Brown, 1973.

Skolnick, A. The myth of the vulnerable child. *Psychology Today,* 1978, *11*(9), 56–65.

Skovholt, T. M. Feminism and men's lives. *The Counseling Psychologist,* 1978, *7*(4), 3–10.

Smith, E. J. The career development of young black females. *Youth and Society,* 1981, *12*(3), 277–312.

Smith, P. K., & Daglish, L. Sex differences in parent and infant behavior. *Child Development,* 1977, *48*(4), 1250–1254.

Smith, S. R. Religion and the conception of youth in seventeenth century England. *History of Childhood Quarterly,* 1975, *2*(4), 493–516.

Smoking and health. News & reports. *Children Today,* 1972, *1*(1), 37.

Snow, C. E., & Hoefnagel-Höhle, H. The critical period for language acquisition: Evidence from second language learning. *Child Development,* 1978, *49*(4), 1114–1128.

Somerville, R. M. The future of family relationships in the middle and older years. *Family Coordinator,* 1972, *21,* 487–498.

Sopchak, A. H., & Sutherland, A. M. Psychological impact of cancer and its treatment, 7: Exogenous sex hormones and their relation to life-long adaptations in women with metastatic cancer of the breast. *Cancer,* 1960, *5,* 857–872.

Sorensen, R. C. *Adolescent sexuality in contemporary America: Personal values and sexual behavior ages 13–19.* New York: World, 1973.

Sorosky, A. D., Baran, A., & Pannor, R. The reunion of adoptees and birth relatives. *Journal of Youth and Adolescence,* 1974, *3*(3), 195–206.

Spekke, A. A. America: The next 200 years. *Intellect,* 1976, *105*(2376), 49–50. (a)

Spekke, A. A. The future of optimism. *Intellect,* 1976, *104*(2375), 605. (b)

Spence, J. T., & Helmreich, R. L. Accentuate the positive. *Contemporary Psychology,* 1979, *24*(1), 3–4.

Spezzano, C., & Waterman, J. The first day of life. *Psychology Today,* 1977, *11*(7), 110–116.

Spinetta, J., Rigler, D., & Karon, M. Personal space as a measure of a dying child's sense of isolation. *Journal of Consulting and Clinical Psychology,* 1974, *42,* 751.

Spingarn, N. D. Tear down the walls. 1974, *4*(7), 78–79.

Sprafkin, J. N., Liebert, R. M., & Poulos, R. W. Effects of a prosocial televised example on children's helping. *Journal of Experimental Child Psychology,* 1975, *20,* 119–126.

Sroufe, L. A. Attachment and the roots of competence. *Human Nature,* 1978, *1*(10), 50–57.

Staffieri, J. R. Body build and behavioral expectancies in young females. *Developmental Psychology,* 1972, *6,* 125–127.

Stafford, R., Backman, E., & DiBona, P. The division of labor among cohabiting and married couples. *Journal of Marriage and the Family*, 1977, *39*(1), 51.

Stearns, M. S. *The effects of preschool programs on disadvantaged children and their families* (report for U.S. Department of Health, Education, and Welfare, Office of Child Development). Washington, D.C.: U.S. Government Printing Office, 1971.

Stegner, W. The writer and the concept of adulthood. *Daedalus*, 1976, *105*(4), 39–48.

Stein, A. H., & Bailey, M. M. The socialization of achievement orientation in females. *Psychological Bulletin*, 1973, *80*(5), 345–366.

Stein, P. J. *Single in America*. Unpublished manuscript, Rutgers University, 1973.

Stein, P. J. Singlehood: An alternative to marriage. *Family Coordinator*, 1975, *24*(4), 489–503.

Stein, P. J. *Single*. Englewood Cliffs, N.J.: Prentice-Hall, 1976.

Stevens, J. H. Jr., & Baxter, D. H. Malnutrition in children's development. *Young Children*, 198, *36*(4), 60–71.

Stickle, G. The health of mothers and babies: How do we stack up? *Family Coordinator*, 1977, *26*(3), 205–210.

Stinnett, N., Carter, L. M., & Montgomery, J. E. Older persons' perceptions of their marriages. *Journal of Marriage and the Family*, 1972, *34*(4), 665–670.

Stoddart, K. The facts of life about dope: Observations of a local pharmacology. *Urban Life and Culture*, 1974, *3*(2), 179–204.

Strauss, M. E., Lessen-Firestone, J. K., Starr, R. H., & Ostrea, E. M. Behavior of narcotics-addicted newborns. *Child Development*, 1976, *46*(4), 887–893.

Strehler, B. L. A new age for aging. In S. H. Zarit (Ed.), *Readings in aging and death: Contemporary perspectives*. New York: Harper & Row, 1977.

Streib, G. F. Social stratification and aging. In R. H. Binstock & Shanas, E. (Eds.), *Handbook of aging and the social sciences*. New York: Van Nostrand Reinhold, 1976, pp. 160–185.

Streib, G. F., & Schneider, C. J. *Retirement in American society: Impact and process*. Ithaca, N.Y.: Cornell University Press, 1971.

Strom, R., Rees, R., Slaughter, H., & Wurster, S. Child-rearing expectations of families with atypical children. *American Journal of Orthopsychiatry*, 1981, *51*(2), 285–296.

Sudnow, D. *Passing on*. Englewood Cliffs, N.J.: Prentice-Hall, 1967.

Swanson, B. R., Massey, R. H., & Payne, I. R. Ordinal position, family size, and personal adjustment. *Journal of Psychology*, 1972, *81* (first half), 53–58.

Tabachnick, N. Sexual aspects of the automobile. Medical aspects of sexuality, *Medical Aspects of Human Sexuality*, 1973, *7*, 138–166.

Talking with Dorothy Kispert. *Merrill-Palmer News*, 1973, *14*(2).

Tanner, J. M. The regulation of human growth. *Child Development*, 1963, *34*, 817–847.

Taub, H. B., Goldstein, J. M., & Caputo, D. V. Indices of neonatal prematurity as discriminators of development in middle childhood, *Child Development*, 1977, *48*(3), 797–805.

Tavris, C. "Male supremacy is on the way out. It was just a phase in the evolution of culture." *Psychology Today*, 1975, *8*(8), 61–69.

Tavris, C. Men and women report their views on masculinity. *Psychology Today*, 1977, *10*(8), 34–42; 82.

Terkel, S. *Working*. New York: Pantheon, 1974.

Thom, P., & Others. The women's resource centre: An educational model for counseling women. *Adult Leadership*, 1975, *24*, 129–132.

Thomae, H. (Ed.). *Patterns of aging: Findings from the Bonn Longitudinal Study of Aging*. Basel, Switzerland: S. Karger, 1975.

Thomas, A., & Chess, S. *Temperament and development*. New York: Brunner/Mazel, 1977.

Thomas, A., & Chess, S. *The dynamics of psychological development*. New York: Brunner/Mazel, 1980.

Thomas, A., Chess, S., & Birch, H. G. The origin of personality. *Scientific American*, August 1970, 102–109.

Thomas, A., et al. *Behavior individuality in early childhood*. New York: New York University Press, 1963.

Thomas, L. On the science and technology of medicine. *Daedalus*, 1977, *106*(1), 35–46.

Thompson, V. D. Family size: Implicit policies and assumed psychological outcomes. *Journal of Social Issues*, 1974, *30*(4), 93–124.

Thornton, A. Children and marital stability. *Journal of Marriage and the Family*, 1977, *39*(3), 531–540.

"Three R's" in schools now: Retrenchment, results, realism. *U.S. News & World Report*, September 6, 1976, pp. 50–51.

Thurnher, M., Spence, D., & Lowenthal, M. W. Value confluence and behavioral conflict in intergenerational relations. *Journal of Marriage and the Family*, 1974, *36*(2), 308–320.

Timiras, P. S. *Developmental physiology and aging*. New York: Macmillan, 1972.

Tobin, J. D. Normal aging—The inevitability syndrome. In S. H. Zarit (Ed.), *Readings in aging and death: Contemporary perspectives*. New York: Harper & Row, 1977, pp. 39–47.

Toffler, A. *Future shock*. New York: Bantam, 1970.

Toffler, A. The American future is being bumbled away. *The Futurist*, 1976, *10*(21), 97–102.

Toman, W. Family constellation as a basic personality determinant. *Journal of Individual Pscyhology*, 1959, (15), 199–211.

Toman, W. Birth order rules all. *Psychology Today*, 1970, *4*(7), 45–49; 68–69.

Trainer, F. E. A critical analysis of Kohlberg's contributions to the study of moral thought. *Journal of Social Behavior*, 1977, *7*(1), 41–63.

Transracial adoptions. *Children Today*, 1975, *4*(4), 33.

Treas, J., & Van Hilst, A. Marriage and remarriage rates among older Americans. *Gerontologist*, 1976, *16*, 132–136.

Trickett, E. J. Toward a social-ecological conception of adolescent socialization: Normative data on contrasting types of public school classrooms. *Child Development*, 1978, *49*(2), 408–414.

Troll, L. E. *Early and middle adulthood*. Monterey, Calif.: Brooks/Cole, 1975.

Trotta, J. Open versus traditional education: Some effects on elementary school children. *Journal of the New York School Board Association*, April 1974, pp. 24–30.

Turiel, E. *Conflict and transition in adolescent moral development*. Unpublished manuscript, Harvard University, 1973.

Udry, J. R., Bauman, K. E., & Morris, N. M. Changes in premarital coital experience of recent decade-of-birth cohorts of urban American women. *Journal of Marriage and the Family*, 1975, *37*(4), 783–787.

Udwin, O., & Shmukler, D. The influence of sociocultural, economic, and home background factors on children's ability to engage in imaginative play. *Developmental Psychology*, 1981, *17*(1), 66–72.

United Nations population and vital statistics report. *Statistical Papers* (Series A), 1976, *28*(1).

U.S. Bureau of the Census. *Census of the population: General social and economic characteristics* (No. SRS 73-03100 NCSS Report A-2, 1/73). Washington, D.C.: U.S. Government Printing Office, 1970.

U.S. Bureau of the Census. Women by number of children ever born. 1970. *Census of the population* (Vol. 2, 3A). Washington, D.C.: U.S. Government Printing Office, 1973.

U.S. Bureau of the Census. Household and family characteristics: March 1975. *Current population reports* (P-20, No. 291). Washington, D.C.: U.S. Government Printing Office, 1976. (a)

U.S. Bureau of the Census. Number, timing, and duration of marriages and divorces in the United States: June 1975. *Current population reports* (P20, No. 297). Washington, D.C.: U.S. Government Printing Office, 1976. (b)

U.S. Department of Health, Education, and Welfare. *Life tables: Vital statistics of the United States, 1973* (Vol. 2, Section 5). Rockville, Md.: National Center for Health Statistics, 1975.

U.S. Department of Labor. Youth and the meaning of work (Manpower Research Monograph No. 32). Washington, D.C.: U.S. Government Printing Office, 1974.

U.S. House of Representatives, Special Subcommittee on Education Discrimination against Women. *Hearings* (2 vols.). Washington, D.C.: U.S. Government Printing Office, 1970.

U.S. Public Health Service. *Vital statistics of the United States, 1970* (Vol. 2). Rockville, Md.: U.S. Department of HEW, Public Health Service, 1974.

Vaillant, G. E. The climb to maturity: How the best and the brightest came of age. *Psychology Today*, 1977, *11*(4), 34–38; 41; 107–108; 110.

Van Dusen, R. A., & Sheldon, E. B. The changing status of American women: A life cycle perspective. *American Psychologist*, 1976, *31*(2), 106–116.

Veevers, J. E. Declining childlessness and age at marriage: A test of a hypothesis. *Social Biology*, September 1972.

Veevers, J. E. The child-free alternative: Rejection of the motherhood mystique. In M. Stephenson (Ed.), *Women in Canada*. Toronto: New Press, 1973, pp. 183–199. (a)

Veevers, J. E. Voluntary childlessness: A neglected area of study. *Family Coordinator*, 1973, *23*, 199–201. (b)

Veevers, J. E. Voluntary childlessness and social policy: An alternative view. *Family Coordinator*, 1974, *23*(4), 397–406.

Veevers, J. E. The life style of voluntarily childless couples. In L. Larson (Ed.), *The Canadian family in comparative perspective*. Toronto: Prentice-Hall, 1975.

Verbrugge, L. M. Females and illness: Recent trends in sex differences in the United States. *Journal of Health and Social Behavior*, 1976, *17*, 387–401.

Verbrugge, L. *Sex differentials in morbidity and mortality in the United States*. Paper presented at the annual meeting of the Population Association of America, 1975.

Veysey, L. Rejoice! Some of what ails us may not be so. *The National Observer*, May 1, 1976, pp. B1–B2.

Von Senden, M. *Space and light*. New York: Free Press, 1960.

Vreeland, R. S. Is it true what they say about Harvard boys? *Psychology Today*, 1972, *5*(8), 65–68.

Vriend, T. J. The case for women. *Vocational Guidance Quarterly*, 1977, *25*(4), 329–331.

Waldrop, M. F., & Halverson, C. F. Intensive and extensive peer behavior: Longitudinal and cross-sectional analyses. *Child Development*, 1975, *46*(1), 19–26.

Wax, J. Sex and the single grandparent. In S. H. Zarit (Ed.), *Readings in aging and death: Contemporary perspectives*. New York: Harper & Row, 1977, pp. 147–151.

Waxenberg, S. E. Psychotherapeutic and dynamic implications of recent research on female sexual functioning. In G. D. Goldman & D. S. Milman (Eds.), *Modern woman: Her psychology and sexuality*. Springfield, Illinois: C C Thomas, 1969, pp. 3–24.

Weber, R. Another view of career education at the K-12 level. *New Generation*, 1976, *58*(1), 4–7.

Weinraub, M., Brooks, J., & Lewis, M. The social network: A reconsideration of the concept of attachment. *Human Development*, 1977, *20*(1), 31–47.

Weir, A. Value judgments and personality in old age. *Acta Psychologica*, 1961, *19*, 148–149.

Weisman, A. *On dying and denying*. New York: Behavioral Publications, 1972.

Weiss, R. S. *Marital separation.* Basic Books, 1976.

Weitzman, L. J., Eifler, D., Hokada, E., & Ross, C. Sex-role socialization in picture books for pre-school children. *American Journal of Sociology,* 1972, 77, 1125–1150.

Welford, A. T. Motor performance. In J. E. Birren & K. W. Schaie (Eds.), *Handbook of the psychology of aging.* New York: Van Nostrand Reinhold, 1977, pp. 450–496.

Welsh, R. S. Severe parental punishment and delinquency: A developmental theory. *Journal of Child Clinical Psychology,* 1974, 3, 24–30.

Wessel, J. A., & Van Huss, W. D. The influence of physical activity and age on exercise adaptation of women, 20–69 years. *Journal of Sports Medicine,* 1969, 9, 173–183.

White, B. L. The first three years of life. Englewood Cliffs, N.J.: Prentice-Hall, 1975.

White, B. L. Guidelines for parent education. Paper prepared for the planning education conference. Flint, Mich., September 29, 1977.

Whitley, E., Duncan, R., & McKenzie, P. Adopted grandparents: A link between the past and the future. *Educational Gerontology,* 1976, 1(3), 243–249.

Why millions hate their jobs—And what's afoot to help. *U.S. News & World Report,* September 27, 1976, pp. 87–90.

Willerman, L. Activity level and hyper-activity in twins. *Child Development,* 1973, 44, 285–293.

Williams, S. Stress and longevity—The thriving top executive. *Psychology Today,* 1974, 8(3), 30.

Williamson, N. E. *Sons or daughters: A cross-cultural survey of parental preferences.* Beverly Hills, Calif.: Sage Publications, 1977.

Wilson, G., & Nias, D. Beauty can't be beat. *Psychology Today,* 1976, 10(4), 96–98; 103.

Wilson, K. L., Zurcher, L. A., McAdams, D. C., & Curtis, R. L. Stepfathers and step-children: An exploratory analysis from two national surveys. *Journal of Marriage and the Family,* 1975, 37(3), 526–536.

Wilson, R. S. Twins and siblings: Concordance for school-age mental development. *Child Development,* 1977, 48(1), 211–216.

Winetsky, C. S. Comparisons of the expectations of parents and teachers for the behavior of preschool children. *Child Development,* 1978, 49(4), 1146–1154.

Winikoff, B. Changing public diet. *Human Nature,* 1978, 1(1), 60–65.

Winter, D. G., Stewart, A. J., & McClelland, D. C. Grading the effects of a liberal arts education. *Psychology Today,* 1978, 12(4), 69–74; 106.

Women on words and images. *Dick and Janes as victims.* Princeton, New Jersey: Annual Review of Psychology, Vol. 28. M. R. Rosenzweig & L. W. Porter (Eds.). Palo Alto: Annual Review Inc., 1977, 173.

Woodruff, D., & Birren, J. E. Age changes and cohort differences in personality. *Developmental Psychology,* 1972, 6, 252–259.

Woolsey, S. H. Pied piper politics and the child-care debate. *Daedalus,* 1977, 127–145.

Work in America. Boston: M. I. T. Press, 1973. In Jones, R. *The other generation: The new power of older people.* Englewood Cliffs, N.J.: Prentice-Hall, 1977.

Working women. *Children Today,* 1977, 6(4), 28.

Yankelovich, D. *The changing values on campus.* New York: Simon & Schuster, 1972.

Yankelovich, D. *The new morality: A profile of American youth in the '70s.* New York: McGraw-Hill, 1974.

Yankelovich, D., & Clark, R. College and noncollege youth values. *Change,* 1974, 6(7), 45–46; 64.

Yarrow, M. R., Scott, P. M., & Waxler, C. Z. Learning concern for others. *Developmental Psychology,* 1973, 8, 240–260.

Yarrow, M. R., & Waxler, C. Z., with Barrett, D., Darby, J., King, R., Pickett, M., & Smith, J. Dimensions and correlates of prosocial behavior in young children. *Child Development*, 1976, *47*(1), 118–125.

Yorburg, B. *The changing family*. New York: Columbia University Press, 1973.

Youmans, E. G. Family disengagement among older urban and rural women. *Journal of Gerontology*, 1967, *22*, 209.

Youmans, E. G., & Yarrow, M. Aging and social adaptation: A longitudinal study of healthy old men. In S. Granick & R. D. Patterson (Eds.), *Human aging 2: An eleven-year follow-up biomedical and behavioral study* (U.S. Department of Health, Education, and Welfare Publication No. HSM 71-9037). Washington, D.C.: U.S. Government Printing Office, 1971.

The younger moderates. *Human Behavior*, 1977, *6*(10), 62.

Zajonc, R. B. Family configuration and intelligence. *Science*, 1976, *192*, 227–236.

Zarit, S. H. (Ed.). *Readings in aging and death: Contemporary perspectives*. New York: Harper & Row, 1977.

Zelazo, P. R., Zelazo, N. A., & Kolb, S. Walking: In the newborn. *Science*, 1972, *176*, 314–315.

Zepelin, H. Age differences in dreams. I: Men's dreams and thematic apperceptive fantasy. *International Journal of Aging and Human Development*, 1980–81, *12*(3), 171–180.

Zeskind, P. S., & Ramey, C. T. Fetal malnutrition: An experimental study of its consequences on infant development in two caregiving environments. *Child Development*, 1978, *49*(4), 1155–1162.

Zimbardo, P. G., & Ruch, F. L. *Psychology and life* (19th ed.). Glenview, Ill.: Scott, Foresman, 1979.

Zinberg, N. E. The war over marijuana. *Psychology Today*, 1976, *10*(7), 45–52; 102–106.

AUTHOR INDEX

469

Hockey, L., 387
Hoffman, L. W., 100, 257
Hokada, E., 133
Holcomb, W. L., 378, 387, 391
Horn, J., 165, 219, 306
Horn, P., 166, 230
Horner, M., 257
Hornung, C. A., 257
Hotch, D. F., 204
Howell, F. M., 204
Hoyer, W. J., 358
Huesman, L. R., 98
Hultsch, D. F., 230
Hunt, M., 184, 225

Illich, I., 392
Irving, H. W., 296
Itzin, F., 335

Jacklin, C. N., 104
Jackson, J. W., 241
Jackson, W., 294
Jacob, P. E., 174
Jacobs, J., 339
Jaffe, D., 126
Jalali, M., 169
James, W., 311
Jantz, R. K., 72
Jaquish, G. A., 252
Jensen, R. E., 104
Johnson, M. M., 111
Jones, M., 361
Jones, P. A., 99
Jones, W. H., 194
Josselson, R., 157
Jung, C. G., 240, 287

Kagan, J., 103, 121, 122, 127, 128, 136,
    222, 224
Kahn, A., 288, 361, 362, 370
Kalish, R. A., 309, 334, 336, 340, 367,
    369, 370, 372, 385, 387, 388, 389
Kalter, N., 143
Kandel, D., 168
Kangas, J., 404
Kanter, R. M., 124, 126
Kantner, J. F., 226
Kaplan, H., 310
Karon, M., 345
Karp, E., 370
Karson, M., 191, 192
Kass, L. R., 315, 384
Kasschau, P. L., 306
Katchadourian, H., 400
Kauffman, J. M., 421

Kay, H., 290
Kearsley, R. B., 45, 103
Keen, S., 392
Keith, P. M., 268
Keller, J., 232
Kellogg, M. A., 365
Kelly, J. R., 293, 298, 410, 419
Kendrick, C., 122
Keniston, K., 116, 123, 149, 150, 151,
    204, 407
Kenshalo, D. R., 315
Kerckhoff, R. K., 260, 268
Kieffer, C., 232
Kimmel, D. C., 245
Kimsey, L. R., 381
King, D., 329
King, S., 110, 149, 171
Kinsey, A. E., 253
Kispert, D., 133
Kivett, V. R., 248
Knapp, J. R., 191
Knox, D., 188
Kobrin, F. E., 332, 333
Kohlberg, L., 94, 95, 97, 100, 173
Komarovsky, M., 257
Korner, A. F., 129
Kosberg, J. I., 341
Kriesberg, L., 278
Krolick, G., 131
Kübler-Ross, E., 386
Kuhn, D., 113
Kunz, P. R., 267
Kutz, S. L., 406
Kuypers, J. A., 369

Labeff, E., 257
Labouvie-Vief, G., 323
LaDriere, L., 167
Lakoff, S. A., 420, 422
Lance, W. D., 133
Langer, J., 97
Larossa, R., 20
Lauducina, E. V., 258, 260
Lawler, E. E., 215, 272
Lawton, M. P., 317
Lazarus, R. S., 121
Leaf, A., 244, 450
Lear, J., 288
Lebovici, S., 162
Lee, P. C., 260, 267
Lefkowitz, M. M., 98
Lehr, U., 344
LeMasters, E., 229
Lerner, R. M., 191, 192
Levin, H., 97

SUBJECT INDEX